THE 100 BEST STOCKS YOU CAN BUY 2007

John Slatter, C.F.A.

BUSINESS
Adams Media
Avon, Massachusetts

Dedication

To my nephew, Jack Gerard

Acknowledgments

Writing a book is far easier than finding a publisher. My first book, *Safe Investing,* didn't find a home until I latched on to my dutiful agent, Edythea Ginis Selman. Edy knows how to find a publisher, and she knows how to convince the editor that I am worth paying a living wage.

My publisher, Adams Media, has treated me like a king. That could be because my editors are Shoshanna Grossman and Larry Shea, easy people to do business with.

Also, a vote of thanks to George G. Morris, CFA, my broker with Wachovia Securities, who helped me gather research. If you need a full-service broker, George is your man in Cleveland at (800) 537-4105.

Published by Adams Media, an F+W Publications Company
57 Littlefield Street
Avon, MA 02322
www.adamsmedia.com

ISBN 10: 1-59337-707-X
ISBN 13: 978-1-59337-707-6

Printed in the United States of America.

J I H G F E D C B A

Library of Congress Cataloging-in-Publication Data
is available from publisher.

Contents

I. THE ART AND SCIENCE OF INVESTING IN STOCKS 1

Is This the Right Investment Book for You? 2

How to Avoid Portfolio Blunders 5

The Essentials of Successful Investing 9

Twenty-One Ways to Reduce Investment Risk 12

Basic Terminology 17

How to Choose a Broker 26

A Novel Approach to Asset Allocation 30

The Double-Check-a-Month Plan 33

A Word about My Record 37

When to Sell 40

II. 100 BEST STOCKS YOU CAN BUY 43

Index of Stocks by Category 360

PART I

THE ART AND SCIENCE OF INVESTING IN STOCKS

Is This the Right Investment Book for You?

The last time I stopped by the investment section of my local bookstore, there was no shortage of books about investing in the stock market. Fortunately, several copies of the latest edition of *The 100 Best Stocks You Can Buy* were prominently displayed.

However, I saw only one lonely soul trying to find a book to his liking. I was tempted to suggest that mine was the best one on the shelf. But I refrained. I recalled that on my previous trip to the bookstore I made a similar suggestion and had been totally ignored. He didn't even look up to see who was offering him this sage advice. (I was tempted to report that recalcitrant cad to the manager but thought better of it.)

Since you have the book in your hands and are wondering whether this is the one for you, let me give you a song and dance that will convince you that your search has ended; you don't need to look any further.

To begin, let me congratulate you on making the decision to educate yourself on the intricacies of the stock market. Many people totally ignore the importance of saving money for the future. It could be that they believe their company 401(k), along with Social Security, will do the job. The odds are that you will need more, particularly if you work for a firm that insists your 401(k) should be stuffed with your employer's company stock.

If you want to build a solid portfolio, it makes better sense to buy stocks on a regular basis—at least once a year. I suggest setting aside at least 10 percent of your gross income every year for stock purchases. And don't skip a year because you don't like the antics of the stock market at that particular time. Forecasting the market is a no-no. You can't do it—nor can anyone else.

Why People Don't Read About Investing

One reason that people don't read about investing is that they are overwhelmed by the complexity of the financial scene. I heartily concur—it *is* overwhelming. That's because there are thousands of mutual funds, common stocks, preferred stocks, certificates of deposit, options, bonds, annuities, and assorted investment products.

Even if you simply confined your search to the stocks listed on the New York Stock Exchange, the task would be daunting, since some 3,000 stocks are traded there. Or you might decide to "Let George do it," by investing in mutual funds. There, too, you will encounter infinite decisions, since there are over 14,000 mutual funds—most of which underperform such market indexes as the Dow Jones Industrial Average (called the Dow, Dow Jones, or DJIA) or the Standard & Poor's 500 (S&P 500).

If you are like many buyers of my books, you are not a sophisticated investor. You have a good job, have an income that is well above average, and you are serious about your career. That means that you spend time improving yourself by reading trade journals and taking courses at a local college.

Why Not Burn the Midnight Oil?

In other words, your day is already taken up with reading. How can you possibly start poring over annual reports, Standard & Poor's reports, *Fortune, Value Line Investment Survey,* the *Wall Street Journal, Forbes,*

BusinessWeek, Barron's, and a half-dozen books on the stock market? Easy. Drink lots of coffee and stay up until two in the morning.

If you object to this routine, you will be better off with my book, since I try to make investing a lot simpler than you thought it would be. For one thing, my style of writing is easy to understand. At least that's what people tell me.

Incidentally, I am one of the few authors who take calls from readers. My address and phone number are at the end of the book. I assume you will confine your calls to regular business hours, based on Eastern Standard Time, since I live in Vermont.

Whenever I buy a book, I always check to see if the writer has good credentials. For my part, I have been on the investment scene for a good forty years. I started as a plain vanilla stockbroker and then became editor of a publication devoted to mutual funds, followed by several years as a securities analyst for a brokerage firm. I spent a few years as a portfolio manager and started operating my own firm, managing portfolios on a fee basis for investors with assets of $150,000 or more.

During these years, I did a lot of writing, first for *Barron's Financial Weekly,* and later for such publications as *Physician's Management* and *Better Investing.* During the same period, I wrote tons of reports on stocks for the brokerage firms that paid my salary. In recent years, I have written a slew of books: *Safe Investing, Straight Talk About Stock Investing,* and ten previous editions of *The 100 Best Stocks You Can Buy.*

I also wrote two great novels, but no publisher seems to agree that they are great, so I am not currently getting royalties on those.

As I mentioned previously, the number of stocks and mutual funds out there is infinite. Besides the 3,000 stocks on the New York Stock Exchange, plus the thousands of mutual funds, there are also thousands of stocks listed on the Nasdaq and thousands more traded on markets in Europe, Asia, Latin America, and Canada.

The beauty of my book is that I whittle the number of stocks you need to know about down to 100. Among those 100 are four types of stocks, depending on your particular temperament: Income, Growth and Income, Conservative Growth, and Aggressive Growth.

Diversification, the First Rule of Investing

Of course, there is no need to confine your investing exclusively to one category. A well-diversified portfolio could have half a dozen from each sector. Incidentally, diversity is the key to investing. Whenever you concentrate on one type of stock, such as technology, energy, banks, utilities, or pharmaceuticals, you expose yourself to extra risk. Don't do it. Let me emphasize that again—don't do it.

When I was a portfolio strategist in Cleveland a few years ago, I examined portfolios submitted to our firm for analysis. About 100 percent of them were not diversified. They were typically concentrated in only three industries: public utilities, banks, and oil.

Before you make up your mind about which stocks to buy, you will want to collect some information. If you have access to a brokerage house, you can easily get a copy of a report called *Value Line Investment Survey.* You can also subscribe yourself, but be prepared to spend over $500 a year for this service, which covers about 1,700 well-known stocks. A less expensive alternative is the same service limited to 600 stocks. Still another good source is Standard & Poor's tear sheets, which can be obtained from a broker or library. Finally, most brokerage houses have a staff of analysts that turn out reports on a multitude of stocks.

My Sources of Information

A final source of information is this book, which is updated every year. I believe that my write-ups are valuable in ways that the other sources are not. When I first began writing this series of books, I obtained my information from each company's annual report, as well as from the two services mentioned. Now, I go much further afield. On a daily basis, I collect information on these companies from such sources as *Barron's, Forbes, Better Investing, BusinessWeek,* and other monthly investment publications. In addition, I consult well-known newspapers across the country, including the *Boston Globe,* the *New York Times,* as well as papers in Chicago, Philadelphia, Atlanta, Denver, St. Louis, Houston, Milwaukee, Los Angeles, Detroit, San Francisco, Miami, and Dallas.

Whenever I see an article on one of my companies, I clip it out and file it for future reference and examine it again when I sit at my computer to prepare a report. Using this vast collection, I sift through the facts to find the reasons that this stock is attractive. I also look for factors that have a negative tone. In other words, I don't want to give you a purely one-sided view of this stock. By contrast, if you read the company's annual report, you will only hear about the attributes of the company and not about its problems and deficiencies.

Similarly, if you read a report from a brokerage house, it is rarely negative. The analyst normally tells you to buy—rarely to sell. One reason for this is the tie brokerage houses have to these companies that can lead to extremely lucrative underwriting and corporate finance deals. If the analyst tells investors to avoid the stock, the company may decide to avoid the brokerage house and give its business to someone else.

Obviously, I have no reason to be anything but unbiased.

Forty Years of Experience Is the Key

Finally, the 100 stocks have to be selected. The publisher is not the one who picks the stocks. I do. My forty years of varied experience on the investment scene give me an edge in this regard. And, of course, I am intimately involved in stock selection from a personal perspective. I have a large portfolio of stocks, over fifty at present, which have made my wife and me millionaires.

If you would like to reach the same comfortable plateau, why not invest $14.95 and start reading?

Oh, and here's one more thing. If you read the rest of these introductory chapters, you will see that I have provided a helpful glossary that explains all the terms you need to know to understand the fundamentals of investing.

I also have a chapter on asset allocation that will tell you what percentage of your holdings should be in stocks and how much in such fixed-income vehicles as bonds and money-market funds. Finally, there also are chapters on how I select my stocks, an intriguing way to reduce risk, and still another on how to analyze stocks. There is also a short chapter that focuses on the four essentials of successful investing. You'll be surprised at how simple investing can be if you read this chapter.

How to Avoid Portfolio Blunders

When I first met Hans Gelderland, he had just finished an inspiring talk to a large group of Vermont's professional and aspiring freelance writers. As you are no doubt aware, he is the author of the highly acclaimed modern classic, *How to Make Up to $37,000 a Year As a Full-time Freelance Writer.*

Since Mr. Gelderland lives in nearby Colchester, I had no trouble getting in touch with him. "I haven't read your book, Mr. Slatter, but I certainly would like to talk shop with you some time."

"Super idea," I said. "How about dinner at my favorite restaurant, The Windjammer?"

After we filled our plates at the salad bar, we sat down at our booth. I started the ball rolling with a question. "What is your latest project, Mr. Gelderland?"

"Please, it's Hans. I've been struggling with a magazine article on the pre-Socratics. I assume you know something about philosophy."

"A smattering," I said. "As I recall, those were the philosophers who lived before Socrates, such as Anaximander, Thales, Heraclitus, and Parmenides."

"That's right. There was quite a stable of them, and I wanted to do a piece to educate people about this little-known group. But the editor said it was too big a project, and he suggested it would be better to concentrate on just one. I chose Pythagoras and interviewed everybody in sight—I think I spent six solid weeks doing my research."

"Great. I can't wait to read it," I said.

"You'll have a long wait. It was rejected. 'Too sophisticated for our audience,' the editor told me."

"That happens, even to the best of us," I said.

"I had better luck on the one on beetles," Hans said. "But the editor told me it was too general. So I put more focus into it, and called it "The Veins in the Hind Wings of an Unborn Beetle." The editor told me to go ahead, but when I had finished a month of research and submitted my manuscript, he said it was perfect, except for one thing. He wanted a few quotes from the leading expert on the topic. So I called this professor in New Mexico, but he insisted I fly out for the interview—at my expense, of course."

"So you finally landed a good one, right?"

"I was hoping for at least $250, but the editor said his magazine was a small quarterly and could go no higher than $175. What's more, I won't get my money till the article appears, about nine months from now."

"That's how the ball bounces," I said, trying to be sympathetic to his plight. "I have an idea that might work, assuming you have an interest in the stock market."

"Always ready to tackle something new," said Hans. "What do you have in mind?"

"I have been dealing with investors for many years, and I see them doing some pretty stupid things. Maybe you could do a piece and call it "The 10 Most Heinous Goofs Made by Investors." How's that for a title?"

"Almost perfect," he said. "Just one change. Make it 'mistakes' instead of 'goofs.' That's a little less intimidating. What's a good mistake to begin with, Mr. Slatter?"

"Since I put my phone number in my book, I get quite a few calls from readers. Not infrequently, they want my opinion on some obscure stock that is not in my book, and often not even in the *S&P Stock Guide.* Really off-the-wall questions. My advice is to pick one of the 100 great stocks in my book, and forget about some stock they discovered under a rock."

"In other words, pick great companies, not ones that may not be here five years from now. What else?"

"Next is diversification. Rarely do I come across a portfolio that is adequately diversified. Most people are aware that stocks have risk, and so they usually own several stocks. But they are often from a narrow sector of the market. For instance, they may have a penchant for medical stocks, such as Lilly, Abbott, Medtronic, Cardinal Health, Becton, Dickinson, or Varian Medical. All these stocks are fine, but they are not immune to the vagaries of the market. I would suggest that in a twenty-stock portfolio, investors should not own more than two from any one sector. And that includes tech stocks. In recent years, the biggest blunder made by unsophisticated investors was to own a portfolio stuffed with tech stocks. In the sagging market since early 2000, those stocks have been a total disaster."

"In other words, Mr. Slatter, what you are saying is that a good portfolio could have two oil stocks, a couple medical stocks, one or two real estate investment trusts, maybe a beverage stock, a couple machinery stocks, a utility or two, a food company, and so forth. How does that sound?"

"You're a quick study, Hans," I said.

"I guess that means I don't have to read your book."

"I intend to give you a copy, Hans, so I think someone in your family better read it. Which reminds me, another goof made by investors is not doing their homework. If you were going to buy a house, you would not buy the first one you looked at. You would go out with a realtor and look at a couple dozen before making your purchase. Why not spend as much time when you buy a stock?"

"You're trying to make investing sound time-consuming. Doesn't that take the fun out of it?"

"Investing is not fun, Hans. Not if you want to be successful. I would say you had better read the company's annual report, as well as the *Value Line* analysis and the Standard & Poor's tear sheet. Once you have the facts, you are ready to decide if the stock is priced right for immediate purchase."

"This interview is getting complicated, Mr. Slatter. I hope you will read my drivel after I finish my rough draft. Okay, what else shall we tell these people?"

"Once you start building a portfolio, you should keep yourself up to date by reading such periodicals as the *Wall Street Journal,* the *New York Times, Barron's, Forbes, BusinessWeek,* the *AAII Journal, Fortune, Better Investing,* or *Money.*"

"I am beginning to wonder if I am qualified to write this article. It really sounds complicated. Maybe I had better read your book, after all. What's the next blunder?"

"If you can write an article on the veins in the hind wings of an unborn beetle, I think you have the ability to do one on the stock market. It's pretty simple stuff, once you get the hang of it.

"The most important part of investing is starting early in life. If you wait until you're fifty or fifty-five, you don't have enough years to build up a portfolio. I suggest starting in your thirties, if possible. If you start at thirty-five, for instance, and invest $10,000 a year and earn 12 percent a year, you'll have over $2.4 million when you reach sixty-five. If, however, you start at age fifty and invest the same $10,000 a year, you'll have only $373,000 when they hand you the proverbial gold timepiece."

"Where am I going to get $10,000?"

"You had better quit buying new cars, for one thing. That's one of the blunders that people make. They spend every cent they make, and even hit their credit card for a few thousand more. Being a spendthrift is the surest path to poverty at age sixty-five or seventy. If you are depending on Social Security to keep you afloat during retirement, you had better plan on eating a lot of hot dogs and hamburgers. And throw in a few bunches of celery and carrots, for good measure."

"You mean I have to give up the good life, Mr. Slatter?"

"I happen to be rich, Hans. My wife and I own well over fifty stocks, we own our home free and clear, and my bookshelves are loaded with hundreds of books I haven't yet read. And I drive a 1998 Cadillac, which I bought used. So, I'm not sure living a frugal life means you have to suffer."

"I assume you inherited your vast wealth."

"Not a penny came from my deceased relatives. My wife and I earned it all."

"You have convinced me I had better change a few things if I hope to be able to retire in style. As soon as I get my check from my article on beetles, I will buy my first stock. Now, what else shall we tell these eager investors?"

"Whenever I meet someone new, the first question they ask me is what I think of the market. For example, one lady I met the other day at a garage sale said, 'This market has been really crazy. You're a professional, Mr. Slatter. Where do you think it's headed?' I told her I didn't have the faintest idea."

"I assume that didn't convince her to become one of your clients. She must really think you're stupid," said Hans Gelderland.

"I sold her a book, so maybe that will convince her otherwise. Most of my clients come from people who have read my book. But, getting back to predicting the market—it can't be done. I realize, of course, that everyone keeps trying, but I defy you to name one analyst or portfolio manager who has consistently predicted what the market will do. There ain't any. So quit trying. My best advice is to invest when you have the money—not when you think the market is poised for a big run. Forget about forecasting. If you buy stocks once or twice a year—and are patient—you'll end up a millionaire like me."

"Well, I think I've got enough for a solid article, Mr. Slatter. Shall we flip to see who pays the tab?"

"I'm not through. One of the most important aspects of picking stocks is not to pay too much. The woods are filled with companies that are doing well and increasing their earnings like clockwork. The trouble is that everybody knows they're great, and you have to pay too much for them."

"What's too much?" asked Hans Gelderland.

"There's no good answer, but the gauge to use is the price/earnings ratio, or P/E ratio. Some people call it the multiple. It's calculated by dividing the annual earnings per share into the price. For instance, if Johnson Controls is priced at $85.60 (which it was at the end of June in 2003), you would divide their latest twelve-month earnings into that figure. That means dividing $6.75 into $85.60, and you get a P/E of 12.7. That was a remarkably low P/E for a company with an exceptional growth record. As it happens, I bought that stock at that time, and a month later it was up at the $95 level. Stocks with good records are rarely available at such a bargain price, but when you find one, latch onto it."

"No wonder you're rich. So I am to assume that 12.7 is a low multiple. But what would you consider a high one?"

"I prefer to buy stocks with a P/E of less than 30, and I certainly would never buy one above 40. On the other hand, you can find stocks with a low multiple that would not be worth pursuing. If their earnings are lackluster and going nowhere, they are not attractive, no matter how low the P/E ratio."

"My notebook is getting overloaded with your maxims, Mr. Slatter. And I'm wondering when the waiter will get fed up with us and toss us out on our ears. We are just taking up space."

"Relax, Hans. The Windjammer has never tossed me out yet. They know I'm a faithful customer, and I bring lots of new people here who later return. One more piece of advice for your notebook. Bear in mind that you can't buy stocks unless you have a broker. It pays to be a careful shopper. The one *not* to deal with is the one who calls you out of the blue to solicit your business. These brokers are often rookies who are still learning the business. *Never* do business with a stranger who calls you.

"The best way to find a broker is by word of mouth. Check with your friends and find out who has done a good job for one of them. And make sure that broker is not suggesting a lot of trades. Trading is the surest way to the poorhouse."

"Is that it?"

"Not quite. The most important rule of thumb is to be alert to when my book is published each year. Normally, it comes out around October 1. If you don't buy every edition and read it carefully, you are destined to suffer the consequences."

"Do you want to flip to see who pays?" asked Hans Gelderland.

"No, I'm rich. Let me handle it."

The Essentials of Successful Investing

You don't have to be a brilliant stock-picker to become a successful investor. Here are a few factors that matter more.

Start Early

Starting your program at an early age wins hands down. Let's say you want to reach age sixty-five with investments worth a million dollars. If you buy your first stock at age thirty-five and pick stocks that appreciate at a rate of 10 percent (dividends included), you will have to set aside $6,079 each year. But if you delay until age forty-five, the amount needed leaps to $17,460. Waiting until you're fifty-five boosts your annual contribution to a real back-breaker—$62,746.

Don't Be a Spendthrift

Also important is your ability to set aside money out of your current income. You will have a lot of trouble if you buy a new car every two or three years. In fact, if you buy new cars at all, you will have trouble. I buy used cars, usually Buicks that are three years old but are in top condition. And don't buy the best house in town and saddle yourself with a huge mortgage. Buy an older home that has been well taken care of. And never fail to pay off your credit card balance before it includes interest charges. In short, don't be a spendthrift. If you need help, read *The Millionaire Mind,* by Thomas J. Stanley.

Stocks Are the Answer

Next, make sure you invest mostly in common stocks. Over the years, stocks have provided 11 or 12 percent a year in total return. If you buy bonds, CDs, preferred stocks, or leave your cash in a money-market fund, you may not be able to pay your bills during retirement. On the other hand, you may want to have a portion of your investment money—let's say 30 percent—in short-term bonds, particularly if you are retired.

Still another alternative to be avoided are mutual funds. Why? Because the people who manage mutual funds scoop off about 1.5 percent of your holdings each year. They call it the "expense ratio." In addition, picking a good fund is made difficult because there are many thousands to choose from—and no effective way to separate the wheat from the chaff. In fact, there are not very many good ones. The average fund underperforms the market. Finally, mutual funds trade stocks as if they were going out of style, which means they distribute capital gains to you that are subject to income tax.

The Keys to Picking Stocks

And now we come to the final factor: picking a good list of stocks.

The most important factor is diversification. I suggest owning at least twenty to thirty stocks. However, that doesn't mean you have to accomplish this objective on day one. Let's say you have $5,000 and will be able to save $5,000 each year. In the first year, you buy one or two stocks. That certainly is not a diversified portfolio—but don't let that worry you. If you start investing at age forty and buy one stock a year, you will have twenty-five stocks at age sixty-five.

The one thing you want to avoid is buying too many stocks that are similar. In 1998 and 1999, many investors were convinced that tech stocks were the wave of the future, so they loaded up on them, often to the exclusion of everything else—no oil stocks, no bank stocks, no drug stocks, no utilities, no REITs, no food stocks, and so forth—just tech stocks. Well, as you know, they crashed big time. Many were down 90 percent, and some didn't even survive the bear market of 2000–2002.

As far as picking stocks is concerned, don't fret over picking all winners. You can't do it. Don't worry about it. Just keep picking stocks from my book, *The 100 Best Stocks You Can Buy,* that appeal to you, and time will take care of the rest.

If you don't want to invest $14.95 in my book, you may find it helpful to use the Dow Jones Industrial Average to make your selections. That list contains thirty blue-chip stocks, such as Procter & Gamble, Merck, General Electric, Microsoft, Home Depot, Boeing, DuPont, Johnson & Johnson, United Technologies, and Coca-Cola. You can find this list on page C2 of the *Wall Street Journal.*

Incidentally, the list of thirty stocks, which remains relatively constant, does change from time to time. On average, about one stock each year is dropped and a new one inserted. Quite often, these changes are not made singly. For instance, on April 8, 2004, three stocks were cast aside: Eastman Kodak, AT&T, and International Paper, which were replaced with Pfizer, American International Group, and Verizon. Before these latest changes, the last time new stocks were added was November 1, 1999, when four stocks were booted out: Goodyear Tire, Chevron, Union Carbide (now part of Dow Chemical), and Sears, Roebuck. Those added in 1999 were Home Depot, SBC Communications, Microsoft, and Intel.

If you are a busy person, this short list may appeal to you, since it reduces the number of stocks you might like to keep track of. By contrast, there are about 3,000 stocks listed on the New York Stock Exchange.

A Few Guidelines

But whichever route you care to traverse, you still have to make up your mind which stock or stocks you will purchase. Ideally, a stock should have these characteristics:

- A rising trend of earnings, dividends, and book value
- A balance sheet with less debt than other companies in its particular industry
- A Standard & Poor's Rating of B+ or better
- A price/earnings ratio no higher than average
- A dividend yield that suits your particular needs
- A below-average dividend payout patio. (For instance, if a company has annual earnings per share of $4.00, I would prefer that it pays out $2.00 or less in the form of dividends.)
- Company's return on shareholders' equity is 15 percent or higher

Sources of Information

You can obtain this information from *Value Line Investment Survey,* which is available at most brokerage offices and some libraries. *Value Line* covers about 1700 stocks with one page devoted to each stock; these are revised every three months. What's more, all the stocks in a given industry are presented together.

An equally helpful source of information is Standard & Poor's, which publishes a two-page report on nearly any stock you can think of. You can also find these sheets online. For instance, I have an account at Charles Schwab, so I merely bring up my portfolio and click on News/Chart, then scroll down Select a Report until I see S&P Stock Report. I click Go, and the report appears on the screen, which I can print out.

Finally, there's no law against calling the company and ordering the latest annual report. Or, if you are computer literate, you can find a wealth of information on the company's Web site. The easiest way to get to the Web site is to bring up the financial section of the *New York Times* and enter the ticker symbol where it offers to give you a quote. When that comes on your screen, you will see a place to click on the company's Web site. Then click Investor Relations, and the rest is easy.

Once you sink your hard-earned cash into a stock, you will immediately start wondering when to sell. This is not an easy decision, but I think you should use the list of characteristics that I discussed above, such as the trend of earnings, the P/E ratio, and the return on equity. If your stock no longer measures up, it may be time to sell. Even so, the more you tinker with your holdings, the worse your performance will be. Buy and hold is the best strategy.

Twenty-One Ways to Reduce Investment Risk

No matter where you invest your money, there is always risk. Even bonds are not safe from inflation and rising interest rates. CDs also suffer from inflation. Stocks, as everyone knows, are regarded as the riskiest investments. However, they are also the most profitable—at least in the long run. In the short run, who knows what they will do.

Based on my long experience in the stock market, I have figured out twenty-one ways you can reduce this risk. Since I use most of them myself and for my clients, I have emerged from the recent bear market relatively intact. Since more bear markets are not out of the question, here are my thoughts on ways to mitigate your discomfort.

You will find some of these same ideas discussed in greater detail in other chapters of this book. This may seem repetitive, but sometimes repetition is one of the best ways to cram new knowledge into your gray matter. Here are the twenty-one ways to reduce your risk, presented for the first time:

1. The first rule of investing is *diversification.* Although most investors are aware of this concept, most do not know how to implement it. Of course, the most grievous blunder is to invest your whole portfolio in one stock. I have seen what this can do.

A few years ago, I met an architect after delivering a lecture. He had more than a million dollars invested in an obscure stock called Comdisco, which was selling around $30 a share. I convinced him to sell $300,000 worth and have me manage that portfolio, which is now worth about $500,000. Meanwhile, Comdisco climbed to $57 a share, which made the architect happy. However, by the end of 2001 it was worth only fifty-two cents a share, and my client had failed to sell it.

Still another investor came to me with all his money invested in WorldCom. He had bought the shares much lower and was well ahead of the game. He agreed to sell it all and have me manage his portfolio by buying twenty-five stocks. It's no secret what has happened to WorldCom.

When I was in Cleveland, I had the task of evaluating portfolios for a firm's clients. Almost without exception, these customers had some diversification. They often had twenty, thirty, or forty stocks, which is considered adequate. But most of these stocks were in three industries: oil, utilities, and banks. That's certainly a far cry from prudent diversification.

2. Not to be forgotten is asset allocation. This concept is similar to diversification, but it goes one step further. Instead of investing all your money in stocks, you should spread it around in such assets as bonds, foreign stocks, and money-market funds. No one knows what the market is going to do, so it makes sense to hedge your bets with prudent asset allocation. In the past three years, bonds have far outperformed stocks. That doesn't mean you should sell all your stocks and concentrate in bonds. Who knows? Now may be the time to be in stocks. Still, it pays to have some money in fixed-income assets, even if you think a new bull market is just ahead.

3. One way to measure whether a stock is overpriced is to calculate its price-earnings ratio (known as the P/E ratio). Simply divide the stock price by the company's most recent twelve-month earnings per share. P/E ratios can vary all the way from 10 to 100 or more. In most instances, a high ratio indicates a company with good prospects for the future. A low P/E ratio often means the company has a lackluster future. Although I am not suggesting that you stuff your portfolio with low P/E stocks, I am suggesting that you avoid stocks that are selling at very high P/E ratios. I would avoid any stock with a ratio of 40 or higher. In the long run, they don't do well. Many studies prove this point.

4. Many investors ignore real estate investment trusts, usually known as REITs. They look stodgy and dull and typically have a dividend yield of 5 percent or higher. In the past two years, REITs have not only avoided the debacle that has engulfed most other stocks, but they have also actually risen in value. That's because REITs act counter to the market. In a rising market, for instance, they would not do as well as growth stocks.

For my own part, I own several of them, such as Washington Real Estate Investment Trust and Equity Office Properties. REITs are not all alike. Some invest in apartment buildings, some in office buildings, and some in shopping malls. And there are others, as well. Most REITs are well diversified geographically.

5. In recent years, dividends have largely been ignored. Historically, however, dividends have played a prominent role in investing. Approximately half of the 11- or 12-percent annual return that investors enjoy can be attributed to dividends. Lately this has not been the case, as companies have tended to buy back their own shares, rather than pay out profits to shareholders. Even so, when I pick stocks, I look for a dividend and a history of regular increases. Stocks that pay a dividend are less likely to plunge in value than those that prefer to reinvest their profits in growth.

6. A strong balance sheet is an essential for a company that you want to consider. It's simply a relationship between the amount of debt as a percentage of capitalization. My preference is for 75 percent in equity (the book value of the common stock). A strong balance sheet makes it easier for the company to finance an acquisition. If you have access to *Value Line Investment Survey*, it's easy to find out this percentage.

7. If you elect to buy bonds, don't look for the highest yield. For one thing, a high yield is often characteristic of a weak company. When the yield gets too large, the bonds are referred to as "junk bonds." The safest bonds are those issued by the federal government. In today's market, you can't get much more of a return than 4 percent, and that's for bonds that mature in twenty or thirty years. Shorter maturities are as low as 3 percent or less. It's best to stick to maturities of five years or less. The reason is that the bond will sink like a stone if interest rates start climbing. This does not happen for bonds due in less than five years, since all you have to do is wait and you'll get the face value of the bond. A bond due in thirty years, by contrast, will drop, and you may not live long enough to get the face value.

8. In an effort to avoid the risk of owning stocks, some people think it pays to buy preferred stocks, convertible bonds, annuities, or commodities, or to sell short. None of these vehicles are recommended—at least not by me. Here's why:

• **Preferred stocks sound safe and sound? Not necessarily.** A preferred stock is somewhat like a bond, in that the dividend is paid regularly and never changes. But a preferred stock—unlike a bond—never matures. In other words, you can't get your money back by waiting for the maturity date. Unlike a common stock, the dividend will never be increased. But if the company has problems, the dividend can be cut. If interest rates go up, the value of a preferred stock will decline.

• **Convertible bonds** appeal to some investors because they have a higher yield than the same company's common stock. They can also be converted into the company's common stock. On the other hand, unless you really know what you are doing, you may find that the company calls in the convertible when it suits their purposes. If you are bound and determined to buy convertibles, I advise you to do it by investing in a mutual fund that is managed by professionals. Even so, I'm not so sure you will be a happy camper.

• **Annuities** are issued by insurance companies. There are two main types. The more conservative is invested in such things as bonds and mortgages. When you are ready to retire, the insurance company will set up a monthly payment plan that will assure you of the same amount each month until you die. Assuming you leave behind a husband or wife, the income will not continue to that survivor. However, if you are willing to take a smaller monthly payment, the company will continue paying that amount to your survivor until his or her death, too. Finally, insurance companies charge a pretty penny for their products, since they have to pay the agent for talking you into it.

• **Variable annuities** are another version of annuity, called "variable" since it is invested in common stocks and other assets of your choosing. Here again, the cost of these products is high. You would be better off buying a conventional mutual fund. The costs are usually about 1.5 percent a year.

• **If you are a speculator, you may find an interest in options, such as puts and calls, and many variations.** A call enables you to buy a particular common stock some weeks or months in the future at today's price. If the stock goes up substantially, this works out fine. But if it drops or advances only modestly, you lose the price of the option. "Puts" work for stocks that are expected to decline. But if they don't decline, you lose. In short, options are best avoided.

• **Commodities** have to do with speculating in such agricultural items as corn, wheat, soybeans, and pork bellies. It is possible to make a lot of money quickly in commodities. But very few people actually do because Mother Nature has a hand in your results. If you think a drought will help the price of your commodity, you might get rich—unless it starts raining, which can lead to a surplus and too much of that commodity, thus reducing prices drastically. This is no game for amateurs.

• **Selling short is similar to calls and puts.** If you think a stock is likely to decline in price, you can make money by selling short. You simply instruct your broker to borrow the shares from one of the firm's accounts. You then sell those shares at today's price. Let's say the stock is selling for $50 a share. Then, when the price drops to $30, you buy shares in the market and give them back to the investor who loaned them to you. Thus, you make a tidy profit of $20 a share. The catch is that the price may very well shoot up to $75, and what do you do then? If you buy back at this level, you lose $25 a share. There is no limit to the amount you can lose when you sell short. If you wait until the price goes to

$150, you lose $100 a share. This is not my idea of having fun.

9. The biggest problem with investing is its vast scope. There are thousands of mutual funds and tens of thousands of stocks, both domestic and foreign. A simple way to get rid of the clutter is to concentrate your investing on a small universe, the thirty stocks that make up the Dow Jones Industrial Average. They include such blue chips as General Electric, Johnson & Johnson, Procter & Gamble, ExxonMobil, and Coca-Cola. Over the years, the Dow has performed well, so why not buy all thirty stocks, rather than hunt under every rock looking for the stock that will make you a millionaire? Another advantage is knowing when to sell. My strategy is sell only when a stock is removed from the Index, about one stock a year. This cuts down on your capital gains taxes, since most of the stocks you remove from your portfolio are losers, not winners.

10. Some investors can't stand inaction. Instead of buying and holding, they insist on selling winners and holding losers. All you do that way is end up with a portfolio of losers. It's better to let your winners run. The more you buy and sell, the more taxes you will have to pay.

11. Be careful in selecting a stockbroker. Most people start with a traditional full-service firm, since their salespeople are aggressively seeking new clients. Brokerage firms can supply you with research material, but these firms rely heavily for their profits on investment banking and their analysts may not be impartial. For their part, the salespeople make their money from commissions, which are much higher than such discount firms as Schwab or Scottrade. Even worse, they tend to recommend products that have a high commission and limited prospects.

12. If you invest in stocks, avoid companies that are losing money. Instead, look for companies with a long history of profitable operation, with a rising trend in earnings per share. If you buy stocks that are losing money, you are a speculator, not an investor.

13. Stocks are traded on the New York Stock Exchange, the American Stock Exchange, and Nasdaq. The leading companies are usually listed on the New York Stock Exchange. Those traded elsewhere are less mature and often of lower quality.

14. If you buy mutual funds, make sure you examine the "expense ratio." Even no-load funds are not free. To pay the salary of analysts and other employees, along with expenses like advertising, rent, and travel, mutual funds subtract these costs from your profits. The average expense ratio is about 1.5 percent per year. Studies show that funds with the highest expense ratios perform worst, while those with the lowest perform the best.

15. Although I am not a fan of mutual funds, if advising on how to invest in them, I would say avoid those with new management. Before you invest, call the company and ask the age of the manager and how long he has been in charge. I would prefer a manager at least forty years of age and a tenure of at least five years.

16. Avoid stocks with excessively high yields, at least in relation to other companies in that industry. Those with high yields are often in trouble and are likely to cut their dividend.

17. Seek companies that are financially strong. This can be determined in two ways. Standard & Poor's rates stocks by letter. The highest rating is A+. An average rating is B+. Avoid those with a rating below B+. *Value Line* uses a similar rating, but its highest rating is A++, and an average one is B++. Again, don't go below B++.

18. Examine the dividend payout ratio. It's calculated by dividing the annual dividend by the annual earnings per share for the past twelve months. If the dividend is $1, and the earnings per share are $4, the payout ratio would be 25 percent. That signifies a company that is plowing back earnings into research, new products, stock repurchase, debt reduction, or acquisitions. If the payout ratio is high, let's say 75 percent, this is an indication that that the company has limited growth potential.

19. The economy has an impact on most companies, but there are some industries that are considered cyclical, such as chemicals, autos, appliances, machinery, metals and mining, paper, and railroads. Most of these have limited long-term growth. The only way to make money is by buying them when they are in trouble and selling them when money is rolling in. It's not that easy to be able to jump in and out with any consistency. Instead of cyclical stocks, concentrate on industries that are more stable, such as food processors, banks, REITs, utilities, food supermarkets, life insurance, medical supplies, and household products.

20. When a major company buys another major company, avoid the buyer. A good case in point is the purchase of Compaq by Hewlett-Packard. Rarely is there an exception to this rule.

21. Most investors are busy people, such as doctors, accountants, executives, and business owners. That means their time is limited. Even so, some time must be allotted for reading annual reports, the *Wall Street Journal, BusinessWeek,* and *Value Line.* To be a successful investor, you have to know how the game is played. This should also include reading at least one book on investing every year. I'll send you a list of good books if you call me or send me an e-mail (for contact information, see "About the Author" on page 362). I will also include a list of great books on other topics, such as biographies.

Basic Terminology

If you are new to the investment arena, you may have difficulty understanding parts of this book. To get you over the rough spots, I have listed some common expressions that appear frequently in books on investing. You will also encounter them in the *Wall Street Journal, Forbes, BusinessWeek, Barron's*, and other periodicals devoted to investing.

This is not a glossary but merely a brief list of terms essential to understanding this book. If you would like a more complete glossary, refer to either of my previous books: *Safe Investing* (Simon & Schuster, 1991) or *Straight Talk About Stock Investing* (McGraw-Hill, 1995).

Analyst

In nearly every one of the 100 articles, you will note that I refer to "analysts" and what they think about the prospects for a particular stock. Analysts are individuals who have special training in analyzing stocks. Typically, they have such advanced degrees as M.B.A. or C.F.A. Many of them work for brokerage houses, but they may work for banks, insurance companies, mutual funds, pension plans, or other institutions. Most analysts specialize in one or two industries. A good analyst can tell you nearly everything there is to know about a particular stock or the industry it's part of.

However, analysts can be dead wrong about the future action of a stock. The reason: surprises. Companies are constantly changing, which means they are acquiring, divesting, developing new products, restructuring, buying back their shares, and so forth. When they make a change and announce this change to Wall Street, the surprise can change the course of the stock. In short, analysts can be helpful, but don't bet the store on what they tell you.

As you can see, analysts are usually intelligent, hardworking, and conscientious. Even so, they don't always succeed in guiding you to riches. Perhaps the biggest beef most people have is the tie that analysts have to the companies they follow. They know these people well and may be reluctant to say anything negative.

One reason for this is economic. Most brokerage firms make a ton of money from their investment banking division. If the analyst antagonizes the company, that company may give its investment banking business to a firm that says nice things rather than pointing out its warts and all.

This reluctance to see no evil and speak no evil can be seen when you examine the number of times that analysts advise investors to sell. According to the research firm First Call, more than 70 percent of the 27,000 recommendations outstanding in November 2000 were strong buys or buys. Fewer than 1 percent were sells or strong sells. To recap: Of the 27,000 recommendations, 26.6 percent were holds, 36.8 percent were buys, 35.7 percent were strong buys, and a mere 0.9 percent were sells or strong sells. I rest my case.

Annual Report

If you own a common stock, you can be certain that you will receive a fancy annual report a couple of months after the close of the year. If the year ends December 31, look for your annual report in March or April. If the fiscal year ends some other time of the year, such as September 30, the annual report will appear in your mailbox two or three months later.

Not all investors read annual reports, but they might be better off if they did. Although most companies will not list their problems, you can usually get a pretty good idea how things are going. In particular, read the report by the president or CEO. It's usually one, two, or three pages long and is written in language you can understand.

If you want detailed information on the company's various businesses, the annual report will often overwhelm you with details that may be difficult to fathom. If you are really curious about what they are trying to say, feel free to call the investor contact. I have provided the phone number of this person for all 100 stocks listed. Have a list of questions ready, and call during the person's lunch hour, leaving your name and phone number. This sneaky little strategy means the cost of the call back will be paid by the company, not you. By the way, don't assume you will be intimidated by the investor contact. Investor contacts are usually quite personable and helpful.

Argus Research Company

Argus is an independent research organization that provides information on stocks to institutions, such as brokerage houses, banks, mutual funds, and banks. It is normally not available to individual investors. However, you may be able to obtain *Argus* reports through your broker. You will note that I have quoted liberally from *Argus* in the analysis of my 100 stocks. You should be able to obtain this information from a brokerage house, such as Charles Schwab & Company. Analysts with *Argus* typically revise their reports quite often, depending on changes in earnings and important developments.

Asset Allocation

This is not the same as diversification. Rather, it refers to the strategy of allocating your investment funds among different types of investments, such as stocks, bonds, or money-market funds. In the long run, you will be better off with all of your assets concentrated in common stocks. In the short run, this may not be true, since the market occasionally has a sinking spell. A severe one, such as that of 2000–2002, can cause your holdings to decline in value by 20 percent or more. To protect against this, most investors spread their money around. They may, for instance, allocate 50 percent to stocks, 40 percent to bonds, and 10 percent to a money-market fund. A more realistic breakdown might be 70 percent in stocks, 25 percent in bonds, and 5 percent in a money-market fund.

Balance Sheet

All corporations issue at least two financial statements: the balance sheet and the income statement. Both are important. The balance sheet is a financial picture of the company on a specific date, such as December 31 or at the end of a quarter.

On the left side of the balance sheet are the company's assets, such as cash, current assets, inventories, accounts receivable, and buildings. On the right side are its liabilities, including accounts payable and long-term debt. Also on the right side is shareholders' equity. The right side of the balance sheet adds up to the same value as the left side, which is why it is called a balance sheet.

In most instances, corporations give you figures for the current year and the prior year. By examining the changes, you can get an idea of whether the company's finances are improving or deteriorating.

Bonds

Entire books have been written on the various kinds of bonds. A bond, unlike a stock, is not a form of ownership. A bond is a contractual agreement that means you have loaned money to some entity and that entity has agreed to pay you a certain sum of money (interest) every six months until that bond matures. At that time, you will also get back the money you originally invested—no more, no less. Most bonds are issued in $1,000 denominations. The safest bonds are those issued by the U.S. government. The two advantages of bonds are safety and income. If you wait until the maturity date, you will be assured of getting the face value of the bond. In the meantime, however, the bond will fluctuate, because of changes in interest rates or the creditworthiness of the corporation. Long-term bonds, moreover, fluctuate far more than short-term bonds. But enough about bonds. This book is about stocks.

Capital Gains

When you buy common stocks, you expect to make money in two ways: capital gains and dividends. Over an extended period of time, about half of your total return will come from each sector. If the stock rises in value and you sell it above your cost, you are enjoying a capital gain. The tax on long-term capital gains is a maximum of 15 percent if the stock is held for twelve months.

Chief Executive Officer (CEO)

This is the executive of a company who reports to the board of directors. That corporate body can terminate the CEO if he or she fails to do an effective job of managing the company. In some instances, the CEO may also have the title of either president or chairman of the board, or both.

Closed-End Investment Company

A managed investment portfolio, similar to a mutual fund, a closed-end investment company is generally traded on a stock exchange. The price fluctuates with supply and demand, not because of changes in the assets within the trust. An open-end investment trust, or mutual fund changes in size as investors buy new shares or surrender their shares for cash. A closed-end trust, by contrast, does not permit new money to be invested, nor can shares be redeemed by the company. Thus, the number of shares remains the same once the trust begins trading. One feature of the closed-end trust is worth mentioning: They often sell at a discount to their asset value. An open-end trust always sells at precisely its asset value.

Common Stocks

We might as well define what a common stock is, since this whole book is devoted to them. All publicly owned companies—those that trade their shares outside of a small group of executives or the founding family—are based on common stocks. A common stock is evidence of partial ownership in a corporation. Most of the stocks described in this book have millions of shares of their stock outstanding, and the really large ones may have in excess of 100 million shares. When you own common stock, there are no guarantees. If the company is successful, it will probably pay a dividend four times a year. These dividends may be raised periodically, perhaps once a year. If, however, the company has problems, it may cut or eliminate its dividend. This can happen even to a major company, such as IBM, Goodyear, or General Motors. As I said, there are no guarantees.

Investors who own common stock can sell their shares at any time. All you do is call your broker, and the trade is executed a few minutes later at the prevailing price—which fluctuates nearly every day, sometimes by a few cents or sometimes two or three points.

Current Ratio

The current ratio is calculated by dividing current assets by current liabilities. Current assets include any assets that will become cash within one year, including cash itself. Current liabilities are those that will be paid off within a year. A current ratio of 2 is considered ideal. Most companies these days have a current ratio of less than 2.

Diversification

Since investments are inherently risky, it pays to spread the risk by diversifying. If you don't, you may be too heavily invested in a stock or bond that turns sour. Even well-known stocks such as Alcoa, International Paper, Eastman Kodak, and American Express can experience occasional sinking spells.

To be on the safe side, don't invest more than 5 percent of your portfolio in any one stock. In addition, don't invest too heavily in any one sector of the economy. A good strategy is to divide stocks among ten sectors: drugs and health care, industrials, materials, energy, telecommunications, utilities, consumer staples, consumer discretionary, financials, and information technology.

Here's a rule of thumb that will keep you out of trouble: Invest at least 4 percent in each sector but not more than 12 percent. That means that you should own at least ten stocks so that you have representation in all ten sectors.

Dividends

Unlike bonds, which pay interest, common stocks may pay a dividend. Most dividends are paid quarterly, but there is no set date that all corporations use. Some, for instance, may pay on January 1, March 1, July 1, and September 1. Another company may pay on February 10, May 10, August 10, and November 10. If you want to receive checks every month, you will have to make sure you buy stocks that pay dividends at different times of the year. The Standard & Poor's *Stock Guide* is a source for this information, as is the *Value Line Investment Survey*. Most companies like to pay the same dividend every quarter until they can afford to increase it. Above all, they don't like to cut their dividends, since investors who depend on this income will sell their shares, and the stock will decline in price. If you use good judgment in selecting your stocks, you can expect that your companies will increase their dividends nearly every year.

Dividend Payout

If a company earns $4 a share in a twelve-month period and pays out $3 to shareholders in the form of dividends, it has a payout ratio of 75 percent. However, if it pays only $1, the payout ratio is 25 percent. In the past, many investors looked favorably on a low payout ratio. The thinking was that such a company was plowing back its earnings into such projects as research, new facilities, acquisitions, and new equipment. It sounds logical.

Now, there is evidence that you are better off buying a company with a higher payout ratio. Mark Hulbert, who writes frequently for the Sunday *New York Times*, has come up with some studies that focus on this concept. According to work done by Michael C. Jensen, currently an emeritus professor of business administration at the Harvard Business School, "The more cash that companies have now (beyond what is needed for current projects), the less efficient they will be in the future."

Two other scholars concur that a higher payout ratio serves investors better than a low one. They are Robert D. Arnott of First Quadrant and Clifford S. Asness of AQR Capital Management. For one thing, they found that "For the overall stock market between 1871 and 2001, corporate profits grew fastest in the ten years following the calendar year in which companies had the highest average dividend payout ratio." What's more, their study showed that in the period from 1946 to 1991, there was a strong correlation that demonstrates conclusively that companies with a high payout ratio performed far better than the ones who were stingy with their dividend distributions.

Mr. Hulbert concludes that "The common theme that emerges from these various studies is a very unflattering portrait of corporate management: give executives lots of rope and they too often end up hanging themselves. It would appear that a high dividend payout ratio is an effective way to reduce the length of that rope."

Dividend Reinvestment Plans

Unless you are retired, you might like to reinvest your dividends in more shares. Many companies have a dividend reinvestment plan (also known as a DRIP) that will allow you to do this, and the charge for this service is often minimal. Most of these companies also allow you to mail in additional cash, which will be used to purchase new shares, again at minimal cost.

In recent years, a few companies have created "direct" dividend reinvestment plans. Unlike most plans, direct plans enable you to buy your initial shares directly from the company. To alert you to which companies have direct plans, I have inserted the word *direct*. Companies with such plans include ExxonMobil, McDonald's, Procter & Gamble, Merck, and Lilly. Incidentally, you can rarely buy just one share. Many companies have a minimum purchase amount, such as $500.

This may sound like a good way to avoid paying brokerage commissions, but there are some drawbacks to bear in mind. For one thing, you can't time your purchases, since it may be a week or more before your purchase is made.

Even worse is calculating your cost basis for tax purposes. By the time you sell, you may have made scores of small investments in the same stock, each with a different cost basis. Make sure you keep a file for each company so that you can make these calculations when the time comes. Or, better still, don't sell.

Dollar-Cost Averaging

Dollar-cost averaging is a systematic way to invest money over a long period, such as ten, fifteen, or twenty years. It entails investing the same amount of money regularly, such as each month or each quarter. If you do this faithfully, you will be buying more stock when the price is lower and less stock when the price is higher. This tends to smooth out the gyrations of the market. Dollar-cost averaging is often used with a mutual fund, but it can just as easily be done with a company that has a dividend reinvestment plan (DRIP).

Income Statement

Most investors are more interested in the income statement than they are in the balance sheet. They are particularly interested in the progress (or lack of it) in earnings per share (EPS). The income statement lists such items as net sales, cost of sales, interest expense, and gross profit. As with the balance sheet, it makes sense to compare this year's numbers with those of the prior year.

Inflation-Indexed Treasury Bonds

Conventional bonds—those that pay a fixed rate of return, such as 5 percent—have one big drawback: They are vulnerable to rising interest rates. For example, if you buy a bond that promises to pay you 5 percent for the next fifteen or twenty years, you will lose principal if interest rates climb to 7 percent. The reason is that new bonds being issued give investors a much better return. Thus, those that pay only 5 percent will sag in price until they hit a level that equates them to the new bonds that pay 7 percent. The loss of principal, moreover, is much greater with long-term bonds, such as those due in fifteen, twenty, or thirty years.

By contrast, short-term bonds, those coming due in three or four years, are much less volatile because you can often hold the bonds until the maturity date. Thus, you are certain to receive the full face value. Of course, you can do the same thing with a twenty-year bond, but twenty years is a long time.

The way to beat this disadvantage is to buy the relatively new bonds being issued by the U.S. government, since they are indexed to inflation. For this reason, you are unlikely to lose principal. To be sure, they pay less initially, currently 3.8 percent. But the ultimate return may be much better if inflation continues to impact the economy.

Suppose you invested $1,000 in inflation bonds at the current yield of 3.8 percent. If consumer prices rose 2.5 percent over the next year, your principal would climb to $1,025, and you would earn interest equal to 3.8 percent on this growing sum. Thus, if you spent the interest but didn't cash in any bonds, you would enjoy a rising stream of income while keeping your principal's spending power intact.

One thing to bear in mind is that with inflation-indexed treasury bonds, you have to pay federal income taxes each year on both the interest you earn and also the increase in the bonds' principal value. One way to take the sting out of this tax is to use these bonds in a tax-deferred account, such as an IRA.

Despite the tax implications, inflation bonds may be useful outside an IRA. Because these bonds don't perform as erratically as conventional bonds, they can be a good place to park money you may need if something unexpected comes along, such as a medical bill not fully covered by insurance. If inflation-indexed bonds ring a bell, ask the teller at your bank to get you started. She won't charge you a fee, and there is no red tape.

Investment Advisor

Investors who do not have the time or inclination to manage their own portfolios may elect to employ an investment advisor. Most advisors charge 1 percent a year. Thus, if you own stocks worth $300,000, your annual fee would be $3,000. Advisors differ from brokers, since they do not profit from changes. Brokers, by contrast, charge a commission on each transaction, which means they profit from changes in your portfolio. Advisors profit only when the value of your holdings increases. For instance, if the value of your portfolio increases to $500,000, the annual fee will be $5,000. You, of course, will be $200,000 richer.

Moving Average

Some investors use the moving average to time the market. The strategy is to buy a stock when it is selling above its moving average and sell when it falls below. A popular moving average is the 200-day version. A dotted line is drawn, taking the average price of the stock over the previous 200 days. The actual price of the stock is plotted on the same graph. Studies show that this method of timing the market does not work on a consistent basis.

PEG Ratio

The PEG ratio is supposed to be helpful in determining if a stock is too expensive. It is calculated by dividing the price-earnings ratio by the expected earnings growth rate. Let's say the P/E ratio of American International Group is 34.39, which is calculated by dividing the price ($98) by the expected EPS in 2001 of $2.85. Meanwhile, the earnings per share in the 1989–1999 period expanded from $0.67 to $2.18, a compound annual growth rate of 12.52 percent. When you divide 34.39 by 12.52, the PEG ratio is 2.75. According to Michael Sivy, a writer for *Money* magazine, "Stocks with a PEG ratio of 1.5 or less are often the best buys."

By that rule, you would avoid American International Group. Curiously, Mr. Sivy includes AIG on his list of "100 Stocks for Long-Term Investors," published in January 2001. By his calculation, AIG had a PEG ratio at that time of 2.5.

Once again, I am a doubting Thomas. Who is to say what a company's future growth rate will be? You can easily determine what it has been in the past. And that may give you some indication of the future, but it is far from reliable. The P/E ratio is also a slippery number, since you are expected to base it on the EPS for the year ahead. I prefer to base it on the most recent twelve months, since that is a figure that does not depend on a crystal ball.

Preferred Stock

The name sounds impressive. In actual practice, owning preferred stocks is about as exciting as watching your cat take a bath. A preferred stock is much like a bond. It pays the same dividend year in and year out. The yield is usually higher than a common stock. If the company issuing the preferred stock does well, you do not benefit. If it does poorly, however, you may suffer, since the dividend could be cut or eliminated.

Price-Earnings Ratio (P/E)

This is a term that is extremely important. Don't make the mistake of overlooking it. Whole books have been written on the importance of the P/E ratio, which is sometimes referred to as "the P/E" or "the multiple."

The P/E ratio tells you whether a stock is cheap or expensive. It is calculated by dividing the price of the stock by the company's earnings per share over the most recent twelve months. For instance, if you refer to the *Stock Guide,* you will see that Leggett and Platt had earnings of $2.23. At the time, the stock was selling for $52. Divide that figure by $2.23, and you get a P/E of 23.32.

A high P/E ratio tends to indicate a stock with good prospects for the future. However, this evaluation tends to be overdone. In an article written by Mark Hulbert for the *New York Times* on January 25, 2004, Mr. Hulbert said, "Although the stock market is not as expensive as it was in 2000, it has many 'pockets of craziness,' in the view of Josef Lakonishok, a finance professor at the University of Illinois at Urbana-Champaign.

Professor Lakonishok bases his assessment on a historical study that found that companies trading at high price-to-earnings ratios almost never grow as quickly as they need to justify their valuations."

The study was conducted by the above professor and two other academics. Mr. Hulbert went on to say, "The professors concluded that very high P/E ratios were hardly ever justified."

Profit Margins

Profit margins fall into two categories: Net Profit Margin and Operating Profit Margin.

Net Profit Margin is simply net income divided by sales. It measures profitability after all expenses and taxes have been paid—and after all accounting adjustments have been made.

Operating Profit Margin is operating income divided by sales. It measures profitability after only those expenses related to current operations have been paid.

Reverse Stock Split

Stock splits are normally a happy occasion. If you have 100 shares of a stock selling for $80 a share, the company may announce a two-for-one stock split. In due course, you will have 200 shares, each worth $40. You are no richer, but you may be happier.

A reverse stock split, however, is *not* good news. If you have 200 shares of a stock selling for $1.25, the company may be contemplating upgrading your shares by announcing a reverse stock split. They will issue new shares worth, say, ten times as much. Now you have only twenty shares, each one worth $12.50. Again, you are no richer. But you may be unhappy. You should be. Studies show that a reverse stock split is a bad omen.

In July 1997, the *Journal of Business* measured all reverse stock splits from 1926 to 1991. The authors were two professors of accounting, Hemang A. Desai of Southern Methodist University and Prem C. Jain of

Georgetown. According to an article in the *New York Times* by Mark Hulbert (dated November 3, 2002), "They found that, over the year after the announcement, the average stock undergoing a reverse stock split performed 8.5 percent worse than the stock market."

Mr. Hulbert explained why some companies resort to this device. "David L. Ikenberry, a finance professor at the University of Illinois at Urbana-Champaign, and Sundaresh Ramnath, an accounting professor at Georgetown, have developed a theory that does explain it. They believe that when management lacks confidence in its company's stock, it is more likely to use a reverse split. By contrast, they say, if management believes that the low price is just temporary, it will be more likely to leave the stock alone."

Standard & Poor's Stock Reports

S&P is a major provider of financial information, primarily to institutions, such as stock brokers, mutual funds, and banks. However, individuals can tap into this information by requesting a "tear sheet" on almost any stock. You will note that I have quoted liberally from *Standard & Poor's* in the analysis of my 100 stocks. S&P stock tear sheets are revised quite frequently, depending on earnings changes and important developments.

Stock Split

Corporations know that investors like to invest in lower-priced stocks. Thus, when the price of the stock gets to a certain level, which varies with the company, they will split the stock. For instance, if the stock is $75, they might split it three-for-one. Your original 100 shares now become 300 shares. Unfortunately, your 300 shares are worth exactly the same as your original 100 shares. What it amounts to is this: Splits please small investors, but they don't make them any richer. One company, Berkshire Hathaway, has never been split. It is now worth a huge amount per share: over $70,000. It also pays no dividend. The company is run by the legendary Warren Buffett and has made a lot of people very wealthy without a stock split or dividend.

Technician

There are two basic ways to analyze stocks. One is *fundamental;* the other is *technical.*

Fundamental analysts examine a stock's management, sales and earnings potential, research capabilities, new products, competitive strength, balance sheet strength, dividend growth, political developments, and industry conditions.

Technicians, by contrast, rarely consider any of these fundamental factors. They rely on charts and graphs and a host of other arcane statistical factors, such as point-and-figure charts, breadth indicators, head-and-shoulders formations, relative strength ratings, and the 200-day-moving average. This technical jargon is often difficult for the average investor to fathom. The fundamental approach predominates among professional portfolio managers, although some institutions may also employ a technician.

The question is, Do technicians have the key to stock picking or predicting the trend of the market? Frankly, I am a skeptic, as are most academic analysts. Among the nonbelievers is Kenneth L. Fisher, the longtime columnist for *Forbes* magazine whom I mentioned earlier. His columns are among my favorites. Here is what Mr. Fisher says about technicians: "One of the questions I hear most often is, 'Can charts really predict stock prices?' Naturally, there is only one answer: a flat 'No.'"

Mr. Fisher goes on to say, "There is virtually nothing in theory or empiricism to indicate anyone can predict stock prices based solely on prior stock price action.

Nevertheless, a big world of chartists continues to exist, amplified by recent Internet day trading. Yet the world of investors with long-lasting success is devoid of them."

Such eminently successful portfolio managers as Peter Lynch and Warren Buffett, for instance, don't resort to charts and other technical mumbo jumbo.

Value Line Investment Survey

Value Line provides one-page reports on about seventeen hundred stocks. It is normally available in brokerage houses and libraries. You will note that I have quoted liberally from *Value Line* in the analysis of my 100 stocks. Although *Value Line* is too expensive for most individual investors, the company does have a much less expensive version that covers 600 major corporations. Stocks are revised by *Value Line* every three months.

Yield

If your company pays a dividend, you can relate this dividend to the price of the stock to calculate the yield. A $50 stock that pays a $2 annual dividend (which amounts to 50 cents per quarter) will have a yield of 4 percent. You arrive at this figure by dividing $2 by $50. Actually, you don't have to make this calculation, since the yield is given to you in the stock tables of the *Wall Street Journal*. Here are some typical yields: Coca-Cola, 1.5 percent; ExxonMobil, 2.0 percent; General Electric, 1.3 percent; Illinois Tool Works, 1.2 percent; Kimberly-Clark, 1.8 percent; and 3M Company, 2.0 percent. Although the yield is of some importance, you should not judge a stock by its yield without looking at many other factors.

Yield Curve

The yield curve is a graphic representation of yields on U. S. Treasury securities. Most of the time, the yield is less on short-term debt and higher on bonds that mature ten or fifteen years from now. If this difference is represented by a graph, you will see a curve going to the right of the graph, gradually rising as it proceeds toward the future.

Ordinarily, short-term bonds carry lower yields to reflect the fact that an investor's money is under lower risk. The longer you tie up money, the theory goes, the more you should be rewarded for the extra risk you are taking. After all, who knows what's going to happen over the next two or three decades? In that period, there may be such developments as high inflation, a recession, or devastation from war.

If this curve does not act in this way, it is referred to as an "Inverted Yield Curve." Such a curve means that short-term rates are higher than long-term rates. Analysts tend to think an inverted yield curve is a sign of a pending recession. In May of 2005, the curve was approaching an inverted status. The difference between short-term rates (overnight federal funds rates) and long-term rates on 10-year Treasury notes was only 112 basis points (or just over 1 percent). By contrast, in June of 2004, the spread was more normal, at 387 basis points, or close to 4 percent.

Although analysts are cautious when they see a flat or inverted yield curve, at least one observer did not agree. "Be careful how you interpret a very narrow yield curve in the context of structural forces that may have flattened it," said former Fed Governor Laurence Meyer in early June 2005. "It doesn't mean the same thing that it used to mean."

How to Choose a Broker

According to my wife and family, I'm a compulsive book-buyer. Even though I already own several hundred books, (including three encyclopedia sets) on such topics as baseball, tennis, philosophy, economics, politics, biography, geography, the Supreme Court, medicine, Greek, Roman, and American history, and U.S. presidents, I still buy more. It all started in high school when I bought a used edition of *The Harvard Classics* for $25. They are still unread.

However, I rarely buy a book without considerable study and investigation (unless it's at a library sale or garage sale). Usually, I cruise around Barnes & Noble and pick up books that appear interesting and then settle down in one of their incredibly comfortable overstuffed chairs to read a few pages here and there. And I also read the biography inside the back cover to see if the author has good credentials. If I go through a half dozen books while I am making these assessments, I rarely buy more than one book, and sometimes none.

Of course, I am not the only bookworm in Barnes & Noble who is hunkered down with a book or two under consideration. I rarely notice what they are reading, but one day I was caught by surprise when I noticed a auburn-haired lady in her midthirties who was studiously absorbed in a copy of *The 100 Best Stocks You Can Buy.* She seemed intent on giving the book a thorough going-over. I was hesitant to interrupt her perusal, for fear she might not buy the book. And so I went back to studying the books piled in front of me.

Finally, I could not restrain myself any longer. I said, "I see you are reading a book on investing. Would you like me to introduce you to the author?"

She looked up in amazement. "You mean the author lives in Vermont? And you know him personally?"

"Well, not exactly," I said. "I happen to be John Slatter. But don't let me disturb you from examining my book. I need all the customers I can get so that the publisher will keep sending me royalty checks. So far, the book has been selling well for the past ten years, and I am currently working on the next edition."

"I can't believe you are the author. Do you have a business card? I'm a tough person to convince."

When she had examined my card, she said, "I like your introductory chapters, but there is one that seems to be missing. I haven't come across one on how to pick a broker. I am new to the investment game, and I haven't the faintest idea how to find someone that I could have confidence in."

"After ten years of writing my book, I seem to have neglected to provide that information. Is now a good time to give you a few ideas on that subject?" I asked her.

"Are you trying to tell me that a busy author like you is willing to spend his time to indoctrinate a total novice and do it free of charge?"

"Before I begin, it might be helpful if I knew your name, since you already know mine."

"Oh, I'm sorry; my name is Valletta Hamamett. I'm a nurse, and this is my day off."

"Let me tell you how I picked a company to put a new roof on my house," I told her. "That will give you a hint on how my mind works. Whenever I need someone to fix a problem in our house, I call a pal down the street who is also a client of mine. I'll call him Fred. In this instance, Fred called a roofer who does work for him. Fred happens to own a lot of rental real estate, so he has a stable of plumbers, electricians, carpenters, and the like. When I call these people and tell them Fred recommended them, they usually come to my rescue. On this occasion, the man never called. Of course, it was early August, and he probably was already swamped with work, so he never got around to me.

Next, I checked with some of my neighbors, mostly those I have met when I jog along Beech Street getting some exercise. Mostly, they are out walking their dogs, and they notice me and strike up a conversation. One lady said she had had her roof replaced a couple years earlier and was satisfied with the results. I called the roofing contractor she recommended and got a quote for $12,800. That seemed too high, so I next talked to my next-door neighbor who was in the midst of having his roof replaced. I accosted the person in charge and told him my roof was in dire straits, and that I would like to get an idea of what he could do to alleviate my predicament. He said he would come over to my house later that afternoon. Over the next three weeks, he failed to make an appearance. I was beginning to get desperate.

"I checked with my friend Fred again, and he gave me another name. I called him and left my name on his answering device but got no response. A week or so later I called him again and finally got to talk to him. He said he was too busy but gave me the name of his cousin, and he promised he would make an appraisal and give me a quote. I am still waiting.

"I was about ready to burn down my house and collect on the insurance when I had a lucky break. One of my neighbors had recently sold their house and moved to New Mexico. One Saturday morning, I decided I had better introduce myself and welcome the new family into the community. During the conversation, I happened to mention that I was about to burn down my house, and he gasped in disbelief—apparently he was unaware that I was joking. When I told him my problem, he immediately said, 'Heavens, I am sure I can solve your problem. My good friend and former partner, Clint Sandhaven, is an experienced, capable roofer. I'll have him give you a call.'"

At that point, Valletta interrupted. She said, "That's quite a tale of frustration, Mr. Slatter. I hope getting a broker is not that difficult."

"I haven't quite finished my story, Valletta. Let me continue. A few days later, Clint called and made an appointment with my wife and me. We were both convinced beyond the shadow of a doubt that Clint Sandhaven was our man. His price was a couple thousand lower than the other guy, and his whole manner impressed us to the extent that we now have a new roof—and my insurance company is unaware of my plans to resort to the torch on our dandy five-bedroom abode."

"I'm beginning to get the idea that I should not pick a broker by leafing through the yellow pages," said Valletta Hamamett.

"Exactly. And another thing. Don't deal with a rookie who calls you on the telephone. Such brokers have a purchased list of prospects in front of them and are 'cold calling' one after another, looking for clients. You don't need someone who is just getting started in the business. I assume you have friends or associates who are investors. Talk with them and find out if they have enjoyed good results with brokers who are not trying to sell you a mutual fund or some product their company has dreamed up that has a fat sales commission tied into it. What you want is a broker who deals in stocks and not one who tries to sell you something else or who tries to convince you that you should have your portfolio managed on a fee basis, which is often 2 percent or so."

"You are right, Mr. Slatter. I do know a number of people who are investing in the stock market. I'm an RN, so I know nurses and doctors who might give me some ideas. Anything else?"

"Yes, there is one more decision you have to make, Valletta. There are two types of brokers. The better known are full-service brokers, such as Edward Jones, Smith Barney, UBS Financial, A. G. Edwards, and Wachovia Securities. Most people start with a full-service broker since they have a staff of brokers who are well-trained and are willing to answer your questions and offer suggestions on how to build a portfolio.

"The advantages of dealing with a full-service broker are several. For one thing, the brokerage firm usually has a staff of research analysts who can provide reports on stocks you may have an interest in. Secondly, their account executives may be quite knowledgeable and experienced. On the negative side, the cost of doing business with them is quite high, often two or three hundred dollars per trade, with a minimum of at least $50.

"The other type of broker is quite different. They are called discount brokers and include ScotTrade, Charles Schwab, E*Trade, Ameritrade, and Fidelity. And there are scores of others.

"The chief advantage of a discount broker is the low cost of buying or selling a stock, often $25 or less. ScotTrade is at the low end, only $7, regardless of the number of shares involved in the trade. The disadvantages are primarily an absence of a research department. In addition, you won't get much sophisticated help from your account executive. They will execute your trade and answer questions concerning how to make trades on the Internet, which is typically less costly than on the phone or in person.

"If you are in doubt as to which route to take, there's no reason why you can't have a full-service broker as well as a discount broker. In my own case, I have an account with Wachovia Securities and two discount brokers: Schwab and Fidelity."

"I am beginning to get an understanding of what's out there, Mr. Slatter. But before you head downstairs to pay for your books, can you outline again what I should look for when I select a full-service broker? I forgot to take notes."

"Glad to. Here are the types of broker to avoid:

- Those who sell mostly mutual funds, rather than stocks.
- Those who are new in the business. Make sure the broker you select has at least five years of experience.
- Those who call you once or twice a month with the hot stock of the week. You are better off making your own selections.
- Those who tell you that you need a professional adviser on a fee basis. The annual fee for such advisory firms is often 2 percent per year, and your portfolio is rarely managed with you in mind. It is typically invested in the same stocks that everyone else is getting. Even worse, such portfolios are not likely to outperform the market—at least not on a consistent basis—particularly when you take the 2 percent fee into account."

"On a more positive note, what you want is a broker who will alert you to poor diversification in your list of holdings. There are ten sectors in the economy—at least according to Standard & Poor's—and you should invest in a minimum of six or seven sectors, or better still, all ten. The sectors include:

1. *Industrials*, such as United Technologies, Caterpillar, and General Electric.
2. *Utilities*, such as Piedmont Natural Gas, FPL Group, and MDU Resources.
3. *Telephone*, such as Alltel, Verizon, and BellSouth.
4. *Financials*, such as Bank of America, Kimco Realty, and Washington REIT.
5. *Consumer Staples*, such as PepsiCo, McCormick, and Procter & Gamble.
6. *Consumer Discretionary*, such as Home Depot, and Staples.
7. *Materials*, such Bemis, Praxair, and Ecolab.
8. *Drugs and Health*, such as Eli Lilly, Pfizer, and Medtronic.
9. *Information Technology*, such as Intel, IBM, and Microsoft.
10. *Energy*, such as ExxonMobil, Chevron, and Devon Energy."

After listening to my lengthy and erudite lecture on investing and sector diversification, Valletta Hamamett said, "I can't thank you enough, Mr. Slatter, for such a professional and interesting lesson in common stock investing. If I follow your advice, I should be able to be one of the few nurses in Vermont who can retire with a million-dollar portfolio. Now, I am wondering whether I really need to buy a copy of your book. For the time being at least, I think I'll return it to the shelf."

A Novel Approach to Asset Allocation

I'm not sure whether my neighborhood is characteristic of Vermont as a whole, but Beech Street in Essex Junction seems to teem with dog-walkers. One dog-walker, in particular, is a real puzzle. The lady who leads this little canine is an attractive widow who looks younger than her fifty-eight years.

But Brutus Kutch III, her little overwrought monster, is about as big as an *Alley Cat Felis domestica*. I am convinced this diminutive wretch is bent on having me for lunch. As soon as he sees me—even from a block away—he starts to yap with ferocity and petulance. Apparently, he is convinced that I am guilty of some heinous crime. Fortunately, the other dogs in the area are unaware of my crimes against the family *Canidae*, since rarely do any of them bare their fangs or utter a word of discontent when I encounter them on my daily walk through the streets of Essex Junction.

I have not tried petting Brutus (I value my hands), but I have offered him some delicious morsels of fancy dog food. But to no avail—I am still his mortal enemy. It's too bad, because I enjoy chatting with Alice Hardleigh, the lady at the other end of the leash who lives nearby on Taffeta Trail. She tells me that Brutus is the only Mongolian toy mastiff in Chittenden County. That's certainly good news!

One day, when Brutus had finally calmed down after Ms. Hardleigh held the little cuss in her arms, she said, "Mr. Slatter, I have been reading your book, but I'm not sure how I should set up my portfolio. I wonder whether you could have lunch with me at the Lincoln Inn sometime and get me headed in the right direction."

"I assume you'll bring Brutus with you," I said.

"Only if you insist. He's never liked the Lincoln Inn."

Once the waiter had taken our orders for Diet Cokes, Alice opened the conversation about her situation. (She doesn't like me to call her Ms. Hardleigh but persists in addressing me as Mr. Slatter. It must be my gray hair. Hers is auburn, with no trace of old age.)

"I know you have a chapter in your book on asset allocation, but somehow I thought I would feel more comfortable getting your thoughts on my particular situation. Does that make sense?"

"Everyone is different, Alice. I assume that your late husband left you with adequate finances. Can you give me an idea of what your holdings are?"

"Yes, you're right, Mr. Slatter, I'm not exactly a pauper. Besides a pension, Fillmore left me an insurance policy worth $300,000. Right now, I don't have to touch the principal, since I manage to keep the bills paid from my piano lessons. I have a waiting list, so I guess it has paid to keep my fingers limber over the years. Fillmore and I used to entertain our friends with my playing and his singing."

"I get the feeling that your $300,000 is still in cash," I said.

"In a money market, which is yielding practically nothing. I know I should put this money to work, but I think I need a little nudge."

"Unfortunately, there is no secret formula for asset allocation," I said. "A few people invest entirely in stocks or mutual funds, with no bonds and very little cash. If you start investing young enough, let's say in your twenties or thirties, stocks are the best way to go. Over the years, stocks (including dividends) have returned about 11 percent a year, compounded. By contrast, bonds, CDs, and other fixed-income vehicles have rarely done much better than 6 percent. That's quite a difference. Let's say you were thirty-five years of age and had $300,000 to invest, and you put it all in stocks. By age sixty-five, your nest egg would be worth more than $8.8 million. On the other hand, if you invested the same $300,000 at 6 percent, you would have only $2.5 million when you reached retirement age."

"Are you suggesting that I invest all my money in common stocks, Mr. Slatter? That sounds a little scary to me. I think Fillmore would turn over in his grave."

"I'm not surprised. Most people know that stocks involve risk—sometimes a lot of risk—and they simply can't stand the worry that it may involve. Of course, diversification can help some. If you own twenty or thirty stocks, you are spreading the risk of owning only a half dozen. However, the risk of stock ownership is still there.

"There are a number of formulas that have been devised. A simple rule of thumb is to invest 70 percent in stocks and the rest in fixed income, such as bonds. This percentage might be suitable for an average investor. But for someone who tends to be conservative, a more suitable breakdown might be 60 percent stocks, with the rest in bonds and money-market funds. Finally, for those who are ultraconservative, the best formula would be to balance stocks and fixed income fifty-fifty."

"I'm not sure which camp I might fall into. Do you have any other magic formulas?" asked Alice, as she munched on her Caesar salad.

"Another one that I devised is based on age. My thinking is that younger people should be more aggressive than older people. At fifty-eight, you're kind of in the middle."

"How does it work?"

"It's quite simple and revolves around the investor who is sixty-five years old. At that age, I suggest having 65 percent in stocks and the rest in bonds and other fixed-income vehicles. But if you are older than sixty-five, you should edge toward the fixed-income sector. My formula says to deduct 1 percent each year from the common stock sector, so that when you reach seventy, you will have 60-percent invested in stocks. Going a step further, when you reach eighty, you'll be fifty-fifty."

"I can't see how that works for me. I'm only fifty-eight," said Alice, as she broke her club sandwich into small portions.

"I was just getting to that. For those younger than sixty-five, the strategy is to add to the percentage invested in common stocks. For each year younger, add 1 percent. That means that for you we would add 7 percent, bringing the total to 72 percent. How does that sound?"

"I can see the logic of your formula, but somehow I don't think I would sleep at night knowing I had more than $200,000 in stocks. How could I afford food for Brutus if the stock market went into a tailspin? I think we had better go to plan C. Do you have any more strategies?"

"Just one more. If you don't like this one, I'm afraid there is no plan D."

"I see you have finished off your prime rib," she said. "Why don't we get another cup of coffee before you start?"

When the coffee arrived, I began my explanation of plan C. "Incidentally, this strategy is not in any of my other books. So, pay close attention."

"I guess I had better takes notes. Okay, my pen is ready to record your words of wisdom. If I like this one, I will give specific orders to Brutus Kutch III to stop barking at you."

"Thanks. Now I won't have to carry a gun when I walk by 36 Taffeta Trail. I think you'll like this one—it's got a little bit of everything. Let's take your $300,000. We divide it into three equal segments, with $100,000 in each. The first $100,000 is invested in twenty blue-chip stocks, with $5,000 in each. These are all huge companies, most of them in the Dow Jones Industrial Average—stocks like General Electric, United Technologies, Coca-Cola, Citigroup, ExxonMobil, Home Depot, IBM, Johnson & Johnson, Merck, 3M Company, Procter & Gamble, Wal-Mart, Anheuser-Busch, Colgate-Palmolive, Costco, FedEx, United Parcel, Lowe's, and Walgreen. How does that sound so far?"

"Great. I think we're onto something. I will alert Brutus that you are not all bad."

"On to the second part. There are those who think that index funds are the best way to invest. They contend that actively managed mutual funds can't compete against them because of the high cost of management, usually about 1.5 percent a year. I agree. A good index fund is the Standard & Poor's 500. You can buy it on the American Stock Exchange. It trades there as an exchange-traded fund with a ticker symbol of IVV. In effect, you are buying all 500 stocks, so diversification is outstanding. One big advantage of an index fund is the low cost. Those managed by Vanguard have an expense ratio of less than 0.25 percent, compared with 1.5 percent for a typical managed mutual fund. I suggest putting $33,000 in IVV.

"The next $33,000 should go into another index fund. This one is called DIAMONDS, or DIA. It invests in the thirty stocks that make up the Dow Jones Industrial Average.

"The third $33,000 goes into a very broad group of stocks that are not in the S&P 500. In other words, they are stocks that are smaller. Many smaller companies may not be familiar, but they are nonetheless worth owning for their future growth. If past history is any indication of the future, small stocks are somewhat more volatile (or more risky), but they tend to perform better than industry giants over the long haul. This index fund is called the Vanguard Extended Market Index and has a symbol of VXF.

"According to my friend Don Dempsey, an investment advisor in Burlington, Vermont, the Extended Market Index is designed to track the performance of the Wilshire 4500 Completion Index, a broadly diversified index of small and medium-size U.S. companies. The Wilshire 4500 Index contains all of the U.S. common stocks regularly traded on the New York and American Exchanges and the Nasdaq over-the-counter market, except those stocks included in the S&P 500.

"By investing in these three market indexes, Alice, you should do well—assuming the stock market does well."

"I'm beginning to like your idea," said Alice Hardleigh. "That still leaves $100,000. So far, we have lots of stocks."

"Right. The rest is left in a money-market fund or in U.S. treasury bonds that mature in less than five years. Bonds that mature within a few years, as opposed to those that mature twenty or thirty years from now, are much less volatile and are far better to hold when interest rates start back up.

"Thus, if stocks have a temporary sinking spell, you will still have an anchor to the windward to preserve a good part of your holdings. To be sure, this is a conservative strategy, but I think it fits the bill for you and Brutus. But before we go ahead with it, you will want to consult with him. After all, he's the one that wants to have me for lunch."

"I still can't understand why he has such a loathing for you, Mr. Slatter. He's normally such a mild-mannered pooch—like all the other Mongolian toy mastiffs. They're a wonderful breed."

The next day I walked by her house on Taffeta Trail and heard the familiar yapping of Brutus Kutch III. It was coming from inside the house, so I knew I was safe from attack.

The Double-Check-a-Month Plan

You've no doubt heard the phrase, *publish or perish.* To be sure, university professors have to conduct lectures, correct term papers and administer examinations to keep the students occupied. But they also have to turn out scholarly articles and books to keep from being sacked.

One such professor that I talked with is Helen Grackle, Ph.D. In recent years, Dr. Grackle has been plying her trade as an English professor at Schumpeter State College.

She called me one day to discuss a plan to augment her income. "Like most professors, I'm not exactly rich, Mr. Slatter—and I don't have a husband to share my household overhead. Fortunately, I have some money coming from my publisher. Since I am impressed with your book, I thought you might give me some of your sage advice on how to devise a stock portfolio with the advance from my publisher."

"I'm not too sure it's sage advice," I said. "But I will be happy to talk to a fellow writer. If I'm not being too personal, what does your book deal with?"

"My field of expertise is English literature, so Shakespeare is part of my curriculum. The title of my book is *Edward de Vere, alias William Shakespeare.* Would you like a copy when it hits the bookstores?"

"That's a tantalizing title. I assume you are one of the mavericks who thinks Shakespeare's plays were written by a noted intellect such as Francis Bacon or Christopher Marlow, rather than the man from Stratford-on-Avon. I thought that whole idea had been shot down long ago."

"Exactly. Most of my colleagues still think Shakespeare is the real McCoy. And, anyway, what does it matter who wrote his plays and sonnets? They are still the greatest literary masterpieces ever created. I agree, it probably doesn't matter. Even so, I have devoted the last two years in an effort to establish that Edward de Vere, the seventeenth Earl of Oxford, is the real author."

"You seem really convinced, Dr. Grackle. Can you give me a few hints as to what makes you so sure that the country bumpkin from Stratford was a phony?"

"There are a host of reasons, all of which are outlined in my book, but here are just a few. For one thing, his parents, his wife, and his children were all illiterate. I can understand that his parents might not know how to read—after all, Abraham Lincoln came from an illiterate background. But certainly no one with the erudition of Shakespeare would marry a dummy, nor would he put up with kids who didn't do their homework."

"That sounds like sound reasoning to me," I said. "I think that alone puts you on first base. What else?"

"In his will he makes no mention of his writings, nor does he even hint that he was a writer. In fact, no one in his hometown had ever mentioned his name as someone connected with literature. What's even more astounding—there is no record of Shakespeare having attended grammar school in Stratford. And certainly no evidence that he had a university degree. On the other hand, de Vere was highly educated and a member of the nobility, which would have given him the knowledge of court life necessary to write his plays. In fact, de Vere mentions a number of incidents from his own life in his plays. That is a distinct characteristic of most fiction writers."

"I'm beginning to see the light, Dr. Grackle. One more question. What got you started on this quest?"

"I first became curious when I read *The 100, a Ranking of the Most Influential Persons in History*. The author is Michael H. Hart. In turn, that led me to a serious book on the subject, *The Mysterious William Shakespeare,* by Charlton Ogburn. Oh, one more convincing piece of evidence. In 1586, Queen Elizabeth awarded the Earl of Oxford an annual lifetime pension of 1,000 pounds, equal in today's purchasing power to $100,000. What's more, when she died in 1603, her successor, King James I, honored the pension until de Vere's death in 1604. Nor were there any strings attached to the pension. There was no indication as to the reason for the pension. Presumably, Edward de Vere wanted to remain anonymous. In those days, nobility thought it somewhat below their dignity to work for a living."

"Wow. You have given me something to think about," I said. "But I'm sure you didn't call me to promote your book. You said something about income. Can you elaborate?"

"My publisher is convinced my book will be on the best-seller list, even though most of my writing in the past has been of the scholarly variety. I'm expecting a check for $60,000 in the next month or so. Can you dream up an idea that will bring me some steady income?"

"How would you like to receive two checks each month, one on the first of the month and the other at the middle of the month?"

"That sounds like a good start, since the college pays me that way now. What do you have in mind?"

"As you know, not all companies pay a dividend—or else pay very little—so you probably would not consider such stocks as Barnes & Noble, Bed Bath & Beyond, Costco Wholesale, or Patterson Companies. In addition, very few companies pay dividends monthly. Typically, they send out checks every three months, so investing your $60,000 in a single company would not give you a monthly income."

"I assume you have a better way."

"Fortunately, there is no set date or month that all companies adhere to. Some schedule dividends to be paid in January, April, July, and October. Similarly, others have schedules that begin in February or March. What's more, they don't all pay on the first of the month. Some pay the tenth or fifteenth. But by combining a half dozen companies, I can set you up to receive checks on the schedule that will coincide with Schumpeter State College. Here is one such plan, which would involve the purchase of $10,000 in each of six stocks: Alltel, Piedmont Natural Gas, National City, Cedar Fair, ConAgra, and Emerson Electric. Each of these stocks has an above-average dividend yield—none less than 2 percent and some more than 5 percent. Let me e-mail you the table, and then you can call me back with your response."

Here is the table of the six stocks I sent Dr. Grackle and when they pay their quarterly dividends. I was able to find out the date of these dividends by consulting the *Standard & Poor's Stock Guide*. The same information is also available in the S&P tear sheets.

Alltel (AT)	January 3, April 3, July 3, October 3
Piedmont N. G. (PNY)	January 15, April 15, July 15, October 15
National City (NCC)	February 1, May 1, August 1, November 1
Cedar Fair (FUN)	February 15, May 15, August 15, Nov. 15
ConAgra (CAG)	March 1, June 1, September 1, December 1
Emerson Elect. (EMR)	March 10, June 10, September 10, December 10

After she had received my e-mail, she called me to make her comments.

"I noticed that one company, Alltel, paid its dividend on the third of the month, not on the first. What bothers me a little is the lack of diversification, with only six stocks. On the other hand, it appears that each is in a different sector. Alltel is a telephone company, National City is a financial, Piedmont is a utility, Emerson is an industrial, Cedar Fair is a consumer discretionary, and ConAgra is a consumer staple. I like that. Even so, it concerns me that my whole $60,000 would be tied up in only six stocks. Do you have any defense of your strategy?"

"Nothing in the field of investing is perfect, Dr. Grackle, but I do have an alternative plan. Since you have $60,000 to invest, you could allocate $5,000 to each of twelve stocks, which would spread the risk a bit better. I have a second plan, which I will e-mail to you."

Here is the second plan:

Coca-Cola (KO)	January 1, April 1, July 1, October 1
Kimco Realty (KIM)	January 18, April 18, July 18, October 18
Bristol-Myers Squibb (BMY)	February 1, May 1, August 1, November 1
Kinder Morgan (KMP)	February 12, May 12, August 12, Nov. 12
Bemis (BMS)	March 1, June 1, September 1, December 1
FPL Group (FPL)	March 15, June 15, September 15, December 15

And here is a look at the twelve-stock portfolio, along with the sector of each company:

	Sector Dividend	Yield
Alltel (AT)	Telephone	2.4%
Piedmont N. Gas (PNY)	Utility	3.8
National City (NCC)	Financials	4.1
Cedar Fair (FUN)	Consumer Discretionary	5.7
ConAgra (CAG)	Consumer Staples	4.7
Emerson Elect. (EMR)	Industrials	2.7
Coca-Cola (KO)	Consumer Staples	2.7
Kimco Realty (KIM)	Financials	4.1
Bristol-Myers Squibb (BMY)	Drugs, Health	4.5
Kinder Morgan (KMP)	Energy	6.0
Bemis (BMS)	Materials	2.7
FPL Group (FPL)	Utilities	3.4

When she called back, Helen Grackle seemed happier with my enhanced strategy. "I'm about convinced that you have solved my problem, Mr. Slatter. It isn't perfect, of course, since there are only nine of the ten sectors represented, with nothing from the Information Technology sector. On the other hand, you have added a food stock, a public utility, an energy company, and a company with a stake in packaging. All in all, I am comfortable with what you have dreamed up. I assume that your efforts are worth some financial reward. Shall I send you a check?"

"Well, I would certainly hope that all my toil would not have been in vain. If I were an auctioneer selling the contents of your house, I would have you sign a contract to pay me 25 percent of the proceeds. Translating that into this situation, how about sending me 25 percent of your dividends for the next twenty-five years?"

Helen Grackle gasped when I presented my compensation package. She said, "I think I'll give up teaching and become an auctioneer. Or should I switch to writing books on the stock market? I assume you are not serious about tapping into my dividend income for the next twenty-five years. After all, I am just a poor, struggling English professor."

"Okay, you win, Dr. Grackle. Since I am already rich, I suppose I can take pity on someone who is less fortunate. However, I do need a favor to compensate me for all the work I have done to keep you solvent. By any chance, do you know of a good biography of either Winston Churchill or Benjamin Disraeli?"

"That sounds a lot better, since it won't drive me into bankruptcy. A history professor here at Schumpeter State has two dandies that he recommends. But both are hundreds of pages long and are written by scholars who have done their homework. Shall I call him and get the exact titles?"

"By all means. And if I like the books, I will cancel the contract to tap into your dividend income."

The next day she called back. "The one on Churchill is called *Churchill: A Life,* by Martin Gilbert. It's 959 pages and available in paperback. The other one is entitled, *Disraeli* by Robert Blake. It's a hardcover edition, with 766 pages. So you have your work cut out for you. I hope that puts me back in your good graces."

"Thanks for doing me that favor, Dr. Grackle. I hope you will be able to live better on your dividend income. I'll be in touch when my next book comes out."

The next day I ordered both books from Amazon.com. Since I like to save money, I bought a used copy of the Churchill book, which was in mint condition, for $7.28, including shipping. The Disraeli biography was okay except for a few pages that had some lines underscored. It cost me a total of $6.49.

Surprisingly, my mailbox contained a book about three days later. I couldn't believe a used book from Amazon had arrived so soon; it usually takes a week or two. But this book was not from Amazon. It was from Helen Grackle. A note inside said, "Mr. Slatter, you gave me some sage advice, so I thought you deserved a modest reward. If your two books on the British monarchs are tough going, I'm sure you can switch to the enclosed collection of anecdotal biographies of British and American writers. My students love *A Dab of Dickens & a Touch of Twain* by Elliot Engel." She was right, it is the best book of brief biographies I have ever read, and I read a lot of them.

A Word about My Record

I was working out in my exercise room when the phone rang. It was J. Dirndl Smith, calling from upstate New York. He said his wife had purchased a copy of my book for his birthday, and he had read it cover to cover. Apparently, he really liked it; he asked me to reserve a copy of my next edition—and to "make sure you autograph it."

"I've never understood why some people ignore their first name and prefer to be called by their middle name," I said. "Or, am I being too personal?"

"I got sick and tired of seeing half the phone book devoted to guys named John Smith. I wanted to be different. My first name happens to be John—like yours. I notice that you prefer to be called Slats."

"I see what you mean. There are definitely far too many Johns in this world. I assume that you have some questions. I thought my book explained everything that an investor would want to know. But I guess I left out a few things."

"Nothing is perfect, Mr. Slatter. But your book comes pretty close. For one thing, your manner of writing appeals to me. No big words or fancy lingo. Every chapter is understandable, even for a novice like me. Still, there is one thing that I wanted to clear up, and your willingness to let me call you is appreciated. I hope this is not a bad time."

"Well, I was just finishing up with my seven torture machines. I am a fiend for daily exercise. Most of my seven machines were purchased at garage sales for no more than $25—two of them for a paltry $5. And they're not cheap machines. Bought new, they probably cost several hundred each. Apparently, a lot of people have good intentions, but then give it up and want to get rid of the beast for a song. Normally, I prefer that people call during business hours, but the Red Sox game was rained out tonight, so I guess I'll make an exception."

"I'm a Yankee fan, so I suppose we're enemies," said J. Dirndl Smith, but I didn't denote any evidence of a smile.

"Not anymore, Mr. Smith."

"Just call me Dirndl, Slats. My question is why don't you publish your record? I assume it isn't very good, or you would be bragging about it."

"I've been asked that question many times, Dirndl. There are several reasons why I don't brag about how well my 100 stocks have performed over the past nine or ten years. For one thing, I am never sure when I should begin counting. Normally, the book hits the bookstores in early October. Should I assume that this is when everyone buys the book and then calculate how each stock performed a year later, or should I start counting on January 1 and end with January 1 the following year? On the other hand, why should I confine my calculation to one year? Most investors don't buy my stocks for a few months or a year. They often hold them for several years, which is fine—that's what they *should* do. So, one year is not necessarily indicative of how my stocks are performing."

"I see what you mean," said Dirndl Smith. "Any other reasons?"

"One reason is time. I have better things to do than make a zillion calculations. Then, too, my 100 stocks are not the same from one year to another. In a typical year, I delete twenty-five or thirty stocks and replace them with a similar number that look attractive to me. Some people ask me if they should sell the deleted stocks, and I usually tell them that my stocks are long-term recommendations and that there is not necessarily any reason to make wholesale switches every year."

"I see what you mean; anything else?"

"Most of the people who buy my book seem happy as clams with their results. And they keep buying more copies, year after year. It is one of the strongest selling books published by Adams Media. Here's what one satisfied customer told me in an e-mail on August 2004:

'I have purchased many copies of your 2003 and 2004 *100 Best Stocks You Can Buy* book. I have used your book myself to significantly diversify my stock portfolio. I have also given many copies to friends, advising them to use the book as a guide as how to get into the market. I look forward to the 2005 edition!'

"That sounds like a satisfied customer, Slats, but he doesn't say it has made him rich. Frankly, I am beginning to have my doubts."

"From time to time, I have made spot checks on my stocks, just to satisfy my own curiosity. In many instances, my record outperforms the market, but not always. What it tells me is this: In all likelihood, my record would not outperform the Dow Jones Industrial Average or the Standard & Poor's 500 every year. By the same token, if you examined a random list of mutual funds, you would find the same pattern. Every portfolio manager has a particular method of picking stocks. Some prefer growth stocks, for instance; some like value stocks; while still others look for momentum. There are plenty of other strategies, as well. None of those strategies is a consistent winner. To give you an idea how difficult it is to outperform the market (such as the Dow Jones Average or the Standard & Poor's 500), I selected five major funds and calculated their total return (growth plus dividends) for the years 1999 through the most recent year. Not one of these funds outperformed the S&P 500 in all of these years. And four of them failed to equal or exceed the market twice during this brief span of time. Let me e-mail you these results. I have marked with an asterisk the years in which those funds failed to equal the S&P 500.

"Then, I picked five more common stock mutual funds—essentially at random—that had been in business at least ten years. Only one of them had a perfect record during the same five-year period: Gabelli Value Fund outperformed the S&P 500 throughout. The other four each had at least two years of failure, and three of them failed to do as well as the Index on three or four separate occasions:

	2003	2002	2001	2000	1999
Fidelity Magellan	+24.7*	−23.3*	−11.6	-9.1	+23.5
Inv. Co. of America	+24.8*	−14.3	−6.2	+3.6	+15.9*
Washington Mutual	+26.2*	−14.9	−1.3	+7.1	+1.0*
Fidelity Contrafund	+28.1	−9.1	−12.6*	−6.7	+14.7*
Dodge & Cox Stock Fund	+30.6	−8.9	+9.2	+1.9	+13.4*
S&P 500 Index	+27.0	−21.7	−12.1	−9.2	+20.0

	2003	2002	2001	2000	1999
AIM Aggressive Growth	+27.4	−22.6*	−26.0*	+ 2.7	+43.5
Burnham Fund Class A	+21.4*	−24.8*	−20.8*	+ 2.1	+25.5
Fidelity Blue Chip	+24.7	−25.3*	−16.6*	−14.3*	+23.8
Gabelli Value Fund	+31.9	−15.6	+5.1	+0.9	+31.7
MassMutual Inv. Trust	+21.8*	−22.4*	−16.2*	−0.3	+4.3*
S&P 500 Index	+27.0	−21.7	−12.1	−9.2	+20.0

"I am certain that my stocks won't be world beaters every year," I told Mr. Smith, "so why go to the trouble of advertising it?"

"Thanks for your thoughts, Mr. Slatter," said J. Dirndl Smith. "I think I can understand your position. Please cancel my order for your next book."

The phone went dead. I wasted no time in hopping back on my rowing machine. I switched on my headset and began listening to *Eisenhower*, written by Geoffrey Perret and narrated by Nelson Runger, my absolute favorite *Recorded Books* reader.

When to Sell

Deciding when to sell is often a wrenching experience. Not long ago, I was fretting over whether to sell Eli Lilly. For one thing, it was not acting well, often sagging when the rest of the market was moving ahead. For another, I was concerned that Lilly was hurting my overall performance, since it was my largest holding. Those are two good reasons to sell a stock—or at least part of it. I ended up selling 300 shares.

Over the years, I have read a number of articles on when to sell, such as one written by Manuel Schiffres for *Kiplinger's Personal Finance Magazine* in February of 1994. He said, "There are some general rules for when to sell a stock—such as when it reaches preposterous valuation levels or when the reason you bought it no longer applies. For example, if you bought a stock because you had high hopes for a new product, you should sell if the product is a lemon. Or, if you owned a stock for its high dividends—as many IBM investors did—and the company slashes the payout, that is also a strong signal to sell.

"Consider selling if your goals change, you desire a more defensive investment posture or you want to establish a gain or loss for tax reasons. Also consider selling if a more attractive opportunity comes along. Always ask yourself, 'What's my potential for this stock over the next twelve months?'" says Michael DiCarlo, who runs the John Hancock Special Equities fund. "If it's 15 percent, and you have something you think can make 50 percent, that's an easy swap to make."

Advice from *Better Investing*

To be sure, there are any number of reasons to sell one of your holdings. Here are seven that are enumerated by the National Association of Investors Corporation (NAIC), which gives assistance and advice to the nation's investment clubs. NAIC also publishes an outstanding monthly magazine, *Better Investing*—I am a faithful subscriber. Here are the sell signals featured by NAIC:

- Sell because an issue of equal or better quality offers the potential for higher returns.
- Sell because of an adverse management change.
- Sell because of declining profit margins or a deteriorating financial structure.
- Sell because direct or indirect competition is affecting the prosperity of the company.
- Sell because a company has great dependence on a single product whose cycle is running out.
- Sell to increase quality or decrease quality as circumstances dictate.
- Sell companies that have become cyclical and have low-growth-rate issues because prosperity is about to succumb to recession.

Helpful Criteria to Use When Judging a Stock

If those reasons for selling don't cover all the bases, perhaps you should consider some of my own ideas on the subject. In an earlier chapter, I discussed what to look for when you are buying a stock. If you examine that list of factors—a version of which is given below—and find that the stock in question does not measure up, that could be a signal to sell:

- A rising trend in earnings, dividends, and book value per share. This information can be obtained from such publications as *Value Line Investment Survey* or Standard & Poor's tear sheets. You'll find them at most brokerage offices and some libraries.
- A balance sheet with less debt—compared with equity—than other companies in its particular industry. In most instances, I look for 75 percent or more in shareholders' equity, and the rest in long-term debt.
- An S&P quality rating of B+ (which is average) or better. If you refer to *Value Line,* their average financial strength rating is B++.
- A P/E ratio (defined below) no higher than average for that industry.
- A dividend yield—such as 2 percent or 3 percent—that suits your particular needs. If a $30 stock has an annual dividend of $.75, that's a yield of 2.5 percent ($.75 divided by $30).
- A stock that insiders—such as officers and board members—are not selling in significant quantities.
- A below-average dividend payout ratio. For instance, if a company earns $4 a share and pays out $3 in dividends, it doesn't have much left to invest in new facilities, acquisitions, research, or marketing. A payout ratio of 25 percent would be far better.
- A history of earnings and dividends not pockmarked by erratic ups and downs.
- Companies whose return on equity is 15 or better.
- A ratio of price to cash flow that is not too high when compared to other stocks in the same industry. Here again, you can obtain this information from *Value Line* or Standard & Poor's.

To be sure, you are not likely to find a company that fits all of those criteria precisely. But if the stock you are worried about misses the mark on the majority of those benchmarks, perhaps the time has come to make a switch. What's more, if you already have a stock in mind that *does* fit the above criteria, you have a good reason to sell the one that doesn't.

Is the Stock Priced Too High?

One good reason to sell a stock is price. Even though the company has most of the other features, if it has climbed to a level that doesn't make sense, it may be prudent to unload it. One of the best gauges to determine price level is the price/earnings ratio. If you bought the stock when it had a P/E of 22, for example, and it is now in the high 30s, it may be a good time to find something that's more reasonably priced, assuming it also fits the pattern described above. The P/E is calculated by dividing the price by the annual earnings per share. If a stock sells for $40 and earned $1.32 in the past twelve months, that works out to a P/E of 30.3—which is much higher than stocks in general. But if the earnings were $2.75, that would be a multiple of 14.6, which is below the market, and might be a bargain if it has the features described above.

Don't Fall in Love with a Stock

You may recall that one reason I sold 300 shares of Eli Lilly was because I owned too much of the stock. A good rule of thumb is to invest no more than 5 percent of your portfolio in any single stock. That means that you should own at least twenty stocks. I own more than fifty stocks.

I can appreciate you may be reluctant to pare back one of your large holdings, since the price has risen appreciably, and you would have to cough up a chunk of cash for the tax collector. That used to make sense, but no more. The maximum capital gains tax is now a mere 15 percent.

One thing to bear in mind when you are giving thought to selling a stock is portfolio turnover. Most conservative investors should avoid too much trading. Buy and hold is a good strategy. Most mutual funds, however, don't adhere to this dictum. They often hold their stocks for no more than twelve months. According to an article in *Fortune* magazine on August 23, 2004: "As it turns out, most of that activity is not paying off for investors. Quite the opposite, in fact," says the author Janice Revell. "A recent Morningstar study shows that managers who adhere to a buy-and-hold strategy—and stifle the impulse to react to short-term market gyrations—tend to outperform their faster-fingered rivals.

"Morningstar analyst Kerry O'Boyle first screened the universe of actively managed equity funds for 1992–98 to find those that fell into the lowest quartile for both portfolio turnover and the number of stocks held. He then went back and tracked the five-year performance for each fund, year by year, from 1992 through 2003. The result: Among all style categories, the concentrated low-turnover funds overwhelmingly beat their peers."

My thought is to make occasional changes, but don't get carried away with change. If your annual turnover is 10 or 20 percent, that should be sufficient. On the other hand, if you *never* bother to update your portfolio, you will end up with too many dogs that should have been sold long ago.

PART II

100 BEST STOCKS YOU CAN BUY

100 Best Stocks

In the following table are listed the 100 stocks discussed in this book. A brief description of the stock appears here.

The ticker symbol is given so that you can use the quote machine in your broker's office. Or, if you call your broker on the phone, it makes it easier if you know the ticker symbol, since your broker may not.

In the table, "Industry" refers to one of the company's main businesses. This is not always easy to express in one or two words.

For instance, United Technologies is involved in such industries as aircraft engines, elevators, and air conditioning equipment. To describe the company succinctly, I arbitrarily picked the designation, "aircraft engines."

Similarly, General Electric presents an even more daunting problem since it owns NBC, makes appliances, aircraft engines, medical devices, and a host of other things.

The designation "Sector" indicates the broad economic industry group that the company operates in, such as Energy, Financial, Drug & Health Care, Consumer Staples, Consumer Discretion, Information Technology, Industrials, Materials, Telecommunications, and Utilities. A properly diversified portfolio should include at least one stock in each of the ten sectors.

"Category" refers to one of the following: 1. Income (Income); 2. Growth & Income (Gro Inc); 3. Conservative Growth (Con Grow); or 4. Aggressive Growth (Aggr Gro). As above, it might make sense to have some representation in each category, even though you have a strong preference for only one.

I have not included the page numbers because of space limitations. In any event, it is easy enough to find a particular stock, since they appear alphabetically in the book.

Company	Symbol	Industry	Sector	Category
-A-				
Abbott Laboratories	ABT	Med. supplies	Health Care	Gro Inc
Air Products	APD	Gases	Materials	Con Grow
Alcoa	AA	Aluminum	Materials	Aggr Gro
Apache *	APA	Exploration	Energy	Aggr Gro
AvalonBay	AVB	REIT	Financials	Gro Inc
-B-				
Bank of America	BAC	Money center bank	Financials	Gro Inc
Banta	BN	Printing	Industrials	Gro Inc
Bard, C. R.	BCR	Hosp. prod.	Health Care	Con Grow
Becton, Dickinson	BDX	Med. supplies	Health Care	Con Grow
Bemis Company	BMS	Packaging	Materials	Gro Inc
Biomet, Inc.	BMET	Orthopedic	Health Care	Aggr Gro
Black & Decker	BDK	Power tools	Cons Discret.	Con Inc
Boeing Company	BA	Aerospace	Industrials	Aggr Gro
Brinker Internat'l	EAT	Restaurants	Cons Discret.	Aggr Gro

Company	Symbol	Industry	Sector	Category
-C-				
Canadian National	CNI	Railroad	Industrials	Con Grow
Carnival Corp.	CCL	Cruise lines	Cons Discret.	Aggr Gro
Caterpillar	CAT	Machinery	Industrials	Aggr Gro
Chevron Corporation	CVX	Gas and oil	Energy	Income
Cintas	CTAS	Uniforms	Industrials	Aggr Gro
Clorox	CLX	Household pd.	Cons Staples	Con Grow
Colgate-Palmolive	CL	Household pd.	Cons Staples	Con Grow
ConocoPhillips	COP	Oil and gas	Energy	Gro Inc
Costco Wholesale	COST	Wholesale	Cons Staples	Aggr Gro
CVS Corporation	CVS	Pharmacy	Cons Staples	Con Gro
-D-				
Deere & Company	DE	Farm equipment	Industrials	Aggr Gro
Dell, Inc.	DELL	Computers	Inform. Tech.	Aggr Gro
Dentsply Int'l	XRAY	Dental products	Health Care	Con Gro
Devon Energy	DVN	Oil and gas explor.	Energy	Aggr Gro
Dominion Resources *	D	Gas and electric	Utilities	Gro Inc
Donaldson	DCI	Filtration	Industrials	Con Grow
Dover	DOV	Ind. machinery	Industrials	Aggr Gro
Dow Chemical	DOW	Chemicals	Materials	Gro Inc
DuPont *	DD	Chemicals	Materials	Gro Inc
-E-				
Eaton Corporation	ETN	Machinery	Industrials	Gro Inc
Ecolab	ECL	Specialty chem.	Materials	Con Grow
Emerson Electric	EMR	Elect. equip.	Industrials	Grow Inc
EnCana Corporation *	ECA	Oil and gas	Energy	Aggr Gro
Energen	EGN	Oil and gas	Utilities	Con Grow
ExxonMobil	XOM	Petroleum	Energy	Gro Inc
-F-				
FedEx Corporation	FDX	Air freight	Industrials	Aggr Gro
-G-				
General Dynamics	GD	Aerospace	Industrials	Con Grow
General Electric	GE	Elect. equip.	Industrials	Gro Inc
Grainger, W. W. *	GWW	Supplies	Industrials	Con Grow

Company	Symbol	Industry	Sector	Category
-H-				
Home Depot	HD	Retail	Cons Discret.	Con Grow
Hormel Foods	HRL	Food	Cons Staples	Con Grow
-I-				
Illinois Tool Works	ITW	Machinery	Industrials	Con Grow
Ingersoll-Rand *	IR	Equipment	Industrials	Aggr Gro
Intel	INTC	Computers	Inform. Tech.	Aggr Gro
Int'l Business Mach	IBM	Computers	Inform. Tech.	Aggr Gro
-J-				
Johnson Controls	JCI	Elect. equip	Cons Discret.	Con Grow
Johnson & Johnson	JNJ	Med. supplies	Health Care	Con Grow
-K-				
Kellogg	K	Packaged foods	Cons Staples	Con Grow
Kimco Realty	KIM	REIT	Financials	Gro Inc
Kinder Morgan	KMP	Oil and gas	Energy	Gro Inc
-L-				
Lilly, Eli	LLY	Pharmaceuticals	Health Care	Grow Inc
Lockheed Martin *	LMT	Aerospace	Industrials	Aggr Gro
Lowe's Companies	LOW	Retail	Cons Discret.	Con Grow
Lubrizol	LZ	Specialty chem.	Materials	Gro Inc
-M-				
Marshall & Ilsley *	MI	Regional banks	Financials	Con Grow
McCormick & Co.	MKC	Spices	Cons Staples	Con Grow
McGraw-Hill	MHP	Publishing	Cons Discret.	Con Grow
MDU Resources	MDU	Oil and gas	Utilities	Gro Inc
Medtronic	MDT	Med. devices	Health Care	Aggr Gro
Meredith	MDP	Publishing	Cons Discret.	Con Grow
Microsoft	MSFT	Comp. software	Inform. Tech.	Con Grow
Motorola	MOT	Comm. equip.	Inform. Tech.	Aggr Gro

Company	Symbol	Industry	Sector	Category
-N-				
Nabors Industries *	NBR	Oil and gas drill	Energy	Aggr Gro
New Jersey Res. *	NJR	Natural gas	Utilities	Income
Norfolk Southern *	NSC	Railroads	Industrials	Con Grow
-O-				
OshkoshTruck	OSK	Trucks	Industrials	Aggr Gro
-P-				
Parker Hannifin *	PH	Industrial mach.	Industrials	Aggr Gro
Patterson Companies	PDCO	Dental	Health Care	Aggr Gro
PepsiCo	PEP	Beverages	Cons Staples	Con Grow
PetSmart *	PETM	Pet stores	Cons Discret.	Aggr Gro
Pfizer	PFE	Drugs	Health Care	Aggr Gro
Piedmont Nat'l Gas	PNY	Nat'l Gas	Utilities	Income
Pitney Bowes	PBI	Office equip.	Industrials	Gro Inc
Praxair	PX	Indust. gases	Materials	Con Grow
Procter & Gamble	PG	Household pd.	Cons Staples	Con Grow
-Q-				
Questar *	STR	Gas utility	Utilities	Con Grow
-R-				
Ruby Tuesday	RI	Restaurants	Cons Discret.	Con Grow
-Q-				
St. Jude Medical	STJ	Medical devices	Health Care	Aggr Gro
Staples	SPLS	Office prod.	Cons Discret.	Aggr Gro
Stryker	SYK	Med. supplies	Health Care	Aggr Gro
Sysco Corporation	SYY	Food distrib.	Cons Staples	Con Grow
-T-				
T. Rowe Price	TROW	Asset manage.	Financials	Aggr Gro
Target Corp. *	TGT	Gen. merchandise	Cons Discret.	Aggr Gro
Teva Pharmaceutical	TEVA	Pharmaceuticals	Health Care	Aggr Gro
Textron	TXT	Conglomerate	Industrials	Gro Inc
3M Company	MMM	Diversified	Industrials	Con Grow

Company	Symbol	Industry	Sector	Category
-U-				
UnitedHealth	UNH	Health Care	Health Care	Con Grow
United Parcel	UPS	Expr. carrier	Industrials	Con Grow
United Technologies	UTX	Aircraft eng.	Industrials	Con Grow
-V-				
Valspar	VAL	Coatings	Materials	Con Grow
Varian Medical	VAR	Med. devices	Health Care	Aggr Gro
-W-				
Walgreen	WAG	Drugstores	Cons Staples	Con Grow
Wal-Mart	WMT	Retail	Cons Staples	Aggr Gro
WellPoint*	WLP *	Blue Cross	Health Care	Aggr Gro
Wells Fargo	WFC	Divers. bank	Financials	Gro Inc
Wrigley *	WWY	Confectionery	Cons Staples	Con Grow

*New in this edition.

GROWTH AND INCOME

Abbott Laboratories

100 Abbott Park Road ❑ Abbott Park, IL 60064-6400 ❑ (847) 937-3923 ❑ Direct dividend reinvestment plan available (888) 332-2268 ❑ Web site: *www.abbott.com* ❑ Ticker symbol: ABT ❑ Listed: NYSE ❑ S&P rating: A ❑ Value Line financial strength rating: A++

On September 15, 2005, Abbott announced it had received U.S. Food and Drug Administration (FDA) approval for a new minimally invasive device to treat patients with carotid artery disease, a risk factor for stroke. Abbott received FDA approval for the Xact® Carotid Stent and 510(k) clearance for the Emboshield® Embolic Protection System to treat patients at risk of stroke who are not favorable candidates for surgery. With this, Abbott becomes the second company to enter the U.S. carotid stent market.

"Surgery, or carotid endarterectomy, has proven a reliable method for treating carotid artery disease, but it is not the ideal treatment for everyone," said Gary S. Roubin, Ph.D., MD, chairman of the department of interventional cardiology at Lenox Hill Hospital in New York. "Some patients may stand to benefit more from a minimally invasive procedure with a carotid artery stent and embolic protection that avoids the risk associated with general anesthesia, eliminates the risk of cranial nerve injury and neck scarring. The Xact Carotid Stent and Emboshield Embolic Protection System provide a truly advanced minimally invasive treatment alternative for these patients."

"The launch of our carotid stent system in the United States is further evidence of the innovative line of vascular products Abbott has built that is gaining momentum in the interventional community," said Robert B. Hance, president of Abbott Vascular. "We are delighted to see the benefits of clinical and scientific advancement at Abbott result in an important new treatment for patients at risk of stroke."

The new system features a stent specifically designed to treat diseased carotid arteries—arteries in the neck that have become clogged or partially blocked due to the buildup of fatty plaque and debris (atherosclerosis). The Xact stent is self-expanding and has a closed-cell design that creates a tightly knit yet highly flexible mesh intended to help restore the inner diameter of a carotid artery, promote a smooth inner vessel surface, and potentially reduce the release of fatty debris (emboli) from a diseased vessel when it is treated, which can lead to stroke.

The Xact stent is designed for use in combination with the fully retractable Emboshield filter. Emboshield is designed to capture emboli that can break off during a carotid stenting procedure, and it is the only filter to feature Barewire™, a proprietary technology developed to allow for better control of stent placement once the filter is in place and fully apposed against the vessel wall.

Abbott established an exclusive agreement to market and distribute Emboshield in February 2001 with Mednova Limited in Galway, Ireland, which developed the stent and filter.

Abbott received approval and clearance for the Xact Carotid Stent and Emboshield Embolic Protection System based on its submission of SECuRITY Registry Study data in a Premarket Approval application filed in 2004. Both Emboshield and Xact already have CE Mark approval and were launched in the European Union at the end of 2003.

Company Profile

Abbott Laboratories is one of the largest diversified health-care manufacturers in the world. The company's products are sold in more than 130 countries, with about 40 percent of sales derived from international operations. ABT has paid consecutive quarterly dividends since 1924.

Abbott's major business segments include Pharmaceuticals & Nutritionals (prescription drugs, medical nutritionals, and infant formulas) and Hospital & Laboratory Products (intravenous solutions, administrative sets, drug-delivery devices, and diagnostic equipment and reagents).

The company's leading brands are the following:

- AxSym systems and reagents (immunodiagnostics)
- Biaxin/Biaxin XL/Klalcid/Klaricid (macrolide antibiotic)
- Depakote (bipolar disorder; epilepsy; migraine prevention)
- Depakote ER (migraine prevention)
- Ensure (adult nutritionals)
- Humira (rheumatoid arthritis)
- Isomil (soy-based infant formula)
- Kaletra (HIV infection)
- MediSense glucose monitoring products
- Mobic (to control pain)
- Similac (infant formula)
- Synthroid (hypothyroidism)
- Tricor (a lipid-control agent)
- Ultane/Sevorane (anesthetic)

Although revenue growth in Abbott's infant formula and diagnostics businesses has slowed in recent years, new drugs (such as the antibiotic clarithromycin), the launch of disease-specific medical nutritionals, and cost-cutting (diagnostics and hospital supplies) continue to boost the company's profits.

Shortcomings to Bear in Mind

- "A panel of outside advisers to the Food and Drug Administration voted unanimously against approval of a new drug for advanced prostate cancer made by Abbott Laboratories," said Leila Abboud, writing for the *Wall Street Journal* on September 14, 2005. "In a scathing assessment, the panel members said Abbott hadn't proved that the drug, which is called Xinlay, slowed the progress of the disease, nor shown what subset of patients benefited from the therapy.

"The vote is a blow to the Abbott Park, Illinois, drug maker. But the company says it will keep trying to get Xinlay approved by completing a continuing clinical trial and planning others. Abbott has been counting on Xinlay to break into the lucrative cancer-drug market, a central part of its corporate strategy."

- "Tricor, one of Abbott's biggest sellers, fell short of expectations when it failed to significantly reduce a composite of heart problems common among people with diabetes," according to a *Wall Street Journal* article written by Leila Abboud and Ron Winslow on November 15, 2005. The study was presented in Dallas at the annual scientific meeting of the American Heart Association.

"Tricor, one of a class of drugs called fibrates that lower blood fats called triglycerides, did show benefit on a number of secondary measures, such as reducing non-fatal heart attacks and cutting down on the need for procedures to open up clogged arteries, as well as slowing nerve damage and blindness that affects people with advanced diabetes.

"Investors had hoped that stronger results from the trials would pave the way for quick approval of Simdax and boost sales of Tricor to more than $1 billion from current annualized global sales of $779 million."

Reasons to Buy

- *New York Times* reported that five analysts gave Abbott a STRONG BUY rating on March 21, 2006; four said the stock was a MODERATE BUY; five called it a HOLD; and one preferred to rate Abbott a SELL. *Somebody* has got to be wrong.
- Argus Research Company gave Abbott a BUY rating on February 3, 2006. Martha Freitag, CFA, said, "We anticipate that Abbott's continued investment in pharmaceuticals and acquisitions of higher-growth hospital products business in 2004 and ongoing cost-cutting measures will translate into higher growth for the company. We expect that sales and earnings growth in 2006 will be driven by continued strength in pharmaceuticals (particularly the rheumatoid arthritis drug Humira, which recently received approval for two additional uses) and medical products (including devices, diabetes monitoring, and diagnostics)."
- In 2004, Abbott paid $1.2 billion for TheraSense, Inc., a fast-growing and innovative maker of blood glucose-monitoring test and equipment for people with diabetes. This move made Abbott a strong number-three player in the glucose-monitoring market, behind Roche Holding AG and Johnson & Johnson.
- Abbott is ranked among the top companies in the world for financial strength and workplace excellence by leading national publications, including these:

  - *Fortune* magazine ranked Abbott third among the "Most Admired Companies" in the pharmaceutical sector and also included Abbott among the "50 Best Companies for Minorities" in the United States for the seventh consecutive year.
  - *Forbes* magazine ranked Abbott 149 on the *Forbes* 2000 list (by sales, profits, assets, and market value).
  - *Working Mother* magazine named Abbott one of the "100 Best Employers for Working Mothers."
  - *Science* magazine listed among the top twenty employers for scientists in a

ranking of the world's most respected biotechnology and pharmaceutical companies.

- TAP Pharmaceutical Products, Inc., established in 1977, is a joint venture between two global pharmaceutical leaders, Abbott and Takeda Pharmaceutical Company Limited of Japan. TAP is one of the leading pharmaceutical companies in the United States. The company is unique in that it does not have its own internal discovery and/or manufacturing organization. Instead, the company teams up with outside organizations and applies its expertise in research and development, quality assurance, and sales and marketing to develop new compounds.

TAP focuses its drug development in four major areas: gastroenterology, rheumatology, urology, and women's health. The company develops and markets pharmaceuticals for sale in the United States and Canada, and it licenses international rights for some of those products to Abbott International.

TAP's current products include Prevacid, a proton pump inhibitor for gastroesophageal reflux disease (GERD), ulcers, and other acid-related disorders; and Lupron for the treatment of advanced prostate cancer, endometriosis, and anemia associated with uterine fibroid tumors in combination with iron and central precocious puberty.

SECTOR: **Health Care** ◆ BETA COEFFICIENT: **.85**
10-YEAR COMPOUND EARNINGS PER SHARE GROWTH: **7.4%**
10-YEAR COMPOUND DIVIDENDS PER SHARE GROWTH: **10.1%**

		2005	2004	2003	2002	2001	2000	1999	1998
Revenues (millions)		22,338	19,680	19,681	17,685	16,285	13,746	13,178	12,513
Net income (millions)		3,351	3,566	3,479	3,243	1,550	2,786	2,446	2,334
Earnings per share		2.16	2.27	2.21	2.06	.99	1.78	1.57	1.50
Dividends per share		1.10	1.03	.97	.92	.82	.76	.68	.60
Price	high	50.0	47.6	47.2	58.0	57.2	56.2	53.3	50.1
	low	37.5	38.3	33.8	29.8	42.0	29.4	27.9	32.5

CONSERVATIVE GROWTH

Air Products and Chemicals, Inc.

7201 Hamilton Boulevard ❑ Allentown, PA 18195-1501 ❑ (610) 481-5775 ❑ Direct dividend reinvestment plan available (877) 322-4941 ❑ Web site: *www.airproducts.com* ❑ Listed: NYSE ❑ Fiscal year ends September 30 ❑ Ticker symbol: APD ❑ S&P rating: B+ ❑ Value Line financial strength rating: B++

On November 29, 2005, Air Products announced that it had entered into a joint marketing agreement with Houghton International to provide a broad range of products and technologies to the U.S. metals processing industry, deployed through a unique industrial gas and fluids management service. The complementary mix of offerings includes a full line of metalworking fluids and a variety of industrial gases, services, technology, and atmosphere generating equipment. The agreement leverages each company's industry leadership position to deliver cost-effective manufacturing and after-sale services sustained by expanded industry skill and technical expertise.

"The joint marketing approach allows both of our companies to strengthen our market leading positions and respond to the growing demand from industrial operations for complete solutions," said Meri Lazar, metals market manager at Air Products.

"By bringing together our respective capabilities in this way, we will be able to provide even greater value for both new and existing customers," added Kevin Baker, director of marketing for North America Gases.

About Houghton International

Houghton supplies chemicals and metalworking fluids to the automotive, aerospace, and primary metals industries, as well as to other metal processing arenas. Air Products is a major supplier of industrial gases used in the metals industry. Among the products supplied are bulk and gaseous nitrogen, hydrogen, oxygen, argon, and helium. Air Products also provides services, complementary equipment, and technologies to the industry.

Since 1865, Houghton International, Inc., has been serving the metalworking, automotive, and steel industries, along with a variety of other markets, with the development and production of specialty chemicals, oils, and lubricants. Headquartered in Valley Forge, Pennsylvania, Houghton maintains manufacturing and research facilities throughout the world. Unequaled in the industry for technical support, Houghton's unique FLUIDCARE® chemical management program gives customers new ways to save on overall processing and disposal costs and increase processing performance. Houghton International continues to expand its Pacific Rim operations and grow its worldwide facilities.

Company Profile

Here is a solid view of the company that I extracted from the company's Web site on the Internet. To be sure, it's a bit self-serving.

"Air Products touches the lives of consumers around the globe in positive ways every day. We serve customers in health care, technology, energy, and industrial markets worldwide with a unique portfolio of products, services, and solutions, providing atmospheric gases, process and specialty gases, performance materials, and chemical intermediates. The company has built leading positions in key growth markets, such as semiconductor materials, refinery hydrogen, home health-care services, natural gas liquefaction, and advanced coatings and adhesives.

"Founded more than sixty years ago, Air Products is recognized for its innovative culture, operational excellence, and commitment to safety and the environment. In fact, we are the safest company of our kind in the nation. With annual revenues of $8.1 billion and operations in more than thirty countries, Air Products' more than 20,000 employees build lasting relationships with their customers and communities based on understanding, integrity, and passion."

Over Sixty Years of Growth

"Air Products was established in 1940 in Detroit, Michigan, on the strength of a simple, but then revolutionary, idea: the "on-site" concept of producing and selling industrial gases, primarily oxygen. At the time, most oxygen was sold as a highly compressed gas product in cylinders that weighed five times more than the gas itself. Air Products proposed building oxygen gas-generating facilities adjacent to large-volume users, thereby reducing distribution costs. The concept of piping the gas directly from the generator to the point of use proved sound and technically solvable.

"Today, Air Products ranks 281st in sales and 276th in total assets among *Fortune* magazine's April 2005 list of the 500 largest corporations in the United States. Corporate headquarters are at the company's 600-acre campus in eastern Pennsylvania's

Lehigh Valley, near Allentown; European headquarters are at Hersham, near London; and Asian headquarters are in Singapore, with offices in Tokyo and Hong Kong."

Serving a Diversity of Markets

"Air Products is one of the world's largest industrial gas producers, supplying a broad range of industrial gases—chiefly oxygen, nitrogen, argon, hydrogen, and helium and related equipment for their production, distribution, and use—to hundreds of thousands of customers throughout the world. These gases are used in most industries, including food and metal processing, semiconductor manufacturing, health care, aerospace, and chemical production.

"Air Products' $1.9 billion chemicals business includes polymers, polyurethane intermediates and additives, amines, and specialty and epoxy additives used in applications such as adhesives, coatings, polyurethane foams, textiles, herbicides, pesticides, water treatment chemicals, reinforced composites, and inks."

Positioned for Growth

"As international competition continues to intensify, Air Products is well positioned to compete with the best anywhere in the world. In addition to a broad product line and invested presence in more than thirty countries, the company has world-class production and applications technology and a long-standing commitment to safety, efficiency, and cost-effectiveness in every facet of its operations. The corporation also has firmly established continuous improvement processes which will yield further productivity gains and even higher levels of customer satisfaction—ensuring a future for Air Products as bright as its past."

Shortcomings to Bear in Mind

- Air Products has a somewhat leveraged balance sheet. Its common stock represents only 69 percent of capitalization. My preference is for common stock to represent 75 percent of capitalization.
- On January 3, 2006, *Standard & Poor's Stock Reports* cast a negative vote on Air Products. According to analyst Richard O'Reilly, CFA, "Our recommendation is SELL, based on our view of an excessive premium valuation. The shares are trading at a P/E [price earnings] multiple of 18, based on our calendar 2005 EPS [earnings per share] estimate, above the level of the S&P 500 of 16."

Reasons to Buy

- On February 27, 2006, the *New York Times* looked at the opinions of nineteen financial analysts. Five rated APD a STRONG BUY; nine thought it should be a MODERATE BUY; four called it a HOLD; and one was even less enthusiastic, dubbing it a MODERATE HOLD.
- On January 26, 2006, Argus Research Company had a positive spin on the stock. Bill Selesky said, "We are maintaining our BUY rating on Air Products & Chemicals, Inc. We still believe the potential exists for solid revenues and better earnings and margins in the future, as the company continues to benefit from the cost-reduction program started in fiscal 2003. In addition, Air Products is benefiting from better price realizations and strong top-line [sales] growth."
- On October 26, 2005, CEO John P. Jones, said, "Our strategies paid off in fiscal 2005, as we posted significant improvements in sales, earnings, and return on capital. Despite the impact of several unprecedented natural disasters, soaring energy, and raw material costs, and pricing pressure in Electronics, we delivered on our commitments and positioned ourselves for further improvement in 2006.

"We have a significant amount of growth already under contract for next year. Some examples are the six hydrogen plants we are bringing on line, the eleven

LNG [liquid natural gas] heat exchangers we have in backlog, and the new contracts we have secured to supply Electronics customers in Asia."

- "As a global gases, specialty chemicals, equipment and services provider, Air Products is unique," according to a company official. "We serve many of today's highest-growth markets, including technology, performance materials, energy, health care, and other industries."

Leading Supply Positions

- "We supply atmospheric gases, process and specialty gases, performance materials, and chemical intermediates to customers throughout the world. With our culture based on innovation, operational excellence, and a commitment to safety and the environment, we have built leading supply positions in key growth markets, including semiconductor and flat-panel display materials, refinery hydrogen, home healthcare services, natural gas liquefaction, and advanced coatings and adhesives."

Global Scope

- "We are geographically diversified, with operations in over thirty countries and half our revenues outside of the United States. Our 19,900 employees differentiate Air Products by building lasting relationships with customers and communities based on understanding, integrity and passion."

Earnings Stability

- "There is a high degree of stability in our earnings. We have a strong balance sheet with 'A' bond ratings, and we generate strong cash flow. We also have attractive business models in how we go to market. For example, the majority of our business is supplied under long-term contracts. We have energy and raw material pass-through capability for the vast majority of the company's sales."

Growing with Discipline

- "And most importantly, we're growing. We have substantial operating leverage as we load our existing assets with good business. We are driving increased productivity across our businesses at all levels. We are focused on growth businesses: Electronics, Performance Materials, Refinery Hydrogen, Healthcare, and Asia. And we remain disciplined in our capital spending, pursuing leadership positions and choosing only the best opportunities. Each and every day, we work hard to improve our business portfolio, shifting it toward a higher-growth, higher-return mix for our shareholders."

SECTOR: **Materials** ◆ BETA COEFFICIENT: **1.00**
10-YEAR COMPOUND EARNINGS PER SHARE GROWTH: **6.6%**
10-YEAR COMPOUND DIVIDENDS PER SHARE GROWTH: **9.4%**

		2005	2004	2003	2002	2001	2000	1999	1998
Revenues (millions)		8,144	7,411	6,297	5,401	5,858	5,467	5,020	4,919
Net income (millions)		712	604	397	525	466	533	451	489
Earnings per share		3.08	2.64	1.78	2.42	2.12	2.46	2.09	2.22
Dividends per share		1.25	1.04	.88	.82	.78	.74	.70	.64
Price	high	65.8	59.2	53.1	53.5	49.0	42.2	49.3	45.3
	low	53.0	46.7	37.0	40.0	32.2	23.0	25.7	33.2

AGGRESSIVE GROWTH

Alcoa Inc.

201 Isabella Street at 7th Street Bridge ❑ Pittsburgh, PA 15212-5858 ❑ (212) 836-2674 ❑ Direct dividend reinvestment plan available (800) 317-4445 ❑ Web site: *www.alcoa.com* ❑ Listed: NYSE ❑ Ticker symbol: AA ❑ S&P rating: B+ ❑ Value Line financial strength rating: A

"Entering 2005, we anticipated significant pressures from rising input, energy costs, and other cost inflation, but actual increases were even higher, nearly $900 million for the year," said CEO Alain Belda.

"To meet that challenge, we took aggressive action, passing through significant price increases to downstream customers, improving our mix of value-added products, continuing productivity gains, and lowering taxes. That management action helped offset cost pressures and drove the top-line to the highest level in Alcoa's 117-year history," said Mr. Belda. "In the year ahead, we don't foresee the same sharp spikes on input prices, and our initiatives will gain further momentum to offset inflation and improve the bottom line.

"As we enter 2006, the vast majority of our primary metal production will benefit from the highest metal prices in more than fifteen years," Mr. Belda added. "And we are working to secure future growth in attractive markets with customers around the world."

"We have the most aggressive growth strategy in the industry and the best growth projects around the world. We continue to achieve the highest returns in the industry, generating the cash we need to fund our growth and maintain a strong balance sheet."

Company Profile

Alcoa (formerly Aluminum Company of America), founded in 1888, is the world's leading integrated producer of aluminum products. The company is active in all major aspects of the industry—technology, mining, refining, smelting, fabricating, and recycling.

Alcoa's aluminum products and components are used worldwide in aircraft, automobiles, beverage cans, buildings, chemicals, sports and recreation, and a wide variety of industrial and consumer applications, including such Alcoa consumer brands as Alcoa wheels, Reynolds Wrap aluminum foil, and Baco household wraps.

Related businesses include packaging machinery, precision castings, vinyl siding, plastic bottles and closures, fiber optic cables, and electrical distribution systems for cars and trucks.

Even though it has some admirable qualities, aluminum is expensive and has difficulty competing against steel. Consequently, it might appear to be a rare element. Not so.

Aluminum is an abundant metal; in fact, it's the most abundant in the earth's crust. Of all the elements, only oxygen and silicon are more plentiful. Aluminum makes up 8 percent of the crust. It is found in the minerals of bauxite, mica, and cryolite, as well as in clay.

Until about 100 years ago, aluminum was virtually a precious metal. Despite its abundance, it was very rare as a pure metal because it was so difficult to extract aluminum from its ore. Aluminum is a reactive metal, and it cannot be extracted by smelting with carbon.

To solve the enigma, displacement reactions were tried, but metals such as sodium or potassium had to be used, making the cost prohibitive. Electrolysis of the molten ore was tried, but the most plentiful ore, bauxite, contains aluminum oxide, which does not melt until it reaches 2050°C.

The solution to the problem of extracting aluminum from its ore was discovered by Charles Hall in the United States and by Paul Heroult in France—both working independently. The method now used to extract aluminum from its ore is called the Hall-Heroult process.

I won't bore you with the steps taken to effect this process. The important fact to remember is that it is far from cheap. Even so, it can be done economically enough to make aluminum the second most widely used metal. However, aluminum is not likely to replace iron and steel any time soon. Iron makes up more than 90 percent of the metals used in the world.

The main cost in the Hall-Heroult process is electricity. So much energy is required that aluminum smelters have to be situated near a cheap source of power, normally hydroelectric dams. The price of entry into the business is so high that it discourages most upstarts from taking the plunge.

On the other hand, this frustrating effort to produce commercial aluminum is worth the cost, since the white metal has a number of valuable attributes. It has a low density. It is highly resistant to corrosion. It is lightweight—one-third the weight of steel. It is an excellent reflector of heat and light.

It is nonmagnetic. It is easy to assemble. It is nontoxic. It can be made strong with alloys. It can be easily rolled into thin sheets. It has good electrical conductivity. It has good thermal conductivity. Aluminum doesn't rust.

Shortcomings to Bear in Mind

- Alcoa is not a classic growth company. Rather, it is a cyclical company, and earnings fluctuate with the economy. What's more, its beta coefficient is 1.40, which means that the stock rises and falls 40 percent more than the market. That's why I have classified the stock as aggressive growth.
- On January 9, 2006, Prudential Equity Group rated the stock as UNDERWEIGHT, which is similar to a SELL. "We rate Alcoa UNDERWEIGHT as the company suffers from classic manufacturing cost-price pressures common to past high inflation periods over twenty-five years ago. Further, higher energy prices could damage demand in some sectors, like large SUVs, adding to a 'stagflation' environment. We expect Alcoa's future earnings will be penalized by various higher costs, such as higher interest rates, which could also crimp demand."

Reasons to Buy

- Alcoa makes a very sustainable product. Almost 70 percent of the aluminum ever produced is still in use, equaling 480 million metric tons (529 million tons) of a total 690 million metric tons (761 million tons) manufactured since 1886.
- The company is seeking to bolster its production capacity overseas. In addition to building a 322,000-metric-ton smelter in Eastern Iceland, Alcoa is investigating the possibility of building additional smelters in Brunei and the Kingdom of Bahrain. Sites such as these fit into Alcoa's long-term plan of shifting its smelting capacity to lower-cost regions.
- During periods when the aluminum industry suffers through a protracted slump in aluminum prices, Alcoa has seen its profits rise. Part of that is due to the effects of recent acquisitions. But much of the improvement can be traced to a new corporate philosophy, called the "Alcoa Business System." Essentially, it calls for plants to produce more aluminum, produce it faster, and not let it sit on the docks for too long. The new production processes are "deceptively simple and seemingly obvious," says one analyst. But, on top of other

cost-cutting efforts already in the works, they are helping Alcoa weather what otherwise might be a dismal year. As aluminum prices recover—either because of growing demand or because excess capacity is shuttered—Alcoa stands to see earnings jump dramatically. Analysts say that each penny increase in the LME price (the spot price of aluminum ingots on the London Metals Exchange) of aluminum boosts Alcoa's per-share earnings by about 12 cents. Normally, the prevailing world price of aluminum is an important determinant of aluminum companies' profits. From 1982 through 1995, Alcoa's earnings and the LME price moved in lockstep. Since then, however, the LME price has dropped while Alcoa's earnings have held steady or drifted up. According to the company's chief financial officer, Richard Kelson, "We are breaking away from the LME pricing."

- On March 4, 2006, the *New York Times* reviewed the opinions of twenty-two financial analysts. Five of them rated Alcoa as a STRONG BUY; nine regarded the stock as a MODERATE BUY; six called it a HOLD; and two said it was a MODERATE HOLD. There were no SELLS.
- "Alcoa has plenty of growth projects in the works," said *Value Line Investment Survey* on January 20, 2006. Stuart Plesser said, "The projects consist of both smelter expansion and new facilities. For example, the company is in the midst of building a 346,000-metric-ton facility in Iceland which should be completed in early 2007. It also has plans for new plants in Norway, Brazil, and Ghana. The increased output from these plants should enable the company to deliver double-digit per annum earnings growth over the coming three to five years."
- *Argus Research Company* had some upbeat comments on the stock on January 11, 2006. Bill Selesky said, "Our rating on Alcoa, Inc., remains BUY despite the 2005's fourth quarter earnings shortfall. When we upgraded the shares on April 8, 2005, we had begun to see a new emphasis on cost controls at the company. Since that report, Alcoa has announced several restructurings that should allow it to become more cost-competitive with its peers. In our view, this is a step in the right direction. In addition, we believe that the company's end markets remain relatively healthy, with the exception of the automotive and European markets. We still believe Alcoa offers an extremely attractive valuation."

SECTOR: **Materials** ◆ BETA COEFFICIENT: **1.40**
10-YEAR COMPOUND EARNINGS PER SHARE GROWTH: **2.4%**
10-YEAR COMPOUND DIVIDENDS PER SHARE GROWTH: **10.1%**

		2005	2004	2003	2002	2001	2000	1999	1998
Revenues (millions)		26,159	23,478	21,504	20,351	22,859	22,936	16,323	15,340
Net income (millions)		1,233	1,310	938	420	908	1,484	1,054	859
Earnings per share		1.40	1.49	1.08	.49	1.05	1.80	1.41	1.22
Dividends per share		.60	.60	.60	.60	.60	.50	.40	.38
Price	high	32.3	39.4	38.9	39.8	45.7	43.6	41.7	20.3
	low	22.3	28.5	18.4	17.6	27.4	23.1	18.0	14.5

AGGRESSIVE GROWTH

Apache Corporation

One Post Oak Central ❑ 2000 Post Oak Boulevard ❑ Suite 100 ❑ Houston, TX 77056-4400 ❑ (713) 296-6662 ❑ Direct dividend reinvestment plan available (800) 468-9716 ❑ Web site: *www.apachecorp.com* ❑ Listed: NYSE ❑ Ticker symbol: APA ❑ S&P rating: B+ ❑ Value Line financial strength rating: B++

"As part of our acquisition from ExxonMobil in September of 2004, we farmed-in nearly 400,000 acres in central Alberta, supplementing our existing 65 million acres of prospective properties in Canada," said CEO G. Steven Farris. "The ExxonMobil acquisition also added production of about 8,000 barrels of oil and 7 MMcf [million cubic feet] of gas per day in the Permian Basin of West Texas and New Mexico. We also acquired rights to 66,000 undeveloped acres in the Permian Basin, where we currently produced about 24,000 barrels of oil and 53 MMcf of gas per day.

"In the Gulf of Mexico, we added to our already sizable position with the acquisition of Anadarko Petroleum's Gulf of Mexico Outer Continental Shelf properties, comprising 232 offshore blocks (664,000 net acres) which should provide additional drilling opportunities in the years ahead." Mr. Farris went on to say, "Apache is now the largest acreage holder on the Shelf, where we operate 395 platforms.

"In Egypt, we were awarded four new concessions in the Western Desert, where we are the largest oil producer and the second-largest natural gas producers. The new concessions will add 1.7 million gross prospective acres to our existing base of 14.3 million gross acres. With the appraisal and development of Apache's Qasr discovery—our largest ever—we expect significant production growth. Discovery of the deep-Jurassic Qasr field with estimated reserves of 2 trillion cubic feet of gas and 40 million barrels of condensate, provides encouragement that we will continue to find new Jurassic fields in the Western Desert with significant gas and condensate potential."

Company Profile

Established in 1954 with $250,000 of investor capital, Apache Corporation has grown to become one of the world's top independent oil and gas exploration and production companies, with $155 billion in assets.

Apache's domestic operations are focused in some of the nation's most important producing basins, including the Outer Continental Shelf of the Gulf of Mexico, the Anadarko Basin of Oklahoma, the Permian Basin of West Texas and New Mexico, the Texas-Louisiana Gulf Coast, and East Texas.

In Canada, Apache is active in British Columbia, Alberta, Saskatchewan, and the Northwest Territories. The company also has exploration and production operations in Australia's offshore Carnarvon, Perth, and Gippsland basins, Egypt's Western Desert, the United Kingdom sector of the North Sea, China, and Argentina.

Shortcomings to Bear in Mind

- "Worldwide, Apache has many opportunities, but the flip side of higher oil and gas prices has been a steady increase in costs," said a company official in 2005. "Service costs and steel costs have grown significantly over the past year. Unless these costs level out, we may reduce our drilling expenditures as we did in 2001. This is the case especially in the lower forty-eight U.S. states, where reserve targets continue to decrease in size."

Reasons to Buy

- On January 12, 2006, *Standard & Poor's Stock Reports* had this to say, according to its analyst, Charles LaPorta, CFA: "We have a BUY recommendation on the shares. While APA has been among the companies most affected by the Gulf hurricanes, we believe its global asset base will mitigate the effect on the overall enterprise; and since its production effectively hits the market unhedged, we believe the spike in hydrocarbon prices should overwhelm the negative impact from lost production."
- On January 23, 2006, Argus Research Company had a BUY rating on Apache. Jeb Armstrong said, "Apache took a pounding at the hands of Katrina and Rita, and while it will take time to make repairs and get back to normal, we believe the company is in a strong position to grow production and earnings. We also expect stronger results in 2006 than in 2005."
- "Six years ago, Apache Chairman Raymond Plank set a goal of doubling the stock price within four years," said Christopher Helman, writing for *Forbes* magazine on January 9, 2006. "When that goal was met in 2004, Plank and Chief Executive G. Steven Farris awarded every employee a stock grant equal to at least one year's salary. Generous performance-based awards like that have helped build teamwork and results: Earnings per share are up an average 34 percent in each of the last five years."
- On August 24, 2005, Apache announced that it had signed a new contract to supply gas to a major west Australian power station to be built at Kwinana, south of Perth. The gas will be supplied from the John Brookes field, jointly owned by Apache (55 percent) and Santos (45 percent). The fifteen-year term of the contract with the plant's developers, Wambo Power Ventures, calls for the delivery of about 215 billion cubic feet of natural gas (118 Bcf net to Apache) at a daily rate of 39 million cubic feet (21 MMcf net). The term can be extended an additional ten years by mutual agreement. The first gas delivery is expected by the second half of 2008. The John Brookes field is situated offshore in the Carnarvon Basin, some thirty-five miles northwest of Apache's operated facilities on Varanus Island.
- On July 28, 2005, Apache announced that its Mohave-1H new-field discovery in the Carnarvon Basin offshore western Australia is onstream. Part of Apache's 2005 program to increase Lower Cretaceous flag sandstone oil production, the well is flowing 10,690 barrels of oil per day from a 398-foot horizontal interval.

  The Mohave field is located in twenty-six feet of water 4.5 miles southeast of Apache's Varanus Island production hub. "Development of new oil production from the Flag Sandstone is a key component of Apache's 2005 Australian drilling program," said Eve Howell, regional vice president and managing director of the company's Australian operations. "Proximity to existing Varanus Island infrastructure and our ability to fully develop the field with a single horizontal well enhance the economies of this project." The Mohave field is part of the Harriet Joint Venture, which Apache operates with a 68.5-percent interest. Its partners are Kufpec, with 19.3 percent, and Tap Oil with 12.2 percent.
- In mid-2005, Apache announced that the Tanzanite-2 well on Egypt's West Mediterranean Onshore Concession flowed 2,846 barrels of oil and 640 thousand cubic feet (Mcf) of gas per day in the first test of the Cretaceous-age Alamein dolomite formation in the Tanzanite Field.

  The Tanzanite-2, located about 2,000 feet northeast of the Tanzanite 1X discovery, was drilled to a total depth of 9,075 feet. The test was conducted on the top twelve feet of the targeted Alamein dolomite formation on a one-inch choke with 205 pounds per square inch of flowing wellhead pressure. An additional twenty-two feet of net pay was logged in the overlying Dahab formation.

■ ExxonMobil and Apache signed an agreement in mid-2005 to expand their successful exploration and development activities in the western Canadian province of Alberta, building on a broader program announced in 2004. This work, like the previously announced program, will capitalize on each company's strengths.

ExxonMobil's subsidiary, ExxonMobil Canadian Energy, will farm out its interest in about 650,000 acres of additional undeveloped property interests in Apache Canada Ltd. over and above the more than 370,000 acres conveyed in 2004. Under this latest agreement, Apache will test additional horizons on about 140,000 acres of the property conveyed in 2004. Apache has access to 1,234 sections under this agreement.

"This agreement will enable our companies to more closely work together to develop a larger portfolio of exploration acreage in Western Canada," said Morris Foster, president, ExxonMobil Production Company. "It allows us to create more shareholder value from these assets by taking advantage of the relative strengths of both companies to increase both the near-term and long-term value of these prospects."

"Apache is pleased to have the opportunity to expand our relationship with ExxonMobil in Canada," said Mr. Farris. "This latest extension allows Apache to add almost 800,000 acres to our existing 6.9 million acres on which to explore in one of the most prolific natural gas basins in North America."

Since the final agreement was signed in August 2004, Apache has drilled eighty-six wells and completed seventy-three wells with tested capacity of 52 million cubic feet per day.

■ In mid-2005, Apache announced the development of its Rose gas/condensate field with the completion of the Rose 4 development well, which is on stream, flowing at a daily rate of 101 million cubic feet (MMcf) of natural gas and 3,500 barrels of condensate from the Brigadier and Mungaroo formations.

The Rose is part of the Harriet Joint Venture. "Development of Rose significantly enhances the joint venture's gas deliverability," said Eve Howell. "Production from Rose-4 will be sold into the thirteen dedicated contracts and, along with the John Brooks development scheduled to come on line in August, should substantially increase the region's second-half gas volumes over previously reported levels."

■ On February 13, 2006, the *New York Times* surveyed twenty-nine securities analysts as to their views of Apache. Eleven rated the stock a STRONG BUY; twelve said it was a MODERATE BUY; and six called it a HOLD.

SECTOR: **Energy** ◆ BETA COEFFICIENT: **.85**

10-YEAR COMPOUND EARNINGS PER SHARE GROWTH: **32.8%**

10-YEAR COMPOUND DIVIDENDS PER SHARE GROWTH: **11.6%**

		2005	2004	2003	2002	2001	2000	1999	1998
Revenues (millions)		7,584	5,333	4,190	2.560	2,791	2,291	1,300	877
Net income (millions)		2,618	1,670	1,246	566	764	721	201	29
Earnings per share		7.84	5.03	3.74	1.84	2.50	2.48	.74	.12
Dividends per share		.36	.26	.22	.19	.17	.09	.12	.12
Price	high	78.2	52.2	41.7	28.9	31.5	32.1	21.6	16.8
	low	47.4	36.8	26.3	21.1	16.6	13.9	7.6	9.1

GROWTH AND INCOME

AvalonBay Communities, Inc.

2900 Eisenhower Avenue ❑ Suite 300 ❑ Alexandria, VA 22314 ❑ Listed: NYSE ❑ (703) 317-4632 ❑ Dividend reinvestment plan not available ❑ Web site: *www.avalonbay.com* ❑ Ticker symbol: AVB ❑ S&P rating: A ❑ Value Line financial strength rating: B+

"The real estate boom has been very good to property owners of all types," said Michael Corkery, writing for the *Wall Street Journal* on November 30, 2005. "But apartment landlords have largely missed the party as low interest rates and the prospect of rising home prices turned thousands of would-be renters into buyers.

"Vacant apartments often stayed empty until the landlord lowered the rent. Now that is slowly changing. Vacancy rates are dropping, and rents are rising in many parts of the country."

According to Mr. Corkery, "One of the few bright spots during the rental downturn was that landlords could sell their buildings to condo-converters at sky-high prices. In the third quarter, apartments being turned into condos sold for an average of $166,000, compared to $99,000 for units in buildings that were sold but remained as rentals, according to Real Capital Analysts, a New York-based real estate research and consulting firm.

"Apartment REITs embraced the condo craze. Over the past two years, for example, AvalonBay Communities, Inc., a Virginia-based REIT, has sold $750 million of apartments across the country—about three times as many properties as it bought, mostly to condo converters. The company is putting a lot of the money from sales into developing new high-end rental apartment buildings."

Company Profile

AvalonBay Communities, Inc. is in the business of developing, redeveloping, acquiring, and managing high-quality apartment communities in the high barrier-to-entry markets of the United States. These markets are located in the Northeast, Mid-Atlantic, Midwest, Pacific Northwest, and Northern and Southern California regions of the country.

As of December 31, 2004, AvalonBay owned or held interest in 148 apartment communities containing 42,810 apartment homes in ten states and the District of Columbia. Of those, ten communities were under construction and four communities were under reconstruction. In addition, the company held future development rights for forty-nine communities.

The company elected to be taxed as a REIT for federal income tax purposes for the year ending December 31, 1994, and it has not revoked that election. AvalonBay was incorporated under the laws of the State of California in 1978 and was reincorporated in the State of Maryland in June 1995. Management's principal executive offices are located at 2900 Eisenhower Avenue, Suite 300, Alexandria, Virginia 22314. ABV also maintain regional offices and administrative or specialty offices in or near the following cities: San Jose, California; New Canaan, Connecticut; Boston, Massachusetts; Chicago, Illinois; Newport Beach, California; New York, New York; Woodbridge, New Jersey; and Seattle, Washington.

Some Historical Dates

Here's how AVB has developed over time:

- August 24, 1993: Avalon Properties, Inc. is incorporated in the State of Maryland to continue and expand the multifamily apartment community acquisition, construction, development, and management operations of the Trammel Crow Residential Mid-Atlantic and Northeast Groups.

• November 18, 1993: Avalon Properties, Inc., completes its initial public offering (IPO) at $20.50 per share on the New York Stock Exchange. At the IPO, Avalon Properties has a portfolio of twenty-two communities containing 7,044 apartment homes in the Mid-Atlantic and Northeast.

• March 17, 1994: Bay Apartment Communities, the successor apartment business of Greenbriar Homes, completes its IPO at $20 per share on the New York Stock Exchange. At the IPO, Bay Apartment Communities has a portfolio of fourteen communities containing 3,481 apartment homes in Northern California.

• June 4, 1998: AvalonBay Communities, Inc., is formed by the merger of Avalon Properties, Inc., with and into Bay Apartment Communities, Inc.

• December 31, 2000: AvalonBay Communities, Inc., achieves its best operating performance in the history of the Company, with $3.70 funds from operations per share (14.9% growth), 8.9% same-store rental revenue growth, and 10.7% same-store net operating income.

• December 31, 2001: AvalonBay Communities, Inc., has another successful year, achieving $4.06 funds from operations per share (9.7% growth), 6.6% rental revenue growth, and 7.5% same-store net operating income.

• December 31, 2002: AvalonBay Communities, Inc., reports funds from operations of only $3.65 per share due to the difficult economic operating environment. Despite the challenging times, the company successfully completed ten communities with a total capitalization of approximately $470 million, completed $140 million in acquisitions, and issued $450 million of long-term debt at an average interest rate of 5.8%.

• December 31, 2003: AvalonBay Communities, Inc., celebrates its ten-year anniversary by ringing the closing bell on the NYSE and generates total shareholder return in 2003 of 30%, outperforming the S&P 500 and the apartment sector.

Shortcomings to Bear in Mind

■ Royal Shepard, CFA, writing for *Standard & Poor's Company Reports* on February 3, 2006, had this negative thought: "Our SELL recommendation is based on valuation. AVB recently traded at 24.5 times our funds-from-operation estimate, well above the apartment REIT peer average of about nineteen times. We think historically low interest rates have spurred private market demand for rental properties, primarily for condominium conversion. AVB shares have benefited, in our view, from investors' assessment of increasing net asset values. We view the shares as overvalued."

Reasons to Buy

■ "Value creation begins with market selection," said an AvalonBay spokesman in 2005. "We operate in premier apartment markets located in the Northeast, Mid-Atlantic, Midwest, Pacific Northwest, and California. These markets are characterized by long and arduous permitting and development processes that limit competition and restrict new apartment supply. Historically, new supply as a percentage of inventory in our markets has been half that of new supply levels in the United States. In addition, high single-family housing costs in our markets lead to a higher propensity to rent, with 37 percent of the population renting, as compared to 31 percent in the nation as a whole.

"Importantly, we believe these markets are now beginning a new cycle of out-performance. Of our sixteen markets, twelve are ranked in the top twenty markets nationwide, based on expected total revenue growth."

The official goes on to say, "Our long-established presence in these markets allows us to get an early look at opportunities for new development as they emerge, enabling us to establish a pipeline of future development rights that will provide value creation for years to come. In-house market research gives us timely market data and analysis that helps us re-allocate capital to those markets with the strongest demand/supply fundamentals, sustaining and optimizing value creation opportunities."

■ AvalonBay Communities, Inc., has been recognized by the National Association of Home Builders (NAHB) in several prestigious categories. These awards include the following:

- 1996 Property Management Firm of the Year
- 1998 Best Mid- or High-Rise Development of the Year
- 1998 Development Firm of the Year
- 1999 Development Firm of the Year
- 1999 Best Rehabilitation of a Multifamily Property
- 1999 Best Mid- or High-Rise Apartment Community
- 1999 Best Mid- or High-Rise Development of the Year
- 2000 Best Multifamily Community by a REIT
- 2001 Best Luxury Multifamily Development
- 2003 Best Corporate Web Site
- 2004 Best Luxury Rental Apartment, Avalon at Newton Highlands, Newton, Massachusetts

Also, AvalonBay Communities was the recipient of the 2004 *Multifamily Executive* magazine's prestigious "Builder of the Year" award. The company also received the award for "Project of the Year, Resort/Luxury Category" for Avalon at Mission Bay in San Francisco, California.

■ "After market selection, the quality and diversity of our portfolio become the next key components to creating and sustaining shareholder value," said a company officer in 2005. "The quality of four portfolios of more than 40,000 apartment homes in over 140 communities is among the highest in the multifamily sector. Our communities are generally young in age (eight years on average), with locations and amenities that our residents value. These assets are largely unencumbered with debt or tax protection, allowing us to achieve higher prices upon sales."

The spokesman goes on to say, "Our communities consist of a diverse mix of garden, townhouse, mid-rise, and high-rise apartments in urban and suburban locations. We use market and customer research to determine the products and amenities to offer. Customer needs are always changing. We use our core competencies to develop, acquire, and sell assets to adjust our portfolio to help ensure our product meets current demand. In this way, we are able to quickly adapt to the changing needs of the customer, improve quality, and position assets for maximum valuations."

SECTOR: **Financials** ◆ BETA COEFFICIENT: **.70**
9-YEAR COMPOUND EARNINGS PER SHARE GROWTH: **-1%**
10-YEAR COMPOUND DIVIDENDS PER SHARE GROWTH: **4.6%**

		2005	2004	2003	2002	2001	2000	1999	1998
Revenues (millions)		671	648	610	632	639	573	504	371
Net income (millions)		322	211	88	132	186	170	142	98
Earnings per share		1.35	1.16	1.30	1.49	3.12	2.53	1.55	1.35
Funds from operations		3.75	3.38	3.27	3.65	4.06	3.70	3.22	2.87
Dividends per share		2.84	2.80	2.80	2.80	2.56	2.24	2.06	2.00
Price	high	93.0	75.9	49.7	52.7	51.9	50.6	37.0	39.3
	low	65.0	46.7	35.2	36.4	42.4	32.6	30.8	30.5

GROWTH AND INCOME

Bank of America Corporation

Bank of America Corporate Center ❑ Charlotte, NC 28255 ❑ (704) 386-5667 ❑ Direct dividend reinvestment plan available (800) 642-9855 ❑ Web site: *www.bankofamerica.com* ❑ Listed: NYSE ❑ Ticker symbol: BAC ❑ S&P rating: A- ❑ Value Line financial strength rating: A+

"It looks as if Bank of America struck a good deal in acquiring credit-card specialist MBNA," said Andrew Bary, writing for *Barron's* on July 4, 2005. "Bank of America agreed last week to pay about $34 billion for MBNA, a maverick that focuses on so-called affinity cards that are issued in conjunction with colleges, professional groups, sports teams, and other organizations.

"Bank of America, based in Charlotte, NC, is buying MBNA for about thirteen times projected 2005 profits, not an unreasonable price considering that financial stocks generally trade for eleven to twelve times estimated 2005 profits."

Mr. Bary goes on to say, "After the deal, Bank of America will have $143 billion of domestic credit-card loans, putting it at the top of the industry, just ahead of Citigroup, which has a $140-billion portfolio."

Company Profile

Bank of America is one of the world's largest financial institutions, serving individual consumers, small businesses, and large corporations with a full range of banking, investing, asset management, and other financial and risk-management products and services.

The company provides unmatched convenience for consumers in the United States, serving one in three American households with 6,000 banking centers, more than 17,000 ATMs, and an award-winning Internet site, with more than 12.4 million active online users.

The Small Business Administration rates Bank of America as the number-one Small Business Administration Lender in the United States. The company serves clients in 150 countries and has relationships with 94 percent of the U.S. *Fortune* 500 companies and 76 percent of the Global *Fortune* 500.

The seventh most profitable company in the United States, Bank of America had $1,045 billion in assets, $6,275 billion in deposits, and a market capitalization of $190 billion.

How a Bank Makes Money

The following is excerpted from an article by Ann Cuneaz in the June 2004 issue of *Better Investing*:

"To understand the banking industry, it's helpful to understand how a bank makes money. The banking industry uses a somewhat different language from that of manufacturing or industrial companies, so it's necessary to learn a few new terms.

"When you think about it, a bank's main product really is money. Banks borrow money from their depositors, paying them the lowest possible interest rate that competition and current market conditions will allow. This payment is an example of what banking companies call **interest expense.**

"Banks also loan money to customers, charging them the highest possible interest rate that competition and current market conditions will allow. This is an example of **interest income.** Interest income minus interest expense is known as the **net interest income**, and this tends to make up the majority of new earnings for most banks.

"The difference between the interest rates a bank charge to its loan customers and the interest rates a bank pays its depositors is known as the **interest rate spread,** or **net interest margin**. It's the spread that generates much of a bank's income, and banks with the highest spread are generally the most profitable.

"Banks also make money from collecting all kinds of fees from customers. As banks offer more and more services, they have more opportunities to charge fees, such as for ATM usage, online bill payment, and trust and brokerage services. Any income not related to lending is known as **non-interest income.**"

Highlights of 2005

- During 2005, Bank of America announced its plan to merge with MBNA, and on January 1, 2006 the bank completed its merger, creating the largest credit card issuer in the United States as measured by balances.
- The bank added a record 2.3 million net new retail checking accounts and now has a portfolio of over 52 million accounts, including checking and savings accounts.
- Average total deposits grew more than 14 percent, to $632 billion.
- Average total loans and leases grew more than 13 percent, to $537 billion.
- Debit card revenue increased 32 percent due to a 29-percent increase in purchase volume.
- The client-coverage partnership between Global Commercial Banking and Global Investment Banking helped Banc of America Securities improve its market share rankings in investment banking.
- Home equity production volume increased 27 percent to a record $72 billion in 2005. Bank of America is one of the nation's leading home-equity loan providers as measured by outstanding balances.
- Sales of products through e-commerce totaled 3.8 million units in 2005, an increase of 69 percent. This included 2.3 million online activations, 380,000 new savings accounts, 375,000 new credit card accounts, and 298,000 new checking accounts. Bank of America is the worldwide leader in online banking, with 14.7 million subscribers and 7.3 million online bill payers.
- Total assets under management grew nearly 7 percent to $482 billion.
- Based on assets under management weighted over three years, 82 percent of Columbia Management Group's funds (equity, fixed income, money market funds) are in the top thirty-fifth percentile of Lipper's overall rankings of the mutual fund industry.
- Of Columbia Management's equity and fixed income funds that are rated by Morningstar, 39 percent are rated four or five stars as of December 31, 2005.

Shortcomings to Bear in Mind

- According to a July 5, 2005, article in the *Wall Street Journal,* written by Valerie Bauerle, Robin Sidel, and Ann Carrns, "With Bank of America Corp.'s $35 billion deal to buy MBNA Corp., the acquisition-hungry lender again has a lot on its plate. Some shareholders and analysts worry the bank could get indigestion."

The article goes on to say, "Because the Bank of America-MBNA deal was put together in a matter of days, many key issues remain unresolved. Bank of America will have to sort out its relationship with Visa USA, Inc., and MasterCard International, Inc., the two card associations that have thousands of banks as members. Bank of America has strong associations with Visa. The combined company is expected to maintain alliances with both associations."

Reasons to Buy

- "Bank of America is a breed apart," said Shawn Tully, writing for *Fortune* magazine on September 5, 2005. "Citigroup and J.P. Morgan rely more on corporate and investment banking and have strong operations in Asia and Europe. By contrast, BofA derives 95 percent of its revenues from the United States and does two-thirds of its business with consumers and small companies. It harvests revenues through millions of tiny transactions each day, from garnering fees on credit cards and mortgages to making car and home-equity loans.

"Nor does BofA have much in common with its two biggest rivals specializing in consumer banking. Wells Fargo and Wachovia are powerhouses mainly on the West and East Coasts, respectively. The recent deal to purchase credit card giant MBNA for $35 billion set BofA further apart. When the deal closes, it will be the country's biggest credit card provider."

■ In an interview with *SmartMoney* in October 2005, CEO Kenneth D. Lewis said, "Initially, investors react negatively to virtually any acquisition, but if you look at our stock performance, we've outperformed our peers on a one-year, five-year, and ten-year basis. While our price/earnings multiple has not improved, our earnings growth has been so good that we've moved the stock price with the sheer muscle of our earnings."

The *SmartMoney* interviewer goes on to say that "Bank of America has more than tripled its dividend over the past ten years. Some say that the baby boomers are going to become more interested in income-producing stocks as they grow older. Do you think the market will eventually recognize that?"

Mr. Lewis said, "We've increased our dividend at an annualized 13-percent compound growth rate for twenty-eight straight years. We're very proud of that. For the reasons you just outlined, I think dividend-paying stocks will become more and more attractive. And if you look at our yield at the moment, it's over 4.5 percent."

■ "Our recommendation is STRONG BUY," said Mark Hebeka, CFA, writing for the *Standard & Poor's Stock Reports* on November 11, 2005. "We believe BAC shares offer an attractive risk/reward trade-off at current valuation levels, and an above-average dividend yield."

■ The company's Global Corporate and Investment Banking group has offices in thirty cities, serving clients in more than 150 countries, with associates in major business centers in the Americas, Europe, and Asia.

■ A pioneer in debit-card transactions, Bank of America is the number-one debit card issuer in the United States, with some 17 million cards outstanding. Debit cards give people an alternative to checks or cash at the point of sale for goods and services, and their popularity is growing dramatically.

■ "When Bank of America announced its $47-billion deal for FleetBoston Financial in October 2003, Wall Street groaned," according to an article that appeared in *BusinessWeek* on April 4, 2005. "Bank of America's stock plunged 10 percent that day. But in its first year with Fleet, Bank of America wrung out $909 million in cost savings even while making a hard push to bring in new customers. The result: Bank of America added 184,000 new consumer checking accounts and 196,000 new savings accounts last year in Fleet's Northeast stronghold. Bank of America's profits rose 31 percent last year. Its shares have returned 61.9 percent over the past three years—not bad for what was once considered a terrible deal."

■ In January 2006, *SmartMoney* had these comments: "Neil Eigen, manager of the Seligman Large Cap Value fund, likes B of A for its three-decade run of double-digit dividend increases as well as its geographically diverse franchise. 'You want to own this stock and put it away,' Eigen says. It's among his largest holdings in the Seligman Large Cap Value fund."

■ On February 15, 2006, the *New York Times* surveyed twenty-seven financial analysts on their view of BAC. Six rated the stock a STRONG BUY; ten called it a MODERATE BUY; and eleven said Bank of America was a HOLD.

SECTOR: **Financials** ◆ BETA COEFFICIENT: **1.15**
10-YEAR COMPOUND EARNINGS PER SHARE GROWTH: **9%**
10-YEAR COMPOUND DIVIDENDS PER SHARE GROWTH: **13.8%**

		2005	2004	2003	2002	2001	2000	1999	1998
Loans (millions)		537,221	515,463	371,463	342,755	322,278	385,355	363,834	350,206
Net income (millions)		16,886	14,143	10,810	9,249	8,042	7,863	8,240	6,490
Earnings per share		4.15	3.67	3.57	2.96	2.48	2.36	2.34	1.82
Dividends per share		1.90	1.70	1.44	1.22	1.14	1.03	0.93	0.80
Price	high	47.4	47.5	42.4	38.5	32.8	30.5	38.2	44.2
	low	41.1	38.5	32.1	27.0	22.5	18.2	23.8	22.0

GROWTH AND INCOME

Banta Corporation

225 Main Street ❑ P.O. Box 8003 ❑ Menasha, WI 54952-8003 ❑ (920) 751-7713 ❑ Dividend reinvestment program is available (800) 278-4353 ❑ Web site: *www.banta.com* ❑ Listed: NYSE ❑ Ticker symbol: BN ❑ S&P rating: B ❑ Value Line financial strength rating: B++

Banta Corporation, a technology and market leader in printing and supply chain management, has a solid foundation for growth:

- Superior business mix
- Strong, predictable cash and earnings generation in the print sector
- Higher growth potential supply-chain management sector to drive top-line growth
- Strong balance sheet
- 18 percent debt to total capital
- Unrelenting cost reduction and continuous improvement
- Technology and systems integration capabilities in both print and supply-chain management
- Blue-chip customer base
- Customer-focused value chains differentiate Banta
- Multiple layers of diversification
- Strong leadership team
- 104-year history of superior performance and values-based management

Company Profile

Banta is much more than a leading provider of printing and digital imaging services. The supply-chain management business, the fastest-growing segment of Banta's operations, offers important value-added products and services to support the growth of Banta's core printing businesses.

Although you've probably never given it much thought, the last time you opened a carton containing a new computer, VCR, or other piece of electronic gear, there's a good chance that Banta printed the instruction booklet, installation guide, warranty cards, and other printed matter inside; provided the how-to video- or audiotape; supplied the software kit, including diskettes; and provided all of the packaging, whether plastic, cardboard, or paper.

Banta Corporation is a market leader in two primary businesses: printing and supply-chain management. The company has more than thirty-five operations in North America, Europe, and the Far East. Founded in 1901, Banta became a public company in 1971.

Business, trade, and special-interest magazine publishers turn to Banta for the production of nearly 800 titles. Three modern facilities provide a focused production environment for printing and mailing short- to medium-run publications.

Its publishing market products include the following:

- Educational, trade, juvenile, professional, and religious books
- Business, trade association, and consumer special-interest magazines
- Journals and newsletters
- Technical manuals
- Calendars
- Directories
- Multimedia kits
- Instructional games
- CD-ROMs
- Video- and audiocassettes
- Web sites

Banta provides a full spectrum of direct marketing materials and personalization technologies that maximize the effectiveness of direct-response print. The company is the leader in the production and distribution of specialty and retail catalogues.

Finally, Banta holds a leadership position in each of its market segments.

Banta health-care products extend the company's reach beyond the traditional printing and digital-imagine segments. Three manufacturing facilities produce sterile and nonsterile products used in hospitals, outpatient clinics, and dental offices. These specialized products are composed of paper, nonwoven materials, and polyethylene film. The product line also extends to related applications in the foodservice industry, such as disposable bibs, tablecloths, and gloves.

The health-care segment was sold to Fidelity Strategic Investments on February 14, 2005, for $67 million. The proceeds were used to buy back some of Banta's own shares, so as to increase earnings per share.

Shortcomings to Bear in Mind

- "These high-quality, neutrally ranked shares have below-average appreciation potential," said Sigourney B. Romaine, writing for *Value Line Investment Survey* on November 18, 2005. "Banta has a good position in printing and generates some free cash flow. Moreover, supply chain management offers higher growth prospects than printing as companies increase their outsourcing. But the shares' recent price anticipates some of the growth we foresee."
- "We recently downgraded our recommendation to HOLD, from BUY, on valuation," said James Peters, CFA, writing for *Standard & Poor's Company Reports* on February 10, 2006. "In the fourth quarter of 2005, the company suspended share repurchases while it pursued strategic acquisitions. Although no purchases were completed, we think BN is likely to broaden its global presence and deepen existing segment penetration through acquisitions in 2006." (This doesn't sound like a bad situation to me. I prefer acquisitions to share repurchase.)

Reasons to Buy

- On March 5, 2006, the *New York Times* put out a dragnet for analysts who keep tabs on Banta. Only two surfaced. One rated the stock a STRONG BUY, and the other said it was a HOLD.
- Banta's strategy is to structure highly focused business units around key industry market segments to support each segment's unique needs. A superior understanding of, and position in, carefully selected markets gives Banta the ability to better allocate capital resources and develop solutions, greater customer loyalty, and continuing growth opportunities.

Watt Publishing, an internationally recognized and respected publisher of seventeen agribusiness, food processing, woodworking, and furniture magazines, is a good example of Banta's ability to provide customized solutions to special-interest magazine publishers. After acquiring Chartwell Communications, Wall Publishing had to manage production in four printing facilities at two different companies, each with a different prepress workflow system. To cope, Watt Publishing used an independent prepress house for converting customer design files to each printer's workflow requirements.

Quickly sensing a need to streamline the process, Watt Publishing invited Banta and the incumbent suppliers—one of which had a thirty-one-year relationship with Watt—to propose a solution. Banta won the business handily by recommending a unique solution: the adaptation of a new prepress system, still in the concept stage, that was actually being designed for smaller print shops. Banta helped install the equipment and led the training of personnel at two Watt Publishing facilities. Watt Publishing will enjoy savings of several hundred thousand dollars in prepress costs during the next few years, while Banta enjoys the business of yet another growing special-interest magazine publisher.

■ "Our Supply-Chain Management Services Sector had an exceptional year in 2004," said CEO Stephanie A. Streeter in 2005. "Both revenue and operating earnings reached all-time highs, surpassing the prior year's record performance. Revenue rose 15 percent and operating earnings increased to $46.7 million, 3 percent above the prior year's $45.4 million, before last year's special charge of $9.6 million. Healthy market demand and our reputation for excellent execution enabled us to both expand relationships with existing customers and win new customers. We also benefited from higher productivity and improved facility utilization.

"Over the past two years, our Supply-Chain Management Services Sector has generated increases of 41 percent in revenue and 68 percent in operating earnings. Moreover, we remain very encouraged by the growth potential in this business, as we aggressively pursue additional opportunities to apply our considerable expertise in material procurement, product assembly, order fulfillment, and distribution."

SECTOR: **Industrials** ◆ BETA COEFFICIENT: **.75**
10-YEAR COMPOUND EARNINGS PER SHARE GROWTH: **4.7%**
10-YEAR COMPOUND DIVIDENDS PER SHARE GROWTH: **6.6%**

		2005	2004	2003	2002	2001	2000	1999	1998
Revenues (millions)		1,544	1,523	1,418	1,366	1,453	1,538	1,278	1,336
Net income (millions)		73	68	47	44	50	59	54	53
Earnings per share		2.76	2.67	2.34	2.35	2.31	2.35	2.02	1.80
Dividends per share		.70	.68	.68	.64	.62	.60	.52	.51
Price	high	52.5	47.5	41.0	39.1	31.0	25.7	27.4	35.3
	low	39.2	36.7	27.0	29.0	22.5	17.2	16.8	21.8

C. R. Bard, Inc.

730 Central Avenue ❑ Murray Hill, NJ 07974 ❑ (908) 277-8413 ❑ Direct dividend reinvestment plan available: (866) 238-5345 ❑ Web site: *www.crbard.com* ❑ Listed: NYSE ❑ Ticker symbol: BCR ❑ S&P rating: B+ ❑ Value Line Financial Rating: A

In 2005, CEO Timothy M. Ring described some of C. R. Bard's endovascular products that augur well for the future. He said, "Patients undergoing chronic hemodialysis often develop a partial or complete blockage in their vessels used for vascular access. Angioplasty balloons are commonly used to reopen the blockage. Our Conquest product combines a low-profile balloon with an ability to reopen the vessel, making it a popular choice for this application. The global market for dialysis access repair is anticipated to reach $60 million in 2005, and we expect our products and technologies to continue to play an important role in this market expansion."

Fluency Stent Graft

Mr. Ring went on to say, "Our Fluency product is Bard's first stent graft introduction. In the United States, it is used to treat the narrowing of the airway connecting the mouth and nose to the lungs. Such narrowing is usually due to either a benign or malignant tissue growth. In Europe, the Fluency stent graft is indicated for opening arteries in the upper part of the leg. The global market for stent grafts is currently $75 million and anticipated to grow to more than $100 million in the near future."

Recovery Vena Cava Filter

Mr. Ring went on to discuss another promising product.

"Vena cava Vacora filters are designed to prevent blood clots from traveling to the lungs. Our Recovery filter is removable, the first of its kind in the United States. The Recovery filter was fully introduced into the domestic market in early 2004 and drove net sales growth of 96 percent in our vena cava filter business in 2004."

Vacora Vacuum–Assisted Biopsy System

"Our new Vacora vacuum–assisted biopsy system is used in breast biopsies, 2.3 million of which are performed globally each year. Vacora is a minimally invasive biopsy device that obtains high-quality tissue samples and can be used in conjunction with X-ray, ultrasound, and MRI procedures. It is proving to be a very versatile tool for physicians."

Nor does this complete a listing of many other promising products in Bard's other businesses, including its Urology, Soft-tissue Repair, Specialty Access, and Endoscopic Technologies businesses.

Company Profile

Founded in 1907 by Charles Russell Bard, the company initially sold urethral catheters and other urinary products. One of its first medical products was the silk urethral catheter imported from France.

Today, C. R. Bard markets a wide range of medical, surgical, diagnostic, and patient-care devices. It does business worldwide to hospitals, individual health-care professionals, extended-care facilities, and alternate site facilities. In general, Bard's products are intended to be used once and then discarded.

The company offers a complete line of urological diagnosis and intervention products (about one-third of annual sales), including the well-known Foley catheters, procedure kits and trays, and related urine monitoring and collection systems; urethral stents; and specialty devices for incontinence.

Urology

This business accounts for about 30 percent of revenues. The Foley catheter, introduced by Bard in 1934, remains one of the most important products in the urological field. Foley catheters are marketed in individual sterile packages, but, more importantly, they are included in sterile procedural kits and trays, a concept pioneered by Bard. The company is the market leader in Foley catheters, which currently are Bard's largest-selling urological product.

Newer products include the Infection Control Foley catheter, which reduces the rate of urinary tract infections; an innovative collagen implant and sling materials that are used to treat urinary incontinence; and brachytherapy services, devices, and radioactive seeds to treat prostate cancer.

Oncology

This business accounts for about 23 percent of revenues. In the realm of oncology, C. R. Bard's products are designed for the detection and treatment of various types of cancer. Products include specialty access catheters and ports; gastroenterological products (endoscopic accessories, percutaneous feeding devices and stents); biopsy devices; and a suturing system for gastroesophageal reflux disease. The company's chemotherapy products serve a well-established market in which Bard holds a major market position.

Vascular Products

This business accounts for about 23 percent of revenues. The company's line of vascular diagnosis and intervention products includes peripheral angioplasty stents, catheters, guide wires, introducers, and accessories; vena cava filters and biopsy devices; electro physiology products, such as cardiac mapping and laboratory systems and diagnostic and temporary pacing electrode catheters; fabrics and meshes; and implantable blood-vessel replacements.

Bard's memotherm nitinol stent technology from the company's Angiomed subsidiary established the company as a major player in this peripheral growth market. With the acquisition of Impra, Inc., in 1996, Bard has the broadest line available of vascular grafts.

Surgical Products

This business accounts for about 19 percent of revenues. Surgical specialties products include meshes for vessel and hernia repair; irrigation devices for orthopedic and laparoscopic procedures; and topical hemostatic devices.

The innovation of Bard's PerFix plug and Composix sheet has significantly improved the way hernias are repaired and has reduced the time needed for repair from hours to minutes. Hernia operations can now be done in an outpatient setting in about twenty minutes. What's more, the patient generally can return to normal activity with little or no recovery time.

The balance of sales (about 4 percent) fall into the "other" category.

International (30 percent)

Bard markets its products through twenty-two subsidiaries and a joint venture in ninety-two countries outside the United States. Principal markets are Japan, Canada, the United Kingdom, and continental Europe.

Shortcomings to Bear in Mind

- One analyst thinks the company's business may take a modest breather in 2006. Growth will continue, but at a slower pace.

Reasons to Buy

- On March 21, 2006, the *New York Times* tabulated what analysts were saying about Bard. Four analysts rated the stock a STRONG BUY, two said it was a MODERATE BUY, and four considered Bard a HOLD.

■ C. R. Bard has an acquisition strategy that targets small research or developing companies as well as larger established companies with market leadership positions. In addition to acquiring companies, Bard has expanded its business in the medical field by acquiring product lines, entering into licensing agreements and joint ventures, and making equity investments in companies with emerging technologies.

On January 12, 2005, C. R. Bard announced that it had acquired certain assets of Genyx Medical, Inc., of Aliso Viejo, California, related to the Uryx® implantable bulking agent for the treatment of stress urinary incontinence. The Uryx product has received premarket approval from the U.S. Food and Drug Administration, and Bard launched it in the first half of 2005. The company's Urological division, located in Covington, Georgia, markets the product.

Stress urinary incontinence is an often-debilitating condition that affects an estimated 50 million people globally, 85 percent of whom are women. Minimally invasive bulking agent therapy can be a first-line treatment choice and is often used for patients who are not candidates for surgery. The Uryx product is a proprietary polymer implanted into the tissue surrounding the urethra to reduce or eliminate this form of urinary incontinence.

CEO Timothy M. Ring commented, "With the aging population and the increasing demand for more effective, minimally invasive therapies for stress urinary incontinence, we view this acquisition as an important opportunity for Bard. We believe that the addition of the Uryx device will further strengthen our broad product line and enhance our position in the incontinence market."

■ *Value Line Investment Survey* had some encouraging words about Bard on March 3, 2006. George Rho said, "We still like this equity as a long-term vehicle for risk-adjusted total returns. Bard has an extremely diversified product portfolio. It also has the financial wherewithal to bolster R&D efforts with acquisitions, as well as to boost returns to shareholders via stock repurchases and/or dividend increases."

SECTOR: **Health Care** ◆ BETA COEFFICIENT: **0.75**
10-YEAR COMPOUND EARNINGS PER SHARE GROWTH: **13%**
10-YEAR COMPOUND DIVIDENDS PER SHARE GROWTH: **4.9%**

		2005	2004	2003	2002	2001	2000	1999	1998
Revenues (millions)		1,771	1,656	1,433	1,274	1,181	1,099	1,037	1,165
Net income (millions)		327	263	204	177	143	125	118	96
Earnings per share		3.03	2.45	1.94	1.68	1.38	1.23	1.14	0.86
Dividends per share		.50	.47	.45	.43	.42	.41	.39	.37
Price	high	72.8	65.1	40.8	32.0	32.5	27.5	29.9	25.1
	low	60.8	40.1	27.0	22.0	20.4	17.5	20.8	14.3

CONSERVATIVE GROWTH

Becton, Dickinson and Company

1 Becton Drive ❑ Franklin Lakes, NJ 07417-1880 ❑ (201) 847-5453 ❑ Direct dividend reinvestment plan available (866) 238-5345 ❑ Web site: *www.bd.com* ❑ Fiscal year ends September 30 ❑ Ticker symbol: BDX ❑ S&P rating: A ❑ Value Line financial strength rating: A+

Robert Rennie, Ph.D., one of Canada's senior clinical microbiologists, wanted to equip his laboratory at the University of Alberta in Edmonton with the most advanced technology for identification and antimicrobial susceptibility testing (ID/AST). Dr. Rennie compared three competing automated microbiology systems to investigate which system would enable him to provide physicians with the fastest, most reliable diagnoses of patients' bacterial infections and help to direct effective drug therapy.

Dr. Rennie concluded that the BD Phoenix Automated Microbiology System offered an opportunity for a new technology that would rapidly identify pathogens and give rapid and accurate identification of the most important antimicrobial resistance markers. Dr. Rennie placed a BD Phoenix system in his laboratory—the first to be installed in a North American hospital.

The BD Phoenix Automated Microbial System detects bacterial resistance rapidly and assists with optimal patient therapy. The system can perform up to 200 simultaneous identification and susceptibility tests and can deliver accurate results in four to sixteen hours—rapid for the microbial world.

Among its competitive advantages, the BD Phoenix system identifies more than 300 organisms—significantly more than that of the nearest competitor. When certain organisms unique to Canada proved difficult to identify, BD worked with Dr. Rennie to design tests that provided the solution.

Company Profile

Becton, Dickinson is a medical technology company that serves health-care institutions, life science researchers, clinical laboratories, industry, and the general public. BD manufactures and sells a broad range of medical supplies, devices, laboratory equipment, and diagnostic products.

Becton, Dickinson focuses strategically on achieving growth in three worldwide business segments: BD Medical (formerly BD Medical Systems), BD Biosciences, and BD Diagnostics (formerly BD Clinical Laboratory Solutions). BD products are marketed in the United States both through independent distribution channels and directly to end users. Outside the United States, BD products are marketed through independent distribution channels and sales representatives and, in some markets, directly to end users.

BDX generates close to 50 percent of its revenues outside the United States. Worldwide demand for health-care products and services continues to be strong, despite the ongoing focus on cost containment. The health-care environment favors continued growth in medical delivery systems due to the growing awareness of the need to protect health-care workers from hazards like accidental needle-sticks and legislative/regulatory activity favoring conversion to safety-engineered devices.

BD Biosciences, one of the world's largest businesses serving the life sciences, provides research tools and reagents to study life—from normal processes to disease states—and to accelerate the pace of biomedical discovery. Throughout the world, clinicians and researchers use BD Biosciences' tools to study genes, proteins, and cells to better understand disease, improve technologies for diagnosis and disease management, and facilitate the discovery and development of novel therapeutics.

BD Diagnostics offers system solutions for collecting, identifying, and transporting specimens, as well as advanced instrumentation for quickly and accurately analyzing specimens. The business also provides services that focus on customers' process flow, supply chain management, and training and education.

BD Medical holds leadership positions in hypodermic needles and syringes, infusion therapy devices, insulin injection systems, and prefillable drug-delivery systems for pharmaceutical companies. It offers the industry's broadest, deepest line of safety-engineered sharps products, as well as surgical and regional anesthesia, ophthalmology, critical care, and sharps disposal products.

According to a company spokesman, "BDX is dedicated to producing solutions—and the best solution of all is helping all people live healthy lives. Our vision is to become a great company, defined by great performance, great contributions made to society, and being a great place to work."

Shortcomings to Bear in Mind

- Nearly half of the company's sales come from abroad. This exposes BDX to the risks associated with foreign current rates, which could create increased volatility in reported earnings. On the other hand, the company has done a good job of managing foreign currency exposure, and the impact on earnings has typically been limited to only 1 or 2 percent.
- On March 5, 2006, of the thirteen analysts polled by the *New York Times,* a dozen considered BDX a HOLD. Two rated the stock a STRONG BUY, and two analysts gave it a MODERATE BUY rating.

Reasons to Buy

- "Our recommendation on the shares is BUY," said Robert M. Gold, writing for the Standard & Poor's *Company Reports* on February 17, 2006. "We think the stock should continue to benefit from improved revenue visibility amid signs of recovering end user demand in the life sciences industry and momentum in the diagnostics and diabetes management areas."
- *Value Line Investment Survey* also had positive comments on March 3, 2006. Erik A. Antonson said, "Good-quality BD shares are suited for conservative investors. Their Timeliness rank of 3 (Average) indicates that business fundamentals should allow the equity to at least keep pace with the market in the coming six to twelve months. Moreover, the stock is ranked 1 (Highest) for Safety, and its Price Stability score is 90. This, coupled with an increasing dividend and sizable cash flow, makes this equity a good selection for more reserved, income-oriented investors."
- In fiscal 2006, CEO Edward J. Ludwig said, "We've come a long way over the past five years. Our 2005 achievements were the latest affirmation that our strategy to drive innovation and operating effectiveness is working. By continuing on this course, we are confident that 2006 will be another year of progress.

"Even now, we are increasing our investments in innovation to address even bigger health-care challenges in the future. For example, we are working toward:

- Employing micron needles and needle-free technologies to provide safer, more effective and painless drug delivery systems.
- Addressing the problem of health-care–associated infections with superior devices, diagnostics, and know-how.
- Developing rapid and more accurate diagnostic systems that will improve therapy and patient health.

- Helping people with diabetes live healthier lives by developing advanced drug delivery, glucose-sensing, and information management systems, and making significant contributions to finding a cure for diabetes with our investments in cellular therapeutics.
- Continuing our fight against the spread of infectious diseases, particularly HIV/AIDS, with safer drug delivery systems, advanced immunization practices, and real-time, accurate diagnostics.
- Further improving the effectiveness of life science researchers by providing advanced discovery systems, bionutrients, and reagents."

■ The company's use of computer-aided design and manufacturing technology enables BDX to bring quality products to market faster and at a lower cost. One such technology is stereo lithography, which uses a laser system to quickly create a three-dimensional physical object from a computer-aided design model. Engineers can use this extremely accurate model as a prototype, improving both the quality of the product design and the speed of the product-development process.

Becton, Dickinson has the technology to help reduce the medical errors that have received attention of late. A U.S. government scientific panel found that about 75,000 hospital patients die each year from medical mistakes. Yet only 9 percent of the facilities have invested in equipment to address the problem.

For its part, BDX is offering two handheld devices, based on 3Com's Palm Computing technology. One tracks drugs from the initial order through their administration. The other serves a similar purpose for specimen collection, testing, and patient file management.

■ Domestic sales of insulin needles and syringes are expected to increase in the high-single digits during the next few years, fueled by the estimated 5 percent annual growth in the number of Americans suffering from diabetes, plus the trend toward multiple insulin injections. Recent scientific studies have shown that the use of multiple daily injections of insulin reduces the severity of the disease's longer-term deleterious effects.

Becton, Dickinson accounts for about 90 percent of the domestic insulin syringe market. The company has entered into an arrangement with Eli Lilly, the largest domestic producer of insulin products, and Boehringer Mannheim, a major manufacturer of glucose monitoring devices, to provide information to diabetics regarding the best manner in which to control their disease. Over time, this program should accelerate the trend toward multiple daily insulin injections.

The company is also reviewing a number of noninvasive techniques to monitor glucose levels in diabetics. This device could reach the market before the end of the decade and further enhance the company's overall position in the diabetic sector.

SECTOR: **Health Care** ◆ BETA COEFFICIENT: **.75**
10-YEAR COMPOUND EARNINGS PER SHARE GROWTH: **12.3%**
10-YEAR COMPOUND DIVIDENDS PER SHARE GROWTH: **13.1%**

		2005	2004	2003	2002	2001	2000	1999	1998
Revenues (millions)		5,415	4,935	4,528	4,033	3,746	3,618	3,418	3,117
Net income (millions)		692	582	547	480	402	393	386	360
Earnings per share		2.66	2.21	2.07	1.79	1.63	1.49	1.46	1.37
Dividends per share		.72	.60	.40	.39	.38	.37	.34	.29
Price	high	61.2	58.2	41.8	38.6	39.3	35.3	44.2	49.6
	low	49.7	40.2	28.8	24.7	30.0	21.8	22.4	24.4

GROWTH AND INCOME

Bemis Company, Inc.

222 South Ninth Street, Suite 2300 ❑ Minneapolis, MN 55402-4099 ❑ (612) 376-3030 ❑ Direct dividend reinvestment plan available (800) 468-9716 ❑ Listed NYSE ❑ Web site: *www.bemis.com* ❑ Ticker symbol: BMS ❑ S&P rating: A ❑ Value Line financial strength rating: A+

"At Bemis, innovation is the keystone of our business strategy," said a company official in 2006. "Using our expertise in material science, we develop unique materials designed to deliver superior performance in packaging and pressure-sensitive applications. Our engineers custom-blend materials and use proprietary processes to create new products. Applications of our material science knowledge are constantly evolving.

"Creative solutions originally developed for one market can provide opportunities to strengthen our product offering in other markets. For instance, the materials designed to extend shelf life for meat and cheese markets can now be applied to oxygen-sensitive, drug-coated medical devices. Anti-fog film, developed for lunchmeat packaging, can be used to reduce condensation in produce packaging."

The spokesman goes on to say, "Our products are designed to maximize the performance of the materials on our customers' production lines, to achieve superior seal strength that reduces waste and extends shelf life, and to optimize the appeal of our customers' products in the retail stores."

Company Profile

Dating back to 1858, Bemis is a leading manufacturer of flexible packaging and pressure-sensitive materials. More than 75 percent of the company's sales are packaging related.

Flexible packaging refers to product packaging that can be easily bent, twisted, or folded. The opposite is rigid packaging, which includes things like glass and plastic bottles, metal cans, and cardboard boxes. Examples of flexible packaging include candy bar wrappers, pouches for shredded cheese, bread bags, and dog food bags.

Flexible packaging (about 80 percent of company revenue) is an attractive means of packaging a wide variety of products because of its light weight and strength, as well as the manufacturer's ability to use small amounts of material in most applications. That results in lower costs for the package itself and less material to be disposed of after the package is used.

The primary market for the company's products is the food industry. Other markets include medical, pharmaceutical, chemical, agribusiness, printing, and graphic arts, as well as a variety of other industrial end uses. Bemis holds a strong position in many of its markets and actively seeks new market segments where its technical skill and other capabilities provide a competitive advantage.

Bemis has a strong technical base in polymer chemistry, film extrusion coating, and laminating, printing and converting, and pressure-sensitive adhesive technologies. These capabilities are being integrated to provide greater innovation and accelerated growth in the company's core businesses.

Business Segments

Bemis's business breaks down into two main segments: flexible packaging and pressure-sensitive materials.

FLEXIBLE PACKAGING

Bemis is the leading manufacturer of flexible packaging in North America. The company provides multinational and North American food and consumer products companies with packaging solutions that protect contents during shipment, extend shelf life, and offer attractive, consumer-friendly designs. Over 60 percent of Flexible Packaging sales are printed film materials. The balance is sold as plain film for retail and institutional food as well as a variety of other markets.

This segment breaks down into three smaller pieces:

- High Barrier Products includes controlled and modified atmosphere packaging for food, medical, personal care, and non-food applications consisting of complex barrier, multilayer polymer film structures, and laminates. Primary markets are processed and fresh meat, liquids, snacks, cheese, coffee, condiments, candy, pet food, personal care, and medical packaging.
- Polyethylene Products include monolayer and coextruded polymer films that have been converted to bags, roll stock, or shrink wrap. Primary markets are bakery products, seed, retail, lawn and garden, ice, fresh produce, frozen vegetables, shrink-wrap, tissue, and sanitary products.
- Paper products include multiwall and single-ply paper bags, balers, printed paper roll stock, and bag closing materials. Primary markets are pet products, seed, chemicals, dairy products, fertilizers, feed, minerals, flour, rice, and sugar.

PRESSURE-SENSITIVE MATERIALS

Bemis is a major worldwide manufacturer of pressure-sensitive adhesive coated materials for a variety of markets. Under the brand name of MACtac, Bemis delivers advanced product performance to the pressure-sensitive industry. Examples include labeling for cold temperature food packaging, harsh environment conditions, wet manufacturing processes, miniature electronic components, tamper-evident packaging, and technologically advanced fastener applications.

This segment is divided up as follows:

- Roll Label Products include unprinted rolls of pressure-sensitive adhesive coated papers and film. These products are sold to converters who print labels for bar coding, product decoration, identification, safety marking, and product instructions. Primary markets are food packaging, personal care product packaging, inventory control labeling, and laser/ink jet printed labels.
- Graphics and Distribution Products include unprinted rolls or sheets of pressure-sensitive adhesive coated papers and films. Offset printers, sign makers, and photo labs use these products on short-run and/or digital printing technology to create labels, sign, or vehicle graphics. Primary markets are sheet printers, shipping labels, indoor and outdoor signs, photograph and digital print over-laminates, and vehicle graphics.
- Technical and Industrial Products include pressure-sensitive adhesive coated tapes used for mounting, bonding, and fastening. Tapes sold to medical markets feature medical-grade adhesives suitable for direct skin contact. Primary markets are batteries, electronics, medical, and pharmaceuticals.

Shortcomings to Bear in Mind

- The *New York Times* polled eight leading analysts on March 3, 2006. Only one said Bemis was a STRONG BUY, and only two rated the stock a MODERATE BUY. The other five viewed it as a HOLD.
- "These shares do not provide wide capital appreciation potential out to 2008–2010," said Eric M. Gottlieb, writing a report for

Value Line Investment Survey on January 6, 2006. "However, future acquisitions within Flexible Packaging are likely, which may render out three- to five-year estimates conservative. Indeed, management stated that it would sacrifice short-term profits for deals that made long-term financial sense. This risky strategy may prove detrimental to Bemis's short-run stock value."

Reasons to Buy

- *Standard & Poor's Company Reports* had some favorable comments on February 7, 2006. According to analyst Stewart Scharf, "Based primarily on our valuation metrics, which indicate attractive potential on a total-return basis [dividends plus appreciation], in what we see as a better pricing environment, we maintain our BUY recommendation on BMS share. We expect the company to continue to buy back stock."
- On February 2, 2006, Lehman Brothers gave the stock an OVERWEIGHT rating, similar to a BUY. The analyst said, "Bemis is a leading manufacturer of flexible packaging and pressure-sensitive materials. BMS has secured a niche for itself in the technologically advanced barrier/multilayer film segment."
- "Our attention to maintaining a world-class manufacturing organization has rewarded our customers with competitive edge and flexibility in packaging options," said a company spokesman. "Over the past five years, Bemis has devoted substantial resources to improving capacity and expanding world-class operating facilities to meet the increasing demand for sophisticated barrier films.

"Since the majority of the packages we sell in the Flexible Packaging business are printed, graphics capabilities are a significant source of expertise and competitive edge for Bemis. We are vertically integrated, offering customers our graphic design and color separation expertise. Bemis manufacturing operators work directly with graphic designers to create the highest-quality printed package. Our state-of-the-art printing presses significantly improve our manufacturing efficiencies with robotics to reduce press idle-time during change over to new colors."

- The key to market leadership is cutting-edge technology and innovation, based primarily upon material science. At Bemis's Flexible Packaging operations, differing grades of polymers, such as polyethylene, polystyrene, polypropylene, nylon, and polyester, are combined in a variety of ways to create films that are stronger, shinier, clearer, abuse-resistant, peelable, easier to print, sterilizable, and easier to process on machinery.

What's more, the company's recent acquisition of a shrink-packaging business introduced a patented technology that was not previously available to Bemis. The combination of this shrink film technology and "our material science expertise creates sizable opportunities for a variety of new innovations for our Flexible Packaging operations," said a company spokesman.

"Our research and development efforts go beyond the laboratory to the manufacturing floor, designing films that work better on even the newest high-speed machinery. We go into customer plants to design innovative solutions for their packaging and marketing needs. Bemis consistently devotes a significant effort to the development of new products and processes that will keep us at the forefront of the industry and keep our customers anticipating the next generation of packing innovation."

- In 2005, Bemis acquired majority ownership of Dixie Toga, one of the largest packaging companies in South America. Headquartered in Sao Paolo, Brazil, Dixie Toga recorded annual sales in excess of $300 million in 2004.

"The Dixie Toga business is an exciting addition to Bemis Company and further strengthens our position as the leading flexible packaging supplier in North America and South America," said CEO Jeff Curler. "The Dixie Toga operations are well-managed, growing businesses with leading market positions and strong customer relationships. This business is achieving strong revenue growth and profit margins through a combination of new product introductions, focused cost control, and improved production efficiencies."

SECTOR: **Materials** ◆ BETA COEFFICIENT: **.95**
10-YEAR COMPOUND EARNINGS PER SHARE GROWTH: **6.3%**
10-YEAR COMPOUND DIVIDENDS PER SHARE GROWTH: **8.4%**

		2005	2004	2003	2002	2001	2000	1999	1998
Revenues (millions)		3,474	2,834	2,635	2,369	2,293	2,165	1,918	1,848
Net income (millions)		162	180	147	166	140	131	115	111
Earnings per share		1.51	1.67	1.36	1.54	1.32	1.22	1.09	1.04
Dividends per share		0.72	0.64	0.62	0.52	0.50	0.48	0.46	0.44
Price	high	32.5	29.5	25.6	29.1	26.2	19.6	20.2	23.4
	low	23.2	23.2	19.6	19.7	14.3	11.4	15.1	16.7

AGGRESSIVE GROWTH

Biomet, Incorporated

56 East Bell Drive ❑ Warsaw, IN 46582-0587 ❑ (574) 267-6639 ❑ Dividend reinvestment plan not available ❑ Fiscal year ends May 31 ❑ Listed: Nasdaq ❑ Web site: *www.biomet.com* ❑ Ticker symbol: BMET ❑ S&P rating: A ❑ Value Line financial strength rating: A

In 1977, the company's first year of operation, Biomet recorded sales of $17,000—and a net loss of $63,000. Today, the company is a leader in the musculoskeletal marketplace, with sales not far from $1.9 billion. Its products include the design and manufacture of four major product groups: reconstructive devices, fixation products, spinal products, and other products.

Favorable demographics and a shift to technologically advanced products are fueling the estimated 12-percent growth in the $7.62-billion domestic musculoskeletal market. The demand for musculoskeletal products continues to grow with the aging of the baby boomer generation. According to the U.S. Census Bureau projections, the population of people aged fifty-five to seventy-five is expected to grow about 70 percent in the next twenty years, to 74.7 million people. What's more, the traditional orthopedic implant population (again, ages fifty-five to seventy-five) continues to expand below age fifty-five and above age seventy-five.

Procedures are now being recommended for patients at younger ages, as skilled engineering of new products and increasingly effective technology directly contribute to the greater probability of successful implant performance and longevity. In addition, the elderly are leading more active lifestyles than in past generations, resulting in stronger, healthier individuals who are excellent candidates for reconstructive implant procedures, creating a greater need for products and services to treat musculoskeletal disorders.

Company Profile

Biomet ranks among the world's largest orthopedic manufacturers. The company offers a wide variety of products that are used primarily by orthopedic medical specialists in the surgical replacement of hip and knee joints and in fracture fixation procedures as an aid in healing. They include reconstructive implants, electrical bone stimulators, and related products.

Reconstructive devices, which accounted for 67 percent of sales in fiscal 2005, are employed to replace joints that have deteriorated because of such diseases as osteoarthritis or injury. These include implants for replacement of hips, knees, shoulders, ankles, and elbows.

Fixation products accounted for 13 percent of revenues in 2005. These devices are used to treat stubborn bone fractures that have not healed with conventional surgical or nonsurgical therapy. In addition, some external fixation devices are used for complicated trauma, limb-lengthening, and deformity correction uses, and fracture repair. Internal fixation devices include nails, plates, screws, pins, and wires to stabilize bone injuries.

Spinal products made up 11 percent of sales in 2005. These include implantable, direct-current electrical-stimulation devices that provide an adjunct to surgical intervention in the treatment of nonunions and spinal fusions.

Other products (9 percent of 2005 revenues) include orthopedic support devices, arthroscopy products, operating room supplies, casting materials, general surgical instruments, and related items.

Biomet now operates more than fifty facilities, including eighteen manufacturing centers, with a marketing arm of about 1,850 sales representatives. The company's products are distributed in more than 100 countries.

Shortcomings to Bear in Mind

- "Our opinion is HOLD," said Robert M. Gold, writing for *Standard & Poor's Stock Reports* on January 5, 2006. "We see Biomet capturing share in the knee implant and spine segments in coming quarters. Although competitive pressures are high, we think some modest market share gains will also occur in the hip market following the launch of the company's recently approved ceramic-on-ceramic offering. In our opinion, however, meaningful valuation expansion will prove difficult amid protracted investor concerns regarding pricing pressure throughout the orthopedic device industry."

Reasons to Buy

- On March 29, 2006, the *New York Times* reported on the views of twenty-seven financial analysts concerning Biomet. Three rated the stock a STRONG BUY; five said it was a MODERATE BUY; seventeen relegated it to the HOLD category; one called it a MODERATE HOLD; and one lone wolf said it was a SELL—a warrant is out for his arrest.
- Beginning early in Biomet's history, the company focused on management's strength in research and development, specifically in the field of biomedical engineering, to produce improved products and technologies.

The company pioneered the use of titanium as a material of choice for hip stems, due to its biocompatibility and elasticity. Biomet designed and introduced tapered hip stems as a means to reduce stress shielding to ensure bone viability, promoting improved long-term fixation.

The company's porous plasma spray-coating technology was created by heating the titanium spray coating for application to the implant, rather than heating the device to create the bond, which can sacrifice the integrity of the implant.

For improved wear characteristics, Biomet produces direct-compression molded polyethylene tibial bearings (rather than machined polyethylene) for knee systems.

During the past six fiscal years, Biomet has introduced more than 500 new products.

These products will make a significant positive impact on long-term clinical outcomes for surgeons and their patients.

■ On July 13, 2004, the company announced the signing of a definitive agreement with Diamicron, Inc., of Orem, Utah, to develop and distribute, on a worldwide basis, diamond articulation technology for total hip arthroplasty. Based on Diamicron's proprietary polycrystalline diamond composite technology, diamond wear couples offer an alternative to conventional wear couples with both structural integrity and superior wear properties.

Under the terms of the agreement, Biomet has been granted semiexclusive rights, along with Exactech, Inc., to distribute initial hip products. In addition, the agreement provides Biomet with option rights to develop and market other extremity joint replacement products, including knee replacements, based on Diamicron's proprietary polycrystalline diamond composite technology.

Dane A. Miller, Ph.D., president and CEO of Biomet, said "This strategic partnership with Diamicron strengthens Biomet's development pipeline for alternative bearing technology. Diamond-on-diamond technology will be complementary to Biomet's existing programs in metal-on-metal articulation and ceramic-on-ceramic articulation bearing technologies. We believe that Biomet's development efforts in alternative bearing technologies comprise the most comprehensive product pipeline in the industry."

■ On June 18, 2004, the company announced the completion of the acquisition of Interpore International, Inc., for $280 million. Interpore's three major product groups include spinal implants, orthobiologics, and minimally invasive surgery products used by surgeons in a wide range of applications.

■ Biomet was one of the first companies to use and promote the use of titanium alloy for its orthopedic implants. Titanium alloy is now the material of choice because of its high biocompatibility, strength, durability, and elasticity, which is more similar to that of natural bone than other metals. Biomet also pioneered the utilization of a proprietary titanium porous coating, known as plasma spray, to encourage bone growth onto the implant for stability.

■ According to the Arthritis Foundation, the number of Americans with arthritis or chronic joint problems in 2005 was nearly one in three adults, or 66 million people, including 23 million adults who report symptoms but are currently undiagnosed. Osteoarthritis is the most prevalent form of arthritis, with more than 21 million adults diagnosed with this form of degenerative joint disease.

The majority of orthopedic implant patients are between fifty-five and seventy-five years of age, with surgical intervention primarily due to osteoarthritic changes. The U.S. Census Bureau currently estimates the target population of fifty-five to seventy-five-year-old individuals to be greater than 48 million people; this number is expected to grow by about 37 percent over the next ten years, to more than 66 million people. With the first of the 78 million baby boomers having entered this age range during the past five years, a significant expansion of this target population group is occurring.

■ The largest category of domestic musculoskeletal products market is the orthopedic reconstructive device market, valued at more than $5.4 billion, with growth estimated to be 12 to 14 percent annually. Biomet is the fourth-largest participant in the orthopedic reconstructive device market. The knee market, estimated to exceed $3 billion, is experiencing the greatest demand, with annual growth of 16 to 18 percent. The hip market is about $2.2 billion and growing at an estimated 6 to 8 percent annually. Biomet maintains the second-largest position in the estimated $160 million domestic shoulder market, growing at a rate of about 13 to 15 percent per year.

SECTOR: **Health Care** ◆ BETA COEFFICIENT: **.80**
10-YEAR COMPOUND EARNINGS PER SHARE GROWTH: **15.9%**
8-YEAR COMPOUND DIVIDENDS PER SHARE GROWTH: **22.3%**

		2005	2004	2003	2002	2001	2000	1999	1998
Revenues (millions)		1,880	1,615	1,390	1,192	1,031	921	757	651
Net income (millions)		352	326	287	240	198	174	116	125
Earnings per share		1.38	1.27	1.10	.88	.73	.65	.46	.49
Dividends per share		.20	.15	.10	.09	.07	.06	.05	.05
Price	high	45.7	49.6	38.0	33.3	34.4	27.8	20.3	18.3
	low	32.5	35.0	26.7	21.8	20.5	12.1	10.9	10.5

CONSERVATIVE INCOME

The Black & Decker Corporation

701 East Joppa Road ❑ Towson, MD 21286 ❑ (410) 716-3979 ❑ Direct dividend reinvestment plan available (800) 432-0140 ❑ Web site: *www.bdk.com* ❑ Listed: NYSE ❑ Ticker symbol: BDK ❑ S&P rating: B+ ❑ Value Line financial strength rating: B+

"During the 1940s, Al Decker, Jr., son of one of this venerable tool company's founders, noticed that workers were borrowing factory tools to do repairs and remodeling at home, so he came up with a home-utility line," said Nicole Bullock and Reshma Kapadia, writing for *SmartMoney* in October 2005. "Today Black & Decker has a team that tours job sites, asking workers what they like and don't like about their products and passing out prototypes to try. That kind of close attention to changing tastes should help the company thrive—even after the housing market cools down."

The *SmartMoney* article goes on to say, "The company gets more than 70 percent of its revenue from power tools and accessories, and it holds nearly 30 percent of both the professional and consumer markets in power tools—making it the global leader in each category."

The *SmartMoney* authors also said, "Black & Decker has an edge that should help it keep growing, even in a quiet market: Some 30 to 35 percent of its sales come from newly introduced products, up from the high 20s a few years ago. Ron Muhlenkamp, manager of the Muhlenkamp Fund, sees that at a sign of strength. 'I don't know many people who wear out power tools—you buy a new one because it's more productive,' he notes, adding that as long as its tools fit that description, Black & Decker 'will continue to grow earnings regardless of what the industry is doing.'"

Company Profile

In 1910, Duncan Black and Alonzo Decker launched the company on a shoestring in Baltimore, initially producing candy dippers and milk-bottle capping machines. In 1916, they brought out the company's first major power tool, a portable electric drill.

Black & Decker is a global manufacturer of quality power tools and accessories, hardware, and home-improvement products. BDK also has a stake in technology-based fastening systems. The company's products and services are marketed in more than 100 countries, and it has thirty-nine manufacturing operations, including ten outside the United States.

Black & Decker has established a reputation for product innovation, quality, end-user focus, design, and value. Its strong brand names and new product development capabilities enjoy worldwide recognition, and the company's global distribution is unsurpassed in its industries. Black & Decker operates three business segments: Power Tools and Accessories, Hardware and Home Improvement, and Fastening and Assembly Systems.

Power Tools and Accessories

This segment manufactures and markets products under three brand names: Black & Decker, Momentum Laser, and Dewalt. They include consumer power tools, accessories, electric lawn-and-garden tools, and electric cleaning and lighting products. In addition, this segment produces high-performance power tools, accessories, and industrial equipment, as well as laser products and air compressors.

Hardware and Home Improvement

This segment consists of Kwikset security hardware, Price Pfister plumbing products, and three security hardware companies in Europe. Kwikset, a world leader in the manufacturing of residential door hardware, markets products in North America, Australia, and Asia under the brand names Kwikset Security, Kwikset Maximum Security, Kwikset UltraMax Security, Black & Decker, and Geo. Price Pfister is a major competitor in the North American faucet and plumbing products market with products sold under the Price Pfister and Bach brands.

Fastening and Assembly Systems

Serving the global automotive and industrial markets, the Fastening and Assembly Systems segment, known as Emhart Teknologies, is the originator of several highly recognizable brands, including Pop blind rivets, Parker-Kalon screws, Gripco locknuts, HeliCoil wire inserts, Dodge inserts, Tucker stud welding equipment, and Warren plastic and metal fasteners.

Shortcomings to Bear in Mind

- Insiders, such as executives of the company and board members, have been heavy sellers of the Black & Decker stock. In a recent nine-month period, there were nineteen instances of selling and none of buying.

Reasons to Buy

- On January 27, 2006, Black & Decker announced that net earnings from continuing operations for the fourth quarter of 2005 were $101.8 million, or $1.28 per diluted share. Excluding $51.2 million of incremental tax expense to repatriate foreign earnings under the American Jobs Creation Act of 2004, net earnings from continuing operations were $1.93 per diluted share, a 21-percent increase from $1.60 in the fourth quarter of 2004.

For the full year 2005, net earnings from continuing operations were a record $544 million or $6.69 per diluted share. Excluding the incremental tax expense in the fourth quarter and a favorable insurance settlement in the first quarter, net earnings from continuing operations were $6.88 per diluted share, a 27-percent increase from $5.40 in 2004. The corporation generated a record $529 million of free cash flow, up from $526 million in 2004.

Sales from continuing operations increased slightly for the quarter to a record $1.7 billion, including a 1-percent negative impact of foreign currency translation. For the full year, sales increased 21 percent, to a record $6.5 billion. Acquisitions contributed 14 percent to sales for the full year, and foreign currency translation had a positive impact of 1 percent.

CEO Nolan D. Archibald commented, "Black & Decker increased earnings per share from continuing operations more than 23 percent for the fourth straight year in 2005. We extended our record of outstanding performance through excellent organic sales growth, aggressive cost reduction efforts, and effective use of our strong free cash flow. Despite raw material inflation, challenging comparisons to prior-year results, and an uneven global economic environment, in the fourth quarter we delivered 16-percent operating income growth and earnings above our guidance.

"Sales in the Power Tools and Accessories segment increased 2 percent for the quarter. The U.S. Industrial Products Group grew sales at a mid single-digit rate, driven by a double-digit growth rate for DEWALT tools and accessories. DEWALT construction tools, including cordless products and the new line of miter saws, sold particularly well. Sales in the U.S. Black & Decker consumer business decreased slightly, due to order patterns that drove a double-digit rate of increase in the third quarter. European sales decreased at a mid single-digit rate and fell short of our expectations due to a weaker economic environment in the U.K. Operating margin for the Power Tools and Accessories segment increased 50 basis points to 13.2 percent this quarter. Our U.S. businesses led the improvement, through continued integration cost savings and favorable mix.

"For the full year, sales in the Power Tools and Accessories segment increased 26 percent, including the 19-percent contribution from the Porter-Cable and Delta Tools Group acquisition. Organic sales growth was driven by the U.S. businesses, which posted a double-digit rate of increase for DEWALT and a mid single-digit growth rate in the consumer division. Operating margins in the segment improved 40 basis points to 13.3 percent, including a negative impact of approximately 90 basis points from the acquisition. Full-year margins of existing businesses increased significantly in all geographic regions, and exceeded 10 percent in Europe.

"Sales in the Hardware and Home Improvement segment decreased 4 percent for the quarter. Sales in the lockset business decreased at a mid single-digit rate, reflecting flat sales at Kwikset and decreases for Baldwin and Weiser against difficult comparisons to prior-year sales. Price Pfister grew sales at a low single-digit rate, as increases at a key retailer were partly offset by a decline in the wholesale channel. Operating margin was flat to the prior year at 13.4 percent, as cost savings from the manufacturing rationalization roughly offset raw material inflation.

"For the full year, sales in the Hardware and Home Improvement segment increased 5 percent, reflecting a double-digit growth rate at Price Pfister and a slight increase in lockset sales. Operating margin decreased 100 basis points to 14.2 percent, primarily due to raw material inflation and manufacturing inefficiencies.

"The Fastening and Assembly Systems segment increased sales 3 percent for the quarter, primarily due to growth in its international automotive divisions. Operating margin increased significantly to 16.6 percent, due to price increases and expense control. For the full year, sales increased 7 percent, driven by strong sales in the automotive divisions and a 1-percent contribution from the MasterFix acquisition. Volume leverage and pricing increases outweighed commodity cost pressure, enabling the segment to improve its full-year operating margin 60 basis points to 14.4 percent.

"Each of our segments made significant efforts to manage costs and expenses, which were key to our earnings growth this quarter. Selling, general, and administrative expenses decreased $13 million, most of which was reflected in corporate expense. For the full year, expenses rose at roughly half the sales growth rate in existing businesses, resulting in significant volume leverage.

"We continued to generate outstanding free cash flow and use our cash wisely in 2005. Free cash flow of $529 million set a record for the fourth straight year. This cash enabled us to repurchase 6.3 million shares of stock, or nearly 8 percent of shares outstanding, while maintaining a strong balance sheet.

"In addition to outstanding free cash flow, the year-end balance sheet reflects repatriation of $888 million of foreign earnings associated with the American Jobs Creation Act of 2004. We utilized $321 million of existing foreign cash and increased both cash and foreign subsidiary borrowings by the remaining $567 million. Also, as expected, the corporation recorded $51.2 million of one-time income tax expense related to the repatriation.

"Looking ahead, we expect another strong year in 2006. We are especially encouraged by the initial market reaction to DEWALT's 36-volt line of lithium-ion cordless tools, which will be available in the second quarter of 2006. We are confident that our lithium-ion technology is superior to our competition's, and that we will remain the leader in cordless power tools. After averaging 7 percent organic sales increases over the last two years, however, and facing a particularly difficult comparison in the first half of 2006, we expect sales growth will moderate to a low single-digit rate. Our cost saving initiatives should drive operating margin improvement despite raw material inflation and higher pension costs."

- The *New York Times* surveyed fifteen securities analysts on March 21, 2006, and found that three were convinced that BDK was a STRONG BUY; four said it was a MODERATE BUY; and eight preferred to rate it a HOLD.

SECTOR: **Consumer Discretionary** ◆ BETA COEFFICIENT: **1.05**
10-YEAR COMPOUND EARNINGS PER SHARE GROWTH: **31.3%**
10-YEAR COMPOUND DIVIDENDS PER SHARE GROWTH: **10.8%**

		2005	2004	2003	2002	2001	2000	1999
Revenues (millions)		6,524	5,398	4,483	4,394	4,333	4,561	4,520
Net income (millions)		544	441	287	261	179	296	300
Earnings per share		6.69	5.40	3.68	3.23	2.20	3.51	3.40
Dividends per share		1.12	.84	0.57	0.48	0.48	0.48	0.48
Price	high	93.7	87.5	49.9	50.5	46.9	50.2	64.6
	low	75.7	48.1	33.2	35.0	28.3	27.6	41.0

AGGRESSIVE GROWTH

The Boeing Company

100 North Riverside ❑ Chicago, IL 60606 ❑ (312) 544-2140 ❑ Direct dividend reinvestment plan available (888) 777-0923 ❑ Web site: *www.boeing.com* ❑ Ticker symbol: BA ❑ Listed: NYSE ❑ S&P rating: B+ ❑ Value Line financial strength rating: B++

"The global market for commercial aircraft is booming, fueled by strong demand from Asia," said Jay Palmer, writing for *Barron's* on December 19, 2005. Both Boeing and EADS (the parent of Europe's Airbus) have been snapping up orders left and right. Last week, Australia's Qantas Airways said it would order as many as 115 of Boeing's new twin-aisle 787 Dreamliners. That announcement came just one week after Airbus took an order from the Chinese government for 150 single-aisle A320 planes, the workhorse of the fleet. In all, EADS and Boeing each have received more than 800 orders this year, leaving both with record backlogs that should keep their manufacturing facilities running at full capacity for several years.

"Few of this year's orders came from U.S. airlines, reflecting cutthroat fare competition and the American carriers' perilous financial state. Instead, the new demand is coming mainly from Asia, particularly from India and China, where airline deregulation is spurring a big travel boom. Asia as a whole is expected to remain strong, with China's air traffic forecast to grow at 8.5 percent a year over the next twenty years, nearly double the average world rate. And U.S. airlines could return to the buying block by the end of this decade, if only because by then aging fleets will need modernization.

"Boeing is the best-known beneficiary of all this, and *Barron's* has been bullish on its stock."

Company Profile

With a heritage that mirrors the first 100 years of flight, the Boeing Company provides products and services to customers in 145 countries. Boeing has been the premier manufacturer of commercial jetliners for more than forty years and is a global market leader in military aircraft, satellites, missile defense, human space flight, and launch systems and services.

Boeing continues to expand its product line and develop new technologies to meet customer needs. Creating new models for its family of commercial airplanes; developing, producing, supporting and modifying aircraft for the U.S. military; building launch vehicles capable of lifting more than fourteen tons into orbit; and improving communications for people around the world through an advanced network of satellites, Boeing is carrying forward a long tradition of technical excellence and innovation.

Boeing is organized into four major business units: Boeing Capital Corporation, Boeing Commercial Airplanes, Connexion by BoeingSM, and Boeing Integrated Defense Systems. Supporting these units is the Boeing Shared Services Group, which contributes common services and efficient infrastructure services that enable the company's business units to concentrate on profitable growth. In addition, Phantom Works provides advanced research and development, including advanced concepts for air traffic management. Phantom Works partners with the company's business units to identify technology needs and address them with innovative and affordable solutions.

Boeing has been the premier manufacturer of commercial jetliners for more than forty years. With the McDonnell Douglas merger in 1997, Boeing's legacy of leadership in commercial jets now is joined with the lineage of Douglas airplanes, giving the combined company a seventy-year heritage of leadership in commercial aviation. Today, the main commercial products consist of the 717, 737, 747, 767, and 777 families of airplanes and the Boeing Business Jet. New product development efforts are focused on the Boeing 7E7, a super-efficient airplane that is expected to be in service in 2008. The company has nearly 13,000 commercial jetliners in service worldwide, which is roughly 75 percent of the world fleet. And through Boeing Commercial Aviation Services, the company provides unsurpassed, round-the-clock technical support to help operators maintain their airplanes in peak operating condition; further, through Commercial Aviation Services, Boeing offers a full range of world-class engineering, modification, logistics, and information services to its global customer base, which includes the world's passenger and cargo airlines as well as maintenance, repair, and overhaul facilities. Boeing also trains maintenance and flight crews in the 100-seat-and-above airliner market through Alteon, the world's largest and most comprehensive provider of airline training.

Boeing Integrated Defense Systems provides end-to-end services for large-scale systems that combine sophisticated communication networks with air-, land-, sea-, and space-based platforms for global military, government, and commercial customers. The company offers an extraordinary range of defense and space systems products and services. It designs, produces, modifies, and supports fighters, bombers, transports, rotorcraft, aerial refuelers, missiles, and munitions and is on the leading edge of military technology through its unmanned systems development efforts. Boeing Integrated Defense Systems also supports the U.S. government on several programs of national significance, including the Missile Defense Agency's Ground-Based Midcourse Defense program, the National Reconnaissance Office's Future Imagery Architecture, the Air Force's Evolved Expendable Launch Vehicle program, and NASA's International Space Station. The company has become the systems integrator for several new programs, including the U.S. Army's Future Combat Systems and Joint Tactical Radio Systems, the Family of Advanced Beyond Line-of-Sight Terminals for the Department of Defense, and the Explosive Detection Systems for the Department of Transportation.

Boeing's Shared Services Group allows business units to focus on profitable growth by providing the infrastructure services required to run their global operations. The group provides a broad range of services worldwide, including computing and network operations, e-business, facilities services, employee benefits and programs, security, transportation, and the purchase of all nonproduction goods and services. It also gives direction to safety, health, and environmental planning and offers comprehensive travel services to Boeing employees and corporate customers through the Boeing Travel Management Company. In addition, the Shared Services Group manages the sale and acquisition of all leased and owned property through the Boeing Realty Company. By integrating services, the Shared Services Group delivers greater value, creates "lean" processes and operations, leverages buying power, and simplifies access to services.

Shortcomings to Bear in Mind

- The company has a rather tarnished image that its new CEO, Jim McNerney, will have to address. According to a July 18, 2005, article in *BusinessWeek* by Stanley Holmes, "For McNerney, cleaning up Boeing's toxic culture is Job One. Yes, the company has made progress improving relations with the Defense Department and key congressional leaders following a string of procurement scandals.

  "But insiders say a bureaucracy that stifles innovation, resists change, and tolerates rule-bending remains largely intact. Adds Lehman Brothers aerospace analyst Joseph F. Campbell Jr., 'This is the Boeing that tolerated behavior that led to sexual harassment suits, debarment, and criminal prosecution.'"

Reasons to Buy

- "The Chicago-based aerospace company has been on a roll of late, racking up orders at a phenomenal pace for its 787 Dreamliner—and the new jet could account for half of the Asia-Pacific orders," according to an article in *BusinessWeek* on November 7, 2005, by Stanley Holmes and Carol Matlack. "But Boeing also is getting some unexpected lift from another plane: the 777. Thanks to the rise of its two most fuel-efficient widebody jets at a time of rising energy prices, Boeing has a potent one-two punch that could knock European rival Airbus into second place for years to come. Says Randy Baseler, Boeing vice president for marketing, 'We feel very confident about our strategy.'"

The *BusinessWeek* article goes on to say that "Boeing's resurgence comes at a time when Airbus is stalling badly. Delivery delays of its 555-seat A380 super-jumbo jet have angered key customers. And an inability to settle on the final design of its new A350 has given the 787 and 777 an even bigger head start."

- On March 21, 2006, the *New York Times* reported on the opinions of twenty-four financial analysts. Seven viewed Boeing as a STRONG BUY; five said it was a MODERATE BUY; nine called the stock a HOLD; two rated it a MODERATE HOLD; and one was convinced it was a SELL. It would appear that analysts are a crazy bunch.
- On February 2, 2006, Prudential Equity Group analyst Byron Callan said, "Our OVERWEIGHT opinion on Boeing rests on assumptions that operating margin in Commercial Airplane can reach record levels on relatively stable production rates, that IDS is stable, and that the company continues to generate $4.50 to $6.50 per share in free cash flow annually."
- On November 21, 2005, a *Wall Street Journal* article by Bruce Stanley said, "In what could shape up as a record aircraft deal for Boeing Company in China, Chinese aviation officials have signed a letter of intent to purchase seventy 737 jetliners and pledged verbally to buy an additional eighty of the single-aisle planes.

"China's pledge to purchase seventy commercial planes—a mix of 737–700s and 737–800s—is valued at about $4 billion, based on list prices, Boeing spokesman Mark Hooper said yesterday. Buyers usually get significant discounts, especially for orders as large as this one."

- In a *Wall Street Journal article* on October 27, 2005, J. Lynn Lunsford said, "Despite the machinists' strike that resulted in the loss of about $1.5 billion in revenue, Boeing's Commercial Airplanes unit still reported a 6-percent increase in revenue, to $4.91 billion and operating profit of $238 million, up 42 percent from the same quarter a year earlier. The company delivered 62 planes in the quarter, five fewer than a year earlier. Boeing said its commercial airplanes unit still is on track to post a record year in aircraft orders, with a total of 616 aircraft orders during the first nine months of 2005, compared with 191 orders in the year-earlier period."
- The *Wall Street Journal* had this to say on October 17, 2005: "Aircraft leasing giant International Lease Finance Corporation (ILFC) has quietly ordered twenty Boeing 787 Dreamliner jets valued at a total of $2.4 billion, becoming the first major leasing company to sign up as a launch customer for Boeing's newest jetliner."

The article goes on to say that "The race for orders between Boeing 787 and the Airbus A350 will likely be one of the hottest competitions between the two manufacturers for the next several years. With an estimated 2,500 to 3,000 twin-aisle jetliners nearing replacement age, both jet makers hope to win as much of the market as possible for midsize, long-haul jets.

"So far, Boeing is leading the race with its 787, which it is billing as an all-new, ultra-efficient airplane that will be 20 percent cheaper to fly and cost a third less to maintain than existing airplanes of its size. Airbus responded by saying that it would update its A330 jetliner with the same fuel-efficient engines and other modifications that would reduce Boeing's competitive advantage, calling it the A350."

"With the ILFC order, Boeing has 293 commitments for 787s from twenty-four customers. Of those, 194 are listed as firm orders. Airbus, which began officially selling the A350 in December, has 143 commitments from ten customers."

SECTOR: **Industrials** ◆ BETA COEFFICIENT: **1.10**
10-YEAR COMPOUND EARNINGS PER SHARE GROWTH: **8.8%**
10-YEAR COMPOUND DIVIDENDS PER SHARE GROWTH: **7.2%**

		2005	2004	2003	2002	2001	2000	1999	1998
Revenues (millions)		54,845	52,457	50,485	54,069	58,198	51,321	57,993	56,194
Net income (millions)		2,572	1,872	809	2,275	2,316	2,511	2,030	1,120
Earnings per share		3.20	2.30	1.00	2.82	2.79	2.84	2.19	1.15
Dividends per share		1.00	0.77	0.68	0.68	0.68	0.59	0.56	0.56
Price	high	72.4	55.5	43.4	51.1	69.9	70.9	48.5	56.3
	low	49.5	38.0	24.7	28.5	27.6	32.0	31.6	29.0

AGGRESSIVE GROWTH

Brinker International, Inc.

6820 LBJ Freeway ❏ Dallas, TX 75240 ❏ (972) 770-7228 ❏ Dividend reinvestment plan not available ❏ Web site: *www.brinker.com* ❏ Listed: NYSE ❏ Fiscal year ends last Wednesday in June ❏ Ticker symbol: EAT ❏ S&P rating: B+ ❏ Value Line financial strength rating: A

"As the casual dining segment continues to grow, so do Brinker's opportunities to expand our market share," said CEO Douglas H. Brooks in fiscal 2006. "And as people dine out more often, they're becoming increasingly sophisticated consumers—particularly when it comes to casual dining. They want greater selection, innovative menu choices, and great value for their money. The Brinker family of restaurants is committed to delivering on all counts."

Mr. Brooks also said, "As part of our new guest-satisfaction initiatives, Brinker has taken steps to become a much more consumer-driven company. More than ever, we're relying on research and consumer input to help us make the most of every dollar we invest in marketing efforts, menu innovation, new store prototypes—anything and everything that impacts our guests.

"Our Consumer Insights department is actively involved in researching and rigorously testing consumer attitudes and behaviors toward Brinker brands and identifying opportunities for improvement.

"We have also established a Consumer Center of Excellence made up of business professionals from each brand to implement standard processes and systems for new product development. In addition, we've expanded the responsibilities of our key marketing staff to include everything that touches the consumer, from menus to advertising to restaurant design."

Company Profile

In little more than two decades, Brinker International (formerly Chili's) has grown from a single restaurant in Dallas to multiple casual dining concepts. The company provides dining experiences for nearly 500,000 people every day. Its strategy is to aggressively expand concepts that exceed its high expectations for return on invested capital and to reposition or divest those concepts that fail to measure up. As a result, the company continues to develop new concepts. What's more, over the years, Brinker International has acquired restaurant concepts, using shares of its own stock in payment.

Among the company's concept restaurant chains are Chili's Grill & Bar (1074 units), Romano's Macaroni Grill (235 units), On The Border's (135 units), Maggiano's Little Italy (thirty-three units), the Corner Bakery Café (ninety units), and Rockfish Seafood Grill (twenty-one units).

Chili's is committed to "providing our guests with new and exciting menu items," said management, "while keeping the sizzle of our Famous and Favorites, such as Big Mouth Burgers, Baby Back Ribs, Fajitas, and the Presidente Margarita."

Romano's Macaroni Grill has a "distinctive chef-driven menu," according to the company's annual report. It features imported Italian ingredients such as olive oil, sun-dried tomatoes, balsamic vinegar, prosciutto, and Parmesan and buffalo mozzarella cheeses. "A newly redesigned menu showcases favorites like the Mama's Trio and Spaghettini and Meatballs, while featuring signature dishes like Chicken Portobello and Filet Firenze."

The company's On The Border Mexican Grill & Cantina has a menu that features such items as quesadillas, enchiladas, fajitas, and "our famous Border Sampler." These dishes have been augmented recently by such items as Salmon Mexicano, Blackened Chicken Salad, and Carnitas.

The Rockfish Seafood Grill features such menu items as "our generous Shrimp Basket, Fish Tacos, Stuffed Fish, Rock-a-Rita Margarita, 18-ounce beer schooner, and award-winning Mexican Shrimp Martini."

Shortcomings to Bear in Mind

- Up until 2005, the company had never paid a cash dividend, which prompted me to classify EAT as aggressive growth.
- According to a company publication, "The restaurant business is highly competitive with respect to price, service, restaurant location, and food quality. What's more, it is often affected by changes in consumer tastes, economic conditions, population, and traffic patterns."

The publication goes on to say, "The company competes in each market with locally owned restaurants as well as national and regional restaurant chains, some of which operate more restaurants and have greater financial resources and longer operating histories than the company.

"There is active competition for management personnel and for attractive commercial real estate sites suitable for restaurants. In addition, factors such as inflation, increased food, labor, and benefit costs, and difficulty in attracting hourly employees may adversely affect the restaurant industry in general and the company's restaurants in particular."

- *Standard & Poor's Stock Reports* had this comment on March 14, 2006: "Our recommendation is HOLD," said Dennis P. Milton. "We expect favorable longer-term demographic trends in the United States to continue to boost customer traffic in the casual dining sector. We see the company continuing to benefit from the expansion of its restaurant concepts, particularly the Chili's brand, which we view as well positioned in what we regard as the attractive bar-and-grill sector. However, we believe that the stock's current valuation fairly reflects EAT's growth prospects." The price at that time was $42.86.

Reasons to Buy

- On March 5, 2006, the *New York Times* published a survey of twenty-four financial analysts and their views of Brinker International. Three dubbed the company a STRONG BUY; eight called it a MODERATE BUY; twelve said it was a HOLD; and one rated it a MODERATE HOLD.
- On January 25, 2006, Lehman Brothers, a leading brokerage firm, had this comment: "Broadly speaking, Brinker remains our top pick in the mature casual dining segment of the restaurant industry, with long-term guidance for 15-percent EPS growth, driven primarily by Chili's new unit growth, both domestically and internationally."

■ A recent "Hot Concept of the Year" award winner, Big Bowl has also been recognized for its child-friendly menu atmosphere. According to management, "The kids' menu comes tucked inside a Chinese carry-out carton containing a fortune cookie, toy, and children's chopsticks, designed for young fingers."

■ Over the past twenty years, the company has had explosive growth. In 1983, Chili's had twenty-three outlets in six states, with 1,800 employees and annual sales of $30 million. Today, Brinker International has grown to more than 1,475 restaurants in forty-nine states and twenty-two countries, with 90,000 employees and annual sales approaching $4 billion. Industry analysts have dubbed the EAT portfolio "the mutual fund of casual dining."

■ According to a Brinker spokesman, "The company purchases certain commodities such as beef, chicken, flour, and cooking oil. These commodities are generally purchased based upon market prices established with vendors. These purchase arrangements may contain contractual features that limit the price paid by establishing certain price floors or caps. The company does not use financial instruments to hedge commodity prices because these purchase arrangements help control the ultimate cost paid, and any commodity price aberrations are generally short term in nature."

■ "Eating away from home has become such an important part of everyday life. Currently, close to half the dollars spent on food are spent on meals away from home. This is a dramatic shift over the last three or four decades," said Joseph Buckley in an interview conducted by Kenneth N. Gilpin for the *New York Times*. Mr. Buckley is a restaurant analyst with Bear Stearns, a major brokerage firm.

He went on to say, "The move to two-wage-earner families, and the fact that baby boomers have grown up with chains, many of which are about to celebrate their fiftieth birthdays, are other reasons. In short, dining out has become so ingrained in the American lifestyle that it is cut back very grudgingly, if at all."

In answer to another question, the Bear Stearns analyst said, "In the casual dining sector, which is defined as an average check of $10 to $20 with full service and having alcohol as an option, growth has been great. As America has shifted its food budget to spending more and more away from home, they have become more sophisticated in their spending."

■ For the past four years, *Forbes* magazine has listed Brinker International, Inc., in their annual list of the "400 Best Companies in America." In 2004, *Fortune* magazine recognized Brinker as a *Fortune* 500 company. From 1999 to 2003, Romano's Macaroni Grill won the Dinner House Category in the Restaurant & Institutions annual Choice in Chains Award. And Maggiano's Little Italy is a past "Hot Concept of the Year" winner by Nation's Restaurant News.

SECTOR: **Consumer Discretionary** ◆ BETA COEFFICIENT: **.85**
10-YEAR COMPOUND EARNINGS PER SHARE GROWTH: **12.6%**
10-YEAR COMPOUND DIVIDENDS PER SHARE GROWTH: **no dividend prior to 2006.**

		2005	2004	2003	2002	2001	2000	1999	1998
Revenues (millions)		3,920	3,707	3,285	2,887	2,407	2,100	1,818	1,529
Net income (millions)		198	212	184	166	145	118	79	69
Earnings per share		2.13	2.17	1.85	1.65	1.42	1.17	0.88	0.68
Dividends per share		—	—	—	—	—	—	—	—
Price	high	42.4	39.8	37.2	36.0	41.3	28.9	20.4	19.5
	low	33.2	28.9	26.3	24.1	21.3	13.8	13.3	10.0

CONSERVATIVE GROWTH

Canadian National Railway Company

935 De la Gauchetiere Street West ❑ Montreal, Quebec, Canada H3B 2M9 ❑ (514) 399-0052 ❑ Dividend reinvestment plan not available ❑ Web site: *www.cn.ca* ❑ Ticker symbol: CNI ❑ Listed: NYSE ❑ S&P rating: A- ❑ Value Line financial strength rating: B++

"As the railroad industry copes with a severe capacity crisis, CN [Canadian National Railway Company] has another take on the issue," said John Gallagher, writing for *Traffic World* in 2005.

"'We have freight capacity, we have line capacity, we have car and locomotive capacity, and we're leveraging all of that,' said CN's president and CEO Hunter Harrison. 'We're not metering freight, we're not talking about rate increases to manage capacity. We are taking modest rate increases, in the 2- to 4-percent range, which we think is very appropriate.'"

Mr. Gallagher goes on: "At a time when demand for transportation services has never been higher, and its rivals are jacking up rates and turning away business for lack of space, CN's perspective runs counter to industry wisdom. But Harrison's approach is not surprising, given that he runs the tightest operating plan in the industry. While some railroads are just now developing a pricing discipline to take advantage of higher demand brought on by a recovering economy, Harrison has been at this for years."

"Harrison honed his precision railroad philosophy over years of practice. He began his career in 1964 with the St. Louis-San Francisco Railroad, known as the Frisco, working his way through school in Memphis as a carman-oiler. Frisco was acquired by Burlington Northern Railroad in 1980, and Harrison was vice president of both transportation and service design before joining Illinois Central in 1989.

"It was at the IC—as senior vice president of transportation in 1991, senior vice president of operations in 1992 and president and CEO in 1993—where his precision railroading concept kicked into gear. By keeping trains on a tight schedule and maintaining a sharp focus on operations and asset utilization, he drove down the railroad's operating ratio 30 points to the low 60s, the best in the industry."

Company Profile

Canadian National Railway, which was controlled by the Canadian government until 1995, operates the largest Canadian railroad. The acquisition of Illinois Central in 1999 made CNI the only railway to cross the continent both east-west and north-south, serving ports on the Atlantic, Pacific, and Gulf coasts while linking customers in the three NAFTA nations of Canada, the United States, and Mexico.

Since late 1998, the company has offered scheduled train service. Railroads typically hold trains until enough cars accumulate. The time schedule means that CNI must run shorter trains, but the company has also realized greater operating efficiency and timeliness, with service peaks and valleys smoothed out. CNI's operating ratio is among the best in the industry, and the company is committed to moving more freight more quickly and with fewer assets.

Canadian National Railway is a leader in the North American rail industry. Following its acquisition of Illinois Central in 1999, WC in 2001, and GLT in 2004, as well as its partnership agreement with BC Rail in 2004, CNI has been able to provide shippers with more options and greater reach in the rapidly expanding market for north-south trade.

CNI is a more diverse railroad. The company's revenues derive from the intermodal movement of a diversified and balanced portfolio of goods, including petroleum and chemicals, grain and fertilizers, coal, metals and minerals, forest products, and automotive parts and supplies. Canadian National has a strong stake in intermodal transportation, which combines a number of different means of transportation to get goods economically from origination to their destination. For instance, a shipment of goods that starts out from Asia on a ship could be loaded onto a railroad flatcar—still in its original container—for several hundred miles and then be transferred to a trucking company for its final destination.

Quick Facts About Canadian National Railway

- CNI operates the largest rail network in Canada and is the only transcontinental network in North America. The company operates in eight Canadian provinces and sixteen U.S. states.
- CNI's railways span Canada and mid-America from the Atlantic and Pacific oceans to the Gulf of Mexico, serving the ports of Vancouver and Prince Rupert, British Columbia; Montreal, Quebec; Halifax, Nova Scotia; New Orleans, Louisiana, and Mobile, Alabama; and the key cities of Toronto, Buffalo, Chicago, Detroit, Duluth (Minnesota)/Superior (Wisconsin), Green Bay, Minneapolis/St. Paul, Memphis, St. Louis, and Jackson (Mississippi), with connections to all points in North America.
- Canadian National has the shortest route from the Atlantic coast to the U.S. Midwest through the St. Clair Tunnel, which connects Sarnia, Ontario, and Port Huron, Michigan.
- CNI originates approximately 85 percent of traffic, allowing the company to capitalize on service advantages, efficient asset utilization, and negotiations with other carriers on revenue division arrangements.

Shortcomings to Bear in Mind

- Although the company has had an impressive record of growth in recent years, it must be remembered that railroads—like chemical companies, car companies, home builders, and paper companies—belong to a very cyclical industry whose profitability depends on the health of the economy.

Reasons to Buy

- On March 28, 2006, the *New York Times* reviewed the opinions of eleven analysts, of which three rated the stock STRONG BUY. Six called it a MODERATE BUY, and two said it should be a HOLD.
- On March 10, 2006, *Value Line Investment Survey* gave the stock a 2 rating (which is above average) for Timeliness. Craig Sirois said, "Intermodal business should be healthy for years to come. Fourth-quarter intermodal revenues jumped 13 percent, thanks to tight truck capacity and strong import/export markets."
- "Our recommendation is BUY," said Andrew West, CFA, writing for *Standard & Poor's Stock Reports* on January 26, 2006. "We think CNI—as the most efficiently run railroad we cover—will be able to maintain its competitive strength through strict cost controls and efficiency-boosting measures."
- Intermodal transportation is by far the company's most complex challenge, with a high degree of randomness, uneven flow of traffic, and numerous points in the chain for delays to occur. In 2003, CNI launched Intermodal Excellence (called IMX), an operating methodology intended to smooth traffic flows, increase speed and reliability, and improve asset utilization and margins.

At the heart of IMX is the application of scheduled railroading's discipline and precision to intermodal transportation. IMX requires shippers to make reservations to get on trains, while pricing encourages a shift in traffic to off-peak days. This, along with required gate reservations at the company's largest terminals, enables Canadian National to align traffic with equipment and gate capacity and improve speed and asset utilization. Even though implementation throughout the entire CNI system was not complete until year-end, the company has already seen improvements in profit margins. What's more, customers are aware of the benefits, primarily better speed and reliability of service.

■ In 2005, Mr. Harrison summarized his philosophy of management: "I remember one of the turning points of my career. I was a young man, in my first management job at BN's Memphis yard. W. F. Thompson, a great railroader who would eventually become a mentor of mine, was visiting the facility. He looked out at a rail yard packed with cars and asked me, 'Son, what do you see out there?' I was young, and he was a big, intimidating man. I wanted to say the right thing. My answer was, 'Sir, that's a lot of business out there in the yard.'

"Mr. Thompson's answer changed forever my view of railroading. He said, 'You know, that's the problem. You look at a crowded yard and see a lot of business. I see a lot of delayed trains.'

"It's been a tradition throughout CN's history as a publicly held corporation to look beyond the conventions of traditional railroading to drive excellence. Those of you familiar with CN's track record know that is our central theme.

"Since that moment in the Memphis yard long ago, getting the absolute maximum out of rail assets has been a major focus of mine, and it's a passion here at CN. It's one of the five guiding principles of successful railroading:

- The first is providing good service—consistently doing what you say you'll do.
- The second is controlling your costs.
- The third is asset utilization.
- The fourth is to make sure operate safely.
- The fifth is developing your people.

"I've always believed if I focus 90 percent of my time as a leader on the fifth principle, the other four will follow naturally."

SECTOR: **Industrials** ◆ BETA COEFFICIENT: **.90**
9-YEAR COMPOUND EARNINGS PER SHARE GROWTH: **21.6%**
9-YEAR COMPOUND DIVIDENDS PER SHARE GROWTH: **18.1%**

		2005	2004	2003	2002	2001	2000	1999	1998
Revenues (millions)		7,240	6,548	4,531	3,874	3,555	3,637	3,613	2,651
Net income (millions)		1,556	1,258	782	667	615	590	531	359
Earnings per share		2.77	2.17	1.35	1.11	1.03	0.98	0.84	0.67
Dividends per share		.43	.32	.26	.18	.17	.16	.14	.12
Price	high	41.4	31.0	21.3	17.9	16.5	11.0	12.2	11.2
	low	27.7	18.3	13.2	12.0	9.6	7.5	6.9	5.7

Carnival Corporation & PLC

3655 N.W. 87th Avenue ❑ Miami, FL 33178-2428 ❑ (305) 406-4832 ❑ Direct dividend reinvestment plan available (800) 568-3476 ❑ Fiscal year ends November 30 ❑ Web site: *www.carnivalcorp.com* ❑ Listed: NYSE ❑ Ticker symbol: CCL ❑ S&P rating: A+ ❑ Value Line financial strength rating: B+

Carnival Corporation & PLC announced on December 14, 2005 that it had reached an agreement with Italian shipbuilder Fincantieri for the construction of four new cruise ships worth more than $2 billion.

Along with the four new vessels, one each for Holland America Line, Carnival Cruise Lines, Princess Cruises, and Costa Crociere, with the agreement includes options for two additional vessels, one each for Carnival Cruise Lines and Holland America Line.

The four new ships will add a collective 11,756 lower berths to the cruise operator's fleet. Two of the orders have been placed in U.S. dollars and two others are in euros.

According to Carnival CEO Micky Arison, the agreement extends Carnival's new building program through 2009 while enabling the company to execute its strategy of expanding its North American and European brands.

"Fincantieri constructs some of the world's most beautiful and technically advanced ships and this agreement enables us to expand our core North American and European brands at very competitive prices considering today's unfavorable U.S. dollar/euro ratio," he said.

The New Ships and Options

- The 2,044-passenger ship on order for Holland America Line will be the largest ever constructed for the North American premium operator. With an estimated all-in cost of $450 million, the 86,000-ton Panamax vessel will be built at Fincantieri's Marghera shipyard. The ship is expected to enter service in summer of 2008. There is also an option for a sister ship scheduled to debut in spring of 2010.
- The 3,100-passenger ship ordered for North American premium brand Princess Cruises is set to debut in fall 2008. A sister to the *Emerald Princess,* the 116,000-ton vessel will be built at Fincantieri's Monfalcone shipyard at an approximate all-in cost of $570 million.
- The 3,608-passenger cruise ship ordered for Carnival Cruise Lines represents the largest vessel ever constructed for the contemporary North American operator. The 130,000-ton vessel, to be built at Fincantieri's Monfalcone shipyard at an estimated all-in cost of 560 million euro, is expected to enter service in fall of 2009. There is also an option for a sister ship scheduled to enter service in summer of 2010.
- The 3,004-passenger ship ordered for the Costa Crociere line, based in Genoa, Italy, is expected to debut in summer of 2009. A sister ship to the Costa *Concordia,* the 112,000-ton vessel will have an estimated all-in cost of 485 million euro and will be built at Fincantieri's Sestri shipyard.

Company Profile

Carnival Corporation is a global cruise company with a portfolio of twelve distinct brands, comprised of the leading cruise operators in North America, Europe, and Australia. Included in this group are Carnival Cruise Lines (twenty ships), Holland America Line (thirteen), Princess Cruises (fourteen), AIDA (four), Costa Cruises (ten), Cunard Line (three), P&O Cruises (four),

Windstar Cruises (three), Seabourn Cruise Line (three), Ocean Village (one), Swan Hellenic (one). All told, these seventy-nine vessels have more than 137,000 lower berths.

The company has sixteen new ships scheduled for delivery between February 2006 and the fall of 2009.

Carnival also operates two tour companies, which include seventeen hotels or lodges in Alaska and the Canadian Yukon, more than 500 motor coaches, twenty domed rail cars, and two day-boats.

Some History Background

Although the name Carnival Corporation didn't come into existence until 1993, the foundation for the company was laid when its flagship brand, Carnival Cruise Lines, was formed in 1972 by the late cruise industry pioneer Ted Arison.

After achieving its position as the world's most popular cruise line, Carnival made an IPO of 20 percent of its common stock in 1987, which provided the influx of capital that enabled the company to begin expanding through acquisitions.

Over a fourteen-year span, Carnival acquired representation in virtually every market segment of the cruise industry, including premium operator Holland America Line in 1989 (in a purchase that also included niche cruise line Windstar Cruises and Alaskan/Canadian tour operator Holland America tours); luxury brand Seabourn Cruise Line in 1992; contemporary operator Costa Cruises, Europe's leading cruise company, in 1997; and the premium/luxury Cunard Line in 1998, which built the world's largest ocean liner, the 150,000-ton *Queen Mary 2*.

On April 17, 2003, agreements were finalized to combine Carnival Corporation with P&O Princess Cruises, PLC, creating a global vacation leader with twelve brands and making Carnival one of the largest leisure travel companies in the world.

Shortcomings to Bear in Mind

- If you're an investor looking for a conservative stock, you may decide that Carnival is not for you. It has a beta coefficient of 1.25, which means that its stock price is 25 percent more volatile than the general market. However, if you have a yen for speculation, this might be an ideal stock.
- "Our HOLD opinion on the shares reflects our view that the stock is appropriately priced," said Tom Graves, CFA, writing for *Standard & Poor's Stock Reports* on January 18, 2006 (when the stock was priced at $53.98). "We look for expectations of increasing consumer interest in cruise ship vacations, plus prospects for free cash flow generation by the company, to offset concerns about higher fuel costs and what we viewed as a disappointing near-term outlook from the company for ticket prices for its ships in the North American market. We think that Carnival's competitive standing, including its ability to attract more cruise customers, is being helped by its addition of new ships."

Reasons to Buy

- On March 17, 2006, the *New York Times* polled twenty-one financial analysts who specialize in such stocks as Carnival. Five rated the stock a STRONG BUY; eleven preferred to tag it a MODERATE BUY; and five were content to be neutral, with a HOLD.
- "We are reiterating our BUY rating on Carnival Corp.," said John Staszak, CFA, writing for Argus Research Company on March 6, 2006. "In late February 2006, Carnival Cruise Lines held an analyst day in New York. Management emphasized initiatives to increase bookings and lower costs. To increase sales, Carnival is adding destinations and ports of departure, targeting long-time customers, and attempting to increase food and beverage revenue. Additional destinations and points of departure include Africa, India, and Asia."

■ Net income for the year ended November 30, 2005, was $2.3 billion, or $2.70 diluted EPS, on revenues of $11.1 billion. This compared to net income of $1.9 billion, or $2.24 diluted EPS, on revenues of $9.7 billion for the same period in 2004.

Fourth-quarter revenues increased by 14.4 percent, driven by both a 9.1-percent increase in cruise capacity and a significant increase in cruise revenue yields (revenue per available lower berth day), partially offset by a stronger U.S. dollar relative to the euro and sterling. Net revenue yields for the fourth quarter of 2005 increased 5.9 percent compared to the prior year. Net revenue yields as measured on a local currency basis (constant dollar basis) increased 6.8 percent over the same period last year, primarily due to higher cruise ticket prices and onboard revenues. Gross revenue yields increased 4.5 percent.

For the 2005 year, net revenue yields increased 6.5 percent (6.1 percent on a constant dollar basis). Gross revenue yields increased 4.9 percent.

Net cruise costs per available lower berth day (ALBD) for the fourth quarter of 2005 were up 3.8 percent compared to costs for the same period last year. On a constant dollar basis, net cruise costs per ALBD increased 4.9 percent from the same period last year primarily due to an approximate 50-percent increase in fuel prices. Excluding higher fuel costs, the company's 2005 fourth quarter net cruise costs per ALBD were approximately equal to the same period last year on a constant dollar basis. Gross cruise costs per ALBD increased 2.5 percent compared to the prior year.

Carnival's CEO Micky Arison said that he was pleased with the company's performance during the period. "It is a testament to the resilience of our cruise business that despite an approximate 50-percent increase in fuel costs for the quarter and the worst hurricane season in our history, we were still able to grow earnings by 20 percent to achieve record fourth-quarter results."

For the full year, Arison said that increased pricing and a continued sharp focus on cost controls more than offset a $180 million year-over-year rise in fuel costs. He further stated, "All facets of our business, from contemporary to luxury, performed well overall during the past year, with guests booking in record numbers."

Looking forward to 2006, Arison said, "We expect continued revenue yield growth in 2006 although probably not at the levels experienced during the last two years. As it stands today, advance booking levels for 2006 are ahead of the prior year on a capacity adjusted basis, with average pricing also higher than last year."

■ With an array of brands, Carnival can offer something for every breed of cruise fanatic. There's the high-end Yachts of Seabourn, which feature onboard lectures by Ivy League professors. At the other end of the spectrum are the Carnival Fun Ships, which offer midnight buffets and dancing until 4 A.M.

■ "Free cash flow should be strong over the next several years," said Marina Livson, writing for *Value Line Investment Survey*, on November 18, 2005. "The available funds may be used for dividend payments, share repurchases, and debt repayments. For as long as interest rates remain relatively low, the company will likely concentrate on returning cash to shareholders versus debt reduction. Indeed, the board of directors recently increased the quarterly dividend payout by 25 percent, to $0.25 per share. This is the second increase this year."

■ The company has three ships scheduled for delivery in 2006—Holland America Line's 1,918-passenger *Noordam* in January, Princess Cruises's 3,100-passenger *Crown Princess* in May, and Costa Cruises's 3,000-passenger Costa Concordia in June—which represent a 5.5-percent increase in capacity.

SECTOR: **Consumer Discretionary** ◆ BETA COEFFICIENT: **1.25**
10-YEAR COMPOUND EARNINGS PER SHARE GROWTH: **12.9%**
10-YEAR COMPOUND DIVIDENDS PER SHARE GROWTH: **17.5**

		2005	2004	2003	2002	2001	2000	1999	1998
Revenues (millions)		11,087	9,727	6,717	4,368	4,536	3,778	3,497	3,009
Net income (millions)		2,257	1,854	1,194	1,016	926	965	1,027	836
Earnings per share		2.70	2.24	1.66	1.73	1.58	1.60	1.66	1.40
Dividends per share		.80	.52	.44	.42	.42	.42	.36	.32
Price	high	59.0	58.3	39.8	34.6	34.9	51.3	53.5	48.5
	low	45.8	39.0	20.3	22.1	17.0	18.3	38.1	19.0

AGGRESSIVE GROWTH

Caterpillar, Inc.

100 N. E. Adams Street ❑ Peoria, IL 61629-5310 ❑ (309) 675-4619 ❑ Direct dividend reinvestment plan available (800) 842-7629 ❑ Web site: *www.cat.com* ❑ Listed: NYSE ❑ Ticker symbol: CAT ❑ S&P rating: B+ ❑ Value Line financial strength rating: A

On October 31, 2005, Caterpillar CEO Jim Owens told a group of financial analysts and institutional shareholders that as a global leader, it was time for Caterpillar to take on new challenges and position itself for future success. At a meeting in New York, Owens presented the company's new enterprise strategy and goals, which are focused on delivering Caterpillar's Vision 2020.

"Now is the time to define the next set of hills to conquer. We have a clear blueprint to build on our successes and strengths," said Owens. In his presentation, Owens commented that the company is operating in an environment that is conducive to industry growth and higher sales for years to come.

"We have set challenging but realistic goals for 2010 and beyond, and are committed to achieving success that will reward customers, stockholders, and employees," said Owens. "It's about being number one in every endeavor we pursue, affirming our leadership in technology and innovation, and creating a great place to work. These are the things that will take Caterpillar performance to the next level."

During the event, Owens provided an overview of Caterpillar's key goals for 2010:

- Achieve breakthroughs in factory-delivered product quality
- Be number one for every major product group on every continent in the markets Caterpillar serves
- Achieve $50 billion in sales and revenues by 2010
- Deliver EPS growth that averages 15 to 20 percent annually through 2010

Company Profile

Caterpillar's distinctive yellow machines are in service in nearly every country in the world. About 48 percent of the company's revenues is derived from outside North America. Europe/Africa/Middle East contributes 27 percent, Asia/Pacific accounts for 13 percent, and Latin America makes up 8 percent. What's more, about 71 percent of CAT's 220 independent dealers are based outside the United States.

Headquartered in Peoria, Illinois, Caterpillar is the world's largest manufacturer of construction and mining equipment, diesel and natural gas engines, and industrial gas turbines. It is a *Fortune* 50 industrial company with more than $37 billion in assets.

Caterpillar's broad product line ranges from the company's new line of compact construction equipment to hydraulic excavators, backhoe loaders, track-type tractors, forest products, off-highway trucks, agricultural tractors, diesel and natural gas engines, and industrial gas turbines. CAT products are used in the construction, road-building, mining, forestry, energy, transportation, and material-handling industries.

Caterpillar products are sold in more than 200 countries, and rental services are offered through more than 1,200 outlets worldwide. The company delivers superior service through its extensive worldwide network of 220 dealers. Many of these dealers have relationships with their customers that have spanned at least two generations. More than 80 percent of Caterpillar sales are to repeat customers.

Caterpillar products and components are manufactured in forty-one plants in the United States and forty-three plants in Australia, Brazil, Canada, England, France, Germany, Hungary, India, Indonesia, Italy, Japan, Mexico, The Netherlands, Northern Ireland, China, Poland, Russia, South Africa, and Sweden.

The company conducts business through three operating segments: Machinery, Engines, and Financial Products.

Machinery

As Caterpillar's largest segment, the Machinery unit (60 percent of revenues, and 74 percent of operating profits) makes the company's well-known earthmoving equipment. Machinery's end markets include heavy construction, general construction, mining quarry and aggregate, industrial, waste, forestry, and agriculture.

End markets are very cyclical and competitive. Demand for Caterpillar's earthmoving equipment is driven by many volatile factors, including the health of global economies, commodity prices, and interest rates.

Engines

For decades, Caterpillar's Engine unit (32 percent of sales and 11 percent of operating profits) made diesel engines solely for the company's own earthmoving equipment. Now, the Engine unit derives about 90 percent of sales from third-party customers, such as Paccar, Inc., the maker of well-known Kenworth and Peterbilt brand tractor/trailer trucks. Engine's major end markets are electric power generation, on-highway truck, oil and gas, industrial original-equipment manufacturers (OEMs), and marine.

Financial Products

The Financial Products unit (7.6 percent of revenues and 20 percent of operating profits) primarily provides financing to Caterpillar dealers and customers. Financing plans include operating and finance leases, installment sales contracts, working capital loans, and wholesale financing plans.

Shortcomings to Bear in Mind

- "Caterpillar's basic business is extraordinarily cyclical, as Owens, a Ph.D. economist, knows all too well," said Michael Arndt, writing for *BusinessWeek* on December 5, 2005. "Behind today's turbocharged results, another industrial bust may already be in the offing. Owens foresees the domestic market for big-rig truck engines peaking in 2006. The mining sector will top out in 2009 if not sooner, he adds, with an outright recession possible as soon as 2011.

  "To offset the slowdown, Owens wants to make more acquisitions, particularly in fast-rising markets such as China, and to double the pace of new rollouts to grab market share. He's also pushing dealers to cut inventories. That would reduce orders now, but should keep factories busier when retail sales slacken. And for as long as demand holds up, he's hiking prices."

Reasons to Buy

- On February 14, 2006, the *New York Times* tabulated the opinions of sixteen analysts who actively follow Caterpillar. Five rated the stock a STRONG BUY; two said it was a MODERATE BUY; and nine preferred to call it a HOLD.
- In a move that will better position the company to respond to customer needs and provide greater value, Caterpillar announced on October 27, 2005, that it had signed definitive agreements to enter into a global alliance with JLG Industries, Inc., to produce a full lineup of Caterpillar-branded telehandlers. The alliance is a strong strategic fit for both companies and will give Caterpillar dealers and customers greater access to a quality range of CAT-branded telehandler products.

  "This alliance leverages our respective strengths, combining Caterpillar's global brand, distribution expertise, and component capabilities with JLG's strong design capabilities in the telehandler and lift industry, to deliver world-class telehandler product to our customers," said Ed Rapp, vice president of Caterpillar's Building Construction Products (BCP) Division.

  Caterpillar's telehandler products are currently produced at BCP's plant in Leicester, England, along with four other machine product groups. Under the alliance agreement, JLG will develop and manufacture a lineup of Cat-branded telehandlers for global distribution. Caterpillar will retain responsibility for the B-Series telehandlers and earlier models that were manufactured and sold by Caterpillar prior to the transition of production to JLG, including warranty and service.
- Jim Owens joined Caterpillar in 1972 as a corporate economist and held management positions worldwide before becoming chief financial officer in 1993 and group president in 1995. According to former CEO Glen Barton, "Jim has a broad understanding of Caterpillar's business strategy, having served as group president for a diverse set of business units—human services, component manufacturing, product support, logistics, information technology, and Latin American operations."
- Over the years, Caterpillar has earned a reputation for rugged machines that typically set industry standards for performance, durability, quality, and value. The company's goal is to remain the technological leader in its product lines. Today, thanks to accelerated design and testing, computer-based diagnostics and operations, and greatly improved materials, the company can more speedily deliver new and better products to its customers.
- Caterpillar is an innovator and spends heavily on research and development. Historically, the company invests about 3.1 percent of annual revenues on R&D.
- Caterpillar's commitment to customer service is demonstrated by the fastest parts-delivery system in its industry. Caterpillar's customers can usually obtain replacement parts from their dealers upon request. If not, Caterpillar ships them anywhere in the world within twelve hours, often much sooner.
- In 2004, Caterpillar acquired Turbomach S.A., a Swiss packager of industrial gas turbines and related systems. Turbomach's power-generation packages incorporate gas turbines manufactured by San Diego–based Solar Turbines Incorporated, a wholly owned subsidiary of Caterpillar.

  Solar Turbines is a world leader in the design, manufacture, and service of industrial gas turbine engines in its size range. More than 11,000 Solar gas turbine engines and turbo machinery systems are used on land and offshore in ninety nations for the production and transmission of crude oil, petroleum products, and natural gas and for generating electricity and thermal energy for a wide variety of industrial applications.

  "Turbomach has distributed Solar brand turbines and equipment to the industrial power-generation market for almost twenty years," said Caterpillar Group President Rich Thompson. "This acquisition will benefit both Caterpillar and its customers by assuring the continuity of this relationship and enhancing our ability to sell and support such systems, particularly in the expanding markets in Europe, Africa, and Asia."

SECTOR: **Industrials** ◆ BETA COEFFICIENT: **1.20**
10-YEAR COMPOUND EARNINGS PER SHARE GROWTH: **10.9%**
10-YEAR COMPOUND DIVIDENDS PER SHARE GROWTH: **12.3%**

		2005	2004	2003	2002	2001	2000	1999	1998
Revenues (millions)		36,339	30,251	22,763	20,152	20,450	20,175	19,702	20,977
Net income (millions)		2,854	2,035	1,099	798	805	1,051	946	1,513
Earnings per share		4.04	2.88	1.57	1.15	1.16	1.51	1.32	2.06
Dividends per share		0.96	0.78	0.72	0.70	0.70	0.67	0.63	0.58
Price	high	59.9	49.4	42.5	30.0	28.4	27.6	33.2	30.4
	low	41.3	34.3	20.6	16.9	19.9	14.8	21.0	19.6

INCOME

Chevron Corporation (Formerly ChevronTexaco)

6001 Bollinger Canyon Road ❑ San Ramon, CA 94583-2324 ❑ (925) 842-5690 ❑ Direct dividend reinvestment plan available (800) 842-7629 ❑ Web site: *www.chevroncorp.com* ❑ Listed: NYSE ❑ Ticker symbol: CVX ❑ S&P rating: B+ ❑ Value Line financial strength rating: A++

"We are at a strategic inflection point in our industry," said CEO Dave O'Reilly in 2005. "The convergence of growing demand, challenging resource locations such as the deep water and oil sands, a need for greater diversity of energy supplies, a complex geopolitical environment, and a shifting competitive landscape have created a fundamentally new energy equation.

"Chevron is strongly positioned to succeed in this new environment. We have robust strategies that have been tested under a variety of market conditions. We are committed to achieving and maintaining world-class levels of operating and capital discipline. We are leveraging technology to create operating efficiencies in the near term and develop promising new energy sources for the long term. We are continuing to build on our efforts to be the partner of choice in strategic energy regions of the world."

Company Profile

Chevron is the world's fourth-largest publicly traded, integrated energy company based on oil-equivalent reserves and production. It is engaged in every aspect of the oil and gas industry, including exploration and production; refining, marketing, and transportation; chemicals manufacturing and sales; and power generation.

The corporation traces its roots to an 1879 oil discovery at Pico Canyon, north of Los Angeles. This find led to the formation, in the same year, of the Pacific Coast Oil Company. Active in more than 180 countries, Chevron has reserves of 11.9 billion barrels of oil and gas equivalent and daily production of 2.6 million barrels.

In addition, it has global refining capacity of more than 2.3 million barrels a day and operates more than 24,000 retail outlets (including affiliates) around the world. The company also has interests in thirty power projects now operating or being developed.

Chevron's upstream success includes the following:

- The number-one oil and gas producer in the U.S. Gulf of Mexico Shelf; number two in the Permian Basin
- The number-one oil producer in California's San Joaquin Valley
- The number-one oil and natural gas producer in Kazakhstan
- The number-one oil producer in Indonesia and Angola
- The number-one natural gas resource holder in Australia
- The number-one deepwater leaseholder and number-three oil and gas producer in Nigeria
- One of the top producers and leaseholders in the deepwater Gulf of Mexico

Chevron's downstream business includes the following resources:

▪ The company's four refining and marketing units operate in the following regions: North America; Europe and West Africa; Latin America; and Asia, the Middle East, and southern Africa. Downstream also has five global business units: aviation, lubricants, trading, shipping, and fuel and marine marketing.

▪ The company's global refining network comprises twenty-three wholly owned and joint-venture facilities that process more than 2 million barrels of oil per day.

▪ Chevron sells more than 2 million barrels of gasoline and diesel per day through more than 24,000 retail outlets under three well-known consumer brands: Chevron in North America; Texaco in Latin America, Europe, and West Africa; and Caltex in Asia, the Middle East, and southern Africa.

▪ Chevron is the number-one jet fuel marketer in the United States and number three worldwide, marketing 550,000 barrels per day in eighty countries.

▪ The company's industrial and consumer lubricants business operates in more than 180 countries and sells more than 3,500 products, from specialized hydraulic fluids to leading branded products such as Delo, Havoline, Revtex, and Ursa.

▪ Chevron's global trading business buys and sells more than 6 million barrels of hydrocarbons per day in some sixty-five countries.

▪ The company's fuel and marine marketing business is a leading global supplier and marketer of fuels, lubricants, and coolants to the marine and power markets, with about 500,000 barrels of sales per day.

▪ Chevron's shipping company manages a fleet of thirty-one vessels and annually transports more than a billion barrels of crude oil and petroleum products.

Shortcomings to Bear in Mind

▪ According to one analyst, "Risks to our recommendation and target price include geographical risks associated with its international operations, oil and gas price volatility, and CVX's ability to improve returns and achieve synergies amid its recent merger with Unocal."

Reasons to Buy

▪ "Chevron, the world's fourth-largest oil company, is riding the oil boom," said David Dreman, writing for *Forbes* magazine on February 27, 2006. "Beyond that, it has acquired Unocal, which adds 15 percent to its reserves. Chevron also is upgrading refineries, a move that will boost production. The company is strong financially, with debt comprising merely 17 percent of capital, making prospects for stock buybacks and dividend hikes high."

▪ On April 4, 2005, Chevron announced that it had acquired Unocal is a deal worth about $18 billion, including net debt. To finance the deal, Chevron issued about 210 million shares of its own stock and paid $4.4 billion in cash. Some industry analysts say Chevron was wise to buy the company mostly with its own stock, since the move reduced the company's risk of overpaying in a high-price environment.

Unocal is based in El Segundo, California. Acquiring Unocal gives Chevron a portfolio of attractive fields in Azerbaijan, Bangladesh, Thailand, Indonesia, and the Gulf of Mexico, all of which are to begin producing in 2005. These projects, if successful, could increase Unocal's production as much as 10 percent a year through 2010, making it one of the industry's best performers.

■ In 2005, Russell Gold, writing for the *Wall Street Journal*, said, "Chevron Corp. said it will increase capital spending by 35 percent next year. The second-largest U.S. oil company by market value after Exxon-Mobil Corp. plans to ramp up spending on expensive projects to develop new energy sources at the same time it faces steep inflation for oil-field services."

The article goes on to say, "Chevron is stepping up its spending to fund giant capital projects required to extract oil and natural gas from the earth, but the billion-dollar increase in spending wasn't accompanied by an announcement that Chevron would raise its production goals. Chevron told investors in April (2005) that it would increase production by 5 percent a year through the end of the decade, including the boost from Unocal assets."

The article also said, "The company also will increase its budget for refineries and other projects to turn raw fuels into usable products by 47 percent, to $2.8 billion. This will help it increase production of gasoline and upgrade its facilities to produce cleaner fuels."

■ Chevron's upstream business, encompassing exploration and production activities, is the company's primary source of value growth. Its upstream portfolio is rich and broadly based, with premier resource, reserves, and production positions in many of the world's largest and most abundant oil and natural gas regions, including Angola, Australia, Indonesia, Kazakhstan, Nigeria, the United States, and Venezuela.

■ Chevron is one of the world's largest producers of heavy crude oil, which represents about one-third of the world's hydrocarbon reserves. Industry production of heavy oil is projected to grow by 30 percent by the end of this decade. Because the company is committed to extracting greater value from its extensive heavy-oil resource base, it is implementing improved technologies and processes for producing, transporting, refining, and marketing this challenging resource.

Meanwhile, Chevron has made significant advances in using steam to enhance recovery as well as in upgrading heavy oil to lighter crude and crude products. Its heavy-oil assets include fields in California's Joaquin Valley, where the company is the largest heavy-oil operator; the Duri Field in Indonesia, the world's largest steamflood project; the Hamaca project in Venezuela, which alone contains nearly 2 billion barrels of recoverable oil; and the Athabasca Oil Sands in Canada, where bitumen is extracted for upgrading into synthetic crude oil.

■ "Our recommendation is STRONG BUY," said T. J. Vital, writing for *Standard & Poor's Stock Reports* on February 1, 2006. "While the recovery of CVX's Gulf operations is expected to extend into the 2006 first quarter, CVX's long-term fundamentals are strong."

■ On March 29, 2006, the *New York Times* said that seven analysts rated Chevron a STRONG BUY; five regarded the stock as a MODERATE BUY. Nine said it was a HOLD, and one called the stock a MODERATE HOLD. There were no analysts who believed Chevron was a SELL.

■ On January 30, 2006, Lehman Brothers said, "CVX appears to be successful in refilling its pipeline and building the foundation for long-term growth. We forecast

Chevron's production will rise 5.3 percent between 2005–2009, while 2006 production will jump by 9.1 percent. We think Chevron continues to offer a very attractive risk/reward ratio, despite the poor fourth-quarter results in 2005."

- "Chevron Corp. says it plans to develop a giant oil-sands project in northern Canada, the latest in a string of investments that is quickly turning the region around Fort McMurray into one of the world's fastest-growing oil-producing regions," said Russell Gold, writing for the *Wall Street Journal* on March 3, 2006.

"Chevron acquired leases for 75,000 acres from the provincial government in two separate sales. The company said there could be 7.5 billion barrels of oil in tar-like deposits there. Chevron plans to get the oil to flow into wells by using a steam-flooding technique that typically recovers between 20 percent and 40 percent of the oil, says James Bates, vice president of operations for Chevron's Canadian unit."

SECTOR: **Energy** ◆ BETA COEFFICIENT: **0.90**
10-YEAR COMPOUND EARNINGS PER SHARE GROWTH: **15.8%**
10-YEAR COMPOUND DIVIDENDS PER SHARE GROWTH: **6.2%**

		2005	2004	2003	2002	2001	2000	1999	1998
Revenues (millions)		198,200	150,865	121,761	98,913	106,245	52,129	36,586	30,557
Net income (millions)		14,099	13,034	7,230	1,132	3,288	5,185	2,070	1,339
Earnings per share		6.54	6.14	3.48	0.54	1.55	3.99	1.57	1.02
Dividends per share		1.75	1.53	1.43	1.40	1.33	1.30	1.24	1.22
Price	high	66.0	56.1	43.5	45.8	49.2	47.4	57.0	45.1
	low	49.8	41.6	30.7	32.7	39.2	35.0	36.6	33.9

AGGRESSIVE GROWTH

Cintas Corporation

P.O. Box 625737 ❑ Cincinnati, OH 45262-5737 ❑ (513) 573-4013 ❑ Dividend reinvestment plan not available ❑ Web site: *www.cintas.com* ❑ Fiscal year ends May 31 ❑ Listed: Nasdaq ❑ Ticker symbol: CTAS ❑ S&P rating: A+ ❑ Value Line financial strength rating: B++

"You'd think a company with thirty-six consecutive years of sales and earnings growth would be shown a little love," said Beverly Goodman, writing for *SmartMoney* in October 2005. "Yet Cintas, the top U.S. provider of uniform rental, cleaning, and related services, has been in a stock-market slump since the economy slowed early this decade. Rather than dwell on this setback, however, this onetime investor's darling has invested in new businesses and is poised for a comeback.

"Cintas's stock soared 900 percent in the 1990s, but as hiring sputtered, so did its shares. 'The market views this as a very cyclical company, and it is,' says Joe Milano, manager of T. Rowe Price's New America Growth fund. 'A component of their growth hinges on the economy. But there are other drivers of revenue growth that investors are largely ignoring.'

"Those other areas provide customers with essential if mundane services, from floor-mat rentals to replacing towels, air freshener and soap in restaurants. 'They're already there delivering the uniforms,' says ABN AMRO Growth fund manager Rick Drake. 'For another $5, they can throw a mat down. As a result, the customer becomes even more dependent on them.'

"Cintas is moving into areas like stocking first-aid stations and ensuring compliance with safety regulations. 'They have an efficient business model they can replicate for these businesses,' Drake says. First aid sales grew 25 percent in the last quarter, and document management was up 40 percent."

Company Profile

Cintas is North America's leading provider of corporate identity uniforms through rental and sales programs, as well as related business services, including entrance mats, hygiene products, clean-room services, and first aid and safety supplies.

Cintas serves businesses of all sizes, from small shops to large national companies employing thousands of people. Today, more than 5 million people go to work wearing a Cintas uniform every day. That is well over 3 percent of the nonfarm, civilian work force in the United States and Canada.

Cintas provides its award-winning design capability and top-quality craftsmanship to the high end of the market—hotels, airlines, cruise ships, and the like. The company delivers the proper uniform to anyone in any job classification from the doorman to the cocktail waitress in a hotel; from the mechanic to the pilot at the airlines; and even people working in the retail sector.

According to a Cintas spokesman, "Companies use Cintas uniforms to identify their employees to their customers. An employee who wears a clean, crisp, and attractive uniform is always viewed as more professional than someone in ordinary work clothes. Uniforms also complement a company's esprit de corps by building camaraderie and loyalty. Bottom line—we don't just sell uniforms—we sell image, identification, teamwork, morale, pride, and professionalism." Put another way, Cintas believes that when people *look* good, they *feel* good. And when they feel good, they work better. What's more, their improved attitude results in a decline in absenteeism and turnover.

Shortcomings to Bear in Mind

- I had a tough time coming up with a negative comment on this stock. However, one analyst had some concern about a "slower-than-anticipated growth in employment levels and uniform rentals, as well as an increased rate of lost business (about a 7.4-percent rate in fiscal 2005) and unexpected increases in labor, medical, and material costs."

Reasons to Buy

- On March 29, 2006, the *New York Times* polled thirteen analysts for their ranking of Cintas. Three rated the stock a STRONG BUY, three said it was a MODERATE BUY; and seven called it a HOLD.
- "Cintas Corporation delivered another year of record-setting sales and profits in fiscal 2005," said CEO Scott D. Farmer. "It was our thirty-sixth consecutive year of such growth. Wal-Mart is the only public company to match that, according to our research."

Mr. Farmer went on to say, "The numbers tell part of the story. During fiscal 2005, Cintas's revenue increased 9 percent, to $3.07 billion, with profits rising 10 percent, to $301 million. Earnings per diluted share grew 10 percent, to $1.74.

"We added new plants, locations, and products in each of our business services. Cintas in fiscal 2005 was 60 percent larger that the size of Cintas in fiscal 2000, a reflection of the many new ways we now deliver service. No longer just the leading uniform company in the industry, Cintas, The Service Professionals, now leads the way with a broad range of products and services delivered to a broader range of customers.

"As our offerings increase, so does our business. Today, Cintas provides products and services to more than 700,000 business customers, or approximately 5 percent of the total number of businesses in the United States and Canada.

"In fiscal 2005, Rentals revenue grew 6.8 percent on an organic basis [which does not include acquisitions]. Despite higher energy costs, gross margins improved to 42.5 percent, from 42.2 percent in fiscal 2004. We also continued to strengthen our balance sheet. Debt to total capitalization declined to 18 percent at May 31, 2005, compared with 20 percent at May 31, 2004. Shareholders' equity reached $2.1 billion versus $1.9 billion in fiscal 2004."

■ According to an analytical report issued by Robert W. Baird & Co. (a brokerage firm with offices in the United States, France, Spain, Germany, and the United Kingdom), "In addition to the current market served, there are another roughly 25 million employees (according to *American Apparel Manufacturer*) that currently purchase work apparel specific for their occupation through retail outlets, which we believe could potentially be served by the industry.

"Furthermore, we believe that there are another 20–25 million employees in occupations that could be conducive to a uniform program, but that do not currently utilize one. If the industry penetrated these two potential markets, we estimate that the direct sales market could potentially reach $11 billion."

■ Many large corporations are re-engineering all aspects of their business, and they are consolidating their source of supply of products and services. They prefer to deal with fewer suppliers to reduce purchasing and administrative costs. They often prefer to do business with Cintas because the company is a complete uniform service, whether the customer wants to rent, lease, or buy their uniforms. In addition, Cintas also provides on-line ordering, inventory control, and paperless systems.

■ According to the company, "When on-the-job injuries occur, businesses need to handle them. Cintas can help by delivering our Xpect line of first aid and safety products and services.

"Cintas regularly and reliably stocks first aid cabinets, provides safety and emergency products, and conducts training to ensure that work places are safer and more prepared. Our products and services run the gamut—everything from pain relievers to defibrillators, from back injury prevention to emergency oxygen, from ergonomics to OSHA compliance."

■ Cintas is a proven performer and has earned a strong reputation as a caring citizen. In fiscal 2005, Cintas earned the following awards:

- Named "Most Admired Company" in the diversified outsourcing industry, according to *Fortune*, for the second consecutive year
- Ranked among "America's Most Admired Companies," per *Fortune*, for the fifth consecutive year
- Highlighted as one of the "World's Most Attractive Big Public Companies For Investors," according to *Forbes* magazine
- Recipient of top uniform design "Image of the Year" honors for the eleventh consecutive year
- Named "Best Uniform Supplier" to the food industry by *Food Processing* magazine
- Honored for donating more than 6 million pounds of humanitarian aid to people around the world and for donating more than $2.3 million in clothing and financial aid to tsunami victims
- Recognized by United Way for outstanding service to the community
- Ranked as one of "Oregon's Top Employers" for the fifth consecutive year
- Named one of the "Best Employers" in British Columbia

■ On February 8, 2006, *Standard & Poor's Stock Reports* had some good things to say. According to analyst Richard O'Reilly, CFA, "We have a BUY opinion on the shares, which recently traded at what we view as an historically low premium P/E [price/earnings ratio], relative to the S&P 500. The company has an attractive EPS [earnings per share] record, in our view, and we think Cintas can achieve its thirty-seventh consecutive year of sales and profit growth in 2006."

SECTOR: **Industrials** ◆ BETA COEFFICIENT: **1.10**
10-YEAR COMPOUND EARNINGS PER SHARE GROWTH: **14.5%**
10-YEAR COMPOUND DIVIDENDS PER SHARE GROWTH: **16.4%**

		2005	2004	2003	2002	2001	2000	1999	1998
Revenues (millions)		3,067	2,814	2,687	2,271	2,161	1,902	1,752	1,198
Net income (millions)		301	272	249	234	222	193	139	123
Earnings per share		1.74	1.58	1.45	1.36	1.30	1.14	.82	.79
Dividends per share		.32	.29	.27	.25	.22	.19	.15	.10
Price	high	45.5	50.5	50.7	56.2	53.3	54.0	52.3	47.5
	low	37.5	39.5	30.6	39.2	33.8	23.2	26.0	26.0

CONSERVATIVE GROWTH

The Clorox Company

1221 Broadway ❑ Oakland, CA 94612 ❑ (510) 271-2270 ❑ Direct dividend reinvestment plan available (888) 259-6973 ❑ Web site: *www.clorox.com* ❑ Listed: NYSE ❑ Fiscal year ends June 30 ❑ Ticker symbol: CLX ❑ S&P rating: A ❑ Value Line financial strength rating: B++

When Clorox researchers set out to design a new tub- and shower-cleaning tool, they knew they had their work cut out for them. Cleaning the bathroom ranks among the most difficult and unpopular household chores, and for good reason: Recent studies show people can actually get injured from common tasks like scrubbing the tub or shower.

"That's why our researchers designed the Clorox BathWand system to make cleaning not only faster and easier, but also an ergonomic improvement over traditional methods," said a Clorox spokesman in 2005. "While observing consumers, the team learned that people spent less time kneeling and cleaning with the wand than an old-fashioned sponge and cleaner. In addition, because women tend to clean the tub and shower more frequently than men, the team designed the BathWand handle to fit a female hand, making it more comfortable than other household tools, according to a survey of test subjects. So, although cleaning the tub and shower may never be most people's idea of a good time, the Clorox BathWand system helps make do so a lot easier."

Company Profile

Clorox has a solid stake in the manufacture and marketing of cleaning products. It offers laundry products, which include liquid bleaches, laundry stain removers, and dry and liquid color-safe bleaches, as well as water filtration systems and filters.

Some of its better-known brands include Formula 409, Handi-Wipes, Clorox Bleach, Lestoil, Liquid-Plumr, Pine-Sol, Tilex, Kingsford and Match Light charcoal,

Kitchen Bouquet, Fresh Step, Armor All, Glad, Hidden Valley, Brita, and S.O.S.

The company's home-care cleaning products primarily comprise disinfecting sprays and wipes, toilet bowl cleaners, carpet cleaners, drain openers, floor mopping systems, toilet and bath cleaning tools, and premoistened towelettes.

Clorox also provides professional products for institutional, janitorial, and food service markets, which include bleaches, toilet bowl cleaners, disinfectants, food-storage bags, trash bags, barbecue sauces, mildew removers, soap scum removers, and bathroom cleaners.

Its auto care products consist of protectants, cleaners and wipes, tire- and wheel-care products, washes, gel washes and waxes, and automotive fuel and oil additives.

The cat litter products include clumping cat litter and scoopable and silica-gel crystals cat litter.

In addition, the company offers food products, which include salad dressings and dip mixes, seasoned minicroutons, seasonings, sauces, and marinades. Clorox sells its products to grocery stores and grocery wholesalers primarily through a network of brokers; the company uses a direct sales force to sell to mass merchandisers, warehouse clubs, and military and other retail stores in the United States. It also sells its products outside the United States through subsidiaries, licensees, distributors, and joint-venture arrangements with local partners.

The company was founded in 1913 as Electro-Alkaline Company and changed its name to Clorox Chemical Corporation in 1922. It changed its name to Clorox Chemical Co. in 1928 and then to the Clorox Company in 1957.

Shortcomings to Bear in Mind

- *Standard & Poor's Stock Reports* had an unenthusiastic view of Clorox on January 5, 2006. Analyst Howard Choe said, "Our HOLD opinion reflects our view the shares are fairly valued in light of CLX's near-term prospects, due to the seasonal nature of some businesses and the diverse categories in which they operate. We expect this trend to continue as long as CLX retains this mix of businesses.

  "We also believe the timing of new product introductions adds to the volatility. However, the level of product innovation is respectable, in our view, and bolsters the company's pricing power, as well as its competitive stance."
- Prudential Equity Group gave Clorox an UNDERWEIGHT rating on February 2, 2006. The analyst said, "Though margin pressure might ease into 2006, it is possible that Clorox's raw materials cost considerably more in the second half of fiscal 2006 than they did in the same period last year. While we feel the price increases and restructuring initiatives would have provided expected results in a normal cost environment, we're not confident they will be able to offset the unusual cost pressure the company now faces."

Price Increases Not Enough

- "The biggest challenge we faced in fiscal 2005 was the sharp increase in energy-related costs such as oil and natural gas," said CEO Jerry Johnston in 2005. "This drove our raw-material and packaging costs up substantially, along with other operating costs such as transportation. While we executed our cost-savings program effectively and took selective price increases throughout the year, those actions were not enough to overcome our cost pressures. As a result, we fell short of our gross margin and operating improvement goals for the year. Nonetheless, I am very proud of the results Clorox people around the world achieved during the year."

Reasons to Buy

- *Value Line Investment Survey* had some favorable comments on October 7, 2005. Jerome H. Kaplan said, "Clorox's finances are in good shape. Like Procter &

Gamble and others in this sector, Clorox operates with lean inventories and low costs. This enables it to achieve strong cash flows, which support the ability to buy back shares, repay debt, and make capital expenditures."

■ Said Mr. Johnston in 2005, "Our company had another good year in fiscal 2005:

- Sales grew more than 5 percent, to $4.4 billion, ahead of our annual goal of 3-percent to 5-percent growth.
- We grew all-outlet market share with our brands in each of our eight categories in the U.S.
- We grew sales and gross profit by double-digit percentages in our International business.
- We generated more than $100 million in cost savings.
- Earnings per diluted share from continuing operations grew 26 percent, to $2.88.
- Return on invested capital increased about 40 basis points [there are 100 basis points in 1 percent].
- Total shareholder return grew 6 percent in fiscal 2005, on top of 29-percent growth last year."

A Trash Bag with Muscle

■ "Glad ForceFlex trash bags are a great example of how Clorox translates consumer insights into products that make life easier," said a company officer in 2005. "Introduced in fiscal 2005, ForceFlex trash bags address the single most important consumer need related to garbage disposal: strength. Consumers needed a trash bag that didn't tear, so the Glad team created an innovative bag with patented technology that uses deep embossing to make it more elastic. Pressure is diverted away from the point of impact so the trash bag absorbs force and stretches to help prevent rips and punctures. The result? Stretchable strength that takes on the toughest trash challenges with the greatest of ease—even the dreaded pizza box. ForceFlex trash bags have quickly become a consumer favorite, surpassing the company's expectations. More than a year after it hit store shelves, the market has yet to see a similar product."

Making Germs Squirm

■ In 2001, Clorox commissioned a study of germs on surfaces, and the findings were astounding. On average, a desk harbors 400 times more germs than a toilet seat. "Since then, we've built a powerful health and wellness platform on two key insights: Consumers are increasingly motivated to protect their families against germ-related illnesses, and Clorox disinfecting products can reduce exposure to germs that can cause many such illnesses," according to the 2005 annual report.

"Last year, our retail consumer marketing group partnered with a national retailer to help drive shoppers to the home-care aisle by promoting Clorox disinfecting wipes in the high-traffic pharmacy area. During the promotional period, the retailer's wipes category sales grew nearly 11 percent. The program has been expanded to other retail partners, who targeted events that put illness intervention front of mind when it matters most, such as the back-to-school season. Our health and wellness platform is striking a chord: Fiscal 2005 marked the fifth consecutive year we delivered record shipments of Clorox disinfecting wipes."

The Best View in the House

■ "The facts are compelling: Brita water-filtration products reduce chlorine, sediment, lead, mercury, and other contaminants from the tap to deliver better-tasting, cleaner drinking water," said a company spokesman in 2005. "In fact, Brita's claims are certified true by a leading independent test lab.

"But sometimes seeing is key to believing. So in fiscal 2005, Brita introduced the AquaView faucet-mount filtration system, the only filter with a window that lets consumers see what it's removing. The filter changes color over time as it traps sediment, offering visible proof that the water is cleaner. Like our popular Brita water-filtration pitchers, the AquaView system also features an electronic indicator light that reminds consumers when it's time to change the filter. And Brita water tastes better than tap. Now that's refreshing."

SECTOR: **Consumer Staples** ◆ BETA COEFFICIENT: **.65**
10-YEAR COMPOUND EARNINGS PER SHARE GROWTH: **11.7%**
10-YEAR COMPOUND DIVIDENDS PER SHARE GROWTH: **8.6%**

		2005	2004	2003	2002	2001	2000	1999	1998
Revenues (millions)		4,388	4,324	4,144	4,061	3,903	4,083	4,003	2,741
Net income (millions)		517	546	514	322	325	394	246	298
Earnings per share		2.88	2.43	2.33	1.37	1.63	1.75	1.63	1.41
Dividends per share		1.10	1.08	0.88	0.84	0.80	0.72	0.64	0.58
Price	high	66.0	59.4	49.2	47.9	40.8	56.4	66.5	58.8
	low	52.5	46.5	37.4	31.9	30.0	28.4	37.5	37.2

CONSERVATIVE GROWTH

Colgate-Palmolive Company

300 Park Avenue ❑ New York, NY 10022-7499 ❑ Listed: NYSE ❑ (212) 310-2291 ❑ Direct dividend reinvestment plan available (800) 756-8700 ❑ Web site: *www.colgate.com* ❑ Ticker symbol: CL ❑ S&P rating: A+ ❑ Value Line financial strength rating: A++

"We enjoyed outstanding top-line [sales] growth this quarter, particularly in North America, Latin America, Eastern Europe, and Africa," said Colgate-Palmolive CEO Reuben Mark on July 27, 2005. "Also, we are encouraged by volume growth in Western Europe, excluding the GABA acquisition, despite the challenging retail environment in that region.

"Toothpaste market shares are strong and getting stronger in the U.S. and abroad, reaching a record high worldwide. Colgate's global leadership in manual toothbrushes also expanded during the quarter with manual toothbrush market shares reaching record highs in the U.S., Mexico, Venezuela, France, and other key countries around the world."

"We're delighted that in addition to market share growth, it appears that our heavier level of advertising spending has accelerated the growth of the toothpaste market in a considerable number of overseas countries."

The GABA Acquisition

Concerning the GABA acquisition, Colgate-Palmolive president William S. Shanahan had this comment in mid-2005: "GABA, a leading European oral care company, is a great strategic fit for Colgate because of its strong relationships with the dental profession and the academic community and its strength in the important pharmacy distribution channel. When combined with Colgate's strong mass market presence, market shares in toothpaste in the region now exceed 33 percent, further strengthening Colgate's category leadership.

"This is just the beginning. Oral care, as we have stated, is a high-margin priority business for Colgate, and we see much more opportunity for additional growth, including geographic expansion of GABA products into Eastern Europe and further leveraging GABA's strong professional and academic relationships."

Company Profile

Colgate-Palmolive is a leading global consumer products company that markets its products in over 200 countries and territories under such internationally recognized brand names as Colgate toothpaste and brushes, Palmolive, Mennen Speed Stick deodorants, Ajax, Murphy Oil Soap, Fab and Soupline/Suavitel, as well as Hill's Science Diet and Hill's Prescription Diet.

With two-thirds of its sales and earnings coming from abroad, Colgate is making its greatest gains in overseas markets. Travelers, for instance, can find Colgate brands in a host of countries:

- They'll find Total toothpaste, with its proprietary antibacterial formula that fights plaque, tartar, and cavities, in more than seventy countries.
- The Care brand of baby products is popular in Asia.
- Colgate Plax makes Colgate the number-one producer of mouth rinse outside the United States.
- The Colgate Zig Zag toothbrush, popular in all major world regions outside the United States, helps make Colgate the number-one toothbrush company in the world.
- Axion is an economical dishwashing paste popular in Asia, Africa, and Latin America.

Shortcomings to Bear in Mind

▪ Colgate's balance sheet is very leveraged, with far more debt than common equity. About 74 percent is debt, which is well above the ideal. I prefer at least 75 percent in common equity and only 25 percent in long-term debt. With this much debt, it is far more difficult for the company to make acquisitions, since adding to debt would make the balance sheet even more leveraged.

Reasons to Buy

▪ On February 26, 2006, the *New York Times* said that five analysts awarded Colgate-Palmolive a rating of STRONG BUY; nine called it a MODERATE BUY; and six preferred a HOLD rating.

▪ Howard Choe, an analyst writing for *Standard & Poor's Company Reports,* had this comment on February 3, 2006, "We are maintaining our STRONG BUY opinion on the shares, reflecting our belief that CL's recently announced restructuring program is likely to drive improved profitability, and that the shares will likely trade at least on par with peer levels. We believe savings derived from the restructuring program will be reinvested in R&D and marketing in an effort to drive product sales. The program will also allocate more resources to faster-growing markets, in our view. We believe these efforts will culminate in greater gross margin expansion and EPS [earnings per share] growth in the low double digits from 2006 on."

▪ In early 2006, Argus Research Company gave Colgate a BUY rating. Lehman Brothers called it an OVERWEIGHT, as did Prudential Equity Group.

▪ Technology-based new products and veterinary endorsements are driving growth at Hill's, the world's leader in specialty pet food. Hill's markets pet foods mainly under two trademarks: Science Diet, which is sold through pet supply retailers, breeders, and veterinarians, and Prescription Diet for dogs and cats with disease conditions. Hill's sells its products in eighty-five countries.

Recent introductions gaining wide acceptance are Science Diet Canine and

Feline Oral Care, Science Diet Canine Light Small Bites, and new Prescription Diet Canine b/d, a clinically proven product that reduces the effects of canine aging.

■ Colgate concentrates research expenditures on priority segments that have been identified for maximum growth and profitability. For example, the fast-growing liquid-body-cleanser category has benefited from continuous innovation. As a result, European sales of Palmolive shower gel have nearly tripled during the past four years. The latest innovation, Palmolive Vitamins, uses unique technology to deliver two types of vitamin E to the skin, thus providing both immediate and long-lasting protection.

In another sector, focused R&D at Colgate's Hills subsidiary has resulted in a superior antioxidant formula that helps protect pets from oxidative damage, including potential damage to the immune system. This discovery led to a significant nutritional advance of Hill's Science Diet dry pet foods, introduced to the United States in 2000. The product has gained excellent reception from vets, retailers, and their customers, aided by national media advertising. Hill's scientists have also developed a new Prescription Diet brand formulation that nutritionally helps avoid food-related allergies.

■ Adding to region-specific initiatives is the company's vast consumer intelligence. Colgate interviews over 500,000 consumers in more than thirty countries annually to learn more about their habits and usage of the company's product.

■ Colgate's global reach lets the company conduct consumer research in countries with diverse economies and cultures to create product ideas with global appeal. The new product development process begins with the company's Global Technology and Business Development groups, which analyze consumer insights from various countries to create products that can be sold in the greatest possible number of countries. Creating "universal" products saves time and money by maximizing the return on R&D, manufacturing, and purchasing. To ensure the widest possible global appeal, potential new products are test-marketed in lead countries that represent both developing and mature economies.

■ To best serve its geographic markets, Colgate has set up regional new-product-innovation centers. From these centers, in-market insight from thousands of consumer contacts is married with R&D, technology, and marketing expertise to capitalize on the best opportunities. Early on, the consumer appeal, size, and profitability of each opportunity are assessed. Once a new product concept is identified, it is simultaneously tested in different countries to ensure acceptance across areas. Then, commercialization on a global scale takes place rapidly.

A prime example is Colgate Fresh Confidence, a translucent gel toothpaste aimed at young people seeking the social benefits of fresh breath and oral health reassurance. The process from product concept to product introduction in Venezuela took only one year. Within another six months, Colgate Fresh Confidence had been expanded throughout Latin America and began entering Asia and Europe. Today, less than a year after its first sale, Colgate Fresh Confidence is available in thirty-nine countries and is gaining new Colgate users among the targeted age group. Colgate Fresh Confidence, moreover, has expanded even faster than Colgate Total, the most successful toothpaste introduction ever.

The U.S. Surgeon General recently cited oral disease as a "silent epidemic," of which the primary victims are inner city children. Initially designed to improve the oral health of urban youngsters in the United States, Colgate's Bright Smiles, Bright Futures program has expanded to address oral care needs in eighty countries.

In the midst of expanding the company's reach, Colgate dental vans are stopping in cities across the country. New York, Houston, Atlanta, Chicago, and Los Angeles are examples of the many cities where children benefit from the expertise of volunteer dental professionals. Colgate's partnership with retail giants such as Wal-Mart and Kmart reaches children and their families outside stores across the United States. Each year, this campaign reaches 5 million children in the United States as well as another 49 million around the world.

- "Colgate's leadership of the U.S. toothpaste market continues to grow, with its ACNielsen market share reaching 35.6 percent year to date, up 150 basis points versus the year-ago period and over 3 share points ahead of the number-two competitor," said a company official on July 27, 2005.

"In the U.S., new products and increased commercial investment are generating strong volume and market-share growth. Key categories continuing to gain market share year to date versus prior year include toothpaste, manual and powered toothbrushes, hand dishwashing liquid, bar soap, and fabric conditioners.

"In oral care, new testimonial advertising for Colgate Total toothpaste and the recently launched Colgate Max Fresh Cinnamint toothpaste and Colgate 360 manual toothbrush contributed to the share gains. Other new products contributing to growth in other categories include Palmolive Oxy Plus Citrus Purity dishwashing liquid, new Mennen Speed Stick and Lady Speed Stick 24/7 multiform deodorants with Micro-Absorber technology, Irish Spring Micro Clean bar soap, and Fabuloso Orange Burst liquid cleaner."

SECTOR: **Consumer Staples** ◆ BETA COEFFICIENT: **.60**
10-YEAR COMPOUND EARNINGS PER SHARE GROWTH: **10.4%**
10-YEAR COMPOUND DIVIDENDS PER SHARE GROWTH: **9.7%**

		2005	2004	2003	2002	2001	2000	1999	1998
Revenues (millions)		11,397	10,584	9,903	9,294	9,084	9,358	9,118	8,972
Net income (millions)		1,351	1,327	1,421	1,288	1,147	1,064	937	849
Earnings per share		2.43	2.33	2.46	2.19	1.89	1.70	1.47	1.31
Dividends per share		1.11	.96	.90	.72	.68	.63	.59	.55
Price	high	57.2	59.0	61.0	58.9	64.8	66.8	58.9	49.4
	low	48.2	42.9	48.6	44.1	48.5	40.5	36.6	32.5

GROWTH AND INCOME

ConocoPhillips

600 North Dairy Ashford ❑ Houston, TX 77079-1175 ❑ (212) 207-1996 ❑ Direct dividend reinvestment plan available (888) 887-2968 ❑ Web site: *www.conocophillips.com* ❑ Ticker symbol: COP ❑ S&P rating: B ❑ Value Line financial strength rating: B++

"ConocoPhillips could be the best value in the energy sector, following last week's sell-off in its shares," said Andrew Bary, writing for *Barron's* on December 19, 2005. "The stock fell 5.72 to 57.35, on the week, after the company announced a deal to buy Burlington Resources, a big North American natural-gas producer, for $35 billion in cash and stock."

Mr. Bary goes on to say, "Critics say Conoco is overpaying for Burlington, whose reserves are heavily weighted toward natural gas, at what could be the top of the gas cycle."

The *Barron's* article countered this thinking: "While the acquisition of Burlington is expected to have little impact on Conoco's 2006 per-share profits, Conoco

CEO Jim Mulva argued in a conference call that the deal will benefit the company by making it the largest natural-gas producer in North America. It will also balance some of the risks in Conoco's portfolio, which includes investments such as a stake in Russian oil giant Lukoil. Given Conoco's strong cash flow, Mulva said the company may be able to pay off all $17 billion of debt associated with the deal in two to three years."

Company Profile

ConocoPhillips is an international integrated energy company. It is the third-largest integrated energy company in the United States, based on market capitalization, oil and gas proved reserves, and production, and the largest refiner in the United States. Worldwide, of nongovernment-controlled companies, ConocoPhillips has the eighth-largest total of proved reserves and is the fourth-largest refiner in the world.

ConocoPhillips is known worldwide for its technological expertise in deepwater exploration and production, reservoir management, and exploitation, 3D seismic technology, high-grade petroleum coke upgrading, and sulfur removal.

Headquartered in Houston, Texas, ConocoPhillips operates in more than forty countries. The company has about 35,800 employees worldwide and assets of $86 billion. ConocoPhillips stock is listed on the New York Stock Exchange under the symbol COP.

The company has four core activities worldwide:

- Petroleum exploration and production
- Petroleum refining, marketing, supply, and transportation
- Natural gas gathering, processing, and marketing, including a 30.3-percent interest in Duke Energy Field Services LLC
- Chemicals and plastics production and distribution through a 50-percent interest in Chevron Phillips Chemical Company LLC

In addition, the company is investing in several emerging businesses—fuels technology, gas-to-liquids, power generation, and emerging technologies—that provide current and potential future growth opportunities.

Exploration and Production (E&P)

ConocoPhillips explores for and produces crude oil, natural gas, and natural gas liquids on a worldwide basis. The company also mines oil sands to produce Syncrude. A key strategy is to accelerate growth by developing legacy assets—very large oil and gas developments that can provide strong financial returns over long periods of time—through exploration, exploitation, redevelopment, and acquisition, and by focusing exploration on larger, lower-risk areas.

At year-end 2003, ConocoPhillips held a combined 52.6 million net developed and undeveloped acres in twenty-five countries and produced hydrocarbons in thirteen. Crude oil production in 2003 averaged 934,000 barrels per day (BPD), gas production averaged 3.5 billion cubic feet per day, and natural gas liquids production averaged 69,000 BPD.

Key regional focus areas include Australia, the North Slope of Alaska, Southeast Asia, Canada, the Caspian Sea, offshore China, the Middle East, Nigeria, the North Sea, the Timor Sea, the lower forty-eight United States, including the Gulf of Mexico, and Venezuela.

Refining and Marketing (R&M)

R&M refines crude oil and markets and transports petroleum products. ConocoPhillips is the largest refiner in the United States and, of nongovernment-controlled companies, is the fourth-largest refiner in the world.

ConocoPhillips owns twelve U.S. refineries, owns or has an interest in five

European refineries, and has an interest in one refinery in Malaysia. At year-end 2003, ConocoPhillips refineries had a combined net crude oil refining capacity of 2.6 million barrels of oil per day.

ConocoPhillips's gasoline and distillates are sold through about 17,300 branded outlets in the United States, Europe, and Southeast Asia. In the United States, products are primarily marketed under the Phillips 66, 76, and Conoco brands. In Europe and Southeast Asia, the company markets primarily under the Jet and ProJET brands. ConocoPhillips also markets lubricants, commercial fuels, aviation fuels, and liquid petroleum gas. The company also participates in joint ventures that support the specialty products business.

R&M owns or has an interest in about 32,800 miles of pipeline systems in the United States.

R&M's strengths include branded wholesale marketing; refining technologies; aviation gasoline sales; and refining capabilities.

R&M's customers include independent marketers and the consuming public.

Midstream

Midstream consists of ConocoPhillips's 30.3-percent interest in Duke Energy Field Services (DEFS), as well as certain ConocoPhillips assets in the United States, Canada, and Trinidad. Midstream gathers natural gas, extracts and sells the natural gas liquids (NGL), and sells the remaining (residue) gas. Headquartered in Denver, Colorado, DEFS is one of the largest natural gas gatherers, natural gas liquids (NGL) producers, and NGL marketers in the United States.

DEFS's gathering and transmission systems include some 58,000 miles of pipelines, mainly in six of the major U.S. gas regions, plus western Canada. DEFS also owns and operates, or owns an equity interest in sixty-six NGL extraction plants. Raw natural gas throughput averaged 6.7 billion cubic feet per day, and NGL extraction averaged 365,000 BPD in 2003. In addition to its interest in DEFS, ConocoPhillips owns or has an interest in an additional eleven gas processing plants and six NGL fractionators.

DEFS's strengths include assets in major gas-producing regions; efficient, reliable low-cost operations; and critical mass for growth transactions.

DEFS's customers are primarily major and independent natural gas producers, local gas distribution companies, electrical utilities, industrial users, and marketing companies. Among DEFS's customers for NGL are Chevron Phillips Chemical Company and ConocoPhillips's R&M operations.

Chemicals

ConocoPhillips participates in the chemicals sector through its 50-percent ownership of Chevron Phillips Chemical Company (CPChem), a joint venture with Chevron. Headquartered in The Woodlands, Texas, its major product lines include olefins and polyolefins, including ethylene, polyethylene, normal alpha olefins, and plastic pipe; aromatics and styrenics, including styrene, polystyrene, benzene, cyclohexane, paraxylene, and K-Resin® styrene-butadiene copolymer; and specialty chemicals and plastics.

CPChem's major facilities in the United States are at Baytown, Borger, Conroe, La Porte, Orange, Pasadena, Port Arthur, and Old Ocean, Texas; St. James, Louisiana; Pascagoula, Mississippi; and Marietta, Ohio. The company also has nine plastic pipe plants and one pipefitting plant in eight states, as well as a petrochemical complex in Puerto Rico. Major international facilities are in Belgium, China, Saudi Arabia, Singapore, South Korea, and Qatar. CPChem also has a plastic pipe plant in Mexico.

CPChem is one of the world's largest producers of ethylene, polyethylene, styrene, and alpha olefins and is one of the largest marketers of cyclohexane. Customers are primarily companies that produce industrial products and consumer goods.

Shortcomings to Bear in Mind

- ConocoPhillips's fortunes are closely tied to the price of oil, which in 2006 was in the stratosphere. In the event of a recession, demand for energy would suffer, and the price of oil would sink back—far below the $50-a-barrel level.
- "Investors worry about operations in politically dodgy Russia and Venezuela, but the ventures are highly profitable," said an article in *SmartMoney* in January 2006. "A. G. Edwards energy analyst Bruce Lanni expects Conoco's investment in Russia's Lukoil to bring in $820 million in 2006, up from $74 million in 2004."

Reasons to Buy

- "Many energy industry CEOs don't know what to do with the gusher of money flowing into their tanks," said Harry Maurer, writing for *BusinessWeek* on December 26, 2005. "They've resorted mostly to paying down debt, buying back stock, and watching the cash pile up. Not ConocoPhillips's James Mulva. The fifty-nine-year-old boss, already one of the biggest spenders on new supplies, put his princely profits on the line on December 12 by agreeing to pay $35.6 billion for gas producer and Houston neighbor Burlington Resources." The author also said, "It may be that rivals ultimately quail, however. Mulva figures his company will catapult over six giants, including ExxonMobil, BP, and Royal Dutch/Shell, to become number one in the white-hot North American natural gas market. Conoco is banking on buoyant gas prices over the next few years and beyond that sees the deal opening the way for lucrative plays in liquefied natural gas and Arctic gas."
- *Standard & Poor's Stock Reports* concurs with the move. On January 31, 2006, T. J. Vital said "We have a STRONG BUY on the shares. We believe the proposed transaction to acquire Burlington Resources is reasonable, and should add high-quality, low-risk, and long-lived North American gas reserves to COP's upstream portfolio and boost COP to the super-major ranks."
- *Value Line Investment Survey* also had good things to say. On March 17, 2006, Michael P. Maloney wrote, "Impressive performance should prevail through 2006 and into 2007. The E&P division should continue to generate hefty profits. Though we do not look for the price of oil to break the $70-a-barrel level that it did in 2005, there is a good possibility that the average price will be higher in 2006 than 2005. Downstream, we anticipate healthy refining margins, as demand forces plants to operate near full capacity."
- On March 21, 2006, the *New York Times* surveyed twenty financial analysts. Seven rated ConocoPhillips a STRONG BUY; three called it a MODERATE BUY; nine gave it a HOLD RATING; and one said it was a MODERATE HOLD.

SECTOR: **Energy** ◆ BETA COEFFICIENT: **.90**
10-YEAR COMPOUND EARNINGS PER SHARE GROWTH: **24%**
10-YEAR COMPOUND DIVIDENDS PER SHARE GROWTH: **7%**

		2005	2004	2003	2002	2001	2000	1999	1998
Revenues (millions)		183,400	135,076	104,196	56,748	26,729	20,835	13,571	11,545
Net income (millions)		13,640	8,107	4,591	1,511	1,709	1,916	548	389
Earnings per share		9.55	5.79	3.35	1.56	2.90	3.74	1.08	0.75
Dividends per share		1.18	0.90	0.82	0.74	0.70	0.68	0.68	0.68
Price	high	71.5	45.6	33.0	32.1	34.0	35.0	28.7	26.6
	low	41.4	32.2	22.6	22.0	25.0	18.0	18.9	20.1

AGGRESSIVE GROWTH

Costco Wholesale Corporation

999 Lake Drive ❑ Issaquah, WA 98027 ❑ (425) 313-8203 ❑ Direct dividend reinvestment plan available (800) 249-8982 ❑ Web site: *www.costco.com* ❑ Listed: Nasdaq ❑ Fiscal year ends Sunday nearest August 31 ❑ Ticker symbol: COST ❑ S&P rating: A- ❑ Value Line financial strength rating: A

The CEO of Costco is sixty-nine-year-old James D. Sinegal. "A lifelong retailer, Sinegal opened the first Costco warehouse in 1983 in Seattle, with Jeffrey H. Brotman, who is chairman," according to an article in *BusinessWeek*. "Their strategy was to offer lower prices and better value by stripping away everything they deemed unnecessary, including deluxe store fixtures, salespeople, even delivery and backup inventory. And it works. Over the past five years, sales have grown 10.5 percent compounded annually, as earnings climbed 9.6 percent a year.

"Their original concept has led to some revolutionary behavior. One of Sinegal's rules, for example, is to strictly limit markups to 12 percent on national brand items and 14 percent for private-label, Kirkland Signature goods."

Costco's strategy of retailing has grown in popularity among consumers and small-business owners in recent years. As a consequence, it has taken market share from such traditional retailers as supermarkets and drugstores. As the leader in its field, Costco should be able to strengthen its position further by broadening its line of products and services, coupled with further penetration into new markets, both at home and abroad.

A reputation for merchandising excellence and quality are a hallmark of Costco operations. These attributes have not gone unnoticed. The American Customer Satisfaction Index survey conducted by the University of Michigan Business School showed that Costco had the highest customer satisfaction rating of any domestic traditional national retailer.

Company Profile

Costco Wholesale Corporation operates an international chain of membership warehouses, mainly under the "Costco Wholesale" name, that carry quality brand-name merchandise at substantially lower prices than are typically found at conventional wholesale or retail sources. The warehouses are designed to help small-to-medium-sized businesses reduce costs in purchasing for resale and for everyday business use. Individuals may also purchase for their personal needs.

Costco's warehouses present one of the largest and most exclusive product category selections to be found under one roof. Categories include groceries, appliances, television and media, automotive supplies, tires, toys, hardware, sporting goods, jewelry, watches, cameras, books, housewares, apparel, health and beauty aids, tobacco, furniture, office supplies, and office equipment. Costco is known for carrying top-quality national and regional brands, with 100-percent satisfaction guaranteed, at prices consistently below traditional wholesale or retail outlets.

Members can also shop for private label Kirkland Signature products, designed to be of equal or better quality than national brands, including juice, cookies, coffee, tires, housewares, luggage, appliances, clothing, and detergent. The company also operates self-service gasoline stations at a number of its U.S. and Canadian locations.

Additionally, Costco Wholesale Industries, a division of the company, operates manufacturing businesses, including special food packaging, optical laboratories, meat processing, and jewelry distribution. These businesses have a common goal of providing members with high-quality products at substantially lower prices.

According to CEO Jim Sinegal, "Costco is able to offer lower prices and better values by eliminating virtually all the frills and costs historically associated with conventional wholesalers and retailers, including salespeople, fancy buildings, delivery, billing, and accounts receivable. We run a tight operation with extremely low overhead which enables us to pass on dramatic savings to our members."

Costco is open only to members and offers three types of membership: Business, Gold Star (individual), and Executive. Business members qualify by owning or operating a business and pay an annual fee ($45 in the United States) to shop for resale, business, and personal use. This fee includes a spouse card. Business members may purchase up to six additional membership cards ($35 each) for partners or associates in the business. A transferable company card may also be purchased.

Gold Star members pay a $45 annual fee (in the United States) and membership is available to those individuals who do not own a business. This fee includes a free spouse membership.

The company also has a third membership level, called the Executive Membership. In addition to offering all of the usual benefits, it allows members to purchase a variety of discounted consumer services (auto and homeowner insurance, real estate and mortgage services, long-distance telephone services, auto buying, personal check printing, financial planning) and/or discounted business services (merchant credit card processing, health insurance, business lending, payroll processing, communication solutions, check and forms printing) at substantially reduced rates. Executive members also receive a 2-percent annual reward (up to $500) on most of their warehouse purchases. Executive members pay an annual fee of $100.

Costco warehouses generally are open seven days per week for all members.

KEY INFORMATION

Number of warehouses: 469 (as of November 17, 2005)

Areas of operation: 344 locations in thirty-seven U.S. States and Puerto Rico

66 locations in nine Canadian provinces

17 locations in the United Kingdom

4 locations in Taiwan

5 locations in Korea

5 locations in Japan

28 locations in eighteen Mexican states

Membership Data (as of August 28, 2005): 45.3 million cardholders

24.8 million households

16.2 million Gold Star

5.1 million Business

3.5 million Business add-ons

Warehouse sizes: 70,000 to 160,000 square feet

Average 137,000 square feet

Shortcomings to Bear in Mind

- On November 11, 2005, *Value Line Investment Survey* rated the stock "untimely." Deborah Y. Fung said, "High petroleum prices are likely to persist, which will hurt margins in a couple of ways. First, the company experiences a negative mix shift, as low-margin gasoline sales increase as a percentage business. Also, hauling freight becomes more expensive."

- "Costco is feeling the heat from Sam's Club," said Steven Greenhouse, writing for the *New York Times* on July 17, 2005. "When Sam's Club began to pare prices aggressively several years ago, Costco had to shave its prices—and its already thin profit margins—ever further.

"'Sam's Club has dramatically improved its operation and improved the quality of their merchandise,' said Bill Dreher, the Deutsche Bank analyst. 'Using their buying power together with Wal-Mart's, it forces Costco to be very sharp on their prices.'"

Reasons to Buy

- On December 28, 2005, *Standard & Poor's Stock Reports* said, "We have a BUY recommendation on the shares." Analyst Joseph Agnese went on to say, "We expect COST to maintain or capture additional market shares in fiscal 2006, reflecting what we view as a strong value proposition and a relatively upscale product mix that appeals to a more affluent customer base. Although we believe that quickly rising gasoline prices may negatively affect gross margins in the near term, with labor cost controls in place and store expansion accelerating, we think the company is well positioned to generate future earnings growth."
- Costco warehouses generally operate on a seven-day, sixty-eight-hour week and are open somewhat longer during the holiday season. Generally, warehouses are open between 10 A.M. and 8:30 P.M., with earlier closing hours on the weekend. Because these hours of operation are shorter than those of traditional discount grocery stores and supermarkets, labor costs are lower relative to the volume of sales.
- Costco's policy generally is to limit advertising and promotional expenses to new warehouse openings and occasional direct-mail marketing to prospective new members. These practices result in lower marketing expenses as compared to typical discount retailers and supermarkets.

In connection with new warehouse openings, Costco's marketing teams personally contact businesses in the region that are potential wholesale members. These contacts are supported by direct mailings during the period immediately prior to opening.

SECTOR: **Consumer Staples** ◆ BETA COEFFICIENT: **.90**
10-YEAR COMPOUND EARNINGS PER SHARE GROWTH: **14.4%**
10-YEAR COMPOUND DIVIDENDS PER SHARE GROWTH: **not meaningful**

		2005	2004	2003	2002	2001	2000	1999	1998
Revenues (millions)		52,035	48,107	41,693	37,993	34,797	32,164	27,456	24,269
Net income (millions)		999	882	721	700	602	631	545	460
Earnings per share		2.03	1.85	1.53	1.48	1.29	1.35	1.18	1.02
Dividends per share		.45	.20	Nil	—	—	—	—	—
Price	high	51.2	50.5	39.0	46.9	46.4	60.5	46.9	38.1
	low	39.5	35.0	27.0	27.1	29.8	25.9	32.7	20.7

CVS Corporation

One CVS Drive ❑ Woonsocket, RI 02895 ❑ (914) 722-4704 ❑ Direct dividend reinvestment plan available (877) 287-7526 ❑ Web site: *www.cvs.com* ❑ Listed: NYSE ❑ Ticker symbol: CVS ❑ S&P rating: B ❑ Value Line financial strength rating: A+

"CVS is the nation's largest retail drugstore chain, with 5,474 stores in thirty-eight states," said Richard Karp, writing for *Barron's* on December 5, 2005. "On Wall Street, however, the company has long played second fiddle to Walgreen, which operates about 5,000 stores."

Mr. Karp goes on to say, "Through the years, there were reasons aplenty for investors to take a dimmer view of Woonsocket, RI-based CVS than its Deerfield, Ill., arch-rival. But those reasons are far fewer today. The company's integration of 1,268 Eckerd drugstores, which CVS purchased last year (2004) from J. C. Penney for $2.15 billion—a real 'steal,' in view of one money manager—has proceeded faster and more efficiently than expected. CVS is now number one or number two in all its markets. Margins are widening, same-store sales are up sharply."

The *Barron's* article goes on to ask, "Given these and other recent achievements, isn't it time the Street showed more respect? That's likely to come in the next year or so."

Company Profile

Stanley and Sid Goldstein were distributing health and beauty products in the early 1960s when they decided to branch out into retailing. The brothers opened their first Consumer Value Store in Lowell, Massachusetts, in 1963. The CVS chain had grown to forty outlets by 1969, the year they sold the business to Melville Shoes. Melville underwent a restructuring in the mid-1990s, spinning off CVS and other retail units.

CVS Corporation is now the largest domestic drugstore chain, based on store count. CVS operates 5,474 retail and specialty pharmacy stores in thirty-eight states and the District of Columbia. The company holds the leading market share in thirty-two of the 100 largest U.S. drugstore markets, or more than any other retail drugstore chain.

Stores are situated primarily in strip shopping centers or freestanding locations, with a typical store ranging in size from 8,000 square feet to 12,000. Most new units being built are based on either a 10,000- or 12,000-square-foot prototype building that typically includes a drive-through pharmacy. The company says that about one-half of its stores were opened or remodeled over the past five years.

Celebrating more than forty years of dynamic growth in the pharmacy retail industry, CVS is committed to being the easiest pharmacy retailer for customers to use. CVS has created innovative approaches to serve the health-care needs of all customers through nearly 4,200 CVS/pharmacy® stores; its online pharmacy, CVS.com®; and its pharmacy benefit management and speciality pharmacy subsidiary, PharmaCare Management Services. The pharmacy industry has some of the best long-term growth dynamics in all of retail, and CVS is extremely well positioned to seize further growth opportunities.

Some Recent History

Here are a few of the significant events in the history of CVS:

- 2004: In April of that year, J. C. Penney sold its Eckerd drugstore chain of 2,800 units to two purchasers: Canada's Jean Coutu Group, Inc., and CVS. Of the 1,260 stores allocated to CVS, 622 are in Florida, a favorite home of retirees, and

437 are in Texas, a large, fast-growing state. The rest are also situated in the South. CVS also received Eckerd's pharmacy benefits management and mail-order businesses. CVS paid $2.15 billion for its share of the Eckerd stores. Coutu was awarded the remaining 1,540 outlets, situated mainly in thirteen Northeast and Mid-Atlantic states.

- 2002: CVS continues to enter and open new stores in new, high population growth markets such as Dallas, Houston, Phoenix, and Las Vegas.
- 2001: CVS has sales that exceed $22 billion and operates over 4,000 stores in thirty-two states and the District of Columbia. CVS is a leading pharmacy retailer in many markets in the Northeast, Mid-Atlantic, Midwest, and Southeast regions. The company also begins its expansion into high-growth markets, including Central and South Florida.
- 1999: CVS launches CVS.com, the first fully integrated online pharmacy in the United States.
- 1998: CVS acquires Arbor Drugs, Inc., of Michigan. Tom Ryan is named president and CEO of CVS. Ryan began working for CVS in 1978 as a pharmacist and is only the third CEO in the history of the company.
- 1997: CVS completes its acquisition of the Revco pharmacy chain—the largest and most successful acquisition in the history of the U.S. retail pharmacy industry. The acquisition of Revco gives CVS new key store locations in the Midwest, Southeast, and other parts of the country.
- 1994: CVS launches PharmaCare, a pharmacy benefit management company providing a wide range of pharmacy management benefit services to employers and insurers.
- 1990: CVS acquires Peoples Drug, which put CVS into new markets, including the District of Columbia, Pennsylvania, Maryland, and Virginia.
- 1985: CVS hits the $1-billion milestone in sales.
- 1980: CVS becomes the fifteenth-largest pharmacy chain in the United States, with 408 stores and $414 million in sales.
- 1974: CVS hits the $100-million milestone in sales.

Shortcomings to Bear in Mind

- Drugstores face growing competition from major retailers. Wal-Mart, Target, and Costco, for instance, are among the big chains that have added pharmacies.
- Mail-order prescriptions are still a small segment of all drug sales. On the other hand, consumers who need maintenance drugs to treat chronic health ailments, such as hypertension, diabetes, and arthritis, may find that their health plans now require that they use mail-order suppliers.
- "We are maintaining our BUY recommendation on CVS," said Christopher Graja, CFA, writing for Argus Research Company on February 6, 2006. However, on a negative note, the analyst said, "But we intend to watch the stock very closely, because we believe the additional debt the company will add in its planned acquisition of 700 drugstores from Albertson's will reduce the company's financial flexibility. Another reason to watch CVS closely is because investors have a lot of confidence in CVS management. That could make the consequences of an unanticipated stumble greater if one should occur."

Reasons to Buy

- In December 2005, a company official said, "CVS is well positioned to capitalize on industry trends as the long-term outlook of the industry is extremely positive. Generic prescriptions, which carry more gross profit dollars per pill than branded drugs, are expected to grow faster over the next several years, thanks to over $40 billion in branded drug patent protection losses. Additionally, we expect to benefit from the implementation of the Medicare Part D drug benefit, which we anticipate will drive incremental volume to our stores as drug utilization increases after the program's launch in January 2006."

- David B. Rickard, executive vice president and chief financial officer of CVS, was named in the August 2004 issue of *Corporate Finance Magazine* (U.K.) as one of the twenty most influential CFOs of the last twenty years. Rickard was recognized for his role in establishing CVS as the industry leader in sales performance, productivity, and earnings growth, as well as his role in the successful restructuring of RJR Nabisco in the 1990s.
- On March 21, 2006, the *New York Times* checked the thinking of seventeen analysts who keep tabs on CVS. Six regarded the stock as a STRONG BUY; seven said it was a MODERATE BUY; and four were less enthusiastic and labeled it a HOLD.
- "We like CVS as a long-term holding," said Andre J. Costanza, writing for *Value Line Investment Survey* on December 30, 2005. "Although the swirling political winds limit the stock's near-term appeal, it holds above-average three- to five-year total-return potential." The analyst goes on to say, "The Eckerd acquisition greatly improved its position in the rapidly growing Florida and Texas markets, as well as in the mail-order business. That said, CVS looks to be well-situated to benefit from favorable trends, such as aging demographics and increased generic drug utilization rates."
- *Standard & Poor's Stock Reports* had good things to say, as well. On February 7, 2006, Joseph Agnese said, "We have a STRONG BUY on CVS shares, based on our view of the potential for significant earnings benefits following the integration of 1,100 former Eckerd drugstores which were acquired in July 2004."
- In a November 2005 issue of *SmartMoney*, CEO Tom Ryan said, "Walgreens stores are about 30 percent larger and carry very general merchandise. We focus on pharmaceutical, health, beauty, and photography-related products. That's how we differentiate ourselves. One of the biggest decisions we make is what we don't want to sell."

Mr. Ryan also said, "We signed an exclusive deal with a Minnesota company called Minute Clinic to manage in-store clinics. They staff nurse practitioners and physician's assistants who can handle basic primary-care needs like ear infections, sore throats, colds, flu shots, anything of that sort. Most of the people we see don't have primary-care physicians, and only about 50 percent have health insurance. This is about making it easier to get health care, and it works. People are usually in and out in about twenty minutes. This is another way to differentiate ourselves and another reason for the customer to come: They think of us as a resource for health care. That's what I want. It's what differentiates us from the Wal-Marts and Walgreens."

SECTOR: **Consumer Staples** ◆ BETA COEFFICIENT: **.80**
10-YEAR COMPOUND EARNINGS PER SHARE GROWTH: **21.9%**
8-YEAR COMPOUND DIVIDENDS PER SHARE GROWTH: **3.1%**

		2005	**2004**	**2003**	**2002**	**2001**	**2000**	**1999**	**1998**
Revenues (millions)		37,006	30,594	26,588	24,182	22,241	20,088	18,098	15,274
Net Income (millions)		1,220	959	847	719	638	734	635	510
Earnings per share		1.45	1.15	1.03	0.88	0.78	0.90	0.78	0.63
Dividends per share		.14	.13	0.12	0.12	0.12	0.12	0.12	0.12
Price	high	31.6	23.7	18.8	17.9	31.9	30.2	29.2	28.0
	low	22.0	16.9	10.9	11.5	11.5	13.9	15.0	15.2

Deere & Company

One John Deere Place ❑ Moline, IL 61265 ❑ (309) 765-4491 ❑ Direct dividend reinvestment plan available (800) 727-7033 ❑ Web site: *www.deere.com* ❑ Listed: NYSE ❑ Fiscal year ends October 31 ❑ Ticker symbol: DE ❑ S&P rating: B ❑ Value Line financial strength rating: A

With residential building space getting tighter and tighter, operating heavy machinery in subdivisions has become more difficult than ever. That's why Mike Brock, owner of Brock Construction in Lenexa, Kansas, relies heavily on four John Deere 50C ZTS compact excavators to do all of his smaller excavating jobs on residential work sites.

"Being small machines, our 50C ZTSs can fit into tight areas," said Mr. Brock on December 13, 2005. "That's important in residential areas, where we're working between trees, or between a tree and a house."

Mr. Brock does mainly residential work, including digging basements and additions, grading yards, and building retaining walls, along with the occasional light commercial work, such as digging building pads and ponds. In addition to digging and other odd jobs, he uses the four compact excavators for building stacking-rock retaining walls. A John Deere Worksite Pro™ hydraulic-thumb attachment on the bucket enables the machine to lift rocks into place.

Building retaining walls is not exactly light work—the stones weigh anywhere from 500 to 5,000 pounds each. With 41.5 horsepower and a lift capacity of 5,190 pounds, the 50C ZTS handles it easily, according to Mr. Brock.

"It's compact, but it has enough power to lift these rocks," he said. "It's got longer tracks and a wider stance than other brands, so it doesn't tip easily. It's just a more stable machine. It has the same lifting capacity and power as some of the larger compacts, but it's smaller, more versatile, and more productive."

The design of the 50C is what makes it so perfectly suited to this type of work. Able to rotate fully without banging their tails, the 50C ZTS slips comfortably into extremely tight quarters. The independent swing boom and 360-degree rotation allow operators to position themselves better and be more productive. "We're always working right up against houses, so if you don't have zero tail swing, it makes it a lot harder to maneuver around," said Mr. Brock.

Maintenance also is a strong point of the 50C ZTS, according to Mr. Brock. All doors open wide, with easy access to daily service points, cooling system, fuel filters, and battery. But one of the clearest advantages of the machine is lower daily operating costs.

Company Profile

Deere & Company, founded in 1837, grew from a one-man blacksmith shop into a worldwide corporation that today does business in more than 160 countries and employs more than 40,000 people around the globe. Deere consists of three equipment operations, a credit operations unit, and four support operations.

Equipment Operations

Equipment operations consist of the following segments: Agricultural Equipment, Construction & Forestry Equipment, and Commercial & Consumer Equipment.

John Deere has been the world's premier producer of agricultural equipment since 1963. Products include tractors; combines, and cotton and sugarcane harvesters; tillage, seeding, and soil-preparation machinery; hay and forage equipment; materials-handling equipment; and integrated agricultural management systems technology for the global farming industry.

Through its Construction & Forestry Equipment operations, John Deere is the world's leading manufacturer of forestry equipment and a major manufacturer of construction equipment. The company's key products are backhoes, four-wheel-drive loaders, graders, excavators, crawler dozers, log skidders, skid steer loaders, wheeled and tracked harvesters, forwarders, and log loaders.

In its Commercial & Consumer Equipment operations, Deere is the world leader in premium turf-care equipment and world vehicles. The company produces a broad range of outdoor power products for both homeowners and commercial users, including tractors, mowers, utility vehicles, golf and turf equipment, and handheld products.

Credit Operations

John Deere Credit is one of the largest equipment-finance companies in the United States, with more than 1.8 million accounts and a managed asset portfolio of nearly $16 billion. It provides retail, wholesale, and lease financing for agricultural, construction and forestry, and commercial and consumer equipment, including lawn and ground care, as well as revolving credit for agricultural inputs and services. John Deere Credit also provides financing in Argentina, Australia, Brazil, Canada, Finland, France, Germany, Italy, Luxembourg, Spain, and the United Kingdom.

Support Operations

Support Operations consist of the following segments: Parts, Power Systems, Technology Services, and Health Care.

Through its Parts operation, John Deere is a major supplier of service parts for its own products as well as those of other manufacturers.

Through its Power Systems operation, John Deere is a world leader in the production of off-highway diesel engines in the 50- to 600-horsepower range. In addition to John Deere equipment operations, the company supplies heavy-duty engines and drive train systems for OEM (original-equipment manufacturer) markets.

Through its Technology Services operations, John Deere offers a wide range of electronic, wireless-communication, information system, and Internet-related products and services to its own and outside customers.

Through its Health Care operations, John Deere Health Care subsidiaries provide health-care management services to about 4,400 employer groups and more than 515,000 members.

Shortcomings to Bear in Mind

- Deere is not a typical growth stock, with steady gains in earnings per share and dividends that follow along. Rather, Deere is a cyclical company with earnings that can vary from year to year. For instance, EPS dropped sharply in 1999 to $1.02, compared with $4.16 the prior year. Similarly, EPS fell from $2.06 in 2000 to $0.65 in 2001. Nor were dividends anything to boast about. In the six-year span from 1998 through 2003, the annual dividend remained at $0.88.
- "We have a HOLD recommendation on the shares," said Anthony M. Fiore, writing for *Standard & Poor's Stock Reports* on February 21, 2006. "Our enthusiasm for the stock is tempered by our belief that near-term profitability will be limited by the projected decline in unit production volumes of agricultural equipment and also due to what we see as difficult earnings comparisons."

Reasons to Buy

- On March 3, 2006, the *New York Times* surveyed sixteen leading securities analysts on how they view Deere as an investment. Three gave the stock a STRONG BUY rating; four said it was a MODERATE BUY; eight called Deere a HOLD; one said it was a MODERATE HOLD.
- On February 23, 2006, Andrew Casey, an analyst with Prudential Equity Group, said, "In our opinion, management continues to target low double-digit average earnings growth, improved cash generation consistency, and 20 percent operating return on identifiable asset average performance through a business cycle. We continue to like DE's improve internal processes, strong new product order book, continued strong cash flow generation, very strong balance sheet, strong demand in its non-agricultural businesses and a potentially longer-than-discounted North American agricultural equipment cycle." The stock was rated OVERWEIGHT.
- "Outdoor tasks for homeowners and professional landscapers just got easier and more affordable with the introduction of the new John Deere 2000 TWENTY Series small-chassis tractors," said a company official on January 20, 2006.

During the previous year and a half, John Deere had redesigned its total compact utility tractor offering with the introduction of the 4000 TWENTY Series large-chassis and 3000 TWENTY Series mid-chassis tractors. The 2000 TWENTY Series offers two new models, the 2320 and 2520, at competitive prices. These machines are built for commercial-grade use, featuring 24- and 26.5-hp EPA Tier II-compliant Yanmar engines, best-in-class mower decks, and attachments. Their ease of use and versatility make these tractors equally ideal for homeowners.

"More customers are in need of a machine that can perform large mowing jobs, in addition to light-duty chores that can't be done with standard lawnmowers, such as loader and/or box blade work," said Sean Sundberg, Brand Manager for John Deere Compact Utility Tractors. "John Deere responded with our new small-chassis tractors that help customers select the right tractor for the right job at the right price.

"While homeowners will appreciate their versatility, ease-of-use, and maneuverability, commercial customers will value the comfort, stability, efficiency, and power of the new 2000 TWENTY Series Tractors. And, with everyday low prices and high-resale value, buying these tractors has never been easier or more affordable."

- On January 20, 2006, a Deere spokesman said, "When it comes to outdoor tasks, thinking small can deliver big results. The new John Deere 2305 compact utility tractor, the entry-level model in the John Deere tractor lineup, is the most powerful tractor in its class with its 24-hp rating. Plus competitive pricing and a wide variety of attachments make it a perfect fit for homeowners with large properties to maintain.

"The 2305 replaces the very popular John Deere 2210 tractor, offering customers a higher horsepower engine, innovative styling, ease-of-use, comfort, and versatility. The new 24-hp Yanmar engine is 11 percent larger and EPA Tier II-compliant, making it more powerful and environmentally friendly than the previous engine. The sloped hood provides greater visibility—especially helpful with loader work—and its two-piece design is engineered for easier access to all major service points."

"The 2305 is a small but powerful tractor, which makes it ideal for lawn chores, pasture maintenance, work in tight spaces, and a variety of other property tasks," said Mr. Sundberg. "Whether it's mowing, hauling, loading, or tilling, the 2305 has the versatility and power to tackle most any job easily and efficiently, and at a significantly lower price than what was previously available."

Mr. Sundberg says a critical component of the 2305 is the ease-of-use and operator comfort. Simple design features make it easy for first-time buyers to acclimate to the tractor's full range of capabilities, while seasoned operators will appreciate a more comfortable ride, thanks to the contoured high-back seat. Additional best-in-class features include automatic transmission, power steering wet disk brakes, Twin Touch™ dual pedal foot control, and Roll Over Protective Structure (ROPS).

SECTOR: **Industrials** ◆ BETA COEFFICIENT: **1.05**
10-YEAR COMPOUND EARNINGS PER SHARE GROWTH: **8.0%**
10-YEAR COMPOUND DIVIDENDS PER SHARE GROWTH: **4.9%**

		2005	2004	2003	2002	2001	2000	1999	1998
Revenues (millions)		21,931	19,635	13,349	11,703	11,077	11,169	9,701	11,926
Net income (millions)		1,447	1,406	643	319	153	486	239	1,021
Earnings per share		5.87	5.56	2.64	1.33	.64	2.06	1.02	4.16
Dividends per share		1.21	1.06	0.88	0.88	0.88	0.88	0.88	0.88
Price	high	74.7	74.9	67.4	51.6	46.1	49.6	45.9	64.1
	low	57.0	56.7	37.6	37.5	33.5	30.3	30.2	28.4

AGGRESSIVE GROWTH

Dell, Inc.

One Dell Way ❑ Round Rock, TX 78682 ❑ (512) 728-7800 ❑ Dividend reinvestment plan not available ❑ Web site: *www.dell.com* ❑ Fiscal year ends on Friday nearest January 31 ❑ Listed: Nasdaq ❑ Ticker symbol: DELL ❑ S&P rating: B+ ❑ Value Line financial strength rating: A++

On September 28, 2005, Dell announced comprehensive, top-of-the-line home-entertainment offerings giving U.S. consumers the ability to combine the ultimate in performance, experience, and service that has made the company the leader in computing.

At a press conference led by CEO Michael Dell, the company unveiled the XPS brand of high-performance computers matched with an unrivaled buying and support experience and two digital televisions, including the company's first fifty-inch plasma HDTV.

"We're consistently hearing a call for performance, power, and style as more consumers see the value of expanding the computer's use for productivity and entertainment," Mr. Dell said. "We're delivering superior technology, design, and service coupled with an enhanced personalized experience so consumers can get the most out of everything they want from Dell."

Dell will ramp its XPS portfolio with the XPS 600, XPS 400, and XPS 200 desktop computers and the XPS M170 notebook computer; additional models will be introduced over time. Available now in the United States, the new XPS models are aimed at tech enthusiasts, gamers, and buyers who prefer the best products, services, and individualized support. Desktop pricing begins at $1,099; the notebook computer starts at $2,699.

All XPS systems are equipped with leading-edge technologies, high standard features, and stylistic designs. They include

Microsoft® Windows® XP Media Center Edition 2005, a fifteen-month security subscription for virus and spyware protection, and seventeen-inch displays (flat panel monitors for desktop computers). Shipping and one year of XPS limited warranty support is included, too.

Whether consumers are looking for the most power, expandability, or portability in their computers, the range of customizable XPS products is unequaled. According to CEO Dell, the new products address the growing sophistication of consumers who are using computers for advanced multimedia and entertainment applications in environments ranging from dens and offices to living rooms, gaming rooms, and home theaters.

Company Profile

Dell, Inc., is a trusted and diversified information-technology supplier and partner that sells a comprehensive portfolio of products and services directly to customers worldwide. Dell's climb to market leadership is the result of a persistent focus on delivering the best possible customer experience by directly selling standards-based computing products and services. Revenue for the last four quarters totaled $49.2 billion, and the company employs approximately 55,200 team members around the globe.

Dell was founded in 1984 by Michael Dell, the computer industry's longest-tenured chief executive officer, on a simple concept: that by selling computer systems directly to customers, Dell could best understand their needs and efficiently provide the most effective computing solutions to meet those needs. This direct business model eliminates retailers that add unnecessary time and cost, or can diminish Dell's understanding of customer expectations. The direct model allows the company to build every system to order and offer customers powerful, richly configured systems at competitive prices. Dell also introduces the latest relevant technology much more quickly than companies with slow-moving, indirect distribution channels, turning over inventory every four days on average.

Harnessing the Internet

In its own business, Dell has enhanced and broadened the fundamental competitive advantages of the direct model by applying the efficiencies of the Internet. Dell led commercial migration to the Internet, launching its site (*www.dell.com*) in 1994 and adding e-commerce capability in 1996. The following year, Dell became the first company to record $1 million in daily online sales. Today, Dell operates one of the highest volume Internet commerce sites in the world based on Microsoft's Windows operating systems. The company's Web site, which runs entirely on Dell PowerEdge servers, receives more than 2 billion page requests per quarter from eighty-one country sites in twenty-eight languages/dialects and twenty-six currencies.

The company is increasingly realizing Internet-associated efficiencies throughout its business, including procurement, customer support, and relationship management. At *www.dell.com,* customers may review, configure, and price systems within Dell's entire product line; order systems online; and track orders from manufacturing through shipping. At its business-to-business site, Dell shares information with its suppliers on a range of topics, including product quality and inventory. Dell also uses the Internet to deliver industry-leading customer services. For instance, thousands of business and institutional customers worldwide use Dell's targeted premier site to do business with the company online.

Dell's high return to shareholders has been the result of a focused effort over time to balance growth with profitability and liquidity. Dell has consistently led its largest competitors in each of those categories.

Shortcomings to Bear in Mind

- In a report issued January 12, 2006, *Standard & Poor's Stock Reports* had this comment, according to its analyst, Megan Graham-Hackett, "We continue to recommend HOLDING the shares. Dell's results have recently been challenged by a shift in the industry toward lower-end PC products, in our view. While Dell has been able to take advantage of a lower cost structure versus peers, reflecting the cost advantage of its direct sales model, we believe the company is witnessing new and more aggressive competition due to changes in the competitive landscape, such as the sale of IBM's PC business."
- "All tech companies have some unhappy customers, of course, but recent surveys suggest the ranks of frustrated Dell owners are growing," said Louise Lee and Emily Thornton, writing for *BusinessWeek* on October 10, 2005. "Complaints to the Better Business Bureau rose 23 percent in 2004 from the year before. And Dell's customer-satisfaction rating fell 6.3 percent to a score of 74, in a survey by the University of Michigan. Dell's score puts it right at the PC industry average for the study, in which Apple Computer, Inc., led the way with an 81. Still, it's a big decline, especially for a company that has often topped the list. 'We've never seen a drop like this,' says professor Claes Fornell, who ran the survey."

Reasons to Buy

- In October of 2005, *SmartMoney* magazine had a favorable view of Dell, according to writers Nicole Bullock and Reshma Kapadia. "As personal computers became a fixture in every household, Dell rose to dominance with a business model that founder Michael Dell came up with two decades ago in his University of Texas dorm room.

  "Using two key concepts—building to order and eliminating the middleman—Dell has kept inventories low and margins high while undercutting its competitors' prices. It takes orders directly, via the Internet and phone, and doesn't even assemble the computer until a customer buys one. 'That's a huge advantage over someone like Hewlett-Packard, who has to build the box, drop it at Best Buy, and wait for a customer to buy it,' says David Daoud, an analyst at technology research firm IDC. It's no surprise that by 2003 Dell had unseated HP as the leader in PC sales worldwide: It now accounts for 19 percent of all PCs sold in the world and 34 percent of those sold in the U.S."
- "In the computer business, it's known as the Dell effect," said Daniel Lyons, writing for *Forbes* magazine on June 6, 2005. The Round Rock, Texas, computer maker spots a market where others are making fat profits, figures out how to deliver the same stuff for less, and then drains the profits right out of the pool. Starting with lowly PCs, Dell has moved on to make conquests in computer servers, data storage systems, and printers.

  "Now the Wal-Mart of computing is muscling into professional services and consulting. Unfortunately for rivals like IBM and Hewlett-Packard, Dell's low-cost method appears to be working. With customers like Boeing, ExxonMobil, and Ford Motor Company, Dell's services division grew 34 percent last year, to $3.7 billion, and now employs 10,000 people. Dell expects the group to keep growing at a 30-percent clip for the next several years.

  "'We've been tremendously successful in applying the 'Dell direct' model to the product business. Now we see an opportunity to apply it to the services business,' says Gary Cotshott, services division vice president."
- On February 17, 2006, the *New York Times* reviewed the opinions of thirty-three analysts who follow Dell. Seven viewed the company as a STRONG BUY; thirteen called it a MODERATE BUY; twelve said it was a HOLD; and one rated the stock a MODERATE HOLD.

- On February 14, 2006, Steven Fortuna, writing for Prudential Equity Group, said, "We believe Dell is the best-positioned company in the IT industry. As the enterprise hardware industry continues to commoditize and move increasingly toward standards-based computing, we think Dell's cost model advantage could drive significant additional share gains not only in PCs but also in higher-margin areas such as servers, storage, and services."
- On February 7, 2006, Wendy Abramowitz, writing for Argus Research Company, said, "We are maintaining our BUY on Dell, Inc." She goes on to say, "We continue to find Dell attractive, as its valuations are reaching levels not seen in some time. Furthermore, we do not expect the company's earnings to stall or decline anytime soon; rather, we think growth will slow a bit."
- On February 17, 2006, Thaddeus Herrick, writing for the *Wall Street Journal*, said, "Computer maker Dell, Inc., said its fiscal fourth-quarter profit rose 52 percent, reflecting growth in sales and services outside the United States. The results, coming after two consecutive disappointing quarters, reflect the resiliency of the company's low-cost, direct-sales strategy developed by founder Michael Dell."

SECTOR: **Information Technology** ◆ BETA COEFFICIENT: **1.20**
10-YEAR COMPOUND EARNINGS PER SHARE GROWTH: **32.1%**
10-YEAR COMPOUND DIVIDENDS PER SHARE GROWTH: **no dividend**

		2005	2004	2003	2002	2001	2000	1999	1998
Revenues (millions)		55,910	49,205	41,444	35,404	31,168	31,888	25,265	18,243
Net income (millions)		3,570	3,043	2,645	2,122	1,780	2,310	1,860	1,460
Earnings per share		1.46	1.18	1.01	0.80	0.65	0.84	0.68	0.53
Dividends per share		—	—	—	—	—	—	—	—
Price	high	42.4	42.6	37.2	31.1	31.3	59.7	55.0	37.9
	low	28.6	31.1	22.6	21.9	16.0	16.3	31.4	9.9

CONSERVATIVE GROWTH

Dentsply International, Inc.

221 West Philadelphia Street ❑ York, PA 17405 ❑ (717) 849-4370 ❑ Dividend reinvestment plan not available ❑ Web site: *www.dentsply.com* ❑ Listed: Nasdaq ❑ Ticker symbol: XRAY ❑ S&P rating: A ❑ Value Line financial strength rating: B++

More than 50 percent of all dental restorations today are repairs of previously placed fillings, indicating a strong market need for a dental filling material that performs more satisfactorily. The major reason for the failure of existing dental materials is secondary caries that develop due to the access of bacteria at the interface of the restoration and the tooth.

Dentsply recently completed a comprehensive licensing agreement with Doxa AB to develop and commercialize products within the dental field, based on Doxa's bioactive ceramic technology. The novel technology was originally developed in Sweden in cooperation with the Department of Engineering Sciences at the University of Uppsala's world-renowned Angstrom Laboratory. Doxa, a

Swedish biomaterial technology company, also located in Uppsala, is an ideal business partner for Dentsply. They have since undertaken significant work to advance the unique calcium aluminate hydrate and bioactive ceramic technology to the point where physical properties and product handling and delivery are supportive of its use in dentistry.

The Doxa technology is designed to induce chemical integration between the bioactive ceramic material and dentition, or bone structure. The bioactive calcium aluminate induces the formation of a substance similar to hydroxyapatite, the main mineral component of teeth. This leads over time to microstructural integration with dentin, enamel, and bone, providing a long-lasting material seal.

With virtually no microleakage at the interface with tooth structure, the new technology will provide a breakthrough platform for the introduction of new and advanced restorative dental materials and cements and may also have application for improved dental implant surface coatings and endodontic root canal filling materials. In the words of a company spokesman, "Our market leadership, global strength, and strategic focus uniquely position the company to successfully bring this new technology to market."

Company Profile

Dentsply designs, develops, manufactures, and markets a broad range of products for the dental market. The company believes that it is the world's leading manufacturer and distributor of dental prosthetics, precious metal dental alloys, dental ceramics, endodontic instruments and materials, prophylaxis paste, dental sealants, ultrasonic scalers, and crown and bridge materials; the leading United States manufacturer and distributor of dental X-ray equipment, dental handpieces, intraoral cameras, dental X-ray film holders, film mounts, and bone substitute/grafting materials; and a leading worldwide manufacturer or distributor of dental injectable anesthetics, impression materials, orthodontic appliances, dental cutting instruments, and dental implants.

Dentsply International, Inc., is among the largest manufacturers of dental products in the world. The company has a presence in more than 120 countries, though its main operations take place in Canada, Germany, Switzerland, Italy, the United Kingdom, Japan, and Italy. The company markets its products under the brand names Caulk, Cavitron, Ceramco, Dentsply, Detrey, and Gende.

The company has an extensive sales network of around 1,800 sales representatives, distributors, and importers. Its products are manufactured both domestically and internationally and include some of the most established brand names in the industry, such as Caulk, Cavitron, Ceramco, Dentsply, Detrey, Midwest, R&R Rinn, and Trubyte.

The company operates under the following segments: dental consumables; endodontics/professional division dental consumables; Africa/European dental laboratory business; Australia/Canada/Latin America/U.S. pharmaceutical; U.S. dental laboratory business/implants/orthodontics and all others.

Dental Consumables

This segment, which operates in the United States, Europe, and Japan, designs and produces nondental equipment, such as chair-side consumable products and laboratory products. Dental consumables operations are concentrated in Germany, Scandinavia, the United States, Iberia, Eastern Europe, and Japan.

Endodontics/Professional

This segment designs and manufactures endodontic products for the Switzerland, Germany, and U.S. markets. It also produces small equipment and chair-side consumable products for the domestic market; for the Chinese market, it produces laboratory products. The segment also sells and distributes all Dentsply products to the

Asian market and sells endodontic products to Canada, Switzerland, Scandinavia, Benelux, and the United States.

Pharmaceutical

Dentsply's pharmaceutical segment focuses largely on the design, production, sale, and distribution of the company's dental anesthetics. This segment caters to the demand for dental anesthetics demand in the U.S. and Brazil markets. Furthermore, the segment also handles the selling and distribution of all the company's products to Canada, Australia, Mexico, and Latin America.

Dental Laboratory

The U.S. dental laboratory business/implants/orthodontics segment caters to the U.S. market's demand for laboratory products. The segment is primarily focused on the design, manufacture, sale, and distribution of laboratory products. It also handles the global sale and distribution of the dental implant, bone generation, and orthodontic products of the company.

Shortcomings to Bear in Mind

- "Based on recent conversations with German dental manufacturers, we believe that dental procedure volumes have not improved, following reimbursement changes at the beginning of the year," said a report issued by FTN Midwest Securities Corporation on July 26, 2005. "Moreover, we are increasingly concerned that weak dental procedure volumes in Germany are at least partially due to a fundamental problem—higher out-of-pocket payments for patients—rather than simply reimbursement startup issues."
- On March 3, 2006, *Value Line Investment Survey* analyst George Rho said, "This issue remains unexciting at the current price. Earnings growth out to 2009–2011 is likely to lag behind that achieved over the past five years."

Reasons to Buy

- At the end of the second quarter in 2005, Dentsply CEO Gary Kunkle said, "Our continuous flow of new products remains a driving force in growing our businesses around the world. We have made considerable progress in our major product categories and markets during the second quarter. The German market, however, remains weak relative to 2004, but has shown significant improvement versus the first quarter of 2005."
- On March 4, 2006, the *New York Times* tabulated the opinions of eight financial analysts who keep track of Dentsply. Four rated the stock a STRONG BUY; two said it was a MODERATE BUY; and two settled for a HOLD.
- On February 16, 2006, *Standard & Poor's Company Reports* had kind words to say about the company. According to analyst Richard Tortoriello, "We have a STRONG BUY recommendation on the stock. Cash-flow generating ability is strong, in our view, with free cash flow per share of $2.25 in 2003, $3.05 in 2004, and $2.86 in 2005."
- On January 4, 2005, the company announced that it had acquired rights to a unique compound, called Satif, from the Sanofi-Aventis Group for an undisclosed amount. Gary Kunkle, Dentsply's CEO stated, "Satif is another excellent example of the progress our Office of Advanced Technology has made in their efforts to locate and acquire new technologies with potential applications in dentistry. Satif is a unique titanium-fluoride derivative, which has demonstrated in studies the ability to protect the tooth surface, which could be of particular value in preventive and aesthetic dentistry. We believe that the potential applications from this technology could be seen as a significant innovation in oral healthcare, similar to the discovery of the benefits of fluorides."

■ Dentsply has joined forces with the Georgia Institute of Technology's Dental Technology Center (DenTeC) to partner on several innovative research projects. DenTeC is a nonprofit, multidisciplined research center focused on advancing dental science and technology.

The institute brings engineering expertise to dentistry by integrating engineering and dental science to introduce new products and technology for dentists through research, testing, and education. What's more, DenTeC will pursue dentistry-related research in other related fields, such as nanotechnology, photonics and optics, imaging, rapid prototyping, material development and testing, tissue-material interface evaluation, and software and hardware development.

SECTOR: **Health Care** ◆ BETA COEFFICIENT: **.70**
10-YEAR COMPOUND EARNINGS PER SHARE GROWTH: **14.9%**
10-YEAR COMPOUND DIVIDENDS PER SHARE GROWTH: **9.1%**

		2005	2004	2003	2002	2001	2000	1999	1998
Revenues (millions)		1,715	1,694	1,571	1,514	1,129	890	831	795
Net income (millions)		215.5	195.8	172.6	146.1	109.9	101.0	89.9	80.2
Earnings per share		1.34	1.20	1.07	0.92	0.70	0.65	0.57	0.50
Dividends per share		.12	.11	.10	.09	.09	.09	0.08	0.07
Price	high	29.2	28.4	23.7	21.8	17.4	14.5	9.8	11.7
	low	25.4	20.9	16.1	15.7	10.9	7.7	6.9	6.7

AGGRESSIVE GROWTH

Devon Energy Corporation

20 North Broadway, Suite 1500 ❑ Oklahoma City, OK 73102-8260 ❑ (405) 552-4526 ❑ Dividend reinvestment plan not available ❑ Web site: *www.devonenergy.com* ❑ Ticker symbol: DVN ❑ Listed: NYSE ❑ S&P rating: B+ ❑ Value Line financial strength rating: B++

Devon's portfolio of oil and gas properties provides stable production and a platform for future growth. The company's oil and gas properties are concentrated in the areas where Devon can be most competitive. By concentrating its properties, Devon has become a dominant operator in most of its core producing areas.

Concentrating operations results in strong relationships with suppliers, service providers, and the purchasers of the company's oil and gas.

Devon's production is weighted toward natural gas, and most of its operations are in North America.

■ 60 percent of production is natural gas.

■ 40 percent is oil and natural gas liquids, such as propane, butane, and ethane.

■ More than 80 percent of both production and proved reserves are in North America, including the United States, Canada, and the Gulf of Mexico.

■ The majority of Devon's international production and proved reserves are found in West Africa, Egypt, Azerbaijan, and China.

■ Devon produces 2.4 billion cubic feet of natural gas each day, or nearly 4 percent of all gas consumed in North America.

■ About 40 percent of Devon's gas production is from unconventional sources, such as the Barnett Shale Field in north Texas, and coalbed natural gas fields in New Mexico, Wyoming, and Canada.

Company Profile

Devon Energy Corporation is the largest U.S.-based independent oil and gas producer and one of the largest independent processors of natural gas and natural gas liquids in North America.

The company's portfolio of oil and gas properties provides stable, environmentally responsible production and a platform for future growth. About 86 percent of Devon's production is from North America. The company also operates in selected international areas, including Brazil, West Africa, the Middle East, and China. The company's production mix is about 60 percent natural gas and 40 percent oil and natural gas liquids, such as propane, butane, and ethane.

Headquartered in Oklahoma City, Devon has about 4,000 employees worldwide. Devon is a *Fortune* 500 company and is included in the S&P 500 index.

The company's primary goal is to build value per share by the following means:

- Exploring for undiscovered oil and gas reserves
- Purchasing and exploiting producing oil and gas properties
- Enhancing the value of its production through marketing and midstream activities
- Optimizing production operations to control costs
- Maintaining a strong balance sheet

On January 20, 2005, Devon Energy Corporation announced that it had completed a multiyear program to divest noncore midstream assets. The midstream divestiture program was launched in 2002 and has involved nine separate transactions. The final transaction took place in mid-2005. Aggregate proceeds from these transactions are about $330 million.

"Devon's midstream operations continue to perform exceptionally well," said Darryl G. Smette, senior vice president of marketing and midstream. "These divestitures, which are in addition to the divestitures of producing oil and gas properties we announced in September, have allowed us to bring increased focus to our core midstream assets."

The divested assets include six gas processing plants and about 7,000 miles of gas gathering pipelines. The assets are situated in Oklahoma, Texas, Louisiana, Kansas, and Wyoming. The midstream assets sold in 2004 and expected to be sold in 2005 contributed about $48 million to Devon's marketing and midstream operating margin in 2004."

Following the divestitures, Devon is still one of the largest independent gas processors in North America. The company retains ownership in sixty-four gas-processing plants in the United States and Canada, with aggregate net processing capacity of nearly 2.1 trillion cubic feet of natural gas per day. The company also owns an interest in 11,320 miles of gas gathering pipelines.

Shortcomings to Bear in Mind

- On February 2, 2006, Jason Gammel, an analyst with Prudential Equity Group, said "Our NEUTRAL WEIGHT rating on DVN reflects an overall slowing in the operating and cash flow levers that had been supporting share appreciation over the last twelve to eighteen months. While we continue to believe that the company will be able to generate solid upstream performance in its core operating areas, the combination of our lowered production expectations, a higher cost structure and a 24-percent increase in capital expenditures that will likely slow the pace of share repurchases leave us with few reasons to believe that DVN's shares will outperform the E&P sector."

■ On February 1, 2006, *Standard & Poor's Stock Reports* lowered its rating on Devon from BUY to HOLD.

Reasons to Buy

■ On March 21, 2006, the *New York Times* reported the opinions of twenty-seven analysts. Nine rated the stock a STRONG BUY; four called it a MODERATE BUY; thirteen regarded it as a HOLD; and one free thinker—who insists that I not reveal his name—said it was a SELL.

■ "We are maintaining our BUY rating on Devon Energy Corp." said Jeb Armstrong, writing for *Argus Research Company* on February 2, 2006.

■ Devon's operating strategy balances lower-risk, near-term investment in the company's gas-weighted, North American asset base with longer-term investment in high-impact exploration projects.

■ Devon's Bridgeport Gas Processing Plant in north Texas has gas processing capacity of 650 million cubic feet per day and natural gas liquids production capacity of 54,000 barrels per day. It serves the largest gas field in Texas, the Barnett Shale Field. Devon produces about 550 million cubic feet of gas equivalent per day from this field.

A decade ago, the Barnett Shale formation in north Texas represented a geological puzzle that had gone unsolved for more than forty years. Geoscientists knew vast energy reserves were sealed inside the tight, black rock formed from organic deposits 325 million years ago. The challenge was recovering them.

The Barnett is not particularly deep or impervious to the drill bit, but it would take more than conventional thinking to recover the gas locked inside the stingy shale known for its low porosity and high complexity.

Devon Energy is a pioneer in the Barnett, using innovations in technology to literally crack open the shale to release the natural gas sealed inside. Engineers are using a method known as fracturing to foster permeability in the rock. Crews inject fresh water and a little sand into the shale at a very high pressure to shatter the surrounding formation and release gas trapped inside. The technology has given Devon access to vast reserves, transforming this challenging play northwest of Fort Worth into one of the nation's most important natural-gas producing zones.

Devon has drilled about 800 wells into the Barnett Shale Field since 2001. Use of fracturing technology has helped Devon increase its Barnett production from 345 million cubic feet of natural gas equivalent per day to nearly 600 million today.

In all, Devon is operating more than 1,700 wells in what is known as the Barnett's core area, where dense layers of limestone separate the shale's gas deposits from the watery Ellenberger formation that lies below. Today, Devon is continuing to confront the most challenging questions in the Barnett. It ventured outside the core with horizontal drilling projects where geological complexities have impeded development in the past. Those projects have shown promise, and Devon geoscientists continue to explore the Barnett's noncore area, where it is a major leaseholder with 390,000 net acres of land.

Through Devon's pioneering effort, the Barnett Shale formation has emerged as the largest natural gas field in Texas and one of the most important gas fields in the nation. With recent inroads into the vast noncore area, the Barnett has potential to remain one of the country's most vital energy resources for years to come. Devon's accomplishments in the Barnett are an example of how technology and innovation are helping to meet growing energy demands by finding new ways to tap North America's remaining reserves.

- About 15 percent of Devon's production comes from the Gulf of Mexico, where it is among the largest producers. The company's operations range from the continental shelf to projects in the deep water nearly 200 miles from the Texas and Louisiana coasts.

Devon holds 1.4 million net acres in the Gulf's deep water, one of the largest among independent producers. The deep Gulf, where depths range from 600 to more than 7,000 feet, is a promising frontier where Devon has made major discoveries on its Cascade, Jack, and St. Malo prospects. Devon's Red Hawk and Magnolia development projects were brought on line in 2004.

Devon holds about 750,000 net acres on the Gulf of Mexico shelf, where production began more than fifty years ago. Today, Devon is participating in a new wave of exploratory projects on the "deep shelf," drilling for oil and gas 15,000 feet below the sea floor.

SECTOR: **Energy** ◆ BETA COEFFICIENT: **.90**
9-YEAR COMPOUND EARNINGS PER SHARE GROWTH: **23.3%**
9-YEAR COMPOUND DIVIDENDS PER SHARE GROWTH: **17.6%**

		2005	2004	2003	2002	2001	2000	1999	1998
Revenues (millions)		10,741	9,189	7,352	4,316	3,075	2,784	734	388
Net income (millions)		2,916	2,176	1,731	549	674	715	87	48
Earnings per share		6.26	4.38	4.04	1.71	2.52	2.73	0.67	0.50
Dividends per share		.30	0.20	0.10	0.10	0.10	0.10	0.10	0.10
Price	high	70.4	41.6	29.4	26.5	33.4	32.4	22.5	20.6
	low	36.5	25.9	21.2	16.9	15.3	15.7	10.1	13.1

GROWTH AND INCOME

Dominion Resources, Inc.

P.O. Box 26532 ❑ Richmond, VA 23261-6532 ❑ (804) 819-2156 ❑ Direct dividend reinvestment plan available: (800) 552-4034 ❑ Web site: *www.dom.com* ❑ Listed: NYSE ❑ Ticker symbol: D ❑ S&P rating: B+ ❑ Value Line financial strength rating: B++

Dominion Resources, one of the nation's largest energy producers, announced on November 22, 2005 that it plans to spend about $500 million to install additional emissions controls on coal-fired power stations in Virginia.

The installation of equipment to reduce sulfur dioxide, nitrogen oxide, and mercury emissions is to meet stringent new emissions reductions required by the federal Clean Air Interstate and Mercury rules. The new equipment will be installed between 2008 and 2015.

"Dominion is proud of its long history of environmental stewardship," said Thomas F. Farrell II, president and chief operating officer. (On January 1, 2006, Mr. Farrell became CEO of the company, replacing Thomas E. Capps, who retired.) "Today, we are setting a new standard in our pledge to be a leader nationally in the effort to improve air quality."

The proposed new environmental controls follow more than $2 billion Dominion has invested or committed to since the 1990s in clean air improvements in Virginia through lowered emissions. The vast majority of these expenses have been borne by the company—not customers—because of capped rates.

"Thanks to the vision of the General Assembly in passing the Virginia Electric Utility Restructuring Act of 1999, Virginians are reaping a truly extraordinary benefit of significantly cleaner air and continued electric reliability with virtually no impact on customer rates for seventeen years," Mr. Farrell said.

With completion of all of the environmental construction by 2015, Dominion will have reduced its sulfur dioxide emissions by an average of more than 80 percent for all of its coal-fired units that serve Virginia. Nitrogen oxide emissions will decrease by 74 percent and mercury emissions by about 86 percent from 2000 levels.

"What's amazing is that we will accomplish these large reductions in emissions while Virginia's economy continues to grow and demand for electricity over the next decade increases by 30 percent," Mr. Farrell said.

Company Profile

Dominion is one of the nation's largest producers of energy. The company's asset portfolio consists of about 28,100 megawatts of power generation, 6,000 miles of electric transmission, about 6 trillion cubic feet equivalent of proved natural gas reserves, 7,900 miles of natural gas pipeline, and the nation's largest natural gas storage system, with more than 965 billion cubic feet of storage capacity. This enables the company to purchase natural gas during the summer when it is cheaper. Dominion also serves retail energy customers in nine states.

Dominion's strategy is to be a leading provider of electricity, natural gas, and related services to customers in the energy-intensive Midwest, Mid-Atlantic, and Northeast regions of the United States, a potential market of 50 million homes and businesses where 40 percent of the nation's energy is consumed.

Dominion Resources has five key subsidiaries.

Dominion North Carolina Power

Dominion North Carolina Power is one of the nation's ten largest investor-owned electric utilities. It delivers power to more than 2 million homes and businesses in Virginia and North Carolina and is active nationally in wholesale power sales and energy services. Dominion's service territory spans an economically healthy region from Northern Virginia to northeastern North Carolina.

Dominion Virginia Power

Dominion Virginia Power is one of the nation's ten largest investor-owned electric utilities. The company delivers power to more than 2 million homes and businesses in Virginia and North Carolina and is active nationally in wholesale power sales and energy services.

Dominion East Ohio

Cleveland-based Dominion East Ohio is the largest gas distribution subsidiary of Dominion. It serves more than 1.2 million residential, commercial, and industrial customers in 400 eastern and western Ohio communities.

Dominion Hope

Headquartered in Clarksburg, West Virginia, Dominion Hope has been providing natural gas service to its customers for more than a century. Using an extensive 2,800-mile pipeline system—with almost 80 percent of its natural gas coming from the Appalachian region—the company supplies thousands of residential, business, and wholesale customers throughout thirty-two counties in West Virginia.

Dominion Peoples

Based in Pittsburgh, Pennsylvania, Dominion Peoples provides natural gas to more than 350,000 homes and businesses throughout the sixteen southwestern Pennsylvania counties.

Other Dominion Companies

Dominion also operates the following:

- Dominion Cove Point LNG, LP: Liquefied natural-gas import facility in Maryland
- Dominion Clearinghouse: Traders and marketers of wholesale gas, electricity, coal, oil, and emissions, and providers of commodity pricing and services to customers in target markets
- Dominion Exploration and Production (E&P): Oil and natural gas exploration and production unit
- Dominion Gathering-Producer Services: Overseas production gas delivery points into the Dominion pipeline system
- Dominion Generation: Managers of the company's generating stations
- Dominion Greenbrier—A sponsor of the Greenbrier Pipeline Company
- Dominion Retail: Retail marketing arm providing energy services in deregulated markets; includes Dominion East Ohio Energy, and Dominion Peoples Plus
- Dominion Technical Solutions, Inc.: Engineering, procurement, and construction services for electric transmission lines, substations, and distribution facilities
- Dominion Transmission: Operators of gas pipelines and gas storage system

Shortcomings to Bear in Mind

■ Although this stock is classified for growth and income, the company's record of dividend increases is suspect. From 1995 through 2003, the annual dividend per share was locked in place at $2.58 and only modestly increased to $2.60 in 2004.

■ "Our recommendation is HOLD," said Yogeesh Wagle, writing for *Standard & Poor's Company Reports* on March 1, 2006. "We view favorably the company's strategy of buying power plants that already serve its utilities. Besides reducing purchased power costs, it provides the company with greater operational flexibility." The analyst went on to say, "Still, we remain concerned about Dominion's ability to get regulatory relief, as well as execution issues, including potential shortfalls in production and unplanned outages. We expect higher prices to lead to declining usage by utility customers."

Reasons to Buy

■ On March 28, 2006, the *New York Times* checked with nineteen securities analysts. Six said that Dominion should be a STRONG BUY; two preferred to tag it a MODERATE BUY; ten said it should be a HOLD; and one called the stock a MODERATE HOLD.

■ On January 30, 2006, Argus Research Company gave the stock a BUY rating. Gary F. Hovis said, "Dominion's cash flow metrics continue to improve, and *Standard & Poor's* recently raised its fixed-income outlook for the company from negative to stable. Our financial strength rating for Dominion is Medium-High, and our long-term estimated EPS [earnings per share] growth rate is 6 percent."

■ "If you've invested with us over the long haul, you know we don't like bandwagons, don't do fads, and aren't wired to make fashionable short-term plays," said CEO Thomas E. Capps in 2005. "Instead, we've spent the last five years building a steadily profitable platform of integrated electric power and natural gas businesses. They serve the energy-hungry mid-Atlantic, Midwest and Northeast. We've hedged our bets and—thanks to our tireless, energetic, and innovative employees—have achieved superior levels of efficiency, safety, and environmental responsibility. These results reflect our embedded values. The businesses we've joined together are widely recognized by investors and industry analysts for their quality and earnings stability."

- Mr. Capps also said, "Our proved gas and oil reserves total nearly 6 trillion cubic feet equivalent (Tcfe). Daily production from more than 25,000 wells is nearly 1.2 billion cubic feet equivalent (Bcfe). Based on these measures, *Oil & Gas Journal*, a top-grade publication, ranked us seventh in U.S. gas production and reserves and thirteenth in oil and gas assets. We ranked second in the total number of U.S. wells drilled, according to the most recently available industry data."
- Mr. Capps goes on to say, "Investors often ask me why Dominion, a gas and electric generation, transmission, distribution, and pipeline company, should invest money in natural gas and oil exploration and production. Regulated and non-regulated energy businesses appear very different. One attracts investors who want to minimize risk and gain reliable, steady growing earnings. The other beckons investors with an appetite for risk and roller-coaster earnings.

"My answer is simple: focus on finding low-risk proved and probable reserves that will contribute to a steady, growing earnings stream. We emphasize production over exploration.

"Dominion's E&P business is dominated by production from low-risk onshore fields. They account for about three-fourths of our gas and oil production and about 80 percent of our proved reserves. The balance lies in our offshore operations in the Gulf of Mexico."

- On December 15, 2005, Dominion Exploration and Production, a wholly owned subsidiary of Dominion, said that it had begun production from the Triton and Goldfinger subsea wells, located 140 miles southeast of New Orleans on Mississippi Canyon Blocks 771, 772, and 728 in the Gulf of Mexico.

Triton/Goldfinger consists of three subsea wells connected to the Devils Tower floating production system via insulated six-inch by ten-inch diameter flowlines. Devils Tower, the world's deepest dry-tree spar, is owned by Williams (NYSE: WMB) and operated by Dominion E&P in 5,610 feet of water on Mississippi Canyon Block 773.

The six-mile tieback was accomplished with a minimal 3.5 days of production shut-in time on the Devils Tower spar, and the wells were ready for commissioning a few days before Hurricane Katrina struck in late August. Since then, sustained production from Devils Tower has been limited by damage to downstream infrastructure owned by other companies.

Dominion E&P owns a 75-percent working interest in Devils Tower, including the Triton and Goldfinger tiebacks. Pioneer Natural Resources Company (NYSE: PXD) owns the remaining 25 percent.

SECTOR: **Utilities** ◆ BETA COEFFICIENT: **.90**
10-YEAR COMPOUND EARNINGS PER SHARE GROWTH: **6.3%**
10-YEAR COMPOUND DIVIDENDS PER SHARE GROWTH: **0.4%**

		2005	2004	2003	2002	2001	2000	1999	1998
Revenues (millions)		18,041	13,972	12,078	10,218	10,558	9,260	5,520	6,086
Net income (millions)		1,560	1,425	1,261	1,378	775	624	639	400
Earnings per share		4.53	3.82	2.98	4.82	2.97	2.50	2.99	1.72
Dividends per share		2.68	2.60	2.58	2.58	2.58	2.58	2.58	2.58
Price	high	87.0	68.9	65.9	67.1	70.0	67.9	49.4	48.9
	low	66.5	60.8	51.7	35.4	55.1	34.8	36.6	37.8

Donaldson Company, Inc.

P.O. Box 1299 ❑ Minneapolis, MN 55440 ❑ (952) 887-3753 ❑ Direct dividend reinvestment plan available: Wells Fargo Bank Minnesota, N.A., Shareholder Services, P. O. Box 64854, St. Paul, MN 55164-0854 ❑ Web site: *www.donaldson.com* ❑ Fiscal year ends July 31 ❑ Listed: NYSE ❑ Ticker symbol: DCI ❑ S&P rating: A+ ❑ Value Line financial strength rating: B++

You can expect to see Donaldson Company's filtration products on the heavy-duty truck traveling the interstate highway, or on the construction equipment on the side of the road. "After all, that's where our company began," said William G. Van Dyke, the company's chairman of the board.

"But you aren't as likely to expect our filters in the camera that captures memories of your daughter's birthday party. Or in the backup generator providing electricity to your computer center or office.

"Donaldson filters and related products are in many unexpected places—in products you see, touch, and use every day. Our long-term, focused investment in filtration technology has created the leverage to carry us into new product lines, new markets, and new geography. This diversification in end markets, linked by a common technology base, has enabled us to smooth out the ups and downs of the various market segments and to achieve our twelfth consecutive year of double-digit earnings growth—no small feat in these turbulent economic times.

"Donaldson holds more than 450 U.S. patents and related patents filed around the world, and our employees are constantly developing new ways to utilize superior filtration and acoustic technology for products that are still years away from market."

Company Profile

Donaldson Company is a leading worldwide provider of filtration systems and replacement parts. Founded in 1915, Donaldson is a technology-driven company committed to satisfying customers' needs for filtration solutions through innovative research and development.

The company's product mix includes air and liquid filters, as well as exhaust and emission-control products for mobile equipment; in-plant air-cleaning systems; air intake systems for industrial gas turbines; and specialized filters for such diverse applications as computer disk drives, aircraft passenger cabins, and semiconductor processing.

Donaldson operates plants throughout the world. Of these, fourteen facilities are in the United States, three in the United Kingdom, and two each are in Germany, Japan, China, South Africa, and Mexico. Finally, the company has one plant in each of the following countries: Australia, France, Hong Kong, Italy, Belgium, and India.

The company has two reporting segments engaged in the design, manufacture, and sale of systems to filter air and liquid and other complementary products.

The Engine Products segment makes air intake systems, exhaust systems, and liquid filtration systems. The company sells to original-equipment manufacturers (OEMs) in the construction, industrial, mining, agriculture, and transportation markets, independent distributors, OEM dealer networks, private-label accounts, and large private fleets. This segment is further subdivided as follows:

- Off-Road Equipment includes products sold to industrial equipment and defense contractor OEMs for agriculture, construction, mining, and military applications.

- The company's Truck operation produces products sold to manufacturers of light-, medium-, and heavy-duty trucks.
- In the Aftermarket sector, Donaldson sells a broad line of replacement filters and hard parts for all of the equipment applications noted above.

The Industrial Products segment consists of dust, fume, and mist collectors, static and pulse-clean air filter systems of industrial gas turbines, computer disk-drive filter products, and other specialized air-filtration systems. DCI sells to various industrial end users, OEMs of gas-fired turbines, and OEMs and users requiring highly purified air. This segment is further broken down as follows:

- Under Industrial Air Filtration, the company sells under such trade names as Donaldson Torit and Donaldson Torit DCE. It provides equipment to control and capture process dust, fumes, and mist in manufacturing and industrial processing plants.
- Under Gas Turbine Systems, Donaldson provides complete systems to deliver clean air to gas-fired turbines. Products include self-cleaning filter units, static air filter units, inlet ducting and silencing, evaporative coolers, chiller coils, and inlet heating and anti-icing systems.
- Under Ultrafilter, the company provides a complete line of compressed air filters and a wide assortment of replacement filters, a complete offering of refrigeration and desiccant dryers, condensate management devices, and after-sale services.
- Under Special Applications, the company provides a wide range of high-efficiency media, filters, and filtration systems for various commercial, industrial, and product applications.

Shortcomings to Bear in Mind

■ Some analysts point out the risk factors for Donaldson because of greater shortages of steel and an inability of the company to recover these higher costs, along with unrest in parts of the world, most notably Iraq.

■ On March 6, 2006, *Standard & Poor's Company Reports* had this lukewarm comment. According to analyst Stewart Scharf, "We maintain our HOLD recommendation, as we believe the shares are fairly priced based on our valuation models, and in light of volatile fuel and other commodity prices, along with some difficult comparisons we see in the second half, due in part to a stronger U.S. dollar against the yen and euro."

Reasons to Buy

■ Donaldson has illustrated the following key investment characteristics:

- Sixteen consecutive years of record earnings growth
- Average annual EPS for sixteen-year period of 16 percent
- Revenue (year ended July 31, 2005) of $1.596 billion
- Consistent earnings growth drivers in its diversified portfolio of filtration businesses, global marketplace coverage, and aggressive cost management
- Strong balance sheet
- Fifty consecutive years of quarterly dividends
- Active share repurchase program has reduced shares outstanding for sixteen consecutive years

■ Donaldson has an enviable record of growth. In the past ten years (1995–2005), earnings per share advanced from $0.36 to $1.27, (with no dips along the way), a compound annual growth rate of 13.4 percent. In the same span, dividends climbed from $0.07 to $0.24, a compound annual growth rate of 13.1 percent.

Despite this fine record of growth, the stock sells at a very reasonable price/earnings multiple.

- In early fiscal 2006, management had these encouraging comments:

- "The company expects NAFTA heavy-duty new truck build rates to remain at their current high levels as truck manufacturers are near capacity. Market share gains should continue to fuel international sales growth."
- "Off-road sales are expected to remain strong worldwide with robust conditions continuing in the production of new construction and mining equipment."
- "Both NAFTA and international aftermarket sales are expected to continue growing as continued strong equipment utilization drives replacement filter sales."

- Commenting on the outlook for fiscal 2006, CEO Bill Cook said, "Demand continues to be strong in most of our end markets. Although we have seen rising oil prices affect our raw material costs for petroleum-based commodities and freight, we are working with our customers to offset these increases through a variety of efforts. We enter fiscal 2006 with continued strong orders and backlogs, giving us confidence of delivering another strong year of results."

SECTOR: **Industrials** ◆ BETA COEFFICIENT: **.95**
10-YEAR COMPOUND EARNINGS PER SHARE GROWTH: **13.4%**
10-YEAR COMPOUND DIVIDENDS PER SHARE GROWTH: **13.1%**

		2005	2004	2003	2002	2001	2000	1999	1998
Revenues (millions)		1,596	1,415	1,218	1,126	1,137	1,092	944	940
Net income (millions)		110.6	106.3	95.3	86.9	75.5	70.2	62.4	57.1
Earnings per share		1.27	1.18	1.05	.95	.83	.76	.66	.57
Dividends per share		.24	.22	.18	.16	.15	.14	.12	.10
Price	high	33.9	34.4	30.8	22.5	20.2	14.4	13.0	13.4
	low	28.6	25.0	16.1	15.0	12.2	9.4	8.5	6.8

AGGRESSIVE GROWTH

Dover Corporation

280 Park Avenue ❑ New York, NY 10017-1292 ❑ (212) 922-1640 ❑ Direct dividend reinvestment plan available (888) 567-8341 ❑ Web site: *www.dovercorporation.com* ❑ Ticker symbol: DOV ❑ S&P rating: A- ❑ Value Line financial strength rating: A

On August 22, 2005, Dover announced that its Dover Electronics subsidiary had signed a definitive agreement to acquire Knowles Electronics for $750 million. Headquartered in Itasca, Illinois, Knowles has significant manufacturing operations in Asia.

Knowles is the leading manufacturer of technologically advanced microacoustic component products. What's more, the company is also the leading manufacturer of MEMS (microelectro mechanical systems) microphones, which provide significant advantages over existing technology, with current applications in the high-end cell phone market. Sales of these products are expected to drive considerable growth in the next several years in a variety of applications.

"We are excited to have the opportunity to acquire Knowles, the market leader in transducer-based components for hearing aids," said Ronald L. Hoffman, CEO of Dover Corporation. "Knowles is an outstanding company with strong brand recognition and significant growth potential. With most of Knowles's sales in the hearing aid industry, this acquisition, combined with the recent purchase of Colder Products, significantly advances Dover's position in the medical and life sciences components markets. Knowles has a strong management team with significant R&D resources and an impressive track record of developing new, patented products and identifying new niche markets—all key elements of future growth."

The Colder Products Company Acquisition

Less than two months earlier, Dover completed the acquisition of Colder Products Company, which also joined the company's Dover Electronics subsidiary on August 5, 2005. Based in St. Paul Minnesota, Colder is the premier designer and manufacturer of plastic quick-disconnect coupling and specialized liquid and gas handling devices for pressure-plastic tubing connections. Colder sells its products into a broad range of applications, including the life sciences/medical, specialty industrial, and chemical/food dispensing markets.

Dover is by no means new to the acquisition realm. In 2005, for instance, Mr. Hoffman said, "We continued our vigorous acquisition program during 2004, purchasing eight add-on acquisitions at an overall cost of $514 million. The largest of these were completed during the third and fourth quarters: U.S. Synthetic, a leading maker of polycrystalline diamond cutters used in drill bits for oil and gas drilling, acquired by Dover Resources's Energy Products Group; Corning Frequency Controls, a leader in oscillators for the telecommunications, military/aerospace test, and instrumentation markets, acquired by Dover Technologies's Vectron (now part of Dover Electronics); and Datamax, a leading manufacturer of bar-coding and RFID equipment, acquired by Dover Technologies, to be operated in close coordination with Imaje."

Company Profile

Dover Corporation is a diversified industrial manufacturer with over $6 billion in annual revenues and is comprised of about fifty operating companies that manufacture specialized industrial products and manufacturing equipment.

Dover's overall strategy is to acquire and develop platform businesses, marked by growth, innovation, and higher-than-average profit margins. Traditionally, the company has focused on purchasing entities that could operate independently (stand-alones). However, over the past ten years, Dover has put increased emphasis on also acquiring businesses that can be added to existing operations (add-ons).

On October 1, 2003, Dover completed its largest-ever acquisition with the $326-million purchase of WARN Industries, the world's most recognized brand in winches and wheel hubs for off-road vehicles. WARN makes equipment and accessories to enhance the performance of four-wheel-drive and all-terrain vehicles. The Oregon-based company, founded in 1948 to manufacture locking hubs to convert World War II Jeeps into on-road vehicles, developed the first recreational winch in 1959. In addition to specialized wheel hubs, WARN makes self-recovery, towing, and utility winches.

A New Breakdown of Operations

In the fall of 2004, Dover announced that it would expand its subsidiary structure from four to six reporting market segments. Concurrently, it realigned its forty-nine operating businesses into thirteen focused business groupings. Management believes that this will better position Dover for "enhanced growth by providing increased management oversight of its operating businesses by expanding the company's acquisition capacity and by supporting the development of future executive management talent."

Effective January 1, 2005, the six subsidiaries and their respective operating company groups were as follows:

- Dover Diversified
  - Industrial Equipment: Crenlo, Performance Motorsports, and Sargent
  - Process Equipment: Graphics Microsystems, Hydratight Sweeney, SWEP, Tranter PHE, and Waukesha Bearings
- Dover Electronics
  - Components: Dielectric, Dow-Key, K&L Microwave, Kurz-Kasch, Novacap, and Vectron
  - Commercial Equipment: Hydro Systems and Triton
- Dover Industries
  - Mobile Equipment: Heil Environmental, Heil Trailer, Marathon, and Somero.
  - Service Equipment: Chief Automotive, Koolant Koolers, PDQ, and Rotary Lift.
- Dover Resources
  - Petroleum Equipment: C. Lee Cook, Energy Products Group
  - Fluid Solutions: Blackmer, OPW Fluid Transfer Group, OPW Fueling Components, RPA Technologies, and Wilden.
- Materials Handling: De-Sta-Co Industries, Texas Hydraulics, Tulsa Winch, and WARN Industries

Shortcomings to Bear in Mind

■ Some analysts point out such risks as the following:

- Dover's reduced industrial capital spending in a rising interest rate environment
- Deterioration in demand for technology products, should the semiconductor cycle peak
- Rising raw material costs

■ Dover does not have a typical pattern of a growth company. Earnings per share have fluctuated widely over the years. For instance, EPS hit a peak in 2000 of $2.57 but retreated to $0.82 the following year. However, earnings per share have made solid progress in each of the years since.

■ In early 2006, both Lehman Brothers and Prudential Equity Group said Dover was an EQUAL WEIGHT, or HOLD.

Reasons to Buy

■ On March 16, 2006, the *New York Times* analyzed eleven opinions of leading analysts. Three called Dover a STRONG BUY; three preferred to tag it as a MODERATE BUY; and five straddled the fence with a HOLD.

■ On January 27, 2006, *Value Line Investment Survey* gave the stock a 2 rating (above average). Praneeth Satish said, "Shares of Dover Corporation are ranked above average for year-ahead performance and have good long-term appeal."

■ Dover has built its group largely through acquisitions. However, management is careful when considering which companies to bring into the fold, following these strict rules to guide its decisions:

- We seek manufacturers of high value-added, engineered products.
- Our focus is on equipment and machinery sold to a broad customer base of industrial and/or commercial users.
- We prefer companies that are niche-oriented market leaders with either a number-one or a strong number-two market position.

- Candidates should have strong national distribution (if not international, which is preferred).
- Dover is decentralized—we will only buy businesses that have strong management teams in place. We expect management of each operating company to behave as the emotional owners of that business and we have longer term financial incentives designed to encourage continued growth of the business.
- Our judgment on the skill, energy, ethics, and compatibility of the top executives at each acquisition candidate is one of the most critical factors in our decision making.
- We expect that operating companies will continue to be run by the management team in place upon acquisition. This reflects our decentralized structure and the fact that Dover buys companies for the long term; we do not have a "portfolio" mentality.
- Since we seek market leaders, we expect outstanding operating financial performance that can be built upon. EBIT's [earnings before interest and taxes] above 15% are the norm in Dover operating companies. We also expect that any business we own will generate significant real growth over time.

SECTOR: **Industrials** ◆ BETA COEFFICIENT: **1.15**
10-YEAR COMPOUND EARNINGS PER SHARE GROWTH: **7.4%**
10-YEAR COMPOUND DIVIDENDS PER SHARE GROWTH: **8.8%**

		2005	2004	2003	2002	2001	2000	1999	1998
Revenues (millions)		6,078	5,488	4,413	4,184	4,460	5,401	4,446	3,978
Net Income (millions)		510	413	285	211	167	525	395	326
Earnings per share		2.50	2.00	1.40	1.04	0.82	2.57	1.87	1.45
Dividends per share		0.65	0.62	0.57	0.54	0.52	0.48	0.44	0.40
Price	high	42.2	44.1	40.4	43.6	43.6	54.4	47.9	39.9
	low	34.1	35.1	22.8	23.5	26.45	34.1	29.3	25.5

GROWTH AND INCOME

The Dow Chemical Company

2030 Dow Center ❑ Midland, MI 48674 ❑ (969) 636-2876 ❑ Direct dividend reinvestment plan available (800) 369-5606 ❑ Web site: *www.dow.com* ❑ Ticker symbol: DOW ❑ Listed: NYSE ❑ S&P rating: B ❑ Value Line financial strength rating: B++

Dow Chemical Company announced on December 13, 2005, that William S. Stavropoulos would retire as chairman of the board, effective April 1, 2006. Dow's board of directors elected Andrew N. Liveris, president and CEO, to succeed Stavropoulos as chairman upon his retirement. Mr. Liveris will retain his role as president and CEO.

Mr. Stavropoulos, aged sixty-six, retired after thirty-nine years of service at Dow. He was elected to Dow's board in 1990 and began serving as chairman in 2000. Mr. Liveris, aged fifty-one, was elected president and CEO by Dow's board of directors in 2004. He had served as president and chief operating officer since 2003.

Harold T. Shapiro, presiding director of Dow's board of directors, said, "We are confident that Andrew will continue to provide the vision and drive necessary to ensure that Dow builds on this strong foundation and delivers on its plans to invest for strategic growth while maintaining strong financial discipline."

Mr. Liveris was elected to Dow's board of directors in 2004. His twenty-nine-year career at Dow has spanned manufacturing, sales, marketing, new business development, and management. He spent the bulk of his career in Asia, where he was general manager for the company's operations in Thailand and later head of all Asia-Pacific operations.

Mr. Liveris was born in Darwin, Australia, and later lived in Brisbane, where he attended the University of Queensland, graduating with a bachelor's degree (first-class honors) in chemical engineering. He began his Dow career in 1976 in Australia. He is a chartered engineer and a Fellow of The Institute of Chemical Engineers.

Mr. Liveris serves on the Board of Directors of Citigroup, Inc. He is an officer of the American Chemistry Council, the industry's trade association, and a member of the following organizations: the American Australian Association, a nonprofit group dedicated to education involving both bilateral and international issues; the Business Council; the Business Roundtable; the Detroit Economic Club; the G100, an association of leading CEOs; the International Business Council; the National Petroleum Council; the Société de Chimie Industrielle; the U.S.-China Business Council; and the World Business Council for Sustainable Development.

Company Profile

Dow is a leader in science and technology, providing innovative chemical, plastic, and agricultural products and services to many essential consumer markets. With annual sales of $46 billion, Dow serves customers in 175 countries and a wide range of markets that are vital to human progress, including food, transportation, health and medicine, personal and home care, and building and construction, among others.

The Dow Chemical Company is a multinational corporation, the second-largest chemical company in the world—DuPont is number one.

Dow is the world's largest producer of plastics, including polystyrene, polyurethanes, polyethylene terephthalate, polypropylene, and synthetic rubbers. It is also a major producer of the chemicals calcium chloride and ethylene oxide, as well as various acrylates, surfactants, and cellulose resins. It produces many agricultural chemicals, perhaps being most famous for its pesticide Lorsban. At the consumer level, the company's best-known products include Saran Wrap, Ziploc bags (which now have been sold to S. C. Johnson), and Styrofoam.

Dow Chemical Company dates back to 1897. At that time, its founder, Herbert Henry Dow, set out to extract chlorides and bromides from brine deposits that were found underground at Midland, Michigan. The company's initial products included bromine and bleach. During those early years, the company established a tradition of rapidly diversifying its product line. Within twenty years, Dow had become a major producer of agricultural chemicals, elemental chlorine, phenol and other dyestuffs, and magnesium metal.

During the Great Depression, Dow began production of plastic resins, which would grow to become one of the corporation's major businesses. Its first plastic products were ethylcellulose, which was made in 1935, and polystyrene, made in 1937.

In 1930, Dow built its first plant to produce magnesium extracted from seawater rather than from underground brine. Growth of this business made Dow a strategically important business during World War II, as magnesium became important in fabricating lightweight parts for airplanes. Also during the war, Dow and Corning began their joint venture, Dow Corning, to produce silicones for military and later civilian use.

Following World War II, Dow began expanding abroad, founding its first foreign subsidiary in Japan in 1952, with several other nations following rapidly thereafter. Based largely on its burgeoning plastics business, Dow opened a consumer products division beginning with Saran Wrap in 1953. Through its growing chemicals and plastics businesses, Dow's sales exceeded $1 billion in 1964, $2 billion in 1971, and $10 billion in 1980.

In September 2004, Dow obtained the naming rights of the Saginaw County Event Center in nearby Saginaw, Michigan, and the facility's new name is now the Dow Event Center. The deal is worth $10 million and is said to last until 2014. The center houses the Ontario Hockey League ice hockey team, the Saginaw Spirit.

Today, Dow is the world's largest producer of plastics, and with its 1999 acquisition of Union Carbide has become a major player in the petrochemical industry as well.

Dow is also a world leader in the production of olefins and styrene, hydrocarbons, and energy. Other businesses include advanced electronic materials and industrial biotechnology.

More than 60 percent of Dow's revenues come from abroad. In fact, most of the company's basic chemicals expansion is being directed at Asia and the Mideast.

Shortcomings to Bear in Mind

- Although this is a Growth and Income stock, you should be aware that dividends have not been raised every year. In fact, in the past ten years (1995–2005), the dividend increased from $0.93 to $1.34, a compound annual growth rate of only 3.7 percent. On the plus side, there is no indication that the company is likely to cut the dividend—even during years when earnings were depressed, as they were in 2001 and 2002.

Reasons to Buy

- "A pickup in the economy has meant strong demand for Dow's chemicals and plastics," said Phyllis Berman, writing for *Forbes* magazine on March 27, 2006. "Its products can be found in everything from solvents to water bottles. Dow, the nation's largest chemical company and number two globally, behind Germany's BASF, was able to raise prices to make up for the enormous hike in its raw material costs. It had the good fortune over the past year of seeing the price of ethylene, a basic component for plastics that is derived from oil and natural gas, rise 35 percent to 55 cents a pound."
- On March 3, 2006, the New York Times polled sixteen analyst who keep tabs on Dow Chemical. Three were convinced that Dow was a STRONG BUY; six were less enthusiastic, but still rated the stock a MODERATE BUY; seven said it was a HOLD.
- On January 20, 2006, *Value Line Investment Survey* had some favorable comments on Dow Chemical. Stuart Plesser said, "We look for 2006 to be another record-breaking year. Based on a pickup in global demand, particularly in emerging market countries, Dow should be able to continue to raise prices for most of its products."
- *Standard & Poor's Stock Reports* was much more bullish. On December 9, 2005, Richard O'Reilly, CFA, said, "We have a STRONG BUY recommendation on the shares. We believe the commodity chemical industry's supply/demand fundamentals will continue to show cyclical improvement over the next two years."
- Steve Schuman, an analyst with Prudential Equity Group, had this comment on January 26, 2006: "We believe Dow is the best way to play the tight world market for chemicals and plastics. Dow is rated OVERWEIGHT [similar to BUY] due to our belief that it can capitalize on the post-hurricane environment and continued strong fundamentals over the next few years."
- Bill Selesky, writing for Argus Research Company on January 27, 2006, said, "We

are maintaining our BUY rating on Dow Chemical Company. Despite the negative impact of escalating input costs on the company's earnings, we believe the stock offers an attractive valuation and has significant upside potential."

- Dow says it has high hopes for a diesel engine emission filtration system that is currently under development. The system reduces particulate matter by more than 90 percent and has fast regeneration at low exhaust temperature, with minimum fuel consumption. Dow also says that further out on the horizon are products that include animal health vaccines and more products based on alternative feed stocks, such as corn sugar and soybean oil.

Dow Product Highlights

- Styrofoam brand insulation is producing more energy efficient homes around the world. In North America alone, over 2 million homes are insulated with Styrofoam, resulting in $200 million per year in energy savings and a significant reduction in fossil fuel consumption and carbon dioxide emissions.
- Dow's manufacturing experts are being contracted to create innovative and life-saving pharmaceutical products such as RenaGel, a promising new drug for kidney failure patients.
- Dow AgroSciences provides farmers globally with crop protection products. New innovations such as biotechnology are reducing environmental risks associated with crop protection products and improving the agricultural industry's ability to feed the world.
- Dow's Ion Exchange resins are used to purify water around the world for drinking water, power plants, wastewater treatment, and pharmaceuticals.
- Dow paper coating polymers are used in the paper and board industry to improve strength, brightness, opacity, and readability for brochures, graphics, and books.
- Dow epoxy technology makes it possible to create lighter, larger, and more durable windmill blades offering higher energy yields and thus increasing the use of renewable energy.
- Innovative Dow thermoplastic resins eliminate the need for paint in consumer products such as televisions, reducing volatile organic compound emissions and making it easier to recycle television cabinets.
- Saran resins provide food protection, extending the food available to the world. In developing countries where refrigeration is scarce, meat products are extruded into a sausage covered with Saran film that can be shipped and stored without refrigeration for up to six months.
- Dow's heat transfer fluids provide freeze and burst protection allowing the U.S. Antarctic Program's McMurdo Station to remain operable in temperatures as low as -60 °F.
- Polyurethane material from Dow offers automobile part manufacturers better cushioning for seats and reduction in noise, vibration, and harshness in interior parts.

SECTOR: **Materials** ◆ BETA COEFFICIENT: **1.20**
10-YEAR COMPOUND EARNINGS PER SHARE GROWTH: **5.3%**
10-YEAR COMPOUND DIVIDENDS PER SHARE GROWTH: **3.7%**

		2005	2004	2003	2002	2001	2000	1999	1998
Revenues (millions)		46,307	40,161	32,632	27,609	27,805	23,008	18,929	18,441
Net income (millions)		4,515	2,797	1,278	299	438	1,513	1,396	1,374
Earnings per share		4.62	2.93	1.38	0.33	0.52	2.22	2.07	2.04
Dividends per share		1.34	1.34	1.34	1.34	1.30	1.16	1.16	1.16
Price	high	56.8	51.3	42.0	37.0	39.7	47.2	46.0	33.8
	low	40.2	36.4	24.8	23.7	25.1	23.0	28.5	24.9

E. I. DuPont de Nemours

1007 Market Street ❑ Wilmington, DE 19898 ❑ (800) 441-7515 ❑ Direct dividend reinvestment plan available (888) 983-8766 ❑ Web site: *www.dupont.com* ❑ Ticker symbol: DD ❑ Listed: NYSE ❑ S&P rating: B ❑ Value Line financial strength rating: A++

On November 21, 2005, leaders of DuPont and the city of Dongying, China, signed a project agreement—a major milestone on the path toward construction of a world-class titanium dioxide plant representing a total investment of $1 billion—in the city's Economic Development Zone. Titanium dioxide is a white pigment widely used in the coatings, plastics, and paper industries.

The plant will be wholly owned by DuPont and will be the company's largest single investment project outside the United States. With a planned completion date of 2010, the plant will have an initial annual capacity of 200,000 tons of titanium dioxide and will employ some 350 workers, most of whom will be hired in the Dongying area.

"The planning and construction of a project of this complexity is not quickly or easily accomplished, yet we have reached this remarkable milestone in just eight months," said Richard C. Olson, vice president and general manager of DuPont Titanium Technologies.

DuPont Titanium Technologies is the world's largest manufacturer of titanium dioxide, serving customers globally in the coatings, paper, and plastics industries. The company operates plants in Mississippi, Tennessee, Delaware, Mexico, Brazil, and Taiwan.

Company Profile

DuPont was founded in 1802 and was incorporated in Delaware in 1915. DuPont is a world leader in science and technology in a range of disciplines, including the following:

- Biotechnology
- Electronics
- Materials and science
- Safety and security
- Synthetic fibers

Recently, the company strategically realigned its businesses into five market- and technology-focused growth platforms:

- Agriculture and Nutrition
- Coatings and Color Technologies
- Electronic and Communication Technologies
- Performance Materials
- Safety and Protection

These growth platforms are designed to address large, attractive market spaces that allow the company to leverage its resources—including its science and technology, products and brands, market access, and global reach—to bring innovative solutions to meet specific customer needs.

Together with the Textiles and the Interiors and Pharmaceuticals segments, the growth platforms comprise the company's seventh reportable segments.

DuPont has operations in about seventy-five countries worldwide, and about 55 percent of consolidated net sales are made to customers outside the United States. Subsidiaries and affiliates of DuPont conduct manufacturing, seed production, or selling activities, and some are distributors of products manufactured by the company.

The company utilizes numerous firms as well as internal sources to supply a wide range of raw materials, energy, supplies, services, and equipment. To ensure availability, the company maintains multiple sources for fuels and most raw materials, including hydrocarbon feed stocks. Large-volume purchases are generally procured under competitively priced supply contracts.

The major commodities, raw materials, and supplies for the company's reportable segments include the following:

- Agriculture and Nutrition: Carbamic-acid related intermediates, polyethylene, soybeans, soy flake, 5-choroindanone, soy lecithin, sulfonamides
- Coatings and Color Technologies: Butyl acetate, chlorine, HDI-based polyalaphatic isocyanates, industrial gases, ore, petroleum coke, pigments
- Electronic and Communications Technologies: Chloroform, fluorspar, hydrofluoric acid, kraton, oxydianiline, perchloroethylene, polyester, polyethylene, precious metals, pyromellitic dianhydride
- Performance Materials: Adipic acid, butanediol, ethane, ethylene glycol, fiberglass, hexamethylenediamine, methacrylic acid, methanol, natural gas, paraxylene
- Safety and Protection: Ammonia, aniline, benzene, high-density polyethylene, isophthaloyl chloride, metaphenylenediamine, methyl methacrylate, natural gas, paraphenylenediamine, polyester fiber, polypropylene, propylene, terephthaloyl chloride, wood pulp
- Textiles and Interiors: Acetylene, adipic acid, ammonia, butadiene, cyclohexane, natural gas, paraxylene, terephthalic acid

Shortcomings to Bear in Mind

- According to the company's form 10-K (similar to an annual report, but much more detailed, sophisticated, and technical), "The company's businesses compete on a variety of factors, such as price, product quality, and performance or specifications, continuity of supply, customer service, and breadth of product line, depending on the characteristics of the particular market involved and the product or service provided.

"Major competitors include diversified industrial companies principally based in the United States, Western Europe, Japan, China, and Korea. In the aggregate, these competitors offer a wide range of products from agricultural, commodity, and specialty chemicals to plastics, fibers, and advanced materials. The company also competes in certain markets with smaller, more specialized firms who offer a narrow range of products or converted products that functionally compete with the company's offerings."

Reasons to Buy

- On January 25, 2006, Bill Selesky, writing for Argus Research Company, said, "Our rating on E. I. DuPont de Nemours & Company remains BUY." The analyst goes on to say, "We continue to expect a moderation in energy costs and believe the weakness in crop protection chemicals is relatively a short-term event."
- On March 17, 2006, the *New York Times* tabulated the ratings provided by seventeen analysts. Five rated DuPont a STRONG BUY; seven said it was a MODERATE BUY; and five relegated the stock to a HOLD.
- According to DuPont's form 10-K, "The company believes that its patent and trademark estate provides it with an important competitive advantage. It has established a global network of attorneys, as well as branding, advertising, and licensing professionals, to procure, maintain, protect, enhance, and gain value from this estate."

What's more, "The company owns approximately 19,600 worldwide patents and approximately 13,600 worldwide patent applications. In 2004, the company was granted almost 490 U.S. patents and about 1,740 international patents."

- On January 5, 2006, DuPont Fire Extinguishants announced that it had signed an agreement with Siemens Building Technologies to deliver DuPont FE-227 fire extinguishant through the Siemens Sinorix fire extinguishing system.

DuPont FE-227 fire extinguishant is a "clean agent," safe for use in applications where people are normally present and in situations where conventional extinguishing agents are unacceptable. Typical applications include the protection of sensitive electronic equipment, network data centers, hospitals, and facilities where there are delicate or irreplaceable materials such as those found in museums, libraries, and historic sites.

"We are pleased to announce this new partnership," said Greg Rubin, global business manager, DuPont Fluorochemicals-Specialties. "DuPont FE-227 fire extinguishant is safe and highly effective, and Siemens is a key global partner that will help us deliver this solution reliably, efficiently, and effectively to benefit more businesses than ever before, on a global scale."

- In 2005, CEO Chad Holliday said "DuPont is a science company. Science is at the heart of everything we do and helps form the capabilities, offerings, and competitive advantages of all our businesses.

"While we are always primed for a blockbuster innovation, we don't depend on that. We realize that exceptional growth can come from dozens of $20-million to $200-million new products. We have an R&D pipeline rich in thousands of new product candidates. Because our approach to innovation is 'market-backed' we now have a higher success rate than ever before. And new products spend a shorter time in the pipeline, which means greater R&D productivity. In 2004, we had nearly 1,700 total patent filings, compared to an annual figure of around 950 as recently as 2001.

"The result is an increased percentage of sales from new products. We have set a goal for ourselves of 35 percent of revenues from products less than five years old by 2007, and to maintain that ratio into the future. We expect to reach 33 percent in 2005, so we are on track."

- In late 2005, DuPont announced a series of initiatives to reduce costs. The company plans to reduce its work force through attrition, for example. Research priorities will be adjusted, and employees and contractors will be reassigned to areas promising better returns. The cost-cutting campaign is expected to reduce expense by about $1 billion over the next three years.

SECTOR: **Materials** ◆ BETA COEFFICIENT: **1.00**
10-YEAR COMPOUND EARNINGS PER SHARE GROWTH: **minus 2.2%**
10-YEAR COMPOUND DIVIDENDS PER SHARE GROWTH: **3.6%**

		2005	2004	2003	2002	2001	2000	1999	1998
Revenues (millions)		26,639	27,340	26,996	24,006	24,726	28,268	26,918	24,767
Net income (millions)		2,100	2,390	1,607	2,012	1,236	2,884	2,843	2,923
Earnings per share		2.32	2.38	1.65	2.01	1.19	2.73	2.58	2.54
Dividends per share		1.46	1.40	1.40	1.40	1.40	1.40	1.38	1.37
Price	high	54.9	49.4	46.0	49.8	49.9	74.0	75.2	84.4
	low	37.6	39.9	34.7	35.0	32.6	38.2	50.1	51.7

GROWTH AND INCOME

Eaton Corporation

Eaton Center ❑ 1111 Superior Avenue ❑ Cleveland, OH 44114 ❑ (216) 523-4501 ❑ Dividend reinvestment plan is available (800) 446-2617 ❑ Listed NYSE ❑ Web site: *www.eaton.com* ❑ Ticker symbol: ETN ❑ S&P rating: B+ ❑ Value Line financial strength rating: A+

Eaton Corporation, a diversified industrial manufacturer, announced on September 13, 2005, that it had reached an agreement with Cobham plc to purchase its aerospace fluid and air division for $270 million.

The aerospace fluid and air division of Cobham, which is based in Wimborne, England, had 2004 sales of $210 million. It employs 1,600 people in five manufacturing locations in the United Kingdom and the United States.

"This acquisition will allow Eaton to capitalize on its recognized strengths in fluid conveyance and pump technology through the products, capabilities, and customers of Cobham's fluid and air division," said CEO Alexander M. Cutler.

Cobham's fluid and air division includes FR-HiTemp, which provides low-pressure airframe fuel systems, electro-mechanical actuation, air ducting, and hydraulic and power generation, and Stanley Aviation, which produces fluid distribution systems for fuel, hydraulics, and air.

"The purchase of Cobham's aerospace fluid and air division will strengthen our position on commercial and defense platforms, expand our European presence, and provide attractive aftermarket opportunities," said Craig Arnold, Eaton senior vice president and president of the company's Fluid Power Group.

Cobham designs and manufactures equipment, specialized systems, and components for the aerospace, defense, homeland security, search-and-rescue, and communications markets. It also operates, modifies, and maintains aircraft for military and commercial purposes.

Company Profile

Eaton Corporation is a globally diversified industrial manufacturer engaged in the design and manufacture of fluid power systems; electrical power quality, distribution, and control; automotive engine air management and power train controls for fuel economy; and intelligent drive train systems for fuel economy and safety in trucks. The principal markets for the company's Fluid Power, Automotive, and Truck segments are original equipment manufacturers (OEMs) and after-market customers of aerospace products and systems, off-highway agricultural and construction vehicles, industrial equipment, passenger cars, and heavy-, medium-, and light-duty trucks. The principal markets for the Electrical segment are industrial, construction, commercial, automotive, and government customers.

Here is a breakdown of the company's segments.

Automotive

Eaton's automotive business segment is a partner to the passenger-car and light-truck industry. The company makes superchargers, engine valves, cylinder heads, locking and limited slip differentials, sensors, actuators, intelligent cruise control systems, tire valves, fluid connectors, and decorative body moldings and spoilers.

The automotive industry faces an ever-increasing list of challenges—from design and aesthetic choices to demands for power and performance. The industry's two main challenges are clear: fuel economy and emissions. Eaton products bridge the gap. With the company's "green machine" focus, its innovative and industry-leading technologies help manufacturers meet tough environmental standards and consumer preferences.

Eaton's vision has been recognized by top manufacturers. It will supply Ford and General Motors with "Smart Transmission" controls and will supply Mercedes and Nissan with superchargers. Both of these Eaton products increase engine power and performance by helping engines to work more efficiently.

Eaton, a partner to seventy of the world's premier vehicle OEMs, operates plants in Brazil, Canada, China, France, Germany, India, Indonesia, Italy, Japan, Korea, Mexico, Monaco, the Netherlands, Poland, Spain, Taiwan, Turkey, the United Kingdom, and the United States.

Fluid Power

Eaton is a worldwide leader in the design, manufacture, and marketing of a comprehensive line of reliable, high-efficiency hydraulic systems and components. ETN's full line of powerful hydraulic component brand names, which include Aeroquip, Char-Lynn, Eaton, Hydro-Line, and Vickers, provide customers with a quality selection of Eaton-engineered products. From a single product to complete systems, Eaton supplies products that keep its customers moving.

Eaton's innovations meet the specific needs of its customers—reducing noise, increasing operating pressure, integrating electromechanical controls, and creating complex integrated solutions. Eaton's fluid power systems are found in earthmoving, agriculture, construction, mining, forestry, utility, and material-handling applications.

Mobile Hydraulics

Mobile hydraulics applications demand speed, reliability, and durability under harsh environmental conditions. Mining equipment performs rigorous cycles at Chilean copper pits 16,000 feet above sea level and South African gold mines 11,000 feet underground. Agriculture machinery works the vast American plains. In coastal cities, earthmoving equipment creates land from sea.

Industrial Hydraulics

Eaton hydraulics provide heavy lifting power in static uses, such as baggage handling and factory equipment. Eaton is also found in leading entertainment venues, creating the motion in virtual reality experiences and bringing inanimate objects to life. Eaton fluid power systems provide the control, quiet operation, and sheer power needed to fuel the most creative minds.

Aerospace

Eaton's aerospace business is a leading designer and manufacturer of hydraulic power generation and fuel fluid management components and systems, hydraulic and electro-mechanical motion control components and systems, fluid conveyance components and systems, electrical power and load management subsystems, cockpit controls and displays, pressure sensors, and fluid monitoring systems for a global group of diverse customers. For more than eighty years, the company has been the innovator and pioneering leader in the development of hydraulic and electronic technology for the aerospace industry.

Electrical

Eaton brings power control and distribution solutions to the utility, industrial, commercial, and residential segments. The company is a global manufacturer of switches, circuit breakers, and power controls that are designed to enhance factory performance. Its control and automation equipment include contactors and motor starters, variable speed drives, photoelectric and proximity sensors, video control panels, microprocessor-based control and protection devices, as well as push buttons and switches. Eaton is well positioned to respond to emerging requirements for power quality and availability that have joined the traditional focus on AC distribution and automation.

ETN's power distribution equipment includes the most complete family of circuit breakers in the industry, ranging from miniature breakers rated from 120 volts to world-class vacuum breakers rated up to 38 kilovolts.

Truck Components

Eaton is the leader in the design, manufacturing, and marketing of drivetrain systems and components for medium-duty and heavy-duty commercial vehicles on the American continents. In concert with the company's manufacturing and marketing partners, principally Dana Corporation, Eaton markets the "Roadranger System"—a complete line of drivetrain components and truck systems, including manual and automatic transmissions, clutches, drive shafts, steer and drive axles, trailer axles and suspensions, brakes, antilock braking systems, tire pressure management systems, and collision warning systems.

Shortcomings to Bear in Mind

- Argus Research Company called the stock a HOLD on January 24, 2006. Dana Richardson said, "We are concerned about decelerating earnings momentum. We note that the company is now forecasting a sales decline of 1 percent in the global auto markets in 2006 and flat truck markets. It seems less likely that the Auto segment will outperform its end markets; this has typically been the case, but not for the last three quarters. If commercial construction does not pick up to counterbalance the coming downturn in residential construction, the electrical segment will be challenged, as well."

Reasons to Buy

- On March 21, 2006, the *New York Times* tabulated what twenty securities analysts were telling investors about Eaton. Three viewed the stock as a STRONG BUY; seven said it was only a MODERATE BUY; nine called it a HOLD; and one timid soul relegated it to a MODERATE HOLD.
- Eaton's electrical products are sold throughout the world and supported by a worldwide distribution-and-service network. Eaton product lines are renowned for their ingenuity, reliability, and quality. Eaton's fast-growing Electrical Services & Systems offers an exciting mix of products, services, and expertise to help companies and facilities improve operations, ensure integrity of power, and utilize capital resources efficiently. Eaton has advanced product development, world-class manufacturing, and global engineering services and support.
- Eaton appears to have successfully transformed itself from reliance on automotive and truck markets to a more diversified, cohesive business that has more consistent earnings growth and lower volatility in total business returns. The company is achieving double-digit revenue and earnings growth and is strengthening its balance sheet and increasing dividends.

In each of its four business groups, ETN has developed products that should enable the business to grow at faster-than-end-market rates over the next five years. There are three trends that should drive ETN's growth above market: the need to increase fuel economy, which is already helping ETN; the need to reduce vehicle emissions, which is bolstering ETN's growth prospects, and continued outsourcing, which will likely drive the company's ability to grow.

- Eaton Corporation currently supplies more than 80 percent of all of the new commercial aircraft platform-hydraulic engine-driven pumps. Its power-generation systems success includes the Raytheon Hawker Horizon, the Airbus A380, the Lockheed Martin F-35, and CargoLifter.

Eaton is the leader in higher-pressure hydraulic systems development, including the Bell/Boeing MV-22 and the Boeing F-18 E/F. Eaton supplies the rudder and aileron flight controls on the Boeing C-17, and the company supplies the electrical power and load management subsystem on the Apache Longbow attack helicopter. In addition, Eaton is the leader in after-market fluid power and motion control customer support around the world.

SECTOR: **Industrials** ◆ BETA COEFFICIENT: **1.10**
10-YEAR COMPOUND EARNINGS PER SHARE GROWTH: **7.4%**
10-YEAR COMPOUND DIVIDENDS PER SHARE GROWTH: **5.2%**

		2005	2004	2003	2002	2001	2000	1999	1998
Revenues (millions)		11,115	9,817	8,061	7,209	7,299	8,309	8,402	6,625
Net income (millions)		805	675	402	315	233	383	439	349
Earnings per share		5.23	4.13	2.67	2.20	1.65	3.26	2.98	2.40
Dividends per share		1.24	1.08	0.92	0.88	0.88	.88	.88	.88
Price	high	72.7	72.6	54.7	44.3	40.7	43.3	51.8	49.8
	low	56.6	52.7	33.0	29.5	27.6	28.8	31.0	28.8

CONSERVATIVE GROWTH

Ecolab, Inc.

370 Wabasha Street North ❑ St. Paul, MN 55102-1390 ❑ (651) 293-2809 ❑ Dividend reinvestment program available (800) 322-8325 ❑ Web site: *www.ecolab.com* ❑ Listed: NYSE ❑ Ticker symbol: ECL ❑ S&P rating: A ❑ Value Line financial strength rating: B++

"If you eat out more than you used to, Douglas Baker thanks you. The forty-six-year-old Ecolab chief executive's glasses fog over when he looks at the increasing concern over food safety and industrial cleanliness in general. No wonder. Ecolab makes countertop sanitizers, floor cleaners, and degreasers, selling them complete with dispensers, installation, and service to outfits like McDonald's, Wal-Mart, and Coors. That's a $36-billion market, of which Ecolab has the largest share, 12 percent."

That comment was made by Chana R. Schoenberger in an article in *Forbes* magazine in 2005; Ecolab was one of the publication's "Best Managed Companies in America."

The author goes on to say, "Baker knows his customers can't afford a hygiene breakdown. 'They have other things to focus on,' he says. To that end, last year, he spent $150 million to buy up six smaller competitors. Ecolab is also giving its field technicians handheld PCs and laptops to feed info back to headquarters quickly. It has also expanded into equipment repair and 'food-safety auditing' (in other words, making sure employees wash their hands.) 'All these guys are doing is selling soap to a thousand Marriotts around the country—and with a high degree of reliability,' says Deutsche Bank analyst David Begleiter, CFA."

Company Profile

According to the company's chairman, Allan Schuman, "When it comes to delivering premium commercial cleaning and sanitizing solutions on a truly global basis,

Ecolab is the one. No other company comes close to rivaling our worldwide reach or the extraordinary breadth of products, systems, and services we offer.

"We meet the varied and specialized needs of thousands of diverse businesses and institutions in North America, Europe, Asia, Latin America, Africa, the Middle East—the list of countries in which we do business reads like an atlas. In 2001, we took decisive actions to ensure that Ecolab remains number one in the world for many years to come."

Founded in 1923, Ecolab is the leading global developer and marketer of premium cleaning, sanitizing, pest elimination, maintenance, and repair products and services for the world's hospitality, institutional, and industrial markets.

In the early years, Ecolab served the restaurant and lodging industries and has since broadened its scope to include hospitals, laundries, schools, retail, and commercial property, among others.

The company conducts its domestic business under these segments:

- The Institutional Division is the leading provider of cleaners and sanitizers for ware-washing, laundry, kitchen cleaning, and general housecleaning, as well as product-dispensing equipment, dishwashing racks, and related kitchen sundries to the foodservice, lodging, and health-care industries. It also provides products and services for pool and spa treatment.
- The Food & Beverage Division offers cleaning and sanitizing products and services to farms, dairy plants, food and beverage processors, and pharmaceutical plants.
- The Kay Division is the largest supplier of cleaning and sanitizing products for the quick-service restaurant, convenience store, and flood retail markets.

Ecolab also sells janitorial and health-care products such as detergents, floor care, disinfectants, odor control and hand care under the Airkem and Huntington brand names; textile care products for large institutional and commercial laundries; vehicle care products for rental, fleet, and retail car washes; and water-treatment products for commercial, institutional, and industrial markets.

Other domestic services include institutional and commercial pest elimination and prevention, as well as the GCS commercial kitchen equipment repair services.

Around the world, the company operates directly in nearly seventy countries. International sales account for 22 percent of sales. In addition, the company reaches customers in more then 100 countries through distributors, licensees, and export operations. To meet the global demands for its products, Ecolab operates more than fifty state-of-the-art manufacturing and distribution facilities worldwide.

Shortcomings to Bear in Mind

- Wall Street seems well aware that Ecolab has a bright future, since it has tagged it with an above-average multiple, typically twenty-five times earnings or higher.

Reasons to Buy

- In 2005 Ecolab introduced Endure 450, a new waterless surgical hand antiseptic that, based on independent testing and available public literature, is not only the strongest formulation on the market but also the mildest for the hands and skin. According to a company official, "Endure 450 Surgical and Healthcare Personnel Hand Antiseptic is a welcome addition to hospital operating rooms, as the brush-free, alcohol-based scrub not only provides long-lasting, persistent antimicrobial protection, but the advanced system of moisturizers and conditioners actually helps to rehydrate and maintain skin health with every application."

John Bucholz, Ecolab marketing manager for the company's Healthcare Division, said "Endure 450, the company's first market entry for waterless hand scrubs for the operating room, incorporates APT™, a patented system of adjuvants and potentiators that works synergistically with ethyl alcohol to extend persistent residual antimicrobial protection for up to six hours.

"The APT™ technology is really a breakthrough because it works very differently than the other water-added or waterless based products on the market. APT™ works by enhancing bacterial cell permeability and susceptibility to alcohol, allowing inactivation and killing of microorganisms on the skin surface and stratum corneum.

"With surgical hand antisepsis, you have to concentrate equally on the complete and speedy removal of bacteria," Bucholz added. "Most importantly, though, is the ability to prevent re-growth under the gloves. A surgery could last six hours, and hands will sweat under the surgical gloves, causing microorganisms to grow. If doctors cut their gloves and are in a sterile cavity, then bacteria could get in the wound and potentially lead to an infection. In a surgical site, you just can't have that."

In addition to providing the prolonged sustainability that allows the product to make the surgical scrub claim, Endure 450 is faster to use than impregnated scrub brushes that doctors have used in the past. It is also effective for the first scrub of the day and for reentry, which allows for product standardization throughout the operating room.

Users of the product appreciate its mildness. "We have received a lot of positive feedback about how the product feels on their hands," said Cheryl Littau, a senior scientist for the Ecolab Healthcare Division. "Our product has excellent spreadability, which is crucial in making sure that users get good, uniform coverage. Best of all, it leaves the skin in great condition. We've done comparative testing showing that Endure 450 is actually more moisturizing than lotion."

- Ecolab is the fourth-best manufacturing company in the United States to sell for, according to *Selling Power* magazine. This monthly sales-management publication annually lists the fifty best companies to sell for in the United States. It ranks the top twenty-five manufacturing companies and the top twenty-five service companies with more than 500 salespeople based on three key categories: compensation, training, and career mobility for their sales people.

"Ecolab's most important asset is our sales-and-service team," said Mr. Baker. "Clearly, this is a terrific recognition for us. Our investments to carefully select, train, compensate, and develop our associates are critical to our company's growth and future."

- "Ecolab was proud to once again be named to *Business Ethics* magazine's list of the '100 Best Corporate Citizens in America,'" said former CEO, Allan L. Schuman in 2004, just before he turned the reins over to Douglas Baker on July 1, 2004. "This recognition, our fourth in as many years, is a reaffirmation of our company's commitment to corporate integrity and good citizenship."
- Despite the company's high P/E ratio, the shares of Ecolab have a low beta coefficient of only 0.90, compared with an average of 1.00 for the S&P 500. This means that it fluctuates less than the general market.
- Ecolab has a highly skilled research-and-development team, which continues to turn out innovative new products. According to a company spokesman, "Never content with the status quo, we strive for constant improvement, so far earning nearly 2,600 patents worldwide. And we boast the industry's most sophisticated R&D facilities—where breakthroughs happen every day."
- On March 22, 2006, the *New York Times* published the opinions of fifteen

securities analysts who follow Ecolab. Three said the stock is a STRONG BUY; five regarded it a MODERATE BUY; six said it was a HOLD; and one pushed it down to MODERATE HOLD.

■ "We think the company has solid 2009–2011 prospects," said Frederick L. Harris, III, writing for *Value Line Investment Survey* on March 17, 2006. "Management's 'Circle the Customer—Circle the Globe' strategy of aggressively cross-selling the various divisions' complementary products (including pest elimination and dishwashing) should continue to pay off handsomely. Too, with a highly skilled team of scientists, Ecolab appears positioned to launch many more innovations."

SECTOR: **Materials** ◆ BETA COEFFICIENT: **.90**
10-YEAR COMPOUND EARNINGS PER SHARE GROWTH: **12.5%**
10-YEAR COMPOUND DIVIDENDS PER SHARE GROWTH: **10.4%**

		2005	2004	2003	2002	2001	2000	1999	1998
Revenues (millions)		4,535	4,185	3,762	3,404	2,321	2,264	2,080	1,888
Net income (millions)		320	310	277	210	188	209	176	155
Earnings per shares		1.23	1.19	1.06	0.80	0.73	0.79	0.66	0.58
Dividends per share		0.35	0.33	0.29	0.27	0.26	0.24	0.21	0.19
Price	high	37.2	35.6	27.9	25.2	22.1	22.8	22.2	19.0
	low	30.7	26.1	23.1	18.3	14.3	14.0	15.8	13.1

GROWTH AND INCOME

Emerson Electric Company

8000 W. Florissant Avenue ❑ P. O. Box 4100 ❑ St. Louis, MO 63136-8506 ❑ (314) 553-2197 ❑ Direct dividend reinvestment plan available (888) 213-0970 ❑ Web site: *www.gotoemerson.com* ❑ Listed: NYSE ❑ Ticker symbol: EMR ❑ Fiscal year ends September 30 ❑ S&P rating: A ❑ Value Line financial strength rating: A++

"After forty-three consecutive years of earnings gains, Emerson Electric hit a giant pothole in 2001, an indirect victim of the dot-com bubble's bursting," said Harlan S. Byrne, writing for *Barron's* on September 19, 2005. "As its customers in the telecommunications and computer industries fell on hard times, the St. Louis-based industrial-equipment manufacturer struggled to make its numbers, as well. To chief executive David N. Farr, barely a year on the job, fell the unenviable task of telling Wall Street that no corks would pop in year forty-four, and that fiscal '01 earnings, including some ugly charges, would fall to $2.40 a share from the prior year's $3.30.

"Well, it's time to ice the champagne. Last fall, after three years of cost-cutting and restructuring, Emerson reported a 24-percent jump in fiscal 2004 earnings, to $2.98 a share, on a 12-percent jump in sales, to $15.6 billion. This year, at last, the company is poised to overtake its old earnings record.

"Based on strong trends in several operating segments, Farr, fifty, is projecting net earnings of $3.45 to $3.50 a share, or $3.31 to $3.36 after special tax charges. 'We are optimistic that we will continue to deliver further growth in sales and profitability in 2005 and beyond,' he says."

Company Profile

Emerson is a leading manufacturer of a broad list of intermediate products such as electrical motors and drives, appliance components, and process-control devices. The company also produces hand and power tools, as well as accessories.

Founded 109 years ago, Emerson is not a typical high-tech capital goods producer. Rather, the company makes such prosaic things as refrigerator compressors, pressure gauges, and In-Sink-Erator garbage disposals—basic products that are essential to industry.

The following sections describe the company's five segments.

INDUSTRIAL AUTOMATION

This segment of the company provides integral horsepower motors, alternators, electronic and mechanical drives, industrial valves, electrical equipment, specialty heating, lighting, testing, and ultrasonic welding and cleaning products for industrial applications. Key growth drivers for the segment include the embedding of electronics into motors and other equipment to enable self-diagnosis and preventative maintenance functionality, as well as alternators for diesel and natural gas generator sets to create reliable distributed power solutions. The Industrial Automation segment brought in 18 percent of Emerson's total sales in 2005.

APPLIANCE AND TOOLS

This operation includes the Emerson Storage Solutions, Emerson Tools, Emerson Appliance Solutions, and Emerson Motors brand platforms. Customer offerings feature an extensive range of consumer, commercial, and industrial storage products; market-leading tools; electrical components and systems for appliances; and the world's largest offering of fractional horsepower motors. Key growth drivers include professional-grade tools serving the fast-growing home-center market, as well as advanced electrical motors, which create entirely new market opportunities for Emerson. In 2005, this business accounted for 22 percent of the company's revenues.

CLIMATE TECHNOLOGIES

This segment is known for leading technologies and solutions for heating, air conditioning, and refrigeration applications that provide homeowners with a whole new level of comfort and efficiency while also lowering their energy bills. Climate Technologies's remote monitoring capabilities help assure food safety and quality for grocery stores. In 2005, this operation accounted for 17 percent of total sales.

PROCESS MANAGEMENT

Award-winning technologies help oil and gas, refining, power generation, chemical, pharmaceutical, and other process businesses increase plant uptime, improve productivity, and identify and eliminate problems before they occur. Emerson offers intelligent control systems and software, measurement instruments, valves, and expertise in engineering, project management, and consulting. In 2005, this segment's sales made up 24 percent of total revenues.

NETWORK POWER

Businesses depend on the company's Network Power for reliable power to run data centers, telecommunications networks, and other mission-critical applications. Emerson leads the industry in the design, manufacture, installation, and service of power solutions such as AC and DC backup systems and precision cooling equipment. In 2005, its revenues represented 19 percent of the company's total.

Shortcomings to Bear in Mind

- On January 13, 2006, *Value Line Investment Survey* was only lukewarm concerning Emerson Electric. Edward Plank said, "Top-quality Emerson stock carries an average rank for Timeliness. While the company boasts diverse product lines, a leading market position, and a commitment to new product development, the shares appear fully priced at present [the stock was $75.24 at the time]. As such, EMR will likely keep pace with the market over the coming year. Capital gains potential out to late decade is about average."

■ Argus Research Company also had a less-than-enthusiastic comment. On February 8, 2006, Dana Richardson said, "We are maintaining our HOLD rating on Emerson Electric Co. as we believe that the company's strong recent performance and solid growth prospects are already priced into the stock."

Reasons to Buy

■ Technology is fundamental to Emerson's sales growth. As a consequence, the company has been increasing its investment in Engineering and Development, notably in such sectors as communications, software, and electronics. E&D investment, moreover, has risen every year since 1973.

■ Emerson is now supplying the world's leading windmill manufacturer with more than 3,000 wind turbine generators, helping deliver electricity to the national grid for twenty-eight different countries.

■ The *New York Times* checked with nineteen analysts on March 3, 2006 and found that five regarded Emerson as a STRONG BUY; six said it looked like a MODERATE BUY; and eight said they were all wrong, since it was clearly a HOLD.

■ "We project an uptick in some of EMR's important end markets and believe that strong growth in emerging markets, particularly in Asia and Latin America, will continue," said John F. Hingher, CFA, writing for *Standard & Poor's Stock Reports* on January 18, 2006.

■ On February 8, 2006, Lehman Brothers gave an OVERWEIGHT rating to Emerson, which is essentially a BUY. The analyst had this comment. "Emerson remains our top large-cap pick for the year, and we think that there could be upside to management's guidance range of $4.10–$4.30, which is meaningfully above consensus of $4.04." "Consensus" refers to the average forecast made by analysts in general.

■ "Emerson had an outstanding year in 2005, as we delivered the second consecutive year of double-digit growth in sales and earnings per share," said Mr. Farr in 2006. "Sales were a record $17.3 billion, up 11 percent from $15.6 billion in 2004. The growth was led by strength in the industrial and technology markets we serve and was also the result of Emerson's continued focus on eight key growth initiatives, which as a group increased by 15 percent in 2005. Earnings per share increased 19 percent to $3.55 for 2005, excluding the tax impact of repatriating foreign earnings under the American Jobs Creation Act (AJCA). Reported earnings per share were $3.40, a 14-percent increase from the $2.98 per share in 2004."

Emerson's CEO goes on to say, "Emerson's cash flow performance in 2005 demonstrates the company's strong commitment to capital efficiency as a means of creating value for shareholders. Operating cash flow was $2.2 billion in 2005, a slight decrease compared with last year's record cash flow. Free cash flow (operating cash flow less capital expenditures) in 2005 was $1.7 billion, an 8-percent decrease from 2004 as we made strategic capital investments throughout the company. Free cash flow was higher than net income for the fifth consecutive year, a testament to Emerson's continued high quality earnings and efficient working capital management. Return on total capital excluding the AJCA impact increased to 16.1 percent from 14.2 percent in 2004, the fourth consecutive annual improvement.

"Emerson's commitment to generating returns for shareholders continues with 2005 marking the forty-ninth consecutive year of increased dividends. Dividends in 2005 were $1.66 per share, and in November 2005, the board of directors increased the dividend to an annualized rate of $1.78 per share."

Mr. Farr also said, "The company's strong cash position also allows us to make strategic acquisitions that strengthen existing businesses and generate long-term returns for shareholders. Process Management and Industrial Automation purchased companies that bring complementary product offerings and expand Emerson's offering of key technologies to the industrial marketplace. Network Power acquired businesses that serve the telecom and data center markets, and an acquisition in the consumer storage business continues to drive to build a billion-dollar storage business. In total, these acquisitions are expected to add about $500 million to revenue to Emerson in 2006."

SECTOR: **Industrials** ◆ BETA COEFFICIENT: **1.10**
10-YEAR COMPOUND EARNINGS PER SHARE GROWTH: **5.8%**
10-YEAR COMPOUND DIVIDENDS PER SHARE GROWTH: **6.6%**

		2005	2004	2003	2002	2001	2000	1999	1998
Revenues (millions)		17,305	15,615	13,958	13,748	15,480	15,545	14,270	13,447
Net income (millions)		1,487	1,257	1,013	1,060	1,032	1,422	1,314	1,229
Earnings per share		3.55	2.98	2.41	2.52	2.50	3.30	3.00	2.77
Dividends per share		1.69	1.60	1.58	1.55	1.53	1.43	1.31	1.18
Price	high	77.8	70.9	65.0	66.1	79.6	79.8	71.4	67.4
	low	60.7	56.2	43.8	41.7	44.0	40.5	51.4	54.5

AGGRESSIVE GROWTH

EnCana Corporation

P. O. Box 2850 ❑ Calgary, Alberta ❑ Canada T2P 2S5 ❑ (403) 645-2194 ❑ Dividend reinvestment plan not available ❑ Web site: *www.encana.com* ❑ Ticker symbol: ECA ❑ Listed: NYSE ❑ S&P rating: B+ ❑ Value Line financial strength rating: B++

On September 20, 2005, EnCana signed an agreement with Methanex Corporation to import up to 25,000 barrels per day of offshore diluent from Methanex's terminal facilities in Kitimat, British Columbia. This move enabled EnCana to transport its growing oil sands production in northeast Alberta to markets in the United States.

"Diluent is a necessary component for the pipeline transportation of heavy oil, but Canadian supply is tight due to increased production from Alberta's vast oil sands," said Bill Oliver, EnCana's President of Midstream & Marketing. "However, cost-effective diluent is readily available on the world market, and this can help us manage transportation costs as we advance our oil sands growth and integration strategy."

Mr. Oliver also said, "With access to the ideally located Kitimat terminal, we expect to be able to import diluent at a competitive cost and move it to where it's most needed—in northeast Alberta—then blend it with our growing oil sands production for transport to key U.S. markets."

Company Profile

EnCana is one of North America's leading independent crude oil and natural gas exploration and production companies. EnCana pursues growth from its portfolio of unconventional long-life resource plays situated in Canada and the United States. The company defines resource plays as large contiguous accumulations of hydrocarbons, located in thick and extensive deposits, that typically have low geological and commercial development risk and low average decline rates.

EnCana's disciplined pursuit of these unconventional assets enabled it to become North America's largest natural gas producer and a leading developer of oil sands through in-situ recovery. The term "in situ" means that the thick bitumen from subsurface oil sands is mobilized through injecting steam into specialized wells.

In an article for *Barron's* October 12, 2005, Andrew Bary said, "It costs about $20 a barrel to transform bitumen, the heavy tar-like heavy oil found in abundance in northern Alberta, into conventional crude oil that can be pumped to refineries in Canada and the U.S. When oil prices stood at $20-to-$30-a-barrel range, the oil sands had limited appeal. But with crude trading above $60 a barrel, the economics of the oil sands becomes compelling."

The *Barron's* writer also said, "Producing crude from oil sands is dirty: The bitumen typically is strip-mined, then separated from the surrounding sands in a process that produces waste water that sits in giant pools. Once separated, bitumen needs to be heated, usually with natural gas, to produce crude oil. Environmental critics decry the strip-mining, its ugly aftereffects, and the energy-intensive upgrading process, which produces greenhouse gases and other emissions."

The company is also engaged in exploration and production activities internationally and has interests in midstream operations and assets, including natural gas storage facilities, natural gas processing facilities, power plants, and pipelines.

EnCana operates under two main divisions: Upstream, and Midstream and Marketing.

Upstream

The Upstream division manages EnCana's exploration for, and development of, natural gas, crude oil, and natural gas liquids and other related activities. Following the merger in 2002, the majority of EnCana's Upstream operations are situated in Canada, the United States, Ecuador, and the United Kingdom's central North Sea. From the time of the merger through early 2004, EnCana focused on the development and expansion of its highest-growth, highest-return assets in those key areas. In 2004, the company sharpened its strategic focus to concentrate on its inventory of North American resource play assets. In focusing its portfolio of assets, EnCana has completed a number of significant acquisitions during the past three years.

Midstream and Marketing

EnCana's Midstream and Marketing division encompasses the corporation's midstream operations and market optimization activities. EnCana's midstream activities are comprised of natural gas storage operations, natural gas liquids processing and storage, power generation operations, and pipelines. The company's marketing groups are focused on enhancing the sale of Upstream proprietary production. Correspondingly, the marketing groups undertake market optimization activities, including third-party purchases and sales of product, which provides operational flexibility for transportation commitments, product type, delivery points, and customer diversification.

Shortcomings to Bear in Mind

- On December 5, 2005, *Standard & Poor's Stock Reports* was less than enthusiastic about this stock. Charles LaPorta, CFA, said, "We have a HOLD recommendation on the shares. While ECA's historical operations have been hurt by relatively low returns on capital (averaging about 8.7 percent in each of the past three years), we believe the asset restructuring undertaken over the past twelve months will lead to significant improvements. However, given the recent production difficulty, the inability to leverage post-hurricane prices due to existing hedges, and continued escalating operating costs, we believe the company needs to demonstrate significant production momentum and cost control before we can become more constructive on the shares."

Reasons to Buy

- On March 21, 2006, the *New York Times* checked with twenty-six analysts and found that six rated the stock a STRONG BUY; ten said it was a MODERATE BUY; eight called it a HOLD; one said it was a MODERATE HOLD; and one bearish analyst insisted it should be regarded as a SELL. He plans to leave the country if he's wrong.
- EnCana's asset base and operating expertise with unconventional resources is focused in North America because this is where "we have the best opportunities to generate long-term, steady, profitable growth," said CEO Gwyn Morgan in 2005. "Those companies focusing on international expansion are doing so because that is where they believe their opportunities lie.

"Historically, North America's natural gas supply came largely from conventional reservoirs. However, we believe that the conventional business model for gas in North America has reached its tipping point. Declines from mature fields can no longer be offset with new conventional discoveries. The future for North American natural gas production lies in unconventional reservoirs—mainly tight gas sands, shale gas, and coalbed methane. In fact, natural gas production from unconventional sources has been increasing to the point where it now represents about one-third of total North American production. The unconventional natural gas potential is estimated to be far larger than the reserves discovered in conventional reservoirs to date. EnCana currently has one of the largest onshore land positions, generally concentrated in contiguous tracts endowed with unconventional natural gas resources which we control and operate at close to a 100-percent basis.

"North America is also one of the world's lowest-risk areas to do business—having a highly developed marketplace and regulation, coupled with an attractive fiscal regime. Furthermore, the demand for North American natural gas is also rising and no external sources are expected to make an material supply impact through at least the end of this decade."

- Mr. Morgan also said, "We are currently North America's leading producer of natural gas, and our land holdings contain huge undeveloped resources. Our large-scale natural gas drilling programs efficiently drive strong internal production growth.

"During our first three years of operation, EnCana's average annual growth in gas sales has been 13 percent, and our 2005 growth is expected to be in the range of 15 percent. Looking forward, we are confident that our existing land base and financial capacity are capable of sustaining internal 10-percent-per-share sales growth annually for at least five years to come."

- Mr. Morgan also said, "The importance of in-situ oil sands production methods is placed into perspective by the fact that less than 10 percent of Canada's oil sands resources are considered accessible by surface mining methods. EnCana's teams have achieved technical and cost leadership in the production of bitumen from in-situ oil sands, and our extensive land holdings are recognized for their high quality and potential. We have compiled the longest and most successful track record in the application of the latest generation recovery process known as steam-assisted gravity drainage."

■ Mr. Morgan goes on to say, "Encana's technical and operating teams have grown up in a company principally focused on resource plays, whereas the main focus of the vast majority of the industry has been on the search for new conventional fields. Successful pursuit of resource plays requires a very different mind set, one trained on assessing the size of previously unproductive resources, finding the technical key to unlocking that potential and acting decisively to acquire very large land blocks containing the play. Then, it requires driving down costs and driving up reserves and production through continually improving technical and operational understanding and thinking creatively over decades of resource play life."

■ The company's CEO also said, "Over a thirty-year history, EnCana and its two predecessor companies have assembled about 18 million net undeveloped acres onshore North America, which contain some of the continent's highest quality unconventional natural gas resources, a position that could not be replicated today."

SECTOR: **Energy** ◆ BETA COEFFICIENT: **.85**
10-YEAR COMPOUND EARNINGS PER SHARE GROWTH: **24%**
10-YEAR COMPOUND DIVIDENDS PER SHARE GROWTH: **6.4%**

		2005	2004	2003	2002	2001	2000	1999	1998
Revenues (millions)		14,266	11,810	10,216	7,064	6,333	4,835	2,672	1,928
Net income (million)		2,715	1,976	1,375	794	822	696	242	81
Earnings per share		3.18	2.11	1.44	0.82	1.58	1.37	0.48	0.16
Dividends per share		0.28	0.20	0.16	0.13	0.13	0.13	0.14	0.13
Price	high	59.8	28.7	20.0	16.2	14.8*			
	low	26.4	19.0	15.0	11.4	11.3*			

* EnCana was formed from a merger between PanCanadian Energy Corporation and Alberta Energy Company on April 5, 2002. Thus, price figures do not extend back to 1998.

CONSERVATIVE GROWTH

Energen Corporation

605 Richard Arrington Jr. Boulevard North ❑ Birmingham, AL 35203-2707 ❑ (205) 326-8421 ❑ Direct dividend reinvestment plan available (800) 654-3206 ❑ Web site: *www.energen.com* ❑ Listed: NYSE ❑ Ticker symbol: EGN ❑ S&P rating: A ❑ Value Line financial strength rating: B++

On January 25, 2006, Energen announced that its oil and gas acquisition and development subsidiary, Energen Resources Corporation, was the dominant driver of the diversified energy company's 35-percent increase in earnings per share in 2005.

Representing 78 percent of Energen's 2005 consolidated earnings, Energen Resources benefited from higher commodity prices and record production of 91 billion cubic feet equivalent (Bcfe). Energen Resources's net income for the year totaled $135.3 million, compared with $94.1 million in 2004.

Energen's utility subsidiary, Alabama Gas Corporation (Alagasco), also contributed to the holding company's higher earnings in 2005, generating net income of $37 million, up from $33.8 million the prior year.

"Our two lines of business continue to perform well," said CEO Mike Warren.

"Not only did each business improve their earnings in 2005, but the acquisition of largely proved undeveloped oil reserves in the Permian Basin late in the year helped set the stage for growth in the future."

Mr. Warren goes on to say, "Energen Resources's proved reserves at year-end topped 1.7 trillion cubic feet equivalent—a new record. And, perhaps, of even greater significance is that 2005 reserve additions from development activities basically replaced our annual production.

"Over the last five years, Energen's earnings have increased at an annual compound growth rate of just under 20 percent a year. At the same time, Energen common stock has generated a five-year annualized total return to shareholders of 20 percent, including a 24.6 percent return in 2005."

Company Profile

Energen is a diversified holding company engaged primarily in the acquisition, development, exploration, and production of oil, natural gas, and natural gas liquids in the continental United States. It also has a stake in the purchase, distribution, and sale of natural gas, principally in central and north Alabama. Its two subsidiaries are Energen Resources Corporation and Alabama Gas Corporation (Alagasco).

Energen was incorporated in Alabama in 1978 in connection with the reorganization of its oldest subsidiary, Alagasco. Alagasco was formed in 1948 by the merger of Alabama Gas Company into Birmingham Gas Company, the predecessors of which had been in existence since the mid-1800s. Alagasco became a public company in 1953. Energen Resources was formed in 1971 as a subsidiary of Alagasco and became a subsidiary of Energen in the 1978 reorganization.

Oil and Gas Operations

Energen's oil and gas operations focus on increasing production and adding proved reserves through the acquisition and development of oil and gas properties. To a lesser extent, Energen Resources explores for and develops new reservoirs, primarily in areas in which it has an operating presence. Substantially all gas, oil, and natural gas liquids production is sold to third parties. Energen Resources also provides operating services in the Black Warrior Basin in Alabama for its partners and third parties. These services include overall project management and day-to-day decision-making, relative to project operations.

At the end of the latest fiscal year, Energen Resources's inventory of proved oil and gas reserves totaled 1,364.9 billion cubic feet equivalent (Bcfe). Substantially all of the company's 1.4 trillion cubic feet equivalent of reserves are situated in the San Juan Basin in New Mexico, the Permian Basin in west Texas, the Black Warrior Basin in Alabama, and the north Louisiana/east Texas region. About 81 percent of Energen Resources's year-end reserves are proved developed reserves. Energen Resources reserves are long-lived, with a year-end reserves-to-production ratio of sixteen. Natural gas represents about 65 percent of Energen Resources's proved reserves, with oil representing about 23 percent and natural gas liquids making up the rest.

Natural Gas Distribution

Alagasco is the largest natural gas distribution utility in the state of Alabama. Alagasco purchases natural gas through interstate and intrastate marketers and suppliers. It then distributes the purchased gas through its distribution facilities for sale to residential, commercial, and industrial customers and other end-users of natural gas. Alagasco also provides transportation services to industrial and commercial customers located on its distribution system. Those transportation customers, using Alagasco as their agent or acting on their own, purchase gas directly from producers, marketers, or suppliers and arrange for the delivery of the gas into the Alagasco distribution system. Alagasco charges a fee to transport such customer-owned gas through its distribution system to the customer's facilities.

Alagasco's service territory is situated in central and parts of north Alabama and includes some 185 cities and communities in twenty-eight counties. The aggregate population of the counties served by Alagasco is estimated to be 2.4 million. Among the cities served by Alagasco are Birmingham, the center of the largest metropolitan area in Alabama, and Montgomery, the state capital. During the most recent year, Alagasco served an average of 427,413 residential customers and 35,463 commercial, industrial, and transportation customers. The Alagasco distribution system includes about 9,810 miles of main and more than 11,494 miles of service lines, odorization and regulation facilities, and customer meters.

Alagasco's distribution system is connected to two major interstate natural gas pipeline systems: Southern Natural Gas Company (Southern), and Transcontinental Gas Pipe Line Company (Transco). It is also connected to several intrastate natural gas pipeline systems and to Alagasco's two liquified natural gas (LNG) facilities.

Shortcomings to Bear in Mind

- Unlike most public utilities, Energen has an extremely low dividend yield of barely 1 percent. Typically, utilities have yields of 3 percent to 5 percent. Thus, this is not a stock you would buy for income.
- Energen has not been particularly generous to investors seeking a rising trend of dividends. In the past ten years (1995 to 2005), the dividend per share advanced from $0.28 to $0.44, for a compound annual growth rate of only 4.6 percent. On a more positive note, the earnings per share growth has been impressive. EPS climbed from $0.44 to $2.35 in the same span, for a growth rate of 18.2 percent.

Reasons to Buy

- "We look forward in 2006 to the start of development drilling associated with our most recent property acquisition," said Mr. Warren on January 25, 2006. "We also are excited about a new coalbed methane drilling program in the Black Warrior Basin, and work continues on more fully developing our extensive San Juan Basin holdings in New Mexico and Colorado. In addition, we continue to rely on Alagasco to contribute modest earnings growth and provide the majority of dividend income for our shareholders."
- On March 21, 2006, the *New York Times* published a tabulation of how leading analysts viewed EGN. Two regarded the stock as a STRONG BUY; two said it was a MODERATE BUY, and one called the stock a HOLD. There were no SELLS.
- Energen Resources attempts to lower the risks associated with its oil and natural gas business. A key component of the company's efforts to manage risk is its acquisition-versus-exploration orientation and its preference for long-lived reserves. In pursuing an acquisition, Energen Resources primarily uses the then-current oil and gas futures prices in its evaluation models, the prevailing swap curve and, for the longer term, its own pricing assumptions.

  After a purchase, Energen Resources may use futures, swaps, and/or fixed-price contracts to hedge commodity prices on flowing production for up to thirty-six months to help protect targeted returns from price volatility. On an ongoing basis, the company may hedge up to 80 percent of its estimated annual production in any given year, depending on its pricing outlook.
- "We think 2006 will be a record-breaking year for Energen Corporation," said Frederick L. Harris, III, writing for *Value Line Investment Survey* on March 17, 2006. "The E&P subsidiary, Energen Resources, ought to enjoy healthy commodity

prices and a moderate rise in output (aided by the purchase of assets in the Permian Basin). Too, the favorable pricing environment has prompted management to hedge a significant portion of output (currently at 64 percent of projected natural gas volumes and 75 percent of estimated oil production). Meanwhile, Alagasco, the Alabama-based natural gas utility, stands to perform reasonably well, as it earns within an allowed range of return on average equity."

- On January 25, 2006, the company's board of directors elected James T. McManus II, age forty-seven, as its new president and chief operating officer. He will also continue to serve as president of the Energen Resources Corporation, the company's oil and gas acquisition and development subsidiary.

"James McManus has been the driving force behind Energen Resources's growth from a small, niche player in coalbed methane development in Alabama to one of the top twenty independent oil and gas producers in the United States," said Mike Warren, Energen's CEO. "In addition, James's broad experience at Alagasco (the company's utility subsidiary) in the financial and rates area and his overall role in strategic planning at all levels of the company will serve him well as he oversees the day-to-day operations of Energen and its two operating subsidiaries."

SECTOR: **Utilities** ◆ BETA COEFFICIENT: **0.75**
10-YEAR COMPOUND EARNINGS PER SHARE GROWTH: **18.2%**
10-YEAR COMPOUND DIVIDENDS PER SHARE GROWTH: **4.6%**

		2005	2004	2003	2002	2001	2000	1999	1998
Revenues (millions)		1,128	937	842	677	785	556	498	503
Net income (millions)		173	127	110	70.6	67.9	53.0	41.4	36.2
Earnings per share		2.35	1.74	1.55	1.05	1.09	0.88	0.69	0.62
Dividends per share		.44	0.38	0.37	0.36	0.35	0.34	0.33	0.47
Price	high	44.3	30.1	21.0	16.0	20.1	16.8	10.6	11.3
	low	27.0	20.0	14.1	10.8	10.8	7.4	6.6	7.6

GROWTH AND INCOME

ExxonMobil Corporation

5959 Las Colinas Boulevard ❑ Irving, TX 75039-2298 ❑ (972) 444-1538 ❑ Direct dividend reinvestment plan available (800) 252-1800 ❑ Web site: *www.exxonmobil.com* ❑ Listed: NYSE ❑ Ticker symbol: XOM ❑ S&P rating: A- ❑ Value Line financial strength rating: A++

"What type of energy will be demanded in the future?" asked Exxon's CEO, Lee R. Raymond, when he addressed the Hong Kong General Chamber of Commerce. Mr. Raymond, who retired at the end of 2005, went on to say, "Without a doubt, for many decades most growth in energy will be for oil, natural gas, and coal. Put simply, these are abundant and affordable, and we have established technologies for finding and using them.

"We project that oil and gas demand will each grow by close to 40 million barrels a day by 2030 and coal by almost 30 million oil-equivalent barrels a day. The rest will come from other sources. These increases will come despite an improvement in global energy intensity, which is the amount of energy used per unit of economic output. That improvement we forecast to average about 1.1 percent per year, or about one-third faster than the pace since 1970."

The Future of Alternative Energy Sources

"And the increase in petroleum and coal energy demanded will come about even as alternative energy sources grow even more rapidly. For example, we believe wind and solar energy may grow at about 10 percent per year, but because they are such small contributors today, they will remain less than 1 percent of total energy in 2030. These alternative energy sources are much discussed in the press, and they will become more important, but we cannot ignore the limitations that each have.

"For example, solar energy has very high costs. Wind and hydroelectric power have siting limitations. And there are constraints to significantly increasing biomass fuels due to economics and competition with alternative needs for food crops and forests."

How About Nuclear Power?

Mr. Raymond continued to say, "Nuclear energy remains an important option, with rapid growth projected in China. However, nuclear power has generated considerable public opposition elsewhere, both to new plants and to waste disposal options. While we think nuclear will grow, with perhaps more upside in the longer term if its costs become more competitive, the factors I just mentioned will certainly constrain growth in many countries in the medium term.

"Another energy type—hydrogen—has been increasingly mentioned as a possible long-term option. However, it is important to remember that hydrogen is more a battery than a primary source of energy. Hydrogen has to be produced from other materials, either hydrocarbons or water, and this process uses lots of energy and is very expensive. In addition, broad consumer use of hydrogen poses important safety and infrastructure issues that will take decades to manage or resolve in the best of circumstances."

The Obvious Conclusion

Mr. Raymond concluded with these words: "The limitations and dilemmas presented by these alternative energy sources are serious and can be overcome only with research, significant investments, and time. Therefore, we are left with the reality that for many decades the vast majority of energy that we will use will be hydrocarbon energy. That is why we must face seriously the issues that arise when obtaining energy from hydrocarbons."

In essence, it seems obvious that companies such as Exxon—the largest in the world—will be around for a long time. Not to have one or two petroleum companies in your portfolio would be a serious omission.

Company Profile

ExxonMobil is engaged in the exploration, production, manufacture, transportation, and sale of crude oil, natural gas, and petroleum products. It also has a stake in the manufacture of petrochemicals, packaging films, and specialty chemicals.

Divisions and affiliated companies of ExxonMobil operate or market products in the United States and some 200 other countries and territories. Their principal business is energy, involving exploration for and production of crude oil and natural gas, manufacture of petroleum products, and transportation and sale of crude oil, natural gas, and petroleum products.

The company is a major manufacturer and marketer of basic petrochemicals, including olefins, aromatics, polyethylene and polypropylene plastics, and a wide variety of specialty products. It also has interests in electric power generation facilities.

In a nutshell, here is ExxonMobil:

- The company conducts oil and gas exploration, development, and production in every major accessible producing region in the world.
- ExxonMobil has the largest energy resource base of any nongovernment company, and it is the world's largest nongovernment natural gas marketer and reserves holder.
- Consumers know the company best by its brand names: Exxon, Mobil, and Esso.
- ExxonMobil is the world's largest fuels refiner and manufacture of lube base stocks used for making motor oils.
- The company has refining operations in twenty-six countries, 42,000 retail service stations in more than 100 countries, and lubricants marketing in almost 200 countries and territories.
- ExxonMobil markets petrochemical products in more than 150 countries. Ninety percent of the company's petrochemical assets are in businesses that are ranked number one or number two in market position.

Shortcomings to Bear in Mind

■ "Lee Raymond, the combative chairman of ExxonMobil (now retired), could be the most successful oilman in a century," said an article in the *Economist* on December 24, 2005. "During his decade and a half at the helm, his firm has outperformed its peers on almost every financial measure. The oil titan will finally step down at the end of 2005 in favor of Rex Tillerson, a company insider who is his handpicked successor. Some worry that the new man cannot possibly fill Mr. Raymond's oversized boots."

"Oilmen are divided over whether Mr. Raymond's departure will herald a change at Exxon. Most observers give him ample credit for the company's performance, but reckon Exxon's culture is now so strong that even Mr. Raymond's departure will not rock the boat."

The *Economist* article also said, "Compared with its peers, Exxon is certainly in an enviable position. But take a broader view of the challenges facing the entire industry, and it appears Mr. Tillerson's job may not prove so easy after all. One astute oil expert insists that 'Lee is getting off the ship at just the right time.' This contrarian argues that there are several factors that could yet trip up Mr. Tillerson as he takes over Exxon.

"The most serious threat to Exxon is replacing reserves. All oil companies must work hard to replace the hydrocarbons they use up. Under Mr. Raymond, Exxon has done better than its peers. Unfortunately, the firm's past success makes today's task even harder. Because Exxon is now such a Goliath, it now must replace many more barrels each day than it used to. Where to find those extra barrels?"

Reasons to Buy

■ "Our recommendation is STRONG BUY," said T. J. Vital, writing for *Standard & Poor's Company Reports* on February 2, 2006. "We expect XOM's upstream to benefit from high oil prices, and its complex refineries to benefit from significant cost discounts from its ability to refine lower-quality crude feedstocks."

■ ExxonMobil's world-class, geographically diverse upstream portfolio consists of 72 billion oil-equivalent barrels of oil and gas resources and activities in nearly forty countries. Large, highly profitable oil and gas operations in established areas, including North America, Europe, Asia, and West

Africa, are the foundations of this portfolio. These areas include long-life fields and have significant near-term potential as new opportunities are developed using existing infrastructure. ExxonMobil also holds a strong position in the Caspian, Eastern Canada, the Middle East, and Russia, as well as in the deep waters of West Africa and the Gulf of Mexico. According to a company official, "Our financial strength allows us to pursue all profitable opportunities. We continually invest in our existing assets to extend their economic life and have an industry-leading portfolio of more than 100 major new projects."

- ExxonMobil is the world's largest refiner, with an ownership interest in forty-six refineries in twenty-six countries and a total capacity of 6.3 million barrels per day. It has an extensive transportation network of oil tankers, pipelines, and product terminals. Lube-refining capacity is 150 thousand barrels per day.
- Worldwide, ExxonMobil markets gasoline and other fuels at more than 40,000 service stations, serves more than 1 million industrial and wholesale customers, provides aviation services and products at more than 700 airports, and services ocean-going vessels in more than 300 ports.
- On September 19, 2005, an article in the *Wall Street Journal* said, "Energy giant ExxonMobil Corp. said it signed an agreement with state-owned petroleum company PT Pertamina to tap East Java province's massive Cepu oil field."

The two authors, Phelim Kyne and Deden Sudrajat, went on to say, "'It's a production-sharing agreement for thirty years, and it enables us to work with Pertamina for development of the Cepu block,' said Stephen Greenlee, an ExxonMobil vice president. He told reporters that Cepu is estimated to contain 600 million barrels of crude oil."

- On March 22, 2006, the *New York Times* tabulated the thinking of twenty-one analysts, with this result: eight ranked Exxon as a STRONG BUY; nine regarded it as a MODERATE BUY; and four said it was a HOLD.

SECTOR: **Energy** ♦ BETA COEFFICIENT: **0.85**
10-YEAR COMPOUND EARNINGS PER SHARE GROWTH: **16.1%**
10-YEAR COMPOUND DIVIDENDS PER SHARE GROWTH: **4.3%**

		2005	2004	2003	2002	2001	2000	1999	1998
Revenues (millions)		370,998	291,252	246,738	204,506	187,510	206,083	160,883	100,697
Net income (millions)		36,100	25,330	17,030	11,011	15,105	16,910	8,380	6,440
Earnings per share		5.71	3.89	2.56	1.69	2.18	2.41	1.19	1.31
Dividends per share		1.14	1.06	0.98	0.92	0.91	0.88	0.84	0.82
Price	high	66.0	52.0	41.1	44.6	45.8	47.7	43.6	38.7
	low	49.2	39.9	31.6	29.8	35.0	34.9	32.2	28.3

AGGRESSIVE GROWTH

FedEx Corporation

942 South Shady Grove Road ❑ Memphis, TN 38120 ❑ (901) 818-7200 ❑ Web site: *www.fedex.com* ❑ Direct dividend reinvestment plan available (800) 446-2617 ❑ Fiscal year ends May 31 ❑ Listed: NYSE ❑ Ticker symbol: FDX ❑ S&P rating: B+ ❑ Value Line financial strength rating: B++

"What are going to be the growth markets over the next twenty years?" asked Dean Foust, an editor with *BusinessWeek*, on June 13, 2005.

In answer, FedEx CEO Frederick W. Smith said, "I think Brazil is becoming a major economic force. In all likelihood, if you fly an airline system for more than a couple of days, you'll be on a Brazilian-built airline, Embraer, which is a heck of a plane. Their agricultural economy has really taken off.

"India, same thing. I mean India has deregulated, eliminated a lot of bureaucracy, signed an open-skies agreement with the United States—which is a reason I think that China will do so, too—and their economy is booming. I think Eastern Europe's going to grow. It's inexorable. The demographics of Western Europe are such that they can't really sustain themselves unless they have growth markets and people to come in and work in those societies, and the natural affinity is Eastern Europe."

Company Profile

FedEx Corporation is the world's leading provider of guaranteed express delivery services. Using a $4-million inheritance as seed money, Frederick W. Smith founded FedEx in 1971, when he was only twenty-seven.

The company offers a wide range of express delivery services for the time-definite transportation of documents, packages, and freight. Commercial and military charter services are also offered by FedEx. The company's operations are as follows:

- FedEx Express is the world's largest express transportation company, providing fast, reliable delivery to 214 countries, including every address in the United States.
- FedEx Ground is North America's second-largest ground carrier for small-package business shipments, including business-to-residential service through FedEx Home Delivery.
- FedEx Freight is the largest U.S. regional less-than-truckload freight company, providing next-day and second-day delivery of heavyweight freight within the United States and from key international markets.
- FedEx Custom Critical is the "24/7" option for urgent shipments, proving nonstop, door-to-door delivery in the contiguous United States, Canada, and Europe.
- FedEx Trade Networks facilitates international trade as the largest-volume customs filer in the United States, and a one-stop source for freight forwarding, advisory services, and trade technology.

Shortcomings to Bear in Mind

■ Over the years, the relationship between FedEx managers and some of its 4,000 pilots has been strained, in part because of CEO Fred Smith's opposition to unions.

"We had started with the dream that if the company rose to Fred's vision, we'd be at the top as well," said Don Wilson, a twenty-eight-year company veteran who helped organize the FedEx Pilots Union in 1992. "The company has exceeded beyond what anyone expected, but our pay and benefits have not," Mr. Wilson said.

On the other hand, the company has had a reputation as a great place to work, with employees claiming they "bleed purple and orange"—the company's colors—and living by Smith's mantra: "People, service, profit." FedEx has repeatedly been on *Fortune* magazine's list of the "100 Best Companies to Work For" and its lists of best places for minorities and women to work.

- "FedEx can deliver just about anything these days—except happy investors," said Dimitra Defotis, writing for *Barron's* on August 8, 2005. "Competition and higher costs, especially for fuel, have weighed on the shares of the world's largest express air-package carrier. The stock is nearly 16 percent off its March all-time high, and it has trailed the Standard & Poor's 500 by about 8 percentage points over the past year. Clearly, high oil prices, price competition, and increased capital investments have taken their toll."

The *Barron's* article went on to say, "But FedEx isn't getting credit for its international growth opportunities, especially in China. The company also continues to pass on fuel surcharges to customers and add profitable package sales at Kinko's, which it acquired for $2.4 billion last year."

Reasons to Buy

- On March 25, 2006, the *New York Times* reported on the opinions of seventeen financial analysts and their view of FedEx. Five rated the stock a STRONG BUY; five said it was a MODERATE BUY; and seven called the stock a HOLD.
- "We recently upgraded the shares to STRONG BUY, from BUY," said Jim Corridore, writing for *Standard & Poor's Stock Reports* on December 21, 2005. "We think FDX is likely to continue to experience operating margin improvement, which should help drive strong net income and free cash flow growth, in our view."
- Similarly, Argus Research Company liked the stock on December 21, 2005. Suzanne Betts said, "BUY-rated FedEx Corp. posted top-line growth of 10 percent in the second quarter of fiscal 2006, with operating margins improving to 9.8 percent. As the company continues to focus on its strategy of cross-selling the full suite of FedEx services, as well as improving margins and seeking out global growth opportunities, we see continued upside in the stock."
- "As the digital revolution took hold in the late 1990s, FedEx didn't sit by and wait for its overnight delivery business to be eroded by e-mail and other new technologies," said the author of a *BusinessWeek* article on April 4, 2005. "It went on the offensive, snapping up major trucking outfits and extending its 'just in time' service into heavier freight and package delivery. Last year, FedEx acquired the Kinko's chain to position itself as the shipping and printing service of choice for home-based entrepreneurs. So even as its overnight document business has slipped, FedEx's diversification paid off in spades. Profits doubled in 2004."
- "FedEx transportation services provide the single most important element that every shipper needs—certainty," said the company's CEO Frederick W. Smith. "We deliver both shipments and the related information about them exactly as customers need, virtually anywhere in the world. We provide a broad portfolio of service options. And all of this is becoming crucial to businesses striving to transform complex supply chains into more efficient engines of growth and profitability."
- Increasingly, businesses are seeking strategic, cost-effective ways to manage their supply chains—the series of transportation and information exchanges required to convert parts and raw materials into

finished, delivered products. According to FedEx management, "Experience tells us that customers prefer one supplier to meet all of their distribution and logistics needs. And FedEx has what it takes: Our unique global network, operational expertise and air route authorities cannot be replicated by the competition. With FedEx, our customers have a strategic competitive weapon to squeeze time, mass, and cost from the supply chain."

- In December of 2003, FedEx invested $2.4 billion to buy Kinko's, Inc., "a one-stop back office" for small and midsize businesses. By acquiring Kinko's, FedEx is adopting a strategy of UPS, which bought MailBoxes, Inc., in 2001 to reach more small businesses. At the end of fiscal 2005, Kinko's had more than 1,400 stores—an increase of more than 200 since it was acquired—in eleven countries. The acquisition is expected to lead to a major expansion of the Kinko's network. FedEx said there is room to "easily double" the number of Kinko's stores in the United States.

- FedEx has invested heavily in recent years to develop an international infrastructure. It presently can reach locations accounting for 90 percent of world GDP, with twenty-four- or forty-eight-hour service. International delivery services for documents and freight have been growing faster than domestic business in recent years.

- According to CEO Frederick W. Smith, "The new strategy we have put in place of the past several years has made us a full-service transportation company, offering the broadest array of services. With FedEx Express, FedEx Ground, FedEx Freight, FedEx Custom Critical, and FedEx Trade Networks, we can offer our customers an unprecedented array of shipping and supply chain services quickly and conveniently across the globe."

- FedEx has been a part of the China free-trade success story for twenty years, helping build the air transportation infrastructure needed to support China's growing economic demands. Over that time, FedEx Express has grown to become the largest international express carrier in the country, with service to more than 220 cities and plans to expand to 100 more during the next five years.

With eleven flights every week through three major gateways—Beijing, Shanghai, and Shenzhen—FedEx serves its customers with more flights into and out of China than any other U.S.-based cargo carrier. "FedEx is benefiting enormously from the surge in China trade," said Michael L. Ducker, executive vice president of FedEx Express. "But we're also helping drive it. For the economic revolution to continue, China will need greater access to the global marketplace. That's what FedEx provides."

SECTOR: **Industrials** ◆ BETA COEFFICIENT: **1.10**
10-YEAR COMPOUND EARNINGS PER SHARE GROWTH: **14.2%**
10-YEAR COMPOUND DIVIDENDS PER SHARE GROWTH: **no dividend prior to 2003**

		2005	2004	2003	2002	2001	2000	1999	1998
Revenues (millions)		29,363	24,710	22,487	20,607	19,629	18,257	16,773	15,703
Net income (millions)		1,449	838	830	710	663	688	531	526
Earnings per share		4.72	2.76	2.74	2.39	2.26	2.32	2.10	1.75
Dividends per share		.32	.22	.20	—	—	—	—	—
Price	high	105.8	100.9	78.0	61.4	53.5	49.8	61.9	46.6
	low	76.8	64.8	47.7	42.8	33.2	30.6	34.9	21.8

General Dynamics Corporation

2941 Fairview Park Drive ❑ Suite 100 ❑ Falls Church, VA 22042-4513 ❑ (703) 876-3195 ❑ Dividend reinvestment plan not available ❑ Web site: *www.generaldynamics.com* ❑ Ticker symbol: GD ❑ S&P rating: A ❑ Value Line financial strength rating: A++

On November 29, 2005, the U.S. Army awarded Signal Solutions, Inc., a subsidiary of General Dynamics Network Systems, the Total Engineering and Integration Services contract to provide information technology (IT) engineering and technical support. The indefinite delivery/indefinite quantity multiple-award contract has a performance period of one base year and four option years with a ceiling value of approximately $800 million. General Dynamics Network Systems is a business unit of General Dynamics.

Signal Solutions, an incumbent provider on the predecessor contract, will continue to provide IT support services to the U.S. Army's Communications-Electronics Life Cycle Management Command and the Information Systems Engineering Command (USAISEC), as well as other federal agencies. Work will be performed in Fort Huachuca, Arizona, the National Capital Region, and at USAISEC customer sites worldwide.

"We are proud to continue providing enterprise engineering services, information assurance, and integration services in support of the army war-fighter," said Philip Jones, the Signal Solutions vice president responsible for the program. "We welcome this opportunity to build upon our partnership with USAISEC to provide new and innovative solutions to the army."

Since the first TEIS contract was awarded in 2000, Signal Solutions has partnered with the USAISEC to provide the army with rapid response and global support in transforming its information systems enterprise. During that time, Signal Solutions has been awarded 500 task orders, totaling more than $440 million.

USAISEC's primary mission is system engineering and integration of information systems for the U.S. Army. Their mission includes the design, engineering, integration, testing, and acceptance of information systems. USAISEC provides matrix support to the program executive officer and program manager structure for systems engineering and integration of assigned information systems.

About Signal Solutions, Inc.

Signal Solutions, Inc., a General Dynamics company, is a diversified high-technology services company headquartered in Fairfax, Virginia, and operating in more than sixty offices throughout the country. More than 85 percent of the 1,900 employees have engineering or technical backgrounds, making Signal Solutions a leader in providing IT and engineering and management products and services to industry and government.

Company Profile

General Dynamics was officially established in February 21, 1952, although it has organizational roots dating back to the late 1800s. The company was formed after its predecessor and current operating division, Electric Boat, acquired the aircraft company Canadair Ltd. and began building the first nuclear-powered submarine, USS *Nautilus.*

Through the years, General Dynamics has applied the wisdom of its experience and insight to recognize and act on change to build its position in the defense and technology business sectors. Building upon its marine business, the company added its first Combat Systems business unit, Land Systems, in 1982; its first Information Systems and Technology business unit, Advanced Technology Systems, in 1997; and returned to the aerospace business with Gulfstream in 1999.

Today, General Dynamics has leading market positions in business aviation and aircraft services, land and amphibious combat systems, mission-critical information systems and technologies, and shipbuilding and marine systems. The company is a leading supplier of sophisticated defense systems to the United States and its allies, and it sets the world standard in business jets.

General Dynamics has four main business segments. The Aerospace segment designs, manufactures, and provides services for midsize, large cabin, and ultra-long-range business aircraft. Combat Systems supplies land and amphibious combat machines and systems, including armored vehicles, power trains, turrets, munitions, and gun systems. Information Systems and Technology's expertise lies in specialized data acquisition and processing, in advanced electronics, and in battlespace information networks and management systems. Marine Systems designs and builds submarines, surface combatants, auxiliary ships, and large commercial vessels.

Information Systems & Technology

General Dynamics Information Systems and Technology is a leading integrator of transformational, network-centric command-and-control, communications, computing, intelligence, surveillance, and reconnaissance (C4ISR) systems using digital information-sharing technologies. These systems provide today's war-fighters with secure, on-demand access to more mission-critical information than ever before, enabling U.S. forces and allies to prevail on the battlefield.

Combat Systems

General Dynamics Combat Systems is a market-leading provider of tracked and wheeled armored combat vehicles, armament systems, and munitions for customers in North America, Europe, the Middle East, and the South Pacific—and the only producer of America's main battle tanks.

Marine Systems

General Dynamics Marine Systems designs, develops, manufactures, and integrates the complex naval platforms that are central to the U.S. Navy's transformation to a more lethal, flexible, network-centric sea force of the future. Its three advanced shipyards apply decades of development innovation, experience, and expertise to produce the world's most sophisticated maritime surface, subsurface, and support systems.

Aerospace

General Dynamics Aerospace is one of the world's leading designers and manufacturers of business-jet aircraft and is a leading provider of services for private aircraft in select markets globally. Gulfstream business jets are among the most technologically advanced aircraft available, and the company provides a broad selection of planes to meet the demanding requirements of business and government customers alike.

Shortcomings to Bear in Mind

- "The good news is mostly reflected in the share price," said Ian Gendler, writing for *Value Line Investment Survey* on March 25, 2006. "Patient investors may want to look elsewhere since this issue has increased by about 14 percent over the last three months, and now offers below-average appreciation potential out to 2009–2011."
- On December 21, 2005, *Standard & Poor's Stock Reports* had this comment: "We are maintaining our HOLD opinion on GD, as the stock is trading near our

discounted cash flow target price of $115 a share," said Robert E. Friedman, CPA.

Reasons to Buy

- On March 25, 2006, the *New York Times* surveyed twenty-three securities analysts concerning General Dynamics. Five rated the stock a STRONG BUY; ten said it was a MODERATE BUY; and eight gave it a HOLD rating. None suggested it was a SELL.
- On January 27, 2006, Suzanne Betts had this comment, writing for the Argus Research Company: "The company is expected to post another strong year in 2006, despite defense spending concerns."
- On November 28, 2005, National Steel and Shipbuilding Company, a wholly owned subsidiary of General Dynamics, delivered the *Alaskan Navigator,* the third of four Alaska-class double-hull crude oil tankers being built for BP Oil Shipping Company, USA, a subsidiary of BP plc.

"We are now focused on completion of the fourth ship in the class, which is progressing well in the shipyard as we have ramped up production on both the BP tankers and Navy new construction work," said Richard Vortmann, NASSCO president.

The Alaskan Navigator will join her sister ships, the *Alaskan Frontier* and the *Alaskan Explorer,* which were delivered in August 2004 and March 2005, delivering crude oil from Alaska to BP's refineries in Los Angeles and Cherry Point, Washington. The fourth ship will be delivered in late 2006.

The state-of-the-art Alaska-class tankers are the most environmentally friendly oil tankers ever built. Their double hull construction has been designed for a life of thirty-five years and their deck structure has a life of fifty years—a robust configuration that will perform at peak efficiency for decades in the rigors of the Gulf of Alaska's waters. The diesel-electric propulsion system, with redundant engines, shafts, and screws, significantly increases reliability and reduces air emissions and maintenance downtime. The ships use seawater instead of oil to cool and lubricate their propeller shafts, eliminating the possibility of accidental oil leaks. Cargo piping, normally installed on the deck, is run inside the cargo tanks to reduce the risk of small spills.

The ships are 287 meters (941 feet) long, with a beam of 50 meters (164 feet) and a capacity of 1.3 million barrels of crude oil.

The *Alaskan Navigator* will be part of the largest oil-industry-owned oil and natural gas shipping fleet in the world and will be operated by the Alaska Tanker Company of Portland, Oregon, which operates BP-chartered tankers used in the Alaska North Slope trade and is 25 percent owned by BP.

BP is the single global brand formed by the combination of the former British Petroleum, Amoco Corporation, Atlantic Richfield (ARCO), and Burmah Castrol. BP is a global producer, manufacturer, and marketer of oil, gas, chemicals, and renewable energy sources. Every day, BP provides energy solutions to approximately 13 million customers in more than 100 countries. In addition to the remaining BP oil tanker, NASSCO has contracts with the U.S. Navy for eight dry cargo/ammunition ships and holds options for an additional four ships. The first ship in the T-AKE program, a new class of combat logistics force ships designated the Lewis and Clark class, was launched in May. The program is expected to run through 2010.

- On December 14, 2005, the company said it would buy Anteon International Corporation for $2.1 billion in cash. According to Ellen McCarthy, writing for the *Washington Post,* "The deal is the fifth for General Dynamics this year, a sign that the Falls Church firm now values defense computer networks and software as much as it has traditionally regarded tanks, ammunition, and submarines. While Pentagon spending on major weapons is expected to slide in coming years, spending on information technology—including building computer networks and designing battlefield simulation software—is on an upward trend, with $200 billion in contracts to be awarded next year.

Anteon was founded in 1996 by industry veteran Joseph M. Kampf. The company grew quickly by acquiring smaller contractors and has gobbled up nine companies in its nine years of existence. Anteon has 9,500 employees—about 65 percent have secret or top-secret security clearance, which makes it easier for the company to bid on intelligence contracts offered by the government."

SECTOR: **Industrials** ◆ BETA COEFFICIENT: **.80**

10-YEAR COMPOUND EARNINGS PER SHARE GROWTH: **14%**

10-YEAR COMPOUND DIVIDENDS PER SHARE GROWTH: **7.6%**

		2005	2004	2003	2002	2001	2000	1999	1998
Revenues (millions)		21,244	19,178	16,617	13,829	12,163	10,356	8,959	4,970
Net income (millions)		1,461	1,203	998	1,051	943	901	715	364
Earnings per share		3.63	2.99	2.50	2.54	2.33	2.24	1.77	1.43
Dividends per share		0.78	0.70	0.63	0.60	0.55	0.51	0.48	0.44
Price	high	61.2	55.0	45.4	55.6	48.0	39.5	37.7	31.0
	low	48.8	42.5	25.0	36.7	30.3	18.2	23.1	20.2

GROWTH AND INCOME

General Electric Company

3135 Easton Turnpike ❑ Fairfield, CT 06828 ❑ (203) 373-2468 ❑ Direct dividend reinvestment plan available (800) 786-2543 ❑ Web site: *www.ge.com* ❑ Ticker symbol: GE ❑ S&P rating: A+ ❑ Value Line financial strength rating: A++

"Technology is the foundation of GE's growth," said CEO Jeffrey R. Immelt in 2005. "Today we invest considerably more in technology than we did in 2000. We have a rich pipeline of new products, based on key market trends, that can win.

"GE leads in energy efficiency through more economical power-producing systems, including those that use renewable resources. In 2004, we and Bechtel began feasibility studies with Cinergy Corporation and American Electric Power for coal gasification power plants. This 'Cleaner Coal' technology will generate power in a cost-effective way using abundant coal resources, with dramatically fewer emissions than traditional coal plants.

"GE leads in personalized health care through a technical focus on prediction, diagnosis, and information linked to treatment. In our product pipeline today are advanced technologies capable of extremely early detection of cancer, heart disease, and Alzheimer's disease.

"GE leads in advanced water technology. With ionics, we will have a broad array of filtration systems and membranes. We are taking this in two directions: toward the sea with desalinization projects and into the home with advanced filtration systems.

"GE leads in advanced security systems. We are the only company that can combine digital surveillance, advanced detection, and bioscience. We have been awarded funding by the U.S. Transportation Security Administration for the next generation of security systems, which will combine material and explosives detection."

Mr. Immelt goes on to say, "Our technical leadership is supported by four Global Research Centers where we can spread ideas across the GE businesses. Good examples are the transfer of our leading medical imaging technology to new uses in homeland defense and the leveraging of our materials technologies across our locomotives, aircraft engines, and turbines. Global Research filed for more than 450 patents in 2004, including twenty-five for nanotechnology."

Company Profile

General Electric, a superbly managed company, provides a broad range of industrial products and services. Under the stewardship of CEO Jack Welch (now retired), GE transformed itself from a maker of diverse industrial equipment into a provider of a broad range of commercial and consumer services.

In 1980, manufacturing operations generated about 85 percent of operating profits; currently, services operations generate 70 percent of total operating profits. GE Capital (the company's enormous financing arm, and the world's largest nonbank financial operation) alone generates nearly 30 percent of operating profits.

General Electric is one of the world's largest corporations. Although GE can trace its origins back to Thomas Edison, who invented the light bulb in 1879, the company was actually founded in 1892.

The company's broad diversification is clearly evident if you examine its components. Operations are divided into two groups: product, service, and media businesses, and GE Capital Services (GECS).

Product, service, and media includes eleven businesses: aircraft engines, appliances, lighting, medical systems, NBC, plastics, power systems, electrical distribution and control, information services, motors and industrial systems, and transportation systems.

In 2002, the company—often criticized for the complexity of its structure and the resulting opacity of its numbers—said it would break up GE Capital, by far its largest business, into four businesses. The new businesses are GE Commercial Finance, GE Insurance, GE Consumer Finance, and GE Equipment Management.

Shortcomings to Bear in Mind

- General Electric is one of the world's largest companies, which might impair the company's ability to increase in size, as compared to a smaller or medium-size company. Also, GE is followed by dozens of analysts, which makes it difficult for any surprises to pop up. Studies indicate that companies that are ignored by analysts or covered by only a handful are likely to outperform those that are covered by every brokerage house on Wall Street. On the other hand, if a company is ignored by the analysts, it could be that it is being neglected for good reason: it has some obvious flaws.

Reasons to Buy

- "Jeff Immelt's GE is built more on biotech and wind power than old-economy ovens and light bulbs," said Suzanne Woolley, writing for *BusinessWeek* on December 19, 2005. "It's also firmly focused on emerging markets such as China, and its senior ranks are starting to reflect the world's diversity. Now in his fifth year as chairman, Immelt's focus on innovation has transformed GE into a model for how to thrive in the twenty-first century, much as Jack Welch's GE was an icon in the century before."
- "General Electric's $6.8-billion sale of most of its insurance operations to Swiss Reinsurance Company marks a turning point in Chairman Jeffrey Immelt's long-term

strategy for the conglomerate portfolio," said Kathryn Kranhold, writing for the *Wall Street Journal* on November 21, 2005.

"The deal with Swiss Re will leave GE temporarily with a small stake in the insurance industry, a volatile market that Mr. Immelt has been methodically exiting since 2002. It will allow GE to redeploy its money into units like energy and transportation, and into its newer businesses such as water treatment, information technology for health care, and security."

- "We expect cash flow from operating activities to grow annually at double-digit rates over the next several years," said Edward Plank, writing for *Value Line Investment Survey* on January 13, 2006. "GE plans to use this strong cash flexibility ($24 billion expected in 2006) to continue to invest in its businesses and return value to shareholders."
- The key to GE's business plan is the requirement that businesses be first or second in market share in their industries. Those that fail to achieve this status are divested.
- Jack Welch, the previous CEO, developed a defect-reduction program called Six Sigma. Six Sigma contributes mightily to GE's earning growth. Think of sigma as a mark on a bell curve that measures standard deviation. Most companies have between 35,000 and 50,000 defects per million operations, or about 3 sigma. For GE, a defect could be anything from the misbilling of an NBC advertiser to faulty wiring in locomotives. Four years ago, engineers determined that the company was averaging 35,000 defects per million operations—or about 3.5 sigma. (The higher the sigma, the fewer the errors.) That was a better-than-average showing, but not enough for Welch's restless mind. He became maniacal about hitting his goal of reducing defects to the point where errors would be almost nonexistent; 3.4 defects per million, or 6 sigma.
- Since taking the reins in late 2001, CEO Jeffrey Immelt has overhauled the company's portfolio of businesses, investing more than $40 billion to expand into industries such as water services and security systems, as well as health-care information technologies and the film industry. What's more, Mr. Immelt has also scaled down the company's volatile—once giant—insurance business and focused on GE's consumer- and commercial-lending businesses.
- "General Electric Co., looking to expand its role in health-care information technology, said it agreed to acquire software maker IDX Systems Corp., for $1.2 billion," said Kathryn Kranhold, writing for the *Wall Street Journal* on September 20, 2005. "IDX of Burlington, VT, makes software to track patient records and billing. The acquisition will roughly double GE's health-care information business at a time when health-care leaders and government officials are urging hospitals and physicians to adopt electronic medical records, in lieu of paper charts, to improve patient care and efficiency."

GE Evolution Locomotive

- GE's Evolution locomotive redefines efficiency. The Evolution generates sixteen cylinders' worth of horsepower with only twelve, cuts key emissions by up to 40 percent, and is the first locomotive to meet new EPA emissions standards—all while delivering as much as 10 percent lower lifecycle costs to customers.

Collaborating with customers, GE tested fifty pre-production models for the equivalent of forty-five years of testing in twenty-one months. The outcome? An evolution in performance and growth, with orders placed for more than 1,200 units.

Biodetection

- It takes sixteen to seventy-two hours on average to respond fully to a potential biological threat, with much of that time spent identifying what has been encountered. And yet every second counts in treating those who are exposed. GE's new suite of biodetection products includes an innovative, nanotechnology-based sampler and analyzer that decreases the average response time to minutes while minimizing false alarms.

Such speed can accelerate treatment and help limit a threat's ability to spread. In 2005, GE added these biodetection capabilities to GE StreetLab, a portable device that detects both drugs and explosives. Biodetection is an estimated $500 million segment of the security industry that is growing at better than 10 percent annually.

Cleaner Coal

■ Coal is the world's most abundant fossil fuel, with nearly 200 years of recoverable reserves, compared with about forty years of oil and seventy of natural gas. GE's innovative Cleaner Coal process used breakthrough technology to convert coal into a gas that can fuel a gas turbine.

By removing undesirable compounds such as mercury, particulates, and sulfur before the fuel is burned—and by reducing the production of nitrogen oxides—the process is significantly cleaner than traditional coal plants. GE and Bechtel have begun feasibility studies for the construction of cleaner coal plants with American Electric Power and Cinergy Corporation. According to GE spokesman, "The technology has the potential for annual sales of $200 million in the next few years and $1 billion by the end of the decade."

Desalinization

■ By 2025, nearly 50 percent of the world's population will live in water-stressed areas, according to the World Meteorological Organization, and conservation and reuse alone will not solve global water scarcity. Desalinization removes saline from brackish or seawater and creates fresh water for drinking, irrigation, and industrial use.

GE's unique total system approach helps decrease both the capital investment required and the cost of water production, and it also optimizes energy efficiency. "GE is combating today a significant problem of tomorrow: the global market for desalinization is projected to be $4.5 billion in 2005, escalating to $10 billion by 2014 and then doubling or even tripling by 2025," said a company official in 2005.

SECTOR: **Industrials** ◆ BETA COEFFICIENT: **1.25**
10-YEAR COMPOUND EARNINGS PER SHARE GROWTH: **10.3%**
10-YEAR COMPOUND DIVIDENDS PER SHARE GROWTH: **12.1%**

		2005	**2004**	**2003**	**2002**	**2001**	**2000**	**1999**	**1998**
Revenues (millions)		149,702	151,299	134,187	131,698	125,913	129,853	111,630	100,469
Net income (millions)		16.400	16,593	15,589	14,118	13,684	12,735	10,717	9,296
Earnings per share		1.73	1.59	1.55	1.51	1.41	1.27	1.07	0.93
Dividends per share		.88	.82	.77	.73	.64	.57	0.48	0.42
Price	high	37.3	37.8	32.4	41.8	53.6	60.5	53.2	34.6
	low	32.7	28.9	21.3	21.4	28.5	41.6	31.4	23.0

W. W. Grainger, Inc.

100 Grainger Parkway ❑ Lake Forest, IL 60045 ❑ (847) 535-0881 ❑ Dividend reinvestment plan not available ❑ Web site: *www.grainger.com* ❑ Ticker symbol: GWW ❑ Listed: NYSE ❑ S&P rating: A- ❑ Value Line financial strength rating: A+

Grainger's 1.6 million customers comprise about 8 percent of the businesses and institutions in the United States. While each customer has unique facilities to run and different problems to solve, they share the same needs when maintaining those facilities. Those customers have two main questions: Does Grainger carry the products? If Grainger has it, can I get it from them faster and easier than from anyone else?

Customer purchases typically aren't planned. When something breaks and needs repair, customers may not know where to find the right product. Most facilities maintenance products aren't expensive. What's expensive is the time spent finding and buying them.

Customers work with Grainger in a number of ways that save them time and money. First, they can refer to one of Grainger's many catalogs, the largest of which is 3,818 pages containing 82,431 different products grouped in eleven categories. Grainger also has the industry's leading Web site with more than 200,000 products that customers can access. Once the item is identified, customers can place an order. Trained customer-service professionals can help customers determine which product is right for their needs, connecting them with technical service people or specialists in repair parts. Finally, customers can stop by a branch where experienced employees can help diagnose the problem and find a solution.

No matter how they access the company, customers can choose the way their order gets fulfilled: they can have it shipped to them or they can buy it at a branch, either over the counter or as a will-call. About half of all transactions are picked up at a branch and half are shipped, mainly from the distributions centers. Because the size of the order is typically larger when a customer requests a shipped order, the ratio of sales dollars is roughly two-thirds shipped and one-third picked up.

Company Profile

Grainger is North America's leading broad-line supplier of facilities maintenance products, providing quick and easy access to products through a network of 582 branches, sixteen distribution centers, and the company's award-winning Web sites.

Grainger offers repair parts, specialized product sourcing, and inventory management. Grainger sells principally to industrial and commercial maintenance departments, contractors, and government customers. Sales are made to about 1.3 million customers.

Acklands-Grainger, Inc., is Canada's leading broad-line distributor of industrial, fleet, and safety products. It serves a wide variety of customers through 166 branches and five distribution centers across Canada. It also offers bilingual Web sites and catalogs.

Grainger, S.A. de C.V. is Mexico's leading facilities maintenance supplier, offering customers more than 40,000 products. Local businesses have access through a Spanish-language catalog, either online at *www.grainger.com.mx* or over the counter at one of six branches.

Lab Safety Supply (LSS) is a leading business-to-business direct marketer of safety and other industrial products in the United States and Canada. LSS primarily reaches its customers through the distribution of multiple branded catalogs and other marketing materials distributed to targeted markets. It is a primary supplier for many small and medium-size companies in diverse industries, including manufacturing, government, and agriculture.

Grainger serves customers in eight categories that contain diverse businesses. Here's a snapshot of each:

- Government customers include government offices, schools, and correctional institutions on the state and local levels and office building, many military installations, and the U.S. Postal Service on the federal level.
- Heavy manufacturing customers are usually involved in the textile, lumber, metals, or rubber industries.
- Light manufacturing includes food, pharmaceutical, and electronic customers.
- Transportation customers are involved in the shipbuilding, aerospace, and automotive industries.
- Retail customers include grocery stores, restaurants, and local gas stations.
- Contractor includes contracting firms involved in maintaining and repairing existing facilities.
- Reseller customers offer Grainger products to customers in different markets.
- Commercial customers include hospitals, hotels, and theaters.

Many of Grainger's customers are corporate account customers, primarily *Fortune* 1000 companies that spend more than $5 million annually on facilities maintenance products. Corporate account customers represent about 25 percent of Grainger's total U.S. sales. Both government and corporate account customer groups typically sign multiyear contracts with facilities maintenance products or a specific category of products, such as lighting or safety equipment.

Shortcomings to Bear in Mind

- The company's record of growth is not particularly steady or dependable. In the past ten years, earnings have declined three times. On the other hand, these declines have been modest, not precipitous.
- *Value Line Investment Survey* doesn't speak highly of Grainger. According to Marina Livson, in an assessment dated January 13, 2006, "This good-quality stock is neutrally ranked for Timeliness. Grainger shares also do not stand out as a long-term investment selection despite the likelihood that earnings will expand at a decent rate over the next three to five years. At the recent quotation, this issue's price appreciation potential is below the *Value Line* average."

Reasons to Buy

- On the other hand, *Standard & Poor's Company Reports* takes issue with Ms. Livson's comment. On February 2, 2006, Stewart Scharf said, "We reiterate our STRONG BUY on the stock, based on our view of favorable market trends and valuations. We think the company's strategic initiatives, which include new plants, additional branches, and a new billing system, will enhance the distribution network and aid operating results."
- On March 1, 2006, the *New York Times* tabulated the thinking of a dozen analysts who keep track of Grainger. A half dozen said it was a STRONG BUY; one called it a MODERATE BUY; four said is was a HOLD; and one settled for a MODERATE HOLD.
- The company's record of dividend increases is good. Its dividend has been increased in each of the past ten years, and the payout ratio is quite modest, which means further dividend increases are likely.

- Grainger has a "clean" balance sheet, which means it has no debt. That enables the company to make acquisitions without resorting to bank loans or bond sales.
- In 2005, Acklands-Grainger expanded its branch presence in eastern Canada, consolidating smaller branches in western Canada and designing a new system infrastructure to improve service and reduce costs.
- Through its expanded presence, Web site enhancements, and improved telesales efforts, Grainger aims to gain market share in the $10-billion facilities maintenance market in Mexico.
- LSS continues to pursue strategic acquisitions to expand the number of markets it serves. In 2005 it acquired AW Direct, Inc., a $28-million direct marketer of products to the $3-billion service vehicle accessories market for tow trucks and service stations.
- Customers buy facilities maintenance supplies in four basic ways. First, they buy the things they use every day, like janitorial supplies and light bulbs, looking to purchase these items in bulk for the lowest price. Second, they buy key products that keep their business running, such as a highly specialized motor for a production line. This type of product is often purchased at a premium and requires technical assistance from the manufacturer. Third, they buy simple products that they use frequently in their businesses, like belts for an auto mechanic or air filters for an HVAC (heating, ventilation, and air conditioning) contractor. They're looking for product specialists who can offer uninterrupted availability.

While Grainger provides products in all of these instances, its value to the customer is in helping in the fourth instance: unplanned, infrequently purchased items. A recent study of Grainger customers revealed that 40 percent of their facilities maintenance spending is on such items.

Over the period of a year, these customers purchased on average about 13,000 unique items from Grainger. Of these, 7,000 were purchased only twice. That's almost 75 percent of their purchases. Sourcing these products from many suppliers is very costly. By consolidating with Grainger, customers are able to get a great level of service from one source and save time and money.

SECTOR: **Industrials** ◆ BETA COEFFICIENT: **1.15**
10-YEAR COMPOUND EARNINGS PER SHARE GROWTH: **7.6%**
10-YEAR COMPOUND DIVIDENDS PER SHARE GROWTH: **7.4%**

		2005	2004	2003	2002	2001	2000	1999	1998
Revenues (millions)		5,527	5,050	4,667	4,644	4,754	4,977	4,534	4,341
Net income (millions)		346	277	227	236	211	175	181	239
Earnings per share		3.78	3.02	2.46	2.50	2.23	1.86	1.92	2.44
Dividends per share		0.92	0.79	0.74	0.72	0.70	0.67	0.63	0.59
Price	high	72.4	67.0	53.3	59.4	49.0	56.9	58.1	54.7
	low	51.6	45.0	41.4	39.2	29.5	24.3	36.9	36.4

CONSERVATIVE GROWTH

The Home Depot, Inc.

2455 Paces Ferry Road, N.W. ❑ Atlanta, GA 30339 ❑ (770) 384-2666 ❑ Direct dividend reinvestment plan available (877) 437-4273 ❑ Web site: *www.homedepot.com* ❑ Fiscal year ends Sunday closest to January 31 of following year ❑ Listed: NYSE ❑ Ticker symbol: HD ❑ S&P rating: A+ ❑ Value Line financial strength rating: A++

Home Depot, the world's largest home improvement retailer, and Hughes Supply, Inc., a leading distributor of construction, repair, and maintenance products, announced on January 10, 2006, a definitive agreement for Home Depot to acquire Hughes Supply for an aggregate consideration of $3.47 billion, including the payment of $46.50 per outstanding share and the assumption of $285 million in net debt.

Hughes Supply will be part of The Home Depot Supply, a division that has built a leadership position in a range of markets serving business-to-business customers, such as homebuilders, professional contractors, municipalities, and maintenance professionals. The addition of Hughes Supply more than doubles the size of The Home Depot Supply, with projected 2006 combined sales about $12 billion. Together, the two companies will serve a $410-billion market, addressing the continuum from infrastructure and construction to maintenance, repair, and remodel.

"By acquiring Hughes Supply, a company with a long and established reputation for excellence and service, we continue to execute our growth strategy laid out five years ago to enhance our core retail business, extend our business into adjacent areas, and expand into new markets," said Home Depot CEO Bob Nardelli. "As part of our expand strategy, The Home Depot and Hughes Supply are an ideal strategic and operational fit for each other, and we look forward to welcoming the Hughes Supply team into The Home Depot family."

Founded in 1928, Hughes Supply is one of the nation's largest diversified wholesale distributors of construction, repair, and maintenance-related products, with over 500 locations in forty states. Hughes Supply's leading position in many of the professional markets will add new platforms to The Home Depot Supply portfolio, while also providing additional scale to the division's positions in water works, professional construction supply, and multifamily home maintenance. The combination will deliver purchasing synergies; enhance overall operating effectiveness through scale, simplification, and knowledge transfer; and accelerate growth by providing professional customers exceptional value, convenience, and choice.

"Hughes Supply, our largest acquisition thus far, will accelerate the execution of The Home Depot Supply strategy of repeating in the professional space the same type of market transformation The Home Depot pioneered and executed in the do-it-yourself retail space," said Joe DeAngelo, executive vice president, The Home Depot Supply. "Together, we can better serve local, national, and government customers, offer the broadest range of products and services, and drive synergies by leveraging our combined purchasing power and customer service. We are looking forward to working closely with Tom Morgan, president and CEO of Hughes Supply, and the company's leadership team to establish an integrated professional business of motivated associates that focus on service, growth and shareholder value."

"Home Depot Supply is well-positioned in the marketplace and possesses a wealth of resources to thrive in an industry where there are tremendous opportunities for growth," said Morgan. "This combination is positive for all of our constituents: creating significant shareholder value, increasing the opportunities available to our employees, continuing our commitment to superior service to customers, and building on the foundation of strong vendor relationships. We have accomplished a great deal since our company's founding in 1928 due to the dedication and hard work of our people. Together with Home Depot Supply, we are positioned to achieve even more. We have a bright future ahead."

About Hughes Supply

Headquartered in Orlando, Florida, Hughes Supply, Inc., employs about 9,600 associates and generated revenues of $4.4 billion in its last fiscal year ended January 31, 2005. Hughes Supply is a *Fortune* 500 company and was named the number-one Most Admired Company in America in the Wholesalers: Diversified Industry segment by *Fortune* magazine and was named to the *Forbes* Platinum 400, an exclusive list of the best managed publicly traded companies in America.

Company Profile

Founded in 1978, Home Depot is the world's largest home-improvement retailer and the second-largest domestic retailer.

Home Depot operates more than 2,000 stores, including 1,602 Home Depot units in the United States, 110 Home Depot stores in Canada, and forty-two Home Depot stores in Mexico. The company also operates fifty-four EXPO Design Centers, eleven Home Depot Landscape Supply stores, five Home Depot Supply stores, and two Home Depot Floor stores.

The company's Home Depot stores are full-service warehouse-style outlets offering between 40,000 and 50,000 different kinds of building materials, home-improvement supplies, and lawn-and-garden products to do-it-yourselfers, home-improvement contractors, tradespeople, and building-maintenance professionals.

What's more, Home Depot operates EXPO Design Center stores, which offer products and services essentially related to design and renovation projects; Home Depot Landscape Supply stores, which service landscape professionals and garden enthusiasts with lawn, landscape, and garden products; and Home Depot Supply stores, serving primarily professional customers. Finally, HD operates one Home Depot Floor Store, a test operation that offers only flooring products and installation services.

In addition, Home Depot has its fingers in a number of other pies. For instance, it offers its products through direct marketing channels. Its Maintenance Warehouse unit is a leading direct mail marketer of maintenance, repair, and operations products, doing business with the multifamily housing and lodging facilities management market.

Nor has the company ignored the Internet. In fiscal 2001, HD began selling some 20,000 products online at its e-commerce site, *www.homedepot.com*. Finally, Home Depot also operates several subsidiaries. Atlanta-based Georgia Lighting offers an extensive collection of decorative lighting fixtures and accessories to commercial and retail customers. Apex Supply Company is a wholesale distributor of plumbing, HVAC, appliances, and other related products. More recently, in the fall of 2002, Home Depot acquired three residential construction-flooring businesses, making the company the largest supplier in a $12-billion market segment.

Shortcomings to Bear in Mind

- Interest rates have been low, which has been a spur to home ownership and home-improvement projects, which helps Home Depot. However, interest rates are starting to climb, and mortgage rates are following suit. This is not good news for Home Depot and Lowe's.

- Lowe's push into major U.S. metro areas, where Home Depot has long dominated, could help Lowe's more than Home Depot. What's more, the smaller company's focus on enhancing customer experience through improved store layout, faster service, and brand name appliances and fixtures could be a thorn in the side of Home Depot.

Reasons to Buy

- "Concerns about rising interest rates and pricey gas are nibbling, like termites, at Home Depot stock—but the house that Nardelli rebuilt is as sturdy as ever, as evidenced by recent better-than-expected quarterly results," said Christopher C. Williams, writing for *Barron's* on October 10, 2005. "'We are evolving into a company with multiple platforms for growth,' Chief Executive Officer Robert Nardelli told analysts in an August conference call."

  The *Barron's* writer goes on to say, "With rival Lowe's focused on opening new stores, Home Depot is enjoying an open-field dash in the $410 billion market that, according to analysts, could lift Supply to between 7 percent and 8 percent of sales in three years. Supply 'has reduced HD's cyclicality and will provide HD with a steady stream of cash flows over the foreseeable future,' says Standard & Poor's analyst Michael Souers, who recently raised his rating on the stock to STRONG BUY, betting Hurricane Katrina–related rebuilding will accelerate earnings growth."

- "The Home Depot is extending its business through installation services," said a company official in 2005. "We assist customers with their home-improvement projects every step of the way. Our services revenue, including flooring, window, appliance, and countertop installation, grew 28 percent last year, and we had more than 11,000 installs per weekday. We believe this growth will continue as more customers prefer to have products installed by certified installers.

  "To benefit our retail customers and professional contractors, we expanded our Tool Rental Centers. We opened our 1,000th Tool Rental Center, making us the largest in the industry by number of locations.

  "Currently, we serve professional contractors in a variety of ways. We have more than 1,560 stores featuring contractor services desks, and our Home Depot Supply, Inc., offers facilities maintenance professionals next-day delivery of thousands of maintenance, repair, and operating products from its twenty distribution centers."

- On March 17, 2006, the *New York Times* reported that seven analysts rated Home Depot a STRONG BUY; eight said it was a MODERATE BUY; eight called it a HOLD; and one rated the stock a MODERATE HOLD.

- "These shares are ranked 1 (Highest) for Timeliness," said William W. Lee, writing for *Value Line Investment Survey* on January 6, 2006. The company's strong balance sheet (A++) and history of share repurchases are also notable. This issue offers wide capital gains potential over the coming three to five years."

- Argus Research Company gave Home Depot a BUY rating on January 11, 2006. Christopher Graja, CFA, said, "Our recommendation is based on the company's return on capital, its high financial strength, and its reasonable valuation. We're also encouraged that HD's investments in technology are allowing the company to redeploy staff to help customers."

SECTOR: **Consumer Discretionary** ◆ BETA COEFFICIENT: **1.15**
10-YEAR COMPOUND EARNINGS PER SHARE GROWTH: **23.1%**
10-YEAR COMPOUND DIVIDENDS PER SHARE GROWTH: **25.9%**

		2005	2004	2003	2002	2001	2000	1999	1998
Revenues (millions)		81,511	73,094	64,316	58,247	53,553	45,738	38,434	30,219
Net income (millions)		5,780	5,001	4,304	3,664	3,044	2,581	2,320	1,614
Earnings per share		2.72	2.26	1.88	1.56	1.29	1.10	1.00	.71
Dividends per share		.40	.34	.28	.21	.17	.16	.11	.08
Price	high	44.0	44.3	37.9	52.6	53.7	70.0	69.8	41.3
	low	34.6	32.3	20.1	23.0	30.3	34.7	34.6	18.4

CONSERVATIVE GROWTH

Hormel Foods Corporation

1 Hormel Place ❑ Austin, MN 55912-3680 ❑ (507) 437-5007 ❑ Direct dividend reinvestment plan available (877) 536-3559 ❑ Fiscal year ends on the last Saturday of October ❑ Listed: NYSE ❑ Web site: *www.hormel.com* ❑ Ticker symbol: HRL ❑ S&P rating: A ❑ Value Line financial strength rating: A

"In a fresh assault on bacterial contamination of food, some major meat processors have embraced a high-pressure processing technique that they say makes cold cuts, fruit, and other edibles safer without affecting taste," said Janet Adamy, writing for the *Wall Street Journal* in 2005.

"Hormel Foods Corporation, Perdue Farms, Inc., and others are dunking pre-wrapped foods into tanks of pressurized water—a process that kills salmonella, E. coli, and listeria and allows food makers to add fewer preservatives. It also enables vendors to keep deli ham, pre-cooked chicken strips, and other meats in the food pipeline a lot longer. Hormel says its lunch meat now lasts for as long as 100 days—more than twice as long as before.

"Experts say it may be the most significant bacteria-killing breakthrough in years." The author also said, "Food-borne illnesses kill about 5,000 Americans annually, estimates the Centers for Disease Control and Prevention. Salmonella accounts for about 1.4 million reported cases of food poisoning in the U. S. annually and more than 500 reported deaths. Listeria, less prevalent but deadlier, accounts for another 500 or so reported deaths a year."

Janet Adamy goes on to say, "Last fall, Hormel, of Austin, Minnesota, started pressurizing the deli meat it sells to restaurants and cafeterias. Workers stack slabs of meat in metal cages that they lower into massive cannon-like tanks at the company's Iowa and Minnesota processing plants. The water in the tanks can be made to exert as much as 87,000 pounds per square inch of pressure on the meat—roughly equivalent to that exerted by three elephants standing on a dime.

"The pressure kills bacteria by disrupting cell functions. But the food stays intact because the machines exert the pressure equally on all sides. Hormel says its consumer tasting panels think the pressurized meat tastes better than the non-pressurized type."

Company Profile

Founded by George A. Hormel in 1891 in Austin, Minnesota, Hormel Corporation is a multinational manufacturer of consumer-branded meat and food products, many of which are among the best-known and trusted in the food industry. The company, according to management, "enjoys a strong reputation among consumers, retail grocers, and food service and industrial customers for products highly regarded for quality, taste, nutrition, convenience, and value."

The company's larger subsidiaries include Jennie-O Turkey Store, the nation's largest turkey processor; Vista International Packaging, Inc., a manufacturer of casings; and Hormel Foods International Corporation, which markets Hormel products throughout the world.

The company's business is reported in five segments: Refrigerated Foods (accounting for 51.7 percent of total Hormel Foods sales in 2005 and 29 percent of operating profits), Grocery Products (14.8 percent and 29.4 percent), Jennie-O Turkey Store (20.1 percent and 30.4 percent), Specialty Foods (9.6 percent and 6.1 percent), and All Other (3.8 percent and 5.0 percent).

The company's products include hams, bacon, sausages, franks, canned luncheon meats, stews, chili, hash, meat spreads, shelf-stable microwaveable entrees, salsas, and frozen processed meats.

These selections are sold to retail, foodservice, and wholesale operations under many well-established trademarks that include Black Label, By George, Cure 81, Always Tender, Curemaster, Di Lusso, Dinty Moore, Dubuque, Fast'n Easy, Homeland, Hormel, House of Tsang, Jennie-O-Kid's Kitchen, Layout Pack, Light & Lean 100, Little Sizzlers, May Kitchen, Old Smokehouse, Peloponnese, Range Brand, Rosa Grande, Sandwich Maker, Spam, and Wranglers.

These products are sold in all fifty states by a Hormel Foods sales force assigned to offices in major cities throughout the United States. Their efforts are supplemented by sales brokers and distributors.

The headquarters for Hormel Foods is in Austin, Minnesota, along with the company's Research and Development division and flagship plant. Company facilities that manufacture meat and food products are situated in Iowa, Georgia, Illinois, Wisconsin, Nebraska, Oklahoma, California, and Kansas. In addition, custom manufacturing of selected Hormel Foods products is performed by various companies that adhere to stringent corporate guidelines and quality standards.

Hormel Foods International Corporation (HFIC), a wholly owned subsidiary in Austin, Minnesota, has established a number of joint venture and licensing agreements in countries including Australia, China, Colombia, Costa Rica, Denmark, England, Japan, Korea, Mexico, Panama, the Philippines, Poland, Spain, among others. HFIC exports products to more than forty countries.

Shortcomings to Bear in Mind

- *Value Line Investment Survey* had some negative comments in a report dated November 4, 2005. Justin Hellman said, "Margin pressures will probably keep a lid on the bottom line (profits) in the near term. Profits continue to be squeezed by higher fuel, transportation, and marketing expenses, as well as by an uptick in live hog prices and other input costs. In fact, these expense items are partially offsetting the good sales momentum and masking big margin gains in the turkey operations, which have emerged as the company's primary bottom-line catalyst."
- Prudential Equity Group labeled the stock a NEUTRAL WEIGHT on February 27, 2006. John M. McMillin, CFA, said, "We are raising our estimates modestly, but we have trouble paying this multiple for earnings driven partly by turkey prices that we think will eventually decline with chicken prices as calendar 2006 progresses."

Reasons to Buy

- "We had a strong finish to an outstanding year," said Joel W. Johnson, chairman of the board and CEO (who retired the end of calendar 2005). "All five segments reported year-over-year improved earnings in the fourth quarter, despite an extra week in last year's quarter. The Jennie-O Turkey Store operation led the way with the largest operating-profit improvement compared to last year. A combination of high turkey meat markets, lower feed costs, and improved production efficiencies all contributed to the excellent performance," said Mr. Johnson.

"The Grocery Products segment reported another quarter of improved top and bottom line results driven by double-digit growth from our microwave line of products. Also, lower pork costs, which decrease the cost of goods for items like the SPAM family of products, are beginning to benefit this segment. We expect pork costs to be lower in 2006 compared to 2005. Specialty Foods, a segment we have been building over the last couple of years, reported improved operating profits from strong sales of core products like sugar substitutes," said Mr. Johnson.

"Demand for our value-added protein products that are sold through our Refrigerated Foods segment continues to be good, and the two acquisitions that were made earlier in the year, Lloyd's Barbeque Company and Clougherty Packing Co., are meeting expectations. Within the All Other segment, our International division delivered improved operating profits driven by increased sales of the SPAM family of products, STAGG chili, and better results from our China operations.

"All of our segments have momentum going into the new year," Mr. Johnson said. "We will be adopting FAS 123R, Share-Based Payment, in the first quarter of 2006. This non-cash charge will reduce earnings per share by $.04 in the first quarter," said Mr. Johnson.

- Value-added products are helping the Jennie-O Turkey Store. This segment now offers a broad selection of value-added branded products such as Thanksgiving Tonight oven-roasted turkey breast, which "delivers holiday flavor and everyday convenience."

Demand for value-added turkey items, moreover, is growing faster than that for traditional products.

- Developing new products takes some effort. For Hormel, it means asking customers "about features that make their lives better." A case in point is the award-winning kid-friendly plastic packaging "of our popular Kid's Kitchen brand of microwave-ready foods."
- On March 17, 2006, the *New York Times* examined the opinions of thirteen financial analysts who follow Hormel. One said the stock should be a STRONG BUY; four preferred to label it a MODERATE BUY; seven were in the HOLD camp; and one felt comfortable calling it a MODERATE HOLD.
- "We have a BUY recommendation on the stock, as we believe the current valuation does not fairly reflect our expectations for an improving raw material environment in fiscal 2006, coupled with continued marketing investment in growing value-added product lines," said Joseph Agnese, writing for *Standard & Poor's Company Reports* on November 28, 2005. "We believe the company is well-positioned for longer-term growth, with profitability expected to benefit as higher-margin, value-added products become a larger part of the company's business."
- Under the leadership of Mr. Johnson (a former Kraft executive), Hormel has become a leader in the pork industry by focusing on offering more convenient, value-added products. The company has grown sales and earnings primarily by expanding into higher-margin, value-added meat products.
- The company's recent acquisition of Diamond Crystal Brands Nutritional Products and Cliffdale Farms further strengthened Hormel Foods' brand presence in the fast-growing managed health-care foods business. Hormel Foods is among the top providers in this field, which has strong growth prospects. The sixty-plus population worldwide is expected to double between 2000 and 2025.

SECTOR: **Consumer Staples** ◆ BETA COEFFICIENT: **.70**
10-YEAR COMPOUND EARNINGS PER SHARE GROWTH: **8.7%**
10-YEAR COMPOUND DIVIDENDS PER SHARE GROWTH: **6%**

		2005	2004	2003	2002	2001	2000	1999	1998
Revenues (millions)		5,414	4,780	4,200	3,910	4,124	3,675	3,358	3,261
Net income (millions)		254	232	186	189	182	170	160	122
Earnings per share		1.82	1.65	1.33	1.35	1.30	1.20	1.09	.81
Dividends per share		.52	.45	.42	.39	.37	.35	.33	.32
Price	high	35.4	32.1	27.5	28.2	27.3	21.0	23.1	19.7
	low	29.2	24.9	19.9	20.0	17.0	13.6	15.5	12.8

CONSERVATIVE GROWTH

Illinois Tool Works, Inc.

3600 West Lake Ave. ❑ Glenview, IL 60025-5811 ❑ (847) 657-4104 ❑ Direct dividend reinvestment plan available: (888) 829-7424 ❑ Web site: *www.itwink.com* ❑ Listed: NYSE ❑ Ticker symbol: ITW ❑ S&P rating: A+ ❑ Value Line financial strength rating: A+

On September 30, 2005 Illinois Tool Works Inc. announced that it had signed an agreement with Kirtland Capital Partners to purchase Instron Corporation, a leading worldwide supplier of instruments, software, and services for the testing of materials and structures.

Based in Norwood, Massachusetts, Instron has manufacturing facilities and technical centers in thirteen countries throughout North America, Europe, and Asia. The company's products are grouped in three major categories: material testing, structural testing, and service. In 2005, Instron's revenues were about $240 million.

"With an installed base of more than 70,000 instruments worldwide, Instron's brand name is highly valued and recognized as a leader in material testing," said Illinois Tool's CEO, David B. Speer. "We also are excited about the company's long-term growth potential and geographic span, with revenues almost evenly spread across the Americas, Europe, and Asia."

Company Profile

Illinois Tools's record of sustained quality earnings is the result of a very practical view of the world. The company relies on market penetration—rather than price increases—to fuel operating income growth. What's more, the company's conservative accounting practices serve as a reliable yardstick of financial performance. These results then generate the cash needed to fund ITW's growth—through both investing in core businesses and acquisitions.

Illinois Tool Works designs and produces an array of highly engineered fasteners and components, equipment and consumable systems, and specialty products and equipment for customers around the world. A leading diversified manufacturing company with nearly 100 years of history, ITW's some 650 decentralized business units in forty-five countries employ about 49,000 men and women who are focused on creating value-added products and innovative customer solutions.

Engineered Products in North America

A snapshot of the Engineered Products sector shows the following:

- Product categories: Short lead-time plastic and metal components and fasteners, and specialty products such as adhesives, fluid products, and resealable packaging
- Major businesses: Buildex, CIP, Deltar, Devcon, Drawform, Fastex, Fibre Glass Evercoat, ITW Brands, Minigrip/Zip-Pak, Paslode, Ramset/Red Head, Shakeproof, TACC, Texwipe, Truswal, and Wilsonart
- Primary end markets: Construction, automotive, and general industrial.

Engineered Products International

A snapshot of the Engineered Products International sector shows the following:

- Product categories: Short lead-time plastic and metal components and fasteners, and specialty products such as electronic component packaging
- Major businesses: Bailly Comte, Buildex, Deltar, Fastex, Ispra, James Briggs, Krafft, Meritex, Novadan, Paslode, Pryda, Ramset, Resopal, Rocol, Shakeproof, SPIT, and Wilsonart
- Primary end markets: Construction, automotive, and general industrial

Specialty Systems North America

A snapshot of the Specialty Systems North American segment shows the following:

- Product categories: Longer lead-time machinery and related consumables, and specialty equipment for applications such as food service and industrial finishing
- Major businesses: Acme Packaging, Angleboard, DeVilbiss, Gerrard, Hi-Cone, Hobart, ITW Foils, Miller, Ransburg, Signode, Valeron, Unipac, and Vulcan
- Primary end markets: Food institutional and retail, general industrial, construction, and food and beverage

Specialty Systems International

A snapshot of the Specialty Systems International segment shows the following:

- Product categories: Longer lead-time machinery and related consumables, and specialty equipment for applications such as food service and industrial finishing.
- Major businesses: Auto-Sleeve, Decorative Sleeves, DeVilbiss, Elga, Foster, Gema, Gerrard, Hi-Cone, Hobart, ITW Foils, Mima, Orgapack, Ransburg, Signode, Simco, Strapex, and Tien Tai Electrode
- Primary end markets: General industrial, food institutional and retail, and food and beverage

Leasing and Investments

This segment makes opportunistic investments in the following categories: mortgage entities; leases of telecommunications, aircraft, air traffic control, and other equipment; properties; affordable housing; and a venture capital fund.

Shortcomings to Bear in Mind

- The stock has historically traded at a premium to the market, but based on its exceptional performance over the years, its price would appear to be warranted. With some 650 businesses, Illinois Tool offers investors wide diversification by product line, geographic region, and industry. This helps insulate the company from weakness in any one sector. Over the years, this has resulted in consistent performance despite the cyclicality of the automotive and construction sectors.

Reasons to Buy

- "If you're looking for a diversified manufacturer that could benefit from the expanding economy, go no further than Illinois Tool Works," said Mara Der Hovanesian, writing for *BusinessWeek* on September 12, 2005. "From heavy machinery to plastic drink containers, it makes products at 650 companies worldwide. But the stock has been weak on worries that 49 percent of its revenues come from the real estate and automotive industries—both under pressure. But Robert McCarthy of broker Robert W. Baird, who has a price target of 109 on the stock, now at 84, says ITW's U.S. real estate is mainly commercial construction, less vulnerable than homebuilding to falling prices. Automotive revenues, 18 percent of sales, derive mostly from South America."
- There's no doubt that Illinois Tool Works is a superior company. I think CEO W. James Farrell explains why in this statement: "What drives these results? We believe it is our time-tested 80/20 business planning process. Simply put, our business units—big and small, new and old—focus their attention and resources on the 20 percent of customers and products that generate 80 percent of revenues."

Mr. Farrell goes on to say, "A prime example of the 80/20 process in action is ITW's 1999 merger with Premark International, our largest acquisition to date. As part of the five-year simplification process, we divested businesses that didn't fit strategically—most recently, the Florida Tile business in the fourth quarter of 2003. We increased operating margins from 9 percent in 1999 to 16 percent in 2003, despite the fact that growth in Premark's top product lines decreased nearly 10 percent for the past four years due to weak end markets. Now in the final year of our five-year profitability improvement plan, we are on track to double Premark's operating margin and reach our margin goal of 18 percent by the end of 2004. We expect that financial performance of the Premark businesses will continue to improve, driven by new product development and greater operating efficiencies."

- Acquisitions are likely to remain a key component of the company's growth strategy. ITW has grown steadily over the years largely by taking underperforming businesses and turning them into solid performers.

In most years, the company completes a dozen or two "bottom-up" acquisitions—companies that are directly related to or integrated into an existing product line or market. These transactions, typically representing more than $1 billion in combined revenues, are normally initiated by operating management for both North American and international businesses. According to management, "Looking ahead, our pipeline of potential acquisitions remains full."

A second type of acquisition, which the company undertakes far less frequently, is a major, or "top-down," proposition. These transactions are identified by senior management and represent entirely new businesses for ITW. Illinois Tool completed the largest transaction of this type in its history when ITW merged with Premark in 1999.

This merger brought the company nearly eighty decentralized businesses with products marketed in more than 100 countries. Two principal lines of business—commercial food equipment and laminate product used in construction—represent about $2.5 billion in revenues. Their products have strong brand names such as Hobart, Wilsonart, Traulsen, Vulcan, and Wittco, established market positions, and good distribution channels, and they benefit from value-added engineering—all the things ITW looks for in a successful acquisition.

- On August 2, 2005, Illinois Tool Works and Rippey Corporation announced the acquisition agreement under which ITW would acquire Rippey Corporation. The Rippey Corporation and brand will remain as an independent company under the ITW Contamination Control umbrella, which consists of Texwipe, ALMA, and Chemtronics.

Since 1982, Rippey Corporation has been an innovator in the development and advancement of technologies and products supporting the global microelectronics industry. As one of the leaders in the commercialization of the CMP process for the semiconductor industry, Rippey Corporation was instrumental in the development of CMP slurries, polishing pads, and PVA brush rollers; an enabling set of products that has provided manufacturers with the technical ability to continue the advancement of chip-fabrication processes and technology.

The acquisition will strengthen ITW's product offering in contamination control supplies, allowing it to further penetrate the industry. "We look forward to continuing Rippey's product and technology programs to enhance our existing presence in clean-room manufacturing environments," said Dan Miller, President of ITW Contamination Control.

- The *New York Times* surveyed twenty-two financial analysts on March 25, 2006, and found that nine regarded ITW as a STRONG BUY; seven called it a MODERATE BUY; and six tagged the stock as a HOLD.
- "This timely, high-quality stock retains good long-term appreciation potential," said Mario Ferro, writing for *Value Line Investment Survey* on March 24, 2006. "Moreover, high scores for Financial Strength, Price Stability, and Growth Persistence should appeal to conservative investors seeking diversified exposure to the manufacturing sector."
- On February 13, 2006, Andrew Casey, writing for Prudential Equity Group, said, "ITW continues to generate returns on invested capital well in excess of its cost of capital, and the company appears to have very good potential to achieve double-digit earnings growth. We believe that ITW will continue to demonstrate excellent operating performance that, when combined with improving markets for most businesses, should drive strong balance sheet, cash flow, and earnings growth."

SECTOR: **Industrials** ◆ BETA COEFFICIENT: **1.05**
10-YEAR COMPOUND EARNINGS PER SHARE GROWTH: **12.2%**
10-YEAR COMPOUND DIVIDENDS PER SHARE GROWTH: **14.2%**

		2005	2004	2003	2002	2001	2000	1999	1998	1997
Revenues (millions)		12,922	11,731	10,036	9,468	9,293	9,984	9,333	5,648	5,220
Net income (millions)		1,495	1,340	1,040	932	806	958	841	810	587
Earnings per share		2.60	2.20	1.69	1.51	1.32	1.58	1.50	1.34	1.17
Dividends per share		0.59	0.52	0.47	0.45	0.41	0.38	0.32	0.27	0.23
Price	high	47.3	48.4	42.4	38.9	36.0	34.5	41.0	36.6	30.1
	low	39.3	36.5	27.3	27.5	24.6	24.8	29.0	22.6	18.7

AGGRESSIVE GROWTH

Ingersoll-Rand Company Ltd.

Clarendon House ❑ 2 Church Street ❑ Hamilton HM 11 ❑ Bermuda ❑ (201) 573-3113 ❑ Direct dividend reinvestment plan available (800) 524-4458 ❑ Web site: *www.irco.com* ❑ Ticker symbol: IR ❑ Listed: NYSE ❑ S&P rating: A ❑ Value Line financial strength rating: A++

"Ingersoll-Rand helped carve the faces on Mount Rushmore and build the Hoover Dam," said Christopher C. Williams, writing for *Barron's* on August 1, 2005. "But the company's transformation into a diversified industrial-equipment conglomerate from a cyclical maker of heavy construction equipment arguably ranks as one of its most impressive projects since then. The four-year makeover, which involved $3 billion of asset sales and another $3 billion of acquisitions, has bolstered Ingersoll's bottom and made its shares . . . an attractive long-term bet."

The *Barron's* article goes on. "Industrial-equipment makers such as Ingersoll, Caterpillar, Danaher, and Deere are doing a brisk business in earth-moving equipment, cranes, and the like."

On June 1, 2005, Ingersoll-Rand Company Limited, a leading diversified industrial firm, celebrated the 100-year anniversary of the merger of Ingersoll-Sergeant Drill Company and Rand Drill Company, which formed Ingersoll-Rand.

"Among business mergers of the past century, the combination of the predecessor companies of Ingersoll-Rand 100 years ago today is notable for its enduring success and legacy of achievement," said CEO Herbert L. Henkel. "For the past 100 years, Ingersoll-Rand people and products have contributed mightily to the advancement of global industry and commerce and, as a result, have played a vital role in worldwide economic development and social progress."

In connection with the company's annual general meeting, Mr. Henkel reflected on the company's contributions to industry and society, and prospects for future growth:

- Ingersoll-Rand's legacy: "Our technologies have been instrumental in creating many of the world's most remarkable engineering feats and enduring symbols of economic progress, from Mount Rushmore and the Hoover Dam to the English Channel and China's Three Gorges Dam."
- Ingersoll-Rand's influence: "Every day, we help our customers across a range of industries improve the way they do business while enhancing the well being of the lives of millions of our global citizens. Our innovations safeguard the foods people eat, build the roads and bridges people and goods travel on, power industrial progress, and enhance the security of people and property."
- Ingersoll-Rand's future: "Today, we are a diversified industrial company, bearing little resemblance to the heavy equipment manufacturer of our past. Yet, our passion for unleashing the power of technology to generate economic value continues to define who we are. As we step further into IR's next century, our ability to make progress possible for our customers will continue to propel our market leadership and global growth.

Company Profile

Ingersoll-Rand is a global provider of products, services, and integrated solutions to industries as diverse as transportation, manufacturing, construction, and agriculture. The company brings to bear a 100-year-old heritage of technological innovation to help companies be more productive, efficient, and innovative. Examples include cryogenic refrigeration that preserves agricultural produce worldwide, biometric security systems for airports, corporations, and government facilities, the efficient harnessing of air to drive tools and factories, and versatile, compact vehicles for construction and efficient movement of people and goods. In every line of business, Ingersoll-Rand enables companies and their customers to turn work into progress. The company operates five business segments:

- Climate Control Technologies provides solutions to transport, preserve, store, and display temperature-sensitive products, and includes the market-leading brands of Hussmann® and Thermo King®.
- The Compact Vehicle Technologies segment includes Bobcat® compact equipment and Club Car® golf cars and utility vehicles.
- Construction Technologies includes Ingersoll-Rand® road pavers, compactors, portable power products, and general-purpose construction equipment and attachments.
- Industrial Technologies provides solutions to enhance customers' industrial and energy efficiency and provides equipment and services for compressed air systems, tools, fluid and material handling, and energy generation and conservation.
- Security Technologies includes mechanical and electronic security products, biometric and access-control technologies, and security and scheduling software integration and services.

Shortcomings to Bear in Mind

- According to one analyst, risks "include slower-than-expected growth, due to a rising interest rate environment; a deceleration in capital spending in construction equipment; and rising prices for key inputs, including steel, oil, and natural gas."
- The company paid $1.8 billion for the refrigeration firm Hussmann International in 2000, just as spending by supermarket customers such as Safeway went into a deep freeze. "Our timing was horrible," said Mr. Henkel, though he notes a recent $50-million contract to supply display cases to Wal-Mart could help to revive the unit's revenues.

Reasons to Buy

- On March 17, 2006, the *New York Times* said that four analysts rated Ingersoll-Rand as a STRONG BUY; five called it a MODERATE BUY; and nine put it in the HOLD category.
- "Our recommendation is STRONG BUY, based on what we see as a solid macroeconomic environment, internal productivity improvements, product innovations, and on our expectations of further growth in several key end markets," said John F. Hingher, CFA, writing for *Standard & Poor's Company Reports*, on January 27, 2006. "In our view, recent momentum in capital spending should continue in 2006, particularly in construction equipment: we see this boding well for the company's business prospects."
- On January 29, 2006, Andrew Casey, writing for Prudential Equity Group, gave the stock an OVERWEIGHT rating. He said, "While the company is benefiting from a cyclical recovery in some of its end markets, we continue to believe that the company is improving its ability to translate revenue growth into earnings growth. IR has clearly demonstrated an ability to translate revenue growth into significantly higher operating

profit over the past quarters with strong incremental profit margins."

- "Solid earnings and cash flow streams help to ensure strong finances," said David M. Reimer, writing for *Value Line Investment Survey* on January 27, 2006. "Through decade's end, we expect these two performance measures to increase at a faster rate than sales. The global economy should stay reasonably healthy over that period. Management has done a commendable job in lifting sales volume, setting optimal product prices, integrating acquired assets, and building a sizable recurring revenue base."
- On August 8, 2005, Ingersoll-Rand welcomed the passage of the Energy Policy Act of 2005, which calls for new tax credit incentives for the use of microturbine technologies and expands existing renewable electricity production tax credits.

"In light of the soaring demand for energy along with our nation's aging power infrastructure, it is clear that there has never been a greater need for clean, reliable, energy-efficient technologies," said Chip Bottone, president of Ingersoll-Rand's Energy Systems business. "The Energy Policy Act of 2005 will help foster the implementation of innovative energy technologies, such as microturbines, which are playing a vital role in providing environmentally friendly, cost-effective energy solutions for a wide range of environmental, commercial, and industrial businesses, as well as for public utilities, to help reduce demands on the nation's increasingly overburdened power grids."

Microturbines are compact, integrated systems comprised of a gas turbine engine, a recuperator, and a generator that efficiently convert fuel and heat into high-quality electricity and thermal energy. Provisions in the legislation include a 10-percent investment tax credit for the purchase of microturbine-based power systems and an extension of existing renewable electricity production tax credits utilizing microturbine technologies.

- On August 9, 2005, the company acquired Astrum Gesellschaft fur angewandte Informatik mbH, a company based in Erlangen, Germany, that develops and provides personnel scheduling and work-time management software and services. Founded in 1992, Astrum provides its software, business consulting, installation, and maintenance services to a range of institutional, commercial, and industrial organizations, including health care, manufacturing, hospitality, customer service, and transportation logistics. The company's flagship product, SP-EXPERT, is a customizable personnel scheduling and time-management program that has been installed at more than 800 client facilities, spanning twenty-eight markets in thirty-two countries.

"Astrum represents a strong, strategically important business that will significantly enhance our capabilities in the global market for security solutions and work-force management systems," said CEO Herbert L. Henkel.

- On August 19, 2005, Ingersoll-Rand acquired the assets of Dolphin Electromagnetic Technologies Pvt. Ltd., a Mumbai, India–based provider of electronic solutions for security management.

Dolphin supplies security systems design, engineering, installation, and integration products and services, as well as a unique Internet-based access-control system, SENSE, which enables users to manage security systems for multiple remote sites. The business, which has six offices located throughout India, provides its solutions to organizations in hospitality, financial services, and pharmaceutical markets, as well as to airports, seaports, corporate and retail centers, and a range of other institutional, commercial, and industrial facilities.

SECTOR: **Industrials** ◆ BETA COEFFICIENT: **1.30**
10-YEAR COMPOUND EARNINGS PER SHARE GROWTH: **13.8%**
10-YEAR COMPOUND DIVIDENDS PER SHARE GROWTH: **8.6%**

		2005	2004	2003	2002	2001	2000	1999	1998
Revenues (millions)		10,547	9,394	9,876	8,951	9,682	8,798	7,667	8,292
Net income (millions)		1,054	830	594	367	246	546	565	509
Earnings per share		3.09	2.37	1.72	1.08	.74	1.68	1.65	1.54
Dividends per share		.57	.44	.36	.34	.34	.34	.32	.30
Price	high	44.0	41.5	34.1	27.2	25.2	28.9	36.9	27.0
	low	35.1	29.5	17.3	14.9	15.2	14.8	22.3	17.0

AGGRESSIVE GROWTH

Intel Corporation

2200 Mission College Boulevard ❑ Santa Clara, CA 95054-8119 ❑ (408) 765-1480 ❑ Direct dividend reinvestment plan available (800) 298-0146 ❑ Web site: *www.intel.com* ❑ Listed: Nasdaq ❑ Ticker symbol: INTC ❑ S&P rating: A ❑ Value Line financial strength rating: A++

On November 11, 2004, Intel Corporation, the world's largest chip maker, selected Paul Otellini, age fifty-four, to succeed Craig R. Barrett, age sixty-five, as its new CEO. The promotion of Mr. Otellini was not a surprise, since he has been president and chief operating officer of the company since January 2002.

The new CEO, who studied economics at the University of San Francisco and received an MBA from the University of California, is the first Intel chief executive not formally trained as an engineer. However, he has had plenty of on-the-job training, serving in a vast array of positions in marketing and management in his thirty years with the company. As a result of the move, Craig Barrett became chairman of the board, and Andrew S. Grove, age sixty-eight, stepped aside as chairman to assume the role of senior adviser to the board of directors and senior management.

Since joining Intel in 1974, Paul Otellini has held a number of positions, including general manager of the company's chipset business and later serving as an assistant to then-Intel president Andy Grove. In 1990, Mr. Otellini was named to oversee Intel's microprocessor business as general manager, leading the introduction of the Intel Pentium processor in 1993.

Mr. Otellini served from 1992 to 1998 as executive vice president of sales and marketing, where he focused on extending Intel's global presence into emerging markets. In that role, he initiated Intel's leadership in the development and use of e-commerce for transacting business worldwide. From 1998 to 2002, the new chief executive served as executive vice president and general manager of the Intel Architecture Group, responsible for the company's microprocessor and chipset businesses and strategies. What's more, he took charge of Intel's business groups related to enterprise, mobile, and desktop computing.

Company Profile

It has been more than three decades since Intel introduced the world's first microprocessor, making technology history. The computer revolution that this technology spawned has changed the world. Today, Intel supplies the computing industry with the chips, boards, systems, and software that are the building blocks of computer architecture. These products are used by industry members to create advanced computing systems.

Intel Architecture Platform Products

Microprocessors, also called central processing units (CPUs) or chips, are frequently described as the "brains" of a computer because they control the central processing of data in personal computers (PCs), servers, workstations, and other computers. Intel offers microprocessors optimized for each segment of the computing market. Chipsets perform essential logic functions surrounding the CPU in computers. They also support and extend the graphics, video, and other capabilities of many Intel processor-based systems. Motherboards combine Intel microprocessors and chipsets to form the basic subsystem of a PC or server.

Wireless Communications and Computing Products

These products are component-level hardware and software focusing on digital cellular communications and other applications needing both low-power processing and reprogrammable, retained memory capability (flash memory). These products are used in mobile phones, handheld devices, two-way pagers, and many other products.

Networking and Communications Products

These system-level products consist of hardware, software, and support services for e-commerce data centers and as building blocks for communications access solutions. These products include e-commerce infrastructure appliances; hubs, switches, and routers for Ethernet networks; and computer telephone components. Component-level products include communications silicon components and embedded control chips designed to perform specific functions in networking and communications applications, such as telecommunications, hubs, routers, and wide-area networking. Embedded control chips are also used in laser printers, imaging, storage media, automotive systems, and other applications.

Solutions and Services

These products and services include e-commerce data center services as well as connected peripherals and security access software.

Major Customers

Intel's major customers come primarily from within the computer hardware industry and include the following:

- Original equipment manufacturers (OEMs) of computer systems and peripherals
- PC users who buy Intel's PC enhancements, business communications products, and networking products through reseller, retail, and OEM channels
- Other manufacturers, including makers of a wide range of industrial and telecommunications equipment

Shortcomings to Bear in Mind

- "Intel laced on its running shoes this year to catch the fast Intel-compatible processors sold by Advanced Micro Devices," said Bill Alpert, writing for *Barron's* on October 31, 2005. "Unfortunately Intel keeps tying its laces together. It disclosed another stumble last Monday, as it announced delays in its plans to deliver next-generation chips for the large data-center computers known as servers. Now, it'll be 2007 or later before Intel offers much competition at the high-end of the server market—where computers have four or more processors and where

Advanced Micro (AMD) enjoys a dominant share of high-margin chip sales.

"Some of the delays Intel announced last week concerned Itanium chips, a product line of dwindling importance in comparison to the Xeon, the Intel server processor that's compatible with software written for the Pentium. Intel's Itanium bet allowed AMD to sprint out in 2003 with the first Pentium-compatible server chip, the Opteron. Intel also pushed out Xeon chips last week. 'They were pouring all this investment into Itanium, but it was the wrong idea,' says Randy Allen, the AMD vice president for server products. 'And they are still in a state of upheaval in trying to recover from that mistake.'"

Reasons to Buy

- "Intel Corp. and Micron Technology, Inc., announced plans to form a company to make an increasingly popular variety of memory chip, jointly pledged up to $5.2 billion to create a rival to the Asian companies that now dominate the market," said a *Wall Street Journal* article published on November 22, 2005, by Don Clark and Evan Ramstad. "The joint venture will manufacture chips known as NAND flash memory, and starts with significant support from Apple Computer, Inc. The computer maker, which needs huge numbers of NAND chips for its music players, will pay $250 million each to Intel and Micron for a share of the new venture's output, part of $1.25 billion in pre-payments to NAND suppliers that Apple plans to make over the next three months.

"The maneuvering is the latest evidence of the rising importance of flash chips, particularly the NAND variety that has become popular for storing music, photographs, and video. Unlike some other widely used memory chips, flash memory retains data when electrical current is turned off."

- Nearly two-thirds of the world's fastest supercomputers now use Intel Itanium or Intel Xeon processors, according to the twenty-fourth edition of the TOP500 list, illustrating the growing momentum toward the use of standard Intel components for the most demanding high-performance computing applications. The TOP500 project was started in 1993 to provide a reliable basis for tracking and detecting trends in high-performance computing. Twice a year, a list of the sites operating the 500 most powerful computer systems is assembled and released. Intel architecture–based platforms currently make up 64 percent of the top 500 systems, continuing the surge in the use of Intel processors that accounted for only nineteen systems in 2001—essentially a fifteenfold increase in the past three years.
- On March 17, 2006, the *New York Times* checked with a host of brainy analysts to find out their opinion of Intel. Thirteen rated the stock a STRONG BUY; eight said it was a MODERATE BUY; twenty-one were convinced it was only a HOLD; four called the stock a MODERATE HOLD; and one free thinker said it should be dumped, labeling INTC a SELL.
- *Standard & Poor's Company Reports* also has glad tidings for Intel on January 19, 2006, according to Tom Smith. "We have a BUY recommendation on the shares. We believe INTC's scale-based strengths in R&D, manufacturing, and marketing should help it remain competitive with an increasing number of peers that do not control their own production. We believe Intel's marketing clout has played a significant role in the success of its Centrino mobile platform, and we expect a similar marketing push behind the company's platforms for the digital home and the digital enterprises."
- For business PCs, the company introduced the first Intel Professional Business Platform in 2005. It is based on the recently introduced Intel Pentium 4 processor with Intel's Hyper-Threading Technology 600 sequence, the new Intel 945G Express

Chipset, and the Intel PRO/1000 PM network connection. The new platform brings the company's advanced security, management, and collaboration technologies to mainstream business PCs.

What's more, the company introduced five new Intel Celeron D processors in 2005, with 64-bit computing capability for the value PC segment. Intel now has 64-bit capability available throughout its desktop and server microprocessor product lines.

For servers, Intel introduced an entry-level server platform based on the dual-core Intel Pentium D processor and the Intel E7230 chipset. The first of Intel's dual-core platforms for servers, it supports DDR2 memory, PCI Express 1/0, and software RAID.

Finally, in 2005, the company also introduced two Intel Itanium 2 processors with a 667-MHZ front side bus. Itanium-based server bandwidth can be increased by 65 percent using the new bus architecture, which also supports Intel's forthcoming dual-core Itanium processor, code-named "Montecito."

SECTOR: **Information Technology** ◆ BETA COEFFICIENT: **1.35**
10-YEAR COMPOUND EARNINGS PER SHARE GROWTH: **11.1%**
10-YEAR COMPOUND DIVIDENDS PER SHARE GROWTH: **32%**

		2005	2004	2003	2002	2001	2000	1999	1998
Revenues (millions)		38,826	34,209	30,141	26,764	26,539	33,726	29,389	26,273
Net income (millions)		8,700	7,516	5,641	3,117	1,291	10,535	7,314	6,178
Earnings per share		1.40	1.16	.85	.46	.19	1.51	1.17	.89
Dividends per share		.32	.16	.08	.08	.08	.07	.05	.04
Price	high	28.8	34.6	34.5	36.8	38.6	75.8	44.8	31.6
	low	21.9	19.6	14.9	12.9	19.0	29.8	25.1	16.4

AGGRESSIVE GROWTH

International Business Machines Corporation

New Orchard Road ❑ Armonk, NY 10504 ❑ (800) 426-4968 ❑ Direct dividend reinvestment plan available (888) 421-8860 ❑ Web site: *www.ibm.com* ❑ Listed: NYSE ❑ Ticker symbol: IBM ❑ S&P rating: A- ❑ Value Line financial strength rating: A++

"Some techies say PlayStation 3, which may debut by mid-year (2006) and could end up in 100 million homes in five years, will usher in the next microchip revolution," said Daniel Lyons, writing for *Forbes* magazine on January 30, 2006. "The Sony system owes its prowess to a microprocessor called Cell, which was cooked up by chip wizards at IBM (with help from Sony and Toshiba) at a cost of $400 million over five years."

The Cell chip, based on a design inspired by supercomputers, runs at least ten times as fast as Intel's most powerful Pentium. More important, Cell boasts a staggering fiftyfold advantage in handling graphics-intensive applications that will define the next generation of visual entertainment—blindingly fast and seductively immersive games, virtual-reality romps, wireless downloads, real-time video chat, interactive television shows with multiple endings, and a panoply of new services yet to be dreamed up.

"IBM reckons Cell, potent and versatile, can do a lot more than just play games. It sees a role for it in mobile phones, hand-held video players, high-definition television, car design, and more."

Company Profile

Big Blue is the world's leading provider of computer hardware. IBM makes a broad range of computers, notebooks, mainframes, and network servers. The company also develops software (number two, behind Microsoft) and peripherals. IBM derives about one-third of its revenues from an ever-expanding service arm that is the largest in the world. IBM owns Lotus Development, the software pioneer that makes the Lotus Notes messaging system.

The company's subsidiary, Tivoli Systems, develops tools that manage corporate computer networks. Finally, in an effort to keep up with the times, IBM has been making a concerted effort to obtain a slice of Internet business.

Shortcomings to Bear in Mind

- "Cost cutting helped International Business Machines Corp.'s earning rise 13 percent in the fourth quarter of 2005, despite a decline in revenue led by weak performance in Big Blue's key service arm," said Charles Forelle, writing for the *Wall Street Journal* on January 18, 2006. "After a disappointing first quarter last year [2005] in services, IBM embarked on a major program of layoffs and restructuring that has boosted profitability. But revenue growth has proved elusive. IBM saw a particularly significant fourth-quarter falloff in signings of large-scale outsourcing deals, the bread-and-butter of technology services."
- "International Business Machines Corp. said yesterday that it will freeze the pension plans of some 120,000 employees in the United States, effective at the end of next year, and will offer instead an improved 401(k) plan," said *Washington Post* staff writers on January 6, 2006. "IBM's move is part of a corporate stampede away from traditional pension plans. IBM officials called the change essential to remain competitive with foreign and domestic information-technology rivals."

  Albert B. Crenshaw and Amy Joyce also said, "IBM's action adds the company to a growing list of U.S. employers that have frozen or terminated pension plans to cut costs or, in some cases, to emerge from bankruptcy. Such changes are especially common in industries in which foreign competition is tough, such as steel, or in which new domestic competitors have arisen—such as airlines and high-tech—that do not offer traditional pensions."

Reasons to Buy

- On January 17, 2006, CEO Samuel J. Palmisano said: "IBM finished the year with another strong quarter. We had solid performance in systems, middleware, and business transformation services, which grew over 25 percent for the year. Our cash position remains very strong, and we saw impressive growth in important parts of our business. We continued to make gains in emerging markets and in important sectors such as healthcare and transportation, and our microprocessors are powering the fast-growing home entertainment market.

  "Gross profit margin improvement in the quarter of more than 5 points demonstrates the benefit of our strategic focus on more profitable, high-value segments of the IT industry, as well as our continued emphasis on productivity and global integration. IBM's business model is much more balanced and profitable than it was just a few years ago.

  "IBM is ready for 2006, as we continue to deliver on our agenda of driving innovation and transformation for our clients and their businesses."

■ Argus Research Company rated IBM a BUY on January 18, 2006, with these comments from Wendy Abramowitz:

- "We are maintaining our BUY rating on International Business Machines Corp. with a target price of $100.
- For all of 2005, IBM posted GAAP EPS [earnings per share] of $4.91 and non GAAP [generally accepted accounting principles] EPS of $5.32.
- We have increased our 2006 EPS estimate to $5.74, from $5.64. Our estimate for 2007 is $6.33.
- Our financial strength rating is Medium-High, and our long-term growth rate is 12 percent."

■ "We look for further gains in the new year and through decade's end," said George A. Niemond, writing for *Value Line Investment Survey* on January 13, 2006. "Signings of service contracts continued at a good pace in 2005, with backlogs of $113 billion at the end of the September quarter. Demand also should be strong for the new family of mainframes and the company's mid-range servers and storage products. What's more, sales and profits probably will improve at the micro-electronics segment, owing to growing production of chips used in gaming machines."

■ On January 20, 2006, M. Graham-Hackett, writing for *Standard & Poor's Stock Reports*, said, "We continue to view IBM as relatively well positioned compared with peers for the long run, in light of what we view as the company's broad solutions-focused product portfolio. In addition, we believe IBM has gained market share during the technology spending downturn in services, software, and servers."

■ On March 18, 2006, the *New York Times* surveyed twenty-four financial analysts concerning their assessment of IBM's prospects. Eight ranked the company as a STRONG BUY; eleven said it was a MODERATE BUY; four called it a HOLD; and one thought IBM was a SELL—I'm wondering whether he didn't do his homework.

■ "An IBM-built computer that has topped the list of the world's 500 more powerful supercomputers has widened its lead in the latest ranking released Monday," said Matthew Fordahl, writing for the Associated Press on November 15, 2005. The computer, name Blue Gene/L and deployed at Lawrence Livermore National Laboratory, has doubled its performance to 280.6 trillion calculations per second (teraflops), up from 136.8 teraflops from the list released in June.

"The system, which is used to study the U.S. nuclear stockpile and perform other research, was officially completed this summer after it was doubled in size. Researchers expect it will hold the top spot for the foreseeable future."

■ Although IBM is well-known as the titan of computer hardware, the Global Services division is proving to be the company's star performer. While sales for the rest of Big Blue are barely inching ahead, the services division is averaging more than 10-percent sales growth a year. That has helped pull up overall growth at IBM to about 5 percent per year.

■ Competing against everyone from Electronic Data Systems to Big Four accounting firms to boutique shops offering only Web services, IBM has emerged as the world's largest purveyor of technology services, according to *BusinessWeek*. IBM counsels customers on technology strategy, helps them prepare for mishaps, runs all their computer operations, develops their applications, procures their supplies, trains their employees, and even gets them into the dot-com realm.

■ IBM launched a security system that it expects will set the industry standard for protecting confidential documents such as those used in the growing sector of electronic commerce. Unlike previous security measures that rely on software "fireballs" that filter out unauthorized users of information, IBM has developed a security chip embedded within the computer hardware, which adds additional levels of security. "People from outside your organization can get at your software," said Anne Gardner, general manager of desktop systems for IBM. "People from the outside can't get to your hardware."

SECTOR: **Information Technology** ◆ BETA COEFFICIENT: **1.10**
10-YEAR COMPOUND EARNINGS PER SHARE GROWTH: **5.9%**
10-YEAR COMPOUND DIVIDENDS PER SHARE GROWTH: **12%**

		2005	2004	2003	2002	2001	2000	1999	1998
Revenues (millions)		91,134	96,503	89,131	81,186	83,067	88,396	87,548	81,667
Net income (millions)		7,934	8,448	7,583	3,579	7,495	8,093	7,712	6,328
Earnings per share		4.91	4.39	4.34	3.07	4.69	4.44	4.12	3.29
Dividends per share		.78	.70	.66	.60	.55	.51	.47	.44
Price	high	99.1	100.4	94.5	124.0	124.7	134.9	139.2	95.0
	low	71.8	81.9	73.2	54.0	83.8	80.1	80.9	47.8

CONSERVATIVE GROWTH

Johnson Controls, Inc.

P. O. Box 591 ❑ Milwaukee, WI 53201-0591 ❑ (414) 524-2375 ❑ Direct Dividend reinvestment plan available (877) 602-7397 ❑ Fiscal year ends September 30 ❑ Web site: *www.johnsoncontrols.com* ❑ Listed: NYSE ❑ Ticker symbol: JCI ❑ S&P rating: A+ ❑ Value Line financial strength rating: A

On October 11, 2005, Johnson Controls and Saft announced that the companies had signed a memorandum of understanding to form a joint venture for advanced-technology batteries to accelerate their participation in the hybrid vehicle market.

Saft is a world leader in the design, development and manufacture of advanced technology batteries. It has years of experience in providing nickel metal hydride and lithium ion batteries for high performance applications from its facilities in France and the United States.

The joint venture will develop, manufacture, and sell, on an exclusive basis, nickel metal hydride and lithium ion batteries for hybrid electric vehicles (HEVs) and electric vehicles globally. The companies completed the joint venture agreement in early 2006 but began their joint sales and marketing activities immediately in October of 2005.

Nickel metal hydride is the technology used in hybrid vehicles today and for at least the next several years. Lithium ion technology, however, is expected to become the preferred hybrid battery technology in future years because of its smaller size and increased power.

The new joint venture provides global automakers with expanded sourcing options and production capacity for nickel metal hydride battery systems. Each company is also contributing complementary capabilities to the development and commercialization of next generation lithium ion battery systems.

The two companies have combined their development teams within existing locations and are investing in state-of-the-art manufacturing facilities in line with demand.

The rapid rise in fuel prices has substantially increased the outlook for hybrid vehicle production. This new partnership will support the JV's customers' expedited hybrid programs and help ensure the availability of HEV battery systems with best-in-class technology and reliability.

Johnson Controls, a leader in automotive interior systems and the world's largest manufacturer of automotive batteries, has global development and manufacturing capabilities and has been at the forefront of research and development activities to create advanced batteries for HEVs. In September of 2005, Johnson Controls announced the opening of a new Lithium Ion Development Laboratory in Milwaukee, Wisconsin.

Company Profile

"Our mission to exceed customer expectations gives us the latitude to bring a powerful set of capabilities to our markets and tap into emerging needs and trends," said CEO John M. Barth.

"Throughout our 120-year history, Johnson Controls has continued to transform itself for continued success, and 2005 is no exception. The impending acquisition of York International doubles our market opportunity, and by combining our controls expertise with HVAC equipment, we will be advantaged in the marketplace and have strengthened capabilities to penetrate the huge building services market. In the automotive battery market, where we are the undisputed leader, we extended our leadership from the Americas and Europe to Asia, and are prepared to be a strong player in the hybrid vehicle market.

"In automotive interiors, we established a blueprint for continued profitable growth by accelerating cost reductions, leveraging our global footprint and investing in innovative products. We are responsive to the various strategies of our customers, and Johnson Controls has the financial strength to deliver on their expectations."

Johnson Controls is strengthening its market leadership through the company's businesses:

Interior Experience focuses on the world's largest automakers and responds to their individual requirements, providing innovative interior components and systems that offer best-in-class functions and features. Johnson Controls offering includes seats, instrument panels, cockpits, electronics, door and overhead systems, as well as navigation and entertainment systems, designed to make the driving experience more comfortable, safe, and enjoyable.

Building Efficiency enables facility managers to optimize comfort and energy efficiency in their buildings. As rising fuel prices make energy management even more essential, Johnson Controls helps its customers improve their building systems and reduce their energy-related costs by providing a single source of integrated heating/cooling, lighting, fire and security products and services, supported by the largest building services force in the world.

Power Solutions services both automotive original equipment manufacturers and the battery after-market by providing advanced battery technology, coupled with systems engineering, marketing, and service expertise. Johnson Controls produces more than 80 million lead-acid batteries annually and offers nickel-metal-hydride and lithium-ion battery technology to power hybrid vehicles.

Shortcomings to Bear in Mind

- On January 23, 2006, *Standard & Poor's Company Reports* rated JCI a HOLD.

Efraim Levy had this to say, "Risks to our recommendation and target price include changes in cyclical demand, especially for automotive parts, higher raw material costs, failure to achieve expected acquisition synergies, and pricing pressure from customers."

Reasons to Buy

- On March 25, 2006, the *New York Times* commented on the opinions of eighteen analysts who follow the stock. Four gave Johnson Controls a STRONG BUY rating; eight said it was a MODERATE BUY; and six regarded it a HOLD.
- In early 2006, both *Lehman Brothers* and *Prudential Equity Group* called Johnson Controls an OVERWEIGHT, similar to a BUY.
- On August 24, 2005, Johnson Controls and York International Corporation announced that Johnson Controls would acquire York, a global supplier of heating, ventilating, air-conditioning, and refrigeration (HVAC&R) equipment and services.

York, with estimated sales of nearly $5 billion, has become part of the nearly $6 billion Controls Group of Johnson Controls. The combination of the Controls Group and York is expected to increase Johnson Controls rate of growth in the $200 billion industry for global building environments. Johnson Controls fiscal 2005 consolidated sales from continuing operations, including its automotive seating/interiors and battery businesses, are forecast at nearly $28 billion.

Under the definitive agreement unanimously approved by the Boards of Directors of both companies, Johnson Controls acquired York in an all-cash transaction in which York shareholders received $56.50 for each outstanding share of York common stock. The total value of the acquisition was about $3.2 billion, including the assumption of approximately $800 million of York debt. Johnson Controls financed the transaction with short and long-term borrowings.

The transaction was modestly accretive to Johnson Controls earnings per share in fiscal 2006. Over $275 million of annual synergies, primarily related to cost efficiencies and a lower effective tax rate, are anticipated to be achieved by 2008.

The combination of York, a leader in the manufacturing and service of heating and cooling equipment, with Johnson Controls, an industry leader in the technologies that control that equipment, is a natural and strategic growth opportunity.

As a result of the combination, Johnson Controls will:

- Design and sell integrated controls and HVAC&R equipment.
- Become the largest global provider to the high-margin building services market.
- Capitalize on significant opportunities to supply products and services to each other's customers.

In addition, Johnson Controls global market reach will be enhanced, as the businesses collectively serve customers from over 500 sales and service offices and reach more than 125 countries. The two companies are market leaders in North America and Europe and have complementary operations in the faster growing regions of Asia (especially China), Central Europe, the Middle East, and Latin America.

John M. Barth, CEO of Johnson Controls, said, "Johnson Controls and York are ideal partners, and this transaction will bring significant benefits to shareholders, customers and employees of both companies. By joining with York, a market leader with a strong growth outlook, Johnson Controls is staking out a strategic leadership position in the global building environments industry that will offer significant growth potential and synergies with our Controls business. Importantly, Johnson Controls will maintain its strong financial position, while substantially diversifying our business mix."

He added, "The transaction will enable us to become a single source of integrated products and services that building owners want in order to optimize comfort and energy efficiency. With the addition of York, we will have enhanced HVAC&R, controls, fire and security capabilities. Bringing together our two organizations will also create the largest building services force in the world, strongly positioning us to capture an increased share of the fragmented $130 billion global services market for commercial buildings."

- The company's automotive business is expected to expand in the years ahead as automakers continue outsourcing seating and interior systems in North America and Europe, as well as in emerging global markets.

What's more, the company's development of innovative features and application of new technologies for the automotive interior will strengthen the company's leadership position, as Johnson Controls makes its customers' vehicles more comfortable, convenient, and safe.

- The company engineers, manufactures, and installs control systems that automate a building's heating, ventilating, and air conditioning, as well as its lighting and fire-safety equipment. Its Metasys Facility Management System automates a building's mechanical systems for optimal comfort levels while using the least amount of energy. In addition, it monitors fire sensors and building access, controls lights, tracks equipment maintenance, and helps building managers make better decisions.
- The company's Controls Group does business with more than 7,000 school districts, colleges, and universities as well as over 2,000 healthcare organizations. These customers benefit from performance contracting, a solution that lets them implement needed facility repairs and updates without up-front capital costs. Performance contracting uses a project's energy and operational cost savings to pay its costs over time. For instance, using a performance contract, Grady Health System in Atlanta was able to complete energy efficiency upgrades that will generate $20 million in savings over the next ten years.

SECTOR: **Consumer Discretionary** ◆ BETA COEFFICIENT: **1.00**
10-YEAR COMPOUND EARNINGS PER SHARE GROWTH: **15.9%**
10-YEAR COMPOUND DIVIDENDS PER SHARE GROWTH: **9.9%**

		2005	2004	2003	2002	2001	2000	1999	1998
Revenues (millions)		27,883	25,363	22,646	20,103	18,427	17,155	16,139	12,587
Net Income (millions)		909	818	683	601	542	472	387	303
Earnings per share		4.68	4.24	3.60	3.18	2.56	2.55	2.07	1.63
Dividends per share		1.00	0.85	0.72	0.66	0.62	0.56	0.50	0.46
Price	high	75.2	63.2	58.1	46.6	41.4	32.6	38.4	31.0
	low	52.6	49.6	35.9	34.6	24.1	22.9	24.5	20.3

CONSERVATIVE GROWTH

Johnson & Johnson

One Johnson & Johnson Plaza ❑ New Brunswick, NJ 08933 ❑ (800) 950-5089 ❑ Dividend Reinvestment Plan available (800) 328-9033 ❑ Web site: *www.jnj.com* ❑ Listed: NYSE ❑ Ticker symbol: JNJ ❑ S&P rating: A+ ❑ Value Line financial strength rating: A++

"A newly approved treatment for ulcerative colitis, an inflammatory bowel disorder, could save many patients from surgery and allow others to discontinue drugs with powerful side effects," said Daniel Rosenberg, writing for the *Wall Street Journal* on September 26, 2005. "Last week, the Food and Drug Administration approved Johnson & Johnson's Remicade for treatment of ulcerative colitis, which affects more than 500,000 Americans. Doctors expect the drug to be adopted quickly for patients who don't respond to other treatments.

"Remicade, injected intravenously, is already a $2.1 billion drug for Johnson & Johnson. The company expects ulcerative colitis approval will expand Remicade's patient base by 20 percent. Remicade already has been approved for treating other diseases, including rheumatoid arthritis and Crohn's Disease, another digestive ailment."

The article goes on to say, "Gary Lichtenstein, a professor of medicine at the University of Pennsylvania and director of the Inflammatory Bowel Disease Program at the Hospital of the University of Pennsylvania, said Remicade has allowed patients to stop taking steroids and avoid surgery. 'It's not for use right from the start, but its outstanding when it comes to people who aren't responding to conventional agents,' said Dr. Lichtenstein, who has done consultant work for Johnson & Johnson."

Company Profile

Johnson & Johnson is the largest and most comprehensive health care company in the world, with 2005 sales of more than $50 billion.

JNJ offers a broad line of consumer products, and ethical and over-the-counter drugs, as well as various other medical devices and diagnostic equipment.

The company has a stake in a wide variety of endeavors: anti-infectives, biotechnology, cardiology and circulatory diseases, the central nervous system, diagnostics, gastrointestinals, minimally invasive therapies, nutraceuticals, orthopaedics, pain management, skin care, vision care, women's health and wound care.

Johnson & Johnson has more than 200 operating companies in fifty-four countries, selling some 50,000 products in more than 175 countries.

One of Johnson & Johnson's premier assets is its well-entrenched brand names, which are widely known in the United States as well as abroad. As a marketer, moreover, JNJ's reputation for quality has enabled it to build strong ties to health care providers.

Its international presence includes not only marketing but also production and distribution capability in a vast array of regions outside the United States.

One advantage of JNJ's worldwide organization: markets such as China, Latin America, and Africa offer growth potential for mature product lines.

The company's well-known trade names include Band-Aid adhesive bandages, Tylenol, Stayfree, Carefree and Sure & Natural feminine hygiene products, Mylanta, Pepcid AC, Neutrogena, Johnson's baby powder, shampoo and oil, and Reach toothbrushes.

The company's professional items include ligatures and sutures, mechanical wound closure products, diagnostic products, medical equipment and devices, surgical dressings, surgical apparel and accessories, and disposable contact lenses.

Shortcomings to Bear in Mind

- On January 25, 2006, a *New York Times* article said, "Guidant accepted Boston Scientific's $27 billion offer today after abandoning its deal with Johnson & Johnson, which had let lapse a crucial midnight deadline without raising its bid."

The authors, Andrew Ross Sorkin and Stephanie Saul, went on to say, "After a bruising eight-week takeover contest that has pushed up the price of Guidant well above earlier valuations, Johnson & Johnson will receive a $705 million breakup fee for leaving the field of battle."

The article went on to say, "For Johnson & Johnson, the reasons that Guidant held a strong attraction were apparent as Johnson & Johnson reported fourth-quarter results yesterday. Analysts and investors have questioned what Johnson & Johnson's strategy for growth will be if it fails to win Guidant. Medical devices have become increasingly important to Johnson & Johnson's profit in recent years."

- "Johnson & Johnson reported soft fourth-quarter sales, especially for drugs in the United States, amid pressure from generics, competition for anemia treatments and less tolerance for drug risks," said Scott Hensley, writing for the *Wall Street Journal* on January 25, 2006. "Net income rose 79 percent in the quarter, however, mainly because of lower taxes, compared with the year-earlier period."

Reasons to Buy

- *Value Line Investment Survey* had an upbeat comment on March 3, 2006. George Rho said, "This issue remains a solid choice for long-term investors. Guidant was a setback. J&J's track record and its bulging coffers suggest a significant acquisition is not too far away, though. Meantime, we think this well-diversified healthcare concern offers attractive, risk-adjusted total return potential, even as currently constituted."
- "Johnson & Johnson received FDA approval for the first spinal-disc implant to replace deteriorated natural shock absorbers between the bones of the lower back," said Scott Hensley, writing for the *Wall Street Journal* on October 27, 2004. The article went on to say, "The disc from Johnson & Johnson, New Brunswick, NJ, consists of a plastic core that slides between two metal end plates. The product, called the Charite artificial disc, is expected to cost $11,500, not including the surgery. Other companies, including Medtronic Inc., are working on rival implants." One important benefit of the new disc is that it gives the patient greater flexibility, compared with the traditional surgery, which fuses the bones around the degenerated disc.
- *Standard & Poor's Stock Reports* had this positive comment on November 29, 2005. Robert M. Gold said, "Our recommendation is BUY. We anticipate challenging conditions in the drug unit through 2006. However, we think momentum will persist in the consumer products and medical device and diagnostics segments."
- "We are maintaining our BUY rating on Focus List selection Johnson & Johnson, Inc. With a target price of $80," said Martha Freitag, CFA, writing for *Argus Research Company* on November 1, 2005. "In our view, J&J's diversified healthcare business portfolio has the ability to achieve long-term earnings growth of 11 percent. We expect R&D investments to pay off for the pharmaceuticals and devices pipeline."
- Johnson & Johnson has thirty-four drugs with annual sales exceeding $50 million; twenty-four drugs with annual sales of more than $100 million; and more than 100 drugs that are sold in more than 200 countries.
- A revolutionary liquid bandage that is changing the way consumers treat minor

cuts and scrapes was introduced by Johnson & Johnson Consumer Products Company. Band-Aid Brand Liquid Bandage provides superior protection and optimal healing and stays on hard-to-cover areas like fingers and knuckles.

The bandage creates a clear seal that keeps out water and germs to help prevent infection and promote quick healing. It stays on until it naturally sloughs off as the wound heals. Band-Aid Brand Liquid Bandage contains 2-octyl cyanoacrylate, the same base material found in Dermabond Topical Skin Adhesive, a prescription device marketed by Ethicon Products. Both are manufactured by Closure Medical Corporation. Used by physicians to close wounds and incisions in place of stitches or staples, Dermabond adhesive acts as a barrier that seals out bacteria that can lead to infection.

- On March 25, 2006, the *New York Times* reported what twenty-three leading analysts were saying about Johnson & Johnson. Five called the stock a STRONG BUY; eight said it was a MODERATE BUY; eight rated J&J a HOLD; and two said it was a MODERATE HOLD.

- "No single franchise or brand accounts for even 10 percent of our sales," said Robert J. Darretta, chief financial office of JNJ, in 2005. "And while our portfolio is well-balanced across a breadth of areas, most of our brands, in their own right, are leaders in their particular fields.

"As important as consistent performance is, breadth brings us much more. It actually elevates our performance by promoting synergy and collaboration between Johnson & Johnson units in different areas of health care.

"In categories ranging from wound care adhesives to drug-coated devices, experts in pharmaceuticals, devices, diagnostics, and consumer products are finding that collaboration can lead to breakthroughs. Internal collaborations are occurring with increasing frequency throughout Johnson & Johnson.

"Our breadth gives us a unique line-of-sight and close proximity to many advancing areas in the science and technology of human health. This makes us aware of the opportunities that may be missed by others with a narrower focus in their business. In effect, our broad base lets us pursue medical advances no matter what course they take."

SECTOR: **Health Care** ◆ BETA COEFFICIENT: **.70**
10-YEAR COMPOUND EARNINGS PER SHARE GROWTH: **14.0%**
10-YEAR COMPOUND DIVIDENDS PER SHARE GROWTH: **14.9%**

		2005	2004	2003	2002	2001	2000	1999	1998
Revenues (millions)		50,514	47,348	41,862	36,298	32,317	29,139	27,471	23,657
Net Income (millions)		10,411	8,509	7,197	6,651	5,668	4,800	4,167	3,669
Earnings per share		3.46	2.84	2.40	2.18	1.84	1.63	1.47	1.34
Dividends per share		1.28	1.10	.93	.82	.70	.62	.55	.49
Price	high	70.0	64.2	59.1	65.9	61.0	53.0	53.5	44.9
	low	59.8	49.2	48.0	41.4	40.3	33.1	38.5	31.7

Kellogg Company

One Kellogg Square ❑ P. O. Box 3599 ❑ Battle Creek, MI 49016-3599 ❑ (269) 961-6636 ❑ Dividend reinvestment plan available (877) 910-5385 ❑ Web site: *www.kelloggcompany.com* ❑ Ticker symbol: K ❑ Listed: NYSE ❑ S&P rating: B+ ❑ Value Line financial strength rating: B++

Responding to the growing demand for foods without trans fatty acids, Kellogg Company announced on December 9, 2005, a major investment in new technologies that will make it possible to reduce or eliminate trans fatty acids while also minimizing the saturated fat content of its products.

As a major part of this investment, Kellogg is one of the first food manufacturers to use low linolenic soybean oil through an agreement with Monsanto. Kellogg uses Monsanto's Vistive® low-lin soybean oil to reduce or eliminate trans fatty acids in a number of its products.

"Kellogg has a longstanding history of innovation, which is why we are among the first to invest in low-lin oils to reduce or eliminate trans fatty acids in our products," said David Mackay, president of Kellogg. "Our goal is to make use of the most innovative ingredients possible and to encourage the accelerated production and adoption of low-lin oils so the public will benefit from this breakthrough technology. This is one of many steps we are taking to continue to provide healthy alternatives to consumers."

Kellogg introduced some products reformulated with Vistive® oil in early 2006. However, MacKay noted there currently is a significant shortage of low-lin soybean oil. To meet future demand, soybean farms will need to transform their production methods, and food manufacturers will need to signal their intention to use low-lin soybean varieties. According to the United Soybean Board, in 2005, farmers planted about 200,000 acres of low linolenic soybean varieties. Nearly a million acres are expected to be planted in 2006 to meet the anticipated demand for low-lin soybean oil and significantly more will be necessary to replace the more than five billion pounds of partially hydrogenated soybean oil used annually in the United States. Currently, soybean oil accounts for 80 percent—or 17.5 billion pounds—of the oil consumed in the United States and is the most widely used oil in food production.

To help address the shortage, Kellogg will be working with the Bunge/DuPont Biotech Alliance, another producer of low linolenic soybeans, to increase production of Nutrium®, its low-lin soybean oil, for use in 2007 in addition to increased acreage of the Monsanto Vistive® soybean varieties. Kellogg is also taking a leadership role within the food industry by calling for better cooperation among farmers, seed producers, and food manufacturers to create a reliable supply and efficient delivery of soybean varieties with a low linolenic acid profile. These efforts will focus on enlisting more farmers to grow low-lin soybeans under contract with participating soybean processors, who will crush the grain, refine the oil, and market the oil to food companies. It will also require an investment by other food manufacturers to create the market demand necessary for ramping up larger volumes of low linolenic soybean varieties.

"Kellogg is providing the leadership needed to expedite the commercialization of low-lin soybean varieties," said John Becherer, CEO of the soybean industry's QUALISOY™ initiative and the United Soybean Board. "We have long recognized the value of bringing healthier soybeans to the marketplace. With Kellogg's decision to begin reformulating some of its products with low-lin soybean oil, we now have the impetus for expediting production of soybean enhancements that will better meet the needs of the food industry and ultimately the consumer."

Company Profile

Dating back to 1906, Kellogg is the world's leading producer of cereal and a leading producer of convenience foods, including cookies, crackers, toaster pastries, cereal bars, frozen waffles, meat alternatives, pie crusts, and cones.

The company's brands include Kellogg's®, Keebler®, Pop-Tarts®, Eggo®, Cheez-It®, Nutri-Grain®, Rice Krispies®, Special K®, Murray®, Austin®, Morningstar Farms®, Famous Amos®, Carr's®, Plantation®, and Kashi®.

Kellogg icons such as Tony the Tiger™, Snap! Crackle! Pop!™, and Ernie Keebler™ are among the most recognized characters in advertising. The company's products are manufactured in nineteen countries and marketed in more than 160 countries around the world.

Shortcomings to Bear in Mind

- The company has not been growing at a very impressive pace. In the 1995–2005 period, earnings per share inched ahead from $1.74 to $2.36. Similarly, per-share dividends moved at a snail's pace, from $0.75 to $1.06.

Reasons to Buy

"Our company produces some of the world's best-loved and most trusted brands," said CEO James N. Jenness in 2005. "These brands are also a competitive advantage for us, as they provide a point of differentiation and immediate credibility for our new products. Consequently, we devote a meaningful amount of time and resources to the development of our brand-building programs such as advertising and consumer promotion.

"We have increased our spending on brand building at a double-digit rate and created programs that resonated with consumers. For example, most businesses ran a localized version of the two-week Special K challenge campaign. This program has been successful around the world and has helped build Special K into our largest global brand."

Mr. Jenness goes on to say, "Most of our products, from Special K cereal, to Fruit Twistables fruit snacks, to Rice Krispies Treats, are sold in one or perhaps two adjacent aisles in the store. This focus gives us the advantage of concentrating on related businesses without the distraction of being involved in unrelated businesses in different categories. This focus extends into our international businesses, where we sell only cereal and wholesome snacks. Our share owners do not need us to diversify for them, but they do want us to focus on what we know and on those businesses where we can add value."

Finally, Mr. Jenness said, "Our international infrastructure is another of our competitive advantages. We are fortunate that our founder, W. K. Kellogg, had the foresight to invest in many markets around the world early in the last century. Today, our products are produced in seventeen countries and are enjoyed in more than 180 countries around the world. Despite this scale, our products remain very similar in each of these regions. This has allowed us to spread ideas across our businesses. We encourage our employees to take proven ideas from another company and adapt them to local tastes. For example, the idea for our new All-Bran bars originated in Mexico. From there it was adapted, and the bars have already been introduced into both the United States and Canada."

- Heart disease is the leading cause of death in the United States. Most people who suffer from heart disease are victims of its two principal risk factors: high blood pressure and high cholesterol. In response to this serious health crisis, Kellogg introduced Smart Start Healthy Heart in 2005, the only nationally distributed cereal with oat bran, potassium and low sodium, ingredients that can help lower both blood pressure and cholesterol. The cereal has been certified by the American Heart Association.

Kellogg Company's legacy is based on the philosophy that people can improve their health by eating a balanced diet and exercising. Medical experts agree that there are steps that people can take to reduce the risks of heart disease, including making changes to their diets.

"When it comes to heart health, we can literally take our lives into our own hands by making lifestyle changes that can help lower risks of heart disease," said Andrea Pennington, M.D., author of "The Pennington Plan," noted lifestyle expert and past medical director of the Discovery Health Channel. "Smart Start Healthy Heart is an excellent choice for people trying to take simple and immediate steps to improve their heart health."

Smart Start Healthy Heart joins the Smart Start line-up, including Smart Start Antioxidants and Smart Start Soy Protein, products that offer health benefits for people who are actively seeking ways to improve their health. The new cereal is a combination of lightly sweetened toasted oat bran flakes and crunchy whole grain wheat and oat clusters.

To commemorate the introduction of this new product, Kellogg launched "Simple Start to a Healthy Heart," an initiative aimed at increasing Americans' awareness of the risks of heart disease and actions they can take to address those risks.

- On March 18, 2006, the *New York Times* surveyed twenty-one financial analysts concerning Kellogg. Five rated the company a STRONG BUY; eleven called it a MODERATE BUY; and five thought it no better than a HOLD.
- On January 10, 2006, *Standard & Poor's Stock Reports* viewed Kellogg favorably. Richard Joy said, "We have a BUY recommendation on the shares, reflecting our belief that continued strong brand momentum and operating leverage will lead to improved EPS (*earnings per share*) visibility and consistency. The company is seeing strong growth trends in cereal and snack products, which we think will offset concerns about cost inflation and competitive pressures."
- On February 2, 2006, Prudential Equity Group gave Kellogg an OVERWEIGHT (or BUY) rating. The analyst said, "We see the company as the best fusion of quality and a reasonable valuation in our universe. We are impressed by Kellogg's dedication to taking the long-term view of breakfast and striving for consistency and dependability. Eschewing short-term promotions in favor of longer-term brand-building initiatives, we believe that the company is committed to running its business, not for the next quarter, but for the next decade."
- In the words of a company official, "Latin America remains our fastest-growing region in the world. We have leading category shares, a long-standing presence, and a strong local management team that is adept at managing through the volatility inherent in that region. Per capita consumption of ready-to-eat cereal continues to grow, and yet remains well below levels of developed markets. This points to sustainable category growth. Furthermore, rising disposable income and increased snacking suggests very attractive potential for our small, but rapidly growing wholesome snacks business in key markets of Latin America."
- "Sales of Special K have grown very quickly in recent years," according to a company spokesman. "The brand is now our single largest around the world and accounts

for a significant proportion of our business in some regions. This growth is due to very successful brand-building programs such as the 'lose up to six pounds in two weeks' promotion in the United States. In addition, an active innovation program has spurred sales and has led to new products such as Special K bars and new and exciting types of cereal."

SECTOR: **Consumer Staples** ◆ BETA COEFFICIENT: **.60**
10-YEAR COMPOUND EARNINGS PER SHARE GROWTH: **3.1%**
10-YEAR COMPOUND DIVIDENDS PER SHARE GROWTH: **3.5%**

		2005	2004	2003	2002	2001	2000	1999	1998
Revenues (millions)		10,177	9,614	8,812	8,304	8,853	6,955	6,984	6,762
Net Income (millions)		980.4	890.6	787.1	710.7	532.8	651.9	606.2	548.9
Earnings per share		2.26	2.14	1.92	1.73	1.31	1.61	1.50	1.35
Dividends per share		1.06	1.01	1.01	1.01	1.01	1.00	.96	.92
Price	high	47.0	45.3	38.6	37.0	34.0	32.0	42.3	50.2
	low	42.4	37.0	27.8	29.0	24.3	20.8	30.0	28.5

GROWTH AND INCOME

Kimco Realty Corporation

3333 New Hyde Park Road ❑ Suite 100 ❑ New Hyde Park, NY 11042-0020 ❑ Listed: NYSE ❑ (516) 869-7288 ❑ Direct dividend reinvestment plan available (866) 557-8695 ❑ Web site: *www.kimcorealty.com* ❑ Ticker symbol: KIM ❑ S&P rating: A+ ❑ Value Line financial strength rating: B++

Kimco, the nation's largest publicly traded owner of neighborhood and community shopping centers, concentrates on increasing the cash flow and value of its properties through strategic re-tenanting, redevelopment, renovation, and expansion. It also makes selective acquisitions of neighborhood and community shopping centers that have below-market-rate leases or other cash flow growth potential. Kimco's current management has been developing neighborhood and community shopping centers for more than forty years.

Solid Historical Growth

■ Kimco has recorded an annualized total return on investment of 21.3 percent per annum for shareholders in the thirteen years following its IPO (initial public offering) in 1991.

■ Dividends have grown at a compound annual growth rate of 9.4 percent.

Key Strengths

- Long-term track record
- Strong balance sheet
- Stable, recurring and growing cash flow
- Proven, cycle-tested and value-added management
- A solid, rising dividend
- Buying capacity
- Specialized expertise
- Increasing market share

Company Profile

Kimco Realty Corporation is the largest publicly traded real estate investment trust (REIT) that owns and operates a portfolio of neighborhood and community shopping centers (measured by gross leasable area). The company has specialized in the acquisition, development, and management of well-located shopping centers with strong growth potential. Kimco has interests in 720 properties, comprised of 645 shopping centers, 32 retail store leases, and other projects totaling about 104 million square feet of leasable area in forty-two states, Canada, and Mexico.

Since incorporating in 1966, Kimco has specialized in the acquisition, development and management of well-located centers with strong growth potential. Self-administered and self-managed, the company's focus is to increase the cash flow and enhance the value of its shopping center properties through strategic re-tenanting, redevelopment, renovation, and expansion, and to make selective acquisitions of neighborhood and community shopping centers that have below market-rate leases or other cash flow growth potential.

A substantial portion of KIM's income consists of rent received under long-term leases, most of which provide for the payment of fixed-base rents and a pro rata share of various expenses. Many of the leases also provide for the payment of additional rent as a percentage of gross sales.

KIM's neighborhood and community shopping center properties are designed to attract local area customers and typically are anchored by a supermarket, discount department store or drugstore, offering day-to-day necessities rather than high-priced luxury items. Among the company's major tenants are Kmart, Wal-Mart, Kohl's, and TJX Companies.

Kimco's core strategy is to acquire older shopping centers carrying below-market rents. This space is then re-leased at much higher rates.

Funds From Operations

REITs are not valued by earnings per share (EPS), but rather by funds from operations (FFO) per share. FFO is calculated by adding net income and depreciation expense and then subtracting profits from the sale of assets. If a REIT pays out 90 percent or more of its taxable income in dividends, it is exempt from paying federal income taxes. FFO per share is in excess of net income because depreciation is added in. This means that a REIT such as Kimco pays out only about 66 percent of its FFO in dividends, with the balance of 34 percent available for acquisitions and improving existing properties.

Shortcomings to Bear in Mind

- On March 1, 2006, *Standard & Poor's Company Reports* had a HOLD rating on Kimco. R. McMillan said, "Given KIM's position as one of the largest owners and operators of neighborhood and community shopping centers in the United States, its broad array of established relationships, and growing retailer demand for space, we believe that KIM will generate above-average rent growth, and that it deserves to trade at a premium." On a negative note, the analyst concluded with, "We think that after recent share gains, the multiple and valuation on the share are likely to contract."
- As most investors are aware, dividends under a new federal tax law, are now taxed at a maximum rate of 15 percent. Unfortunately, this does not apply to dividends paid out by REITS. That's because real estate investment trusts generally don't pay corporate income tax.

Reasons to Buy

- On March 18, 2006, the *New York Times* poled eighteen analysts and found that five regarded the stock as a STRONG BUY; eight called it a MODERATE BUY; and five said it was a HOLD.
- "Kimco's diversity will likely lead to above-average profit gains out to 2008–2010," said Sigourney B. Romaine,

writing for *Value Line Investment Survey* on January 20, 2006. "Pension funds will probably increase their investments in real estate, which should lead to a growing pool of capital for Kimco."

■ In the past ten years (1995–2005), the company's earnings per share climbed from $0.45 to $1.52, a compound annual growth rate of 12.9 percent, a rather spectacular performance for an income stock. In the same span, dividends per share advanced from $0.49 to $1.27, a growth rate of 10 percent, or far above the rate of inflation. What's more, the dividend was boosted every year during that ten-year period.

■ Kimco's customers include some of the strongest and most rapidly growing chains in the United States, such as Costco, Home Depot, Circuit City, Best Buy, Wal-Mart, Value City, Target, and Kohl's.

■ Nearly all of the company's revenue is contractual. This means that even when a retailer's sales slump, it does not change the rent they must pay to Kimco under the lease agreement or the value of the company's real estate.

■ Knowledge of local markets and trends is crucial to success in the real estate sector. Kimco's decentralized asset management staff—situated in such cities as New York, Los Angeles, Chicago, Philadelphia, Dallas, Phoenix, Tampa, Charlotte, and Dayton–provides knowledge of real estate developments that are analyzed by professionals on the scene.

■ Kimco's success comes not by accident but as the careful product of business principles that have remained firmly in place since the company was founded in the 1950s. The company invests in properties that are undervalued assets, where management knows it will be able to capitalize on the margin between the price at which it can buy the property and the price at which it can lease it. The average rent on properties in Kimco's portfolio remains below the market, providing the company with significant upside potential.

■ To continue growing its portfolio and income, the company has established the following special-purpose ventures to acquire properties:

- The Kimco Retail Opportunity Portfolio, a joint venture with GE Capital Real Estate.
- Kimco formed a joint venture with RioCan real estate investment trust, Canada's largest REIT.
- In 1999, the company launched the Kimco Income REIT, which currently consists of more than $1.2 billion in assets.
- Anticipating new opportunities when the REIT Modernization Act became effective on January 1, 2001, Kimco formed Kimco Developers Inc. (KDI) which operates as a merchant developer. The new legislation allows KDI to immediately sell properties and capture the developer's profit for future reinvestment. KDI generated income of $8.1 million in its first full year of operations.

■ "While you can't be sure whether REITs or rental properties will perform better, REITs do have one undeniable advantage: They are a lot less risky," said Jonathan Clements in the *Wall Street Journal*. Mr. Clements's columns appear nearly every Wednesday in the *Wall Street Journal*. I urge you to read them. His thinking and advice are nearly always exceptionally sound.

His piece on REITs went on to say, "If you invest in rental property, you are banking a ton of money on a single piece of real estate, rather than getting the diversification of REITs. Moreover, there is the problem of collecting those rent checks. 'If it takes you three months to evict a tenant, you're out a quarter of that year's return,' according to Chris Mayer, a finance professor at New York's Columbia Business School.

"The bottom line: Owning REITs is not only less risky, but it also involves far fewer hassles. 'It's easy to describe the difference,' between REITs and rental properties, says William Bernstein, an investment adviser in North Bend, Oregon. 'One is an investment and the other is a job. It also depends on your tolerance for broken toilet bowls and psychopathic tenants.'"

SECTOR: **Financials** ◆ BETA COEFFICIENT: **0.75**
10-YEAR COMPOUND EARNINGS PER SHARE GROWTH: **12.9%**
10-YEAR COMPOUND DIVIDENDS PER SHARE GROWTH: **10%**

		2005	2004	2003	2002	2001	2000	1999	1998
Rental Income (millions)		522	517	480	433	450	459	434	339
Net Income (millions)		363	282	244	226	236	205	177	122
Earnings per share		1.52	1.19	1.11	1.08	1.03	0.96	0.82	0.68
Funds from Operations		2.00	1.78	1.62	1.52	1.50	1.35	1.21	1.01
Dividends per share		1.27	1.16	1.10	1.05	0.98	0.91	0.80	0.83
Price	high	33.4	29.6	22.9	16.9	17.0	14.9	13.6	13.9
	low	25.9	19.8	15.1	13.0	13.6	10.9	10.3	11.1

GROWTH AND INCOME

Kinder Morgan Energy Partners, L.P.

500 Dallas Street ❑ Houston, TX 77002 ❑ (713) 369-9490 ❑ Dividend reinvestment program not available ❑ Web site: *www.kindermorgan.com* ❑ Listed: NYSE ❑ Ticker symbol: KMP ❑ S&P rating: Not rated ❑ Value Line financial strength rating: B+

"For a company to be successful and deliver value to its unit holders (*similar to stockholders)*, it has to have a solid strategy, and it must effectively executive that strategy," said Richard D. Kinder, CEO of Kinder Morgan Energy Partners. "At KMP, our game plan has remained simple and consistent. We own and operate quality midstream energy assets—primarily pipelines and terminals—that are core to the energy infrastructure of growing markets and which produce stable, fee-based cash flow and earnings.

"We run these assets in the most efficient, cost-effective way possible. We increase distributions due to internal volume growth, small rate increases, expansions, and extensions, and we maximize the tax efficiency of the master limited partnership (MLP) structure.

"In addition to a proven strategy, we have employed a philosophy that I believe helps us stand apart from many other companies. I receive $1 a year in salary—with no bonuses, no stock options, and no restricted stock.

"We limit base salaries for the rest of senior management to $200,000 a year, well below industry medians. To keep corporate costs low, we don't own corporate jets or fly first class. However, we don't cut corners in the field where maintenance and safety are key to our operations. We avoid businesses with direct commodity exposure as much as possible and hedge to minimize the risk when there is exposure. And, we have a very hands-on senior management team that pays great attention to detail."

Company Profile

The Kinder Morgan family of companies includes three separate entities—Kinder Morgan, Inc. (now a private company, no longer traded on the NYSE), Kinder Morgan Energy Partners, L.P. (KMP), and Kinder Morgan Management, LLC (KMR).

Kinder Morgan, Inc. is one of the largest energy transportation and storage companies in America, operating more than 35,000 miles of natural gas and products pipelines and approximately 135 terminals. Kinder Morgan, Inc. owns the general partner interest of Kinder Morgan Energy Partners, L.P., the largest publicly traded pipeline limited partnership in the United States in terms of market capitalization.

The general partner of KMP is owned by Kinder Morgan, Inc. (NYSE: KMI), one of the largest energy transportation and storage companies in America. Combined, the two companies have an enterprise value of approximately $26 billion.

Kinder Morgan Management, LLC (KMR) is a limited liability company, and its only significant assets are the partnership units it owns in KMP. KMR shareholders receive distributions in the form of additional shares equivalent in value to the cash distributions received by KMP common unit holders.

Kinder Morgan Energy Partners, L. P.

Kinder Morgan Energy Partners, L.P. (KMP) is America's largest pipeline master limited partnership.

- KMP is the largest independent owner/operator of products pipelines in the country, transporting more than two million barrels a day of gasoline, jet fuel, diesel fuel, and natural gas liquids through more than 10,000 miles of pipelines. The Products Pipelines segment also includes associated storage terminals and transmix processing facilities.
- KMP's Natural Gas pipelines consist of approximately 15,000 miles of pipelines, with the capacity to transport 7.8 billion cubic feet per day (Bcf/d), and include gathering, treating, processing, and storage facilities.
- KMP is the largest independent terminals operator in the United States. The company's nearly 100 terminals handle over 60 million tons of coal and other dry-bulk materials annually and have a liquids storage capacity of approximately 60 million barrels for petroleum products and chemicals.
- KMP is the largest CO2 marketer and transporter in the country. Kinder Morgan CO2 Company, L.P. owns the most prolific source of carbon dioxide in the world and transports and markets more than 1 billion cubic feet per day of CO2 through its network of more than 1,100 miles of pipelines. CO2 is used for enhanced oil recovery projects.
- KMP's strategy is to focus on the development and acquisition of stable, fee-based midstream energy assets and to take advantage of the low-cost capital advantages of the master limited partnership structure. Since 1997, KMP's enterprise value (market equity plus debt) has grown from $325 million to about $13 billion.

Shortcomings to Bear in Mind

- Mr. Kinder pointed out some risks to owning Kinder Morgan Energy Partners. "Let me assure you that all companies have challenges, and KMP is not an exception. We operate more than 25,000 miles of pipelines and more than ninety terminals across America, which exposes us to both regulatory and operational risks. On the regulatory front, we face possible challenges to our rate structure, including the long-running case involving our Pacific system (part of our Products Pipelines businesses segment), along with increasingly stringent and expensive safety regulations. On the operational side, mishaps are possible regardless of how careful we are or how much money we spend to keep our pipelines and terminals operating safely."

Reasons to Buy

- Our recommendation is STRONG BUY, based on total return (*dividends plus stock action*)," said Royal Shepard, CFA, writing for *Standard & Poor's Company Reports* on January 24, 2006. "The units offer an attractive opportunity to invest in one of the largest and most diversified owners of midstream energy assets, in our opinion. We think KMP continues to demonstrate a distinctive ability to identify attractive investment opportunities."
- On March 1, 2006, Lehman Brothers gave the stock an OVERWEIGHT rating.
- On January 27, 2006, Argus Research Company had a BUY rating on Kinder Morgan. Tom Mongan, CFA, said, "Management has extensive experience in the energy industry. The team has been effective in developing markets while improving margins and strengthening the capital structure. The tax advantage of the limited partnership structure has particular appeal to retail investors, because it avoids the double taxation of the typical corporation."
- "Kinder Morgan Energy Partners is widely recognized for having one of the premier management teams in the energy industry. Consequently, its annual presentation is typically the most well-attended conference among MLPs by a wide margin."

This comment was made on January 19, 2005 by analysts with the brokerage firm of Lehman Brothers who rated the stock OVERWEIGHT, which is their term for BUY.

- On March 29, 2006, the *New York Times* checked with fifteen analysts who follow KMP on a regular basis. Four tagged the stock a STRONG BUY; two felt it deserved a MODERATE BUY rating; eight preferred to call it a HOLD; and one analyst labeled it a MODERATE HOLD. In general, securities analysts are a brainy bunch with good credentials and a high IQ. Even so, they rarely agree on anything.
- On December 26, 2005, *Fortune Magazine* had a favorable comment on the company. "Investing in energy stocks seemed like a no-brainer this year, at least until oil fell from $70 to $56 a barrel and dragged down the likes of Chevron and ExxonMobil with it. As the nation's largest independent oil-pipeline company, Kinder Morgan is one energy company whose fortunes aren't directly tied to short-term fluctuations in commodity prices. Whether oil is $70 a barrel or $40 a barrel, crude oil and gasoline still need to be transported from point A to point B."
- The company is aggressive on the acquisition front. Here are its moves in 2004: Southeast Terminals (purchased for $129 million between February and November); Kaston Pipeline ($111 million in August); Global Materials (October for $80 million); TransColorado (November for 275 million); Cochin (November for $11.8 million); and Novolog ($15.8 million in December).

In 2005, Kinder Morgan purchased Terasen Inc. of Vancouver, British Columbia, for $3.1 billion in stock and cash, and the assumption of $2.5 billion in debt. According to a 2005 article in the *Wall Street Journal,* "Houston-based Kinder Morgan operates 35,000 miles of natural gas and oil pipelines across North America, as well as 145 storage terminals. But it lacks a significant presence in Alberta, Canada, where the world's second-largest deposit of oil rests locked in gritty oil-sands deposits.

"Extracting and processing the molasses-like bitumen—the type of crude oil found in oil sands—is much more expensive than producing and refining conventional crude oil, but recent high oil prices have made bitumen projects more viable. Analysts have estimated that oil-sands developments need long-term prices averaging $25 a barrel or more for benchmark crude—well below recent levels."

SECTOR: **Energy** ◆ BETA COEFFICIENT: **0.70**
10-YEAR COMPOUND EARNINGS PER SHARE GROWTH: **13.9%**
10-YEAR COMPOUND DIVIDENDS PER SHARE GROWTH: **17.2%**

		2005	2004	2003	2002	2001	2000	1999	1998
Revenues (millions)		9,787	7,933	6,624	4,237	2,947	816	429	323
Net Income (millions)		552	832	694	608	442	278	175	117
Earnings per share		1.58	2.22	2.00	1.96	1.56	1.34	1.22	1.05
Dividends per share		3.07	2.81	2.58	2.36	2.08	1.60	1.39	1.19
Price	high	55.2	49.1	38.9	39.7	28.9	22.8	19.1	20.6
	low	42.8	37.6	33.5	23.9	25.2	18.2	16.5	14.3

GROWTH AND INCOME

Eli Lilly and Company

Lilly Corporate Center ❑ Indianapolis, IN 46285 ❑ (317) 651-4545 ❑ Direct Dividend reinvestment plan available (800) 833-8699 ❑ Web site: *www.lilly.com* ❑ Listed: NYSE ❑ Ticker symbol: LLY ❑ S&P rating: B+ ❑ Value Line financial strength rating: A++

"Driven by rising demand from an aging population, sales and profits at many health-care companies are projected to grow at double digit rates," according to an article in *Fortune* magazine on December 26, 2005. "Unlike most pharma giants, Lilly has been churning out new drugs at a rapid pace. The Indianapolis company has launched a half-dozen new products in the past two years, including depression drug Cymbalta, which could become a $2 billion blockbuster. Lilly has the best growth prospects in the industry, say Morningstar analyst Tom D'Amore, who forecasts that sales will increase 7 percent a year through 2008.

"Give credit to Lilly's top-notch drug-discovery program. CEO Sidney Taurel pours 20 percent of the firm's $14-billion in annual sales back into research and development, while the industry averages 16 percent. 'You don't find many companies that are spending 20 percent of their sales on R&D,' says Doug Eby, co-manger of the Torray fund, which generated 11 percent annualized returns in the past ten years. 'They're taking a lot of cash and investing it in future growth.'"

Company Profile

Eli Lilly is one of the world's foremost health-care companies. With a solid dedication to R&D, Lilly is a leader in the development of ethical drugs—those available on prescription.

It is well-known for such drugs as Prozac (to treat depression); a number of antibiotics such as Ceclor, Vancocin, Keflex, and Lorabid; insulin and other diabetic care items. Some of its other important drugs include Gemzar (to treat cancer of the lung and pancreas); Evista (to treat and prevent osteoporosis); ReoPro (a drug used to prevent adverse side effects from angioplasty procedures); Zyprexa, its largest-selling drug (a breakthrough treatment for schizophrenia and bipolar disorder); Dobutrex (for congestive heart failure); Axid (a medication that reduces excess stomach acid); and Sarafem (for the treatment of premenstrual dysphoric disorder).

At the end of 2005, these were the company's leading products and their contribution to Lilly's sales that year:

Zyprexa	$4.4198 billion
Gemzar	1.3345 "
Humalog	1.1977 "
Evista	1.0361 "
Humulin	1.0047 "
Cymbalta	679.7 million
Strattera	552.1 "
Actos	493.0 "
Prozac family	453.4 "
Humatrope	414.4 "
Forteo	389.3 "

Highlights of 2005

- Sales increased 6 percent, to $14.645 billion.
- Newer products contributed $2.58 billion to 2005 sales and accounted for 18 percent of total sales, compared with 11 percent of sales in 2004.
- Net income and earnings per share were $1.98 billion and $1.81, respectively, compared with 2004 net income of $1.81 billion and $1.66.

The company is a pioneer in the treatment of diabetes and sells several versions of insulin. Sales of insulin products are well over $2 billion a year.

Lilly also has a stake in animal health and agricultural products.

Like most drug companies, Lilly is active abroad and does business in 120 countries.

Shortcomings to Bear in Mind

- "The Food and Drug Administration and Eli Lilly Co. said Monday the antidepressant Cymbalta shouldn't be used in patients with liver problems because the drug might worsen the underlying condition," said Jennifer Corbett Dooren, writing for the *Wall Street Journal* on October 18, 2005. "The drug was first approved in August 2004 to treat major depressive disorders. It's also approved to treat nerve pain associated with diabetes. More than one million patients have been prescribed Cymbalta, Lilly said.

"The label had already warned of the possibility of liver injury, and doctors were told not to prescribe the drug to patients 'with substantial alcohol use' because the clinical studies showed that some patients experienced liver damage when they consumed Cymbalta and alcohol."

- On January 20, 2006, *Value Line Investment Survey* gave the stock a neutral rating. George Rho said, "We don't have a strong position on these shares. Lilly has a decent pipeline and minimal concerns about patent expires. On the flip side, the company's stock is only neutrally ranked, and the current valuation leaves average three- to five-year capital appreciation potential."

Reasons to Buy

- Lilly is one of a few pharmaceutical companies free of patent concerns—at least until 2011. By contrast, Pfizer and Merck, whose big-selling anticholesterol products face patent expiration.
- On February 7, 2006, Argus Research Company had a BUY rating on Lilly. Analyst Martha Freitag, CFA, had this to say: "The company is rolling out new products and has promising drugs in the pipeline. In our view, earnings growth has the potential to accelerate as newer drugs become a larger portion of revenues and as expense controls leverage the bottom line."

■ On March 3, 2006, the *New York Times* asked twenty-six financial analysts to give their assessment of Lilly. Five called the stock a STRONG BUY; six said it was a MODERATE BUY; fourteen gave it a HOLD rating; and one said it was a MODERATE HOLD. There were no SELLS.

■ On March 13, 2006, *Standard & Poor's Stock Reports* said, "We think LLY is the best-positioned stock in the large-capitalization pharmaceutical sector, based on our view of its solid portfolio of growth products, no significant patent expirations until 2011, and its robust R&D pipeline." Analyst H. B. Saftlas also said, "The company expects nine newer drugs to account for about 18 percent of 2005 sales and 25 percent in 2006."

■ As the developer of the first insulin product and one of the world's major suppliers of insulin, Lilly has long been a global leader in the field. But diabetes, which affects more than 100 million people worldwide, continues to cause severe long-term complications, suffering, lost productivity, and death.

For many patients with this disease, diabetes is also inconvenient. Diabetics have to check their blood glucose several times a day. They may have to give themselves one or more shots of insulin or risk severe complications, such as blindness, poor circulation, amputations, and nerve damage.

Lilly believes that it has an answer that gives patients with diabetes a better quality of life—and a good deal more convenience. Humalog acts faster than traditional insulin to control blood-glucose levels. Patients take it right before a meal, compared with 30 to 45 minutes before with current products. Humalog provides them with more freedom, better health, and fewer complications.

■ On February 7, 2006, a Lilly spokesman said, "Different people with diabetes have different insulin needs, and today Eli Lilly and Company announced the launch of a new pre-mixed insulin, Humalog® 50 percent insulin lispro protamine suspension, 50% insulin lispro. Humalog Mix50/50 is for use in patients with diabetes to control high blood sugar and is available in an easy-to-use pen delivery device.

Humalog Mix50/50 is designed to provide blood sugar control between meals but also includes a higher percentage of rapid-acting insulin for people with diabetes who need more insulin control at mealtime. The Humalog component starts lowering blood sugar more quickly than regular human insulin, allowing for convenient dosing immediately before a meal (within fifteen minutes). Humalog Mix50/50 provides doctors with an additional tool to help their patients better manage blood sugar after meals."

■ The first new drug for ADHD in decades, Strattera is regarded as a potentially important drug because most of the existing treatments for the condition, such as Ritalin, generic methylphenidate, Adderall and Concerta, are stimulants and can interfere with sleep and appetite. What's more, they are controlled substances under federal law. This means that access to them is restricted, and that their sales are monitored by the federal Drug Enforcement Administration.

ADHD, which can be a subjective diagnosis, is believed to be widely over-diagnosed and yet quite prevalent. It is estimated that as many as 5 percent to 10 percent of school-age children have the affliction. ADHD involves compulsive behavior, great difficulty concentrating, and often a learning disability. Finally, the condition tends to be inherited and can continue into adulthood.

■ In 2005, Mr. Taurel said, "Lilly's outstanding R&D productivity continues to set us apart from the crowd. We have several exciting compounds now in late-stage development, including two potential breakthroughs in diabetes, one in cancer, and a drug we believe could become best-in-class in the treatment of acute coronary syndrome and stroke. At the other end of the pipeline, our scientists posted a record-breaking year in 2004. The output from discovery research has increased by more than 50 percent, and the number of candidates entering human clinical studies has increased by more than 40 percent, compared to the average for the four prior years."

SECTOR: **Health Care** ◆ BETA COEFFICIENT: **.80**
10-YEAR COMPOUND EARNINGS PER SHARE GROWTH: **4.6%**
10-YEAR COMPOUND DIVIDENDS PER SHARE GROWTH: **8.7%**

		2005	2004	2003	2002	2001	2000	1999	1998
Revenues (millions)		14,645	13,858	12,583	11,077	11,543	10,953	10,003	9,237
Net Income (millions)		1,980	1,810	2,561	2,763	3,014	2,905	2,721	2,098
Earnings per share		1.81	1.66	2.37	2.55	2.76	2.65	2.28	1.94
Dividends per share		1.52	1.42	1.34	1.24	1.12	1.04	.92	.80
Price	high	61.0	76.9	73.9	81.1	95.0	109.0	97.8	91.3
	low	49.5	50.3	52.8	43.8	70.0	54.0	60.6	57.7

AGGRESSIVE GROWTH

Lockheed Martin Corporation

6801 Rockledge Drive ❑ Bethesda, MD 20817-1877 ❑ (800) 568-9758 ❑ Direct dividend reinvestment plan is available (877) 498-8861 ❑ Web site: *www.lockheedmartin*.com ❑ Listed: NYSE ❑ Ticker symbol: LMT ❑ S&P rating: B- ❑ Value Line financial strength rating: A

On January 17, 2006, the U.S. Navy awarded Lockheed Martin $57.3 million under an existing contract for Aegis Combat System engineering, installation, and integration on new U.S. Navy destroyers, as well as upgrades for Aegis-equipped cruisers and destroyers already in service.

As the U.S. Navy's Combat System Engineering Agent for Aegis, Lockheed Martin is responsible for the shipboard installation, integration, and test of all combat system elements on all Aegis-equipped ships in the U.S. Navy, as well as those in Japan, Spain, Norway, and Korea.

"The complexity of putting a front-line warship to sea relies on teamwork among the Navy, the shipbuilder and Lockheed Martin as the combat system engineering agent," said Orlando Carvalho, vice president and general manager of Lockheed Martin's business in Moorestown. "The Aegis reputation for working every time, all the time is built on a very deliberate process of designing, building and testing at multiple phases during the initial construction, shipboard installation and lifetime support."

The Aegis Weapon System is the world's premier naval surface weapon system. It seamlessly integrates the AN/SPY-1D(V) radar, the Mk 41 Vertical Launching System and a family of U.S. Navy missiles with its own command and control system. Aegis also is at the heart of the U.S. Navy's sea-based missile defense system, one of the first operationally-deployed components of the nation's layered network of defenses against cruise and ballistic missile attack.

Currently, Aegis Weapon Systems are on seventy-six cruisers, destroyers, and frigates in service around the world. Plans are currently underway to install the system on more than twenty-five additional U.S. and international destroyers and frigates.

Company Profile

Lockheed Martin is a world leader in systems integration and the development of air and missile defense systems and technologies, including the first operational hit-to-kill missile defense system. It also has considerable experience in missile design and production, infrared seekers, command and control, battle management, and communications, precision pointing and tracking optics, as well as radar and signal processing. The company makes significant contributions to all major U.S. missile defense systems and participates in several global missile defense partnerships.

Headquartered in Bethesda, Maryland, Lockheed Martin employs about 135,000 people worldwide and is principally engaged in the research, design, development, manufacture, and integration of advanced technology systems, products, and services.

Shortcomings to Bear in Mind

- Lockheed does not have a very impressive dividend record. Until recently, the dividend was not raised on an annual basis and sometimes stayed the same for two or three years. Worst of all, the dividend was slashed from $0.88 in 1999 to $0.44 the following year. On the plus side, the dividend was raised to $0.58 in 2003 from $0.44 in 2002 and was raised in a big jump to $0.91 in 2004 and is now $1.20.

Reasons to Buy

- On January 4, 2006, the company announced that it had achieved key milestones on several critical missile defense programs during 2005 and was the only company to lead the development of new technology for boost-, midcourse- and terminal-phase systems.

"Our friends and allies rely on us to provide products and innovative solutions that enable them to find and engage missile threats with speed, precision and confidence," said David Kier, Lockheed Martin vice president and managing director of missile defense. "Ultimately, these products allow us not only to protect the brave men and women of the armed forces, but also civilian populations and high-value assets throughout the world."

Lockheed Martin is the leader of the Missile Defense Agency's (MDA) Command and Control, Battle Management and Communications (C2BMC) program team, the first ever integrated battle management system for global missile defense. It also serves as the system integrator on other missile defense programs such as THAAD™, MEADS, and the Aegis Combat System. Lockheed Martin systems provide forces with a layered defense capability against ballistic missile threats, contributing to nearly every U.S. air-, land-, sea-, and space-based missile defense initiative.

- On January 11, 2006, Lockheed Martin opened its new Post Production Center of Excellence for the U.S. Navy's Fleet Ballistic Missile (FBM) program at Cape Canaveral Air Force Station. The center consolidates the company's FBM work performed in Florida for the U.S. Navy's Trident ballistic missile submarine fleet.

Lockheed Martin Space Systems FBM operations previously conducted in other facilities at Cape Canaveral and in the surrounding Cocoa Beach area have been consolidated in the center—a renovated 70,000-square-foot government-owned facility. Lockheed Martin employs 185 people at the new center, which is responsible for a variety of

Trident II D5 FBM deployed systems support activities.

"Cape Canaveral long has been an important location for the Navy's FBM program," said Tom Marsh, executive vice president, Lockheed Martin Space Systems Company, who led today's ceremony to mark the opening of the center. "By centralizing our Florida staff, we are achieving greater cost effectiveness while ensuring continued close support to our Navy customers," he noted.

"Our new Post Production Center of Excellence enables us to further increase the focus of our Eastern Range resources on supporting the Navy in its important and highly successful FBM program," said George Olson, director of test and support systems engineering, Lockheed Martin.

Lockheed Martin is the Navy's prime strategic missile contractor and missile system program manager. Approximately 2,500 Lockheed Martin Space Systems employees, principally in California, Georgia, Florida, Washington, and Utah, provide direct support to the design, development, production, test, and operation of the Trident strategic weapon systems.

■ On January 5, 2006, the U.S. Navy has awarded Lockheed Martin a $10.6 million contract modification to integrate a sensor array capable of three-dimensional (3D) obstacle detection and classification, VHF communication and 3D bathymetry into the Navy's Advanced Development Unmanned Undersea Vehicle (ADUUV).

Under the contract modification, Lockheed Martin will provide engineering and manufacturing services to integrate the Littoral Precision Underwater Mapping Array (LPUMA) sensor into the ADUUV. LPUMA is produced by the Applied Research Laboratory in Austin, Texas. The first phase includes the design, fabrication, and testing of a single ADUUV to support risk reduction for the Mission Reconfigurable UUV (MRUUV). Work will be performed in Riviera Beach, Florida, and is expected to be completed by September 2007.

"The LPUMA sensor suite advances the revolutionary ADUUV's capabilities to the next level," said Jim Weitzel, Lockheed Martin Maritime Systems & Sensors vice president for Mission and Unmanned Systems. "By adding the next generation of precise 3D bathymetry and object detection and classification capabilities, the ADUUV can more rapidly change its mission from mine countermeasures to intelligence and surveillance, and expand to other missions as well."

The ADUUV, the first underwater vehicle of its kind designed to accommodate interchangeable modular payloads that can be swapped out for various missions, is the precursor to the revolutionary MRUUV. The system will be deployed from a Virginia-class or Los Angeles-class submarine for launch and recovery through submarine torpedo tubes and be used for clandestine intelligence collection, surveillance, and reconnaissance, as well as mine reconnaissance and tactical ocean survey.

■ On January 4, 2006, Lockheed Martin received a contract from Navantia to work with Navantia and other Spanish industrial leaders to develop the advanced combat system for the SpanishareArmada's new S-80A diesel submarines.

"This new submarine program will establish Spain as a premier developer of modern diesel electric submarine technology," said Charles A. Cantello, vice president of Sensors & Advanced Programs for Lockheed Martin Maritime Systems & Sensors. "Lockheed Martin's open systems architecture model provides flexibility for content while maximizing Spanish industrial participation in the combat system development and integration."

Lockheed Martin has decades of experience working with the United States and international navies to provide high-performance, affordable, and supportable combat systems for nuclear and diesel electric submarines. Its combat system approach focuses on an open systems architecture that leverages commercial technology proven on the U.S. Navy's Virginia, Seawolf, and Los Angeles class submarines. Lockheed Martin's proven open architecture approach enables navies to easily upgrade systems with new commercial technology and capabilities for enhanced performance and greatly reduced cost over the life of the platform.

For the S-80A submarines, Lockheed Martin will support a Spanish industry design and develop the core combat system as a technology partner using experience gained over the last forty years from combat systems design and development work for the U.S. Navy's submarine force.

■ On March 18, 2006, the *New York Times* surveyed the opinions of twenty-two leading analysts. Eight said Lockheed was a STRONG BUY, four called it a MODERATE BUY, while ten analysts said it was a HOLD. There were no SELL decisions.

SECTOR: **Industrials** ◆ BETA COEFFICIENT: **.70**
10-YEAR COMPOUND EARNINGS PER SHARE GROWTH: **5.1%**
10-YEAR COMPOUND DIVIDENDS PER SHARE GROWTH: **4.6%**

		2005	**2004**	**2003**	**2002**	**2001**	**2000**	**1999**	**1998**
Revenues (millions)		37,213	35,526	31,824	26,578	23,990	25,329	25,530	26,266
Net Income (millions)		1,825	1,266	1,053	533	694	432	575	1,184
Earnings per share		4.10	2.83	2.34	1.11	1.60	1.07	1.41	3.11
Dividends per share		1.05	0.91	0.58	0.44	0.44	0.44	0.88	0.82
Price	high	65.5	61.8	58.9	71.5	53.0	37.6	46.0	58.9
	low	52.5	43.1	40.6	45.8	31.0	16.5	16.4	41.0

CONSERVATIVE GROWTH

Lowe's Companies, Inc.

1000 Lowe's Boulevard ❑ Mooresville, NC 28117 ❑ (704) 758-2033 ❑ Direct dividend reinvestment plan available (877) 282-1174 ❑ Web site: *www.lowes.com* ❑ Fiscal year ends Friday closest to January 31 of following year ❑ Listed: NYSE ❑ Ticker symbol: LOW ❑ S&P rating: A+ ❑ Value Line financial strength rating: A+

"Our strength and the strength of the home improvement industry is driven by several factors—demographic, social, and economic," said former CEO Robert L. Tillman in fiscal 2005. Mr. Tillman retired January 28, 2005, having been with Lowe's since 1962.

"First, evolving demographic trends have been, and will continue to be, a positive force for Lowe's and the home improvement industry. The large and influential baby boomer population is entering the peak second-home buying age and is driving a robust second-home market. Driven by this phenomenon, some estimates suggest that 150,000 second homes will be built each year for the rest of the decade. In addition, boomers are more time-strapped than ever and are looking for solutions that make their life easier. One-stop shopping convenience and an ever-expanding array of installation services makes Lowe's a destination to fulfill their needs.

"Generation Xers are in the family formation years and are looking for ways to improve their home's function, safety and appeal. This generation values information that allows it to initiate projects. Our informative signage and knowledgeable employees provide just the resources they're looking for at Lowe's.

"And finally, Echo boomers, also known as generation Y, are focused on customization, frequently changing everything from paint to flooring to faucets to fulfill their desire for distinctiveness. This generation is coming of age and is actively influencing many purchasing decisions today. With over 40,000 products in stock, and hundreds of thousands more available by special order, these customers can find the products they're looking for at Lowe's.

"The second force driving home improvement is diversity. Home ownership among minorities is growing rapidly in the United States, driven by an immigrant population focused on the American dream of owning a home. Harvard's Joint Center for Housing Studies reports that in 2001, minorities accounted for 32 percent of first-time home buyers, and from 1995 to 2001, they represented 60 percent of the increase in households. Bilingual employees, targeted advertising and unique products to meet varying cultural styles are just a few of the things we're doing at Lowe's to meet the needs of our increasingly diverse customers.

"Third, Americans are more focused than ever on the comfort, security and warmth that home has to offer. As Americans deal with a tumultuous geopolitical environment and the stress of everyday life, keeping in touch with the people who matter remains a top priority, and they're doing it at home. Home ownership was a cornerstone of the American dream long before interest rates began their latest decline in 2001, and we believe a focus on the home and home improvement will remain part of the American dream even as interest rates rise.

"Finally, a growing trend in home improvement is a phenomenon know as 'serial remodeling.' Inspired by innovation and energy efficiency, home improvement is being driven less by need and more by a sense of style and a desire to trade up. Many customers are repainting their rooms with the most fashionable new color or replacing a working washer and dryer with new, more efficient appliances that clean better while using less water and energy. Innovation is the key, and we encourage vendors to ensure they are providing inspirational products for our customers."

Company Profile

Lowe's Companies, Inc. is the second-largest domestic retailer of home-improvement products serving the do-it-yourself and commercial business customers. (Home Depot is number one.) Capitalizing on a growing number of U.S. households (about 100 million) the company has expanded from 15 stores in 1962. During the third quarter of 2005, Lowe's opened 33 new stores and temporarily closed one store impacted by hurricane Katrina. As of October 28, 2005, Lowe's operated 1,170 stores in forty-nine states representing 133.0 million square feet of retail selling space, a 13.1 percent increase over the prior year.

The company sells more than 40,000 home-improvement products, including plumbing and electrical products, tools, building materials, hardware, outdoor hard lines, appliances, lumber, nursery and gardening products, millwork, paint, sundries, cabinets, and furniture. Lowe's has often been listed as one of the "100 Best Companies to Work for in America."

The company obtains its products from about 6,500 merchandise vendors from around the globe. In most instances, Lowe's deals directly with foreign manufacturers, rather than third-party importers.

To maintain appropriate inventory levels in stores and to enhance efficiency and distribution, Lowe's operates six highly automated, efficient, state-of-the-art regional distribution centers (RDCs). RDCs are strategically situated in North Carolina, Georgia, Ohio, Indiana, Pennsylvania, Washington, and Texas.

In 2000, the company broke ground in Findlay, Ohio on an $80-million regional distribution center. Completed in October of 2001, the 1.25-million-square-foot facility employs 500 people and supplies products to some 100 stores throughout the lower Great Lakes region.

Lowe's serves both retail and commercial business customers. Retail customers are primarily do-it-yourself homeowners and others buying for personal and family use. Commercial business customers include building contractors, repair and remodeling contractors, electricians, landscapers, painters, plumbers, and commercial building maintenance professionals.

During 1999, Lowe's acquired Eagle Hardware & Garden, a thirty-six-store chain of home-improvement and garden centers in the West. The acquisition accelerated Lowe's West Coast expansion and provided a stepping stone for the company into ten new states and a number of key metropolitan markets.

In recent years, the company has been transforming its store base from a chain of small stores into a chain of home-improvement warehouses. The current prototype store (the largest in the industry) has 150,000 square feet of sales floor and another 35,000 dedicated to lawn and garden products. The company is in the midst of its most aggressive expansion in company history. Lowe's is investing $2 billion a year and opening more than one store each week.

Shortcomings to Bear in Mind

- Interest rates have been low, which has been a spur to home ownership and home improvement projects, which helps Lowe's. If interest rates start to climb and mortgage rates follow suit, that ball game may come to an end.
- By competing head-to-head with Home Depot in large metropolitan markets, Lowe's may find it has a formidable rival to deal with, compared to the small cities where it made its fast-growth reputation.

Reasons to Buy

- On November 14, 2005, CEO Robert A. Niblock said, "Our performance, highlighted by positive comparable store sales in all of our 20 product categories and 19 of our 21 geographic regions, is a clear indication that consumers continue to invest in products and projects to maintain, enhance and improve their homes even in light of concerns about the impact of rising gasoline and home heating costs."

  Mr. Niblock goes on to say, "Continued investments in our business coupled with our culture of customer service have strengthened our competitive position, and we're confident Lowe's has the flexibility to adapt to changes in the marketplace to continue to deliver solid results.

  "Our employees provided exceptional service in a quarter marked by the distractions of three major hurricanes," Mr. Niblock added. "Our focus on serving our customers' needs with innovative and differentiated products and services allows us to continue to capture market share in a fragmented home improvement industry."
- On March 1, 2006, the *New York Times* checked with twenty-two analysts who keep tabs on Lowe's. Five rated the stock a STRONG BUY; seven called it a MODERATE BUY; and the other ten preferred the HOLD category.

- On March 3, 2006, *Standard & Poor's Company Reports* had these favorable comments, according to Michael Sauers, "We have a BUY recommendation on the shares. We believe LOW will be one of the primary beneficiaries of the rebuilding efforts from the devastation caused by Hurricane Katrina. We also expect other positive demographic data, such as the aging of homes, and the increased net worth of baby boomers to help LOW more than offset any slowdown in housing turnover in 2006. In addition, we think the company's expansion plans into Canada will provide another growth avenue as domestic saturation slowly takes place."
- On January 27, 2006, Argus Research Company gave the stock a BUY rating. Christopher Graja, CFA, said, "Lowe's is continuing its aggressive store-building campaign and plans to add 150–160 stores in each of the next two fiscal years."
- To enhance its extensive line of national brands, such as DeWalt, Armstrong, American Standard, Olympic, Owens Corning, Sylvania, Harbor Breeze and Delta, the company is teaming up with vendors to offer preferred brands exclusive to Lowe's. These include Laura Ashley, Sta-Green, Troy-Bilt, Alexander Julian, among others.

In categories where preferred brands are not available, Lowe's has created its own brands, including Kobalt tools, Reliabilt doors and windows, and Top Choice lumber.

SECTOR: **Consumer Discretionary** ◆ BETA COEFFICIENT: **1.05**
10-YEAR COMPOUND EARNINGS PER SHARE GROWTH: **26.1%**
10-YEAR COMPOUND DIVIDENDS PER SHARE GROWTH: **16%**

		2005	2004	2003	2002	2001	2000	1999	1998
Revenues (millions)		43,243	36,464	30,838	26,491	22,111	18,779	15,905	12,245
Net Income (millions)		2,770	2,176	1,844	1,471	1,023	810	673	482
Earnings per share		1.73	1.36	1.18	.95	.65	.53	.45	.34
Dividends per share		.11	.08	.06	.04	.04	.03	.03	.03
Price	high	34.9	30.3	30.2	25.0	24.5	16.8	16.6	13.1
	low	25.4	23.0	16.7	16.3	11.0	8.6	10.8	5.4

GROWTH AND INCOME

Lubrizol Corporation

29400 Lakeland Boulevard ❑ Wickliffe, OH 44092-2298 ❑ (440) 347-1252 ❑ Dividend reinvestment plan available (877) 573-3998 ❑ Web site: *www.lubrizol.com* ❑ Listed: NYSE ❑ Ticker symbol: LZ ❑ S&P rating: B ❑ Value Line financial strength rating: B+

"Lubrizol isn't very glamorous," said Harlan S. Byrne, writing for *Barron's* on October 17, 2005. "The 77-year-old Midwestern company's products—lubricant additives and specialty chemicals—aren't exactly head-turners. But, over the past year, Lubrizol's shares have performed like stars."

The *Barron's* article goes on to say, "The company is a global leader in supplying products that improve the quality, and extend the life, of engine oils, gasoline and diesel fuels—an important mission as the price of petroleum goes up. It also markets chemicals used in consumer items, such as hair and skin-care products, pharmaceuticals and plastics."

Mr. Byrne also said, "Lubrizol has more than one-third of the global market for lubricant additives and is particularly strong among transportation customers. In fact, Lubrizol's products and those of some of its competitors just might be too good. About a decade ago, demand from transportation outfits hit a wall because the modern additives were lasting too long. That's when the company began diversifying into specialty chemicals, through small acquisitions. Specialty chemicals now account for 44 percent of its business."

Company Profile

Lubrizol is an innovative specialty chemical company that produces and supplies technologies that improve the quality and performance of its customers' products in the global transportation, industrial, and consumer markets. Lubrizol's business is founded on technical leadership. "Innovation provides opportunities for us in growth markets as well as advantages over our competitors," according to the Lubrizol 10-K publication (*which is published annually by all public companies and is far more extensive and detailed than an annual report).* From a base of some 2,800 patents, "we use our product development and formulation expertise to sustain our leading market positions and fuel our future growth. We create additives, ingredients, resins and compounds that enhance the performance, quality and value of our customers' products, while minimizing their environmental impact. Our products are used in a broad range of applications, and are sold into stable markets such as those for engine oils, specialty driveline lubricants and metalworking fluids, as well as higher growth markets such as personal care and pharmaceutical products and performance coatings and inks. Our specialty materials products are also used in a variety of industries, including construction, sporting goods, medical products, and automotive industries."

The 10-K goes on to say, "We are an industry leader in many of the markets in which our product lines compete. We also produce products with well recognized brands names, such as Anglamol (gear oil additives), Carbopol (acrylic thickeners for personal care products), Estane (thermoplastic polyurethane) and TempRite (chlorinated polyvinyl chloride resins and compounds used in plumbing, industrial, and fire-sprinkler systems).

"We are geographically diverse, with an extensive global manufacturing, supply chain, technical and commercial infrastructure. We operate facilities in twenty-seven countries, including production facilities in twenty-one countries and laboratories in nine countries, in key regions around the world through the efforts of about 7,800 employees. Including the 2004 acquisition of Noveon International for the period ended December 31, 2004, we derived about 48 percent of our consolidated total revenues from North America, 28 percent from Europe, 18 percent from the Asia/Pacific and the Middle East regions and 6 percent from Latin America. We sell our products in more than 100 countries."

Shortcomings to Bear in Mind

- The company's balance sheet is quite leveraged as a result of considerable borrowing to finance the acquisition of Noveon International in 2004. Debt now equals or exceeds shareholders' equity. This makes it difficult for the company to make future acquisitions, until this debt has been reduced.
- Looking at the company's record of earnings and dividend increases would not convince you that this is a classic growth stock. In 1995, Lubrizol earned $2.08 per share and reached a high of $2.68 in 1997, before falling off to a low of $1.55 in 1998.

Nor have dividends made much headway in that span, rising very modestly from $0.93 in 1995 to a high of $1.04 in 1998, at which level they still remain.

Reasons to Buy

■ On March 25, 2006, the *New York Times* reported that one financial analyst rated Lubrizol a STRONG BUY. However, four said it was a MODERATE BUY; two called it a HOLD; and one rated it a MODERATE HOLD.

■ William W. Lee, writing for *Value Line Investment Survey* on March 17, 2006, had this comment: "These shares are ranked 4 (Below Average) for Timeliness. The rising cost of raw materials has hampered Lubrizol's earnings performance, despite price hikes. However, with crude oil prices expected to moderate, margins should improve. Also, additional acquisitions down the pipeline will likely enhance the company's long-term potential. The stock's three- to five-year total return (*dividends plus price appreciation*) possibilities may interest patient investors."

■ *Standard & Poor's Company Reports* also looked favorably on LZ, according to Richard O'Reilly, CFA, on December 28, 2005. He said, "Our BUY recommendation is based on total return. The mid-2004 acquisition of Noveon greatly changed LZ's business mix, reducing its low-growth lubricant additives business to about 55 percent of sales, and expanding its industrial and consumer-related product lines."

■ The company's 10-K had this comment on its acquisition of Noveon. "On June 3, 2004, we acquired Noveon International, a leading global producer and marketer of technologically advanced specialty materials and chemicals used in the industrial and consumer markets.

"With the acquisition of Noveon International, we have accelerated our program to attain a substantial presence in the personal care and coatings markets by adding a number of higher-growth, industry-leading products under highly recognizable brand names, including Carbopol, to our already strong portfolio of lubricant and fuel additive products and consumer product ingredients.

"Additionally, Noveon International has a number of industry-leading specialty materials businesses, including TempRite chlorinated polyvinyl chloride and Estane thermoplastic polyurethane, that generate strong cash flow. We believe that the Noveon International acquisition meets the core tenets of our stated strategy to:

- Maintain technology leadership.
- Apply our formulation expertise to extend applications into new markets.
- Expand the global breadth of our businesses."

"The lubricant additives segment is the leading global supplier of additives for transportation and industrial lubricant," said the company's recent 10-K publication. "We pioneered the development of lubricant additives over seventy-five years ago and continue to maintain leadership in the $5-billion industry today. Our customers rely on our products to improve the performance and lifespan of critical components, such as engines, transmissions and gear drives for cars, trucks, buses, off-highway equipment, marine engines, and industrial applications."

The 10-K also said, "Our products serve to increase cost-effectiveness by reducing friction and heat, resisting oxidation, minimizing deposit formation, and preventing corrosion and wear. Through our in-house research, development and testing programs, we have the capability to invent and develop a broad range of proprietary chemical components, including antioxidants, anti-wear agents, corrosion inhibitors, detergents, dispersants, friction modifiers and viscosity modifiers."

■ The 10-K goes on to say, "Our engine additives products hold a leading global position for a wide range of additives for passenger car, heavy-duty diesel, marine diesel, stationary gas and small engines. We also produce fuel additives and refinery and oilfield products.

"Our customers, who include major global and regional oil companies, refineries and specialized lubricant producers and marketers, blend our additive products with their base oil and distribute the finished lubricant to end users via retail, commercial or vehicle original equipment manufacturer channels. Passenger car motor oils and diesel engine oils are more than 80 percent of our engine additive sales."

SECTOR: **Materials** ◆ BETA COEFFICIENT: **1.00**
10-YEAR COMPOUND EARNINGS PER SHARE GROWTH: **2.4%**
10-YEAR COMPOUND DIVIDENDS PER SHARE GROWTH: **1.1%**

		2005	2004	2003	2002	2001	2000	1999	1998
Revenues (millions)		4,043	3,156	2,049	1,980	1,839	1,771	1,744	1,615
Net Income (millions)		189	139	91	126	94	103	125	86
Earnings per share		2.63	2.48	2.04	2.45	1.84	1.94	2.30	1.55
Dividends per share		1.04	1.04	1.04	1.04	1.04	1.04	1.04	1.04
Price	high	44.5	37.4	34.4	36.4	37.7	33.9	31.4	40.2
	low	35.2	29.4	26.5	26.2	24.1	18.3	18.0	22.4

CONSERVATIVE GROWTH

Marshall & Ilsley Corporation

770 North Water Street ❑ Milwaukee, WI 53202 ❑ (414) 765-7801 ❑ Dividend reinvestment plan available ❑ Web site: *www.micorp.com* ❑ Ticker symbol: MI Listed: NYSE ❑ S&P rating: A ❑ Value Line financial strength rating: A

"Marshall & Ilsley, a major Midwest banking concern, has a lot going for it: strong markets, steady earnings growth and an opportunity to cash in on some big trends in its industry," said Jim McTague, writing for *Barron's* in 2005.

"The company's stock, however, has been a dud, falling 2 percent this year to a recent $43.3. What gives? 'It's a bank,' says Anthony Davis, an analyst with brokerage Ryan Beck & Co. 'There are a lot of wobbly knees about the banking sector right now, with interest rates headed upward. People are squeamish, and there's not a lot you can do to make them feel better.'

"Marshall & Ilsley could turn out to be just the pill. The Milwaukee-based company, which has $41 billion in assets, is much different from the average regional bank. More than a third of its revenue now comes from a rapidly growing data-processing subsidiary that performs a range of work for other banks, including key tasks in the promising field of paperless check-clearing. Instead of shipping physical checks around the country, banks are starting to process checks by sending digital images to one another.

"The high-tech unit, called Metavante, could see a 20 percent to 30 percent pickup in its revenues this year, in spite of rising rates, because of increased demand for its full line of data and transaction services. The unit, a prime beneficiary of a rise in out-sourcing by banks trying to cut costs, could well see its revenues top $1.2 billion this year."

Company Profile

Marshall & Ilsley Corporation is a diversified financial services corporation headquartered in Milwaukee, Wisconsin, with $45 billion in assets. Founded in 1847, M&I Marshall & Ilsley Bank has the largest banking presence in Wisconsin, with 194 offices throughout the state. In addition, M&I has 37 locations throughout Arizona, 13 offices in metropolitan Minneapolis/St. Paul, Minnesota, and locations in Duluth, Minnesota, Las Vegas, Nevada, and Naples and Bonita Springs, Florida. M&I's Southwest Bank affiliate has seven offices in the St. Louis area and one office in Belleville, Illinois.

Metavante Corporation, Marshall & Ilsley Corporation's wholly owned technology subsidiary, provides virtually all of the technology an organization needs to offer financial services.

M&I also provides trust and investment management, equipment leasing, mortgage banking, asset-based lending, financial planning, investments, and insurance services from offices throughout the country and on the Internet.

M&I's customer-based approach, internal growth, and strategic acquisitions have made M&I a nationally recognized leader in the financial services industry.

Shortcomings to Bear in Mind

- According to a 2005 article in *Institutional Investor*, "On the off-putting side, M&I's hot subsidiary, Metavante Corp., may soon have to struggle with a potential erosion of its core deposit-processing business. The bank, meanwhile, faces intense competition in almost every one of its product and geographic markets, and M&I's every success makes it a potential takeover prize. But chief executive Dennis Kuester sees no reason to change what has been a winning formula.

"'We're a dull story and proud of it,' insists Kuester (pronounced 'Kesster'), the 62-year-old native Milwaukeean and former IBM Corp. salesman who is M&I's president, CEO and chairman. He gained the last title in January, after having become president of the M&I holding company in 1987 and CEO in 2002 upon retirement of James Wigdale, who was chairman through December and remains a director.

"'If there's any kind of culture here, it's that there's no flash,' says Kuester. 'We're real meat-and-potatoes folks.'"

Reasons to Buy

- On March 25, 2006, the *New York Times* said that six analysts rated the stock a STRONG BUY; three called it a MODERATE BUY; and ten said it was a HOLD. There were no analysts lurking in the bushes calling the stock a SELL.
- "The improving geographic and business mix augurs well for 2006," said Theresa Brophy, writing for *Value Line Investment Survey* on March 24, 2006. "Continued strong commercial loan growth should more than offset a little more pressure on the net interest margin. Credit costs may only rise slightly."
- Metavante Corporation celebrated forty-one years of operation in 2005 and began the year committed to providing superior service to its clients and to grow the business internally and through acquisitions. Focused on financial services and payment solutions, Metavante made strategic acquisitions to move the company toward $1 billion in annual revenue.

The first of eight acquisitions beginning in November 2003 was Printing For Systems, Inc. (PSI) a Madison, Connecticut provider of identification cards and related documents to the health-care insurance industry. Metavante saw a fit between its electronic funds transfer (EFT) and card-production services and PSI's customer needs. During 2004, PSI introduced health-care eligibility cards and health-care payment cards and replaced traditional insurance ID cards with magnetic-striped plastic cards, thereby reducing the threat of identity theft by printing less personal data on the card.

In 2005, Metavante completed the acquisition of Prime Associates, Inc. Another New Jersey company that provides antimoney laundering and regulatory-compliance software, which can be sold along with Metavante's enterprise risk-management consulting practices. Financial institutions need such software and consulting to comply with increased regulations driven by the USA Patriot Act and Bank Secrecy Act.

■ According to a company official, "Our Financial Institutions Group (FIG), specialists in serving financial institutions nationwide, are continuing to successfully cross-sell M&I's services. By taking advantage of M&I's comprehensive product selection, customers of FIG—including the smallest institutions—have the tools they need to compete with even the largest banks, to better serve their customers. FIG's success outside the M&I's traditional footprint supports the philosophy that the corporation can grow its business significantly withou traditional bricks-and-mortar facilities. FIG customers can now be found in all fifty states; the FIG initiative has produced more than 600 referrals and resulted in sales of more than 200 new products and services."

■ "More and more, our community banking customers want the convenience of accessing their finances on their own schedule—and from anywhere," said a company spokesman in 2005. "Therefore, we continue to enhance our services and product lines so our customers can check their balances from the comfort of home, pay a bill from work, or transfer funds while on vacation.

"To that end, we've made several enhancements to our customer online banking products, which include a free bill-pay service. A comprehensive online guarantee ensures customers' online banking and bill-pay transactions are processed with the highest level of privacy and security. The results have been significant. Online banking usage is up 60 percent, and online bill payments doubled in one year."

■ On October 21, 2005, Marshall & Ilsley announced that it had signed a definitive agreement to acquire FirstTrust Indiana from First Indiana Bank. The transaction closed in the first quarter of 2006.

FirstTrust Indiana's businesses has been integrated with M&I's Wealth Management unit, which provides trust, asset management, brokerage, and private banking services to individuals, institutions, and corporate clients. All employees of FirstTrust Indiana joined M&I to ensure ongoing continuity of sales and service to their clients. The new M&I Wealth Management office in Indianapolis has continued to serve First Indiana Bank's clients' wealth management and trust needs.

"We are pleased to announce this strategic acquisition and partnership with FirstTrust Indiana," said Kenneth Krei, Senior Vice President, Marshall & Ilsley Corporation, and President of M&I Wealth Management. "We believe this partnership will allow us to expand our wealth management services into an important new marketplace for M&I Wealth Management, while increasing the product capabilities and resources for FirstTrust's client base."

FirstTrust Indiana began operating in 1998 and offers asset management, trust administration, and estate planning services to high-net-worth individuals and institutional customers. FirstTrust Indiana has nearly $1 billion in assets under administration.

"In 1998, we sensed the need for locally provided portfolio management and estate administration in central Indiana. In seven short years, the overwhelming support of our valued clients has made us one of the fastest growing de novo trust departments," said Ralph Nowak, President and Chief Investment Officer for First-Trust. "The combination of our continuing association with First Indiana Bank and our new partnership with M&I Wealth Management, with its comprehensive products and services and long-standing reputation, will help move our local capabilities to the next level."

SECTOR: **Financials** ◆ BETA COEFFICIENT: **.95**
10-YEAR COMPOUND EARNINGS PER SHARE GROWTH: **12.6%**
10-YEAR COMPOUND DIVIDENDS PER SHARE GROWTH: **11.3%**

		2005	2004	2003	2002	2001	2000	1999	1998
Loans (millions)		34,167	29,179	24,801	22,788	18,065	17,352	16,109	13,770
Total Assets (millions)		46,213	40,437	34,373	32,875	27,254	26,078	24,370	21,566
Net Income (millions)		728	627	544	485	406	364	355	318
Earnings per share		3.10	2.77	2.39	2.18	1.86	1.66	1.57	1.38
Dividends per share		.93	.81	.70	.63	.57	.52	.47	.43
Price	high	47.4	44.7	38.5	32.1	32.1	30.4	36.4	31.1
	low	40.0	35.7	24.6	23.1	19.1	27.2	19.7	16.2

CONSERVATIVE GROWTH

McCormick & Company, Inc.

18 Loveton Circle ❑ P. O. Box 6000 ❑ Sparks, MD 21152-6000 ❑ (410) 771-7244 ❑ Web site: *www.mccormick.com* ❑ Direct dividend reinvestment plan available (877) 778-6784 ❑ Fiscal year ends November 30 ❑ Listed: NYSE ❑ Ticker symbol: MKC ❑ S&P rating: A+ ❑ Value Line financial strength rating: B++

"Many people don't care for eggnog. But just try getting through the holidays without being offered a cup," said Robert Barker, writing for *BusinessWeek* on December 5, 2005. "Chances are, the spice in it will be McCormick's, and if that leaves a bad taste in your mouth, you're probably a stock analyst: Of the thirteen who track McCormick, *Standard & Poor's* lists just one who rates it a BUY."

Mr. Barker goes on to say, "Chief Executive Robert Lawless remains undaunted. 'We'll get back on track in 2006,' he told me. 'No one should hold the view of us that we have a damaged business strategy.'

"Chief executives, especially those scrambling to find their way back into investors' good graces, rarely say anything very different. Just the same, the steadiness of McCormick's 116-year-old business, along with its sturdy financial position—debt is 45 percent of capital, down from 59 percent in 2001—lead me to think that the shares represent a buying opportunity. For one thing, the way the Street is treating the stock, you would think McCormick is suddenly losing money on its $2.6 billion in revenues. Instead, growth in earnings per share have slowed abruptly, to 5 percent or so this year from an annual average of 11 percent in the five years ended August 31."

The *BusinessWeek* writer also said, "McCormick has been able to outpace the food industry by diverting its steady excess cash flow—$290 million after capital spending over the past four quarters—in a variety of salutary directions. These include higher dividends; share repurchases, currently a $400 million program that began in June right after a $300 million buyback budget was exhausted; selected acquisitions, such as

2003's $180 million deal for the Zatarain's brand of New Orleans-style food; and the development of higher-margin products, including a group of barbecue sauces, marinades, rubs, and seasonings called Grill Mates. Another new line is Grinders, which are a variety of unground peppers, salts, and herbs that come in bottles with an integrated grinding tool."

Company Profile

McCormick, the world's foremost maker of spices and seasonings, is committed to the development of tasty, easy-to-use new products to satisfy consumer demand.

When investors hear the name McCormick, they think of the spices they use every day. Indeed, McCormick is the world's largest spice company. Yet, the company is also the leader in the manufacture, marketing, and distribution of such products as seasonings and flavors to the entire food industry. These customers include food service and food-processing businesses, as well as retail outlets. This industrial segment was responsible for 49 percent of sales and 33 percent of operating profits. A majority of the top 100 food companies are MKC's customers.

Founded in 1889, McCormick distributes its products in about 100 countries.

McCormick's U.S. consumer business (47 percent of sales and 67 percent of operating profits), its oldest and largest, is dedicated to the manufacture and sale of consumer spices, herbs, extracts, proprietary seasoning blends, sauces, and marinades. They are sold under such brand names as McCormick, Schilling, Produce Partners, Golden Dipt, Old Bay, and Mojave.

Many of the spices and herbs purchased by the company are imported into the United States from the company of origin. However, significant quantities of some materials, such as paprika, dehydrated vegetables, onion and garlic, and food ingredients other than spices and herbs originate in the United States.

McCormick is a direct importer of certain raw materials, mainly black pepper, vanilla beans, cinnamon, herbs, and seeds from the countries of origin.

The raw materials most important to the company are onion, garlic, and capsicums (paprika and chili peppers), which are produced in the United States; black pepper, most of which originates in India, Indonesia, Malaysia, and Brazil; and vanilla beans, a large portion of which the company obtains from the Malagasy Republic and Indonesia.

Shortcomings to Bear in Mind

- On February 3, 2006, *Value Line Investment Survey's* analyst, Iason Dalavagas, said, "Shares of McCormick maintain a Timeliness rank of 4 (Below Average). Continued weakness in the Industrial group, along with increased competitive pressures in Europe, will likely limit any significant earnings rebound in the short run. The equity also offers below-average appreciation potential over the three- to five-year period."
- On March 18, 2006, the *New York Times* surveyed fourteen leading securities analysts; a dozen were lukewarm, rating the stock a HOLD. Only two were positive, one with a STRONG BUY and the other with a MODERATE BUY assessment.

Reasons to Buy

- Not everyone agrees with the dismal tidings outlined above. *Standard & Poor's Stock Reports,* for instance, had this to say on October 14, 2005. Richard Joy said, "Our BUY recommendation on the shares reflects our expectations of 9 percent to 11 percent annual EPS (*earnings per share*) growth and gains for the company's business." The analyst goes on to say, "We expect MKC's financial strength and free cash flow will continue to improve. New product and packaging initiatives should lead to strong growth for the consumer business and aid a rebound in the industrial business in fiscal

2006, in our opinion. We think longer-term growth prospects are attractive, reflecting the company's dominant and expanding U.S. spice market share (over 45 percent), as well as its leading share of the European consumer market (over 20 percent)."

- The market environment for McCormick's consumer products—such as spices, herbs, extracts, propriety seasoning blends, sauces, and marinades—varies worldwide. In the United States, for instance, usage is up, and consumers are seeking new and bolder tastes.

Although many people use prepared foods and eat out, a *Parade Magazine* survey reports that 75 percent of families polled eat dinner together at least four nights a week. A study conducted by *National Panel Diary* indicates that 70 percent of all meals are prepared at home, and a Canned Food Association Survey reports that 51 percent of women eighteen to sixty-four actually "scratch-cook" meals six times a week.

- In the company's industrial business, said Mr. Lawless, "Our customers are constantly seeking new flavors for their products. In this environment, the ability to identify, develop and market winning flavors is essential. We flavor all kinds of products—spaghetti sauce, snack chips, frozen entrees, yogurt, a pack of chewing gum. In restaurants, we provide seasonings for a gourmet meal, salad dressings at a casual dining chain, and coating and sauce for a quick-service chicken sandwich.

"To anticipate and respond to changing tastes in markets worldwide, we are investing in research and development staff, equipment, instrumentation, and facilities. These investments enable us not only to create innovative products but also to use sensory skills to make sure that the flavors we deliver are winners in the marketplace."

- McCormick has paid dividends every year since 1925, which have been raised in each of the past sixteen years. In the 1995-2005 period, dividends climbed from $.26 to $.64, a compound annual growth rate of 9.4 percent.

- Worldwide, the retail grocery industry continues to consolidate, creating larger customers. What's more, in many of McCormick's markets, the company has multiyear contracts with customers to secure the shelf space for its products. McCormick's capabilities in category management and electronic data interchange, along with its high-quality products and service, also forge a link to its increasingly larger customers.

- The company's past successes and future potential are rooted in the strength of the McCormick name. As a consequence, the company is now experiencing a 95 percent brand-awareness rating in the United States. This leadership role in the food industry ensures that consumers will enjoy a McCormick product at nearly every eating occasion. Grocery store aisles present more than 700 well-known products from major processors that rely on McCormick for seasoning or flavor.

- McCormick completed the purchase of C. M. Van Sillevoldt B. V. on November 2, 2004. The company sells spices, herbs, and seasonings under the Silvo brand in The Netherlands and the India brand in Belgium. Silvo dates back to 1833. Today, the brand has a strong heritage and high recognition among consumers in The Netherlands. Net sales have increased at a 5 percent compound annual growth rate since 1999 and reached euro 38 million in 2003. The business is achieving growth through innovative products and packaging, with a focus on convenience, quality, and ethnic flavors. In 2003, Silvo transformed its direct-to-store distribution system that is leading to improvements in product merchandising, customer service, sales information, and distribution logistics.

Silvo is a market leader in the Dutch spices and herbs consumer market. Products are spices, herbs, and seasonings (75 percent of sales) and specialty food items (25 percent). The company has a 63 percent share of spices and herbs in The Netherlands, with distribution in all major food retailers. Silvo also has a strong position in Belgium, with a 30 percent share, including brands and private label.

Robert J. Lawless, CEO of McCormick said, "A primary avenue of growth for McCormick is the acquisition of leading brands in key markets. Since the acquisition of Ducros in 2000, we have directed our efforts to expansion in Europe. The Silvo acquisition fits squarely within this strategy, extending our presence into The Netherlands, with a strong leading brand."

SECTOR: **Consumer Staples** ◆ BETA COEFFICIENT: **0.50**
10-YEAR COMPOUND EARNINGS PER SHARE GROWTH: **10.0%**
10-YEAR COMPOUND DIVIDENDS PER SHARE GROWTH: **9.4%**

		2005	2004	2003	2002	2001	2000	1999	1998
Revenues (millions)		2,592	2,526	2,270	2,045	2,372	2,124	2,007	1,881
Net Income (millions)		215	214	199	180	147	138	122	106
Earnings per share		1.56	1.52	1.40	1.29	1.05	1.00	.85	.72
Dividends per share		.64	.56	.46	.42	.40	.38	.34	.32
Price	high	39.1	38.9	30.2	27.3	23.3	18.9	17.3	18.2
	low	29.0	28.6	21.7	20.7	17.0	11.9	13.3	13.6

CONSERVATIVE GROWTH

The McGraw-Hill Companies, Inc.

1221 Avenue of the Americas ❑ New York, NY 10020-1095 ❑ (212) 512-4321 ❑ Direct Dividend reinvestment program available (888) 201-5538 ❑ Web site: *www.mcgraw-hill.com* ❑ Listed: NYSE ❑ Ticker symbol: MHP ❑ S&P rating: not rated ❑ Value Line financial strength rating: A+

On April 1, 2005, McGraw-Hill announced that it had completed the acquisition of J.D. Power and Associates, a leading provider of marketing information to consumers and businesses worldwide.

"J.D. Power and Associates is an excellent fit with The McGraw-Hill Companies and will enhance the growth prospects of our business information platforms," said CEO Harold McGraw III. "J.D. Power will benefit from our broad global presence, while providing a new direct link to consumers and creating new collaborative opportunities with our existing platforms in financial services, construction, energy and aviation."

J.D. Power and Associates, founded in 1968 by J.D. Power III, is the leading provider of marketing information services for the global automotive industry and has established a strong and growing presence in several other important industries, including finance and insurance, health care, home building, telecommunications, and energy. Its customer satisfaction ratings and market research are recognized worldwide as benchmarks for quality.

J.D. Power III, the founder, will remain actively involved in the strategic direction of the operation, and Stephen Goodall will continue to serve as J.D. Power and Associates president, with responsibility for day-to-day operations. The company, which includes the Power Information Network, LLC, has 787 employees, operates globally in twelve locations and will maintain its Westlake Village, California, headquarters as well as its other regional offices.

Company Profile

The McGraw-Hill Companies is a leading global information services provider aligned around three powerful and enduring forces essential to economic growth worldwide: the need for knowledge, the need for capital, and the need for transparency. MHP has built strong businesses with leading market positions in financial services, education, and business information to meet those needs.

McGraw-Hill Financial Services

- Standard & Poor's sets the standard for the global investment community by providing highly valued investment data, analysis, and opinions to financial decision-makers through its three businesses.
- Credit Market Services, which includes the world's largest network of credit ratings professionals, provides ratings for a wide array of credit obligations, as well as risk management and credit performance evaluation services.
- Investment Services provides institutional and retail investors with a wide range of investment information, analysis, and opinions in equities, fixed-income, foreign exchange, and mutual fund markets. The S&P indexes are used more than any other index group around the world.
- Corporate Value Consulting is the U.S. market leader in providing valuation and value analysis for financial reporting, tax, business combinations, corporate restructuring, capital allocation, and capital structure purposes.

McGraw-Hill Education

- McGraw-Hill Education is a global leader in education and professional information. With a broad range of products—from traditional textbooks to the latest in online and multimedia offerings—the company helps teachers teach and learners learn.
- The School Education Group is the domestic leader in the pre-K to 12 school market, providing educational, supplemental, and testing materials across all subject areas.
- Through its Higher Education, Professional, and International businesses, the company is a leader in the globally expanding market for college and postcollege and postgraduate education, and the company's professional publishing businesses serve the rapidly expanding needs of the global scientific, health care, business, and computer technology fields.

McGraw-Hill Information and Media Services

Information and Media Services provides information, business intelligence, and solutions that business executives, professionals, and governments worldwide use to remain competitive in their fields and in the global economy.

- Well-known brands in this unit include *BusinessWeek*, the number one global business magazine. The franchise also includes *BusinessWeek Online*, conferences and events, and *BusinessWeek TV*.
- This business also includes Platts (the key provider of price assessments with the petroleum, petrochemical, and power markets).
- McGraw-Hill Construction and Aviation Week, which serve the needs of construction, and aviation professionals worldwide, and ABC-affiliated television stations in Bakersfield, California; Denver, Colorado; Indianapolis, Indiana; and San Diego, California.

Shortcomings to Bear in Mind

■ One analyst pointed out that "risks include a sharp rise in interest rates, which could curtail growth in S&P's ratings division, or a prolonged economic slump that could negatively affect the publishing division."

■ "There are some concerns in education," said Simon R. Shoucair, writing for *Value Line Investment Survey* on February 17, 2006. "The prospects for new curriculums and adoptions are slimming in comparison to the robust new adoption markets of 2005. Increased competition for key state new adoptions will present a challenge. However, management notes that McGraw-Hill's programs have been prepared for this and are focused on maximizing opportunities. We remain optimistic that profits will continue to grow, albeit at a slower pace than last year."

Reasons to Buy

■ On March 18, 2006, the *New York Times* checked with twelve analysts who keep track of McGraw-Hill and tabulated that three analysts regarded the stock as a STRONG BUY; five said it was a MODERATE BUY; and four sat on the fence with a HOLD rating. There were no SELLS.

■ "We are raising our rating on McGraw-Hill Companies to BUY from HOLD," said John Eade, writing for Argus Research Company on January 26, 2006. "Our long-term growth rate is 10 percent. We would not be surprised to see MHP raise its outlook as the year goes by."

■ S&P Indexes are the foundation for a growing array of investment funds and exchange-traded products that continue to generate new revenue. The company receives fees based on assets and trading activity. In addition, the recent volatility of the stock market has increased the revenue stream. Currently, more than $700 billion is invested in mutual funds tied to the S&P indexes.

■ Europe contributes almost half of McGraw-Hill's international revenue, growing at a double-digit rate. With a push from the new Monetary Union, the European market will be a springboard for growth in many of the company's key businesses. Here are some expectations:

- European companies that once financed their growth mainly by borrowing from banks are shifting to the issuance of corporate bonds instead, while nontraditional financial instruments also boom. Those are both large opportunities for Standard & Poor's Rating Services, which has built the world's largest network of ratings professionals.
- Increases in investments by Europeans building retirement funds—the result of a transition to privately funded pension plans—will accelerate demand for global financial information. These are pluses for *Standard & Poor's Financial Information Services.*
- The continued growth of English in business communications and as a second language in everyday use widens. These will benefit the company's educational products and the European edition of *BusinessWeek.*
- The promise of the global economy depends on educational training. This is a plus for McGraw-Hill's global publishing activities—most notably the company's business, finance, engineering, and information technology products.

■ In the construction industry, The McGraw-Hill Construction Information Group (MH-CIG) is the foremost source of information crucial to new construction projects and planning. MH-CIG has increasingly turned to the Internet and other electronic tools to gather and distribute information.

Dodge Plans is the latest of several MH-CIG electronic products stemming from print media. It provides access—online or by CD-ROM twice weekly—to the plans, specifications, and bidding requirements for more than 60,000 new construction and renovation projects.

- The McGraw-Hill Professional Book Group publishes nearly 800 titles per year in computing, business, science, technical, medical, and reference markets. The group continues to expand by creating publishing alliances with partners such as Oracle and Global Knowledge, transforming key reference titles into Internet-based services. In addition, the Professional Book Group offers electronic products, ranging from Internet subscription services to CD-ROMs, and is building its capabilities in on-demand publishing.
- On November 8, 2005, McGraw-Hill announced that it had sold its Healthcare Information Group to specialist publisher, Vendome Group, LLC. The Healthcare Information Group comprises the magazines *Physician and Sportsmedicine, Postgraduate Medicine,* and *Healthcare Informatics,* as well as a variety of health care information programs that serve the medical market.

"Divesting this business is consistent with our strategy to direct resources where we have the best opportunities to achieve both financial growth and market leadership," said Scott Marden, president of McGraw-Hill Information and Media Services. "We remain strongly focused on building our key business information and market insight franchises, which include J.D. Power and Associates, *BusinessWeek,* Platts, McGraw-Hill Construction and *Aviation Week.*"

SECTOR: **Consumer Discretionary** ◆ BETA COEFFICIENT: **.80**
10-YEAR COMPOUND EARNINGS PER SHARE GROWTH: **14.5%**
10-YEAR COMPOUND DIVIDENDS PER SHARE GROWTH: **8.2%**

		2005	2004	2003	2002	2001	2000	1999	1998
Revenues (millions)		6,004	5,250	4,828	4,640	4,646	4,308	3,992	3,729
Net Income (millions)		872	736	629	572	380	481	402	342
Earnings per share		2.21	1.91	1.64	1.48	1.23	1.21	1.01	0.86
Dividends per share		0.66	0.60	0.54	0.51	0.49	0.47	0.43	0.39
Price	high	54.0	45.8	35.0	34.9	35.5	33.9	31.6	25.9
	low	40.5	34.3	25.9	25.4	24.4	21.0	23.6	17.2

GROWTH AND INCOME

MDU Resources Group, Inc.

1200 W. Century Avenue ❑ P. O. Box 5650 ❑ Bismarck, ND 58506-5650 ❑ (800) 437-8000 Ext. 1020 ❑ Direct dividend reinvestment plan available: (877) 536-3553 ❑ Web site: *www.mdu.com* ❑ Listed: NYSE ❑ Ticker symbol: MDU ❑ S&P rating: A ❑ Value Line financial strength rating: A+

"MDU Resources achieved record financial results last year," said CEO Martin A. White on February 21, 2006. "Revenues for 2005 totaled $3.5 billion, up 27 percent from $2.7 billion in 2004. We also achieved our highest earnings, $274.4 million, up 33 percent from $206.4 million in 2004. Earnings per common share, diluted, totaled $2.29, up 30 percent from $1.76 in 2004."

Mr. White goes on to say, "This strong performance resulted in an outstanding one-year total return of 26 percent for our shareholders. For the five-year period ending with 2005, our total average annual return was 12 percent, while our peer group average return was 11 percent, and the S&P 500 average return was 1 percent.

"MDU Resources has had an unbroken record of quarterly dividend payments since 1937. We increased our quarterly dividend 5.6 percent in August 2005. With this increase, our annualized dividend grew to 76 cents per share. Our dividend has increased every year since 1990.

"In our natural gas and oil production segment, we continue to increase our proved reserves, which now total 616 billion cubic feet equivalent. We have interests in more than 1.7 million acres of existing leaseholds, which provide future exploitation and exploration opportunities that will serve our shareholders well for years to come. We are the largest producer of natural gas in Montana, where we have legacy fields that have been producing since the 1930s. In fact, production has gone up in those fields because of the implementation of new technologies."

Mr. White also said, "Our construction materials and mining segment targets mid-sized, high-growth markets. We enjoy a distinct competitive advantage in this business as a result of our strong aggregate reserve position of 1.3 billion tons—more than a thirty-year supply—which we also continue to build.

"In our pipeline and energy services segment, we are the owners of the largest natural gas storage field in North America. We connect natural gas in the Rocky Mountain region to lucrative Mid-Continent markets through our Grasslands Pipeline, the largest pipeline project ever undertaken by this company.

"In our two regulated utility segments (electric and natural gas distribution), our customers consistently give high marks to our service. Additionally, our electric generation costs are some of the lowest in the nation with one plant ranking No. 23 out of 297 plants.

"Our independent power production segment completed the first major coal-fired electric generating facility to be built in Montana in twenty years, bringing competitively priced energy to its markets.

"Our construction services group—formerly known as utility services—has successfully targeted niche markets where barriers to entry are high and where it can capitalize on the specialized technical expertise of its employees."

Company Profile

MDU Resources Group, Inc. is a natural resource company. The company's diversified operations, such as oil and gas and construction materials should help MDU Resources grow at a better rate than electric utilities that depend entirely on their electric business.

MDU Resources Group has a number of operations:

Electric Distribution

Montana-Dakota Utilities Company generates, transmits, and distributes electricity and provided related value-added products and services in the Northern Great Plains.

Natural Gas Distribution

Montana-Dakota Utilities Company and Great Plains Natural Gas Company distribute natural gas and provide related value-added products and services in the Northern Great Plains.

Utility Services

Operating throughout most of the United States, Utility Services, Inc. is a diversified infrastructure construction company specializing in electric, natural gas, and telecommunication utility construction, as well as interior industrial electrical, exterior lighting, and traffic stabilization.

Independent Power Production

Centennial Energy Resources owns electric generating facilities in the United States and Brazil. Electric capacity and energy produced at these facilities is sold under long-term contracts to nonaffiliated entities.

Pipeline and Energy Services

WBI Holdings, Inc. provides natural gas transportation, underground storage, and gathering services through regulated and nonregulated pipeline systems and provides energy marketing and management throughout the United States. Operations are situated primarily in the Rocky Mountain, Midwest, Southern, and Central regions of the United States.

Natural Gas and Production

Fidelity Exploration & Production Company is engaged in oil and natural gas acquisition, exploration, and production throughout the United States and in the Gulf of Mexico.

Construction Materials and Mining

Knife River Corporation mines and markets aggregates and related value-added construction materials products and services in the western United States, including Alaska and Hawaii. It also operates lignite and coal mines in Montana and North Dakota.

Shortcomings to Bear in Mind

■ Public utilities are often hurt by rising interest rates, since they have to borrow money to build new facilities. As the economy strengthens, it seems logical to assume that interest rates will climb from the depressed levels of recent years.

■ On February 10, 2006, Paul E. Debbas, CFA had this to say in his analysis for *Value Line Investment Survey*, "This stock's yield and total-return potential to 2008–2010 are just modest. It is now trading within our three- to five-year Target Price Range."

Reasons to Buy

■ Over the past ten years (1995–2005), earnings per share advanced from $0.64 to $2.29, a compound annual growth rate of 13.6 percent, an enviable record for a public utility. To be sure, MDU Resources is not a typical utility, since it has many diverse businesses.

■ MDU Resources has an established position in the coal bed natural gas fields in the Powder River Basin of Wyoming and Montana. This provides the company's natural gas and oil production segment with additional reserve potential of low-cost coal bed natural gas.

In addition, MDU continues enhancing production from its existing gas fields in Colorado and Montana. The company's strong reserve position, both onshore and offshore in the Gulf of Mexico, provides this group a large geographic base upon which to expand.

■ As the corporation has grown, so has the recognition it has received. In 2005, MDU Resources was recognized as follows:

- Named 2005 "Utility of the Year" by Electric Light & Power magazine in its November/December 2005 issue. According to EL&P, MDU Resources was chosen because it has built on an electric and natural gas utility foundation, and it follows a corporate strategy based on integrity and solid, conservative growth.
- Named for the sixth straight year to Forbes magazine's "Platinum 400 Best Big Companies" in America list. Criteria used were corporate governance and accounting practices, as well as financial performance.
- Named by Mergent, a leading provider of business and financial information, as a Dividend Achiever for 2005. This honor, which recognizes

ten or more years of consecutive dividend increases, is bestowed on only 3 percent of listed dividend-paying companies in the United States.

- Ranked number eighteen on Public Utilities *Fortnightly*'s "Fortnightly 40," the magazine's Top 40 list of the best energy companies in America. The "Fortnightly 40" is a financial ranking of electric and gas utilities, pipelines, and distribution companies that appeared in the September 2005 issue of the magazine. The publication dubs its list "a benchmark that highlights the industry's leading companies—its brightest stars proven in performance and exceptional corporate management."

- On March 22, 2006, the *New York Times* asked seven analysts their opinion of MDU Resources. Three gave the company a STRONG BUY rating; two said it was a MODERATE BUY; and two preferred to rate the stock a HOLD.
- On March 17, 2006, Gary F. Hovis, writing for Argus Research Company said, "We continue maintaining our BUY rating on MDU Resources Group." He goes on to say, "Overall, we think MDU's strategically diverse business model will continue to drive EPS growth."

SECTOR: **Utilities** ◆ BETA COEFFICIENT: **.90**
10-YEAR COMPOUND EARNINGS PER SHARE GROWTH: **13.6%**
10-YEAR COMPOUND DIVIDENDS PER SHARE GROWTH: **4.4%**

		2005	2004	2003	2002	2001	2000	1999	1998
Revenues (millions)		3,455	2,719	2,352	2,032	2,224	1,874	1,280	897
Net Income (millions)		275	206	175	148	156	110	83	74
Earnings per share		2.53	1.17	1.03	0.92	1.02	0.80	0.67	0.29
Dividends per share		0.49	.47	0.44	0.42	0.40	0.38	0.36	0.35
Price	high	24.7	18.5	16.3	14.9	17.9	14.7	12.1	12.8
	low	17.0	14.5	10.9	8.0	9.9	7.9	8.3	8.4

AGGRESSIVE GROWTH

Medtronic, Inc.

710 Medtronic Parkway N. E. ❑ Minneapolis, MN 55432-5604 ❑ Listed: NYSE ❑ (763) 505-2692 ❑ Dividend reinvestment plan available (888) 648-8154 ❑ Web site: *www.medtronic.com* ❑ Ticker symbol: MDT ❑ Fiscal year ends April 30 ❑ S&P rating: B+ ❑ Value Line financial strength rating: A+

"Medtronic Inc. has become the third major entrant in the fast-growing business of selling drug-coated stents to open coronary arteries with the approval by European regulators of a device called the Endeavor," said Thomas M. Burton, writing for the *Wall Street Journal* in 2005.

"Stents are wire-mesh cylinders placed in arteries to keep them propped open. The drug-coated versions are the latest incarnation of these products, secreting medicines designed to prevent arteries from reclosing. The $5.5 billion worldwide market for drug-coated stents until now has been dominated by Boston Scientific Corp. and Johnson & Johnson, but analysts say Minneapolis-based Medtronic could make significant inroads if Endeavor proves to be as adept as competitors's devices at keeping arteries clear.

The *Wall Street Journal* article went on to say, "'Endeavor will be the most deliverable product in the marketplace and the easiest one to use,' Scott Ward, president of Medtronic's vascular business, said in an interview. Cardiologists find that some devices are easier than others to maneuver through the curves of arteries, which can be especially tortuous in some patients."

An Update

On October 18, 2005, Daniel Rosenberg, writing for the *Wall Street Journal* said, "Medtronic, Inc. Said its Endeavor III drug-eluding stent trial barely missed its main goal in a patient trial and that secondary goals were met.

"On the whole, the company said, data from the trial put Medtronic's Endeavor stent in the same safety and efficacy category with competitors Johnson & Johnson and Boston Scientific Corp., and will allow Medtronic to file next year (2006) for U.S. approval of its product, with final Food and Drug Administration approval coming sometime in 2007."

Mr. Rosenberg goes on to say, "The main goal of the 436-patient trial was to compare Endeavor with J&J's Cypher stent in the category of in-segment late loss. This refers to the difference in the width of a vessel just after stenting versus several months later. A small narrowing is almost always the case, and is considered relatively benign. But more advanced narrowing can eventually lead to blockage that must be retreated. 'We narrowly missed,' said Scott Ward, president of Medtronic Vascular, referring to narrowing of the vessel width."

Company Profile

Medtronic is the world's leading medical technology company, providing lifelong solutions for people with chronic disease. Here are its key businesses:

Medtronic Cardiac Rhythm Management develops products that restore and regulate a patient's hearth rhythm, as well as improve the heart's pumping function. The business markets implantable pacemakers, defibrillators, cardiac ablation catheters, monitoring and diagnostic devices, and cardiac resynchronization devices, including the first implantable device for the treatment of heart failure.

Medtronic Cardiac Surgery develops products that are used in both arrested and beating heart bypass surgery. The business also markets the industry's broadest line of heart valve products for both replacement and repair, plus autotransfusion equipment and disposable devices for handling and monitoring blood during major surgery, as well as cardiac ablation devices to treat a variety of heart conditions.

Medtronic Vascular develops products and therapies that treat a wide range of vascular diseases and conditions. These products include coronary, peripheral, and neuro-vascular stents, stent graph systems for diseases and conditions throughout the aorta, and distal protection systems.

Medtronic Neurological and Diabetes offers therapies for movement disorders, chronic pain, and diabetes. It also offers diagnostics and therapeutics for urological and gastrointestinal conditions, including incontinence, benign prostatic hyperplasia (BPH), enlarged prostate, and gastroesophageal reflux disease (GERD).

Medtronic Spinal, ENT, and SNT develops and manufactures products that treat a variety of disorders of the cranium and spine, including traumatically induced conditions, deformities, and tumors.

Shortcomings to Bear in Mind

- "Our recommendation is HOLD, said Robert M. Gold, writing for *Standard & Poor's Stock Reports* on December 1, 2005. "We believe the implantable defibrillator market can sustain 18 percent to 22 percent growth over the coming three years and expect Medtronic to remain overall market share leader. However, we see a protracted slowdown in the pacemaker area."

Reasons to Buy

- On March 25, 2006, the *New York Times* poled thirty-seven securities analysts and found that fourteen rated Medtronic a STRONG BUY; twelve said it was a MODERATE BUY; and eleven called the stock a HOLD.
- On December 9, 2005, Larry Biegelsen, writing for Prudential Equity Group, said, "In our view, the stock provides investors with a combination of above-average sales and earnings growth driven by a broad range of market-leading franchises in many of the fastest-growing med-tech markets and a reasonable valuation."
- "In the next year or so, Medtronic expects to launch new products into the growing markets for artificial spinal discs and automated insulin pumps," said Bill Alpert, writing for *Barron's* on December 26, 2005.
- We are reaffirming our BUY rating on Medtronic," said David H. Toung, writing for Argus Research Company on November 30, 2005. "While the cardiac rhythm business continues to be a solid contributor, earnings have also been driven by demand for spinal products."
- Medtronic is a pioneer in the emerging field of medicine that promises to restore normal brain function and chemistry to millions of patients with central nervous system disorders. The company's implantable neuro-stimulation and infusion systems treat disorders by modulating the nervous system with electrical stimulation, chemicals, and biological agents delivered in precise amounts to specific sites in the brain and spinal cord.
- Since its origin, Medtronic has held a clear market leadership in cardiac pacing, chiefly with pacemakers designed to treat bradycardia (hearts that beat irregularly or too slow) and more recently, tachyarrhythmia (hearts that beat too fast or quiver uncontrollably, called tachycardia and fibrillation). Today, more than half the cardiac rhythm devices and leads implanted throughout the world come from Medtronic.
- The worldwide coronary vascular market is estimated at $4 billion and is expected to grow because it serves significant, unmet medical needs. Medtronic's coronary vascular products include several types of catheters used to unblock coronary arteries, stents that support the walls of an artery and prevent more blockage, and products used in minimally invasive vascular procedures for coronary heart disease, the chief cause of heart attack and angina.
- Medtronic's cardiac surgery group offers superior products to support cardiac surgeons, including tissue heart valves that are best represented by the Freestyle stentless valve, the Mosaic stented tissue valve, and the Hall mechanical valve. In addition, the company is expanding its leadership in cardiac cannulae used to connect a patient's circulatory system to external perfusion systems used in conventional and minimally invasive surgeries.
- Medtronic has a pipeline filled with treatments for a number of profitable (but uncrowded) markets. Its Activa, for example, which uses electronic stimulation to alleviate many of the symptoms associated with Parkinson's Disease, received approval in 2002 from the U.S. Food & Drug Administration (USFDA).

Parkinson's Disease impacts the lives of an estimated one million people in the United States and two million worldwide. Activa, according to the company "utilizing our brain pacemaker, can significantly reduce shaking, slowness, and stiffness for patients who live with this debilitating disease. The dramatic benefits of this therapy were vividly demonstrated during an extensive media campaign that followed USFDA approval, including a report that aired on CBS Television's '60 Minutes' in February 2002."

In another realm, Medtronic's InSync ICD system is one of the only treatments for heart failure that does not rely on the use of drugs. Heart failure, the progressive deterioration of the heart's pumping capability, afflicts more than 22 million people worldwide and over five million in the United States.

According to management, the company's InSync and InSync ICD cardiac devices address "one of the largest and fastest-growing new market opportunities. As reported in the *New England Journal of Medicine,* it is estimated that more than three million heart failure patients around the world can experience improved quality of life from this new bi-ventricular pacing therapy.

"Sudden Cardiac Arrest strikes one American every two minutes and is the leading cause of death in the U.S. Research data reported in the *New England Journal of Medicine* shows dramatically reduced mortality from sudden cardiac arrest in the heart attack survivors who receive implantable cardioverter defibrillators (ICDs). This expanded indication for ICDs approximately doubles the market potential to more than 600,000 patients a year in the U.S. alone."

- Diabetes afflicts more than 170 million people worldwide and about 20 million in the United States. It's the most costly chronic condition, with annual expenditures exceeding $130 billion in the United States alone. People with diabetes are also much more likely to suffer from numerous other medical complications, including cardiovascular disease, kidney disease, blindness, and amputation. As the world leader in external insulin pumps, Medtronic is expanding its product offering to help insulin-dependent diabetes patients better manage their glucose levels and their disease.

SECTOR: **Health Care** ◆ BETA COEFFICIENT: **.85**
10-YEAR COMPOUND EARNINGS PER SHARE GROWTH: **19.2%**
10-YEAR COMPOUND DIVIDENDS PER SHARE GROWTH: **20%**

		2005	2004	2003	2002	2001	2000	1999	1998
Revenues (millions)		10,055	9,087	7,665	6,411	5,552	5,015	4,134	2,605
Net Income (millions)		1,804	1,959	1,600	984	1,282	1,111	905	595
Earnings per share		1.48	1.60	1.30	.80	.85	.90	.40	.48
Dividends per share		.29	.28	.25	.20	.12	.15	.12	.10
Price	high	58.9	53.7	52.9	49.7	62.0	62.0	44.6	38.4
	low	48.7	45.5	42.2	32.5	36.6	32.8	29.9	22.7

CONSERVATIVE GROWTH

Meredith Corporation

1716 Locust Street ❑ Des Moines, IA 50309-3023 ❑ (515) 284-2633 ❑ Dividend reinvestment plan not available ❑ Fiscal year ends June 30 ❑ Listed: NYSE ❑ Web site: *www.meredith.com* ❑ Ticker symbol: MDP ❑ S&P rating: A- ❑ Value Line financial strength rating: A

On July 1, 2005, Meredith Corporation announced that it had completed the acquisition of *Parents, Child, Fitness,* and *Family Circle* magazines from Gruner + Jahr for $350 million.

"All four of these titles mesh well with our editorial focus on service journalism and we look forward to serving their loyal readers, as well as attracting new subscribers," said CEO William T. Kerr. "We are also eager to begin offering advertising and marketing clients access to our expanded magazine portfolio, which reaches more American women than any other magazine publisher."

Meredith expects the transaction to generate EBITDA (earnings before interest, taxes, depreciation, and amortization) in the low-to-mid $30 million range and be modestly accretive to earnings per share in fiscal 2006.

A few weeks later, on September 29, Meredith announced that it had purchased the station license assets of KSMO-TV, the WB affiliate in Kansas City, from the Sinclair Broadcast Group for $6.7 million. On November 12, 2004, Meredith purchased the nonlicense assets of KSMO-TV from Sinclair for $26.8 million and received Federal Communications Commission approval earlier this week to complete the acquisition.

"Now we will be able to offer Kansas City viewers a new array of viewing options, including a 9 p.m. prime-time newscast, more local programming and increased sports coverage," said Kirk Black, KCTV/KSMO Vice President/General Manager. Black said the prime-time newscast will debut in mid-October, and expanded Chiefs's coverage on KSMO will begin on Sunday, October 16.

"This positions us to serve advertisers seeking either the younger-skewing WB audience or the powerful CBS audience with its top-rated primetime programming, market-leading sports and Emmy Award-winning local news," Black said.

Kansas City is the nation's thirty-first-largest television market. KSMO airs on channel 62 and is available on cable channel 10.

"This agreement fits well with our existing growth strategy of expanding our presence in growing and vibrant television markets," said Meredith Broadcasting Group President Paul Karpowicz, noting that Meredith has operated KCTV, a market leader in Kansas City, for more than fifty years. "We will continue to grow and expand Meredith Broadcasting Group's portfolio, particularly focusing on duopolies and regional clusters."

Company Profile

Meredith Corporation is one of America's leading media and marketing companies. Its business centers on magazine and book publishing, television broadcasting, interactive media, and integrated marketing. The company's roots go back to 1902, when it was an agricultural publisher.

The Meredith Publishing Group is the country's foremost home and family publisher. The group creates and markets magazines, including *Better Homes and Gardens, Ladies' Home Journal, Country Home, Creative Home, Midwest Living, Traditional Home, WOOD, Hometown Cooking, Successful Farming, MORE, Renovation Style, Country Gardens, American Patchwork &*

Quilting, Garden Shed, Do It Yourself, Garden, Deck and Landscape, Decorating, and about 150 special-interest publications.

In 2002, the company acquired American Baby Group, a publisher with titles geared toward mothers-to-be and young mothers. American Baby's magazines include: *American Baby, First Year of Life, Childbirth, Healthy Kids en Espanol, Pimeros 12 Meses,* and *Espera.* American Baby produces television shows; owns six consumer sampling programs; provides custom publishing; and owns the American Baby Family Research Center and two Web sites. The company expected the acquisition to attract younger readers and to tap the fast growing domestic Hispanic market.

The Publishing Group also creates custom marketing programs through Meredith Integrated Marketing, licenses the *Better Homes and Gardens* brand, and publishes books created and sold under Meredith and Ortho trademarks. Meredith has some 350 books in print and has established marketing relationships with some of America's leading companies, including Home Depot, Daimler-Chrysler, and Carnival Cruise Lines. Meredith's most popular book is the red-plaid *Better Homes and Gardens New Cook Book.*

The Meredith Broadcasting Group includes fourteen television stations in locations across the continental United States, in such cities as Atlanta; Phoenix; Portland, Oregon; Hartford-New Haven, Connecticut; Kansas City, Missouri; Nashville; Greenville-Spartanburg-Anderson, South Carolina; Asheville, North Carolina; Las Vegas; Flint-Saginaw, Michigan; and Bend, Oregon. The network affiliations include CBS (5 affiliates), NBC (one), UPN (one), and FOX (4).

Meredith's consumer database contains more than eighty million names, making it one of the largest domestic databases among media companies. These databases enable magazine and TV advertisers to precisely target marketing campaigns. In addition, the company has an extensive Internet presence, including branded anchor tenant positions on America Online.

Shortcomings to Bear in Mind

- The company's profits depend heavily on advertising revenues. The recession in the early part of the decade was particularly hard on advertising, which can be a volatile factor. When a company's hurting, it often lays off employees and pares back advertising.

Reasons to Buy

- "Fiscal 2005 was an outstanding year for Meredith," said CEO William T. Kerr on July 27, 2005. "We produced the best earnings in our 103-year history, and on July 1, 2005, we completed the most significant publishing transaction as well. The acquisition of *Parents, Child, Fitness, Family Circle* and *Ser Padres* magazines broadens our magazine portfolio to reach younger women and furthers our strategy to serve the Hispanic market. Additionally, we extended our marketing services capabilities and increased audience share at our television stations. These actions enhance our ability to sustain strong earnings growth in fiscal 2006."
- For fiscal 2005, Publishing operating profit increased 10 percent, to $174.3 million, and operating profit margin improved from 18.1 percent to 19.2 percent. This performance reflects profit growth in magazines, books, integrated marketing, and interactive media. What's more, Broadcasting operating profit increase 25 percent, to $86.7 million. Earnings before interest, taxes, depreciation and amortization (EBITDA) grew 20 percent and EBITDA margin improved from 31.8 percent to 35.2 percent.
- The company generated $170.9 million in cash flow from operations in fiscal 2005. During the year, Meredith purchased $97.5 million of its stock, reduced debt by

$50 million, invested $35.4 million to enter a joint sales agreement with the WB affiliate in Kansas City and to acquire the WB affiliate in Chattanooga.

- In the 1995–2005 period, earnings per share advanced from $.62 to $2.50, a compound annual growth rate of 15 percent. In the same ten-year span, however, dividends per share expanded less impressively, from $.19 to $.52, a growth rate of 10.6 percent.
- On March 18, 2006, The *New York Times* said that one analyst called Meredith a STRONG BUY; three said it was a MODERATE BUY, and three preferred to regard it as a HOLD.
- "The company has a big presence online," said Stuart Plesser, writing for *Value Line Investment Survey* on February 17, 2006. "It operates more than thirty Web sites, drawing viewers mostly by leveraging the company's magazine titles. Not only are MDP's Internet sites a source of advertising revenue, they act as a means to promote magazine subscriptions. These high-quality neutrally ranked shares offer good appreciation potential through 2008–2010."
- *Standard & Poor's Stock Reports* also had favorable remarks on January 31, 2006. James Peters, CFA, said, "Our recommendation is BUY. We view positively MDP's strategy of publishing special interest publications (SIPs) and developing new products that target growth segments of the United States, including a growing Hispanic population, as we think this strategy will support continued revenue growth."
- "Americans are coming home," said a company spokesman. "Research shows they are devoting more time to their homes and their families, and the Meredith Publishing Group is ideally positioned to serve them. Through our century-long commitment to quality service journalism, we have built a reputation as a trusted source of information. Our subscription magazines, special interest publications, book, Web sites and other materials are respected resources for Americans seeking to enrich their homes through remodeling, decorating, gardening and cooking."
- Meredith serves more than 80 million American consumers each month through its magazines, books, custom publications, Internet presence, and television stations. What's more, the company's database contains 75 million names, with 300 data points on seven of the ten domestic home-owning households.
- The company's products dominate the industry sweet spot of Americans in the 35–54 age group, the nation's largest purchasers. This age group does a disproportionate amount of spending in Meredith specialties—remodeling, decorating, cooking, and gardening.
- The national recognition of titles such as *Better Homes and Gardens, Ladies' Home Journal, American Baby*, and *Country Home*, combined with the strong local reputation of many of its TV stations, provide a solid foundation for continued growth.

SECTOR: **Consumer Discretionary** ◆ BETA COEFFICIENT: **.85**
10-YEAR COMPOUND EARNINGS PER SHARE GROWTH: **15%**
10-YEAR COMPOUND DIVIDENDS PER SHARE GROWTH: **10.6%**

		2005	2004	2003	2002	2001	2000	1999	1998
Revenues (millions)		1,221	1,162	1,080	988	1,053	1,097	1,036	1,010
Net Income (millions)		128	110.7	91.1	70.1	71.3	71.0	89.7	79.9
Earnings per share		2.50	2.14	1.80	1.38	1.55	1.71	1.64	1.46
Dividends per share		.52	.43	.37	.35	.33	.31	.29	.27
Price	high	54.6	55.9	50.3	47.8	39.0	41.0	42.0	48.5
	low	44.5	48.2	36.9	33.4	26.5	22.4	30.6	26.7

CONSERVATIVE GROWTH

Microsoft Corporation

One Microsoft Way ❑ Redmond, WA 98052-6399 ❑ (425) 706-3703 ❑ Direct Dividend reinvestment plan available (800) 285-7772 ❑ Web site: *www.microsoft.com* ❑ Listed: Nasdaq ❑ Fiscal year ends June 30 ❑ Ticker symbol: MSFT ❑ S&P rating: B+ ❑ Value Line financial strength rating: A++

"Microsoft Corp.'s profit rose 5.5 percent in its second fiscal quarter on strong sales of software for server computers, though tight supplies of the Xbox 360 video game machine tempered overall sales," said Robert A. Guth, writing for the *Wall Street Journal* on January 27, 2006."

Mr. Guth goes on to say, "Revenue reached $11.84 billion, 9.4 percent above the $10.82 billion Microsoft posted for the same period a year earlier—and a record for the company.

"'We're happy for the overall financial performance in the quarter,' said Christopher Liddell, Microsoft's chief financial officer. The results indicate a major transition for Microsoft as it rolls out one of the broadest array of new products in its history. Meanwhile, sales of software for server computers are an increasingly important source of growth for the company as it prepares new versions of its core PC software, *Windows* and *Office*."

Company Profile

Microsoft is the dominant player in the PC software market. It climbed to prominence on the popularity of its operating systems software and now rules the business-applications software market. Microsoft, moreover, has set its sights on becoming the leading provider of software services for the Internet.

By virtue of it size, market positioning and financial strength, Microsoft is a formidable competitor in any market it seeks to enter. Earnings have shown explosive growth in recent years, enhanced by a strong PC market in general, along with new product introductions and market-share gains. Of course, the last couple of years have seen the PC market sag, along with most everything else. But better times should return.

Microsoft is best known for its operating-systems software programs, which run on close to 90 percent of the PCs currently in use. Its original DOS operating system, of course, gave way to Windows, a graphical user interface program run in conjunction with DOS, which made using a PC easier.

The company entered the business-applications market in the early 1990s via a line-up of strong offerings, combined with aggressive and innovative marketing and sales strategies. The company's Office 97 suite, which includes the popular Word (word processing), Excel (spreadsheet), and PowerPoint (graphics) software programs, is now by far the best-selling applications software package.

Shortcomings to Bear in Mind

- "Despite all the hype surrounding the new Xbox 360 video game console, Microsoft won't make money on the machine itself," said Arik Hesseldahl, writing for *BusinessWeek* on December 5, 2005. "A tear-down analysis by market researcher iSuppli of the high-end Xbox 360, which contains a hard drive, found that the materials cost Microsoft $470 before assembly. Chips alone account for 72 percent of that. The console sells at retail for $399, for a loss of $71 per unit. Other items in the box, such as the power supply, cables, and controllers, add $55 more to Microsoft's cost, pushing its loss per unit to $126.
- Insiders, such as officers and board members, have been selling their own stock in recent months. In a recent nine-month period, there were seventeen sales and no purchases.

Reasons to Buy

- "The Xbox 360, released to frenzied hordes of buyers on November 22, 2005, is charged with a dual mission for Microsoft," said Stephen H. Wildstrom, writing for *BusinessWeek* on December 12, 2005. "Coming out several months ahead of Sony's PlayStation 3, the new Xbox is aimed at letting Microsoft dominate the game console market as well as giving the company control over the digital living room. It is more likely to succeed at the former than the latter.

  "Personal computing technology seems as if it has been nearly static for the past few years. But the Xbox 360 displays the great progress in processing power and graphics that has occurred in the four years since the original version shipped. The first Xbox was a bare-bones PC with Pentium chip and a cheap but powerful nVIDIA graphics adapter. The 360 uses an entirely new design built around a custom IBM processor that crams three Power PC processors onto a single chip, plus a custom graphics processor from ATI."
- On March 18, 2006, the *New York Times* poled thirty-four analysts who keep tabs on Microsoft. An amazing number (fifteen) said the stock is a STRONG BUY; fourteen were not quite so sanguine, but still tabbed it a MODERATE BUY; four called MSFT a HOLD; and one lone wolf cried SELL!
- "The good flow of new products should spur sales," said George A. Niemond, writing for *Value Line Investment Survey* on February 24, 2006. "Microsoft loses money on the early versions of the Xbox, though, turning a profit as the product matures and on the sales of games for the machine. Too, expenses associated with developing and marketing vista (the new version of Windows) and Office 12 will also pressure margins in the near term." Mr. Niemond goes on to say, "Good-quality Microsoft shares have some appeal. The issue is ranked to only move with the market during the next six to twelve months, but it has above-average, and well-defined, appreciation potential for the three- to five-year haul."
- *Standard & Poor's Stock Reports* were in the bullish camp on January 27, 2006. G. McDaniel said "We have a STRONG BUY recommendation on the shares, reflecting what we see as MSFT's strong balance sheet, market leadership, and discount to our estimate of intrinsic value, based on our discounted cash flow analysis. The company has continued to diversify its revenue stream into new areas, resulting in solid growth and profitability, in our view, while many competitors were severely affected by the technology downturn."
- Argus Research Company also had a favorable comment on January 27, 2006. Robert K. Becker, CFA, said "We are maintaining our BUY rating on Microsoft Corporation." The analyst goes on to say, "Benefiting from a strong management team and an enormous research and development effort, Microsoft should be able to capitalize on growth opportunities this year. As such, we believe that the company's operating performance has upside potential, particularly in the second half of calendar 2006."
- "We expect Microsoft to grow 50 percent faster than the Standard & Poor's 500 next year (2006)," said David Hilal, a managing director at Friedman Billings Ramsey in Arlington, Virginia, according to an article in the *New York Times* in 2005. "So on a growth-adjusted basis, Microsoft would be actually less expensive than the market multiple. That would probably be the first time that's ever happened."

  The article goes on to say, "The optimism derives from the new-product pipeline, the basis for what Mr. Ballmer, at the company's annual session with financial analysts last month, called 'phenomenal' growth opportunities."
- Xbox is Microsoft's future-generation video game system that gives the game

players experiences they have yet to imagine. With a built-in hard disk drive, Xbox delivers much richer game worlds. And with Dolby Digital 5.1 sound, gamers will actually feel what's happening. Xbox is the only system designed to enable players to compete or collaborate with other players around the world through broadband online gaming.

- Microsoft said it plans to invest $1.7 billion and hire 3,000 additional people in India over the next four years, making it the latest in a line of foreign companies to pledge more than $1 billion each to tap growth and talent in the subcontinent, according to any article in the *Wall Street Journal*, dated late in 2005.

The author, Eric Bellman, said, "Microsoft Chairman Bill Gates said his company was increasing its presence in India because it expects the country to become an increasingly important area of demand for its software as well as a source for the highly qualified but inexpensive engineers Microsoft needs to build its empire.

"'We are keen to increase the growth of Microsoft activities in India,' Mr. Gates told a news conference in New Delhi. 'Microsoft has been in India fifteen years now, and our commitment continues to grow.'"

The article also said, "The high-tech sector is ripe for investment, analysts said, as an increasing number of big international names are outsourcing to India everything from software programming to accounting to telemarketing.

"India also is becoming an increasingly important source of demand, as the country's affluent middle class is buying cell phones, computers, and cars at an unprecedented rate."

SECTOR: **Information Technology** ◆ BETA COEFFICIENT: **1.20**
10-YEAR COMPOUND EARNINGS PER SHARE GROWTH: **22.7%**
10-YEAR COMPOUND DIVIDENDS PER SHARE GROWTH: **no dividend prior to 2003**

		2005	2004	2003	2002	2001	2000	1999	1998
Revenues (millions)		39,788	36,835	32,187	28,365	25,296	22,956	19,747	14,484
Net Income (millions)		12,254	8,168	9,993	7,829	7,785	9,421	7,625	4,786
Earnings per share		1.16	1.04	.97	.94	.90	.85	.70	.45
Dividends per share		.32	.16	.08	Nil	—	—	—	—
Price	high	28.2	27.5	30.0	35.3	38.1	58.6	60.0	36.0
	low	23.8	21.6	22.6	20.7	21.3	20.2	34.0	15.6

AGGRESSIVE GROWTH

Motorola, Inc.

1303 East Algonquin Road ❑ Schaumburg, IL 60196 ❑ (847) 576-6873 ❑ Direct Dividend reinvestment plan available (800) 704-4098 ❑ Web site: *www.motorola.com* ❑ Listed: NYSE ❑ Ticker symbol: MOT ❑ S&P rating: B+ ❑ Value Line financial strength rating: B++

On November 21, 2005, Motorola, a global leader in wireless communications, and Skype, a global Internet communications company, announced the first Skype-certified Bluetooth headset solution in America, the Motorola Wireless Internet Calling Kit.

Available at 3,500 RadioShack stores nationwide, the Motorola Wireless Internet Calling Kit enables Skype users to experience the freedom of wireless while making free, unlimited voice calls over the Internet. Comprised of a Motorola H500 Bluetooth Headset and PC850 PC Adapter, the Motorola Wireless Internet Calling Kit also includes 30 free SkypeOut minutes so users can make Skype calls to mobile and landline phones without additional charges.

To experience wireless communications, users plug in the Motorola PC850 PC Adapter to equip traditional laptops and PCs with Bluetooth technology, load the required software onto the PC and follow a simple, step-by-step procedure to establish the cordless connection between the PC and Motorola H500 headset.

The Motorola Wireless Internet Calling Kit is the latest offering from Motorola and Skype. Leveraging Motorola's strength in seamless mobility, advanced technologies, devices, and accessories along with Skype's rapidly-growing global user base and rich voice and messaging communication tools, the companies aim to provide greater connectivity options and access for Skype's more than 66 million registered worldwide users.

"Motorola and Skype are combining the power of Internet telephone with Bluetooth technology, redefining the ways that consumers can stay in touch," said Bruce Hawver, vice president and general manager, Motorola, Inc., Companion Products. "Multi-taskers will be impressed with the streamlined communications, using the Motorola H500 Bluetooth Headset for either wire-free mobile or Internet-based calls."

"By working with Motorola, we're delivering products that make Skype more accessible to consumers and businesses," said Niklas Zennström, Skype CEO and co-founder. "The Motorola Wireless Internet Calling Kit is the first Skype-recommended Bluetooth solution in America, reinforcing our mission to evolve the Skype solution beyond the desktop for on-the-go communications."

With up to approximately eight hours of talk time and a lightweight, ergonomic fit, the Motorola H500 empowers Skype users to embrace wireless connectivity for Internet calls—up to thirty feet away from a Bluetooth-enabled PC. Skype users can also have calls automatically forwarded to their compatible Bluetooth-enabled mobile phones when away from the PC and use the Motorola H500 Headset to wirelessly conduct cord-free conversations on their mobile phone.

About Skype

Skype allows people everywhere to make free, unlimited, voice calls, chat, and share files. Skype is available in twenty-seven languages and is the fastest growing voice communications offering worldwide. Skype has been downloaded more than 200 million times in 225 countries and territories. Sixty-six million people are registered to use Skype's free services, with over 175 thousand new registered users each day, and more than four million people using Skype simultaneously at any one time. Skype earns revenue through its premium service offerings and has a growing network of global affiliates, and a community of developers working with the Skype APIs.

Company Profile

According to the company's 10-K (an annual publication that is more detailed and sophisticated than its annual report), Motorola is a global leader in wireless, broadband, and automotive communications technology and embedded electronic products.

Wireless

Handsets: Motorola is one of the world's leading providers of wireless handsets, which transmit and receive voice, text, images, and other forms of information and communication.

Wireless Networks: Motorola also develops, manufactures, and markets public and enterprise wireless infrastructure communications systems, including hardware, software, and services.

Mission-Critical Information Systems: In addition, Motorola is a leading provider of customized, mission-critical radio communications and information systems.

Broadband

Motorola is a global leader in developing and deploying end-to-end digital broadband entertainment, communication, and information systems for the home and for the office. Motorola broadband technology enables operators and retailers to deliver products and services that connect consumers to what they want, when they want it.

Automotive

Motorola is the world's largest market leader in embedded telematics systems that enable automated roadside assistance, navigation, and advanced safety features for automobiles. Motorola also provides integrated electronics for the powertrain, chassis, sensors, and interior controls.

Shortcomings to Bear in Mind

- "While most phones were getting plumper to pack in cameras and stereo speakers, Arnholt (*a designer at Motorola*) and top company executives wanted to become what they called 'the kings of thin,'" said Roger O. Crockett, writing for *BusinessWeek* on December 5, 2005. "The result: the wildly popular RAZR, introduced a year ago. Barely a half-inch thick, with sleek lines and a shimmering keypad, it has become a must-have phone for actress Mischa Barton, celeb Denise Richards and more than twelve million cell-phone users across the globe."

  On a negative note, the author went on to say, "Well, it's time to check the rearview. Rivals are coming on fast with their own trim mobile phones to take on Motorola's pacesetter. Korea's Samsung Electronics looks to be the most aggressive. By the first week of December (2005), Sprint Nextel Corp. is expected to start selling Samsung's A900, a similar svelte clamshell phone."
- Motorola has a choppy history, with earnings bobbing up and down from one year to the next. The price of the stock has also been gyrating, from a high of $61.5 in 2000 to a low of $7.3 in 2002 and was still far below its high during 2005. If you're looking for an aggressive growth stock, you have found one. What's more, its beta is indicative of its volatility, at 1.30.
- The dividend has remained stationary at $0.16 per share since 1997.

Reasons to Buy

- On March 19, 2006, the *New York Times* reported the opinions of thirty-eight analysts, of which nine said Motorola was a STRONG BUY; nineteen called the stock a MODERATE BUY; and ten preferred to rate it a HOLD.
- *Standard & Poor's Stock Reports* was gung ho on Motorola, with this comment on January 24, 2006, according to analyst K. Leon, "Our recommendation is STRONG BUY. We believe MOT's major wireless customers will continue to buy higher quantities of handsets and increase network spending in 2006 for 3G system upgrades. In our opinion, MOT is well positioned to grow its handset and broadband businesses and use its free cash flow to retire long-term debt, make some tactical acquisitions, consider some asset sales on non-strategic businesses and possibly repurchase common shares."
- *Value Line Investment Survey* was equally ecstatic over Motorola's prospects on January 13,2006, giving the stock its highest ranking for Timeliness. Edward Plank had this comment:

"Motorola shares are Timely. The company's out to late decade are above average, as well. Competition remains fierce and the battle for market share wages on. But, given the success of its recent product portfolio, Motorola has been able to wrest some additional global market share."

- Nor was management shy about commenting on its current prospects, according to CEO Ed Zander who completed his first year in that post in 2004. He had this comment in 2005, "We captured the world's attention with iconic products like the RAZR, the thinnest mobile device ever made, that is both an engineering and a design marvel. Our vision around Seamless Mobility is redefining the future of mobile communications.

"The progress we made in 2004 is just the beginning, as we continue to deliver increased value to our shareholders. We are moving ahead on the path to transform this great company into the greatest company—with vision, consistent performance and superior financial results."

- On February 1, 2006, the Argus Research Company had a favorable view of Motorola, according to analyst Jim Kelleher, CFA: "BUY-rated Motorola, Inc. continues to gain mobile handset share, based on its very strong third-quarter EPS (earnings per share) report. Motorola was able to boost its handset margins even while ramping up shipments of low-cost handsets for developing markets. The RAZR, an iconic handset that is flying off the shelves, has been joined by other memorably named units, such as the iTunes-enable ROKR and the nubby PEBL. Despite lower gross margins, Motorola raised its overall operating margin. The company also generated strong cash flows while paying down substantial debt in the quarter."

SECTOR: **Information Technology** ◆ BETA COEFFICIENT: **1.30**
10-YEAR COMPOUND EARNINGS PER SHARE GROWTH: **6.4%**
10-YEAR COMPOUND DIVIDENDS PER SHARE GROWTH: **2.1%**

		2005	2004	2003	2002	2001	2000	1999	1998
Revenues (millions)		36,843	31,323	27,058	26,679	30,004	37,580	30,931	29,398
Net Income (millions)		4,578	1,928	581	314	Def.	1,797	1,297	347
Earnings per share		1.82	0.78	0.25	0.14	Def.	0.84	0.69	0.19
Dividends per share		0.16	0.16	0.08	0.16	0.16	0.16	0.16	0.16
Price	high	25.0	20.9	14.4	17.1	25.1	61.5	49.8	22.0
	low	14.5	13.8	7.6	7.3	10.5	15.8	20.3	12.8

AGGRESSIVE GROWTH

Nabors Industries Ltd.

2nd Floor International Trading Center ❑ Warrens ❑ P. O. Box 905E ❑ St. Michaels, Barbados ❑ (281) 775-8038 ❑ Dividend reinvestment plan is not available ❑ Web site: *www.nabors.com* ❑ Listed: NYSE ❑ Ticker symbol: NBR ❑ S&P rating: B ❑ Value Line financial strength rating: B++

"Nabors continues to invest in enhancing the quality and versatility of our assets," said an official of Nabors Industries Ltd. in 2005. "Our goal is to help reduce the increasing costs and difficulties our customers face in finding incremental supplies of oil and gas. To this end, we have continually focused our acquisition efforts on high-specification rigs that lend themselves to reconfiguration for new drilling applications and to the upgrades necessary to fully exploit advancements in technology.

"Recent examples exist in the Rocky Mountains and in Canada where we modified rigs specifically to accommodate the drilling of closely spaced wells on pads to minimize environmental impact. We are also continuing to implement a fleet-wide program to increase individual rig power in order to drive the larger pumps necessary to accommodate new bit technology and the increased use of horizontal drilling. Collectively, these actions are reducing the time required to drill a well, creating the impetus to continue investing in corresponding reductions in rig-moving time to further shorten the drilling cycle. These investments have had a clear and significant positive impact on our customers' drilling economics."

Company Profile

Nabors is the largest land drilling contractor, with about 600 land drilling rigs. The company conducts oil, gas, and geothermal land drilling operations in the lower forty-eight states, Alaska, Canada, South and Central America, the Middle East, the Far East, and Africa. What's more, NBR is one of the largest land well-servicing and workover contractors in the United States and Canada.

Nabors owns about 700 land workover and well servicing rigs in the United States, primarily in the southwestern and western United States and about 215 land workover and well-servicing rigs in Canada. Nabors is also a leading provider of offshore platform workover and drilling rigs and owns forty-three platform, nineteen jack-up units, and three barge rigs in the United States and multiple international markets.

Land Rigs

A land-based drilling rig generally consists of engines, a draw-works, a mast (or derrick), pumps to circulate the drilling fluid (mud) under various pressures, blowout preventers, drilling string, and related equipment.

The engines power the different pieces of equipment, including a rotary table or top drive that turns the drill string, causing the drill bit to bore through the subsurface rock layers. Rock cuttings are carried to the surface by the circulating drilling fluid. The intended well depth, bore hole diameter, and drilling site conditions are the principal factors that determine the size and type of rig most suitable for a particular drilling job.

Platform Rigs

Platform rigs provide offshore workover, drilling, and re-entry services. The company's platform rigs have drilling and/or well-servicing or workover equipment and machinery arranged in modular packages that are transported to, and assembled and installed on, fixed offshore platforms owned by the customer.

Fixed offshore platforms are steel towerlike structures that either stand on the ocean floor or are moored floating structures. The top portion, or platform, sits above the water level and provides the foundation upon which the platform rig is placed.

Jack-up Rigs

Jack-up rigs are mobile, self-elevating drilling and workover platforms equipped with legs that can be lowered to the ocean floor until a foundation is established to support the hull, which contains the drilling and/or workover equipment, jacking system, crew quarters, loading and unloading facilities, storage areas for bulk and liquid materials, helicopter landing deck, and other related equipment. The rig legs may operate independently or have a mat attached to the lower portion of the legs to provide a more stable foundation in soft bottom areas.

Shortcomings to Bear in Mind

- If the high price of oil and natural gas bring on a worldwide recession, the demand for these energy products could recede substantially and lead to a reduction in drilling.

Reasons to Buy

- "We expect 2006 to be another record earnings year for Nabors Industries, as the company's operating fundamentals steam along at all-time highs," said Michael P. Maloney, writing for *Value Line Investment Survey* on February 17, 2006. "Management previously stated that every indication at all of its businesses is reinforcing its belief that the current drilling cycle will be more powerful and enduring than previous cyclical peaks. With record oil and natural gas prices apparently failing to subdue rising global energy demand, we see it increasingly difficult to counter Nabors's claim."
- On February 13, 2006, *Standard & Poor's* analyst Stewart Glickman, said, "We have a STRONG BUY recommendation on the stock, based, in part, on our expectation that strong fundamentals will continue in land drilling for some time. We think NBR should trade at a modest premium to its peers, partly based on its leadership position in the industry and greater presence in fast-growing international regions."
- "We are maintaining our BUY rating on Nabors Industries Ltd.," said Jeb Armstrong, writing for Argus Research Company on February 8, 2006. "Barring an immense collapse in the demand for oil and gas, Nabors will continue to see strong earnings growth, as the need for both new and rehabilitated wells increase. This growing need, coupled with the limited supply of existing rigs and limited rig construction capacity, should provide a strong market for Nabors over the next few years."

  Mr. Armstrong goes on to say, "As one of the largest offshore drilling and well-servicing contractors in North America, Nabors is capturing a good portion of the growth in drilling activity in the United States and Canada. Its sizable fleet of work-over rigs enables it to help production firms maximize production from existing wells."
- On March 19, 2006, the *New York Times* tabulated the results of a survey of leading analysts. Five analysts rated the stock a STRONG BUY; eight called it a MODERATE BUY, five said NBR was a HOLD; two regarded it as a MODERATE HOLD; one had the audacity to call the stock a SELL.
- According to a company spokesman, "Nabors continues to make substantial investments in the latest rig and equipment technology and in the instrumentation systems that facilitate data collection, distribution and processing. A significant portion of this investment is in A/C electrical drive systems and the attendant computer-based programmable logic control systems.

  "These lend themselves to more finite control of the drilling process as well as facilitating remote diagnostics and troubleshooting, including advanced warning of mechanical and electrical failures, and the downloading of remedial software."
- The spokesman also said, "Nabors continues to invest in expanding our current areas of operations and in the penetration of new markets, not only geographically but in rig types and business lines. Our success in this effort is derived from our large, diverse asset base and broad infrastructure that allow us to deploy rigs in whatever demand materializes at favorable capital costs.

  "We continue to adapt existing concepts to new applications, such as in deepwater where we were able to upgrade our MASE and Super Sundowner rigs into Modular Offshore Dynamic Series (MODS) rigs to withstand the dynamic forces generated by wave action. Even in a mature industry like well-servicing, we were able to roll out the Millennium rig, a step-change in safety and efficiency for workover rigs. We were able to expand in our existing markets, significantly increasing the number of units working in Saudi Arabia, the United States Rocky Mountains and Canada. We continue to capitalize on other opportunities to deploy under-utilized assets, particularly the movement of Gulf of Mexico offshore rigs to international venues such as India, Mexico, and Indonesia."

SECTOR: **Energy** ◆ BETA COEFFICIENT: **1.15**
10-YEAR COMPOUND EARNINGS PER SHARE GROWTH: **21.3%**
10-YEAR COMPOUND DIVIDENDS PER SHARE GROWTH: **no dividend**

		2005	2004	2003	2002	2001	2000	1999	1998
Revenues (millions)		3,551	2,394	1,880	1,466	2,121	1,327	638	1,029
Net Income (millions)		660	302	192	108	348	136	28	125
Earnings per share		2.01	0.96	0.63	0.36	1.09	0.45	0.12	0.58
Dividends per share		Nil	—	—	—	—	—	—	—
Price	high	40.0	27.2	22.9	25.0	31.6	30.3	15.7	15.8
	low	23.1	20.0	16.1	13.1	9.0	14.1	5.4	5.9

INCOME

New Jersey Resources Corporation

P. O. Box 1468 ❑ Wall, NJ 07719 ❑ (732) 938-1229 ❑ Dividend reinvestment plan available (800) 817-3955 ❑ Web site: *www.njliving.com* ❑ Fiscal year ends September 30 ❑ Ticker symbol: NJR ❑ S&P rating: A ❑ Value Line financial strength rating: B+

"This year, I had the privilege of serving as the Chairman of our industry trade association, the American Gas Association (AGA), which represents 195 local natural gas distribution companies that deliver natural gas to more than fifty-six million customers throughout the United States," said CEO Laurence M. Downes on December 1, 2005. "The AGA has been a tireless voice in advocating for a comprehensive national energy policy to meet our customers' energy needs now and in the future.

"Through the efforts of the AGA, working in partnership with many others, we were able to help secure the passage of The Energy Policy Act of 2005. For the first time in thirteen years, we have legislation that focuses on the supply, delivery and use of renewable energy, nuclear power and fossil fuels, such as natural gas. It also recognizes the important role that efficiency and conservation will play in the future.

"While the Act addresses some critical issues, it will not have an immediate impact upon energy prices. It does provide certain benefits, including incentives for new pipeline infrastructure, energy efficiency and conservation, as well as expanded resources to help low-income families with their energy bills. More needs to be done, however, in the areas of accessing reserves and pursuing environmental initiatives if we are to make progress in lowering prices for customers."

Company Profile

New Jersey Resources is organized into three primary businesses: New Jersey Natural Gas (NJNG), the company's principal subsidiary; NJR Energy Service; NJR Energy Services; and NJR Home Services.

New Jersey Natural Gas

New Jersey Natural Gas serves more than 462,000 customers in New Jersey's Monmouth and Ocean counties and parts of Morris and Middlesex counties. Since 1952, customers have counted on NJNG for the natural gas that keeps their homes warm and businesses running. Through the service area's outstanding demographics, New Jersey Natural Gas has maintained an average annual customer growth of about 2.5 percent over the past ten years. The company is also a leader in the off-system and capacity-release markets.

NJR Energy Services

NJR Energy Services provides unregulated wholesale energy services to customers in New Jersey, as well as states from the Gulf Coast to New England and Canada. According to a company spokesman, "NJR provides customer service and management of natural gas storage and capacity assets to assist customers maintain their competitive edge. Our natural gas supply, pipeline capacity and storage management services include storage positions in the Gulf Coast, Appalachia, Mid-Continent and Canada."

NJR Home Services

NJR Home Services provides home appliance service, sales, and installations to customers primarily in New Jersey's Monmouth and Ocean counties and parts of Morris and Middlesex counties. The company official goes on to say, "We offer comprehensive appliance service contracts and related products and services, including installing, servicing and repairing natural gas furnaces, hot water heaters, grills, outdoor lights and electric central air conditioning equipment. Our team of skilled, certified technicians offers unparalleled care and service for our customers' comfort at home."

Shortcomings to Bear in Mind

- In fiscal 2006, CEO Laurence M. Downes said, "Rising wholesale natural gas prices have created unprecedented challenges for our industry. Demand for natural gas by home owners, businesses and electric generation remains strong, given its efficiency and cleanliness. At the same time, supply has not kept pace, and the impact of Hurricanes Katrina and Rita has complicated the situation further. Unfortunately, high and volatile prices will persist in our industry unless specific federal policy initiatives are pursued immediately."
- On March 25, 2006, *Value Line Investment Survey* awarded New Jersey Resources a below-average rating (4) for Timeliness. Evan I. Blatter had this comment: "These shares are good quality, and the company's consistent results are reflected in the stock price. Recently, the board increased its share-repurchase program, and coupled with strong customer growth and contributions from the company's wholesale business, this should support steady earnings advances. However, the yield doesn't stand out from the group. The stock is also not favorably ranked for year-ahead performance."
- On March 25, 2006, the views of five financial analysts were tabulated by the *New York Times.* Only one rated the stock a STRONG BUY; three called it a HOLD; and one said it was a MODERATE HOLD. Are they trying to tell us something?

Reasons to Buy

- On February 6, 2006, New Jersey Resources announced improved fiscal 2006 first quarter earnings of $1.24 per basic share, a 14 percent increase over the same period from the prior year. NJR's earnings were $34.3 million, compared with $30.2 million in 2005.

"We are off to a solid start in fiscal 2006," said Mr. Downes. "Our record of earnings consistency is supported by continued strong growth in our successful unregulated wholesale energy services business."

NJR's successful first quarter earnings were driven by the company's wholesale energy services business unit, which saw earnings grow to $14.9 million,, a 127 percent increase over the $6.6 million for the same period in 2005. These strong results more than offset the impact of lower customer usage at New Jersey Natural Gas, the company's largest subsidiary.

■ On January 11, 2006, New Jersey Resources said that it had been named a member of the *Forbes Platinum 400*, the annual list of America's Best Big Companies, published by *Forbes* magazine. A company official said, "This is the fourth consecutive year the company has been placed on the list, due to its strong financial performance."

Each year, *Forbes* magazine searches twenty-six industries for companies that stand out above their peers in several areas. To be considered for the list, a company must have annual revenue of more than $1 billion and rank in the upper half of its industry group for sales and earnings growth, stock market returns, and debt to total capital.

In six of the past seven years, the companies listed in the *Forbes Platinum 400* have outperformed the stock market in the twelve months following the list's announcement.

■ "With an unparalleled record of earnings growth consistency over the past fourteen years—and a rock-solid balance sheet—New Jersey Resources is one of our favorite utilities," said *Morningstar Stock Report* on December 12, 2005. The report goes on to say, "New Jersey Natural Gas—the company's regulated distribution business—accounts for the bulk of NJR's earnings and has been the driving force behind the company's earnings stability and growth. NJNG is one of the fastest-growing local distribution companies in the United States, with customer growth averaging roughly 3 percent over the last ten years—twice the industry average. Population growth in the NJNG's service territory has been the foundation of the company's impressive growth, but it has also benefited from customers converting from competing fuels to natural gas."

■ "We continue to rate the shares of New Jersey Resources a BUY and view the company as one of the best-managed and financially strong companies in the natural gas distribution industry," said David M. Schanzer, an analyst with Janney Montgomery Scott (a leading brokerage firm) on February 6, 2006. The report goes on to say, "New Jersey Resources has historically traded at a premium to its traditional natural gas distribution group. We believe a greater premium for New Jersey Resources is justified, given the company's ability to deliver on its objectives, as demonstrated by its earnings and dividend record over the past fourteen years, as well as its strong balance sheet and credit ratings. Our valuation is also based on New Jersey Resources's well-defined strategy, solid regulated earnings base, above-average customer growth, reasonable regulatory environment, consistent historical and projected earnings and dividend growth, and strong financial position."

■ NJNG currently purchases a diverse gas supply consisting of long-term (more than seven months), winter-term (for the five winter months), and short-term contracts within its portfolio. In fiscal 2005, NJNG purchased gas from eighty-nine suppliers under contracts ranging from one day to ten years. In fiscal 2005, the distributor purchased about 12.9 percent of its natural gas from BP Energy Company, 12.2 percent from Alberta Northeast Gas Limited, and 10.6 percent from Atmos Energy Marketing. No other supplier provided more than 10 percent of NJNG's natural gas supplies. The company believes the loss of any one of all these suppliers would not have a material adverse impact on its results of operations, financial position, or cash flows. What's more, the company believes that its supply strategy should adequately meet its expected firm load over the next several years.

SECTOR: **Utilities** ◆ BETA COEFFICIENT: **.75**
10-YEAR COMPOUND EARNINGS PER SHARE GROWTH: **7.5%**
10-YEAR COMPOUND DIVIDENDS PER SHARE GROWTH: **3%**

		2005	2004	2003	2002	2001	2000	1999	1998
Revenues (millions)		3,148	2,534	2,544	1,831	2,048	1,164	904	710
Net Income (millions)		74.5	71.6	65.4	56.8	52.3	47.9	44.9	43.3
Earnings per share		2.65	2.55	2.38	2.09	1.95	1.79	1.66	1.55
Dividends per share		1.36	1.30	1.24	1.20	1.17	1.15	1.12	1.09
Price	high	49.3	44.6	39.5	33.6	32.5	29.8	27.4	26.8
	low	40.7	36.5	30.0	24.3	24.8	24.1	22.4	21.0

CONSERVATIVE GROWTH

Norfolk Southern Corporation

Three Commercial Place ❑ Norfolk, VA 23510-2191 ❑ (757) 533-4810 ❑ Dividend reinvestment plan available (866) 272-9472 ❑ Web site: *www.nscorp.com* ❑ Ticker symbol: NSC ❑ Listed: NYSE ❑ S&P rating: B ❑ Value Line financial strength rating: B

Freight transportation is undergoing immense change, and it favors railroads. Demand for rail transportation is expanding in all major business sectors: coal, intermodal, and general merchandise.

A dynamic convergence of circumstances is driving this demand, while shaping a structural change in the basic nature of the transportation business:

- Rising freight volumes have strained the capacity of highways, increasing congestion.
- Driver and equipment shortages are increasing costs for trucking companies.
- Fuel prices favor the inherent efficiency advantages of railroads. One intermodal train pulled by two locomotives can haul the equivalent of up to 300 trucks. Trucking companies are converting business to rail, accelerating growth in intermodal traffic. Norfolk Southern meanwhile has built the most extensive intermodal network in the East.
- Intermodal traffic has been very successful for railroads in general. This involves moving truck trailers and containers that normally would be hauled over the highway. In the past, intermodal business did not apply to shorter hauls, those of 500 miles or less. More recently, railroads have even been competing successfully in this sector, as well. One reason for growth in intermodal business is the problem that truckers have had in hiring drivers. Turnover among drivers has been high because drivers are averse to being away from home several weeks at a stretch.
- Changing ocean shipping patterns have led to a surge of intermodal traffic at East Coast ports. Traditionally, Asian imports have moved by ship to the U.S. West Coast, and then by rail inland. Now,

more and more traffic from Asia is routed through the Panama Canal to East Coast ports. Both coasts have seen triple-digit growth of imports from Asia.

- Norfolk Southern has positioned itself to take on additional business and handle it effectively and efficiently. New systems have enhanced operating efficiency, service, and capacity.
- The Thoroughbred Operating Plan and the Coal Transportation Management System are driving improved service and capacity for Norfolk Southern's general merchandise and coal networks.

Company Profile

Norfolk Southern Corporation is one of the nation's premier transportation companies. Its Norfolk Southern Railway subsidiary operates 21,500 route miles in twenty-two states, the District of Columbia, and Ontario, Canada, serving every major container port in the eastern United States and providing superior connections to western rail carriers. NS operates the most extensive intermodal network in the East and is North America's largest rail carrier of automotive parts and finished vehicles.

Shortcomings to Bear in Mind

- Norfolk Southern is a cyclical company, not a growth company. Look at its records of earnings per share for evidence. In the past ten years, earnings per share have fluctuated up and down from a high of $2.70 in 2005 to a low of $0.55 in 2000. Only rarely have EPS risen to $2. The dividend record is equally spotty. For several years, the company paid $0.80, from 1997 through 2000. The following year, the dividend payout was slashed to $0.24 and is only $0.48 at present.
- "These shares are ranked to outperform the broader market in the year ahead," said Garrett Sussman, writing for *Value Line Investment Survey* on March 10, 2006. "The stock's strong earnings and price momentum has led to this favorable rating. The issue offers about average appreciation potential for the 2009–2011 timeframe."
- On January 30, 2006, *Standard & Poor's Stock Reports* was lukewarm. The analyst said, "our HOLD recommendation is based on total return potential. We believe the shares are fairly valued based on our longer-term growth outlook for NSC."

Reasons to Buy

- Norfolk Southern Corporation plans to spend $1.146 billion in 2006 for capital improvements to its railroad operations and subsidiaries.

"Continuing strong demand for rail transportation is driving the need for additional investment in Norfolk Southern's rail network," said CEO Wick Moorman on December 9, 2005. "Our 2006 capital program ensures that our network and assets continue to be well maintained and also provides for increased capacity in terms of infrastructure, locomotives and cars, and new technology. These investments will enable Norfolk Southern to maintain its safe and reliable operations while providing for further improvements in customer service and capacity for continuing growth."

The anticipated spending includes $735 million for roadway projects, $358 million for equipment, and $53 million for small projects and real estate.

In roadway improvements, the largest expenditure will be $484 million for rail, crosstie, ballast, and bridge programs. In addition, $37 million is provided for communications, signal, and electrical projects; $35 million for maintenance of way equipment; $29 million for modifications to a new data center located in Tucker, Georgia, and $15 million for environmental projects and public improvements such as grade crossing separations and crossing signal upgrades.

Equipment spending includes $305 million to purchase 138 six-axle locomotives, upgrade existing locomotives, certify and rebuild 225 multilevel automobile racks, and add supplemental restraints to multilevel racks. Equipment spending also includes $35 million for projects related to computers, systems, and information technology, which will improve operations efficiency and equipment utilization.

Business development initiatives total $103 million and include investments in intermodal terminals and equipment to add capacity to the intermodal network, increased capacity and access to coal receivers, bulk transfer facilities, and vehicle production and distribution facilities.

- On December 5, 2005, Norfolk Southern Corporation and New York Air Brake Corporation announced an agreement to begin deploying a locomotive computer system to improve the fuel efficiency and safe handling of trains in long-haul operations.

The system, developed by New York Air Brake and known as LEADER® (Locomotive Engineer Assist Display and Event Recorder), provides locomotive engineers with real-time information about a train's operating conditions. It consists of an onboard computer that calculates and displays the optimum speed at which to operate the train, depending on the topography and curvature of the track to be encountered, the train's length and weight and other operating conditions.

NS tested LEADER in a 2003 pilot project involving 15 locomotives running coal trains between Winston-Salem, North Carolina, and Roanoke, Virginia. The two-year pilot was a cooperative effort involving General Electric, New York Air Brake, Norfolk Southern and the Federal Railroad Administration.

"The project proved that LEADER could reduce fuel consumption and minimize in-train dynamic forces," said John Samuels, Norfolk Southern senior vice president Operations Planning and Support. "In 2006 we will begin installing the technology on NS' road locomotive fleet."

"Norfolk Southern has been an outstanding partner in helping validate the fuel savings and other benefits provided by LEADER through exhaustive field trials" said J. Paul Morgan, NYAB President. "We are delighted with Norfolk Southern's decision to begin installation of LEADER on its road locomotive fleet in 2006."

LEADER ultimately will be an integral part of the Optimized Train Control (OTC) system, a positive train control program announced earlier this year and currently in testing. OTC will combine data communications, positioning systems, and onboard computers tied to a train's braking systems to enforce speed and operating limits automatically.

New York Air Brake Corporation, a member of the Knorr-Bremse Group, supplies air brake control systems and components, electronically controlled braking systems, foundation brakes, training simulators, and driver information systems to the freight railroad industry. NYAB has facilities in Watertown, New York, where it is headquartered, and in Fort Worth, Texas and Kingston, Ontario, Canada. Knorr-Bremse Group is the world's leading manufacturer of brake systems for rail and commercial vehicles.

- On March 25, 2006, the *New York Times* surveyed a dozen analysts concerning their view of Norfolk Southern. Four called the stock a STRONG BUY, five rated it a MODERATE BUY; and three rated it a HOLD.

- "Shares of BUY-rated Norfolk Southern Corp. jumped recently amid a strong earnings season for the rails," said Suzanne Betts, writing for Argus Research Company on January 26, 2006. "The outlook for rails remains bright for 2006 and 2007, as rate increases and more efficient operations stimulate top- and bottom-line growth."

SECTOR: **Industrials** ◆ BETA COEFFICIENT: **1.00**
10-YEAR COMPOUND EARNINGS PER SHARE GROWTH: **5.5%**
10-YEAR COMPOUND DIVIDENDS PER SHARE GROWTH: **-3.6%**

		2005	2004	2003	2002	2001	2000	1999	1998
Revenues (millions)		8,527	7,312	6,468	6,270	6,170	6,159	5,195	4,221
Net Income (millions)		1,281	870	529	460	362	210	239	630
Earnings per share		3.11	2.18	1.35	1.18	0.94	0.55	0.63	1.65
Dividends per share		.48	0.36	0.30	0.26	0.24	0.80	0.80	0.80
Price	high	45.8	36.7	24.6	27.0	24.1	22.8	36.4	41.8
	low	29.6	20.4	17.3	17.2	13.4	11.9	19.6	27.4

AGGRESSIVE GROWTH

OshkoshTruck Corporation

2307 Oregon Street ❑ P. O. Box 2566 ❑ Oshkosh, WI 54903-2566 ❑ (920) 233-9332 ❑ Web site: *www.oshkoshtruckcorporation.com* ❑ Dividend reinvestment plan available (866) 222-4059 ❑ Fiscal year ends September 30 ❑ Listed: NYSE ❑ Ticker symbol: OSK ❑ S&P rating: A ❑ Value Line financial strength rating: not covered

CEO Robert G. Bohn made these comments in fiscal 2006:

"When we talk about our fierce growth orientation, we mean it. We are getting it done. In fiscal 2005, we drove sales to nearly $3 billion, up more than 30 percent year-over-year. For the first year ever, our operating income margin reached 9 percent as operating income grew 48.1 percent, to $267.2 million, and net income climbed 42 percent, to $160.2 million. Most impressively, our earnings per share growth of 38.9 percent, up from $1.57, to $1.18, capped a five-year period during which we have delivered a 194.6 percent total increase in earnings per share."

"Overall, our defense sector posted the strongest results, with operating income rising 64.4 percent. Fire and emergency quietly delivered an exceptional year as well, with operating income growth of 44.9 percent. The commercial business underperformed but showed signs of improvement late in the fiscal year."

"Several factors contributed to our record performance, but none more than our disciplined approach to business. We plan strategically, always searching for big ideas. We act decisively and aggressively, making things happen rather than waiting to see what happens. Specifically, five strategic areas impacted fiscal 2005 performance.

"First, we were able to step up to the strong defense parts, service and remanufacturing requirements resulting from heavy use of thousands of our trucks in Iraq.

"Second, we drove market share gains in the fire and emergency business, particularly leveraging opportunities for homeland security vehicles.

"Third, we faced challenges in our commercial segment aggressively throughout the year, though we were unable to overcome steel and component cost increases domestically, and European profitability was delayed until the fourth quarter.

"Fourth, we successfully integrated four acquisitions since July 2004, providing $15.4 million of operating income in fiscal 2005. These included JerrDan Corporation, Brescia Antincendi International S.r.l., Concrete

Equipment Company, Inc. and London Machinery, Inc.

"Fifth, our lean initiative took hold, contributing to strong cash flow from operations and cash of $127.5 million at year-end that can be used to continue our acquisition strategy."

Mr. Bohn goes on to say, "Two acquisitions positively impacted the commercial business in fiscal 2005, as we successfully integrated CON-E-CO, a United States manufacturer of concrete batch plants, and London, a Canadian concrete mixer manufacturer. As we move into fiscal 2006, we intend to expand production capacity for batch plants to meet growing demand and leverage London's outstanding service capabilities to enhance support for Canadian refuse-hauling customers.

"Overall, we believe there are several reasons to be optimistic about the outlook for our commercial sector. We expect robust market conditions to continue in the United States into 2006 as a result of prebuys before new engine emissions standards take effect in 2007. In Europe, we expect that our cost reduction initiatives will drive the Geesink Norba Group to modest profitability in fiscal 2006."

Company Profile

OshkoshTruck is a manufacturer of a broad range of specialty commercial, fire and emergency, and military trucks and truck bodies. It sells mostly to customers in domestic and European markets. The company sells trucks under the Oshkosh and Pierce trademarks; truck bodies under the McNeilus, MTM, Medtec, Geesink, and Norba trademarks; and mobile and stationary compactors under the Geesink Kiggen trademark.

Oshkosh began business in 1917 and was among the early pioneers of four-wheel drive technology.

The company's commercial truck lines include refuse truck bodies, rear and front-discharge concrete mixers, and all-wheel drive truck chassis. Its custom and commercial fire apparatus and emergency vehicles include pumpers; aerial and ladder trucks; tankers; light-, medium- and heavy-duty rescue vehicles; wildland and rough-terrain response vehicles; and aircraft rescue and firefighting vehicles and ambulances, and snow-removal vehicles.

As a manufacturer of severe-duty, heavy-tactical trucks for the United States Department of Defense, OshkoshTruck manufactures vehicles that perform a variety of demanding tasks, such as hauling tanks, missile systems, ammunition, fuel, and cargo for combat units. More than 6,500 OshkoshTrucks have been in service in Iraq.

Shortcomings to Bear in Mind

- *Standard & Poor's Company Reports* had the following opinion of OshkoshTruck on February 13, 2006. Anthony M. Fiore, CFA, said, "Our recommendation is HOLD. We believe near-term growth prospects are strong for the company, and we have confidence in management's ability to execute its strategic initiatives over the long term. However, while we expect favorable conditions to continue in many of the end-markets that OSK serves, we believe that our positive outlook is already reflected in the price of the stock."

Reasons to Buy

- On March 5, 2006, the *New York Times* rounded up six analysts who follow OSK and found that three regarded the stock as a STRONG BUY; two said it was a MODERATE BUY; and only one retreated to the HOLD category.
- *Value Line Investment Survey* had these comments on December 2, 2005. Jason A. Smith said, "The U.S.'s continued involvement in Iraq should support the defense segment's top- and bottom-line growth in the near term. Although new military orders will likely slow at some point, Oshkosh ought to be able to offset much of this lost revenue through its re-manufacturing business. In addition, the rise of municipal

spending at home augurs well for the fire and emergency division."

■ In recent years, OshkoshTruck has impressed a host of writers and publications. Here is a sample of their comments:

"Under-promise, over-perform. That seems to be the philosophy of OshkoshTruck, which repeatedly has boosted the shares of the specialty truck maker from about $25 two years ago to a recent $44. And Oshkosh's earnings—along with the share price—appear likely to remain on the upswing over the next year.

"Given the promising outlook for its operations, how much higher could Oshkosh shares go over the next twelve months? While the kind of out-performance seen over the past two years isn't likely, another 10 percent or 15 percent rise could be in the cards." —*Barron's*, December 26, 2005.

"Saddam may have been pried from his hole, but the ongoing military operations in Iraq and Afghanistan continue to deliver a big payload of $1.9 billion (sales) of OshkoshTruck. The U.S. military's need for heavy transport equipment and spare parts in both nations pushed the Oshkosh, Wisconsin-based truckmaker's defense sales to $199 million in 2003's fourth quarter, 18 percent ahead of the year-ago period. Total net income for the full year rose 27 percent, to $76 million, from $60 million."—*Forbes* magazine, January 12, 2004.

"In the past decade at the helm of the top-performing fund at T. Rowe Price, Brian Berghuis has averaged a return of nearly 14 percent annually. He likes to focus on companies flying below the radar because he finds he gets easier access to management. That, in turn, allows him to gain a better understanding of the catalysts that drive the company. Right now, Berghuis is excited about OshkoshTruck. The Wisconsin company makes specialty trucks used by the military, garbage haulers, and cement layers. It also has a 29 percent share of the U.S. fire truck market. And sales are sizzling. Profits have grown 30 percent annually over the past five years." —*Fortune* magazine, December 22, 2003.

"Five years ago, OshkoshTruck was losing money, and its stock was stuck in single digits. Then came a revival. Oshkosh, based in Oshkosh, Wisconsin, borrowed to acquire some specialized businesses with the intention of becoming a rapidly growing manufacturer. Manufacturing isn't usually considered sexy, but consider this: Since October 1997, when Robert Bohn was elevated to CEO, the shares are up by five times, and profits have soared." Kiplinger's Personal Finance, April 2002.

"Since 1997, Oshkosh's earnings have risen from $10 million to about $51 million. Sales have grown to $1.4 billion, from $683 million. And now, the company's growth is about to get a shot in the arm. Given that, the stock appears reasonably valued at 19 times the past four quarter's earnings, 2.6 times book value, and 0.6 times revenue. Though with a market cap of $895 million, the firm is small by my standards, *Forbes* magazine recently named Oshkosh to the number eleven position on its list of best big companies." —*Bloomberg Personal Finance* magazine, April 2002.

■ The development of the ProPulse hybrid electric drive systems exemplifies OshkoshTruck's ability to deliver new technologies to meet the changing demands of all Oshkosh business segments. ProPulse alternative drive technology increases fuel economy up to 40 percent and generates 400 kilowatts of electricity on-board, enough to power an airport, hospital, command center, or an entire city block.

According to a company executive, "Oshkosh was the first company to apply hybrid technology to severe-duty vehicles. With some of the most experienced engineers in the industry working on the project, the Oshkosh team developed many breakthrough technologies for the ProPulse project. Oshkosh has patents pending for many of the technologies incorporated into the ProPulse system.

"The ProPulse technology has applications well beyond the military use, including refuse trucks, fire apparatus, snow removal and other commercial vehicles. In fact, Oshkosh is already adapting the ProPulse technology to a refuse-hauling vehicle."

SECTOR: **Industrials** ◆ BETA COEFFICIENT: **.90**
10-YEAR COMPOUND EARNINGS PER SHARE GROWTH: **25.8%**
10-YEAR COMPOUND DIVIDENDS PER SHARE GROWTH: **10.6%**

		2005	2004	2003	2002	2001	2000	1999	1998
Revenues (millions)		2.960	2,262	1,926	1,744	1,445	1,324	1,165	903
Net Income (millions)		160	113	75.6	59.6	50.9	48.5	31.2	16.3
Earnings per share		2.18	1.57	1.08	0.86	0.74	0.74	0.60	0.32
Dividends per share		.22	.13	.08	.09	.09	.09	.08	.08
Price	high	46.2	34.5	26.4	16.3	12.4	11.0	9.6	5.8
	low	30.3	23.9	13.1	11.5	8.0	5.4	4.8	2.9

AGGRESSIVE GROWTH

Parker Hannifin Corporation

6035 Parkland Boulevard ❑ Cleveland, OH 44124-4141 ❑ (216) 896-3000 ❑ Web site: *www.parker.com* ❑ Dividend reinvestment plan available (800) 622-6757 ❑ Fiscal year ends June 30 ❑ Listed: NYSE ❑ Ticker symbol: PH ❑ S&P's rating: A- ❑ Value Line financial strength rating: B++

"Parker Hannifin has found a winning formula," said Harlan S. Byrne, writing for *Barron's* on January 16, 2006. "In fact, the Cleveland-based maker of industrial motion and control equipment and other products has used what it terms its 'Win Strategy' over the past few years to position itself for growth.

"Parker produces valves, actuators, pumps, cylinders, electronic controls, filters and hundreds of other products used at sites as varied as airplane plants, supermarkets, boatyards, auto factories and car washes. It operates around the globe and employs about 50,000 people. Its products can show up just about anywhere. Remember the climactic scene (at least for the ship) in the movie *Titanic?* Parker Hannifin motion-control equipment helped create the illusion of a monstrous vessel plunging into the frigid Atlantic.

"The aim of the Win Strategy was to make Parker Hannifin strong enough to weather economic downturns well and to accelerate growth in good times. To do this, CEO Donald E. Washkewicz focused on improving profitability, reducing costs, eliminating complexity and reaching long-term, mutually beneficial agreements with suppliers."

Company Profile

In the company's 2005 annual report, its key sectors are outlined:

Aerospace

Parker's cooling technology is used to boost the computing power of mobile military computers by up to five times to facilitate remote intelligence capabilities.

Automation

Parker invented the world's smallest motorized syringe assembly for high throughput autosamplers used in the life sciences market. By synchronizing adaptive fluidic and motion control systems, and by developing strategic partnerships, Parker is delivering pre-engineered solutions that improve precision, and dramatically increase productivity by four times for OEM leaders in the drug discovery process.

Climate & Industrial Controls

Our electronic superheat control system provides temperature control, a wireless interface, a "smart defrost" function for added energy efficiency, and intelligent diagnostic capabilities to keep supermarket refrigeration systems running at optimal performance.

Filtration

Parker's innovative low-pressure fuel systems are getting smarter and lasting longer with new brushless pumps that optimize fuel flow during all engine cycles for agriculture equipment.

Fluid Connectors

Parker assists the oil and gas market with high-pressure capability hoses that provide greater flexibility and safe, economical handling of methanol used to force oil to the surface from subsea wells.

Hydraulics

Parker's next generation hydraulic pumps and motors are quieter, more compact, and more efficient. With our new H1A axial piston pump, we can now offer OEMs in the turf care and similar markets, a complete hydrostatic transmission.

Instrumentation

Process industries extract and analyze pipeline samples to determine their composition and maximize production yields. The sample must then be disposed of properly to ensure environmental compliance. Parker's new vent master system promises to replace complex pumping systems while maintaining stable pressure and flow as the sample is analyzed and discharged through disposal points such as flares and incinerators.

Seal

With our ever-advancing materials and sealing processes, we provide tangible performance benefits in the most critical aerospace, fluid power, energy, oil and gas, and transportation applications. Aggressive fluids, harsh chemicals, high-temperature, and high-pressure are no match for Parker's wide range of sealing systems.

Shortcomings to Bear in Mind

■ The Street is not jumping up and down with enthusiasm about Parker Hannifin. In a tabulation made by the *New York Times* on March 19, 2006, only four out of twenty financial analysts rated the stock a STRONG BUY. Two called the stock a MODERATE BUY, but thirteen rated it a HOLD, and one said it was a MODERATE HOLD.

Reasons to Buy

■ The company achieved record results in fiscal 2005:

- Sales climbed to $8.2 billion, an increase of 17 percent over 2004.
- Income from continuing operations increased to $548 million, or $4.55 per diluted share, compared with $336 million, or $2.82 per diluted share for the prior year.
- Cash flow from operations grew much stronger, too, reaching $872 million, or 10.6 percent of sales.
- The company increased its annual dividend for the forty-ninth consecutive year—one of the longest track records of dividend increases among the Standard & Poor's 500.

■ On January 18, 2006, Parker Hannifin reported second quarter records in sales, income from continuing operations, and cash flow from operations. For the second quarter of fiscal 2006, sales were $2.2 billion, up 13 percent, as compared to sales of $1.9 billion from the same period of the prior year. "The strong sales and income growth over last year's record second quarter results keeps us solidly on track for another record year in fiscal 2006," said CEO Don Washkewicz. "Parker employees across the world continue to execute our Win Strategy, which is providing very clear and positive results in premier customer service, improved operating margins, record cash flows, and profitable growth."

He goes on to say, "As part of our Win Strategy, we have set a goal to grow the company on an organic basis by at least 5 percent each year, and 10 percent overall. I am very pleased to report that of our 13.2 growth in the quarter, more than half came from organic growth (*which means without adding in profits from acquisitions*)."

The CEO also said, "Our growth from acquiring new businesses for the Parker portfolio is the other half of our growth story. Investing in our industry through acquisitions this quarter has added over $490 million in annual revenues to our company. We're especially excited over our recent acquisition of Domnick Hunter, headquartered in the UK. The combination creates a powerful array of filtration, separation, and purification solutions, extending our customer reach in Europe and North America through complementary products and similar cultures of our two organizations."

- On January 19, 2006, Lehman Brothers gave Parker-Hannifin an OVERWEIGHT rating, tantamount to a BUY. The analyst said, "Parker is still one of our favorite ideas in the Machinery space. We think Parker offers a strong combination of actual better performance in this cycle vs. previous cycles."
- Argus Research Company also had good things to say on January 19, 2006. Dana Richardson said, "We are reiterating our BUY rating on Parker Hannifin Corporation. Our expectation that new order growth would accelerate has been validated. Monthly new order growth has risen steadily from a negative 2 percent in February to the positive double digits in December 2005. We expect further acceleration, especially beginning in February, when the company will face easy prior-year comparisons.
- On January 30, 2006, Kenneth L. Fisher, a money manager had this comment in his article in *Forbes* magazine, "In the U.S. Parker Hannifin makes steady profits from motion control systems—the hydraulic parts inside things like backhoes and airplane wings. At thirteen times 2006 earnings, Parker Hannifin can afford to buy back a lot of shares. Before it's done, some acquirer may buy the whole thing."
- Erik M. Manning, writing for *Value Line Investment Survey* on January 27, 2006, had this comment, "Cash flow generation remains robust. We expect funds to be used for acquisitions and the development of new products. Share buybacks appear to be on the minds of the investment community, but higher returns will probably be generated by the investment of capital in automation, filtration and aerospace."

SECTOR: **Industrials** ◆ BETA COEFFICIENT: **1.15**
10-YEAR COMPOUND EARNINGS PER SHARE GROWTH: **8.7%**
10-YEAR COMPOUND DIVIDENDS PER SHARE GROWTH: **6.2%**

		2005	2004	2003	2002	2001	2000	1999	1998
Revenues (millions)		8,215	7,107	6,411	6,149	5,980	5,355	4,959	4,633
Net Income (millions)		548.0	345.8	196.3	130.2	340.8	368.2	310.5	323.2
Earnings per share		4.55	2.77	1.72	1.12	2.98	3.31	2.83	2.88
Dividends per share		.82	.76	.74	.72	.70	.68	.64	.60
Price	high	76.2	78.4	59.8	54.9	50.1	54.0	51.4	52.6
	low	56.8	51.7	35.8	34.5	30.4	31.0	29.5	26.6

AGGRESSIVE GROWTH

Patterson Companies, Inc.
(formerly Patterson Dental Company)

1031 Mendota Heights Road ❑ St. Paul, MN 55120-1419 ❑ (651) 686-1775 ❑ Web site: *www.pattersondental.com* ❑ Dividend reinvestment not plan available ❑ Fiscal year ends last Saturday in April ❑ Listed: Nasdaq ❑ Ticker symbol: PDCO ❑ S&P rating: B+ ❑ Value Line financial strength rating: A

Patterson Dental is the exclusive North American distributor of the CEREC 3D dental restorative system. Reflecting strong ongoing demand for the CEREC system, which is fundamentally changing the way dentists perform crown, inlay, and onlay procedures, the company believes this new technology equipment has gained full clinical acceptance.

Unlike traditional crown procedures that require two office visits for the patient, a CEREC procedure is completed in just one appointment. By strengthening office productivity and enabling the dentist to perform more restorative procedures, CEREC technology is generating new revenue opportunities for dental practices. CEREC procedures also result in improved clinical outcomes with numerous advantages for the patient. It is a conservative treatment that requires no impressions or temporary caps, and the ceramic, metal-free crown is tooth-colored, highly durable, and biocompatible.

Patterson Dental also is the leading provider of digital radiography systems, which rank high on the wish list of most dentists. Unlike traditional film-based X rays, digital systems create instant images. The resulting increase in office productivity enables dentists to treat more patients. The benefits of digital radiography are increased when it is integrated with the appropriate software, including Patterson's proprietary EagleSoft line. This integration creates an electronic database that combines the patient's dental record with digital information from the X ray, intraoral camera, CEREC, and other digital equipment. With a current market penetration of only about 20 percent, it is believed that digital radiography eventually will be installed in most dental offices.

Company Profile

Patterson Companies, Inc. is a value-added distributor serving the dental, companion-pet veterinarian, and rehabilitation supply markets. The company recently changed its name from Patterson Dental Company to reflect its expanding base of business, which now encompasses the veterinary and rehabilitation supply markets, as well as it traditional base of operations in the dental supply market.

Dental Market

As Patterson's largest business, Patterson Dental Supply provides a virtually complete range of consumable dental products, equipment, and software, turnkey digital solutions, and value-added services to dentists and dental laboratories throughout North America.

Veterinary Market

Webster Veterinary Supply is the nation's second-largest distributor of consumable veterinary supplies, equipment, diagnostic products, vaccines, and pharmaceuticals to companion-pet veterinary clinics.

Rehabilitation Market

AbilityOne Products Corp. is the world's leading distributor of rehabilitation supplies and nonwheelchair assistive patient products to the physical and occupational therapy markets. The unit's global customer base includes hospitals, long-term-care facilities, clinics, and dealers.

Shortcomings to Bear in Mind

■ On December 27, 2006, *Lehman Brothers* had this negative comment: "We reiterate our Equal weight rating on PDCO after the company's late Friday announcement that the head of its dental business was resigning. With sales growth moderating and management turnover increasing, we continue to be cautious on the stock."

■ As noted below, Patterson Dental has a most impressive record of consistent growth. It is not surprising that the stock normally sells at a lofty P/E ratio.

Reasons to Buy

■ On March 19, 2006, the *New York Times* checked with eight securities analysts for their views on the stock. Two looked upon Patterson as a STRONG BUY; four said it was a HOLD; and two regarded it as a MODERATE HOLD.

■ "We are raising our rating on Patterson Companies to BUY from HOLD," said David Coleman, writing for Argus Research Company on February 15, 2006. "Valuations are more attractive following a drop in the share price. Despite the difficulty the company faces to regain investor confidence, following a string of disappointing earnings releases, we believe that the company's franchise is solid and that its outlook for sales and margins is improving."

■ "Fiscal 2005 was another year of record operating results for Patterson, with consolidated sales and earnings both increasing 23 percent," said CEO John W. Wiltz. "Our solid performance included contributions from four acquisitions that further strengthened our business platform as a specialty distributor serving the dental, veterinary and rehabilitation supply markets."

Mr. Wiltz also said, "A significant portion of our consolidated results was driven by Patterson Dental, which performed at an exceptionally high level in fiscal 2005. For the year, dental sales rose 13 percent, to $1.8 billion. Substantially all of this growth was internally generated (*or not from acquisitions*).

"Sales of consumable supplies rebounded strongly as the year progressed, reflecting the positive impact of our renewed focus on this aspect of our dental business."

Mr. Wiltz went on to say, "Demand for new-technology equipment was particularly robust, with sales of the CEREC 3D dental restorative system up 39 percent for the year, while sales of digital radiography systems, including related software and hardware, rose 31 percent."

■ Dental market growth drivers:

- Graying of America generating demand for dental services, since older individuals require more dental care than any other age group.
- Consumers are spending more on oral health.
- People are keeping natural teeth longer.
- Technological advances are improving clinical outcomes.
- There is an increased demand for specialty procedures.
- There is a strong demand for new-generation equipment needed to strengthen office productivity.
- Dentists per capita are declining, resulting in more business per dentist.
- There is a growing number of dentists who are updating basic equipment.
- There is an expansion of dental insurance coverage.

■ Webster Veterinary Supply serves the $2.2 billion domestic companion-pet veterinary supply market, which the company believes to be growing at a 6 percent to 7 percent rate. Small-animal or companion-pet veterinarians are the largest and fastest-growing segment of the overall veterinary market.

A variety of factors are driving the growth of this segment, including rising pet ownership. It is currently estimated that about 31 million U.S. households own dogs, while 27 million own cats. Consistent with the growth of pet ownership, annual consumer spending on veterinary care is far higher today than it was a decade ago. The willingness of owners to spend more on their pets is related in part to the advent of new procedures and drugs that significantly improve clinical outcomes.

Patterson Companies entered the estimated $5-billion worldwide rehabilitation-supply market in fiscal 2004 by acquiring AbilityOne Products Corp., the world's leading distributor of rehabilitation supplies, equipment, and nonwheelchair assistive living products. As the only one-stop shop in the rehabilitation marketplace, AbilityOne provides its customers with the convenience of a single source of supply for all of their product needs.

AbilityOne owns many of the leading brands on the global rehabilitation market, including Sammons, Preston, and Rolyan in the United States and Homecraft in Europe. As a result, no competitor comes close to matching the breadth, and leadership positions of AbilityOne's offerings, which include:

- Braces, splints, and continuous passive motion machines for the orthopedic market.
- Dressings, dining, and bathing devices for the assistive living segment.
- A full range of rehabilitation equipment, including treatment tables, mat platforms, and stationary bicycles.
- Clinical products, such as exercise bands, weights, balls, and mats.
- Walkers, canes, and wheelchair accessories in the mobility category.
- Sales of Patterson Medical (formerly AbilityOne Corporation) increased 33 percent in fiscal 2005, to $295.3 million. Excluding the May 2004 acquisition of Medco Supply Company—a leading national distributor of sports medicine, first aid, and medical supplies—and the impact of currency adjustments related to its foreign operations, Patterson Medical's internally generated sales increased about 11 percent during 2005. Given favorable demographics and Patterson Medical's industry-leading position, the company view's the rehabilitation market as an excellent long-term growth opportunity for PDCO. According to a company spokesman, "By extending our proven value-added business model to this unit and by making selective acquisitions, we intend to further build Patterson Medical's position of market dominance."

SECTOR: **Health Care** ◆ BETA COEFFICIENT: **.65**
10-YEAR COMPOUND EARNINGS PER SHARE GROWTH: **22%**
10-YEAR COMPOUND DIVIDENDS PER SHARE GROWTH: **no dividend**

		2005	2004	2003	2002	2001	2000	1999	1998
Revenues (millions)		2,421	1,969	1,657	1,416	1,156	1,040	879	778
Net Income (millions)		184	150	116	95.3	76.5	64.5	49.9	40.8
Earnings per share		1.32	1.09	0.85	0.70	0.57	0.48	0.37	0.31
Dividends per share		Nil	—	—	—	—	—	—	—
Price	high	53.8	43.7	35.8	27.6	21.1	17.3	12.6	11.6
	low	33.4	29.7	17.7	19.1	13.8	8.2	8.3	7.1

CONSERVATIVE GROWTH

PepsiCo, Inc.

700 Anderson Hill Road ❑ Purchase, NY 10577-1444 ❑ (914) 253-3055 ❑ Dividend reinvestment plan available (800) 226-0083 ❑ Web site: *www.pepsico.com* ❑ Listed: NYSE ❑ Ticker symbol: PEP ❑ S&P rating: A+ ❑ Value Line financial strength rating: A++

"Shifting consumer tastes have hurt beverage companies like Coca-Cola, Anheuser-Busch, and Molson Coors, but PepsiCo continues to shine," said Andrew Bary, writing for *Barron's* on June 6, 2005. "Its shares are up 10 percent this year, to a record $57, and have risen 25 percent since we penned a bullish piece on the company last year ('Fat Chance,' Jan. 19, 2004). At the time, Wall Street feared that the popularity of the Atkins diet and other low-carbohydrate regimens would crimp growth at Pepsi's Frito-Lay snack-food unit, but Frito-Lay was unscathed."

Mr. Bary goes on to say, "Pepsi's attractions include Frito-Lay, the dominant U.S. snack-food company with a 60 percent-plus market share, and a beverage business that outclasses arch-rival Coca-Cola in noncarbonated drinks, the source of all the industry's recent growth. Pepsi has the number one sports drink, Gatorade; the top juice brand, Tropicana; the leading iced tea, Lipton; and the biggest water brand, Aquafina. Meanwhile, the company's international snack-food sales are growing at twice the rate of overall Pepsi sales."

Company Profile

The company consists of the snack businesses of Frito-Lay North America and Frito-Lay International; the beverage businesses of Pepsi-Cola North America, Gatorade/Tropicana North America and PepsiCo Beverages International; and Quaker Foods North America, manufacturer and marketer of ready-to-eat cereals and other food products. PepsiCo brands are available in nearly 200 countries and territories.

Many of PepsiCo's brand names are over 100-years-old, but the corporation is relatively young. PepsiCo was founded in 1965 through the merger of Pepsi-Cola and Frito-Lay. Tropicana was acquired in 1998 and PepsiCo merged with The Quaker Oats Company, including Gatorade, in 2001.

Frito-Lay North America and Frito-Lay International

PepsiCo's snack food operations had their start in 1932 when two separate events took place. In San Antonio, Texas, Elmer Doolin bought the recipe for an unknown food product—a corn chip—and started an entirely new industry. The product was Fritos brand corn chips, and his firm became the Frito Company.

That same year in Nashville, Tennessee, Herman W. Lay started his own business distributing potato chips. Mr. Lay later bought the company that supplied him with product and changed its name to H.W. Lay Company. The Frito Company and H.W. Lay Company merged in 1961 to become Frito-Lay, Inc.

Today, Frito-Lay brands account for more than half of the U.S. snack chip industry.

PepsiCo began its international snack food operations in 1966. Today, with operations in more than 40 countries, it is the leading multinational snack chip company, accounting for more than one quarter of international retail snack chip sales. Products are available in some 120 countries. Frito-Lay North America includes Canada and the United States. Major Frito-Lay International markets include Australia,

Brazil, Mexico, the Netherlands, South Africa, the United Kingdom, and Spain.

Often Frito-Lay products are known by local names. These names include Matutano in Spain, Sabritas and Gamesa in Mexico, Elma Chips in Brazil, Walkers in the United Kingdom, and others. The company markets Frito-Lay brands on a global level, and introduces unique products for local tastes.

Major Frito-Lay products include Ruffles, Lay's, and Doritos brands snack chips. Other major brands include Cheetos cheese flavored snacks, Tostitos tortilla chips, Santitas tortilla chips, Rold Gold pretzels, and SunChips multigrain snacks. Frito-Lay also sells a variety of snack dips and cookies, nuts and crackers.

Pepsi-Cola North America and PepsiCo Beverages International

PepsiCo's beverage business was founded at the turn of the century by Caleb Bradham, a New Bern, North Carolina druggist, who first formulated Pepsi-Cola. Today consumers spend about $33 billion on Pepsi-Cola beverages. Brand Pepsi and other Pepsi-Cola products—including Diet Pepsi, Pepsi-One, Mountain Dew, Slice, Sierra Mist, and Mug brands—account for nearly one-third of total soft drink sales in the United States, a consumer market totaling about $60 billion.

Pepsi-Cola also offers a variety of noncarbonated beverages, including Aquafina bottled water, Fruitworks, and All Sport.

In 1992 Pepsi-Cola formed a partnership with Thomas J. Lipton Co. Today Lipton is the biggest selling ready-to-drink tea brand in the United States. Pepsi-Cola also markets Frappuccino ready-to-drink coffee through a partnership with Starbucks.

In 2001 SoBe became a part of Pepsi-Cola. SoBe manufactures and markets an innovative line of beverages including fruit blends, energy drinks, dairy-based drinks, exotic teas, and other beverages with herbal ingredients.

Outside the United States, Pepsi-Cola soft drink operations include the business of Seven-Up International. Pepsi-Cola beverages are available in about 160 countries and territories.

Gatorade/Tropicana North America

Tropicana was founded in 1947 by Anthony Rossi as a Florida fruit packaging business. The company entered the concentrate orange juice business in 1949, registering Tropicana as a trademark.

In 1954 Rossi pioneered a pasteurization process for orange juice. For the first time, consumers could enjoy the fresh taste of pure not-from-concentrate 100% Florida orange juice in a ready-to-serve package. The juice, Tropicana Pure Premium, became the company's flagship product.

In 1957 the name of the company was changed to Tropicana Products, headquartered in Bradenton, Florida. The company went public in 1957, was purchased by Beatrice Foods Co. in 1978, acquired by Kohlberg Kravis & Roberts in 1986, and sold to The Seagram Company Ltd. in 1988. Seagram purchased the Dole global juice business in 1995. PepsiCo acquired Tropicana, including the Dole juice business, in August 1998.

Today the Tropicana brand is available in sixty-three countries. Principal brands in North America are Tropicana Pure Premium, Tropicana Season's Best, Dole Juices, and Tropicana Twister. Internationally, principal brands include Tropicana Pure Premium and Dole juices along with Frui'Vita, Loóza, and Copella. Tropicana Pure Premium is the third largest brand of all food products sold in grocery stores in the United States.

Gatorade sports drinks was acquired by the Quaker Oats Company in 1983 and became a part of PepsiCo with the merger in 2001. Gatorade is the first isotonic sports drink. Created in 1965 by researchers at the University of Florida for the school's football team, "The Gators," Gatorade is now the world's leading sport's drink.

Quaker Foods North America

The Quaker Oats Company was formed in 1901 when several American pioneers in oat milling came together to incorporate. In Ravenna, Ohio, Henry D. Seymour and William Heston had established the Quaker Mill Company and registered the now famous trademark.

The first major acquisition of the company was Aunt Jemina Mills Company in 1926, which is today the leading manufacturer of pancake mixes and syrup.

In 1986, The Quaker Oats Company acquired the Golden Grain Company, producers of Rice-A-Roni.

PepsiCo merged with The Quaker Oats Company in 2001. Its products still have the eminence of wholesome, good-for-you food, as envisioned by the company over a century ago.

Shortcomings to Bear in Mind

- According to one analyst, there is some risk from unfavorable weather conditions in the company's markets, inability to meet volume and revenue growth targets, increased popularity of low-carbohydrate diets, and consumer acceptance of new product introductions.

Reasons to Buy

- "PepsiCo has agreed to acquire Stacy's Pita Chip Co., extending its reach into all-natural snacks to boost its appeal to health-conscious consumers," said Chad Terhune, writing for the *Wall Street Journal* on November 22, 2005. "Stacy's pita chips are baked and have no cholesterol or trans fats. They come in five flavors such as pesto and sun-dried tomato, and qualify for PepsiCo's Smart Spot symbol that designates healthier options."
- The *New York Times* surveyed nineteen analysts on March 19, 2006 and found that six viewed PepsiCo as a STRONG BUY; ten called the stock a MODERATE BUY; and three said it looked like a HOLD. There were no analysts lurking in a thicket calling PEP a SELL.
- "We have a STRONG BUY recommendation on the shares, based on our view of strong profit and free cash flow growth and what we see as solid EPS *(earnings per share)* visibility and consistency," said Richard Joy, writing for *Standard & Poor's Stock Reports*, on February 21, 2006.
- On February 17, 2006, *Prudential Equity Group* called PepsiCo an OVERWEIGHT. Cheryl Gedvila said, "Fundamentally, we favor companies with strong portfolios to address the changing consumer landscape, as well as those companies with significant emerging market exposure. We think PepsiCo, Inc. fits this profile."
- In 2005, CEO Steve Reinemund said, "With sixteen brands that each generate over a billion dollars of retail sales annually, and many more moving in that direction, we have big 'global icon' brands that sit squarely in the sweet spot of convenience. We constantly differentiate those brands in the marketplace by what we do with ingredients and nutrition science, product packaging and processing."

Mr. Reinemund goes on to say, "We have more of these icon brands than any other food and beverage company in the world, and we continue to add new products to the portfolio through internal innovations combined with smaller, tuck-in acquisitions in our international businesses."

SECTOR: **Consumer Staples** ◆ BETA COEFFICIENT: **.65**
10-YEAR COMPOUND EARNINGS PER SHARE GROWTH: **6.8%**
10-YEAR COMPOUND DIVIDENDS PER SHARE GROWTH: **10%**

		2005	2004	2003	2002	2001	2000	1999	1998
Revenues (millions)		32,562	29,261	26,971	25,112	23,512	25,480	20,367	2,348
Net Income (millions)		4,078	4,174	3,494	3,313	2,660	2,540	1,845	1,760
Earnings per share		2.39	2.44	2.01	1.85	1.47	1.42	1.23	1.16
Dividends per share		1.01	.85	.63	.60	.58	.56	.54	.52
Price	high	60.3	55.7	48.9	53.5	50.5	49.9	42.6	44.8
	low	51.3	45.3	36.2	34.0	40.3	29.7	30.1	27.6

AGGRESSIVE GROWTH

PetSmart, Inc.

19601 North 27th Avenue ❑ Phoenix, AZ 85027-4010 ❑ (623) 587-2025 ❑ Dividend reinvestment plan not available ❑ Web site: *www.petsmart.com* ❑ Ticker symbol: PETM ❑ Listed: Nasdaq ❑ Fiscal year ends on the Sunday nearest January 31 ❑ S&P rating: B- ❑ Value Line financial strength rating: B+

Contrary to popular opinion, you *can* teach an old dog new tricks. At least that's the philosophy at PetSmart these days. After eighteen years in business as PETsMART, the company is emphasizing its smarts, now officially calling itself PetSmart.

In the words of a company official on August 25, 2005, "The numbers show why PetSmart is, in fact, so smart: 1,500 accredited trainers each spend 96 hours learning their trade, training more than 300,000 dogs annually; 6,600 pet stylists must complete a safety certification process in order to groom and bathe more than 5 million dogs a year; nearly 32,000 associates are helpful, knowledgeable and passionate about pets; and with more than 760 stores, PetSmart is the smart destination for pet products, service and advice."

The company demonstrates its smarts in other ways, as well. With the SmartPet Promise for all pet training classes, customers are guaranteed 100 percent satisfaction; or they can take the class again for free. All PetSmart PetsHotels offer an exclusive 24-hour PetCare Promise, featuring caregivers who are hand-picked for their love of pets and are on the premises 24 hours a day. PetSmart stores and petsmart.com offer not only more than 12,000 different products at everyday low prices, but with a PetPerks Savings Card, members receive even greater discounts on hundreds of items every month.

"We've earned the right to call ourselves PetSmart," said CEO Philip L. Francis. "When we started in this business, we were a mart, offering a wide selection of pet products at low prices. Today, we also offer superior solutions and services for healthier, happier pets."

"Whether it's finding the right food or the perfect toy, signing up for training or grooming sessions, checking into a PetsHotel, or taking home a newly adopted dog or cat, pet parents will find PetSmart associates who are ready, willing and able to help them make smart decisions," said a company official.

Company Profile

PetSmart, Inc. is the largest specialty retailer of services and solutions for the lifetime needs of pets. The company operates more than 725 pet stores in the United States and Canada, a growing number of PetsHotels, as well as a large pet supply catalog business and the Internet's leading online provider of pet products and information (PetSmart provides a broad range of competitively priced pet food and supplies and offers complete pet training, grooming, and adoption services.

Since 1994, PetSmart Charities, an independent 501(c)3 organization, has donated more than $38 million to animal welfare programs and, through its in-store adoption programs, has saved the lives of more than two million pets.

According to the company's 2004 10-K report:

"The pet product industry serves a large and growing market. The American Pet Products Manufacturers Association, or APPMA, estimated the 2004 market at approximately $34.4 billion, an increase of over 100 percent since 1994. Based on the 2005/2006 APPMA National Pet Owners Survey, more than 69 million households in the United States own a pet. This translates to approximately 91 million cats and 74 million dogs. The APPMA also estimates 63 percent of United States's households own a pet, and 45 percent of those households own more than one type of pet.

"Pet supplies and medicine sales account for approximately 24 percent, or $8.1 billion, of the market. These sales include dog and cat toys, collars and leashes, cages and habitats, books, vitamins and supplements, shampoos, flea and tick control and aquatic supplies. Veterinary care, pet services and purchase of pets represent about 23 percent, 7 percent, and 5 percent, respectively, of the market."

Shortcomings to Bear in Mind

- Conservative investors may prefer to skip this one, since the stock tends to fluctuate over a wide range. For instance, the stock hit a high of $29.9 in 1996 and plunged over a period of years to a low of $2.3 in 2000. From that low ebb, the shares started a long ascent, rising to a high of $36.2 in 2004. Also, the stock has a slim dividend that has a short history, dating back to 2003.
- On October 6, 2005, Mr. Francis had some cautionary comments. "Although we continue to feel quite positive about this business and its long-term growth, we're clearly operating in an uncertain economic environment, and the recent hurricanes had a material short-term impact on our business. We've lost a total of 238 sales days, or at least half a point of comp sales, to stores closed by the hurricanes, and our stores remain closed. In addition, we believe sticker shock at the gas pump, high home interest rates, and general uncertainty mean the consumer is simply shopping less often, and we're losing trips to the car staying in the garage."

Mr. Francis went on to say, "We think these challenges are short term in nature, and we continue to be confident that PetSmart is capable of generating an average of 20 percent earnings per share growth over the long term."

Reasons to Buy

- "After a scrap with Wal-Mart Stores, Inc. during the late 1990s, PetSmart in 2000 switched from a warehouse-style format to a specialty-store strategy that increasingly is focused on services that include grooming, training, and boarding for pets," said James Covert, writing for the *Wall Street Journal* on June 1, 2005. "Looking to steal business from mom-and-pop salons, obedience schools and kennels, PetSmart is devising new ways to offer good, mass-producible services at low prices. The company expects to reap big returns if it can 'convince and train' customers to keep stepping up their pet-related spending—particularly on dogs, says CEO Phil Francis."

The *Wall Street Journal* goes on to say, "By far, the biggest part of the business will always be selling pet food and supplies. (PetSmart as a matter of policy doesn't sell dogs and cats but donates space to pet-adoption services.) When it switched from the warehouse-retailing format, PetSmart began selling more specialized, pricey foods, and accessories that couldn't be found at Wal-Mart, Target Corp., or traditional supermarket chains, which still have a dominant—although steadily shrinking share of the business."

- The 2004 annual report listed some of the features that make PetSmart an attractive investment:

  - "Our flexible store format, which is designed around our customers and how they shop, is a distinct advantage over our competitors.
  - "Our prices are generally 10 percent below other pet specialty stores and within 5 percent of the cheapest discounter.
  - "We focus on selecting, educating and rewarding people who are passionate about pets and who can build a customer-focused culture.
  - "Our store size and configuration gives us tremendous flexibility as we develop and enhance our service offerings as well as grow our product and pet lines.
  - "Nearly one quarter of our stores serve equine customers through our State Line Tack business and more than half offer veterinary services through Banfield, The Pet Hospital.
  - "PetSmart products are also found in our series of leading catalogs and online at the popular pet e-commerce site.
  - "In 2004, PetSmart's accredited pet instructors taught nearly 300,000 dogs good behavior skills.
  - "Our pet services are two times more profitable than the core store and have consistently grown at or above our target of 20 percent. We expect these growth rates to continue at least through 2006.
  - "Since our inception in 1987, we've helped battle the problem of pet overpopulation by refusing to sell cats and dogs. Instead, we donate store space to local animal welfare organizations, who in partnership with PetSmart Charities, help give homeless pets a second chance at life.
  - "PetSmart Charities Adoption Centers on average find homes for more than 7,000 pets weekly.
  - "In 2004, we took our brand loyalty card, PetPerks, from test to full-scale implementation. PetPerks will be in all stores by mid-2005. PetPerks is more than a traditional loyalty card program, it's also a data mining and management system. Early customer response has been positive, with 70 to 80 percent of total transactions and 75 percent of total sales captured by the card.
  - "About 5.4 million dogs were pampered by PetSmart safely certified pet stylists in 2004, nearly one million more dogs than were groomed in 2003.
  - "With more and more pet parents treating their pets like children, grooming services are increasingly being treated as more necessity than luxury.
  - "PetSmart grooming salons are carefully designed and equipped to ensure the highest levels of safety and comfort and groomers must pass a rigorous training and certification program before working in the salon."

- On March 2, 2006, the *New York Times* checked with thirteen analysts who concentrate on such stocks as PetSmart. Five rated the stock a STRONG BUY; another five said it was a MODERATE BUY; and only three straddled the fence with a HOLD.
- "We have a STRONG BUY recommendation on the shares, based on valuation as well as qualitative factors," said Michael Sauers, writing for *Standard & Poor's Company Reports* on March 7, 2006. "We estimate that the overall market for pet-related products and services is growing in the mid-single digits due to favorable demographics such as rising pet ownership and greater expenditures per pet."
- On March 2, 2006, *Lehman Brothers* rated the stock as OVERWEIGHT, similar to a BUY.
- "The company will continue its rapid expansion," said Evan I. Blatter, writing a report for *Value Line Investment Survey* on February 10, 2006. "PetSmart opened about 100 new stores in 2005 and is scheduled to add a similar number this year. The chain continues to gain market share in such key under-penetrated markets as the Northeast and California."

SECTOR: **Consumer Discretionary** ◆ BETA COEFFICIENT: **1.00**
10-YEAR COMPOUND EARNINGS PER SHARE GROWTH: **16.1%**
10-YEAR COMPOUND DIVIDENDS PER SHARE GROWTH: **not meaningful**

		2005	2004	2003	2002	2001	2000	1999	1998
Revenues (millions)		3,760	3,364	2,996	2,695	2,501	2,224	2,110	2,109
Net Income (millions)		182	168	140	102	35	Def	13	22
Earnings per share		1.25	1.12	0.95	0.72	0.31	Def	0.12	0.19
Dividends per share		.12	0.12	0.04	Nil	–	–	–	–
Price	high	35.8	36.2	28.8	21.0	10.2	5.8	11.3	13.1
	low	21.1	23.0	9.9	9.4	2.5	2.3	2.6	4.8

AGGRESSIVE GROWTH

Pfizer Inc.

235 East 42nd Street ❑ New York, NY 10017-5755 ❑ (212) 573-3685 ❑ Direct Dividend reinvestment plan available (800) 733-9393 ❑ Web site: *www.pfizer.com* ❑ Listed: NYSE ❑ Ticker symbol: PFE ❑ S&P rating: A ❑ Value Line financial strength rating: A++

In 2005, CEO Hank McKinnell said, "Because we operate in more than 180 nations, have the world's largest privately funded biomedical research organization, and have earned a reputation for excellence in marketing, we enjoy a special advantage in partnering on new products and technologies with other pharmaceutical companies, biotechs, and other organizations. Pfizer today has hundreds of such alliances, ranging from work with research institutions to global co-marketing agreements with well-known companies."

Mr. McKinnell also said, "Global trends favor Pfizer and our position of industry leadership. The baby-boom generation is well into middle age, demanding help in healthy aging. Widespread chronic conditions, such as hypertension, depression, and lipid imbalances, remain largely undiagnosed and untreated. People are beginning to recognize that it makes far more sense to invest in disease prevention and early treatment rather than to accept the human misery and high cost of events such as heart attacks and strokes."

Company Profile

Pfizer traces its history back to 1849 when it was founded by Charles Pfizer and Charles Erhart. In those early days, Pfizer was a chemical firm. Today, it is a leading global pharmaceutical manufacturer, creating and marketing a wide range of prescription drugs.

In the prescription drug realm, Pfizer has some of the world's best-selling drugs. Principal cardiovascular drugs include Lipitor, the world's largest-selling cholesterol-lowering agent, and antihypertensives such as Norvasc, Cardura, and Accupril. Infectious disease drugs consist of Zithromax broad-spectrum macrolide antibiotic; key central nervous system medicines are Zoloft antidepressant and Neurontin anti-convulsant.

Nor is that all. Pfizer's prescription drugs also include Viagra for male erectile dysfunction, Zyrtec, an antihistamine, and Glucotrol XL for type 2 diabetes.

In the over-the-counter sector, the company's consumer products (sold to JNJ in 2006) include such well-known brands as Ben-Gay, Desitin, Sudafed, Benadryl, Listerine, Trident, Dentyne, Certs, Halls cough drops, and Schick shaving products. In 2003, Schick was sold to Energizer for $930 million.

PFE also has an important stake in hospital products, and animal health products.

Pfizer's growth over the past half century was paced by strategic acquisitions, new drug discoveries, and vigorous foreign expansion. Its most recent move involved the giant acquisition of Warner-Lambert in 2000, making the new firm the largest pharmaceutical company in the world—and even larger when it acquired Pharmacia Corporation in December of 2002.

Shortcomings to Bear in Mind

- When patents expire on important drugs, the price that can be charged for those drugs plummets, as makers of generic copies swoop in for the kill. Like every pharmaceutical company, Pfizer has a few preparations that don't have long to live. On the other hand, it also has a host of products that will be on pharmacist shelves for some time to come. Here is a rundown of major drugs, along with the year in which they lose patent protection:

Zithromax	2005
Zoloft	2006
Norvasc	2007
Zyrtec	2007
Aricept	2010
Lipitor	2010
Viagra	2012
Detrol	2012
Celebrex	2013
Bextra	2015
Genotropin	2015

- In 2005, CEO Hank McKinnell commented on some of Pfizer's challenges. "There can be no doubt that Pfizer, along with other research-based pharmaceutical companies, is facing the headwinds of an operating environment quite unlike any we have ever seen. We face severe pricing pressures, a contentious political atmosphere, and a maze of new regulatory demands. We are in a period of 'discontinuous change'—where many of the assumptions of the last half century no longer hold true. These industry-wide challenges are compounded for Pfizer by the fact that we will lose patent protection on several of our best-selling medicines between this year and the end of 2007."

Reasons to Buy

- "A London court upheld a patent on Pfizer Inc.'s blockbuster anticholesterol drug Lipitor, handing it a victory by blocking India's Ranbaxy Laboratories Ltd. from launching a copycat version of the pill in Britain," according to a *Wall Street Journal* article on October 13, 2005. The authors were John Larkin and Leila Abboud. "In its ruling, the U.K. High Court of Justice agreed with Pfizer that its underlying patent on the Lipitor compound was valid. But it sided with Ranbaxy's argument that a more specific but secondary patent on a component of the same drug was valid.

  "The court's ruling means that Lipitor's active ingredient will main proprietary in the United Kingdom from generic copies until its patent expires in November 2011."
- On December 31, 2004, the U.S. Food and Drug Administration approved Lyrica for the treatment of pain caused by nerve damage from diabetes or shingles. This pain is often described as burning, tingling, sharp, stabbing, or pins and needles in the feet, legs, hands, or arms. "Lyrica is an important new therapy for millions of people suffering from the two most common neuropathic pain conditions, as it provides rapid and sustained pain relief," said Dr. Joseph Feczko, president of Worldwide Development at Pfizer. The company estimates that about three million diabetes patients in the United States will develop this affliction sometime during their diabetic life. Another 150,000 develop nerve damage from shingles each year.
- Zithromax is the world's largest-selling antibiotic as well as the leading branded product in the U.S. respiratory-infection market. Zithromax is first-line therapy for a number of key indications, including acute exacerbations of chronic bronchitis, community-acquired pneumonia, sinusitis, and otitis media.
- Norvasc is the world's most prescribed branded medicine for treating hypertension.
- Viagra remains the leading treatment for erectile dysfunction and one of the world's most recognized pharmaceutical brands.
- Zoloft is the most-prescribed antidepressant in the United States. It is indicated for the treatment of depression, panic disorder, obsessive-compulsive disorder in adults and children, post-traumatic stress disorder, premenstrual dysphoric disorder, and social anxiety disorder.
- Lipitor, for the treatment of elevated cholesterol levels in the blood, is the most widely used treatment for lowering cholesterol and the best-selling pharmaceutical product of any kind in the world.
- Each day, 20,000 people around the world go to work promoting Pfizer products to the medical profession. They fill their "detail" bags with free samples of popular drugs such as Viagra and Zithromax, and they quote favorable conclusions from scientific studies (often company-sponsored) that show how Lipitor is the most potent way to control cholesterol and should be used instead of Merck's Zocor. By nearly all counts, Pfizer is the industry's largest, and most effective, sales force.

  According to Henry A. McKinnell, Ph.D., who became the company's CEO in 2001, "Pfizer has never been stronger and today possesses strengths and capabilities unequaled in the pharmaceutical industry. Our U.S. sales force, for example, was recently ranked as best in class in a survey of physicians, the sixth year in a row for this honor."
- Pfizer's Animal Health Group (AHG) in not only one of the largest in the world but is also noteworthy for the breadth of its product lines and its geographic coverage. Innovative marketing has become an AHG hallmark in its efforts to succeed in a highly competitive market. An independent survey of U.S. veterinarians, for example, named the Pfizer sales force the best in the industry.
- Pfizer regularly makes use of partnerships and licensing agreements to extend its

reach. Although the company must share the profits from any products developed with a partner, the deals take some pressure off Pfizer's research arm. Given its marketing expertise and reputation for successful collaborations, many smaller drug companies are reported to view Pfizer as their first choice as a partner. A recent example is Aricept, a drug developed by Eisai Company of Japan. It was co-promoted by Pfizer and quickly became the leading treatment for Alzheimer's disease in the United States.

- On March 19, 2006, the *New York Times* surveyed twenty-nine analysts as to their opinion of Pfizer. Eight were convinced that the company was a STRONG BUY; nine rated Pfizer a MODERATE BUY, ten said it was a HOLD; and one called the stock a MODERATE HOLD; the bad news is that one disgruntled analyst said it was a SELL.
- On February 15, 2006 *Prudential Equity Group's* rated the stock OVERWEIGHT. The firm's analyst, Timothy A. Anderson, said, "PFE is the cheapest stock of its peers on a P/E multiple basis. It appears to have more cash than it knows what to do with; it should have at least some earnings growth over the next three years; it has a huge potential winner of a pipeline drug (torcetraib); and management says it will continue to outreach to investors."
- In January 2006, the Food & Drug Administration approved the company's new insulin drug, Exubera, the first version of insulin that does not need to be injected—only inhaled. It gives millions of adult diabetics an alternative to the regular injections they now endure. Analysts believe that Exubera could have annual sales of $1 billion.

SECTOR: **Drugs, Health Care** ◆ BETA COEFFICIENT: **.85**
10-YEAR COMPOUND EARNINGS PER SHARE GROWTH: **10.3%**
10-YEAR COMPOUND DIVIDENDS PER SHARE GROWTH: **16.2%**

		2005	2004	2003	2002	2001	2000	1999	1998
Revenues (millions)		51,298	52,516	45,188	32,373	32,259	29,574	16,204	13,544
Net Income (millions)		8,100	11,361	3,910	9,126	7,788	6,495	3,360	2,627
Earnings per share		1.09	1.49	0.54	1.53	1.31	1.02	.87	.67
Dividends per share		.76	.68	.60	.52	.44	.36	.31	.25
Price	high	29.2	38.9	36.9	42.5	46.8	49.3	50.0	43.0
	low	20.3	23.5	27.0	25.1	34.0	30.0	31.5	23.7

INCOME

Piedmont Natural Gas Company, Inc.

P. O. Box 33068 ❑ Charlotte, NC 28233 ❑ (704) 731-4438 ❑ Dividend reinvestment program is available (800) 937-5449 ❑ Fiscal year ends October 31 ❑ Listed NYSE ❑ Web site: *www.piedmontng.com* ❑ Ticker symbol: PNY ❑ S&P rating: A- ❑ Value Line financial strength rating: B++

"Fiscal 2005 proved to be a solid year for your company," said CEO Thomas E. Skains on January 17, 2006. "Some of our many noteworthy accomplishments include:

- Record net income and earnings per share.
- Customer growth in excess of 3 percent.

- Strong performance from our energy-related joint ventures.
- Regulatory approval for the 'roll-in' of NCNG and EasternNC into Piedmont.
- Regulatory approval of new rates in North Carolina and South Carolina.
- Progress on key process improvement initiatives.
- Development and implementation of a customer-focused strategic communications initiative."

Mr. Skains also said, "Our utility customer base grew at a rate in excess of 3 percent during 2005, a growth rate among the highest in the nation for natural gas distribution companies. Gross customer additions were at their highest level since 2000, with particularly strong growth in our residential new construction and small commercial market segments."

Company Profile

Incorporated in 1950, Piedmont Natural Gas is an energy services company, primarily engaged in the transportation, distribution, and sale of natural gas and propane to residential, commercial, and industrial customers in North Carolina, South Carolina, and Tennessee.

The company is the second-largest natural gas utility in the Southeast, serving 960,000 natural gas customers. Piedmont Natural Gas and its nonutility subsidiaries and divisions are also engaged in acquiring, marketing, transporting, and storing natural gas for large-volume customers, in retailing residential and commercial gas appliances.

Other business interests in which the company is engaged that are not subject to state utility regulation include the sale of propane and investments in a natural gas pipeline and an interstate LNG (liquefied natural gas) storage facility and marketing natural gas and other energy products and services to deregulated markets.

PNY's Joint Ventures:

- SouthStar Energy Services LLC—an equity participant (or part owner) in Georgia's largest retail natural gas marketer.
- Pine Needle LNG Company, LLC—an equity participant in a liquefied natural gas facility that's among the nation's largest.
- Cardinal Pipeline Company, LLC—an equity participant in a 102-mile intrastate pipeline serving portions of North Carolina.
- EasternNC Natural Gas—an equity participant in a venture that is expanding natural gas distribution into fourteen counties in eastern North Carolina.

Shortcomings to Bear in Mind

- The company has benefited from extraordinary growth in its service territory. However, customer growth can be a double-edged sword, as it is expensive to continuously expand an underground pipe system to keep up with new construction. On the other hand, Piedmont has effectively lowered its cost to connect a customer to about $1,800, a significant decline over prior years. Analysts, moreover, expect this cost to continue to decline, which would contribute to future earnings growth.
- On March 29, 2006, the *New York Times* published a survey of analytical opinions on PNY. Only one analyst considered the stock a STRONG BUY, or a MODERATE BUY. Five said it was a HOLD, and one rated the stock a MODERATE HOLD.
- Piedmont Natural gas has increased its dividend for twenty-six consecutive years. In the 1995–2005 period, dividends expanded from $0.54 per share to $0.92, a compound annual growth rate of 5.5 percent, or well ahead of the pace of inflation—but not exactly spectacular. If you are looking for growth, this may not be a good choice. That's why I have categorized this stock for "income."

Reasons to Buy

▪ Piedmont Natural Gas has an impressive record of acquisitions:

- Effective January 1, 2001, the company purchased for cash the natural gas distribution assets of Atmos Energy Corporation, situated in the city of Gaffney and portions of Cherokee Country, South Carolina. It added 5,400 customers to PNY's operations.
- Effective September 30, 2002, the company purchased for $26 million in cash substantially all of the natural gas distribution assets of North Carolina Gas Service, a division of NUI Utilities, Inc. This added 14,000 customers to PNY's distribution system in the counties of Rockingham and Stokes, North Carolina.
- Effective September 30, 2003, the company purchased for $417.5 million in cash 100 percent of the common stock of NCNG from Progress Energy, Inc., a natural gas distributor serving some 176,000 customers in eastern North Carolina.
- In 2004, the company completed the permanent debt and equity financing of its acquisition of NCNG. Mr. Skains said, "We established our historically strong capital structure with an equity capitalization of 56 percent, as of October 31, 2004. In April, the rating agencies recognized these accomplishments by raising their outlook for Piedmont to 'stable' along with credit ratings of 'A' and 'A3.' Your company is financially strong and well-positioned to take advantage of future strategic opportunities in a disciplined fashion."

According to another officer of the company, "The primary reasons for these acquisitions are consistent with our strategy of pursuing profitable growth in our core natural gas distribution business in the Southeast. The reasons for the acquisitions and the factors that contributed to the goodwill include:

- A reasonable purchase price, slightly above book value.
- The prospect of entering a market contiguous to our existing North Carolina service areas where, as a combined company, we could realize on-going system benefits.
- The prospect of acquiring an operation that could be integrated into our existing business systems and processes.
- The opportunity to grow within a regulatory environment with which we are familiar."

▪ Piedmont Natural Gas enjoys an economically robust and diverse service area that is among the fastest growing in the nation. The company's three-state service area consists of the Piedmont region of the Carolinas—Charlotte, Salisbury, Greensboro, Winston-Salem, High Point, Burlington, and Hickory in North Carolina and Anderson, Greenville, and Spartanburg in South Carolina—and the metropolitan area of Nashville, Tennessee. Both *Plant Sites and Parks* and *Site Selection* magazines continue to rank the Carolinas and Tennessee among the best in the nation for business relocation and expansion and business climate.

The center of the Piedmont Carolinas area is the Greater Charlotte urban region—sixth largest in the nation—with over six million people within a 100-mile radius. Charlotte is the nation's second-largest financial center. It is headquarters city for Bank of America, the nation's second-largest bank, and for First Union National bank, the sixth largest. Wachovia Corporation, the nation's fifth-largest bank, is headquartered in Winston-Salem.

Charlotte/Douglas International Airport, with over 500 flights per day and 23 million passengers annually, is U.S. Airways' largest hub and the twentieth busiest airport in the World.

The Nashville region is a diverse center of a retail trading area of over two million people, where health care is the largest industry. It is also home to major transportation, publishing, printing, financial, insurance and communications companies as well as twenty colleges and universities.

- An important factor in analyzing any public utility is the region's regulatory environment. In Piedmont's states, regulators have generally been supportive of the company's regulatory needs over the past few years. In the opinion of Daniel M. Fidell and Tracey W. McMillin, analysts with A. G. Edwards, "Our conclusion is based on several factors, such as purchased gas and weather normalization mechanisms in rates that serve to smooth the impact of changes in gas prices and abnormal weather conditions. In addition, PNY has benefited from fair and timely rate relief in the past to recover costs associated with extensive system growth."
- Insiders, such as executives and board members, have been aggressively buying the stock. In a recent nine-month period, there were only five sells, but a massive list of seventy-nine purchases. Although analysts are not enthusiastic, this list of eager buyers tells me maybe the analysts are wrong.

SECTOR: **Utilities** ◆ BETA COEFFICIENT: **0.75**
10-YEAR COMPOUND EARNINGS PER SHARE GROWTH: **6.1%**
10-YEAR COMPOUND DIVIDENDS PER SHARE GROWTH: **5.5%**

		2005	2004	2003	2002	2001	2000	1999	1998
Revenues (millions)		1,761	1,530	1,221	832	1,108	830	686	765
Net Income (millions)		101	95	74	62	65	64	58	60
Earnings per share		1.32	1.27	1.11	0.04	1.01	1.00	0.93	0.98
Dividends per share		.92	.86	0.82	0.79	0.76	0.72	0.68	0.64
Price	high	25.8	24.4	22.0	19.0	19.0	19.7	18.3	18.1
	low	21.3	19.2	16.6	13.7	14.6	14.3	13.9	11.0

GROWTH AND INCOME

Pitney Bowes, Inc.

1 Elmcroft Road ❑ Stamford, CT 06926-0700 ❑ (203) 351-6349 ❑ Dividend reinvestment plan available (800) 648-8170 ❑ Web site: *www.pb.com* ❑ Ticker symbol: PBI ❑ Listed: NYSE ❑ S&P rating: A- ❑ Value Line financial strength rating: A

"Mail has a bright future as a critical communication channel," says CEO Michael J. Critelli. "Contrary to common perceptions, the rise in electronic forms of communication has not led to a reduction in overall mail volumes. While mail is declining as a percentage of overall message volumes, absolute volumes continue to increase."

Mr. Critelli goes on to say, "I believe that stable postal rates can result in even higher mail volumes for the following reasons:

- "Organizations are increasingly finding mail to be an exceptionally effective medium for building and strengthening stakeholder relationships. Businesses that were not large mailers in the past, like small retailers, are learning about the power of mail.
- "The trend toward remote commerce creates another opportunity for mail, since videos, digital photos, prescription drugs and many other items ordered online must be shipped. Our very successful partnership with eBay to provide Internet postage services is a good example of how we are taking advantage of this trend.
- "Transaction mail volumes are proving to be surprisingly resilient. For every consumer who shifts to electronic bill presentment or payment, there seems to be a comparable increase in mailings for health claims, satellite TV or radio subscriptions, gift card mailings, and the like."

Company Profile

Pitney Bowes is the world's leading provider of integrated mail and document management systems, services, and solutions. The $5-billion company helps organizations—both large and small—to efficiently and effectively manage their mission-critical mail and document flow in physical, digital, and hybrid formats.

Its solutions range from addressing software and metering systems to print stream management, electronic bill presentment, and presort mail services. The company's eighty-plus years of technological leadership has produced many major innovations in the mailing industry and more than 3,500 active patents with applications in a variety of markets, including printing, shipping, encryption, and financial services. With about 33,000 employees worldwide, PBI serves more than two million businesses through direct and dealer operations.

Pitney Bowes operates in three business segments, as follows:

- Global Mailstream Solutions, Global Enterprise Solutions, and Capital Services. The Global Mailstream Solutions segment includes worldwide revenue and related expenses from the rental of postage meters and the sale, rental and financing of mailing equipment, including mail finishing and software-based mail creation equipment.
- The Global Enterprise Solutions segment includes Pitney Bowes Management Services and Document Messaging Technologies.
- The Capital Services segment consists of financing for non-Pitney Bowes equipment.

The Company maintains field service organizations in the United States and some other countries to provide support services to customers who have rented, leased, or purchased equipment.

Shortcomings to Bear in Mind

- Here's an excerpt from an article *in Barron's* on January 2, 2006: "Bob Goldsborough, an analyst with Ariel Capital, whose 8.9 million shares made it Pitney Bowes fifth-largest shareholder, says that its acquisitions have positioned the company to grow faster, 'and it is starting to happen.' But, he says, it isn't growing fast enough to fit in the growth category. At the same time, it isn't an income or value stock. Result: 'You get a kind of confused shareholder base,' he argues, and that's hurt the shares."

Reasons to Buy

- On March 19, 2006, the *New York Times* surveyed six analysts who follow Pitney Bowes. Two said the stock was a

STRONG BUY; one regarded PBI as a MODERATE BUY; and three settled for a HOLD. There were no SELLS.

▪ "Our recommendation is BUY, based on our view of PBI's large recurring revenue stream, its leadership position within its market, and the stock's above-average dividend yield of 2.8 percent," said Megan Graham Hackett, writing for *Standard & Poor's Company Reports,* on February 10, 2006. "In addition, we see a strengthening economy, synergies from recent acquisitions, and new product introductions focusing on digital technology leading to steady revenue growth and widening margins in coming periods."

▪ On September 9, 2005, Pitney Bowes Inc. introduced the DM Infinity™ Meter Permit and Graphics Printing Module, which gives customers the flexibility to print permit indicia and graphics—including a town circle and customizable advertising slogans—to personalize mail pieces.

The Permit and Graphics Printing Module, the newest offering in the DM Infinity series family of high-speed digital mailing solutions, also enables customers to further reduce unnecessary costs and improve the performance of their production mailing operations.

"The DM Infinity™ meter series gives mailers unlimited flexibility in a single solution," said David Robinson, vice president, business development of Pitney Bowes Document Messaging Technologies division. "Since the introduction of the Series in January, Pitney Bowes has launched a government meter, the DM Infinity™ Meter Roll-Up System: DDA Solution, and now the Permit and Graphics Printing Module. With the DM Infinity™ series, one meter base can do it all."

The ability to print permit indicia on plain envelopes enables customers to save inventory costs associated with storing large numbers of preprinted, permitted envelopes. In addition, the module gives customers the flexibility to add individualized and customized graphics to a pre-printed envelope.

"With the DM Infinity™ Meter Permit and Graphics Printing Module, mailers can print indicia and graphics on a plain envelope, or add graphics with marketing messages that may improve 'openability' to pre-printed permit envelopes, and switch between those two applications in minutes," Robinson said. "This is an ideal solution for service bureaus, telecommunications companies, utilities and all high volume mailers that place a premium on flexibility."

The DM Infinity™ Meter Permit and Graphics Printing Module also includes workforce productivity features. Printing permit indicia enables mailers to standardize on envelope types, streamline processes, and reduce the potential for human error. Use of a town circle with a configurable date allows them to advance the mail run date to help maximize workforce productivity.

The Permit and Graphics Printing Module was introduced at the Print '05 Conference being held thru September 14 in Chicago and can be seen at booth # 3667. The company today also announced the general availability of the DM Infinity™ meter Roll-Up System: DDA Solution, introduced in June 2005, and the Series' extended support of all Pitney Bowes accounting solutions, including AccuTrac™ HT, Business Manager, OMS-NT, and DFWorks™ Postage Accounting.

The Pitney Bowes DM Infinity™ meter series is the only digital meter family in the world that can meter up to 22,000 mail pieces per hour and meet the demanding reliability and durability requirements of production mailers. It enables mailers to: lower postage costs through its Weigh-on-the-Fly™ technology, which eliminates the costly guesswork associated with overestimating postage; increase throughput, with faster print speeds and fewer jams; reduce return mail costs through improved print quality; simplify postage reconciliation; and reduce maintenance costs.

■ On September 9, 2005, Pitney Bowes Inc. introduced the FPS™ Flexible Productivity Series, a new family of high volume inserting solutions designed to deliver a leading-edge combination of speed, flexibility, and integrity to high volume mailers of transactional and direct mail.

Designed as a single, high performance platform that can handle all production mailing applications for organizations such as financial services companies, telecommunications service providers, utilities, government agencies, and service bureaus, the FPS™ system delivers three key benefits:

- Speed. The FPS™ system is capable of processing up to 14,000 letters per hour.
- Flexibility. It can handle the widest range of applications, insert materials, collations, envelopes or mail piece-finishing requirements.
- Integrity. The FPS™ system helps ensure a high level of mail quality through its ability to scale from simple file audits to complete file-based processing.

"The Flexible Productivity Series sets a new industry standard in terms of performance, agility and integrity in a single platform capable of processing all types of mail, all the time," said Clint Dally, vice president, product line management, Pitney Bowes Document Messaging Technologies. "The performance and flexibility of the FPS™ Flexibility Productivity Series improves productivity and lowers cost per mail piece. For transaction mail and direct mail applications, the FPS™ system provides the superior quality and the monitoring and tracking capability that enables mailers to expand their offerings. From inputs to processing to outputs, the FPS™ system handles the widest variety of inserts, envelopes and applications with ease. We're convinced that it's the most flexible inserter on the market today."

The FPS™ system joins Pitney Bowes' family of high productivity inserters. It features advanced technologies such as Servo motor-driven rotary and friction feeders, which deliver high performance, and ease of set up and use.

SECTOR: **Industrials** ◆ BETA COEFFICIENT: **.90**
10-YEAR COMPOUND EARNINGS PER SHARE GROWTH: **7.3%**
10-YEAR COMPOUND DIVIDENDS PER SHARE GROWTH: **7.5%**

		2005	2004	2003	2002	2001	2000	1999	1998
Revenues (millions)		5,492	4,957	4,577	4,410	4,122	3,881	4,433	4,220
Net Income (millions)		527	594	569	572	556	626	630	568
Earnings per share		2.70	2.54	2.41	2.37	2.25	2.44	2.31	2.03
Dividends per share		1.24	1.22	1.20	1.18	1.16	1.14	1.02	0.90
Price	high	47.5	47.0	42.8	44.4	44.7	54.1	73.3	66.4
	low	40.3	38.9	29.5	28.5	32.0	24.0	40.9	42.2

CONSERVATIVE GROWTH

Praxair, Inc.

39 Old Ridgebury Road ❑ Danbury, CT 06810-5113 ❑ (203) 837-2354 ❑ Dividend reinvestment plan available (800) 368-5948 ❑ Web site: *www.praxair.com* ❑ Listed: NYSE ❑ Ticker symbol: PX ❑ S&P rating: A ❑ Value Line financial strength rating: B++

The largest construction project in Praxair's history—two new hydrogen plants in Texas—started up in 2004 to supply refinery customers along Praxair's 340-mile pipeline. The new plants doubled Praxair's hydrogen capacity on the U.S. Gulf coast.

Demand for the company's hydrogen on the Gulf coast is expected to grow 20 percent annually through 2010 for the following reasons:

- More stringent limits on sulfur content in motor fuels.
- The need to process crude oil containing higher levels of sulfur.
- The role hydrogen can play in expanding existing refining capacity.
- Increased processing of tar sands in Canada.
- New regulatory requirements for locomotives, off-road vehicles, and marine engines scheduled to be implemented later in the decade.

Company Profile

Praxair, Inc. is a global, Fortune 500 company that supplies atmospheric, process, and specialty gases, high-performance coatings, and related services and technologies.

Praxair, which was spun off to Union Carbide shareholders in June 1992, is the largest producer of industrial gases in North and South America; it is the third-largest company of its kind in the world.

Praxair's primary products are: atmospheric gases—oxygen, nitrogen, argon, and rare gases (produced when air is purified, compressed, cooled, distilled, and condensed), and process and specialty gases—carbon dioxide, helium, hydrogen, semiconductor process gases, and acetylene (produced as by-products of chemical production or recovered from natural gas).

The company also designs, engineers and constructs cryogenic and noncryogenic supply systems. Praxair Surface Technologies is a subsidiary that applies metallic and ceramic coatings and powders to metal surfaces to resist wear, high temperatures, and corrosion. Aircraft engines are its primary market, but it serves others, including the printing, textile, chemical and primary metals markets, and provides aircraft engine and airframe component overhaul services.

Praxair adopted its name in 1992, from the Greek word "praxis," or practical application, and "air," the company's primary raw material. PX was originally founded in 1907 when it was the first company to commercialize cryogenically separated oxygen.

Over the near century of its existence, Praxair has remained a leader in the development of processes and technologies that have revolutionized the industrial gases industry. The company introduced the first distribution system for liquid gas in 1917 and developed on-site gas supply by the end of WWII. In the 1960s, Praxair introduced noncryogenic means of air separation and since then has continued to introduce innovative applications technologies for various industries. PX holds almost 3,000 patents.

Praxair serves a wide range of industries: food and beverages, health care, semiconductors, chemicals, refining, primary metals, and metal fabrication, as well as other areas of general industry.

Shortcomings to Bear in Mind

■ On January 5, 2006, *Standard & Poor's Stock Reports* regarded Praxair as a SELL, since the stock appeared overpriced, selling at a premium to the S&P 500. Richard O'Reilly, CFA, said, "PX typically sold at a discount prior to 2004. We are also concerned about any lingering EPS (earnings per share) effects from recent hurricanes. We believe that the company's long-term fundamentals remain sound and that it is concentrating on several less-capital-intensive, faster-growing global markets, such as health care, as well as hydrogen for use by petroleum refiners."

■ For its part, *Value Line Investment Survey* said Praxair should be ranked a 3 (neutral) on March 28, 2006. Eric M. Gottlieb said, "The issue appears adequately priced. Shares of Praxair offer investors average returns to the 2009–2011 period. The company's consistent record of healthy earnings performance, and our expectation of double-digit earnings growth to this period, appears to be already priced into the stock, which is trading near an all-time high."

Reasons to Buy

■ On March 28, 2006, the *New York Times* checked with nineteen securities analysts and found that four regarded Praxair as a STRONG BUY, eight called it a MODERATED BUY; and seven were less enthusiastic, saying it should be a HOLD.

■ "We are maintaining our BUY rating on Praxair, Inc.," said Bill Selesky, writing for Argus Research Company on January 26, 2006. "We continue to believe that the company has the potential to generate better earnings and margins and to be more aggressive on pricing."

■ Lehman Brothers and Prudential Equity Group both gave the stock a solid OVERWEIGHT rating. For his part, Steve Schuman, an analyst with Prudential, said, "Praxair is rated OVERWEIGHT as it should continue to exhibit solid execution and capital discipline, key requirements to growing return on capital, in our view. We believe Praxair is also in a top position to play on our Emerging markets, Energy, and Environmental mega-trends. It is the largest industrial gas company in South America and India, and the second-largest in China."

■ Praxair's applications technologies have improved air and water quality and increased energy efficiency for customers in dozens of industries. Most recently, Praxair and BP opened a hydrogen fueling station at Los Angeles International Airport to supper Governor Schwarzenegger's hydrogen highway initiative. In its own operations, the company is on track to meet its goals of reducing energy intensity* by 18 percent and greenhouse gases emissions intensity by 8 percent over the next ten years.

*Intensity is a per-unit-of-production measure.

■ In 2004, Praxair and CSPC, a joint venture between China National Offshore Oil Corporation (CNOOC) and Shell Petrochemicals Company Ltd., announced an agreement for Praxair to supply CSPC with its oxygen and nitrogen requirements for its new $4.3 billion integrated petrochemical complex in Daya Bay, Huizhou, in Guangdong Province, China.

The heart of the complex is a world-scale condensate or naphtha cracker producing 800,000 tons per year of ethylene and 430,000 tons per year of propylene, integrated with downstream products. It will be the largest capital investment for a Sino-foreign joint venture project in China.

Under the agreement, Praxair will supply high-purity oxygen and nitrogen from new air separation units that will be built adjacent to the CSPC site in the center of the new chemical enclave in Daya Bay Economic and Technical Development Zone. The supply of these products is scheduled to begin in May 2005. Praxair will also produce liquid oxygen, nitrogen, and argon and distribute these products to customers in the rapidly growing Guangdong region.

- Hydrogen is part of a comprehensive portfolio of bulk and specialty gases, technologies, and services Praxair provides refining and chemical customers worldwide. For example, Praxair supplies more than fifty refineries and petrochemical plants from its 280 miles of pipeline along the Texas and Louisiana Gulf Coast. Other Praxair pipeline enclaves serving these industries are situated in Ecorse, Michigan; Edmonton, Alberta, Canada; Salvador, Brazil; Antwerp, Belgium; and Beijing, China.
- Beyond its longstanding supply of pure oxygen and bulk storage equipment to hospitals and other medical facilities worldwide, Praxair delivers respiratory therapy gases and equipment, and a host of on-site gas-management services, including asset, inventory, transaction, and distribution management. Praxair's home oxygen services, moreover, provide respiratory patients with life support, as well as therapies to help with sleep disorders or other illnesses in the home environment.
- The company sees opportunities to differentiate its offering in the food and beverage segment, based on the need for higher standards of food safety. Praxair is bringing the potential to save more than fifteen billion gallons of water and $70 million each year to the U. S. poultry processing industry through a water recycling system that helps increase production and reduce water consumption without compromising food safety.
- The sparkle in soft drinks, the freshness of pastries, the crunch in an apple—chances are, Praxair carbon dioxide or nitrogen had something to do with it. At Praxair's Food Technology Laboratory—the only one of its kind in the industry—technologies and equipment are developed and tested to assist bakers, meat processors, and specialty foods producers deliver products that retain their taste and freshness.
- Taxis, buses, and many private automobiles in Brazil have run on natural gas for decades. Praxair's subsidiary, White Martins, has a growing business producing natural gas cylinders and conversion kits that allow passenger vehicles to run on natural gas. In a bid to reduce the country's oil imports, the state-owned oil company, Petrobras, formed a joint venture with White Martin recently to further increase access to natural gas, particularly at locations not currently supplied by pipelines.

White Martin will build the country's first liquefied natural gas plant in Sao Paulo state and distribute output by truck. Natural gas is liquefied using a cryogenic process, and its distribution requires the same kind of specialized equipment and logistics that are currently used to deliver other industrial gases like oxygen and nitrogen.

- In recent years, Praxair has been the recipient of a host of honors:

- "The Best CEOs in America" from *Institutional Investor* magazine—Praxair's CEO Dennis Reilley tops the basic materials category, January 2004.
- "The Best CFOs in America," *Institutional Investor* magazine—Praxair's CFO, James Sawyer is among the top ten, February 2004.
- "Best Managed Companies in America," *Forbes* magazine—Praxair headlines the chemical company section, January 2004.
- "Leader for the 21st Century," *Treasury and Risk Management* magazine—Praxair's CFO, James Sawyer, is one of the three selected, January 2004.
- "Top Governance Practices Rating," Governancemetrics International, July 2003 and February 2004.
- "Senior Financial Officer of the Year," *Chemical Week* magazine—Praxair's CFO James Sawyer, April 2003.
- "Most Admired Companies," *Fortune* magazine—Praxair ranked third among chemical companies, March 2003 and March 2004.

SECTOR: **Materials** ◆ BETA COEFFICIENT: **1.00**
10-YEAR COMPOUND EARNINGS PER SHARE GROWTH: **9.3%**
10-YEAR COMPOUND DIVIDENDS PER SHARE GROWTH: **16.2%**

		2005	2004	2003	2002	2001	2000	1999	1998
Revenues (millions)		7,656	6,594	5,613	5,128	5,158	5,043	4,639	4,833
Net Income (millions)		726	697	585	548	432	432	441	425
Earnings per share		2.22	2.10	1.77	1.66	1.50	1.49	1.36	1.30
Dividends per share		.72	.60	.46	.38	.34	.31	.28	.25
Price	high	54.3	46.2	38.3	30.6	28.0	27.5	29.1	26.9
	low	41.1	34.5	25.0	22.4	18.3	15.2	16.0	15.3

CONSERVATIVE GROWTH

The Procter & Gamble Company

P.O. Box 599 ❑ Cincinnati, OH 45201-0599 ❑ (800) 742-6253 ❑ Direct Dividend reinvestment plan available (800) 764-7483 ❑ Web site: *www.pg.com* ❑ Listed: NYSE ❑ Fiscal year ends June 30 ❑ Ticker symbol: PG ❑ S&P rating: A ❑ Value Line financial strength rating: A++

In 2005, Procter & Gamble acquired Gillette Company for about $57 billion. "This merger is going to create the greatest consumer products company in the world," said Warren E. Buffett, CEO of Berkshire Hathaway, Inc., Gillette's largest shareholder. "It's a dream deal."

Here is what Gillette looks like:

Founded in 1901, The Gillette Company is the world leader in male grooming, a category that includes blades, razors, and shaving preparations. Gillette also holds the number one position worldwide in selected female grooming products, such as wet shaving products and hair epilation devices.

The company holds the number one position worldwide in manual and power toothbrushes and is the world leader in alkaline batteries.

According to the company, "Our focus is on placing resources behind Gillette's three core businesses: grooming, batteries and oral care. Our core businesses account for nearly 80 percent of our sales and 90 percent of our profits. We are—in all three—the undisputed global leader.

"Some of our core brands include:

- Gillette Mach3
- Gillette for Women Venus
- Gillette Series
- Right Guard
- Duracell Copper Top
- Oral-B
- Braun Oral-B
- Braun"

Gillette manufacturing operations are conducted at thirty-four facilities in 15 countries. Products are distributed through wholesalers, retailers, and agents in over 200 countries and territories.

Company Profile

Procter & Gamble dates back to 1837, when William Procter and James Gamble began making soap and candles in Cincinnati. The company's first major product introduction took place in 1879, when it launched Ivory soap. Since then, P&G has traditionally created a host of blockbuster products that have made the company a cash-generating machine.

Procter & Gamble is a uniquely diversified consumer—products company with a strong global presence. P&G today markets its broad line of products to nearly 5 billion consumers in more than 160 countries.

Procter & Gamble is a recognized leader in the development, manufacturing, and marketing of superior quality laundry, cleaning, paper, personal care, food, beverage, and health-care products, including prescription pharmaceuticals.

Among the company's nearly 300 brands are Tide, Always, Whisper, Didronel, Pro-V, Oil of Olay, Pringles, Ariel, Crest, Pampers, Pantene, Vicks, Bold, Dawn, Head & Shoulders, Cascade, Iams, Zest, Bounty, Comet, Scope, Old Spice, Folgers, Charmin, Tampax, Downy, Cheer, and Prell.

Procter & Gamble is a huge company, with 2005 sales of more than $56 billion. In the same fiscal year (which ended June 30, 2005), earnings per share advanced from $2.32 to $2.53. Dividends also climbed—as they have for many years—from $0.93 to $1.03. The company has nearly 110,000 employees working in more than eighty countries.

Shortcomings to Bear in Mind

- "Retailers are sometimes competitors as well as partners," said CEO A. G. Lafley. "Their own brands are growing as the retailers, themselves, grow. Private labels, or store brands, strive to match innovation quickly and try to present a compelling value alternative in many categories. This is healthy, in my opinion. It requires that we continue to lead innovation and price P&G products competitively. Further, the growing strength of store brands underscores the importance of always being the number one or number two brand in any category. Brands that can't maintain this leadership stature will find it difficult to compete effectively with the best store brands. Based on our internal global share measures, we have the number one or number two brand in seventeen of our nineteen key global categories—categories that account for about 70 percent of sales and earnings. P&G is in a strong position, and ready to become an even better retail partner."
- "It's a more competitive marketplace out there, and at the same time commodity prices are going up," said Amy Bonkoski, a consumer-staples analyst at National City Private Client Group in Cleveland, which owns a little more than seven million P&G shares. She was quoted in the *Wall Street Journal* on August 8, 2005. "In that environment, increasing prices can be difficult, especially in categories like laundry."

Reasons to Buy

- "Since taking the helm of P&G in 2000, A. G. Lafley has led a turnaround that continues to defy expectations," said Suzanne Woolley, writing for *BusinessWeek* on December 19, 2005. "The maker of Pampers and Crest has posted earnings and sales growth that lead the industry and put competitors on the defensive. Lafley capped all this in October with the $57-billion acquisition of Gillette.

  "Lafley, 58, transformed a stodgy, insular culture into one that is nimbler and more open—P&G now gets 35 percent of its product ideas from outside companies or inventors. It has also outflanked rivals in design and innovation: The company had five of the top ten best-selling consumer-product launches in 2005, says market researcher *Information Resources*."
- "At the beginning of this decade, we made several promises to P&G shareholders," said Mr. Lafley on August 9, 2005.

  "We said we would get P&G growing again. We set demanding but realistic growth goals: 4–6 percent sales growth, 10 percent or better earnings per share growth, and free cash flow productivity equal to or greater than 90 percent of earnings. P&G has met or exceeded these growth goals for four consecutive years. Since 2000:

- We've grown sales more than 40 percent, to $57 billion. We've more than doubled profits. We've generated more than $30 billion in free cash flow.
- We have returned $11 billion in cash to shareholders through dividends, and have increased shareholder value another $60 billion by nearly doubling the price of P&G stock.

"We said we would focus on being the global leader in P&G's core categories, with leading global brands.

- P&G is the global leader in all four core categories. Baby Care and Feminine Care both have global share above 35 percent. Fabric Care has more than 30 percent share globally. Hair Care is over 20 percent in a large and fragmented category.
- P&G is growing shares in categories that represent more than two-thirds of company sales.
- Since 2000, we've grown P&G billion-dollar brand lineup from 10 to 17 brands. Pampers is now a $6 billion brand. Tide is a $3 billion brand. Pantene, Always, and Ariel are all $2 billion brands. Dawn became P&G's 17th billion-dollar brand in 2005."

■ In a recent U.S. survey by Cannondale Associates, retailers were asked to rank manufacturers on a number of competencies. P&G was ranked number one in virtually every category:

- Clearest company strategy
- Brands most important to retailers
- Best brand marketers overall
- Most innovative marketing programs

■ Procter & Gamble is known for product innovation. More than 8,000 scientists and researchers are accelerating the pace of new products. The company has a global network of eighteen technical centers in nine countries on four continents. What's more, P&G holds more than 27,000 patents and applies for 3,000 more each year. Not surprisingly, the company is among the ten patent-producing companies in the world—well ahead of any other consumer-products manufacturer.

■ Procter & Gamble believes in product quality. One of the reasons given for the company's problems in 2000 was its refusal to get into the lower-quality, lower-cost private-label business. That just goes against the grain.

P&G believes that the consumer will reward even minor product advantages, and it will not launch a brand if it does not have a competitive advantage. Then, it will continually improve its products and make every effort to maintain that advantage. Tide, for example, has been improved more than seventy times over the years.

■ While most stocks have been a huge disappointment since the market hit a peak on March 24, 2000, Procter & Gamble has made an impressive comeback. Much of its recent success can be attributed to its CEO, Alan G. Lafley who took the reins of the company in June of 2000, when it was "the sort of ink-stained mess you'd find in a Tide commercial," according to Katrina Brooker, writing for *Fortune* magazine.

In the words of Ms. Brooker, "Since he's been P&G's chief, Lafley has managed to pull off what neither of his two predecessors could—turn around the global behemoth. And he did it in the midst of a world economic slowdown to boot."

Ms. Brooker also points out that Mr. Lafley "is a listener, not a storyteller. He's likable but not awe-inspiring. He's the type of guy who gets excited in the mop isle of a grocery store. His plan to fix P&G isn't anything ground-breaking, but rather a straightforward, back-to-the-basics tack. And so far it's worked. He has rallied his troops not with big speeches and dazzling promises, but by hearing them out (practically) one at a time. It's a little dull, perhaps. Workaday dull."

In another part of the *Fortune* article, Katrina Brooker said, "Lafley, who got his start at P&G a quarter century ago as a brand assistant for Joy dishwashing liquid, wouldn't be all that interesting to watch—were it not for the fact that he's so darn good at his job."

- On March 19, 2006, the *New York Times* reported on the opinions of twenty financial analysts. Three rated Procter & Gamble a STRONG BUY; eight said it was a MODERATE BUY; and nine called it a HOLD.
- On February 3, 2006, *Standard & Poor's Stock Reports* gave P&G a five-star rating, it's best. Howard Choe said, "We have a STRONG BUY on the shares, in view of the Gillette acquisition and what we see as PG's own strong fundamentals. Given Gillette's dominant position in the wet shaving category and high margins, and cash flow, we believe the acquisition should provide long-term benefits to P&G."

SECTOR: **Consumer Staples** ◆ BETA COEFFICIENT: **.60**
10-YEAR COMPOUND EARNINGS PER SHARE GROWTH: **11.1%**
10-YEAR COMPOUND DIVIDENDS PER SHARE GROWTH: **11.4%**

		2005	2004	2003	2002	2001	2000	1999	1998
Revenues (millions)		56,741	51,407	43,377	40,238	39,244	39,951	38,125	37,154
Net Income (millions)		7,257	6,481	5,186	4,352	2,922	4,230	4,148	3,780
Earnings per share		2.66	2.32	1.85	1.54	1.04	1.24	1.30	1.28
Dividends per share		1.03	0.93	0.82	0.76	0.70	0.64	0.57	0.51
Price	high	59.7	57.4	50.0	47.4	40.9	59.2	57.8	47.4
	low	51.2	48.9	39.8	37.1	28.0	26.4	41.0	32.6

CONSERVATIVE GROWTH

Questar Corporation

180 East 100 South Street ❑ Salt Lake City, UT 84145-0433 ❑ (801) 324-5077 ❑ Dividend reinvestment plan is available (800) 729-6788 ❑ Web site: *www.questar.com* ❑ Listed: NYSE ❑ Ticker symbol: STR ❑ S&P rating: A- ❑ Value Line financial strength rating: B++

On November 21, 2005, Kinder Morgan Energy Partners, L.P., Sempra Pipelines & Storage, a unit of Sempra Energy, and Questar Corporation announced that Rockies Express Pipeline LLC had signed a binding memorandum of understanding with Overthrust Pipeline Company, a Questar subsidiary, to enter into a long-term capacity lease for up to 1.5 billion cubic feet per day of natural gas to support the extension and expansion of the Entrega Gas Pipeline.

The capacity lease will effectively extend Entrega about 140 miles from the Wamsutter Hub in Sweetwater County, Wyoming, westward to the Opal Hub in Lincoln County, Wyoming. Entrega will connect with the proposed Rockies Express Pipeline to provide seamless transportation from Rocky Mountain production areas to eastern Ohio.

Company Profile

Questar Corporation is a natural gas-focused energy company with three principal subsidiaries—Questar Market Resources (gas and oil exploration, development, and production; gas gathering and processing); Questar Pipeline (interstate gas transportation and storage); and Questar Gas (retail gas distribution).

Questar Market Resources

Questar Market Resources is the corporation's primary growth driver. Market Resources has four major subsidiaries:

- Questar Exploration and Production (Questar E&P) acquires, explores for, develops, and produces gas and oil in two core areas—the Rocky Mountain region of Wyoming, Utah, and Colorado and the Midcontinent region of Oklahoma, Texas, and Louisiana.
- Wexpro develops and produces cost-of-service reserves for affiliated company Questar Gas.
- Questar Gas Management provides midstream services, including gas gathering and processing, primarily in the Rockies.
- Questar Energy Trading sells Market Resources' equity gas and oil in the western United States, provides risk-management services, and operates a natural gas storage facility in the Rockies.

Questar Pipeline

Questar Pipeline is an interstate pipeline company that transports natural gas in Utah, Wyoming, and Colorado and operates gas-storage facilities in Utah and Wyoming. Questar Pipeline is regulated by the Federal Energy Regulatory Commission. Questar Pipeline also owns and operates the eastern segment of the Southern Trails Pipeline, which extends from the Four Corners area to the California state line, and the Overthrust Pipeline in southwestern Wyoming.

Questar Gas

Questar Gas provides retail gas-distribution service to more than 800,000 customers in Utah, southwestern Wyoming, and a small portion of southeastern Idaho. Questar Gas is regulated by the Public Service Commission of Utah and the Wyoming Public Service Commission.

Shortcomings to Bear in Mind

- Insiders, such as executives of the company and board members, have been heavy sellers of the Questar stock. In a recent nine-month period, there were eighteen instances of selling and not a single instance of anyone buying.

Reasons to Buy

- Questar E&P (*exploration and production)* and Wexpro are major operators on the Pinedale Anticline in western Wyoming, one of the nation's most significant onshore natural gas development plays. Questar E&P and Wexpro have a combined 67 percent average working interest in 470 total development locations on about 9,400 productive acres in the Lance Pool (combined Lance and Mesaverde Formations) at Pinedale.

  Pinedale wells target hundreds of stacked, low-permeability Lance and Mesaverde fluvial-sandstone reservoirs from depths of 9,500 to 14,500 feet. These "tight gas sand" reservoirs are completed using state-of-the-art, multiple-stage hydraulic-fracture-stimulation techniques. A typical Pinedale well, spaced on twenty acres, will recover gross reserves of 3.8 to 8.8 bcfe.

Management Philosophy

- "We manage our company to generate acceptable returns on invested capital across the full commodity-price cycle," said Charles B. Stanley, president and CEO of Questar Market Resources. "We strive to protect returns by hedging gas and oil prices and by rigorously maintaining our investment and capital discipline. I think it's important we not change our risk discipline and fundamental perception of pricing in response to current cyclical price strength."

Mr. Stanley goes on to say, "Today's high prices may be here for a while for fundamental reasons—pent-up demand for gas for already-built electric power plants; flat to declining production from most major producing basins; steeper declining rates in new wells due to smaller development targets and a focus on unconventional reservoirs; intense opposition to opening prospective new supply areas; uncertain timing of LNG (liquid natural gas) imports and Arctic gas; and high global oil prices. Even so, history has shown that high prices lead to increased drilling and supply growth, suppressed consumer demand and an inevitable return of prices to normal levels. With that in mind, we test investment decisions in our E&P business for a risk-adjusted 15 percent after-tax return at $3.50 pr Mcf NYMEX gas price, not because that's our forecast, but because it helps us maintain investment discipline in a high-price environment."

Differentiating Market Resources in the E&P Sector

- Mr. Stanley also said, "We have a large inventory of low-cost, low-risk development locations at Pinedale and in the Uinta Basin that should sustain our organic growth rate for the next several years. Another differentiator is our large acreage position in some of the most prospective areas in the Rockies. We've thoroughly reviewed these assets and, with help from our outside reserve engineers, we've quantified the probable and possible reserves and resource potential on our extensive acreage. Think of it as our warehouse of future opportunities."
- On March 29, 2006, the *New York Times* poled fourteen financial analysts who specialize in the analysis of Questar. Four regarded the stock as a STRONG BUY; five said it should be a MODERATE BUY; five preferred to tag it a HOLD.
- "Our BUY recommendation is based on total return potential (*dividends plus capital gains*)," said Yogeesh Wagle, writing for *Standard & Poor's Company Reports* on February 17, 2006.

"While U.S. natural gas production has declined over the past three years, STR has posted steady production gains through an aggressive drilling program at its Rockies and Midcontinent assets. In 2005, production grew 10 percent, to 114.2 billion cubic feet of gas equivalent (Bcfe). Higher production and elevated natural gas prices should drive strong EPS (earnings per share) growth through 2006."

- On February 17, 2006, Lehman Brothers looked upon STR favorably, rating the stock OVERWEIGHT. The analyst said, "The stock has been weak with falling gas prices. Investors have been disappointed by a modest bump in proved reserves and a rollback in guidance. Neither should have been a surprise, nor should they be of lasting importance, in our opinion. More importantly, fundamentals are very strong, and the pace of drilling at Pinedale should increase."
- Questar offers a lower-risk way to invest in the strong fundamentals of natural gas. Questar's primary growth driver is gas and oil exploration and production and gas-gathering and processing. These businesses provide the potential for better growth than regulated business. Questar's regulated businesses—interstate natural gas transportation and storage and retail gas distribution—play an important role in Questar's value proposition. They provide earnings that are not sensitive to commodity prices and help pay the company's dividend.

SECTOR: **Utilities** ◆ BETA COEFFICIENT: **0.85**
10-YEAR COMPOUND EARNINGS PER SHARE GROWTH: **14.3%**
10-YEAR COMPOUND DIVIDENDS PER SHARE GROWTH: **4.4%**

		2005	2004	2003	2002	2001	2000	1999	1998
Revenues (millions)		2,725	1,901	1,463	1,201	1,439	1,266	924	906
Net Income (millions)		326	229	179	144	158	140	95	97
Earnings per share		3.74	2.67	2.13	1.74	1.94	1.74	1.15	1.18
Dividends per share		0.89	0.85	0.78	0.73	0.71	0.69	0.67	0.65
Price	high	89.6	52.1	35.5	29.5	33.8	31.9	19.9	22.4
	low	46.7	33.8	26.0	18.0	18.6	13.6	14.8	15.8

CONSERVATIVE GROWTH

Ruby Tuesday, Inc.

150 West Church Avenue ❏ Maryville, TN 37801 ❏ (865) 379-5702 ❏ Web site: *www.rubytuesday.com* ❏ Dividend reinvestment plan not available ❏ Fiscal year ends first Tuesday after May 30 ❏ Listed: NYSE ❏ Ticker symbol: RI ❏ S&P rating: B+ ❏ Value Line financial strength rating: B++

"I believe there are four P's that are critical to building and maintaining a great brand, whether it is in packaged goods, retailing, or restaurants," said CEO Sandy Beall in fiscal 2006.

People

"We have become more people-centered than ever, with better selection tools, a step-up in the concentrated training our teams receive at Wow-U, our performance development center, along with expanded training for all levels of management, increased base pay for all field management, and bonus programs that reward achievement of high standards and guest-count goals. The result is management turnover, including all trainees, at 26.6 percent, the lowest management turnover since 2001. Team turnover, at approximately 123 percent, is also in good shape, especially considering that we initiated a lot of changes to further raise our standards. Our goal for next fiscal year are for management turnover to be below 20 percent and hourly team member turnover to be below 110 percent."

Product

"Our menu today is more appealing than ever, and we ended the year with the most guest favorites and the best value, variety, and uniqueness, based on our consumer satisfaction scores that include an overall 4.3 rating on a 0-to-5 scale. We made solid progress in differentiating our brand from our direct competitors with menu choices like our thirty famous burgers, twenty-one awesome appetizers, and an enhanced sixty-five-item salad bar—all huge hits with our guests and mainstays that the bar-and-grill segment of casual dining was built on. We also added signature items like Ruby's Stackers, our baked pasta pies, and an expanded Hang-Off-the-Plate ribs category. Our Ruby Tuesday Smart Eating selections offer our guests more than twenty choices that are lower in fat, carbohydrates, or calories."

Price

"We believe we also offer our guests attractive prices and excellent value. We lowered pricing in most categories to be even more competitive as we transitioned into television advertising. Our menu prices today are essentially the same as they were in 2003, and our salad bar is actually less expensive than it was in 2001. Our latest menu is high in value yet has the opportunity to increase the average amount our guests spend when they visit Ruby Tuesday because with greater value and more options, they are more likely to add appetizers or a visit to the salad bar. It is a win-win that allows guests to get more for their money and for us to realize higher sales."

Place

"Our prototypical building creates value by allowing great returns at lower sales volume but has the capability of annual volume of more than $3 million. Expanded versions are built in areas where sales are forecast to be higher. This new, more contemporary prototype ranges in size from 4,600 to 5,100 square feet, has more of a lunch counter than bar, an open kitchen, and a fresher feeling more in sync with today's consumer. Also, after two years of investment in remodeling and upgrades, our existing units are in very good shape."

Company Profile

Ruby Tuesday, Inc. owns and operates Ruby Tuesday casual dining restaurants. The company also franchises the Ruby Tuesday concepts in selected domestic and international markets. As of May 31, 2005, the company owned and operated 579 restaurants, while U.S. franchises and international franchises operated 216 and 36 restaurants, respectively. The Ruby Tuesday chain includes restaurants in forty-four states, Washington, D.C., Puerto Rico, and twelve foreign countries.

The first Ruby Tuesday restaurant was opened in 1972 in Knoxville, Tennessee. The Ruby Tuesday concept, which consisted of sixteen units, was acquired by Morrison Restaurants, Inc. in 1982.

During the following years, Morrison added other casual dining concepts, including the internally developed American Café. In 1995, Morrison completed the acquisition of Tias Inc., a chain of Tex-Mex restaurants. In a spin-off transaction that took place in March 1996, shareholders of Morrison approved the distribution of two separate businesses of Morrison to its shareholders. In conjunction with the spin-off, Morrison was reincorporated in the state of Georgia and changed its name to Ruby Tuesday, Inc.

Ruby Tuesday restaurants are casual, full-service restaurants with warm woods, whimsical artifacts, and classic Tiffany-style lamps that create a comfortable, nostalgic look and feel. The menu is based on variety, with something for just about everyone. Some of Ruby Tuesday's most popular entree items, which are prepared fresh daily are: fajitas, ribs, chicken, steak, seafood, pasta, burgers, soups, sandwiches, the company's signature salad bar, and signature Tallcake desserts in strawberry and chocolate varieties. Entrees range in price from $6.49 to $16.99.

Shortcomings to Bear in Mind

- According to some analysts, there is some risk here, which includes rising food and labor costs that could cause margins to narrow. Then, too, the company might suffer from the aggressive expansion by its competitors, which could hurt operating earnings in the bar and grill segment of the entire casual dining segment.

Reasons to Buy

- On March 27, 2006, the *New York Times* tracked down ten analysts who keep tabs on Ruby Tuesday. Three said that RI was a STRONG BUY; two called the company a MODERATE BUY; and five tagged it a HOLD.
- "Our recommendation is BUY," said Dennis Milton, writing for the *Standard & Poor's Stock Reports* on January 9, 2006. "We

believe the shares are attractively valued." The reports goes on to say, "We believe RI is well positioned within the fast-growing bar-and-grill segment."

- "Ruby stock is an appealing three- to five-year holding, thanks to a stronger profit outlook," said Warren Thorpe, writing for *Value Line Investment Survey* on March 10, 2006. He also said, "Menu changes and improved customer satisfaction should prove beneficial. Ruby has added a number of dishes and increased portion size overall. This, with an increased focus on faster, friendlier service should help to boost business."
- "We think that the rise of dual-income households and consumers' increased desire for convenient meal solutions provide an attractive landscape for long-term sales growth in the restaurant industry," said a report issued by *Wachovia Capital Markets* on October 6, 2005. "It is our view that Ruby Tuesday is distancing itself from its primary competition in key strategic areas such as employee training, restaurant staffing levels, and menu development. We are targeting annualized EPS growth of approximately 16 percent for Ruby Tuesday over the next three to five years."
- "We remain impressed with the company's focus and execution of its strategy shift from coupon-based marketing to media-driven advertising over the last year," said a report issued by Bank of America Securities on October 6, 2005. "Looking ahead, we believe the company has additional initiatives in place to continue its positive momentum, including the rollout of a kitchen display system over the next several months and the opportunity to refocus their attention on its 'go-go' business—possibly toward the end of fiscal 2006 or the beginning of fiscal 2007, which would provide another sales-driven catalyst."
- Mr. Beall commented on the care and training of employees. "Because approximately 80 percent of our managers come from within the ranks of hourly team members, we have to be good at training and development. We are 100 percent committed to take care of the people who take care of our guests. We do that by offering healthcare benefits from the first day an employee joins our team, with performance-based compensation and stock options and a career pathway that certifies competency and enables outstanding performers to become future leaders of the company.

"All of our general managers, district sales and standard partners, regional directors and vice presidents, and the 'A' players in our performance management system spend time throughout the year at Wow University (WOW-U), our training facility in Maryville, Tennessee. They are hands-on participants in skill-development classes and workplace simulations. They are assessed for readiness and tested for certification before they are promoted to new levels of responsibility and ownership. WOW-U is also where new initiatives and processes are presented before being rolled out to our restaurants."

SECTOR: **Consumer Discretionary** ◆ BETA COEFFICIENT: **.90**

9-YEAR COMPOUND EARNINGS PER SHARE GROWTH: **21%**

7-YEAR COMPOUND DIVIDENDS PER SHARE GROWTH: **14%**

		2005	2004	2003	2002	2001	2000	1999	1998
Revenues (millions)		1,110	1,041	914	833	790	798	722	711
Net Income (millions)		102.3	110	88.5	58.3	59.2	36.5	36.5	29.1
Earnings per share		1.56	1.64	1.36	1.15	.91	.72	.54	.42
Dividends per share		.05	.05	.05	.05	.05	.05	.05	.02
Price	high	26.8	33.0	30.0	27.2	21.7	16.6	11.0	10.6
	low	20.5	22.6	15.9	14.2	13.3	7.8	8.2	6.0

St. Jude Medical, Inc.

One Lillehei Plaza ❑ St. Paul, MN 55117 ❑ (651) 766-3029 ❑ Dividend reinvestment program is not available ❑ Web site: *www.sjm.com* ❑ Listed: NYSE ❑ Ticker symbol: STJ ❑ S&P rating: B ❑ Value Line financial strength rating: B++

On October 19, 2005, the company said that data from a clinical trial show that a new device from St. Jude Medical is effective in treating a common condition associated with more than 200,000 strokes worldwide each year. The PFO (patent foramen ovale) CLOSE UP (Closure Using Premere™) Trial results were presented at the Cardiovascular Research Foundation's Seventeenth Annual Transcatheter Cardiovascular Therapeutics (TCT) scientific symposium by Principal Investigator Horst Sievert, M.D., Professor of Internal Medicine, Cardiology, and Vascular Medicine at the CardioVascular Center Frankfurt, Sankt Katharinen, Frankfurt, Germany.

PFOs, or patent foramen ovale, are common defects where a small hole between the upper chambers of the heart can allow unfiltered venous blood to enter the arterial circulation. If the unfiltered blood contains a clot or other debris, it can trigger a stroke or transient ischemic attack (TIA, or "ministroke"). While everyone is born with a PFO and most close naturally during infancy, approximately 25 percent of the adult population has a PFO, which is usually considered benign in most people.

The Premere™ PFO Closure System (20mm) device safely and effectively closed PFOs in 87 percent of cases after six months with no adverse events. The trial included sixty-seven patients at five research sites in Europe.

Premere was specifically designed for PFO closures. During the procedure, physicians deliver the device through the PFO and then open its two sides independently, allowing physicians to precisely place the device and close the PFO. The Premere™ device is implanted through a transcatheter approach, which is far less invasive than open heart surgery.

"The Premere™ design conforms well to PFO anatomy, using materials that minimize complications, limit the body's exposure to foreign material and enable physicians to precisely place the device," said Paul R. Buckman, president of St. Jude Medical's Cardiology Division. "The absence of complications during the trial confirms the device was successful in meeting these important clinical objectives."

Strokes occur when an artery bursts or is blocked, which denies oxygen to the brain and leads to loss of function. It is estimated that more than 2 million patients worldwide suffer strokes each year, 10 percent of which are associated with PFOs. TIAs temporarily interrupt the brain's blood supply. While they do not have lasting effects, they are warning signs of a stroke, and one-third of people with TIAs eventually experience a stroke, too. Medical researchers have observed that patients whose PFOs have been closed appear to have less recurrence of strokes.

In December 2004, Premere™ received European CE Mark approval for sale in Europe and select international markets. Premere™ is only available for investigational use in the United States. There is evidence that PFOs also are associated with migraine headaches; in the United States, the device will be used in the ESCAPE clinical trial (Effect of Septal Closure of Atrial PFO on Events of Migraine with Premere) under an approved Investigational Device Exemption to study the effect of PFO closure on migraine attacks. The ESCAPE trial (*www.ESCAPEmigraines.com*) is expected to begin in late 2005.

Company Profile

St. Jude Medical, Inc. is dedicated to the design, manufacture, and distribution of cardiovascular medical devices of the highest quality, offering physicians, patients, and payers unmatched clinical performance and demonstrated economic value. The company's product portfolio includes pacemakers, implantable cardioverter defibrillators (ICDs), vascular closure devices, catheters, and heart valves.

In the Cardiac Rhythm Management therapy area, St. Jude Medical has assembled a broad array of products for treating heart rhythm disorders—including atrial fibrillation—as well as heart failure. Its innovative product lines include sophisticated ICDs, state-of-the-art pacemaker systems, and a variety of diagnostic and therapeutic electrophysiology catheters.

Atrial fibrillation (AF), a quivering chaotic rhythm in the upper chamber of the heart (atria) is the world's most common cardiac arrhythmia, affecting more than 5 million people worldwide. It reduces the normal output of the heart, is a known risk factor for stroke, is often associated with heart failure, and can greatly impair a person's quality of life. AF is encountered by all of the company's physician customers—and today it remains one of the most difficult conditions for the medical profession to treat.

In addition to its electrophysiology catheters, the company develops catheter technologies for the Cardiology/Vascular Access therapy area. Those products include industry-leading hemostasis introducers, catheters, and the market's leading vascular closure device. From access to closure, those products represent a complete set of tools for vascular access site management.

In the Cardiac Surgery therapy area, the company has been the undisputed global leader in the mechanical heart valve technology for more than twenty-five years. St. Jude Medical also develops a line of tissue valves and valve-repair products. In 2003, the company expanded its presence in cardiac surgery with a minority investment in Epicor Medical, Inc., which is developing a unique surgical approach for atrial fibrillation.

St. Jude Medical products are sold in more than 120 countries. The company has twenty principal operations and manufacturing facilities around the world.

Shortcomings to Bear in Mind

- To be sure, St. Jude is an exceptional company with an impressive record. However, the market knows this and gives it a lofty P/E ratio, typically about thirty times earnings.

Reasons to Buy

- On March 27, 2006, the *New York Times* published the results of a survey, in which the opinions of thirty-two analysts were tabulated. Nine viewed St. Jude as a STRONG BUY; seven called it a MODERATE BUY; and eighteen looked upon the stock as a HOLD.
- "These shares are ranked to outperform the broader market in the coming six to twelve months," said Alex Roomets, writing for *Value Line Investment Survey* on March 3, 2006. "The equity also offers decent appreciation potential out to 2009–2011, with a number of possibly lucrative products in development and slated for approval during that time span."
- "St. Jude Medical, Inc. agreed to pay $1.3 billion to acquire Advanced Neuromodulation Systems, Inc., a major force in the relatively new field of using electrical stimulation to treat pain and other conditions," said Thomas M. Burton, writing for the *Wall Street Journal* on October 17, 2005. "St. Jude, in agreeing to buy the number two maker of such neurostimulation products, will diversify itself and take on the number one company in the field, Medtronic, Inc. of Minneapolis."

Mr. Burton goes on to say, "With its agreement to purchase Advanced Neuromodulation, St. Jude will be entering a market, estimated at $1 billion annually, to treat pain and potentially Parkinson's and the malady called essential tremor. The treatment involves stimulating the nerves and spinal cord."

The *Wall Street Journal* article also said, "'This will be our first platform outside cardiac care,' said St. Jude's CEO, Daniel J. Starks. He said he expects the spinal-cord-stimulation business to grow at a rate of about 20 percent a year, even without approval by the Food and Drug Administration to treat multiple conditions beyond pain."

- On February 15, 2005, St. Jude Medical announced it had signed a definitive agreement to acquire the business of Velocimed, LLC ("Velocimed"), a privately-owned company located in Maple Grove, Minnesota. Velocimed develops and manufactures specialty interventional cardiology devices. Under the terms of the agreement, St. Jude acquired Velocimed's business for a cash purchase price of $82.5 million, less an estimated $8.5 million of cash at Velocimed upon closing, plus additional contingent payments tied to revenues in excess of minimum future targets.

Velocimed was founded in 2001 to develop, manufacture, and market specialty interventional cardiology devices. Velocimed has developed three product platforms: the Premere™ patent foramen ovale (PFO) closure system; the Proxis™ proximal embolic protection device; and the Venture™ guidewire control catheter for accessing difficult anatomy and crossing chronic total occlusions in interventional catheterization procedures.

Commenting on the agreement to acquire Velocimed, St. Jude's CEO Daniel J. Starks said, "The acquisition of Velocimed supports our objective of building on the market leadership of our Angio-Seal™ vascular closure product line through selective investments in emerging therapies that represent significant new growth opportunities for interventional catheterization procedures. We look forward to completing this transaction and welcoming the employees of Velocimed to St. Jude Medical."

Paul R. Buckman, president of the company's Cardiology Division, said, "In July 2004, St. Jude Medical announced the formation of the Cardiology Division. With this transaction, St. Jude Medical gains immediate access to three product platforms that serve growing segments of the interventional cardiology market and that we are particularly interested in bringing to our customers."

About Velocimed's Products: A patent foramen ovale (PFO) is a structural defect of the heart where a small hole at birth between the right and left atria (upper chambers of the heart) fails to close in infancy. An estimated 25% of the adult population has a PFO. Though usually considered benign, this condition has been associated with an elevated risk of a stroke. Over 200,000 patients worldwide who survive a stroke each year have a PFO and are potential candidates for PFO therapy. The Premere™ PFO closure system already is approved in Europe. Efforts to initiate a U.S. clinical study of the Premere™ system under an investigational device exemption (IDE) are underway.

Embolic protection devices are used to help minimize the risk of heart attack or stroke if plaque or other debris are dislodged into the blood stream during interventional cardiology procedures. Interest in the embolic protection market has increased based on recent studies involving saphenous vein grafts (SVG) where a reduction of major adverse coronary events (MACE) occurred when other embolic protection devices were deployed. The Proxis™ device has CE Mark approval for SVG use in Europe and is currently being evaluated in the United States in a clinical study under an approved IDE granted by the FDA.

SECTOR: **Health Care** ◆ BETA COEFFICIENT: **.90**
10-YEAR COMPOUND EARNINGS PER SHARE GROWTH: **8.5%**
10-YEAR COMPOUND DIVIDENDS PER SHARE GROWTH: **no dividend**

		2005	2004	2003	2002	2001	2000	1999	1998
Revenues (millions)		2,915	2,294	1,932	1,590	1,347	1,179	1,114	994
Net Income (millions)		394	410	339	276	203	156	144	129
Earnings per share		1.04	1.10	0.92	0.76	0.57	0.46	0.43	0.38
Dividends per share		Nil	–	–	–	–	–	–	–
Price	high	52.8	42.9	32.0	21.6	19.5	15.6	10.2	9.9
	low	34.5	29.9	19.4	15.3	11.1	5.9	5.7	4.8

AGGRESSIVE GROWTH

Staples, Inc.

500 Staples Drive ❑ Framingham, MA 01702 ❑ (800) 468-7751 ❑ Web site: *www.staples.com* ❑ Direct Dividend reinvestment plan is available (888) 875-9002 ❑ Fiscal year ends Saturday closest to January 31 ❑ Listed: Nasdaq ❑ Ticker symbol: SPLS ❑ S&P rating: B+ ❑ Value Line financial strength rating: A

On October 27, 2005, Staples, the world's largest office products company, announced that the National Joint Powers Alliance (NJPA) had awarded Staples a national office products and classroom supplies contract. NJPA is a member-owned buying cooperative serving public and private schools, state and local governments, and nonprofit organizations. Staples Contract division, which serves midsized and Fortune 1000 companies, will provide office products and classroom supplies to all qualified organizations including more than 8,000 NJPA members nationwide.

"We awarded Staples because in their bid response they demonstrated that they share NJPA's commitment to products and services with exceptional value and great customer service," said Mike Hajek, director of business development and marketing of NJPA. "Through Staples, we'll help our member organizations operate at an efficiency level they would not be able to achieve on their own."

"Staples is honored to work with the NJPA as their strategic supplier of office products," said Steve Mongeau, senior vice president, Staples Business Advantage, Staples Contract division. "Through our operational and customer service excellence, we'll provide a program that makes it easy for NJPA members to get the products and service they need to get their work done."

About NJPA

The National Joint Powers Alliance (NJPA) is a member-owned cooperative that creates business and service relationships between buyers and suppliers. NJPA serves public and nonpublic educational systems and nonprofit and governmental agencies and is governed by publicly elected officials.

About Staples Contract

Staples Contract is Staples's fastest growing business with industry-leading double-digit growth for the past five years. The business serves midsized companies through Staples Business Advantage and Fortune 1000 companies through Staples National Advantage. Staples Contract works collaboratively with its customers enabling procurement professionals to efficiently manage procurement programs with lowest total delivered cost. Staples Contract has been certified by J.D. Power and Associates for delivering "An Outstanding Customer Service Experience" for the second consecutive year.

Company Profile

Staples, Inc. launched the office supplies superstore industry with the opening of its first store in Brighton (near Boston) Massachusetts in May 1986. Its goal was to provide small business owners the same low prices on office supplies previously enjoyed only by large corporations. Staples is now a $16 billion retailer of office supplies, business services, furniture, and technology to consumers and businesses from home-based businesses to *Fortune* 500 companies in the United States, Canada, the United Kingdom, France, Italy, Spain, Belgium, Germany, the Netherlands, and Portugal. Customers can shop with Staples in any way they choose, by either walking in, calling in, or logging on.

Staples is the largest operator of office superstores in the world, serving customers in 1,600 office superstores, mail order catalogs, e-commerce, and a contract business.

The company operates three business segments: North American Retail, North American Delivery, and European operations.

The company's North American Retail segment consists of the company's U.S. and Canadian business units that sell office products, supplies, and services.

Staples North American Delivery segment consists of the company's U.S. and Canadian contract, catalog and Internet business units that sell and deliver office products, supplies, and services directly to customers.

Staples European Operations segment consists of the company's business units that operate 201 retail stores in the United Kingdom (93), Germany (53), the Netherlands (40), Portugal (14), and Belgium (1). The company also sells and delivers office products and supplies directly to businesses throughout the United Kingdom and Germany. The company's delivery operations comprise the catalog business (Staples Direct and Quill Corporation), the contract stationer business (Staples National Advantage and Staples Business Advantage) and the Internet e-commerce business (Staples.com). Quill, acquired in 1998, is a direct mail catalog business, serving more than one million medium-sized businesses in the United States.

In 2002, SPLS acquired, for $383 million, Medical Arts Press, a leading provider of specialized printed products and supplies for medical offices. In 2002, the company acquired Guilbert's European mail order business for about $788 million.

At the retail level, stores operate under the names Staples-The Office Superstore and Staples Express. The prototype store had, up until recently, about 24,000 square feet of sales space, which the company reduced to 20,000 in fiscal 2003. Stores carry about 8,500 stock items.

Express stores are much smaller, with between 6,000 square feet and 10,000 square feet of sales space. They also handle fewer items, generally about 6,000, and are situated in downtown business sectors. By contrast, the larger units tend to be situated in the suburbs.

Sales by product are: North American Retail, 59 percent; North American Delivery, 28 percent; and Europe, 13 percent. Sales by product line are: office supplies and services, 42 percent; business machines and telecommunications services, 30 percent; computers and related products, 21 percent; and office furniture, 7 percent.

Shortcomings to Bear in Mind

- If you are looking for a conservative stock, you had better avoid Staples. It has a beta coefficient of 1.30, which means it is very volatile. In other words, if the stock market rises or falls a certain percentage, SPLS will rise or fall 30 percent more.

Reasons to Buy

- "The aisles of Staples stores are bustling with holiday shoppers snapping up everything from digital cameras to tape for wrapping gifts," said Robin Goldwyn Blumenthal, writing for *Barron's* on November 28, 2005. "Investors might want to grab a shopping cart, too." She also said, "Staples, which already boasts industry-leading efficiency, is pushing into high-margin ventures like copy centers and its own brand of office products."

  The author then quotes an industry source, "'Staples is a quality stock with a compelling valuation,' says Gordon Marchand, a principal of Sustainable Growth Advisers who holds the shares there and in the John Hancock U.S. Global Leaders Growth Fund, which he also advises. 'Staples is in a position right now where they have more control over their business's than Office Depot, he adds.'"

- "As Ronald Sargent was about to assume the chief executive post at Staples Inc. about five years ago, he called a staff meeting to discuss a radical idea: eliminating more than 800 items from the chain's shelves," said Joseph Pereira, in an article that appeared in *The Wall Street Journal* March 5, 2003.

  "The nixed items were aimed at casual shoppers, and included cheap printers, cartoon-themed notepads, and novelty pens adorned with feathers or edible candies.

  "Mr. Sargent argued that the company needed to shift focus, de-emphasizing occasional shoppers, looking for discounts in favor of bigger-spending small businesses and 'power users.' Although a group of Staples sales and merchandising executives balked, arguing that the company couldn't afford to alienate any potential customers in the midst of the post-Sept.11 downturn, Mr. Sargent prevailed."

- Mr. Sargent, now in this seventh year in the corner office, has no plans to let up. He says there's room for 25 percent growth in the industry-wide count of 3,200-plus office superstores in North America. And Staples plans to grow its own base 5 percent for the next few years, as well as opening smaller stores in downtown markets. In total, Sargent figures Staples can add about one hundred stores a year for the next few years.

- Staples has a solid balance sheet, with 88 percent of its capitalization in shareholders' equity. Total interest coverage, moreover, is impressive, at twenty-nine times.

- *Standard & Poor's Company Reports* spoke favorably about the company on January 12, 2006. Michael Sauers said, "We have a BUY recommendation on the shares. We believe greater business spending, particularly by small-to-medium-size businesses, and a solid job market bode well for SPLS. We think strong early returns from new Chicago stores indicate further growth in untapped domestic metropolitan areas, and the company's joint venture in China should provide ample opportunity for future growth with its $25-billion office products market."

- On March 1, 2006, the *New York Times* surveyed seventeen analysts who follow Staples and three were convinced the company should be a STRONG BUY; seven rated the stock a MODERATE BUY; and seven settled for a HOLD.

- David R. Cohen, writing for *Value Line Investment Survey* on January 13, 2006, said "This timely stocks offers good three- to five-year appreciation potential. Moreover, cash assets, currently at $1.3 billion and free cash flow (estimated at $700 million next year) appear ample to fund potential acquisitions, as well as recently expanded stock-repurchase activity."

■ On February 10, 2006, Argus Research Company awarded Staples a BUY rating. Christopher Graja, CFA, said, "We believe that the company has three of the four attributes we like to see in the retail sector. First, we think the company has the ability to boost sales by adding stores, taking market share in the delivery business, expanding internationally and selling Staples-brand product in new venues, including grocery stores. Second, we believe that the company has the ability to lift operating margins by another 200 basis points (*100 basis points equals 1 percent)* in coming years by developing proprietary products, adding copy centers, improving logistics and getting European business turned around. Third, we believe that Staples has the financial strength to enhance shareholder returns by making small dividend increases, completing a recently announced $1.5 billion buyback and using cash flow productively. The fourth area is valuation. While we believe that the shares are reasonably valued at 21-times earnings, we are not forecasting a significant multiple expansion."

SECTOR: **Consumer Discretionary** ◆ BETA COEFFICIENT: **1.35**
10-YEAR COMPOUND EARNINGS PER SHARE GROWTH: **23.1%**
10-YEAR COMPOUND DIVIDENDS PER SHARE GROWTH: **not meaningful**

		2005	2004	2003	2002	2001	2000	1999	1998
Revenues (millions)		16,079	14,448	13,181	11,596	10,744	10,674	8,937	7,132
Net Income (millions)		834	708	552	417	307	264	315	238
Earnings per share		1.12	0.93	0.75	.63	.44	.39	.45	.35
Dividends per share		.17	.13	Nil	—	—	—	—	—
Price	high	24.1	22.5	18.6	15.0	13.0	19.2	23.9	20.5
	low	18.6	15.8	10.5	7.8	7.3	6.9	10.9	7.1

AGGRESSIVE GROWTH

Stryker Corporation

P. O. Box 4085 ❑ Kalamazoo, MI 49003-4085 ❑ (616) 385-2600 ❑ Web site: *www.strykercorp.com* ❑ Listed: NYSE ❑ Dividend reinvestment plan not available ❑ Ticker symbol: SYK ❑ S&P rating: B+ ❑ Value Line financial strength rating: A

On August 22, 2005 Stryker announced that the company had entered into an exclusive U.S. marketing and distribution agreement with Corin Group PLC (traded on the London Stock Exchange), a leading United Kingdom-based manufacturer and supplier of orthopaedic devices, for the Cormet Hip Resurfacing System and Optimom, its large diameter articulation hip system.

The ten-year agreement should enable Stryker to be one of the first companies to offer hip resurfacing technology to patients in the United States.

Interest in hip resurfacing procedures is on the rise globally due to the bone conserving nature of the procedure and anticipated benefits related to postoperative activities and range of motion. In these procedures, surgeons replace the acetabulum in much the same way as a conventional total hip but the femoral head is resurfaced rather than removed.

Resurfacing hip procedures are currently in clinical trials in the United States and are being performed routinely outside of the United States. A PMA (Premarket Approval Application) for the Cormet Resurfacing Hip System has been filed with the Food and Drug Administration and is under consideration for approval.

Michael P. Mogul, President, Stryker Orthopaedics, stated, "Hip resurfacing provides Stryker with yet another alternative to help younger patients return to more active lifestyles. We are committed to providing this option to patients in the U.S. and our international markets."

Company Profile

Stryker Corporation was founded in 1941 by Dr. Homer H. Stryker, a leading orthopedic surgeon and the inventor of several orthopedic products. The company now ranks as a dominant player in a $12-billion global orthopedics industry. SYK has a significant market share in such sectors as artificial hips, prosthetic knees, and trauma products.

Stryker develops, manufactures, and markets specialty surgical and medical products worldwide. These products include orthopedic implants, trauma systems, powered surgical instruments, endoscopic systems, patient care, and handling equipment.

Through a network of 374 centers in twenty-six states, Stryker's Physiotherapy Associates division provides physical, occupational, and speech therapy to orthopedic and neurology patients. The physical therapy business represents a solid complementary business for Stryker, in view of the high number of its surgeon customers who prescribe physical therapy following orthopedic surgery.

A major component of Stryker's success is the optimal use of resources in manufacturing and distribution. Taking advantage of both information technology and leading-edge workflow management practices, the company monitors quality and service levels at its sixteen plants throughout North America and Europe for continuous improvement. This attention to operations has resulted in the inclusion of Stryker facilities in the elite *Industry Week* Best Plants list twice in the last three years. The Stryker Instruments plant in Kalamazoo, Michigan, was named one of the Best Plants in 2000, and the Howmedica Osteonics facility in Allendale, New Jersey, was honored in 1998.

Shortcomings to Bear in Mind

- "Despite the company's track record and the favorable demographics, Wall Street lately has been skittish about this Michigan-based manufacturer of medical devices," said a writer for *Better Investing* in November 2005. "Some observers question the company's ability to sustain its historically high growth rates over the long term. An ongoing government probe of certain industry practices may have dampened investor enthusiasm for Stryker and other implant makers. Pressure from sources such as Medicare and large hospital chains may constrain the company's ability to raise prices." Despite these negative comments, the magazine listed the stock as a Featured Company, giving some favorable reasons for owning the stock.
- On February 8, 2006, *Standard & Poor's Stock Reports* had this view of the company, in the words of Robert M. Gold, "Our recommendation is HOLD. We think the orthopedics group continues to face challenging year-over-year comparisons through 2006, and although Stryker has a favorable new product cycle in place, we believe rising competition and global pricing pressures will make it more challenging to meet the company's planned 20 percent earnings growth objective. We believe Stryker can grow faster than the industry on new product introductions and modest market share gains."

Reasons to Buy

▪ The *New York Times* checked on the thoughts of twenty-seven analysts on March 27, 2006. Six rated SYK a STRONG BUY; four preferred a MODERATE HOLD rating; but the majority of seventeen huddled around a HOLD rating.

▪ Among the optimists was David H. Toung, writing for Argus Research Company on February 17, 2006. "We are maintaining our BUY rating on Stryker Corp. While Stryker delivered a strong performance in orthopedics and surgical equipment in the fourth quarter, we are impressed that the pricing momentum turned out to be more benign than expected three months ago. Through a combination of manufacturing improvements, new product introductions, and sales force expansions, Stryker appears to have the resources to sustain 15 to 20 percent earnings growth."

▪ CEO Stephen P. MacMillan had this comment in 2005, "Stryker is well known for our decentralized structure, which is one of the main sources of our success. In addition, where it makes sense, Stryker increasingly draws on the strength of our entire enterprise, presenting comprehensive solutions as one seamless company. For example, we have the ability to provide world-class orthopedic implants, powered surgical instruments, integrated operating suites and patient handling equipment to a health-care institution or system—all backed by our unparalleled management experience in an environment of accountability, metrics and financial controls."

▪ "These shares are favorably ranked for Timeliness, reflecting Stryker's superior operating and share-price momentum," said George Rho, an analyst with *Value Line Investment Survey,* on March 3, 2006. "Note, too, that the stock still offers above-average three- to-five-year capital appreciation possibilities, despite the remarkable gains achieved over the past decade. Our long-term optimism is based on the company's outstanding record, as well as the worldwide demographic trends that augur well for most healthcare concerns."

▪ Analysts believe that industry trends are setting the stage for continued growth for Stryker in the years ahead. Virtually all market dynamics point in that direction. These are the key factors:

- The population as a whole is aging. In fact, the target population for orthopedic implants for knees and hips is expected to increase 68 percent in the next nine years, according to a report issued by Gerard Klauer Mattison & Company, Inc., a brokerage firm headquartered in New York City.
- Mild inflation in average selling prices for orthopedic implants in the United States compares favorably to the declining price environment of the past decade.
- Consolidation among orthopedic implant and device manufacturers over the past few years has greatly decreased the number of competitors in sectors such as orthopedic implants, spinal devices, arthroscopy products, and other orthopedic products. This serves to consolidate market share and mitigates price competition.
- Advances in orthopedic technology—much of which has taken place in the past decade—have markedly decreased operating and recovery times. These advances have decreased the amount of time a surgeon must spend with each patient, thus giving the surgeon more time to perform more operations in a period. Consequently, according to the Gerard Klauer Mattison report, "we believe that procedural volume will increase."

For its part, Stryker has set itself up to benefit from these microeconomic dynamics, according to the report issued by this same brokerage house. "For example, Stryker has strategically used acquisitions over the past few years to broaden and deepen its product portfolio. Furthermore, innovation in orthopedic implants and instrumentation has provided the company with certain competitive advantages that should be important ingredients for gaining market share in the coming years."

■ The company has achieved these distinctions:

- Ranked #1 in *Fortune* magazine's America's Most Admired Companies in Medical Products and Equipment
- Ranked #11 in *Barron's* 500 Best Companies for Investors
- Ranked #30 overall and #4 in Health Care Equipment & Services in *BusinessWeek*'s Top Fifty Companies of the S&P 500

■ "Total joint arthroplasty has changed radically, thanks in large part to Stryker's leadership," said a company spokesman in 2005. "With novel materials, implant designs and wear-reduction technologies, our reconstructive implants have the potential to improve the longevity and range of motion necessary for younger, more active patients. In addition, new instrument designs and operative techniques make surgeries shorter and less invasive.

"The Triathlon Knee System, which we began selling in 2004, is a prime example of such progress. The development process was grounded in market research. Patients emphasized the need for a more natural-feeling, high-performance implant to meet their expectations for lifestyle recovery. Triathlon features a new geometry and enhanced mechanics to provide both greater stability and greater range of motion. We paid particular attention to the ergonomics of the instrumentation, diving operating room efficiency with fewer and easier-to-use tools of superior quality.

"Triathlon joins other advanced knee options in Stryker's product portfolio, enabling surgeons and their patients to determine the optimal solution for individual situations. Our established Scorpio and Duracon knee systems, both offering high-performance insert options, have recently achieved excellent growth."

SECTOR: **Health Care** ◆ BETA COEFFICIENT: **.75**
10-YEAR COMPOUND EARNINGS PER SHARE GROWTH: **21.7%**
10-YEAR COMPOUND DIVIDENDS PER SHARE GROWTH: **27.1%**

		2005	**2004**	**2003**	**2002**	**2001**	**2000**	**1999**	**1998**
Revenues (millions)		4,872	4,262	3,625	3,012	2,602	2,289	2,104	1,103
Net Income (millions)		675	586	454	346	272	221	161	150
Earnings per share		1.64	1.43	1.12	0.88	0.67	0.55	0.41	0.39
Dividends per share		.11	.09	.07	.05	.04	.035	.035	.03
Price	high	56.3	57.7	42.7	33.8	31.3	28.9	18.3	14.0
	low	39.7	40.3	29.9	21.9	21.7	12.2	11.1	7.8

CONSERVATIVE GROWTH

Sysco Corporation

1390 Enclave Parkway ❑ Houston, TX 77077-2099 ❑ (281) 584-1458 ❑ Web site: *www.sysco.com* ❑ Dividend reinvestment plan available (800) 730-4001 ❑ Fiscal year ends the Saturday closest to June 30 ❑ Listed: NYSE ❑ Ticker symbol: SYY ❑ S&P rating: A+ ❑ Value Line financial strength rating: A++

With the advent of two household incomes, with both husband and wife working outside the home, it is not surprising that no one wants to come home after eight hours at the office and still have to face cooking supper. Not to mention cleaning up after the repast.

Today, about half of Americans' food dollars are spent on meals prepared away from home. That figure far surpasses the 37 percent that was spent on away-from-home meals in 1972. It reveals how heavily our society now depends on food service operations to satisfy consumers' nutritional needs by providing a variety of quality meals at affordable prices.

According to a company officer, "Sysco's $30 billion in sales translates into a 14 percent share of a growing market. We are in a wonderful industry with great upside potential. Two-income families have more disposable income to spend. As the population ages, the fifty- and sixty-five-year-olds also have more time and money to eat meals cooked in someone else's kitchen.

"In addition, retirees are healthier and living longer, and many are in retirement communities that serve meals on site. Of course, the twenty-to-forty-year-old segment has grown up with parents who worked outside the home, so eating out comes naturally to them, and many just don't have the time, skills or desire to cook."

Company Profile

As they go about their lives, many people encounter the familiar Sysco trucks, bearing giant blue lettering, delivering products to customers. Few are aware, however, of Sysco's far-reaching influence on meals served daily throughout North America. As the continent's largest marketer and distributor of food service products, Sysco operates 150 distribution facilities across the United States and Canada (including 84 broadline facilities, 17 hotel supply locations, 16 specialty produce facilities, 15 SYGMA distribution centers, 12 custom-cutting meat locations, and 2 distributors specializing in the niche Asian foodservice market). These distribution facilities serve about 415,000 restaurants, hotels, schools, hospitals, retirement homes, and other locations where food is prepared to be eaten on the premises or taken away and enjoyed in the comfort of the diner's chosen environment.

Sysco is by far the largest company in the food service distribution industry. In 2005, the company's revenue breakdown was as follows: restaurants (64 percent sales), hospitals and nursing homes (10 percent), schools and colleges (5 percent), hotels and motels (6 percent), other (15 percent).

With annual sales in 2005 of $30.3 billion, Sysco distributes a wide variety of fresh and frozen meats, seafood, poultry, fruits and vegetables, plus bakery products, canned and dry foods, paper and disposables, sanitation items, dairy foods, beverages, kitchen and tabletop equipment, as well as medical and surgical supplies.

Sysco's innovations in food technology, packaging, and transportation provide customers with quality products, delivered on time, in excellent condition, and at reasonable prices.

Shortcomings to Bear in Mind

- "The year just ended was a difficult one for Sysco," said CEO Richard J. Schnieders on October 3, 2005. "Sales for the year were $30.3 billion, 3.2 percent above sales in 2004. Fiscal 2004 contained fifty-three weeks, so on a comparable basis, 2005 sales were 5.3 percent higher than adjusted 2004 sales of $28.8 billion. This is below our stated goal of high single-digit to low double-digit sales growth. Sales during the year were negatively affected by higher-than-normal product cost inflation and higher fuel costs. Inflation hurt sales because restaurant customers have to pay more in order to purchase the same number of meals, while higher fuel costs take disposable income out of customers' pockets."

Reasons to Buy

- On a more positive note, Mr. Schnieders had this to say, "Throughout fiscal 2005, we worked diligently on positioning Sysco for future growth, and we have several programs in place which will help produce profitable, sustainable sales growth. Our Business Program is a systematic method of consulting with our very best customers to strengthen and solidify our existing customer relationships. A typical review involves extensive preparation and a meeting of several hours with the customer to review ways that we can contribute to their success. This involves everything from menu analysis to food product testing to access to our value-added services. The results from these business interviews in 2005 were gratifying, and we plan to conduct about 40,000 reviews in 2006."
- Mr. Schnieders also said, "In addition to investing in people for growth, we will also be investing in assets for future growth. During 2005, we spent $390.2 million on capital expenditures, and we will increase that pace somewhat in 2006, with capital spending planned at the $425 million–$450 million range. Spending will be primarily in three areas: 1) for buildings—new and more efficient warehouses; 2) for fleet—both replacement and expansion of our truck fleet; and 3) for systems—to help us operate more efficiently and effectively."
- According to industry sources, there are nearly 900 thousand food service locations in the United States—such as restaurants, hospitals, nursing homes, cruise ships, summer camps, sports stadiums, theme parks, schools, colleges, hotels, motels, corporate dining rooms and cafeterias, and retirement homes—and more than sixty-three thousand in Canada.
- Whether dining in an upscale restaurant or picking up pasta as the entree for a meal at home, people spend less time on food preparation than ever before. They want variety and flavor in the foods they choose to eat, yet their time to prepare meals is constantly in competition with work and leisure activities. More than ever, people are turning to meals prepared away from home for greater convenience, quality, and, most of all, choice.

It is a trend that started in World War II, as women began to work outside the home. Business cafeterias, coffee shops, school lunchrooms and restaurants broadened the range of dining choices for people who were used to much simpler fare. Twenty-five years ago, not many consumers could identify kiwi fruit. During the past three decades, food service offerings have moved from fruit cocktail with a cherry on top to kiwi and other exotic fare; from steak and potatoes to fajitas with all the trimmings.

- As the largest distributor of food service products in North America, Sysco assists customers in creating a vast array of dining choices. Menus have greatly improved since a French chef named Boulanger offered a choice of soups, or "restorative" to patrons who paused at his inn to refresh themselves as they traveled during the 1700s. The sign in French read "restaurant," and his establishment may have been the first to offer a menu.

Today's diverse menu choices could not have been imagined then—raspberries from Australia served fresh in Wisconsin in January; gourmet pesto sauce rich with garlic, fresh basil, and pine nuts delivered to a Vancouver chef's doorstep; or artfully prepared hearts of lettuce served in an Arizona college cafeteria each day. Providing choices from soup to nuts, and everything in between, Sysco leads the way in helping chefs in restaurants, schools, business cafeterias, health care locations, lodging, and other facilities increase the variety and quality of food choices in North America.

- Sysco keeps margins high by selling products under its own label, a strategy it began a year after its founding. It saves on national advertising and passes some of the savings along to its customers. Its private-label business carries an estimated 24 percent gross margin, or 10 percent more than it earns on national brands.
- "Better share-net gains appear likely in 2007 and through decade's end," said George A. Niemond, writing for *Value Line Investment Survey* on February 3, 2006. "The food distributor's diverse initiatives to spur sales and earnings growth ought to bear fruit. It plans to increase the sales force by 6 percent in fiscal 2006. That will allow it to conduct more reviews of customers' businesses. Typically, such a review is followed by an average sales gain in the mid-teens." Mr. Niemond also said, "Sysco is ranked to only move with the year-ahead market, but if our forecast for good annual share-net gains for the three to five-years ahead is near the mark, the equity should best the averages over that span."
- On March 19, 2006, the *New York Times* tabulated the opinions of thirteen analysts who follow Sysco. One viewed the stock as a STRONG BUY; four called it a MODERATE BUY; and eight classified it as a HOLD.

SECTOR: **Consumer Staples** ◆ BETA COEFFICIENT: **.75**
10-YEAR COMPOUND EARNINGS PER SHARE GROWTH: **15.4%**
10-YEAR COMPOUND DIVIDENDS PER SHARE GROWTH: **18.8%**

		2005	2004	2003	2002	2001	2000	1999	1998
Revenues (millions)		30,282	29,335	26,140	23,351	21,784	19,303	17,423	15,328
Net Income (millions)		961	907	778	680	597	454	362	325
Earnings per share		1.47	1.37	1.18	1.01	.88	.68	.54	.48
Dividends per share		.56	.48	.40	.36	.28	.22	.19	.16
Price	high	38.4	41.3	37.6	32.6	30.1	30.4	20.6	14.4
	low	30.0	29.5	22.9	21.2	21.8	13.1	12.5	10.0

AGGRESSIVE GROWTH

T. Rowe Price Group, Inc.

100 East Pratt Street ❑ Baltimore, MD 21202 ❑ (410) 345-2124 ❑ Dividend reinvestment plan not available ❑ Web site: *www.troweprice.com* ❑ Ticker symbol: TROW ❑ Listed: Nasdaq ❑ S&P rating: A ❑ Value Line financial strength rating: A+

"T. Rowe Price investment professionals practice 'bottom-up' investing, exploring fundamental research to uncover promising opportunities," said an official with the company in 2005.

"Ninety-six equity and fixed-income analysts cast a wide net around the globe to research securities and markets first-hand. Meeting with, and evaluating, corporate managers is a key part of the research process, as is analyzing financial data and assessing information from myriad sources.

"Our analysts conduct more than 2,000 visits per year. They discuss companies with their suppliers and clients and even observe the company grounds to glean useful insights. This information, distilled by our staff and combined with rigorous valuation analysis, ultimately determines whether an investment is purchased, held, or sold.

"One benefit of investment experience is the insight it provides into the role of risk management in long-term results. A disciplined, risk-aware approach can help minimize losses during periods of market weakness, seize opportunities when markets are oversold, and maintain focus on sound fundamentals when they may be overvalued. Hands-on research and valuation disciplines, combined with prudent diversification, are key elements of our approach to risk management.

"Our portfolio managers try to avoid performance extremes and may give up potential gains when downside risk appears excessive. This perspective was severely tested during the heady days of the late-1990s bull market, when we were cautious about investing in speculative stocks because they failed one or more of our analysts' tests for value, earnings quality, or management strength and vision. We lost ground to our competitors during that period, but our discipline was rewarded with outstanding results during the subsequent market decline and recovery."

Company Profile

T. Rowe Price is an investment management firm offering individuals and institutions around the world investment management guidance and expertise.

The company's investment approach strives to achieve superior performance but "is always mindful of the risks incurred relative to the potential rewards. Our consistent investment philosophy helps mitigate unfavorable changes and takes advantage of favorable ones. We provide our clients with world-class investment guidance as well as attentive service."

Founded in 1937 by Thomas Rowe Price Jr., the company offers separately managed investment portfolios for institutions and a broad range of mutual funds for individual investors and corporate retirement accounts. Mutual funds are pooled investments representing the savings of many thousands of individuals that are invested in stocks, bonds, and other assets managed by a portfolio manager or managers in the hope of either outperforming a market average—such as the S&P 500 of the Dow Jones Industrial Average—or meeting a similar goal. No-load funds are sold without a sales commission. However, this does not infer there is no cost. All mutual funds have expenses, such as salaries, office rent, advertising, travel, and the like. This averages about 1.6 percent per year but does not include the cost of buying and selling stocks. T. Rowe Price is a low-cost manager.

In founding his firm, Mr. Price followed a very simple principle: What is good for the client is also good for the firm. Rather than charge a commission, as was then the practice in the securities business, Mr. Price charged a fee based on the assets under management. If the client prospered, so did T. Rowe Price.

Mr. Price is best known for developing the growth stock style of investing. Although he was trained as a chemist, he had a passion for investing. Mr. Price believed that investors could earn superior returns by investing in well-managed companies in fertile fields whose earnings and dividends could be expected to grow faster than inflation and the overall economy. The core of Mr. Price's approach, proprietary research to guide investment selection and diversification reduce risk, has remained part of the firm's bedrock principles.

Today, growth stock investing is one of the many investment styles the firm currently follows. T. Rowe Price also employs value-oriented, sector-focused, tax-efficient, and quantitative index-oriented approaches in managing mutual funds and institutional portfolios.

Shortcomings to Bear in Mind

- Although T. Rowe Price is highly regarded, most analysts are not convinced that the stock is on the bargain table. According to a *New York Times* survey of sixteen analysts who covered the stock March 20, 2006, fifteen regarded T. Rowe Price as a HOLD. Only one said the stock was a MODERATE BUY.
- If you are a conservative investor, this may not to be the stock for you. T. Rowe Price has a Beta Coefficient of 1.50, which means it fluctuates 50 percent more than the market, both up and down. A Beta of 1.00, by contrast, would indicate a stock that is much less volatile, or about the same as the overall market.

Reasons to Buy

- "More gains are likely out to 2008–2010," said Stephen Sanborn, CFA, writing for *Value Line Investment Survey* on February 24, 2006. "Stock prices should move higher over the coming three to five years, and, if they do, Price will do well. The company has a good operating record, is very strong financially, and has a diversified line of funds to offer investors. It also has a good record in developing new products, one of the latest being target-date Retirement Funds, which invest in underlying Price funds and automatically shift asset allocations as an investor ages."
- "We have a STRONG BUY recommendation on the shares, based on our view of the company's strong relative investment performance, diversified client base, and high proportion of retirement-related assets under management," said Robert Hansen, CFA, writing for *Standard & Poor's Company Reports* on February 22, 2006.
- "To help investors meet a range of goals, and provide diverse offerings for all market environments, T. Rowe Price has steadily expanded its investment expertise," said a company executive in 2005. "We offer a broad base of investment strategies covering equity styles and small- (*such as Nasdaq stocks*) to large-cap (*such as IBM, GE, ExxonMobil, or Procter & Gamble*), as well as growth, value, and core styles. The firm also offers a wide range of capabilities in fixed-income (*such as bonds and preferred stocks*) sectors, including U.S., non-U.S., and global strategies.

"Our commitment to proprietary fundamental research is extensive and far-reaching. More than 200 investment professionals, including portfolio managers, research analysts, traders, and economists, work on behalf of clients in more than twenty countries. Our world-wide presence enables us to conduct first-hand research on U.S. And non-U.S. equities and fixed-income securities.

"The challenge to distinguish relevant information from the insignificant in market trends and company data places a high premium on experience. Our portfolio managers average more than seventeen years of experience in the industry, and twelve years at T. Rowe Price.

"Our investment professionals, who typically begin as analysts, benefit from a proactive mentoring program that supports their training and development. Analysts work both independently and as part of portfolio management teams, providing them with experience that eventually enables them to assume a portfolio management role. This process serves to deepen relationships, improve communication, and ensure that our best investment ideas impact clients' portfolios."

SECTOR: **Financials** ◆ BETA COEFFICIENT: **1.50**
10-YEAR COMPOUND EARNINGS PER SHARE GROWTH: **17.5%**
10-YEAR COMPOUND DIVIDENDS PER SHARE GROWTH: **18.8%**

		2005	2004	2003	2002	2001	2000	1999	1998
Revenues (millions)		1,516	1,280	996	924	1,028	1,212	1,036	886
Net Income (millions)		431	337	227	194	195	269	239	174
Earnings per share		1.58	1.26	.89	.76	.76	1.04	.93	.67
Dividends per share		.48	.40	.35	.33	.31	.27	.22	.18
Price	high	37.7	31.7	23.8	21.4	22.0	25.0	21.7	21.5
	low	27.1	21.9	11.9	10.7	11.7	15.1	13.0	10.5

AGGRESSIVE GROWTH

Target Corporation

1000 Nicollet Mall ❑ Minneapolis, MN 55403 ❑ (612) 370-6735 ❑ Direct Dividend reinvestment plan available (800) 842-7629 ❑ Web site: *www.target.com* ❑ Fiscal year ends Saturday closest to January 31 of following year ❑ Listed: NYSE ❑ Ticker symbol: TGT ❑ S&P rating: A+ ❑ Value Line financial strength rating: A

"Target has had an incredible run selling 'cheap chic' goods, from polo shirts to pots and pans to patio furniture," said Lawrence C. Strauss, writing for *Barron's* on August 1, 2005. "With its signature red and white bull's eye logo, savvy merchandising and exclusive deals with designers such as Isaac Mizrahi and architect Michael Graves, the company has convinced both the masses and the classes that discount shopping is cool.

"Indeed, its hippest fans, in perfect faux French, call the Minneapolis-based retailer 'Tar-zhay.' Their spending habits have help boost Target/Tar-zhay's profits by an average of 10 per cent a year over the past five years."

The article goes on to say, "The key to Target's success has been low prices—but not as low as Wal-Mart's—and stylish merchandise. The median household income of the company's 'guests'—its preferred word for customers—is approximately $57,000, but there's plenty in its stores to satisfy rich and poor alike.

The *Barron's* writer also said, "The company executes well. Its stores have wide aisles and uncluttered shelves, checkout lines that move quickly and customer-service buttons located throughout. Target also buys merchandise directly from suppliers overseas, which has improved its gross margins and profits. In its latest fiscal year, gross margins widened to 31.2 percent from 30.6 percent, owing to higher mark-ups."

Company Profile

Target Corporation (formerly Dayton Hudson Corporation) was formed in 1969 through the merger of two old-line department store companies, Dayton Corporation and J. L. Hudson Company. In 1990, TGT acquired another venerable retailer, Marshall Field & Company. The department stores (once run separately, but now under the Marshall Field umbrella) have since been eclipsed by TGT's fast-growing Target division, which accounts for the bulk of revenues and profits.

Target is the nation's fourth-largest general merchandise retailer, specializing in large-store formats, including discount stores, moderate-priced promotional stores, and traditional department stores. The company operates Target stores, Marshall Field's, and Mervyn's stores.

At the end of October, 2005, Target operated 1,400 stores in forty-seven states. The Target operation is the company's strongest retail franchise and is its growth vehicle for the future. Most of the remaining units operate under Mervyn's banner. These 266 outlets handle soft goods. Finally, the department store segment consists mostly of 62 Marshall Field's department stores.

Target stores are situated largely in such states as California, Texas, Florida, and the upper Middle West. Mervyn's are clustered largely in California and Texas.

In 2000, the company formed target .direct, the direct merchandising and electronic retailing organization. The business combines the e-commerce team of Target with its direct merchandising unit into one integrated organization. The target.direct organization operates seven Web sites, which support the store and catalog brands in an on-line environment and produces six retail catalogs.

Shortcomings to Bear in Mind

■ Because Target has a greater proportion of trendy, discretionary merchandise and has been rapidly increasing its credit-card business, analysts consider it more sensitive to economic swings than its chief rival Wal-Mart.

■ The retail business is always subject to competitive pressures from such outstanding companies as Bed Bath & Beyond, Wal-Mart, Costco, Lowe's, and Home Depot. Here's what the company has to say, according to its latest 10-K, "Target's retail merchandising business is conducted under highly competitive conditions in the discount segment. Its stores compete with national and local department, specialty, off-price, discount, grocery and drug store chains, independent retail stores and Internet businesses which handle similar lines of merchandise. Target also competes with other companies for new store sites."

On a more positive note, the 10-K goes on to say, "Target believes the principal methods of competing in its industry include brand recognition, customer service, store location, differentiated offerings, value, quality, fashion, price, advertising, depth of selection and credit availability."

Reasons to Buy

■ Since the company's fiscal year ends at the end of January, rather than the end of December, its 2005 annual report was not available in time for this edition of *The 100 Best Stocks You Can Buy.* Thus, I must rely on the 2004 annual report to give you a glimpse of this company. In any event, here are some notable accomplishments that Target's CEO Bob Ulrich mentions in that report:

- "The sale of both our Mervyn's and our Marshall Field's business units for aggregate pre-tax cash proceeds of about $4.9 billion.
- "Our board's authorization of a $3 billion share repurchase program, which we expect to complete within a two to three-year time horizon.
- "Our introduction of a new Target store prototype that enhances our guests' shopping experience and highlights our store's design evolution and innovation.
- "Disciplined execution and integration of Target's strategy within both our retail and credit card operations that fostered greater merchandise differentiation, a more compelling value offering, increased guest loyalty and a growing frequency in guest visits.
- "Continued market share gains and an increase of more than 17 percent, to $2.07, in earnings per share from continuing operations."

■ Mr. Ulrich also said, "In 2004, Target added sixty-five net new general merchandise stores and eighteen new SuperTarget stores, representing net new growth in square footage of 8.2 percent. Barring a substantial real estate acquisition, our 2005 plans for Target envision a similar rate of expansion. While we have sufficient capital capacity to grow more rapidly, we believe that a disciplined program is the best way for us to preserve both our brand integrity and our expected financial returns.

"As a result, we expect to operate about 2000 stores by the end of the decade, an increase in store count of about 50 percent, and we expect to continue to enjoy meaningful gains in market share, reflecting both new store growth and increased sales productivity in existing stores."

■ "To remain relevant in today's dynamic retail environment, we continually test, re-invent, adapt and pursue creative initiatives in merchandising, marketing, store operations, store design, systems, and distribution, even as we adhere to our long-standing financial disciplines," said a company official in 2005.

"Our efforts in 2004, including the rollout of our new store prototype and the introduction of new exclusive merchandise brands such as Simply Shabby Chic and C9 by Champion, reinforced our brand image."

■ The official goes on to say, "We have consistently delighted our guests with a broad assortment of high-quality merchandise that is stylish, yet practical—and well-designed, yet affordable. For example, Target has launched several exciting new merchandise brands in recent months, including:

- C9 by Champion, a line of performance athletic wear and functional basics at about half the price of other premium-quality athletic brands.
- The Isaac Mizrahi Home collection, consisting of home furnishings and accessories such as lighting, furniture, tabletop, bath, bedding, stationery and pet items.
- Fieldcrest, an offering of bed and bath merchandise, such as 400-thread-count Egyptian-cotton sheets and silk quilts, with traditional styling and genuine luxury at extremely attractive prices."

■ On March 19, 2006, the *New York Times* said that four analysts rated the company a STRONG BUY; twelve preferred to call it a MODERATE BUY; and eleven perched on the fence, saying it was a HOLD.

■ "Earnings may well advance around 15 percent per annum through late decade," said David R. Cohen, writing for *Value Line Investment Survey* on February 10, 2006. "Moreover, we don't foresee any narrowing of the stock's P/E ratio. Accordingly, these neutrally ranked shares offer attractive appreciation potential to 2008–2010."

■ On March 19, 2006, Argus Research Company gave the stock a BUY rating. Christopher Graja, CFA, said, "We credit Target for recognizing that consumers of all ages and income levels want products that are stylish and fun, as well as low-priced. We think this good merchandising will help the company to take market share from a range of competitors to outperform the S&P 500 on a risk-adjusted basis."

■ On March 9, 2006, *Standard and Poor's Company Reports* gave Target a BUY rating. Jason N. Asaeda said, "TGT recently posted better-than-expected fourth-quarter fiscal 2006 results. Strong earnings contributions from credit-card operations, coupled with expense leverage on a solid 4.2 percent same-store sales increase, which we believe reflected the company's delivery of unique merchandise at affordable prices, drove a 20 basis-point improvement in margins." (*There are 100 basis points in one percent.*)

■ Lehman Brothers had this comment on February 16, 2006, "We continue to believe that Target is poised to generate 15 percent annual average EPS (*earnings per share*) growth over at least the next five years, driven by 5 percent comp-store sales growth and annual square footage growth of 8 to 10 percent. With 1,400 stores, Target is still only about 40 percent the size of Wal-Mart's U.S. operation, and we believe it has considerable opportunities for continued expansion over the next ten years. We believe the company has the opportunity to double its current store base in the United States."

SECTOR: **Consumer Discretionary** ◆ BETA COEFFICIENT: **1.15**
10-YEAR COMPOUND EARNINGS PER SHARE GROWTH: **17.5%**
10-YEAR COMPOUND DIVIDENDS PER SHARE GROWTH: **10.3%**

		2005	2004	2003	2002	2001	2000	1999	1998
Revenues (millions)		52,620	46,839	48,163	43,917	39,888	36,903	33,702	30,662
Net Income (millions)		2,408	1,885	1,841	1,654	1,419	1,264	1,185	962
Earnings per share		2.71	2.07	2.01	1.81	1.56	1.38	1.27	1.02
Dividends per share		.40	.30	.26	.24	.22	.21	.20	.18
Price	high	60.0	54.1	41.8	46.2	41.7	39.2	38.5	27.1
	low	45.6	36.6	25.6	24.9	26.0	21.6	25.0	15.7

AGGRESSIVE GROWTH

Teva Pharmaceutical Industries, Ltd.

5 Basel Street ❑ P. O. Box 3190 ❑ Petach Tikva ❑ Israel 49131 ❑ (215) 591-8912 ❑ Dividend reinvestment plan not available ❑ Web site: *www.tevapharm.com* ❑ Listed: Nasdaq ❑ Ticker symbol: TEVA ❑ S&P rating: not rated ❑ Value Line Financial Rating: A

"In a deal that will create the world's largest generic drug company, Teva Pharmaceutical Industries, Ltd, said Monday it is acquiring rival Ivax Corporation for about $7.4 billion in cash and stock," said Theresa Agovino, writing for the *Associated Press* on July 25, 2005.

Ms. Agovino goes on to say, "The acquisition comes as the generic drug industry has been benefiting from a drive to lower health care costs and a spate of patent expirations on major medicines. But competition among generic makers is intensifying, and the deal may trigger further consolidation.

"'We have always viewed Ivax as one of the most attractive and most compelling acquisitions strategically,' Teva President and Chief Executive Israel Makov told analysts on a conference call. 'Ivax is both an outstanding company and an unusually excellent fit for Teva.'

"Analysts largely applauded the move, saying the deal made strategic sense as it expanded Teva's operations into Latin America and Eastern Europe while giving it a portfolio of respiratory products."

The Acquisition of Sicor

In 2004, the company completed the acquisition of Sicor, one of the largest acquisitions in the health care industry that year. The move combined Teva's successful oral dose generic drugs franchise with Sicor's leading generic injectable business.

In addition, Sicor's complementary API businesses (see below) enhanced and expanded Teva's portfolio in the industry. The Sicor acquisition further provided Teva with new capabilities for the development and production of biological products.

What Are Generic Drugs?

"All drugs—whether prescription or over the counter—have a nonproprietary name (also called a generic name, it's the name of a drug that's not subject to being trademarked), but only some are sold as generic drugs," said Robert S. Dinsmoor, a Contributing Editor of *Diabetes Self-Management*. The article appeared in the January/February 2004 issue of this leading publication devoted to the treatment of diabetes. "If and when a drug can be sold as a generic depends on when the patent (or patents) held by the developer of the drug expire. A patent gives the drug developer the exclusive right to market the drug under its brand name for a certain amount of time."

Mr. Dinsmoor went on to explain, "Generic drugs usually sell for a fraction of the cost of the brand-name drugs. Generic metformin, for example, costs about two-thirds as much as the brand-name product. The price drop that occurs when generics enter the market is attributable to several factors, including competition and the lower overhead of generic-drug manufacturers. When companies compete with each other to sell the same product, market theory argues that prices will tend to go down. Manufacturers of generics are also able to offer lower price because, unlike the developer of the original brand-name drug, they do not have to recoup large investments in research and development or engage in expensive marketing and advertising campaigns."

Teva and Ivax had combined global sales in 2005 of $6.64 billion. Bigger companies have an edge in the generics industry because they can achieve economies of scale in what is essentially a commodity business.

Company Profile

Teva was founded in Jerusalem in 1901 as a small wholesale drug business that distributed imported medicines loaded onto the backs of camels and donkeys to customers throughout the land. The company was called Salomon, Levin and Elstein, Ltd., after its founders.

Teva Pharmaceutical Industries Ltd. is a global pharmaceutical company specializing in generic drugs. The company has major manufacturing and marketing facilities in Israel, North America, and Europe.

Teva's scope of activity extends to many facets of the industry, with primary focus on the manufacturing and marketing of products in the following categories:

- Human pharmaceuticals. Teva produces generic drugs in all major therapeutic realms in a variety of dosage forms, from tablets and capsules to ointments, creams, and liquids. Teva manufactures innovative drugs in niche markets where it has a relative advantage in research and development.
- Active Pharmaceutical Ingredients (API) competitively distributes its API to manufacturers worldwide as well as supports its own pharmaceutical production. Through its API division, the company offers raw materials used by drug manufacturers. API produces more than 190 different bulk chemicals or active ingredients for use in human pharmaceuticals. Teva's acquisition of Sicor added complementary API operations to its existing capabilities.

These activities, which comprise the core businesses of the company, account for 90 percent of Teva's total sales.

Shortcomings to Bear in Mind

- In 2006, Medicare began providing a drug benefit to senior citizens that will boost the industry sales. Unfortunately, analysts say the generic drug industry is becoming more competitive. Low cost, India-based companies are gaining a bigger foothold in the United States while technological advances lower the barriers to entry in the field. And there's debate over just how lucrative the Medicare drug benefit will be since those implementing it will try to extract the lowest possible prices.

Meanwhile, deals known as "authorized generics" may ultimately hurt the industry. Under the current law, the first generic company to file for approval to make a medicine receives 180 days to sell the product exclusively. This enables the company to make a significant portion of money before competitors enter, driving down costs.

On the other hand, pharmaceutical companies have recently been giving permission to a generic company to make its drug right before the patent expires, effectively ending 180 days of exclusivity for the other company. While two providers means lower prices for consumers, it also means lower profits for generic makers that can ultimately harm their business.

Reasons to Buy

- U.S. generic makers tend to be scrappy upstarts with short histories and sometimes-rapid turnover. At Teva, many employees have been around for decades. The company has a paternalistic streak that would be more familiar at a long-established European company. It pays the tab for employees' vacations and subsidizes their children's educations.

  Being global allows Teva to start manufacturing generic copies of drugs even before they lose patent protection in the United States. For example, the Kfar Saba factory is already making generic versions of Merck & Company's big-selling anticholesterol drug Zocor, even though Zocor's U.S. patents don't expire until 2006. Teva sells the pills in parts of Europe where Zocor patents have expired. When the U.S. market opens, it'll be ready to pounce.
- In addition to the production and sale of finished pharmaceutical products, Teva is a large manufacturer and provider of Active Pharmaceutical Ingredients, the vital raw materials of the drug manufacturing industry. In addition to supplying a major share of Teva's own needs, the API division is an active competitor in world markets, investing both in development of new products and manufacturing processes and in the upgrading of production facilities, it also provides an essential link in Teva's strategic marketing chain. The division also spearheads the company's entry into new drug markets, providing a cost-effective source of materials with which to commence local manufacturing and establishing viable distribution channels.
- In 2005, Mr. Makov said, "Teva's API (active pharmaceutical ingredients) business is thriving, and we are continuing to invest in its further development. Through our API, we are able to supply a large share of Teva's own raw material needs, and we are now one of the largest suppliers of API to third parties. Our portfolio includes some 190 products, and we intend to add about twenty to twenty-five products each year, a rate of productivity which we believe is unprecedented in this industry."
- On March 4, 2006, the *New York Times* reported that five analysts viewed Teva as a STRONG BUY; thirteen considered it a MODERATE BUY; eight viewed it as a HOLD; and one lone wolf regarded it as a MODERATE HOLD.
- "Our opinion is STRONG BUY," said Phillip M. Seligman, writing for the *Standard & Poor's Company Reports* on January 31, 2006. "We are encouraged by what we see as TEVA's expanding product and geographic diversity, its pipeline of 140 ANDAs (valued in excess of $100 billion in annual brand sales)."
- "With IVAX, Teva's generic drug pipeline should be extensive and lucrative," said J. Susan Ferrara, writing for *Value Line Investment Survey* on January 20, 2006. "Notably, IVAX will roll out several

generics later this year, including equivalents of Zoloft (a treatment for depression and anxiety). Teva should also benefit from its own generics that were recently approved by the FDA."

■ Lehman Brothers gave an OVERWEIGHT rating to Teva on March 1, 2006. The analyst said, "Dictating our positive thesis on Teva's industry leadership, further strengthened by the Ivax acquisition and the significant leverage we expect from the combined product pipeline. What's more, there are diversified earnings to be boosted in the coming year by high-profile, financially attractive new generic launches."

■ "We rate Teva OVERWEIGHT because we feel that Teva has the best prospects of any generic company, especially after it completes its recently announced acquisition of IVAX," said David Woodburn, writing a report of Prudential Equity Group on March 2, 2006. "Acquiring IVAX expands Teva's geographic reach (new territory mainly in Latin America) and also brings it expertise in respiratory products, both generic and proprietary."

SECTOR: **Health Care** ◆ BETA COEFFICIENT: **.90**
5-YEAR COMPOUND EARNINGS PER SHARE GROWTH: **40.5%**
10-YEAR COMPOUND DIVIDENDS PER SHARE GROWTH: **29.7%**

		2005	2004	2003	2002	2001	2000	1999	1998
Revenues (millions)		5,250	4,799	3,276	2,519	2,077	1,750	1,282	1,116
Net Income (millions)		1,072	965	691	410	278	148	118	69
Earnings per share		1.59	1.42	1.04	0.76	0.53	0.29	0.24	0.15
Dividends per share		0.22	0.16	0.14	0.09	0.06	0.07	0.03	0.03
Price	high	45.9	34.7	31.2	20.1	18.6	19.7	9.1	6.4
	low	26.8	22.8	17.3	12.9	12.1	8.0	4.9	4.0

GROWTH AND INCOME

Textron, Inc.

40 Westminster Street ❑ Providence, RI 02903 ❑ (401) 457-2353 ❑ Dividend reinvestment program is available (800) 829-8432 ❑ Listed NYSE ❑ Web site: *www.textron.com* ❑ Ticker symbol: TXT ❑ S&P rating: B+ ❑ Value Line financial strength rating: A

Marking a major milestone in aviation, Textron announced on September 28, 2005 that its Bell Helicopter unit had been granted approval by the United States Defense Department for Full Rate Production (FRP) of the Bell Boeing V-22 Osprey tiltrotor aircraft. Current plans include the delivery of 360 aircraft to the U.S. Marine Corps (USMC), 50 for the U.S. Air Force, and 48 for the U.S. Navy. The total program is worth in excess of $19 billion to Bell and Textron through 2018.

With FRP, the U.S. government has authorized Bell and Boeing to increase current low-rate production of eleven aircraft per year up to forty-eight. The 2005 FRP decision by the Defense Acquisition Board (DAB) follows the successful completion of extensive Operational Evaluation testing, conducted last summer by the USMC.

This revolutionary tiltrotor technology combines fixed-wing airplane and vertical lift capabilities into one efficient and extremely capable aircraft that can take off and land like a helicopter and fly like an airplane, providing military customers with significant improvements in combat capabilities—including speeds and range two to three times more than that of conventional helicopters, as well as increased payloads, survivability, and reliability.

"The V-22 Osprey is an unprecedented feat in aviation and an excellent example of how our investments in innovation are fueling organic growth for Textron," said CEO Lewis B. Campbell. "Bell's tiltrotor technology is enabling new capabilities and more operational flexibility for our military customers never before thought possible and will undoubtedly take 21st Century flight to a new dimension. So much so that the Federal Aviation Administration (FAA) is creating an entirely new class of aircraft specifically for the tiltrotor."

"Now that we are authorized for full rate production, U.S. Forces will soon have the most versatile aircraft in the world—which will provide a tremendous advantage in the face of ever-changing future combat challenges around the globe," said Michael A. Redenbaugh, CEO of Bell Helicopter. "Not only is this a pivotal moment for Bell and the literally thousands of employees who helped bring the V-22 to life, but today we mark a truly game-changing advancement in the aviation industry. With this decision, tiltrotor technology has come to life in a big way."

Company Profile

Textron Inc. is one of the world's largest and most successful multi-industry companies. Founded in 1923, the company has grown into a network of businesses with total revenues of $10 billion, and more than 44,000 employees in nearly forty countries, serving a diverse and global customer base. Textron is ranked 194th on the *Fortune* 500 list of largest U.S. companies. Organizationally, Textron consists of numerous subsidiaries and operating divisions, which are responsible for the day-to-day operation of their businesses

Bell

A leader in vertical takeoff and landing aircraft for commercial and military applications and the pioneer of the revolutionary tiltrotor aircraft. This segment also includes Textron Systems, a provider of advanced technology solutions for the aerospace and defense industries, and Lycoming aircraft engines. Bell's revenues are comprised of Bell Helicopter (75 percent of division revenues) and Textron Systems (25 percent). Overall, the Bell segment represents 24 percent of Textron, Inc.

Textron Systems provides innovative, advanced technology solutions to meet the needs of the global aerospace and defense industries. The Textron brand is well-known within these industries for its precision strike weapons, mobility, surveillance systems, specialty marine craft, and Cadillac Gage armored vehicles.

Lycoming is the world leader in the design and manufacture of reciprocating piston aircraft engines for the global general aviation industry. In addition to new engines, Lycoming provides after-market parts and service for its installed base of engines.

Cessna Aircraft

The world's largest manufacturer of light and midsize business jets, utility turboprops, and single-engine business jets, utility turboprops, and single-engine piston aircraft. The segment also includes a joint venture in CitationShares fractional jet ownership business. Cessna's annual revenues make up 23 percent of Textron, Inc.

Fastening Systems

Textron Fastening Systems is the premier full-service provider of value-based fastening solutions, making up 18 percent of Textron, Inc. Its products and services are as follows:

THREADED FASTENERS (TFS)

TFS offers the most comprehensive threaded fasteners product line available in the industry. The TFS line of threaded fasteners is globally recognized in a broad range of markets and includes the Torx Plus Drive System, Taptite, Plastite, PT and Mag-Form thread-forming fasteners and Drillite self-drilling fasteners, as well as nuts and washers.

TFS has more than forty manufacturing facilities in 17 countries and serves customers in more than 100 countries.

ENGINEERED PRODUCTS

To lower assembly costs, manufacturers utilize TFS-engineered products and assemblies, as well as TFS's extensive capabilities in cold forming, metal stamping, plastic molding, die-casting, and modular assemblies. Each TFS-engineered assembly is designed to meet the specific form, fit, and function requirements of the application.

BLIND FASTENERS

The globally recognized Avdel and Cherry brands offer a broad range of installation tools and blind fasteners, including threaded inserts and structural, breakstem, and speed fasteners.

AUTOMATED SYSTEMS

For full fastener assembly automation, TFS offers a vast array of solutions. TFS automation systems enable customers to automate their fastener installation processes to lower costs and greatly improve productivity.

Industrial

The Industrial segment is comprised of five businesses that manufacture and market branded industrial products worldwide. This part of the company is responsible for 29 percent of Textron's revenues. It consists of five groups:

E-Z-GO (11 percent of the segment)

E-Z-GO offers the world's most comprehensive line of vehicles for golf courses, resort communities, and municipalities, as well as commercial and industrial users, such as airports and factories. Products include electric-powered and internal-combustion-powered golf cars and multipurpose utility vehicles.

JACOBSEN (12 percent)

Jacobsen offers the world's most comprehensive line of turf-care products for golf courses, resort communities, and municipalities, as well as commercial and industrial users and professional lawn-care services.

GREENLEE (12 percent)

Greenlee, a leader in wire and cable installation systems, is the premier source for professional grade tools and test instruments to the electrical contractor and voice/data/video contractor markets, as well as the telecommunications and CATV markets.

KAUTEX (50 percent)

Kautex is a leading global supplier of plastic fuel systems, including plastic and metal fuel filler assemblies. Kautex also supplies automotive clear vision systems (windshield and headlamp cleaning), blow-molded ducting, and fluid reservoirs, and other components, such as cooling pipes and acoustic components.

TEXTRON FLUID & POWER (15 percent)

Textron Fluid & Power manufactures industrial pumps, gears, and gearboxes for hydrocarbon processing, polymer processing, industrial mining, mobile equipment, and defense applications.

Finance

Textron Finance is a diversified commercial finance company with core operations in distribution finance, aircraft finance, golf finance, resort finance, structured capital, and asset-based lending. Textron Finance also provides financing programs for products manufactured and services by Textron, Inc. It makes up 8 percent of the company's revenues.

Shortcomings to Bear in Mind

- Textron does not have an impressive record of increases in earnings per share. In the 1995–2005 period, earnings advanced modestly from $2.76 to a high of $4.05 in 1999 but then sagged badly to a low of $1.16 in 2001 and has rebounded from that low ebb in recent years but is still below the $4.05 achieved in 1999. Nor have dividends made significant headway during those years. Dividends per share were $0.78 in 1995 and reached a high of $1.40 ten years later, which amounts to a compound annual growth rate of only 6 percent.

Reasons to Buy

- The *New York Times* surveyed fifteen securities analysts on March 19, 2006, finding six rated the stock a STRONG BUY; five called it a MODERATE BUY; and four said it was a HOLD.
- Cessna Citations are operated in more than seventy-five countries, representing the largest fleet of business jets in the world. In its seventy-five-year history, Cessna has delivered more than 185,000 aircraft, including more than 150,000 single-engine airplanes, more than 1,400 Caravans; more than 2,000 military jets, and more than 4,000 Citation business jets. Cessna has delivered 34 percent more business jets than its closest competitor.
- "Our powerful brands, such as Bell, Cessna, E-Z-GO, Jacobsen, Kautex, Greenlee, and others, continue to lead their industries with technological innovation, generating new products that promise impressive revenue and earnings through the end of the decade and beyond," said Mr. Campbell. "In 2003 alone, we brought more than 120 new and upgraded products and services to market, creating opportunities for our customers to realize benefits unavailable elsewhere in our industries."
- On July 29, 2005, Bell Helicopter, a unit of Textron was awarded a $2.2 billion contract by the United States Army to build its next generation Armed Reconnaissance Helicopter, or ARH. The ARH will replace the Army's OH-58D Kiowa Warrior Helicopter, also produced by Bell. The contract calls for Bell Helicopter to build 368 aircraft for delivery during fiscal years 2006 through 2013.

"We are honored to have been chosen by the U.S. Army to continue our legacy of providing outstanding Armed Reconnaissance Helicopter technology," said Mike Redenbaugh, CEO of Bell Helicopter Textron. "The Army requires a state-of-the-art Armed Reconnaissance Helicopter, and that's exactly what Bell Helicopter will deliver."

Bell's ARH is a militarized version of its highly successful 407 single engine light helicopter. Capable of being equipped with a wide variety of weapons, the Bell ARH will provide the Army with exceptional mission versatility, with the flexibility to accomplish armed reconnaissance, light attack, troop insertion, and special operations missions with a single aircraft. The Bell ARH will also provide greater deployability, interoperability, and survivability.

SECTOR: **Industrials** ◆ BETA COEFFICIENT: **1.20**
10-YEAR COMPOUND EARNINGS PER SHARE GROWTH: **3.2%**
10-YEAR COMPOUND DIVIDENDS PER SHARE GROWTH: **6%**

		2005	2004	2003	2002	2001	2000	1999	1998
Revenues (millions)		10,043	9,792	9,287	10,028	11,612	12,399	11,116	9,316
Net Income (millions)		500	471	281	364	166	277	623	443
Earnings per share		3.78	3.36	2.05	2.60	1.16	1.90	4.05	2.68
Dividends per share		1.40	1.30	1.30	1.30	1.30	1.30	1.30	1.14
Price	high	80.7	74.9	58.0	53.6	60.5	76.3	98.0	80.9
	low	65.2	50.6	26.0	32.2	31.3	40.7	65.9	52.1

3M Company

3M Center, Building 225-01-S-15 ❑ St. Paul, MN 55144-1000 ❑ (651) 733-8206 ❑ Web site: *www.MMM.com* ❑ Listed: NYSE ❑ Dividend reinvestment plan available (800) 401-1952 ❑ Ticker symbol: MMM ❑ S&P rating: A ❑ Value Line financial strength rating: A++

New products are the engine of 3M's growth, as the company continues to develop innovative products that make life better for people around the world. One of 3M's largest and fastest-growing product lines—Vikuiti Display Enhancement Films—make electronic displays brighter, more colorful, and easier to read, while also extending battery life. Vikuiti films are extensively used in notebook computers, color cellular phones, personal digital assistants, and other portable electronic products, as well as in LCD desktop computer monitors. And now they're being used in LCD televisions, too.

Another 3M product platform showing rapid growth is immune response modifiers (IRMs). This unique class of drugs stimulates the body's immune system to fight virus-infected cells and tumor cells. The company's first-approved IRM—Aldara (imiquimod) Cream, 5 percent—is a patient-friendly prescription drug that attacks the virus that causes genital warts, a common sexually transmitted disease. In March 2004, the U.S. Food and Drug Administration granted 3M marketing approval for Aldara cream for the treatment of actinic keratosis, a precancerous skin condition affecting about ten million Americans.

3M ingenuity is transforming a broad range of industries. For example, a new-generation 3M security laminate—combining advanced film, retro-reflective and imaging technologies—makes it virtually impossible to counterfeit or alter passports, driver's licenses, and other security documents. What's more, 3M Composite Conductors, for use in overhead power transmission, represent one of the most important industry advances in nearly a century and were named by *R&D* magazine as one of the 100 most technologically advanced products introduced in 2003.

Company Profile

Minnesota Mining and Manufacturing—now known as 3M Company—is a $21-billion diversified technology company with leading positions in industrial, consumer and office, health care, safety, electronics, telecommunications, and other markets. The company has operations in more than 60 countries and serves customers in nearly 200 countries.

3M has a vast array of products (more than 50,000), including such items as tapes, adhesives, electronic components, sealants, coatings, fasteners, floor coverings, cleaning agents, roofing granules, fire-fighting agents, graphic arts, dental products, medical products, specialty chemicals, and reflective sheeting.

The company's Industrial and Consumer Sector is the world's largest supplier of tapes, producing more than 900 varieties. It is also a leader in coated abrasives, specialty chemicals, repositionable notes, home cleaning sponges and pads, electronic circuits, and other important products.

The Life Sciences Sector is a global leader in reflective materials for transportation safety, respirators for worker safety, closures for disposable diapers, and high-quality graphics used indoors and out. This sector also holds leading positions in medical and surgical supplies, drug-delivery systems and dental products.

3M has a decentralized organization with a large number of relatively small profit centers, aimed at creating an entrepreneurial atmosphere.

Shortcomings to Bear in Mind

■ On January 24, 2006, Prudential Equity Group gave 3M a NEUTRAL rating. Nicholas Heymann said, "3M has established itself as one of the most profitable manufacturers in the industry and its net return on total capital is expected to reach 35 percent in 2005, making it also one of the most proficient companies in generating returns on invested capital. However, in order to convince investors that the company's organic growth rate (*that is, without adding in acquisitions*), relative to global GDP growth, can be truly improved on a sustainable basis (particularly in the face of slowing global GDP), better visibility of the company's plans to sustain mid-single-digit organic revenue growth, independent of an increasingly challenging global economy, must be shared with the investment community—this will be vital."

Reasons to Buy

■ On March 19, 2006, the *New York Times* reported that four securities analysts rated 3M a STRONG BUY; seven preferred to call it a MODERATE BUY; and seven sat on the fence with a HOLD.

■ "Our three- to five-year projections may well prove conservative," said Jeremy J. Butler, writing for *Value Line Investment Survey* on February 17, 2006. "It is difficult to know how the new CEO, George Buckley, will run the company. He has indicated a conservative bent, but shown a willingness to use abundant cash flow and strong finances to consummate acquisitions in arenas with good growth potential."

■ In January of 2006, Lehman Brothers gave the stock an OVERWEIGHT rating, and Argus Research Company agreed with that assessment, giving 3M a BUY rating.

■ "For the second time in five years, 3M is tapping an outsider to fill its corner office," said Michael Arndt, writing for *BusinessWeek* on December 19, 2005. "But this time the new CEO arrives with a lot less fanfare. On December 7, 3M named Brunswick CEO George Buckley chairman and CEO. He succeeds James McNerney, who left St. Paul (Minn.)-based 3M last July to head Boeing. Before becoming the first outsider to lead 103-year-old 3M, McNerney was in the running to head General Electric.

"Buckley, 58, has a low profile even in the Chicago area. He joined Lake Forest (Ill.)-based Brunswick in 1997, from Emerson Electric, and rose to CEO in 2000. He beefed up Brunswick's pleasure-boat brands, which include Boston Whaler and Sea Ray. That helped to nearly double the stock price in three years."

■ MMM has many strengths:

- Leading market positions. Minnesota Mining is a leader in most of its businesses, often number one or number two in market share. In fact, 3M has created many markets, frequently by developing products that people didn't even realize they needed.
- Strong technology base. The company draws on more than thirty core technologies—from adhesives and nonwovens to specialty chemicals and microreplication.
- Healthy mix of businesses. 3M serves an extremely broad array of markets—from automotive and health care to office supply and telecommunications. This diversity gives the company many avenues for growth, while also cushioning the company from disruption in any single market.
- Flexible, self-reliant business units. 3M's success in developing a steady stream of new products and entering new markets stems from its deep-rooted corporate structure. It's an environment in which 3M people listen to customers, act on their own

initiative, and share technologies and other expertise widely and freely.
- Worldwide presence. Minnesota Mining has companies in more than 60 countries around the world. It sells its products in some 200 countries.
- Efficient manufacturing and distribution. 3M is a low-cost supplier in many of its product lines. This is increasingly important in today's value-conscious and competitive world.
- Strong financial position. 3M is one of a small number of domestic companies whose debt carries the highest rating for credit quality.

▪ To sustain a strong flow of new product, 3M continues to make substantial investments—about $1 billion a year—in research and development.

▪ 3M Company is a global leader in industrial, consumer, office, health care, safety, and other markets. The company draws on many strengths, including a rich pool of technology, innovative products, strong customer service, and efficient manufacturing.

▪ The unrelenting drive toward smaller, lighter, more powerful and more economical electronic products creates strong demand for leading-edge 3M Microflex Circuits. 3M is the world's No. 1 supplier of adhesiveless flexible circuitry. 3M microflex circuits connect components in many of the world's ink-jet printers. They also link integrated circuits to printed circuit boards efficiently and reliably, making it possible to develop even smaller cellular phones, portable computers, pagers, and other electronic devices.

▪ 3M supplies a wide variety of products to the automotive market, including high-performance tape attachment systems; structural adhesives; catalytic converter mounts; decorative, functional, and protective films; and trim and identification products.

▪ The Life Sciences Sector produces innovative products that improve health and safety for people around the world. In consumer and professional health care, 3M has captured a significant share of the first-aid market with a superior line of bandages. 3M Active Strips Flexible Foam Bandages adhere better to skin—even when wet—and 3M Comfort Strips Ultra Comfortable Bandages set new standards for wearing comfort. Under development are tapes, specialty dressings, and skin treatments that will reinforce and broaden the company's leading market positions and accelerate sales growth.

▪ In pharmaceuticals, 3M is a global leader in technologies for delivering medications that are inhaled or absorbed through the skin, and the company is expanding its horizons in new molecule discovery.

▪ Hostile conditions lie under any vehicle's hood, but 3M's Dyneon Fluoropolymers withstand the heat. Found in seals, gaskets, O-rings, and hoses in automotive and airplane engines, the company's fluoropolymers outperform the competition when high temperatures and chemicals cross paths. And 3M technology isn't merely under the hood. Minnesota Mining also makes products for the vehicle's body and cabin that identify, insulate, protect, and bond—such as dimensional graphics, Thinsulate Acoustic Insulation, cabin filters, and super-strong adhesives and tapes that replace screws and rivets. The company is also developing window films that help keep the cabin cool by absorbing ultraviolet light and reflecting infrared light.

▪ Post-it Notes were named one of the twentieth century's best products by *Fortune* magazine, and Scotch Tape was listed among the century's 100 best innovations by *BusinessWeek* magazine. Also, 3M ranked as the world's most respected consumer-goods company and fifteenth overall in a survey published by the *Financial Times of London*. Finally, 3M received Achieved Vendor of the Year status from four leaders in the office-supply industry.

SECTOR: **Industrials** ◆ BETA COEFFICIENT: **.95**
10-YEAR COMPOUND EARNINGS PER SHARE GROWTH: **9.9%**
10-YEAR COMPOUND DIVIDENDS PER SHARE GROWTH: **6%**

		2005	2004	2003	2002	2001	2000	1999	1998
Revenues (millions)		21,167	20,011	18,232	16,332	16,079	16,724	15,659	15,021
Net Income (millions)		2,234	2,990	2,403	1,974	1,430	1,782	1,711	1,526
Earnings per share		4.16	3.75	3.09	2.50	1.79	2.32	2.11	1.87
Dividends per share		1.68	1.44	1.32	1.24	1.20	1.16	1.12	1.10
Price	high	87.4	90.3	85.4	65.8	63.5	61.5	51.7	48.9
	low	69.7	73.3	59.7	50.0	42.9	39.1	34.7	32.8

CONSERVATIVE GROWTH

UnitedHealth Group

9900 Bren Road East ❑ Minneapolis, MN 55343 ❑ Listed: NYSE ❑ (800) 328-5979 ❑ Dividend reinvestment plan is not available ❑ Web site: *www.unitedhealthgroup.com* ❑ Ticker symbol: UNH ❑ S&P rating: A ❑ Value Line financial strength rating: A+

"In its three decades, UnitedHealth Group has helped to drive some of the biggest shifts in the U.S. health-care system—and made some hefty profits doing so," said Vanessa Fuhrmans, writing for the *Wall Street Journal* on October 24, 2005. "Now the big health insurer is at the leading edge of the latest trend sweeping the industry—so-called consumer-driven health care.

"The principle of consumer-driven plans is that people will shop for the best care at the lowest price if they have to pay more of the cost themselves. The idea is a response to traditional plans in which employers pay most of the bill after modest deductibles and co-pays, leaving consumers with little incentive to curtail their medical spending.

"UnitedHealth's efforts show how consumer-driven plans are beginning to shake up the way Americans get their health insurance. UnitedHealth has spent hundreds of millions of dollars to buy two pioneering companies in the field that help it offer plans with high deductibles. It wants to help people navigate the health-care system more wisely with information on cost and quality. And with a landmark federal law allowing people to build up a health-care nest egg in tax-free 'health savings accounts,' the company has opened a bank. It hopes to manage the accounts much as Fidelity Investments handles corporate 401 (k) plans."

Company Profile

UnitedHealth Group is a U.S. leader in health care management, providing a broad range of health care products and services, including health maintenance organizations (HMOs), point of service (POS) plans, preferred provider organizations (PPOs), and managed fee for service programs. It also offers managed behavioral health services, utilization management, workers' compensation, and disability management services, specialized provider networks, and third-party administration services. Here are its four segments.

UnitedHealthcare coordinates network-based health and well-being services on behalf of local employers and consumers in six broad regional markets, including commercial, Medicare, and Medicaid products and services.

Ovations offers health and well-being services for Americans age fifty and older and their families, including Medicare supplement insurance, hospital indemnity coverage and pharmacy services for members of the health insurance program of AARP. Ovations also provides health and well-being services for elderly, vulnerable, and chronically ill populations through Evercare.

Uniprise provides network-based health and well-being services, business-to-business infrastructure services, consumer connectivity and service, and technology support services for large employers and health plans.

Specialized Care Services offers a comprehensive array of specialized benefits, networks, services, and resources to help consumers improve their health and well-being, including employee assistance/counseling programs, mental health/substance abuse services, solid organ transplant programs and related services, 24-hour health and well-being information services and publications, dental benefits, vision care benefits, life, accident and critical illness benefits, and chiropractic, physical therapy, and complementary medicine benefits.

Ingenix serves providers, payers, employers, governments, pharmaceutical companies, and medical device manufacturers and academic and other research institutions through two divisions. Ingenix Health Intelligence offers business-to-business publications, and data and software analytic products. Ingenix Pharmaceutical Services is a global drug development and marketing services organization offering clinical trial management services, consulting services, medical education, and epidemiological and economic research.

Shortcomings to Bear in Mind

- UnitedHealth Group has a minuscule dividend and has only been paying a dividend since 2000, then only $.01 per share; it is now only $.03 per share. If you like dividends, this is not the stock for you.
- A recent acquisition of PacifiCare Health Systems, discussed below, was greeted with some skepticism by managed-care experts and consumer groups, concerned that the deal will mean higher costs and fewer choices for consumers.

Reasons to Buy

- On March 27, 2006, the *New York Times* published the opinions of twenty-two financial analysts. Six called the stock a STRONG BUY; twelve said it was a MODERATE BUY; three referred to it as a HOLD; and one rated UnitedHealth as a MODERATE HOLD.
- On January 23, 2006, Phillip M. Seligman, writing for *Standard & Poor's Stock Reports*, said, We have a STRONG BUY on the shares. We believe that UNH has shown strong, consistent performance and continues to have a robust operating outlook. We are encouraged by gains in member growth and productivity, the development of new sales channels and, more importantly, in our view, what we see as good management execution."
- "Barring discovery of the Fountain of Youth, the cost of health care will continue to rise considerably faster than inflation," according to an article in *SmartMoney* in January 2006. "Health care costs jumped 14 percent in 2003 and 11 percent in 2004, according to Kaiser Family Foundation. Core inflation, by contrast, rose less than 2.5 percent a year."
- On February 9, 2006, David Shove, an analyst with *Prudential Equity Group,* rated the stock as OVERWEIGHT. He said, "UnitedHealth Group's role as an industry leader and product pioneer should be well secured."

"This year looks particularly bright for the health care industry, says Motola of Thornburg Core Growth, because several well-managed firms are boosting profits quickly but still trading at compelling valuations.

"UnitedHealth Group is the largest health maintenance organization, dictating what care its 11.4 million customers get and how much it will cost. Company executives expect to attract another half million customers in 2006 and to hold the growth in health care costs down to 7.5 percent."

■ "Insurance juggernaut UnitedHealth Group said Wednesday that it would buy Orange County-based PacifiCare Health Systems in an $8.1 billion deal that would give it a big stake in California and would accelerate consolidation of the health insurance business," according to Debora Vrana and Lisa Girion, writing for the *Los Angeles Times* on July 7, 2005. "UnitedHealth, the nation's second-largest health care insurer with twenty-two million members, would gain ground on industry leader WellPoint Inc. and tap into PacifiCare's strong Medicare business, positioning the company to capitalize on a prescription-drug benefit schedule to start January 1.

Wall Street analysts were enthusiastic about the transaction. "This is a great fit," said Sheryl Skolnick, an analyst with Fulcrum Global Partners in New York. "Clearly United has a made a commitment to the senior market, and it gives them added products and a bigger presence in that area."

The *Wall Street Journal* had this comment on the merger on July 7, 2005. "Acquiring PacifiCare would give UnitedHealth two major growth opportunities. First, UnitedHealth will gain a big presence in the Medicare HMO market, which is poised to grow as the new Medicare drug benefit takes effect next year (2006). PacifiCare's Secure Horizons plans for seniors have been popular alternatives to traditional Medicare coverage for over two decades. Health plans have been rushing to administer the drug benefit and offer comprehensive private-insurance plans to Medicare recipients. UnitedHealth has been among the most aggressive, signing a deal with Walgreen Co. to promote its plans to Medicare beneficiaries at the drug store chain's 4,738 nationwide stores, as well as a branding partnership with AARP.

"Second, the acquisition will give UnitedHealth a presence in California, where it currently has an agreement to share the Blue Shield of California network of doctors and hospitals."

■ Since its inception, UnitedHealth Group and its affiliated companies have led the marketplace by introducing key innovations that make health care services more accessible and affordable for customers, improving the quality and coordination of health care services, and helping individuals and their physicians make more informed health care decisions.

Time Line of Selected Highlights and Innovations

1974: Charter Med incorporated is founded by a group of physicians and other health care professionals.

1977: United HealthCare Corporation is created and acquires Charter Med Incorporated.

1979: United HealthCare Corporation introduces the first network-based health plan for seniors and participates in the earliest experiments with offering a private-market alternatives for Medicare.

1984: United HealthCare Corporation becomes a publicly traded company.

1989: William W. McGuire, M.D. assumes leadership of the company. Annual revenues are just over $400 million. Today they are over $26 billion.

1995: The company acquires The MetraHealth Companies Inc. for $1.65 billion. MetraHealth is a privately held company that was formed by combining the group health care operations of The Travelers Insurance Company and Metropolitan Life Insurance Company.

1996: The company patented artificial intelligence system AdjudiPro, which is entered into the permanent research collection of the Smithsonian Institution, is awarded the CIO Enterprise Value Award.

1998: United HealthCare Corporation becomes known as UnitedHealth Group and launches a strategic realignment into independent but strategically linked business segments—UnitedHealthcare, Ovations, Uniprise, Specialized Care Services, and Ingenix.

1998: The first release of Clinical Profiles takes place. Clinical Profiles, produced by Ingenix, provides network physicians with data comparing their clinical practices to nationally accepted benchmarks for care.

2001: UnitedHealthcare uses Web-enabled technology to simplify and improve service for physicians, enabling them to check benefit eligibility for patients and submit and review claims. The company also launches a Web-based distribution portal to serve small business brokers.

2002: Ingenix continues to introduce new knowledge and information products—including Parallax i iCES and Galaxy clinical and financial insights and improve the quality of health care delivery and administration. (Parallax i iCES aggregates health data from multiple systems, enabling users to identify and analyze multifaceted benefit issues.)

SECTOR: **Health Care** ◆ BETA COEFFICIENT: **.65**
10-YEAR COMPOUND EARNINGS PER SHARE GROWTH: **25.3%**
10-YEAR COMPOUND DIVIDENDS PER SHARE GROWTH: **not meaningful**

		2005	2004	2003	2002	2001	2000	1999	1998
Revenues (millions)		45,365	37,218	28,823	25,020	23,454	21,122	19,562	17,355
Net Income (millions)		3,820	2,587	1,825	1,352	913	705	563	509
Earnings per share		2.48	1.97	1.48	1.07	0.70	0.53	0.40	0.33
Dividends per share		.03	.015	.01	.01	.01	.005	.005	.005
Price	high	64.6	43.8	29.4	25.3	18.2	15.9	8.8	9.3
	low	42.6	27.7	19.6	17.0	12.7	5.8	4.9	3.7

CONSERVATIVE GROWTH

United Parcel Service, Inc.

55 Glenlake Parkway N. E. ❑ Atlanta, GA 30328 ❑ (800) 877-1503 ❑ Direct dividend reinvestment plan is available (800) 758-4674 ❑ Web site: *www.ups.com* ❑ Listed: NYSE ❑ Ticker symbol: UPS ❑ S&P rating: Not rated ❑ Value Line financial strength rating: A+

Internet shoppers say the successful delivery of goods purchased online is critical to their overall satisfaction and loyalty to online retailers, according to a new survey commissioned by UPS in November 2005.

The survey, conducted for UPS by the national opinion research firm Synovate, found online consumers were overwhelming in their demand for high-quality delivery services. Among the findings:

- Online consumers's top three delivery priorities, in order, are reliability, convenience, and speed of shipping.
- 80 percent of online shoppers said a positive delivery experience would

cause them to likely purchase from that online retailer again.

- 69 percent of the respondents said they were more likely to patronize those online retailers that offered package tracking, rates, and service selection online.

"The UPS survey confirms what we hear from our customers, that reliable and on-time shipping is just as important as the ability to easily browse products via our Web site and confidently and securely pay for them," said Patrick M. Byrne, president of Overstock.com., which recently began using UPS as its primary carrier. "We view UPS as an extension of our overall relationship with our own customers."

UPS now is delivering orders fulfilled out of Overstock.com's distribution centers in Salt Lake City and Indianapolis, based on a comprehensive operations plan that will help the online retailer manage its flurry of orders during the holidays.

"As a supply chain provider to some of the world's leading retailers, it's important for UPS to understand what consumers think about the shipping of goods they purchase online," said Kurt Kuehn, senior vice president, UPS worldwide sales and marketing. "This survey tells us there's more to online ordering than just clicking the mouse to 'buy.' The successful fulfillment and delivery of the order has a significant impact on consumer loyalty to online retailers."

UPS long has played a key role in supporting online retailers, serving as the primary delivery arm for many of the nation's largest Web merchants. The new survey was commissioned to study whether the delivery options offered by a retailer are really that critical to building repeat business. While UPS does not attempt to estimate its online retail volume each year, its total holiday season surge will build from roughly fourteen million deliveries a day to a peak day of more than 20 million on December 20.

Over the past decade, UPS has deployed a host of technology tools that help the world's top multichannel and online retailers respond to new customer demands driven by the Internet. As a result, more than 18,000 UPS retail customers have integrated shipping technology to tap into UPS's global IT infrastructure, increasing efficiency while improving customer service. Lands' End, for example, provides its customers 24-hour access to their order status by providing UPS tracking directly on LandsEnd.com.

Company Profile

United Parcel—also known as Big Brown—is one of the largest employee-owned companies in the nation. With a fleet of 88,000 vehicles and 600 aircraft, UPS delivers 13.5 million packages and documents each day, or well over three billion a year.

The company's primary business is the delivery of packages and documents throughout the United States and in over 200 other countries and territories. In addition, UPS provides logistic services, including comprehensive management of supply chains, for major companies worldwide.

United Parcel has built a strong brand equity by being a leader in quality service and product innovation in its industry. UPS has been rated the second-strongest business-to-business brand in the United States in a recent Image Power® survey and has been *Fortune* magazine's Most Admired Transportation Company in the mail, package, and freight category for sixteen consecutive years.

UPS entered the international arena in 1975. It now handles over 1.2 million international shipments each day. What's more, its international package-delivery service (17 percent of revenues) is growing faster than its domestic business, and this trend is likely to continue. The company is also moving to expand its presence in Asia. In 2001, the Department of Transportation awarded UPS the right to fly directly from the United States to China.

Nonpackage businesses, although only 8 percent of revenues, comprise the company's fastest-growing segment. These operations include UPS Logistics Group and UPS Capital Corporation. A truck leasing business was sold in 2000. The logistics business provides global supply chain management, service parts logistics, and transportation and technology services. UPS Capital, launched in 1998, provides services to expedite the flow of funds through the supply chain.

The UPS shares sold in late 1999 represent about 10 percent of the company's total ownership. The rest is still owned by about 125,000 of its managers, supervisors, hourly workers, retires, foundations, and descendants of the company's early leaders. The company sold only Class B shares to the public. Each share has one vote, compared with the Class A stock, which has 10 votes per share.

Shortcomings to Bear in Mind

■ Good companies often have a high price tag. UPS falls into that category. You may find that its P/E ratio is more than thirty. If so, it might pay to delay your purchase until its multiple sags down to twenty-five or so.

Reasons to Buy

■ On March 28, 2006, the *New York Times* surveyed eighteen financial analysts who follow UPS. Six regarded the stock as a STRONG BUY; four said it was a MODERATE BUY; and eight called it a HOLD.

■ "Prospects for the years out to 2009–2011 are bright," said Deborah Y. Fung, writing for *Value Line Investment Survey* on March 10, 2006. "Opportunities overseas are particularly promising, thanks to rising international trade and rapid economic growth in China."

■ "United Parcel Service (UPS) may soon bring shareholders a nice surprise package," said Gene G. Marcial, writing for *BusinessWeek* on February 27, 2006. "The world's largest express company, with an AAA credit rating, is rich in cash and profits. So it might look as if its stock, up from $66 in September to $75 on Feb. 15, already reflects these goodies. Not by a long shot, says Stephen Leeb, who heads Leeb Capital Management, which owns shares. He expects the stock to hit $100 in eighteen to twenty-four months because of its 'supergrowth prospects.' Not only does UPS dominate the U.S. Market, where it picks up 75 percent of its revenues, but it's also building up in China and India. The global delivery market is estimated to be worth more than $100 billion a year."

■ UPS obtains the vast majority of its revenue from small-package deliveries here at home. On the other hand, overseas shipments, finance, and supply-chain management are growing at a fast clip—and that's where the company believes its future is headed.

■ UPS stands out from the crowd in scores of ways:

- The company's mobile radio network transmits more than three million packets of tracking data each day.
- The company's maintenance capacity allows the transmission of more than twenty-two million instructions per second.
- UPS shipping tools are embedded in more than 65,000 customer Web sites.
- Using Global Positioning Satellite technology, has the capacity to pinpoint a package within thirty feet of its location.
- UPS Supply Chain Solutions has operations in more than 120 countries. The Supply Chain Solutions Group provides logistics and distribution services, international trade management, and transportation and freight using multimodal transportation.
- UPS Supply Chain Solutions files more than four million customer entries in the United States, making it the nation's largest broker.

- UPS Supply Chain Solutions has hundreds of engineers to help remap supply chains for greater efficiency and market responsiveness.
- UPS Supply Chain Solutions was rated as the number one logistics provider in Inbound Logistics annual "Top 10 3PL Excellence Award" survey.
- UPS is ranked as the largest third-party logistics provider in North America by *Traffic World* magazine.
- UPS has 4,500 retail locations worldwide—more than all other franchised shipping chains put together.
- In the United States and Canada, UPS has more than 41,000 drop boxes.
- There are 7,500 third-party retail pack-and-ship locations.
- The company operates 1,400 customer centers with its operating facilities worldwide.
- UPS has more than 12,900 in-store shipping locations and commercial counters.
- The company serves more than 850 airports around the world, flying more than 1,800 flight segments each day.
- UPS operates the eleventh-largest airline in the world.
- Local country management people average fourteen years of UPS experience.
- With expanded air rights to Hong Kong, UPS now offers direct service to its two largest hubs in Europe and Asia and enhanced service to China's fastest-growing express and cargo region.
- The company has under construction a $135-million, 30,000-square-meter facility at Cologne/Bonn Airport in Germany. It will be the largest UPS facility outside the United States.
- UPS has a ninety-seven-year history of revenue growth.
- UPS is one of seven companies in the United States that has a triple-A credit rating from both Standard & Poor's and Moody's.
- Active and former employees and their families own more than 50 percent of UPS stock. That may be why you rarely see a UPS driver walking—they insist on running at top speed.

SECTOR: **Industrials** ◆ BETA COEFFICIENT: **.80**
8-YEAR COMPOUND EARNINGS PER SHARE GROWTH: **19.8%**
8-YEAR COMPOUND DIVIDENDS PER SHARE GROWTH: **18%**

		2005	2004	2003	2002	2001	2000	1999	1998
Revenues (millions)		42,591	36,582	33,485	31,272	30,321	29,771	27,052	24,788
Net Income (millions)		3,870	3,333	2,898	3,182	2,425	2,795	2,325	1,741
Earnings per share		3.47	2.90	2.55	2.84	2.10	2.38	2.04*	
Dividends per share		1.32	1.12	.92	.76	.76	.68	.58	
Price	high	85.8	89.1	74.9	67.1	62.5	69.8		
	low	66.1	67.2	53.0	54.3	46.2	49.5		

* United Parcel was a private company prior to 1999, and thus no additional statistics are available.

United Technologies Corporation

One Financial Plaza ❑ Hartford, CT 06103 ❑ (860) 728-7912 ❑ Listed: NYSE ❑ Dividend reinvestment plan available (860) 728-7870 ❑ Web site: *www.utc.com* ❑ Listed: NYSE ❑ Ticker symbol: UTX ❑ S&P rating: A+ ❑ Value Line Financial Strength A++

The country's largest fuel cell power plant in commercial operation was commissioned on September 21, 2005 in Long Island, New York. UTC Power, a division of United Technologies Corporation, provided seven PureCell™ 200s to the project, which generates 1.4 megawatts of primary electrical power and 6.3 million BTUs of useable heat for Verizon Communications, Inc.

The project is the largest fuel cell installation connected to the Long Island Power Authority's massive grid and the latest among UTC Power's fleet of seventeen fuel cells in the area.

The fuel cell power plants are integrated into the energy system of Verizon's 292,000-sq.-ft. Garden City Central Office call-routing center to provide cooling, heating, and power. The call-routing center has 900 employees and serves 35,000 Verizon customers. The units operate as a hybrid system with diesel and dual fuel gas/diesel reciprocating engines that can generate a total of 4.4 megawatts of electrical power.

"This industry-leading fuel cell system that Verizon has installed demonstrates the increasing need for larger, independent power sources," said Jan van Dokkum, president of UTC Power. "We are honored Verizon chose UTC Power to provide clean, reliable energy to their critical call routing center. The PureCell™ 200's durability offers significant, long-term benefits to Long Island residents and the environment."

A fuel cell is an electrochemical device that combines hydrogen or hydrogen-rich fuel, and oxygen to produce electricity, heat, and water. Fuel cells operate without combustion, making them virtually pollution free. While a traditional generating system produces as much as 25 pounds of pollutants to generate 1,000 kilowatt-hours of electricity, the PureCell™ 200 power plant produces less than an ounce.

United Technologies provides high-technology products and services to the commercial building and aerospace industries. Its UTC Power division, based in South Windsor, Connecticut, includes UTC Fuel Cells and is a full-service provider of environmentally advanced power solutions. With more than forty years of experience, UTC Power is the leading developer and producer of fuel cells for on-site power, transportation, and space flight applications.

Company Profile

United Technologies provides high-technology products to the aerospace and building systems industries throughout the world. Its companies are industry leaders and include:

Pratt & Whitney

Large and small commercial and military jet engines, spare parts, and product support, specialized engine maintenance and overhaul and repair services for airlines, air forces, and corporate fleets; rocket engines and space propulsion systems; industrial gas turbines.

Chubb

Security and fire protection systems; integration, installation, and servicing of intruder alarms, access control, and video surveillance, and monitoring, response, and security personnel services; installation and servicing of fire detection and suppression systems.

Hamilton Sundstrand

Aircraft electrical power generation and distribution systems; engine and flight controls; propulsion systems; environmental controls for aircraft, spacecraft, and submarines; auxiliary power units; product support, maintenance, and repair services; space life support systems; industrial products including mechanical power transmissions, compressors, metering devices, and fluid handling equipment.

Sikorsky

Military and commercial helicopters; fixed-wing reconnaissance aircraft; spare parts and maintenance services for helicopters and fixed-wing aircraft; and civil helicopter operations.

UTC Power

Combined heat, cooling, and power systems for commercial and industrial applications and fuel cell systems made by UTC Fuel Cells for commercial, transportation, and space applications, including the U.S. space shuttle program.

Carrier

Heating, ventilating, and air conditioning (HVAC) equipment for commercial, industrial, and residential buildings; HVAC replacement parts and services; building controls; commercial, industrial, and transport refrigeration equipment.

Carrier emphasizes energy-efficient, quiet operation, and environmental stewardship in its new residential and commercial products. The new WeatherMaker residential air conditioner using Puron, a nonozone-depleting refrigerant, provides the domestic market with low operating costs and sound levels—about the same as a refrigerator's. The Puron unit gives Carrier a healthy lead over competitors, as chlorine-free refrigerants become the standard.

Otis

Elevators, escalators, moving walks and shuttle systems, and related installation, maintenance, and repair services; modernization products and service for elevators and escalators.

Shortcomings to Bear in Mind

- "We are maintaining our HOLD rating on UTX, as the stock is trading near our discounted-cash-flow-based twelve-month price," said Robert Friedman, writing for *Standard & Poor's Stock Reports* on December 5, 2005.
- Nicholas P. Heymann, an analyst with Prudential Equity Group, had this comment on January 24, 2006, "We believe our previous largest risk to the company, an accelerated deterioration in the commercial spare parts sales of UTC's Pratt & Whitney engine business has now been replaced by a slowdown in the relatively well-established recovery in commercial spare parts sales."

Reasons to Buy

- The *New York Times* tabulated the opinions of twenty-one analysts on March 20, 2006, and five rated the stock a STRONG BUY; thirteen called it a MODERATE BUY; and only three retreated to the HOLD position.
- "We are reaffirming our BUY rating on United Technologies. Our acquisition-and-margin-expansion thesis remains the same," said Dana Richardson, writing for Argus Research Company on January 24, 2006. "The company is realizing our thesis, and with a $2 billion acquisition placeholder in 2006 and demonstrable margin expansion in new acquisitions in 2005, we expect it will continue to do so."
- On August 3, 2005, United Technologies announced completion of its Rocketdyne Propulsion & Power acquisition from The Boeing Company. Rocketdyne joined Pratt & Whitney's space propulsion business,

creating a company with the most complete product line in the space launch industry. This new company now operates as Pratt & Whitney Rocketdyne, and is headquartered in Canoga Park, California. Pratt & Whitney Rocketdyne has aligned its space power and energy segment with UTC's Hamilton Sundstrand unit.

"We see great strategic value in growing our liquid propulsion space business," said Louis R. Chênevert, president of Pratt & Whitney. "Leveraging synergies, increasing our product breadth and combining our engineering resources will ensure our leadership in space propulsion."

- Pratt & Whitney scored a major coup by being chosen by the Pentagon as the lead engine supplier on both versions of the Joint Strike Fighter, as well as the F-22 fighter, two of the military's highest-profile new programs. Pratt is also tapping into markets it once chose to leave to others, aggressively seeking commercial-engine overhaul and maintenance business that could be valued at more than $1 billion a year. What's more, the company also has seized on an opportunity provided by the nation's power woes: It expects to sell fifty-four modified JT8D engines for industrial electric generation for major power companies in need of cheap and quickly obtainable electric power.
- Otis Elevator Company won the contract to supply elevators and escalators for Beijing's biggest public transit project, a new facility under construction in preparation for the Olympic Summer Games in Beijing in 2008. Otis will supply and install 11 elevators and 38 escalators for the Transit Center.
- The Comanche is a new helicopter under development for the U.S. Army by the Boeing-Sikorsky team. This sophisticated piece of hardware will more accurately and effectively relay critical information from the battlefield to the command center than any other system in place today. Sikorsky is part of United Technologies' Flight Systems, one of the company's four segments.

While it has the ability to carry out light attack missions, the Comanche will mainly serve as a reconnaissance aircraft that will coordinate the many aircraft and ground forces involved in a combat mission. For this reason the U.S. Army has called the Comanche critical to the twenty-first century Objective Force.

The Comanche is designed, manufactured, and tested by the Boeing-Sikorsky team, with help from over fifteen leading aerospace manufacturers. In addition to Sikorsky, another one of UTX's subsidiaries, Hamilton Sundstrand, will provide the electrical power generating system and the environmental control system for the Comanche.

The battlefield of the twenty-first century will be almost entirely digitalized. As such, the Comanche, which carries highly advanced electronic equipment, will be essential for receiving and processing intelligence and sending it on to other assets. This aircraft can visually detect and classify targets seven times quicker than any other U.S. Army surveillance device today, and it can hand off precise coordinates to shooters within seconds. What's more, it can operate any time of the day and in all weather conditions. The Comanche has been undergoing rigorous testing for almost ten years. Initial deployment is scheduled for the end of the decade.

SECTOR: **Industrials** ◆ BETA COEFFICIENT: **1.15**
10-YEAR COMPOUND EARNINGS PER SHARE GROWTH: **16%**
10-YEAR COMPOUND DIVIDENDS PER SHARE GROWTH: **13%**

		2005	2004	2003	2002	2001	2000	1999	1998
Revenues (millions)		42,725	37,445	31,034	28,212	27,897	26,583	24,127	25,715
Net Income (millions)		3,164	2,788	2,361	2,236	1,938	1,808	841	1,255
Earnings per share		3.12	2.76	2.35	2.21	1.92	1.78	0.83	1.27
Dividends per share		0.88	0.70	0.57	0.49	0.45	0.42	0.38	0.35
Price	high	58.9	53.0	48.4	38.9	43.8	39.9	39.0	28.1
	low	48.4	40.4	26.8	24.4	20.1	23.3	25.8	16.8

CONSERVATIVE GROWTH

Valspar Corporation

1101 Third Street South ❑ Minneapolis, MN 55415-1259 ❑ (612) 375-7702 ❑ Web site: *www.valspar.com* ❑ Direct Dividend reinvestment plan is available (800) 842-7629 ❑ Fiscal year ends Friday before October 31 ❑ Listed: NYSE ❑ Ticker symbol: VAL ❑ S&P rating: A- ❑ Value Line financial strength rating: B+

Valspar's sales for 2005 increased 11.2 percent, to $2.7 billion, with revenue growth in all of the company's major business lines. Net income of $147.6 million and earnings per share of $1.42 were up 3.3 percent and 5.2 percent, respectively—remarkable results, given the challenging raw material environment.

Valspar generated $231 million of operating cash flow that was put to work to fund capital spending of $63 million, to acquire the stock of Samuel Cabot for $79 million, and to purchase $82 million of Valspar stock. Reflecting the company's confidence in its future, the board of directors raised the annual dividend 10 percent, to $0.40 per share. That move represents the twenty-eighth consecutive year of dividend increases.

The Coatings business segment generated solid results in 2005, with sales increasing more than 11 percent. By the fourth quarter, this segment had significantly narrowed the gap between raw material cost increases and pricing initiatives. "Building on the company's technologies, technical service and our global presence, packaging coatings grew significantly faster than the market," said CEO William L. Mansfield. "In addition, we introduced new technologies that should enhance growth in 2006 and beyond. Industrial coatings also had a strong year, benefiting from the rebound in the economy, success with new business initiatives and growth in China.

"The Paints business segment had a more difficult year. Sales were solid, increasing more than 8 percent, but operating margins declined due to the lag between price increases and rapidly rising raw material costs."

Mr. Mansfield goes on to say, "The resin, colorant, gelcoat and furniture protection plan businesses generated double-digit growth, reflecting multiple pricing actions and new business. Resins and gelcoats had remarkable performances in the face of raw material shortages earlier in the year and unprecedented raw material and cost increases throughout the year."

Company Profile

Founded in 1806, The Valspar Corporation is the manufacturer of the nation's first varnishes VAL represents the combination of many pioneer coatings firms. Now one of the five largest North American manufacturers of paint and coatings, the company has expanded in recent years largely through a host of acquisitions. More recently, it has moved aggressive abroad, with close to a third of its revenues from that sector. Its largest customer is Lowe's Companies, which accounts for about 10 percent of the company's revenues.

The Valspar Corporation provides coatings and coating intermediates to a wide variety of customers. The company's products include:

- Industrial coatings for wood, metal, and plastic for original equipment manufacturers.
- Coatings and inks for rigid packaging, principally food and beverage cans, for global customers.
- Paints, varnishes, and stains, primarily for the do-it-yourself market.
- Coatings for refinishing vehicles.
- High-performance floor coatings.
- Resins and colorants for internal use and for other paint and coatings manufacturers.

Valspar's long-term objective is 15 percent growth in both sales and earnings through a combination of internal growth and acquisitions to enhance and complement its existing businesses. Management's goal is to be the lowest-cost supplier with the leading customized technology.

Shortcomings to Bear in Mind

■ "This year (2005) presented the most difficult operating environment in recent memory," said Mr. Mansfield. "The unprecedented increase in our raw material costs, combined with supply shortages, challenged the company throughout the year. We responded aggressively by expanding our supply base globally, exercising prudent expense controls, pursuing productivity improvements and increasing our selling prices. These actions resulted in a record year in sales and earnings.

"As we begin 2006, rising raw material costs continue to be our biggest challenge. We will continue our efforts to lower costs, and we will remain focused on implementing pricing actions as required."

Reasons to Buy

■ The company has been very active on the acquisition front, particularly in the past decade. Since 1995, Valspar had made more than a score of acquisitions, including purchases of equity in joint ventures. VAL believes its most important acquisitions were Coates Company (in a series of four transactions, in 1996, 1997, 2000, and 2001); Dexter Packaging (1999); and Lilly Industries (2000).

The Coates acquisitions added to the company's packaging coatings businesses in a number of global locations. The Dexter move added to the company's packaging and industrial coatings businesses in Europe, the United States, and Asia. Lilly, previously one of the five largest industrial coatings and specialty chemical manufacturers in North America, greatly expanded the company's presence in wood, coil, and mirror coatings, as well as in nonindustrial automotive coatings.

More recently, in August 2004, Valspar completed the acquisition of the forest products business of Associated Chemists, Inc. The acquired product line generated sales of about $28 million in 2003 and includes edge-sealers, surface primers, plaints, and stains, inks, and specialty chemicals for oriented strand board manufacturers and others in the forest products industry.

In 2004, Valspar continued its long record of building the company through acquisition and strategic alliances. This time, it is teaming up with Quikrete, the number one name in concrete. Founded in 1940, Atlanta-based Quikrete Companies manufactures an extensive line of cement and concrete-related products for the do-it-yourself and commercial markets. The company has seventy-five manufacturing facilities in the United States, Canada, Puerto Rico, and South America, producing more than 200 products. It is unsurpassed in product depth and distribution.

In the fall of 2004, the two companies announced that they would combine their talents with the manufacture of the market's first complete line of premium concrete coatings. Going on sale in early 2005, the new line is being made and sold jointly by Valspar and Quikrete under the brand name, "Quikrete Professional Concrete Coatings." The line features fourteen technologically advanced products, from sealers to floor coatings to waterproofers. The flagship product of the new line is the Quikrete Epoxy Garage Floor Coating Kit, an all-in-one, easy-to-use kit that features Bond-Lok technology to deliver a coating that is actually twice as strong as concrete itself.

The new product was born out of a mutual desire to leverage a respected brand name to address an underserved sector of the coatings marketplace. "Concrete coatings is currently a fragmented category that is confusing for customers," said Bill Mansfield, Valspar's executive vice president and chief operating officer. "There is definitely a need in the marketplace for a comprehensive program. With the home-improvement industry booming, and Americans investing more in their homes than ever before, the time is ripe for this category to reach into the twenty-first century. With Quikrete, this strategic alliance will create a synergistic force in the concrete coatings category and maximize growth in the retail environment."

For its part, Quikrete's executive vice president, Dennis Winchester, said, "Quikrete and Valspar each bring something unique to this relationship. We bring unparalleled concrete knowledge, and Valspar brings coatings expertise. Utilizing these joint technologies allows us to horizontally diversify our business, and has all the signs of a profitable end result for the companies involved and the retailers we serve."

Finally, in 2005, despite the difficult operating environment, the company completed the acquisition of Samuel Cabot Inc., a privately owned manufacture of premium quality exterior and interior stains and finishes based in Newburyport, Massachusetts. Mr. Mansfield said, "The combination of the Valspar and Cabot brands significantly strengthens our product offering for independent paint dealers. We are optimistic about the prospects for growth in this important channel."

- On March 27, 2006, the *New York Times* poled twelve financial analysts for their take on Valspar. Three rated the stock a STRONG BUY; three said it was a MODERATE BUY; and a half dozen viewed the stock as a HOLD.
- *Value Line Investment Survey* had some favorable comments on Valspar on March 17, 2006. Jeremy J. Butler said, "This stock has above-average long-term capital gains potential. Since we have just rolled out our three- to five-year horizon to 2009–2011, the stock has longer to achieve our Target Price Range of $30–$50. Given the restructuring currently taking place, and our expectation for minor accretive acquisitions, combined with the company's global reach and high-profile customers, the stock has a good chance to attain our expectations."

SECTOR: **Materials** ◆ BETA COEFFICIENT: **.90**
10-YEAR COMPOUND EARNINGS PER SHARE GROWTH: **10.2%**
10-YEAR COMPOUND DIVIDENDS PER SHARE GROWTH: **10.3%**

		2005	2004	2003	2002	2001	2000	1999	1998
Revenues (millions)		2,714	2,441	2,248	2,127	1,921	1,483	1,388	1,155
Net Income (millions)		147.6	142.8	112.5	120.1	51.5	86.5	82.1	72.1
Earnings per share		1.42	1.36	1.09	1.17	.55	1.00	0.94	0.82
Dividends per share		.40	.30	.30	.28	.27	.26	.23	.21
Price	high	26.0	25.8	24.8	25.1	21.0	21.7	20.9	21.1
	low	20.4	22.3	18.8	17.4	13.2	9.9	14.6	12.9

AGGRESSIVE GROWTH

Varian Medical Systems, Inc.

3100 Hansen Way ❑ Palo Alto, CA 94304-1030 ❑ (650) 424-5782 ❑ Dividend reinvestment plan not available ❑ Web site: *www.varian.com* ❑ Fiscal year ends on Friday nearest September 30 ❑ Ticker symbol: VAR ❑ Listed NYSE ❑ S&P rating: B+ ❑ Value Line financial strength rating: A

Increasing demand for more effective and affordable health care solutions, together with a focus on execution and operational efficiency, enabled Varian Medical Systems to grow and achieve excellent financial results in fiscal year 2005. The year was marked by another major revolution in cancer care sparked by products for state-of-the-art radiation oncology and X-ray imaging. The company launched several new and enhanced products for advanced cancer treatments, bloodless neurosurgery, filmless X-ray imaging, and automatic inspection of cargo containers. Varian extended its global leadership in its traditional markets and pushed more deeply into promising new markets.

All in all, it was another successful year in which Varian positioned the company for continued growth.

Profitable Growth

In fiscal year 2005, compared with the previous fiscal year:

- Net orders rose 14 percent, to $1.6 billion.
- Year-end backlog rose 21 percent, to $1.2 billion.
- Revenues increased 12 percent, to $1.4 billion.
- Operating earnings climbed 19 percent, to $305 million.
- Net earnings rose 23 percent, to $207 million.
- Earnings per diluted share climbed 27 percent, to $1.50.

All three of the company's business segments contributed positively to the growth in annual net orders, revenues, and operating earnings. Annual net orders increased 14 percent in Oncology Systems, 11 percent in X-Ray Products, and 20 percent in the "Other" segment that included the Ginzton Technology Center and BrachyTherapy products. Annual revenues rose 10 percent in Oncology Systems, 18 percent in X-Ray Products, and 23 percent in our "Other" segment.

Company Profile

Varian Medical Systems is the world's leading manufacturer of integrated radiotherapy systems for treating cancer and other diseases; it is also a leading supplier of X-ray tubes for imaging in medical, scientific, and industrial applications. Established in 1948, the company has manufacturing sites in North America and Europe and in forty sales and support offices worldwide.

In 1999, the company (formerly Varian Associates, Inc.) reorganized itself into three separate publicly traded companies by spinning off two of its businesses to stockholders via a tax-free distribution.

Since then, the company has significantly broadened its product and business offerings, acquired new businesses, and set records for sales and net orders. More importantly, Varian put itself at the forefront of a radiotherapy revolution that is making a dramatic difference in the struggle against cancer.

About three out of every ten people will be afflicted with some form of cancer. The good news is that their chances of surviving, of beating cancer, have greatly improved, thanks to recent advances in radiation therapy—many of which have been led by Varian Medical Systems. The company has three segments:

Varian Oncology Systems

Varian Oncology Systems is the world's leading supplier of radiotherapy systems for treating cancer. Its integrated medical systems include linear accelerators and accessories, and a broad range of interconnected software tools for planning and delivering the sophisticated radiation treatments available to cancer patients. Thousands of patients all over the world are treated daily on Varian systems. Oncology Systems works closely with health care professionals in community clinics, hospitals, and universities to improve cancer outcomes. The business unit also supplies linear accelerators for industrial inspection applications.

Varian X-Ray Products

Varian X-Ray Products is the world's premier independent supplier of X-ray tubes, serving manufacturers of radiology equipment and industrial inspection equipment, as well as distributors of replacement tubes. This business provides the industry's broadest selection of X-ray tubes expressly designed for the most advanced diagnostic applications, including CT scanning, radiography, and mammography. These products meet evolving requirements for improved resolution, faster patient throughput, longer tube life, smaller dimensions, and greater cost efficiency. X-Ray Products also supplies a new line of amorphous silicon flat-panel X-ray detectors for medical and industrial applications.

Ginzton Technology Center

The Ginzton Technology Center acts as Varian Medical Systems' research and development facility for breakthrough technologies and operates a growing brachytherapy business for the delivery of internal radiation to treat cancer and cardiovascular disease. In addition to brachytherapy, current efforts are focused on next-generation imaging systems and advanced targeting technologies for radiotherapy. The center is also investigating the combination of radiotherapy with other treatment modalities, such as bioengineered gene delivery systems.

Shortcomings to Bear in Mind

- Varian has been a solid performer in recent years which has pushed up the price/earnings multiple to a high level, often more than thirty. Such stocks are sometimes vulnerable to bad news.

Reasons to Buy

- "International orders for Oncology Systems increased 29 percent in fiscal 2005 over last year's levels, while domestic orders rose 3 percent," said Christopher Robertson, writing for *Value Line Investment Survey* on March 3, 2006. "The company sells to clients in many nations, which means that earnings are not dependent on the strength of one exchange rate or foreign economy."

■ "Our recommendation is BUY," said Robert M. Gold, writing for *Standard & Poor's Company Reports* on February 6, 2006. "We think revenue growth in coming quarters will continue to be bolstered by clinical adoption of IMRT in North America and Europe, along with IGRT upgrades to the installed base."

■ On March 29, 2006, the *New York Times* reviewed the opinions of ten financial analysts and found that two rated Varian as a STRONG BUY; five called it a MODERATE BUY; and three said it was a HOLD.

■ According to recent studies, more than six million people worldwide succumb to cancer each year. Nearly twice as many others are diagnosed with the disease. In some countries, cancer is a leading cause of death among children. Mostly though, it is a disease primarily of aging, with people fifty or older—the "baby boomers"—now accounting for nearly 80 percent of diagnosed cases. In the United States, the chances that you'll eventually develop cancer are one in three if you are female, one in two if you are male. In a very real sense, cancer victimizes not only patients, but also their families and friends, colleagues, and neighbors. Ultimately, the disease affects us all. The social and economic costs are staggering.

The fact is that half of U.S. patients receive radiotherapy as part of their treatment. Now, thanks to the new technology that Varian Medical Systems has helped to develop, radiotherapy is poised to play an even stronger role in cancer treatment, and many more patients could be cured by it. It's technology that is being implemented in all corners of the world.

■ With certain cancers, the odds of surviving are improving markedly, thanks to the growing use of a radiotherapy advance called intensity modulated radiation therapy, or IMRT. IMRT is being used to treat head and neck, breast, prostate, pancreatic, lung, liver, and central nervous system cancers. IMRT makes it possible for a larger and more effective dose of radiation to be delivered directly to the tumor, greatly sparing surrounding, healthy tissues. This is expected to result in a higher likelihood of cure with lower complication rates.

The clinical outcomes using IMRT are extremely promising. A study of early stage prostate cancer has shown that the higher radiation doses possible with IMRT have the potential to double the rate of tumor control to more than 95 percent. Using IMRT, clinicians were able to deliver high doses while reducing the rate of normal tissue complications from 10 percent to 2 percent. Similar results have been reported by doctors using IMRT to treat cancers of the head and neck.

Varian Medical Systems has joined forces with GE Medical Systems to combine the latest in diagnostic imaging results with advanced radiotherapy technologies in what are called See & Treat Cancer Care imaging and treatment tools. This approach enables physicians to see the distribution of malignant cells more clearly and treat them more effectively with precisely targeted radiation doses using IMRT.

■ Varian Medical Systems has long been the world's leading supplier of radiotherapy equipment. Now, the company's SmartBeam IMRT system, the culmination of twelve years and $300 million of development effort, is already making a difference for thousands of patients.

Today, a little more than 500 of the world's 5,700 radiotherapy centers for cancer treatment have acquired a set of integrated tools for SmartBeam IMRT from Varian Medical Systems.

Almost one-fifth of them are now offering it to their patients, and many others are close behind.

In addition to promising outcomes and public demand for better care, new Medicare and Medicaid reimbursement rates are expected to help accelerate the rapid adoption of IMRT by both hospitals and free-standing cancer centers in the United States. In international markets, public health systems are under pressure to reduce patients' waiting periods by updating systems with more effective treatment technology that can treat more patients.

SECTOR: **Health Care** ◆ BETA COEFFICIENT: **.80**
10-YEAR COMPOUND EARNINGS PER SHARE GROWTH: **7.2%**
10-YEAR COMPOUND DIVIDENDS PER SHARE GROWTH: **none**

		2005	2004	2003	2002	2001	2000	1999	1998
Revenues (millions)		1,383	1,236	1,042	873	774	690	590	1,422
Net Income (millions)		207	167	131	94	68	53	8	74
Earnings per share		1.50	1.18	.92	.67	.50	.41	.07	.61
Dividends per share		Nil	–	–	–	–	–	.03	.10
Price	high	52.9	46.5	35.7	25.7	19.3	17.8	10.8	14.6
	low	31.6	30.8	23.7	15.8	13.5	7.1	4.1	7.9

CONSERVATIVE GROWTH

Walgreen Company

200 Wilmot Road ❑ Mail Stop #2261 ❑ Deerfield, IL 60015 ❑ (847) 914-2972 ❑ Direct dividend reinvestment program is available (888) 368-7346 ❑ Fiscal year ends August 31 ❑ Web site: *www.walgreens.com* ❑ Ticker symbol: WAG ❑ S&P rating: A+ ❑ Value Line financial strength rating: A++

"It is easy to see why investors might feel more comfortable with Walgreen," said Ian McDonald, writing for the *Wall Street Journal* on November 22, 2005. "The Deerfield, Illinois, company has mostly grown by opening stores, rather than buying competitors. That is a less risky route than acquisitions and keeps a crop of recently opened, fast-growing stores in the pipeline. The company says that more than half of its 5,000 stores are less than five years old.

"Also, Walgreen was a leader in recent years as pharmacies expanded into everything from film processing to soft drinks, and built ever-larger stand-alone locations. Walgreen has the most 24-hour and drive-through stores in the industry, which the company says has been a top differentiator between it and other drugstores for time-strapped customers.

"On average, Walgreen outlets write more prescriptions than CVS pharmacy counters, partly because Walgreen has more senior citizens in a 1.5-mile radius than CVS, according to UBS's Neil Currie. That edge will be tough to chip away, partly because research has shown that consumers are often reluctant to switch pharmacies once a store has their information on file."

Company Profile

Walgreens, one of the fastest-growing retailers in the United States, leads the chain drugstore industry in sales and profits. Sales for fiscal 2005 reached $42.2 billion, produced by 4,953 stores in forty-five states and Puerto Rico (up from 4,582 stores a year earlier).

Founded in 1901, Walgreens today has 179,000 employees. The company's drugstores serve more than 4.4 million customers daily and average $8.3 million in annual sales per unit. That's $747 per square foot, among the highest in the industry. Walgreens has paid dividends in every quarter since 1933 and has raised the dividend in each of the past twenty-five years.

Stand-Alone Stores

Competition from the supermarkets has convinced Walgreens that the best strategy is to build stand-alone stores. Since the rise of managed care, many pharmacy customers now make only minimal copayments for prescriptions. That leaves convenience as the major factor in choosing a pharmacy. The free-standing format makes room for drive-thru windows, which provide a speedy way for drugstore customers to pick up or drop off prescriptions.

On the other hand, the company's stand-alone strategy is more expensive. Walgreens insists on building its units on corner lots near an intersection with a traffic light. Such leases normally cost more than a site in a strip mall.

More Than a Pharmacy

Home meal replacement has become a $100-billion business industry-wide. In the company's food section, Walgreens carries staples as well as frozen dinners, desserts, and pizzas. In some stores, expanded food sections carry such items as fruit, and ready-to-eat salads.

In the photo department, the company builds loyalty through a wide selection of products and the service of trained technicians. Walgreens experimented with one-hour photo service as early as 1982, but it was in the mid-1990s before, according to CEO Dan Jorndt, "We really figured it out." Since 1998, one-hour processing has been available chain-wide, made profitable by "our high volume of business. We've introduced several digital photo products that are selling well and are evaluating the long-term impact of digital on the mass market."

Highlights of 2005:

- "We opened 435 new stores for a total of 4,953 Walgreens in forty-five states and Puerto Rico.
- "We filled 490 million prescriptions—15 percent of the U.S. retail market. Pharmacy is 64 percent of our business.
- "Our drugstores serve 4.4 million customers daily and average $8.3 million in annual sales per store. That's $747 per square foot, among the highest in the drugstore industry.
- "Walgreens has 179,000 employees and about 750,000 share holders. We added 15,700 jobs in fiscal 2005.
- "Walgreens digital photo service now offers customers the ability to upload photos from home and pick up their prints at nearly any store chain-wide in one hour.
- "Walgreens ranks number one among food and drug stores on *Fortune* magazine's Most Admired Companies in America list. We also rank 38th on the Fortune 500 list of the largest U.S. based companies.
- "*Barron's* magazine lists Walgreens as one of the top 10 'most respected' companies in the world.
- "We increased net earnings 15.5 percent, outpacing our 12.5 percent sales increase.
- "We increased our quarterly dividend 23.8 percent. In the past five years, our annual dividend payment has increased nearly 65 percent overall.
- "We now fill more prescriptions than all our grocery competitors . . . combined. And in the front-end—or non-pharmacy side of the store—we gained market share in fifty-four of our top sixty core categories, versus our drugstore, grocery and mass merchant competitors."

Shortcomings to Bear in Mind

- "Walgreens happens to be in the middle of a vicious multifront battle," said Matthew Boyle, writing for *Fortune* magazine on June 13, 2005. First, there's Walgreens's biggest traditional rival, CVS, which has been expanding rapidly—it recently acquired 1,268 Eckerds to push its total store count to 5,415. Scarier still, are the supermarkets and mass merchandisers that have been moving emphatically into the pharmacy business. Wal-Mart, which already has 3,144 stores with pharmacies, is testing 24-hour pharmacies and offers eye exams in many stores. The most dangerous threat of all—and one to which, as we'll see, Walgreens was late to respond—is the rise of low-cost mail-order prescriptions, which represents a profound shift in the way Americans buy their medicines."

Reasons to Buy

- On March 27, 2006, the *New York Times* reported on the opinions of twenty-one leading analysts and their view of Walgreens. Seven said it was a STRONG BUY; eight said it was a MODERATE BUY; and a half dozen regarded the stock as a HOLD.
- "We are reiterating our BUY rating on Walgreen Co., based on the company's track record of using current earnings to finance future growth," said Christopher Graja, CFA, writing for Argus Research Company on January 3, 2006. "Walgreen's shares have historically been much less volatile than the average company in the S&P 500, while its historical earnings stability and expected growth have been higher. We believe these attributes could be assets to the stock as investors grapple with the implications of high energy prices and rising interest rates."
- Favorable demographics include seventy-seven million aging baby boomers (forty-five to sixty-four years old) and their estimated increased usage. For instance, the typical forty-year-old takes six-plus prescriptions annually; at fifty it reaches eight; at sixty the annual rate is eleven; and at seventy the number of prescriptions reaches fifteen.
- Some investors are concerned that the company is diluting sales by putting stores so close together, "just cannibalizing yourself." To that concern, CEO David W. Bernauer replied, "I haven't gone to a party in two years where that question hasn't come up. The answer is yes—when we open a store very near another one, the old store usually sees a drop in sales. But in virtually every case, it builds back to its original volume and beyond. Here's the scenario: as you add stores, overall sales in the market increase, while expenses are spread over a larger base. Bottom line, *profitability* increases. Our most profitable markets are the ones where we've built the strongest market share."
- Investors are also wondering about e-commerce. They ask, "Is there a long-term future?" To this concern, Mr. Bernauer said, "Though there's a lot of carnage on the early e-commerce road, we definitely see a future for *www:walgreens.com.* That's not, however, in "delivered-to-your-door" merchandise. Frankly, we never thought there would be a big demand for prescriptions by mail, and we were correct—well over 90 percent of prescription orders placed through our Web site are for store pickup. It's not convenient, when you need a prescription or a few drugstore items to wait three days for it to show up.

  "What *does* excite us is using the Internet to provide better service and information. We're already communicating by e-mail with nearly 20,000 prescription customers per day."
- The company's new pharmacy system, Intercom Plus, is now up and running in all Walgreens stores across the country. This system—costing over $150 million—has raised Walgreens service and productivity to a new level. While providing increased patient access to Walgreen's pharmacists, it also substantially raises the number of prescriptions each store can efficiently dispense.

■ A high number of drugs are coming off patent over the next few years, which means more generic drugs will come to market and will become a bigger percentage of prescriptions. To be sure, generics have a much lower price, but the drugstore can add on a bigger profit.

■ Recently, a major grocery chain cited drugstores as a reason behind disappointing sales gains: "Fill-in shopping needs," said the grocery CEO, "are increasingly being satisfied in convenience and drug stores." Walgreens, with highly convenient, on-the-way-home locations, is on the receiving end of this trend.

■ With stores in forty-five states and Puerto Rico, Walgreens has a base of customers that covers more of the United States than any other drugstore chain. The company's national coverage is a major advantage in negotiations with managed-care pharmacy companies.

SECTOR: **Consumer Staples** ◆ BETA COEFFICIENT: **.75**
10-YEAR COMPOUND EARNINGS PER SHARE GROWTH: **16.5%**
10-YEAR COMPOUND DIVIDENDS PER SHARE GROWTH: **8.2%**

		2005	2004	2003	2002	2001	2000	1999	1998
Revenues (millions)		42,202	37,502	32,505	28,681	24,623	21,207	17,839	15,307
Net Income (millions)		1,478	1,360	1,176	1,019	886	756	624	514
Earnings per share		1.52	1.32	1.14	.99	.86	.74	.62	.51
Dividends per share		.22	.18	.15	.15	.14	.14	.13	.13
Price	high	49.0	39.5	37.4	40.7	45.3	45.8	33.9	30.2
	low	38.4	32.0	26.9	27.7	28.7	22.1	22.7	14.8

AGGRESSIVE GROWTH

Wal-Mart Stores, Inc.

702 Southwest Eighth Street ❑ P.O. 116 ❑ Bentonville, AR 72716-8611 ❑ (479) 273-8446 ❑ Direct dividend reinvestment plan available (800) 438-6278 ❑ Web site: *www.walmartstores.com* ❑ Listed: NYSE ❑ Fiscal year ends January 31 ❑ Ticker symbol: WMT ❑ S&P rating: A+ ❑ Value Line financial strength rating: A++

Wal-Mart did not appear to be a corporate colossus in 1962. That was the year that Sam Walton opened his first store in Rogers, Arkansas, with a sign saying "Wal-Mart Discount City. We sell for less." In the decades since, Wal-Mart has evolved into a $244-billion-a-year empire by selling—at a discount, of course—prodigious quantities of all manner of items, from clothing, food, hardware, and eye glasses to Kleenex, tooth brushes, pots and pans, and pharmaceuticals.

An essential key to Wal-Mart's success, says H. Lee Scott, the company's CEO, is "driving unnecessary costs out of businesses."

To keep prices at rock bottom, the company insists that its 65,000 suppliers become leaner machines that examine every farthing they spend. This ruthless drive to whittle away fat has clearly reshaped the practices of businesses that deal with Wal-Mart, as well as those that compete against them. Wal-Mart's strategies for holding costs in check—the use of cutting-edge technology, innovative logistics, reliance on imported goods, and a nonunion work force—are becoming industry standards.

Company Profile

Wal-Mart is the world's number one retailer—larger than Sears, Kmart, and J. C. Penney combined. As of January 31, 2006, the company operated 1,209 Wal-Mart stores, 1,980 Supercenters, 567 Sam's Clubs, and 101 Neighborhood Markets in the United States. Internationally, the company operated units in the following countries: Mexico (786), Puerto Rico (54), Canada (278), Argentina (11), Brazil (156), China (56), South Korea (16), Germany (88), and the United Kingdom (315). More than 100 million customers per week visit Wal-Mart Stores.

Wal-Mart operates four different retail concepts:

Wal-Mart Discount Stores. Since founder Sam Walton opened his first store in 1962, Wal-Mart has built more than 1,600 discount stores in the United States. The stores range in size from 40,000 to 125,000 square feet and carry 80,000 different items, including family apparel, automotive products, health and beauty aids, home furnishings, electronics, hardware, toys, sporting goods, lawn and garden items, pet supplies, jewelry, and housewares.

Wal-Mart Supercenters. Developed in 1988 to meet the growing demand for one-stop family shopping, Wal-Mart supercenters today number more than 1,980 nationwide and are open twenty-four hours a day. Supercenters save customers time and money by combining full grocery lines and general merchandise under one roof. These units range in size from 109,000 to 230,000 square feet and carry 100,000 different items, 30,000 of which are grocery products.

Wal-Mart Neighborhood Markets. These stores offer groceries, pharmaceuticals, and general merchandise. Generally, these units are situated in markets with Wal-Mart Supercenters, supplementing a strong food distribution network and providing added convenience while maintaining Wal-Mart's everyday low prices. First opened in 1998, Neighborhood Markets range from 42,000 to 55,000 square feet and feature a wide variety of products, including fresh produce, deli foods, fresh meat and dairy items, health and beauty aids, one-hour photo, and drive-through pharmacies, to name a few.

Sam's Clubs. The nation's leading members-only warehouse club offers a broad selection of general merchandise and large-volume items at value prices. Since 1983, Sam's Club has been the preferred choice for small businesses, families, or anyone looking for great prices on name-brand products. Ranging in size from 110,000 to 130,000 square feet, the 567 Sam's Clubs nationwide offer merchandise for both office and personal use, bulk paper products, furniture, computer hardware, and software, groceries, television sets, and clothing. A nominal membership fee ($30 per year for businesses and $35 for individuals) helps defray operating costs and keeps prices exceptionally low.

Shortcomings to Bear in Mind

- "Wal-Mart Stores, Inc. has become a beacon for bargain-minded shoppers, even as its daunting market power and controversial management practices have made it a lightening rod for criticism," said Joseph Weber, writing for *BusinessWeek* on December 12, 2005. "Investors, though, see a once innovative outfit whose stock has been flat-lining for at least five years. Profitability has slipped since the chain began a national expansion in the mid-1980s. More recent pushes abroad have produced disappointing returns."
- "We are maintaining our HOLD rating on Wal-Mart Stores," said Chris Graja, CFA, writing for Argus Research Company on January 9, 2006. "One reason is because we believe that the company may experience continued margin pressure in the future. Sales of food have been a source of revenue growth, but we believe that many of these categories have lower margins than

the company average. Another issue is that we believe the company's wage cost structure is more likely to rise than fall."

Reasons to Buy

- On January 5, 2006, Lehman Brothers, a major brokerage firm, rated this stock OVERWEIGHT, similar to a BUY. The analyst said, "We believe Wal-Mart represents a compelling long-term investment for several reasons, including our belief that Wal-Mart has a distinct competitive advantage with its low-cost structure and distribution capabilities as well as a highly cohesive, talented, and seasoned management team."
- On January 18, 2006, *Standard & Poor's Stock Reports* said, "We have a STRONG BUY (*its best rating*) on the shares." Joseph Agnese also said, "We believe WMT will remain well positioned to increase its U.S. market share, due to continued low price leadership, an expanding merchandise assortment with improving quality, and strong square footage growth."
- On March 2, 2006, the *New York Times* published a rundown on the opinions of twenty-eight analysts. Eight rated the stock a STRONG BUY; eight also said it was a MODERATE BUY, and twelve called it a HOLD.
- Wal-Mart's success is no secret. The company was named "Retailer of the Century" by *Discount Store News*; made *Fortune* magazine's lists of the "Most Admired Companies in America" and the "100 Best Companies to Work For" and was ranked on *Financial Times* "Most Respected in the World" list.
- Wal-Mart makes a concerted effort to find out precisely what its customers want. To do this, the company relies on information technology. It does this by collecting and analyzing internally developed information, which it calls "data-mining." It has been doing this since 1990.

The result, by now, is an enormous database of purchasing information that enables management to place the right item in the right store at the right time. The company's computer system receives 8.4 million updates every minute on the items that customers take home—and the relationship between the items in each basket.

Many retailers talk a good game when it comes to mining data at cash registers as a way to build sales. Wal-Mart, since it has been doing this for the past dozen years, is sitting on an information trove so vast and detailed that it far exceeds what many manufacturers know about their own products. What's more, Wal-Mart's data base is second in size only to that of the U.S. government, says one analyst. Wal-Mart also collects "market-basket data" from customer receipts at all of its stores, so it knows what products are likely to be purchased together. The company receives about 100,000 queries a week from suppliers and its own buyers looking for purchase patterns or checking a product.

Wal-Mart plans to use the data in its new Neighborhood Markets. Equipped with a drive-through pharmacy and selling both dry goods and perishables, the stores are a little smaller than typical suburban supermarkets. They are much smaller than Wal-Mart's Supercenters, the massive grocery-discount store combinations that Wal-Mart began opening in 1987.

This kind of information has significant value in and of itself. According to management, "Consider Wal-Mart's ability to keep the shelves stocked with exactly what customers want most, but still be able to keep inventories under tight control. Consider the common banana—so common, in fact, that the grocery carts of America contain bananas more often than any other single item. So why not make it easy for a shopper to remember bananas? In Wal-Mart grocery departments, bananas can be found not just in the produce section, but in the cereal and dairy aisles too."

SECTOR: **Consumer Staples** ◆ BETA COEFFICIENT: **.85**
10-YEAR COMPOUND EARNINGS PER SHARE GROWTH: **16.1%**
10-YEAR COMPOUND DIVIDENDS PER SHARE GROWTH: **19.2%**

		2005	2004	2003	2002	2001	2000	1999	1998
Revenues (millions)		315,654	288,189	258,681	244,524	217,799	191,329	165,013	137,634
Net Income (millions)		11,158	10,267	9,054	8,039	6,671	6,295	5,377	4,430
Earnings per share		2.68	2.41	2.07	1.81	1.49	1.40	1.28	0.99
Dividends per share		.58	.48	.36	.30	.28	.24	.20	0.16
Price	high	54.6	61.3	60.2	63.9	58.8	68.9	70.3	41.4
	low	42.3	51.1	46.2	43.7	41.5	41.4	38.7	18.8

AGGRESSIVE GROWTH

WellPoint, Inc.

120 Monument Circle ❑ Indianapolis, IN 46204-4903 ❑ (317) 488-6390 ❑ Dividend reinvestment plan not available ❑ Web site: *www.wellpoint.com* ❑ Ticker symbol: WLP ❑ Listed: NYSE ❑ S&P rating: not rated ❑ Value Line financial strength rating: A

"The blues don't have to bring you down," said Sandra Ward, writing for *Barron's* on July 25, 2005. "Just look at WellPoint, the nation's leading managed-care company and the biggest provider of Blue Cross and Blue Shield health plans. Formed by the November 2004 merger of Anthem and WellPoint Health Networks, WellPoint boasts perhaps the best-recognized brand in the business, a deep management team (no senior executives departed after the merger), dominant share in its markets, favorable industry trends and shares that have run straight up the flagpole."

Ms. Ward also said, "The entire managed-care sector has performed well in the past five years; the Morgan Stanley Healthcare Payors Index quadrupled in that span as the broad market sagged. But many investors consider WellPoint, which split its stock 2-for-1 in May, to be the best positioned to continue rewarding investors."

The *Barron's* article goes on to say, "By providing higher-margin specialty services that include pharmacy, dental, vision, and disability benefits, among others, WellPoint reaps more profits from its customer base. Indeed, one of its hidden assets is WellPoint Pharmacy Management, the fourth-largest pharmacy management company in the country (behind Caremark, Medco Containment and Express Scripts), with thirty million members."

Company Profile

WellPoint, Inc. is the nation's leading health benefits company. More than 38,000 WellPoint associates serve nearly 28 million members through the individual, small group, large group, national accounts, senior, and state-sponsored segments.

No other health benefits company has leading market presence in so many geographic areas. WellPoint is an independent licensee of the Blue Cross Blue Shield Association and serves its members as the Blue Cross licensee for California and the Blue Cross and Blue Shield licensee for Colorado, Connecticut, Georgia, Indiana, Kentucky, Maine, Missouri (excluding thirty counties in the Kansas City area), Nevada, New Hampshire, Ohio, Virginia (excluding the

Northern Virginia suburbs of Washington, D.C.), and Wisconsin.

The company also serves members through UniCare and HealthLink. UniCare serves medical members nationwide with innovative, high-quality health care plans and products. HealthLink is one of the largest managed care networks in the central United States and also operates two prominent networks in the Mid-Atlantic and Texas.

WellPoint's specialty companies provide a full range of benefits and services to its health plan customers, including pharmacy benefit management, vision, dental, and behavioral health benefits; group life and disability insurance benefits; workers' compensation; and long-term-care insurance.

WellPoint is the nation's second-largest Medicare contractor. Its combined operations handle more than 113 million Medicare claims each year. WellPoint companies administer Medicaid and children's health programs in a number of states. In fact, Blue Cross of California is the largest Medicaid managed care provider in the United States.

WellPoint has established one of the most significant social legacies in American industry with the creation or funding of charitable foundations in many states that the company serves. Today, these independent foundations have assets of more than $6 billion. In addition, Anthem, Inc. And WellPoint Health Networks Inc. established corporate foundations that now have total assets of more than $150 million. Through the company's foundations and corporate giving programs, WellPoint contributed a total of $14 million in 2004.

Shortcomings to Bear in Mind

- "What is the cause of risking health insurance premiums?" According to WellPoint, "Premiums have risen to keep pace with the growing cost and use of health care services. Key drivers include the growing health care needs of an aging population, the cost of new technology, and the increased use of prescription drugs. Other factors that add to the cost of health care are legally mandated benefits, unwarranted litigation, and medical malpractice insurance."
- According to the company's Form 10-K, "The managed care industry is highly competitive, both nationally and in our regional markets. Competition continues to be intense due to more aggressive marketing, a proliferation of new products and increased quality awareness and price sensitivity among customers. Significant consolidation within the industry has also added to competition. In addition, with the enactment of the Gramm-Leach-Bliley Act, banks and other financial institutions have the ability to affiliate with insurance companies, which may lead to new competitors in the insurance and health benefits fields."

Reasons to Buy

- "WellPoint, Inc., the nation's largest health insurer, said Tuesday it has agreed to buy WellChoice, Inc., an insurer with about five million customers in New York and New Jersey, for about $6.5 billion in cash and stock," according to an article by the *Associated Press* on September 27, 2005. The author, Ashley M. Heher, goes on to say, "Better known as Empire Blue Cross Blue Shield, New York-based WellChoice is the largest health insurer in New York state."
- All managed-care companies stand to benefit from the Medicare Modernization Act that goes into effect in 2006. WellPoint should see $1 billion in incremental revenue each year in the first few years of the new Medicare prescription-drug benefit known as Part D, as the company offers stand-alone drug plans and also caters to the one million senior members enrolled in its Medicare Advantage program.
- On the other hand, WellPoint isn't as exposed to the Medicare and senior market as some other HMOs. This helps explain why investors have bet more heavily on those companies that stand to gain more

from the act. However, they may be missing one thing: when the government eventually reins in health care spending, WellPoint won't face the same downside risk.

■ WellPoint is benefiting from margin expansion brought about by a sharp decline in operating expenses. Selling, general, and administrative costs now represent 15 percent of revenue, down from 25 percent five years ago, and more improvement is likely.

■ According to the company's form 10-K, "We intend to continue to expand through a combination of organic growth (*that is, without considering acquisitions*) and strategic acquisitions in both existing and new markets. Our growth strategy is designed to enable us to take advantage of the additional economies of scale provided by increased overall membership. In addition, we believe geographic diversity reduces our exposure to local or regional regulatory and competitive pressures and provides us with increased opportunities for expansion.

"While the majority of our growth has been the result of strategic mergers and acquisitions, we have also achieved organic growth in our existing markets by providing excellent service, offering competitively priced products and effectively capturing the brand strength of the Blue Cross and Blue Shield names and marks."

■ On March 28, 2006, the *New York Times* tabulated the opinions of nineteen analysts. Six were convinced that WellPoint was a STRONG BUY; nine said it was a MODERATE BUY; and four regarded the stock as a HOLD.

■ "Our recommendation is STRONG BUY," said Phillip M. Seligman, writing for *Standard & Poor's Stock Reports* on February 3, 2006. "We continue to view WLP's long-term profit prospects as positive. In our view, the Blue Cross Blue Shield name, and what we see as its long-standing reputation for high-quality service, should help WLP attract members at rates above most peers."

■ "WellPoint's prospects over the next three to five years are bright, " said Randy Shrikishun, writing for *Value Line Investment Survey* on March 24, 2006. "With its wider geographic scope, technological advancements, ongoing product and service innovations, and greater contributions from small acquisitions, we believe that the company will be able to achieve modest annual top- and bottom-line gain in the mid-teens out to decade's end."

■ On January 26, 2006, Prudential Equity Group gave the stock an OVERWEIGHT rating, or BUY. David Shove said, "In our view, WellPoint's fourth quarter 2005 performance demonstrates this Blue plan's earnings power resilience. Deploying its sizable footprint and product breadth, WellPoint posted solid organic enrollment growth in national account and the state-sponsored segment. Leveraging its enrollment mass, WellPoint applied purchasing pressure and effective cost controls to further reduce its medical cost trends."

SECTOR: **Health Care** ◆ BETA COEFFICIENT: **.80**

4-YEAR COMPOUND EARNINGS PER SHARE GROWTH: **26.9%**

4-YEAR COMPOUND DIVIDENDS PER SHARE GROWTH: **no dividend**

		2005	2004	2003	2002	2001	2000	1999	1998
Revenues (millions)		45,136	20,460	16,477	12,991	10,120	8,544	*	
Net Income (millions)		2,464	1,046	747	502	314	208	*	
Earnings per share		3.94	3.32	2.63	2.06	1.52	*		
Dividends per share		Nil	–	–	–	–	–	–	
Price	high	80.4	58.9	41.4	37.8	26.0	*		
	low	54.6	36.1	26.5	23.2	20.2	*		

* WellPoint was established in May 1996.

GROWTH AND INCOME

Wells Fargo & Company

420 Montgomery Street ❑ San Francisco, CA 94163 ❑ (415) 396-0523 ❑ Direct Dividend reinvestment plan available (877) 840-0492 ❑ Web site: *www.wellsfargo.com* ❑ Listed: NYSE ❑ Ticker symbol: WFC ❑ S&P rating: A ❑ Value Line financial strength rating: A+

"Wells Fargo proves that you don't have to be the biggest dog to be a top dog," said an article in *SmartMoney* in October 2005. The authors were Nicole Bullock and Reshma Kapadia. "While some banks have garnered impressive results via blockbuster acquisitions, most notably Bank of America, the San Francisco-based Wells Fargo has relied on smaller deals and careful cultivation of its existing customer base. That strategy has helped make Wells Fargo the nation's largest mortgage lender. And it has wowed investors like James Barrow of Vanguard's Windsor II fund, who notes that the company is 'showing consistent earnings growth while lots of banks are not.'"

The *SmartMoney* article goes on to say, "Overall banking-industry market share is hard to calculate because of the array of businesses involved, but Young Im, banking analyst at Robert W. Baird, says Wells Fargo has increased its loans and deposits at a much faster rate than the industry as a whole. And cross-selling—bankerese for deriving more income from existing customers by, for example, getting a checking-account holder to take out a mortgage—has fueled the bank's rise, accounting for about 80 percent of its 2004 revenue growth. Strategies like these help to make Wells Fargo a purebred stock in a pound full of banking mutts."

Company Profile

Wells Fargo & Company is a diversified financial services company, providing banking, insurance, investments, mortgages, and consumer finance from more than 6,250 stores, the Internet (*wellsfargo.com)* and other distribution channels across North America. Wells Fargo Bank, N. A. Is the only "AAA"-rated bank in the United States.

As of the end of 2005, Wells Fargo had $453 billion in assets, was the fifth-largest among its domestic peers, and the market value of the stock ranked third among its peers.

In community banking, Wells Fargo has 3,120 stores in twenty-three states, 23 million customers, and is the nation's most extensive banking franchise.

Wells Fargo Card Services

In the realm of card services, WFC has:

- 6.0 million credit card accounts.
- $6.2 billion in average consumer credit cards outstanding.
- The nation's number two issuer of credit cards.
- 15.48 million debit card accounts.

Wells Fargo is the number one originator of home mortgages and the number two servicer of residential mortgages. Combined, the company's retail and wholesale lending operations fund about one of every eight homes financed annually in the United States.

Here is a summary of the company's home mortgage operations:

- Serving all fifty states through more than 2,000 mortgage and Wells Fargo banking stores, and the Internet.
- The nation's number one retail home mortgage lender.
- 4.9 million customers.
- Originations: $470 billion.
- Servicing: $753 billion.

Credit Card Group

A leading provider of home equity and personal credit accounts with a combined portfolio of $64 billion. Sales channels include Retail Banking, Wells Fargo Home Mortgage, CCG Direct-to-Consumer (Internet/wellsfargo.com, telesales, and direct mail), wholesale and third-party mortgage brokers, finance companies, indirect dealer programs, and other third-party partners. In summary, this is how WFC stacks up:

- One of America's largest and fastest-growing providers of home equity and personal credit.
- Serving more than 2.1 million customer households.
- Largest lender of prime home equity (loans and lines of credit).
- First to introduce Home Asset Management Account, which combines a mortgage and home equity line of credit, enabling customers to finance a home in an all-in-one process.
- Number one in personal credit market share in Wells Fargo banking states.
- Largest provider of auto loans, excluding captive finance companies.

Shortcomings to Bear in Mind

■ In recent years, banks have been finding it increasingly difficult to expand revenues. Those with the broadest product mix are more likely to have an easier time registering top-line growth. In addition, savings from cost-cutting efforts, which have propelled earnings for many large bank in recent years, are becoming more difficult to come by, placing greater emphasis on top-line growth.

■ On February 6, 2006, Mark Hebeka, CFA, an analyst with *Standard & Poor's Company Reports,* said, "Our recommendation is HOLD. Based on the stock's valuation versus peers and what we consider a mixed operating outlook, we expect the shares to be average performers in the year ahead. We view WFC as having solid banking fundamentals, a diverse customer base and look for continued growth in 2006, albeit slower."

Reasons to Buy

■ "The bank is well positioned for growth over the pull to 2008–2010," said Randy Shrikishun, writing for *Value Line Investment Survey* on February 24, 2006. "Commercial and consumer loan activity should rise further during this time as the economy improves. Meanwhile, we believe that the percentage of net charge-offs and nonperforming assets will remain relatively stable over the long haul."

■ As reported by the *New York Times* on March 20, 2006, twenty eight analysts had this view of Wells Fargo: six rated the stock a STRONG BUY, fourteen said it was a MODERATE BUY; seven gave the stock a HOLD rating; and one said it was a MODERATE HOLD.

■ "Despite rising costs for energy, healthcare and housing, one of the bright spots for the U.S. economy is the continued growth of small businesses," said a Wells Fargo spokesman on December 6, 2005. "They are still driving the U.S. economy forward, as evidenced by the latest, most comprehensive government data on small business lending. In 2004, financial institutions lent $93 billion to small business owners nationwide (in loans under $100,000), showing a healthy demand for capital and a strong sense of optimism in their future business prospects.

"With 95 percent of all small businesses generating less than $2 million in annual revenues, tracking loans under $100,000 is an important measurement to gauge how financial institutions are meeting the capital needs of small business owners.

"For the third year in a row, Wells Fargo led this category, extending over 540,000 loans totaling $13.6 billion nationwide—15 percent of the industry total. Wells Fargo was the number one lender to small businesses in Low and Moderate Income neighborhoods (loans under $100,000), with over 114,000 loans totaling more than $3 billion dollars (16% of the industry total), according to the 2004 Community Reinvestment Act (CRA) data. Additionally, Wells Fargo was also the number one lender to businesses with less than $1 million in annual revenue. CRA data provides the industry's most comprehensive set of small business lending figures."

"As uncertainties continue, small businesses are clearly anchoring us through economic ups and downs," said Wells Fargo's president and chief operating officer, John Stumpf. "They are over 20 million strong, have created 55 million jobs, and generate 50 percent of the total U.S. GDP—roughly $5 trillion. There is no denying that small business is big business."

Another spokesman went on to say, "Small businesses represent more than 99 percent of all employers, employ half of all private sector employees, and generate between 60–80 percent of new jobs annually. And they are still growing. According to the latest U.S. Census Data (1997–2002), small businesses overall grew 10 percent, with the diverse segments growing even faster. African American-owned businesses grew 45 percent; Latino-owned businesses grew 31 percent; Asian-owned businesses grew 24 percent; and women-owned businesses grew 20 percent."

■ Wells Fargo's diversity of businesses makes the company much more than a bank. According to a WFC official, "We're a diversified financial services company. Financial services is a highly fragmented and fast-growing industry. Our diversity helps us weather downturns that inevitably affect any one segment of our industry."

Here's how diversified Wells Fargo is:

PERCENTAGE OF EARNINGS

Community Banking	33%
Investments and insurance	15%
Home mortgage and home equity	20%
Specialized lending	14%
Wholesale banking	7%
Consumer finance	7%
Commercial real estate	4%

Wells Fargo is a major player in the banking industry, as noted below:

No. 2 in total stores (6,250 stores)

No. 2 in banking (3,120 stores)

No. 1 in mortgages (1,009 stand-alone stores, 947 Wells Fargo banking stores with mortgage salespeople).

No. 1 in Supermarkets (655 stores)

No. 4 Consumer Finance (1,284 stores)

No. 1 Internet Bank (5.2 million active online customers)

A leading Phone Bank (20 million calls a month)

No. 3 ATM Network (6,363 ATMs)

SECTOR: **Financials** ◆ BETA COEFFICIENT: **.90**
10-YEAR COMPOUND EARNINGS PER SHARE GROWTH: **12.6%**
10-YEAR COMPOUND DIVIDENDS PER SHARE GROWTH: **16.1%**

		2005	2004	2003	2002	2001	2000	1999	1998
Loans (millions)		296,100	269,600	249,182	192,772	168,738	157,405	116,294	104,860
Total Assets (millions)		460,000	427,849	387,798	349,259	307,569	272,426	218,102	202,475
Net Income (millions)		7,670	7,014	6,202	5,710	3,423	4,026	3,747	2,906
Earnings per share		2.25	2.05	1.83	1.66	0.99	1.17	1.12	0.88
Dividends per share		1.00	0.93	0.75	.55	0.50	0.45	0.40	0.31
Price	high	32.4	32.0	29.6	27.4	27.4	28.2	25.0	22.0
	low	28.8	27.2	21.7	19.1	19.2	15.7	16.1	13.8

CONSERVATIVE GROWTH

Wm. Wrigley Jr. Company

Wrigley Building ❑ 410 North Michigan Avenue ❑ Chicago, IL 60611 ❑ (313) 645-4754 ❑ Dividend reinvestment plan available (800) 874-0474 ❑ Web site: *www.wrigley.com* ❑ Listed: NYSE ❑ Ticker symbol: WWY ❑ S&P rating: A+ ❑ Value Line financial strength rating: A++

"Investors in Wm. Wrigley Jr., the globe's top purveyor of gum, have a lot of news to chew on," said Harlan S. Byrne, writing for *Barron's* on June 6, 2005. "For one thing, Wrigley is adding two well-known names, Life Savers and Altoids, to its arsenal of brands. For another, the century-old Chicago company is pursuing an aggressive growth strategy, at home and abroad. And it's enjoying good results."

Mr. Byrne goes on to say, "The company, which already derives almost two-thirds of its sales outside the U.S., has positioned itself nicely for further global expansion. It's in the last stages of digesting Joyco, a Spanish outfit that it bought for 215 million euros ($260 million at the time the deal was done last year). Joyco has a strong position in several European chewing-gum markets, and is number one in India and China, each of which have huge growth potential. Wrigley also is making inroads in Eastern Europe, particularly Russia and Ukraine, and is pushing into Latin America."

The *Barron's* article went on to say, "Wrigley is also benefiting from the growing popularity of pellet gum, such as its Eclipse brand, which sells for 79 cents and costs an estimated 15 cents to make. In contrast, the typical stick gum, such as Juicy Fruit, sells for a quarter and costs an estimated dime to make."

Company Profile

The Wm. Wrigley, Jr. Company is a recognized leader in the confectionery field and the world's largest manufacturer of chewing gum. Founded in 1891, the company has been traded on the New York Stock Exchange since 1924.

Led by four generations of the Wrigley family, the company is committed to providing the world's highest-quality and best-tasting chewing gum and confectionery products for consumers.

Since the introduction of Juicy Fruit and Wrigley's Spearmint gums more than 110 years ago, the company has greatly increased its portfolio of products to include dozens of brands that deliver a wide variety of consumer benefits, including breath freshening, tooth whitening, and oral care.

Brands such as Doublemint, Big Red, Winterfresh, Extra, Eclipse, Freedent, Hubba Bubba, Orbit, and Excel continue to generate excitement in the gum category by meeting consumer needs and supporting the company's strategy of boosting its core chewing gum business.

The Wrigley Company continues to diversify its confectionery products through both internal development and acquisition. Wrigley's development of Orbit Drops, a sugar-free dental candy, Extra, Eclipse and Wintergreen mints, and Airwaves mentholated candies build on the strong equity and high quality of these global brands by extending their reach into new confectionery segments.

Recent acquisitions have also helped Wrigley extend into the broader confectionery marketplace. Brands such as Altoids, Life Savers, Pim Pom, and Solano give consumers a variety of delicious product across numerous confectionery types. From mints to chewy and hard candies to lollipops, these products help Wrigley reach a wide range of consumers around the world.

Wrigley brands are sold in more than 180 countries. In each geographic region, the company's goal is to deliver the quality synonymous with the Wrigley name, while tailoring flavors and product benefits to address the tastes and needs of local consumers. Wrigley has production facilities in fourteen countries, offices in about three dozen countries, and almost 15,000 employees around the globe.

The Americas region, consisting of the United States and Canada, represents 36 percent of Wrigley's sales. The EMEAI region, which is principally Europe, but includes the Middle East, Africa and India, generates about 49 percent of company sales. Representing about 11 percent of Wrigley's sales, Asia is the company's fastest-growing region. Other regions, principally the Pacific (Australia and New Zealand) and Latin America, contribute about 4 percent of Wrigley's sales.

Wrigley's Gum Ingredients

Gum Base: Gum base put the "chew" in chewing gum, binding all the ingredients together for a smooth, soft texture. The Wrigley Company uses synthetic gum base materials that provide longer-lasting flavor, improved texture, and reduced tackiness. Sweeteners: The finest grades of pure powdered cane sugar, beet sugar, and corn syrup are used in the production of Wrigley's sugar-sweetened chewing gums. Several types of high-intensity sweeteners are used in Wrigley's sugar-free products such as flavor enhancers in some other brands. These artificial sweeteners deliver long-lasting, noncaloric taste and do not promote tooth decay: Acesulfame K, Aspartame, Maltilol, Sucralose, Sorbitol, and Xylitol.

Softeners and Bulking Agents: Glycerin and other vegetable oil products help keep the gum soft and flexible by retaining the proper amount of moisture in Wrigley's products. Ingredients like manitol and sorbitol ensure the proper density of a product.

Flavorings and Colorings: The most popular flavors for chewing gums come from the mint plant. Mint flavoring for Wrigley's chewing gums is extracted from fresh mint plants grown on farms in the United States. After plants are harvested, they go through a distillation process that extracts the oils used for flavoring Wrigley brands.

Shortcomings to Bear in Mind

- On February 3, 2006, *Value Line Investment Survey* gave Wrigley a Timeliness score of 4, or below average. Its analyst, Jason A. Smith, said, "The candymaker faces a number of challenges this year. Trends within the domestic chewing gum industry pose some problems for Wrigley's franchise brands. Innovative packaging drove demand at a steady pace from 2004 to early 2005. Still, the honeymoon may be over, since it appears growth has slowed significantly in recent months. Further, the shift from gum sticks, Wrigley's bread and butter, to lower-margined products should also take its toll. Meanwhile, the battle for market share continues to intensify, as innovation and consolidation increase industry-wide."

Reasons to Buy

- *Standard & Poor's Stock Reports* took issue with *Value Line* on this one, giving the stock five stars on February 23, 2006, its highest rating. Richard Joy said, "Our recommendation is STRONG BUY. We believe the shares are attractive, in light of our view of WWY's relatively high and improving operating profitability, clean balance sheet, dominant and growing U.S. market share (about 60 percent), and impressive global distribution infrastructure. Volume and earnings growth have been strong in recent quarters, reflecting, we think, successful new product introductions and strong international growth."
- On March 20, 2006, the *New York Times* poled a dozen securities analysts on their view of Wrigley. Four rated the company a STRONG BUY, five called it a MODERATE BUY, one said Wrigley was a HOLD; one said it was a MODERATE

HOLD; and only one analyst was downright bearish, giving the stock a SELL rating.

- On February 10, 2006, Prudential Equity Group gave the stock an OVERWEIGHT rating. Similarly, another brokerage firm, Lehman Brothers gave it the same rating on February 17, 2006. OVERWEIGHT is an above-average rating, similar to a BUY.
- On December 8, 2006, Wrigley launched eight new confectionery products that hit store shelves in January 2006.

"The recent opening of our Global Innovation Center reinforces Wrigley's focus on new product innovation," said Ralph Scozzafava, Vice President & Managing Director, North America and Pacific. "These new items deliver on Wrigley's commitment to provide consumers with innovations that meet their changing tastes and needs."

The eight new products are:

- New Doublemint Twins Mints—the first innovative extension from the popular ninety-plus-year-old Doublemint brand. Available in single serve sizes, Doublemint Twins Mints come in two flavors: Wintercreme and Mintcreme. Both flavors are a blend of mild mint flavors with a creme.
- Extra "Cool Watermelon"—the latest flavor addition to Extra gum, the number one gum in the United States for over a decade. Extra "Cool Watermelon" provides consumers a unique, long lasting twist to the traditional watermelon flavor.
- Eclipse "Cinnamon Inferno" and "Midnight Cool" gums—two new items from Eclipse that deliver powerful fresh breath through intense, unique flavors.
- Orbit White "Wintermint" gum—the latest flavor of Orbit White not only whitens teeth and removes stains, but also tastes great.
- Life Savers Gummies Wild Berry Sours—available in multiserve bags, Berry Sours contain six "sour" gummy flavors: cherry berry, strawberry, red raspberry, black raspberry, blackberry, and white grape. Life Savers Gummies Wild Berry Sours combine a kick of sour with great tasting, sweet wild berry flavors.
- Creme Savers Tropicals Hard Candy—the latest addition to Creme Savers, which is the number one brand in Dairy Hard Candy. Creme Savers Tropicals are available in a multiserve bag and bring creamy, dreamy great taste in three new tropical flavors: Pina Colada & Creme, Banana & Creme, and Mango & Creme.
- Altoids Mango Sours—a new sour flavor from the leader in Hard Candy Sours. Altoids Mango Sours is a new, and curiously strong, way for adults to enjoy the fruity yet strong taste of Altoids.

"Wrigley's consumers have come to expect the highest quality, value, innovative benefits and fun from Wrigley products," said Martin Schlatter, General Manager, United States. "We have a robust pipeline of innovation across formats, flavors, packaging and new products to exceed these consumer expectations."

Over the past four years, the contribution from new products has averaged nearly 20 percent of Wrigley's global sales, up significantly from the 5–6 percent rate of the 1990s. "There is no doubt that sustainable innovation that adds value is a critical growth driver for our business going forward," said Mr. Schlatter. "What makes Wrigley unique is our focus on ensuring our innovations have staying power in the marketplace."

SECTOR: **Consumer Staples** ◆ BETA COEFFICIENT: **.55**
10-YEAR COMPOUND EARNINGS PER SHARE GROWTH: **9%**
10-YEAR COMPOUND DIVIDENDS PER SHARE GROWTH: **8.4%**

		2005	**2004**	**2003**	**2002**	**2001**	**2000**	**1999**	**1998**
Revenues (millions)		4,159	3,649	3,069	2,746	2,430	2,146	2,062	2,005
Net Income (millions)		517	493	446	402	363	329	308	298
Earnings per share		1.83	1.75	1.58	1.42	1.29	1.16	1.06	0.71
Dividends per share		0.86	0.74	0.70	0.65	0.60	0.56	0.54	0.52
Price	high	59.5	56.0	47.1	47.1	42.6	38.6	40.2	41.8
	low	50.6	43.8	40.9	35.4	34.3	23.9	26.6	28.4

Index of Stocks by Category

Aggressive Growth

Alcoa 55
Apache 58
Biomet, Inc. 79
Boeing 85
Brinker International 89
Carnival 95
Caterpillar 98
Cintas 104
Costco Wholesale 117
Deere & Company 123
Dell 126
Devon Energy 132
Dover Corp. 141
EnCana Corporation 160
FedEx Corporation 170
Ingersoll-Rand 193
Intel 196
Int'l Business Machines (IBM) 199
Lockheed Martin 221
Medtronic 242
Motorola 251
Nabors Industries 254
Oshkosh Truck 263
Parker Hannifin 266
Patterson Companies 269
PetSmart 275
Pfizer 278
St. Jude Medical 300
Staples 303
Stryker 306
T. Rowe Price 312
Target Corporation 315
Teva Pharmaceutical 318
Wal-Mart 347
WellPoint 350

Conservative Growth

Air Products 51
Bard, C.R. 70
Becton, Dickinson 73
Black & Decker 82
Canadian National Railway 92
Clorox 107
Colgate-Palmolive 110
CVS 120
Dentsply 129
Donaldson 139
Ecolab 154
Energen 163
General Dynamics 173
Grainger, W.W. 180
Home Depot 183
Hormel Foods 186

Illinois Tool Works 189
Johnson Controls 202
Johnson & Johnson 206
Kellogg 209
Lowe's 224
Marshall & Ilsley 230
McCormick & Co. 233
McGraw-Hill 236
Meredith 246
Microsoft 249
Norfolk Southern 260
PepsiCo 272
Praxair 288
Procter & Gamble 291
Questar 294
Ruby Tuesday 297
Sysco Corporation 310
3M Company 325
UnitedHealth 328
United Parcel Service 331
United Technologies 335
Valspar 338
Varian Medical 341
Walgreen 344
Wrigley 356

Growth & Income

Abbott Laboratories 48
Avalon Bay 61
Bank of America 64
Banta 67
Bemis Company 76
ConocoPhillips 113
Dominion 135
Dow Chemical 144
DuPont 148
Eaton Corp. 151
Emerson Electric 157
ExxonMobil 166
General Electric 176
Kimco Realty 212
Kinder Morgan 215
Lilly, Eli 218
Lubrizol 227
MDU Resources 239
Pitney Bowes 284
Textron 321
Wells Fargo 353

Income

Chevron Corporation 101
New Jersey Resources 257
Piedmont Natural Gas 281

About the Author

John Slatter has a varied investment background and has served as a stockbroker, securities analyst, and portfolio strategist. He is now a consultant with Prim Asset Management, a firm in Cleveland, Ohio, that manages investment portfolios on a fee basis.

John Slatter has written hundreds of articles for such publications as *Barron's*, *Physician's Management*, *Ophthalmology Times*, *The Writer*, and *Better Investing*, as well as for brokerage firms he has worked for, including Hugh Johnson & Company, and Wachovia Securities. His books include *Safe Investing*, *Straight Talk About Stock Investing*, and nine prior editions of *The 100 Best Stocks You Can Buy*.

John Slatter has been quoted in such periodicals as the *Cleveland Plain Dealer*, the *New York Times*, the *Gannett News Service*, the *Burlington Free Press*, the *Wall Street Journal*, the *Cincinnati Enquirer*, the *Toledo Blade*, the *Christian Science Monitor*, *Money Magazine*, the *Dayton Daily News*, and the *Buffalo News*. He has also been quoted in a number of books, including *The Dividend Investor* and *Stocks for the Long Run*, and he has also been interviewed on a number of radio stations, as well as by the CNBC daily television program *Today's Business*.

In August of 1988, John Slatter was featured in the *Wall Street Journal* concerning his innovative investment strategy that calls for investing in the ten highest-yielding stocks in the Dow Jones Industrial Average. This approach to stock selection is sometimes referred as "The Dogs of the Dow," a pejorative reference that Mr. Slatter does not believe is justified, since the stocks with high yields have, in the past, included such blue chips as Merck, IBM, 3M, General Electric, AT&T, Caterpillar, DuPont, ExxonMobil, J.P. Morgan Chase, and Altria.

John Slatter may be reached by calling (802) 879-4154 (during business hours only) or by writing him at 70 Beech Street, Essex Junction, Vermont 05452. His e-mail address is *john.slatter@verizon.net*.